'*The Indian Empire at War* is  from the perspective of South book provides a vital corrective math that only look at the world author of *The Silk Roads*

'Essential to a proper understanding of the war and of our world of today, in Britain and in India. A much-needed book' Michael Morpurgo, author of *War Horse*

'An extraordinarily original contribution to our understanding of the important Indian role in the First World War' Max Hastings, author of *Catastrophe: Europe Goes to War 1914*

'The Indian Army was of absolutely crucial importance to Britain in the First World War, but that simple fact has too often been neglected. Impeccably researched and very well written, George Morton-Jack's book should go a long way to rectifying this case of historical amnesia' Gary Sheffield, author of *Forgotten Victory: The First World War, Myths and Realities*

'Revelatory ... George Morton-Jack's fluent and colourful account of the Indians' role across the globe shows how crucial they were to Allied success [and] describes the war as a worldwide conflict' Andrew Lycett, *Daily Telegraph*

'George Morton-Jack skilfully presents the reader with the first comprehensive telling of the Indian story and places it in a global context ... Morton-Jack's work is magisterial and yet immensely readable. This is the book for anyone interested in an authentic broad-based account of the role played by India and its soldiers in the defining conflict of the twentieth century ... The book is remarkable in having used, for the first time, thousands of pages of interview transcripts of Indian veterans of the war, recorded in the 1970s' Rana Chhina, *India Today*

'Fills a gap that should have been dealt with long ago' Professor Sir Michael Howard

'A splendid book ... A multi-layered, rigorously researched and empathetically interpreted account of the Indian contribution to the Great War. The author's objective of shining "a more filtered light on the Indian soldiers" is luminously met ... Morton-Jack, to his credit, does not shy away from recording the cruel face of the colonial ruler' Chitrapu Uday Bhaskar, *Hindustan Times*

'Wonderfully written and authoritative ... Global in reach and packed full of fascinating stories, this is an insightful and intimate portrayal' Alexander Watson, author of *Ring of Steel: Germany and Austria Hungary at War, 1914–1918*

'An outstanding book that brings to life the experiences of Indian soldiers in all of the theatres of the First World War, from German colonies in China and Africa to the Middle East and the Western Front . . . Morton-Jack restores the Indian Army to its rightful place in the history of the Great War' Eugene Rogan, author of *The Fall of the Ottomans: The Great War in the Middle East*

'An impressive, humane, and myth-busting book' Allan Mallinson, *Spectator*

'*The Indian Empire at War* offers fascinating insight into a conflict that was both imperial and global. The true scale and scope of Indian involvement in the First World War remains underappreciated, even in India itself. Morton-Jack's compelling account explains how 1.5 million Indian soldiers fought on three continents, what difference this made to the war, to them and to India' Peter H. Wilson, Chichele Professor of the History of War, All Souls College, University of Oxford

'This is narrative military history at its most impressive. There is no other work so comprehensive on the Indian Army at war overseas – from fighting on the Pacific rim, the dreadful British failures in Iraq and desert warfare in North Africa, to U-boat attacks in the Mediterranean, the war in Italy and POWs in Germany' Thomas R. Metcalf, Professor of History Emeritus at the University of California, Berkeley

'A lively history of the Indian Army in all its tragedies, difficulties and occasional triumphs ... reveals the touching humanity of the Indian soldier' Ian Jack, *Guardian*

'A comprehensive analysis of the Indian Army's experience between 1914 and 1918. Covering every theatre of conflict, painstakingly researched and vividly written, *The Indian Empire at War* is full of colour and interest' David Stevenson, author of *1914–1918: The History of the First World War*

'Morton-Jack has given a voice to hundreds of thousands of soldiers who fought overseas for an Empire and would be widely forgotten from the UK to India and Pakistan. Important and moving' Dan Snow, History Hit

'Every chapter contains a wealth of evocative contemporary reflections from and about men who represented a "uniquely multicultural" army ... A fascinating socio-cultural history' Chandrika Kaul, *BBC History Magazine*

THE INDIAN EMPIRE AT WAR

From Jihad to Victory, The Untold Story of the
Indian Army in the First World War

GEORGE MORTON-JACK

ABACUS

First published in Great Britain in 2018 by Little, Brown
This paperback edition published in 2020 by Abacus

1 3 5 7 9 10 8 6 4 2

Copyright © George Morton-Jack 2018

Maps by John Gilkes

The moral right of the author has been asserted.

A CIP catalogue record for this book
is available from the British Library.

ISBN: 978-0-349-14184-8

Typeset in Sabon by M Rules
Printed and bound in Great Britain by
Clays Ltd, Elcograf S.p.A.

Papers used by Abacus are from well-managed forests
and other responsible sources.

Abacus
An imprint of
Little, Brown Book Group
Carmelite House
50 Victoria Embankment
London EC4Y 0DZ

An Hachette UK Company
www.hachette.co.uk

www.littlebrown.co.uk

CONTENTS

MAPS

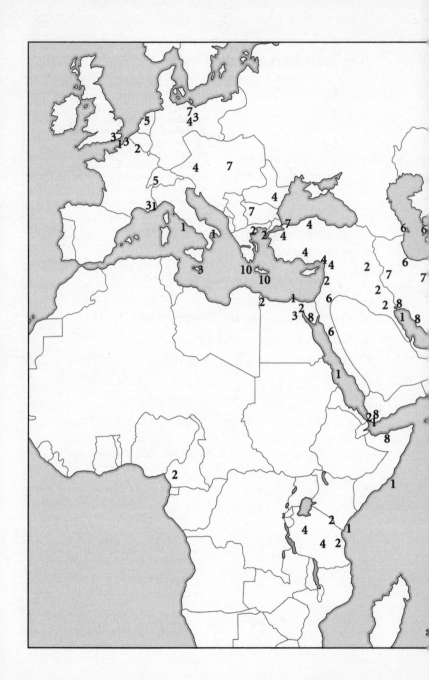

The Indian Army in the First World War, 1914–18

1: In transit by sea
2: Battlefronts
3: Hospitals
4: Indian POW camps
5: Medical cases interned (released from enemy captivity)
6: With secret British missions
7: With secret German missions
8: Imperial garrisons
9: Imprisoned mutineers
10: Troopships sunk by U-boats

INTRODUCTION

'A splendid gathering'

In 1911, the Indian Empire put on its most dazzling ever display of pomp and pageantry to celebrate George V's accession as its King-Emperor. He embarked on a public tour to show himself to the Indian people as their absolute ruler in the tradition of Akbar, Shah Jahan and the other Mughal emperors, and its climax was the Delhi Durbar in December at a vast purpose-built amphitheatre outside the city. Here 200,000 spectators, many of them sitting in stands arranged like flowerbeds according to the colour of their turbans – snow-white, orange, yellow or green – saw him make a spectacular entry in the winter sunshine as an authority second only to God.

To the thunder of artillery fire and flourishes of silver trumpets, George appeared in a horse-drawn maroon carriage in purple robes and a crown of 6100 diamonds, the Queen-Empress Mary at his side, and footmen in their wake with fans of peacock feathers and yak tails, and golden maces with king cobra heads. After processing to a throne under a red velvet canopy topped with a golden dome and small minarets, he presided over an afternoon of slick ceremonials in his honour. To kettle-drum rolls, claps and cheers, bowing maharajahs laid swords at his feet, and scroll-clutching civil servants read out proclamations of his semi-divine and supreme will, before the British national anthem rang out.

The spectators were mostly civilians, but standing in the middle of the amphitheatre, set among the red clay roads criss-crossing it, the empire's professional Indian Army was on show: 15,000 of its men under their British officers, standing bolt-upright in immaculately turned out regimental blocks, from towering Sikhs, six-foot tall in their khaki breeches and tunics with turbans, brown leather belts and boots, down to Gurkhas, five-foot-five in green uniforms with their cowboy-style felt hats and Himalayan curved knife, the *khukuri*, alongside a smaller number of British Army troops in scarlet and blue with spotless white pith helmets.

Watching on from the King-Emperor's cavalry escort was Thakur Amar Singh, an observant and quietly spoken Hindu officer in his early thirties, on a plumed horse with a snow leopard skin draped under his saddle. 'I wanted to see it thoroughly,' he wrote enthusiastically in his diary of the amphitheatre's great spectacle. 'Just as we entered the pace was reduced from a trot to a walk and we were able to see what a splendid gathering it was.' For him, the Delhi Durbar was 'great & historic [and] will be remembered for ages ... worthy of the illustrious sovereign'. Among the standing Indian soldiers, meanwhile, was a bearded Muslim soldier named Mir Dast. He had enlisted in 1894, been decorated for bravery in action in 1908, and in the amphitheatre joined the rest of the Indian troops in a flawless rifle fire salute that rippled from them to troops outside lining the road for several miles to the King-Emperor's camp, and then back again. According to Mir Dast's British officer, he was just the kind of man British recruiters looked for: 'always outstanding' and 'intensely "imperialist"'.

With men like Mir Dast in its ranks, the British generals in the stands seemed to have every confidence in the Indian Army. There was the Chief of the Indian General Staff – a Scotsman,

Douglas Haig – who considered the Durbar 'a wonderful show'. And sitting near him was the Indian Army's most senior field commander, James Willcocks, who also happened to be the British soldier most decorated for active service. The Durbar, Willcocks was sure, confirmed the Indian troops' visible allegiance to their King-Emperor. 'It left its imprint deeper than any event that took place during my long service in India,' he wrote. 'It was used by the Indians as the date to describe occurrences by, i.e. "before" or "after" the Durbar ... The King was the only power the Indians understood thoroughly ... he alone could finally say "yea" or "nea".'

To all appearances, therefore, when the First World War broke out in 1914 the British, and by extension the Allies, had in the Indian Army a professional force ready, willing and able to fight for its King-Emperor. Up to 1918, a total of 1.5 million Indian recruits would serve in the Indian Army, seven times the pre-war number. They were to fight far and wide, on Flanders fields, rocky ridges above Turkish beaches, coral island shores with swaying coconut trees, golden grasslands with roaming giraffe, lion and rhino, in steaming tropical rainforests on mountain slopes wandered by gorillas, and the sun-baked deserts of the Islamic world.

In fact, the Indian Army was the Allies' most widespread army of 1914–18, serving in foreign lands across Africa, Asia and Europe that today number some fifty different countries. This book is the first single narrative of it on all fronts, a global epic not only of the Indians' part in the Allied victory over the Central Powers, but also of soldiers' personal discoveries on their four-year odyssey. It retraces Indian Army footsteps from front to front, following the Hindu diarist Thakur Amar Singh, the Muslim Mir Dast (who was to be one of eighteen Indian Army Victoria Cross winners), Douglas Haig, James Willcocks and others. In exploring the Indians' war, this book reveals their differing experiences of the worldwide tragedy of 1914 to 1918, whether as villagers or travellers, fighting men or prisoners of war, secret agents or lovers across cultural divides. So far as possible, the story is told in the words of the Indian Army's officers and men, using wartime letters and veteran interviews, many previously unpublished, to revisit the First World War as never before.

The 'Indian' Army

The Indian Army of 1914–18 was uniquely multicultural, combining such a variety of humankind into a single brotherhood-in-arms that it was really a modern wonder of the world. Its officers and men were a breathtaking array worshipping more gods and speaking more languages than any other army on the planet. They were a mix of Muslims, Hindus, Sikhs, Buddhists, Christians, Jews, Zoroastrians and pagans, and they spoke not just Hindustani, the army's official vernacular blending Hindi and Urdu, but also their separate home languages. These were numerous and some Indian servicemen not fluent in Hindustani could only understand each other if they knew the right language: Hindi, Urdu, Punjabi, Pushtu, Dari, Bengali, Marathi, Tamil, Burmese, Nepali or a number of other tongues, uttered in local dialects beyond count.

In having such stunning diversity, the Indian Army reflected the society that produced it. It came not from the country we know today as India but from a much bigger, sprawling imperial society with double its total surface area. On a map of the world of 2018, the Indian Army's Indian and British recruits' homelands are in ten nation states including India. In 1914, however, their homes fell within the borders of a quite different international landscape where many of those nation states did not exist, the bulk of their territories being in the colonial chains of the British Empire's most prized possession: its great Asian bloc, the Indian Empire.

The Indian Empire was the region of South Asia now covered mainly by Pakistan, India, Bangladesh and Burma, excluding Goa and other coastal enclaves that belonged to French or Portuguese

India. Its isolated outposts stretched as far west as the Arabian Peninsula's port of Aden opposite Somalia, and eastwards to the Andaman Islands in the Bay of Bengal. The British shorthand for it all was 'India', and the Indian Army was its principal security force, based in its biggest sector – British India, the two thirds under the direct rule of the British autocracy nicknamed the Raj.

The majority of the Indian Army's Indian recruits of 1914–18 – some 1.28 million, or 85 per cent – came from British India's provinces, above all Punjab. The other 15 per cent were immigrants to British India, slightly over half of whom, or around 115,000 recruits, came from the Indian Empire's third that was not under direct British rule and consisted of the princely States of India. These were spread in their hundreds the length and breadth of the Indian Empire, from Kashmir, Bikaner and Jaipur in the north to Hyderabad in the south. Their rulers were a constellation of fabulously wealthy hereditary monarchs dubbed 'princes' for colonial ease of reference, their panoply of royal titles ranging from Hindu or Sikh rajas, maharajahs and begums to Muslim khans, nawabs and nizams. Although formally independent of British India, they were bound by treaty into allegiance to the King-Emperor. The arrangement extended to some of their own domestic regiments, collectively known as the Imperial Service Troops, being liable for active service abroad alongside the Indian Army.

The final tranche of the Indian Army's Indian recruits of 1914–18, numbering 100,000 or so, came from independent foreign lands neighbouring the Indian Empire. Several thousand were Muslims either from Afghanistan, ruled by its Emir at Kabul, or from an internationally anomalous Islamic territory wedged between Afghanistan and British India's North-West Frontier Province. This was the independent tribal areas of the Pukhtun tribes, divided into Waziristan, Tirah and other constituent lands encompassing 25,000 square miles and with a population of over a million Pukhtun. They were stateless, with

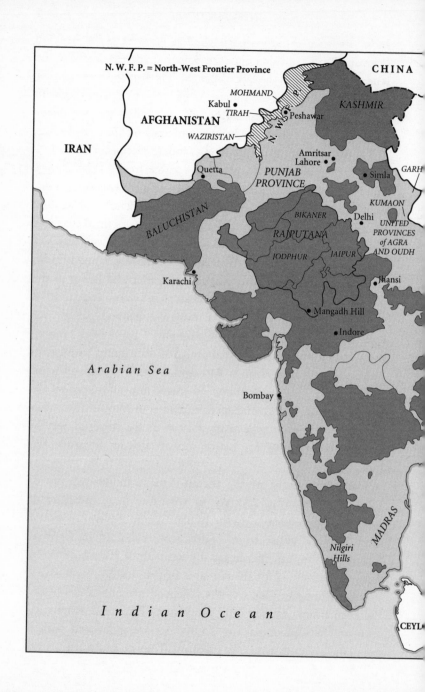

N.W.F.P. = North-West Frontier Province

CHINA

AFGHANISTAN

IRAN

MOHMAND
Kabul •
TIRAH
WAZIRISTAN

KASHMIR

Peshawar

N. W. F. P.

• Quetta

PUNJAB
PROVINCE

Amritsar
Lahore •

• Simla

GARH

KUMAON

BALUCHISTAN

BIKANER

RAJPUTANA

JODPHUR   JAIPUR

Delhi •

UNITED
PROVINCES
of AGRA
AND OUDH

Karachi •

• Jhansi

• Mangadh Hill

• Indore

Arabian Sea

Bombay •

MADRAS

Nilgiri
Hills

Indian Ocean

CEYL•

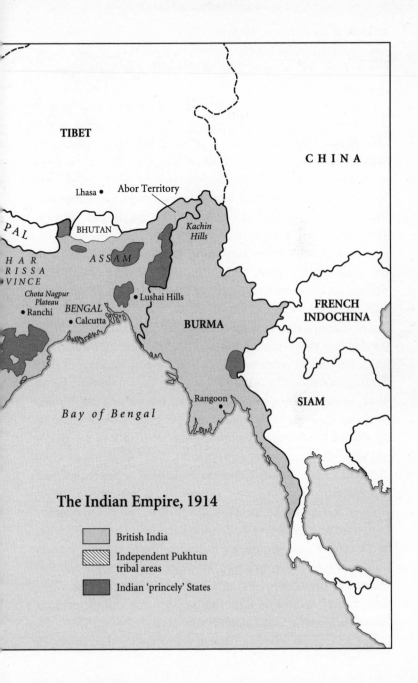

TIBET

CHINA

Lhasa •   Abor Territory

PAL

BHUTAN

Kachin Hills

H A R RISSA VINCE

A S S A M

Chota Nagpur Plateau
• Ranchi

BENGAL

• Lushai Hills

• Calcutta

BURMA

FRENCH INDOCHINA

Bay of Bengal

Rangoon •

SIAM

The Indian Empire, 1914

British India

Independent Pukhtun tribal areas

Indian 'princely' States

no central government, no taxes and no passports; so protective were their tribes of their traditional autonomy and society, no one had ever taken the trouble of trying to rule them according to international norms.

The remaining Indian recruits were Gurkhas from Nepal, along with a few Tibetans. Meanwhile the Indian Army's white British officers came from all corners of imperial Britain – Englishmen, Welshmen, Scotsmen and Irishmen. But they also came from elsewhere around the British Empire. Some were recruited from British India itself, including a number born there, and some came from Ceylon (now Sri Lanka), Australia, Canada and Jamaica. The Indian Army's Asian recruits were called 'Indian', therefore, not so much after where they came from but after the name of the army itself. Indeed, their white officers were often called 'Indian' on the same basis, and talked of their men as 'native' to set them apart.

The Indian Army's exclusively British officer-led units broadly divided into two types: on the one hand fighting (or combatant) units, and on the other hand logistical (or non-combatant). The fighting variety had a total of 1 million Indian soldiers up to 1918, mostly infantrymen spoken of as 'sepoys' and cavalrymen as 'sowars', along with some engineers and artillery gunners; they filled five hundred battalions that divided into thousands of companies, squadrons and batteries. The logistical units had 500,000 men, officially classed as 'followers' or 'labourers', not as soldiers.

Over the course of the First World War, there were twenty Indian infantry and cavalry divisions, the war's standard higher battle unit; at any one time, each division had 12–14,000 soldiers divided between three brigades. However, following pre-war tra-dition, the divisions were 'Indian' in only a limited sense. They were created not simply from the Indian Army and the princely States' Imperial Service Troops, but from the 'Army in India' – the official title of the entire garrison of British India, which included

British Army regiments on rotation from the garrison of the British Isles, designated the Home Army. Accordingly, the Indian divisions were usually 25 per cent British Army.

From 1914, the Army in India produced seven Indian Expeditionary Forces, labelled A to G and containing the majority of the Indian divisions. Their destinations were dictated by the British Cabinet at No. 10 Downing Street, and depended on a fundamental split in the British Empire's war effort. The Indian Army was deployed either for the primary British cause, to defeat Germany as the Central Powers' linchpin, or for the secondary, to defeat the Ottoman Empire, 'Turkey' for short and their sole Islamic member.

'We are unsheathing our sword in a just cause'

The British took the Indian Empire to war in 1914 as Germany and Austria-Hungary, the co-founding Central Power, invaded the free nations of Belgium, France, Serbia and Montenegro, and Poland as partitioned within the Tsarist Russian Empire. 'We are unsheathing our sword in a just cause,' Britain's brandy-loving Prime Minister Herbert Asquith told Parliament on 6 August in his first war speech, 'in defence of principles the maintenance of which is vital to the civilisation of the world.' To the British government, Germany was possessed by a toxic militarism personified by the hawkish Kaiser Wilhelm, emperor of the Second Reich. He had inherited the crown of Germany's leading constituent state, Prussia, whose ruling elite dominated the German government and army. Under them the German people appeared in British minds spellbound by *Kultur*, a national spirit demanding the individual's subservience to the community, and bent on carrying out an aggressive programme of national expansion by military means.

The apparent pitilessness of Prussian militarism was plain to see from August 1914 during the invasion of Belgium where the German Army burned down villages, towns, a university library and even a cathedral, and killed several thousand civilian men, women and children, many of them lined up and shot in town squares. As German troops rampaged into France, killing hundreds more civilians on the road to Paris, at stake in British eyes was civilisation itself on the basis that Europe had been its cradle since the ancient Greeks invented democracy. The ultimate British fear was that any German hegemony imposed on Europe by Prussian militarism would be authoritarian, thereby threatening democracy's status as the high road of human progress, and eclipsing its sacred values of liberalism, freedom and the rule of law. 'Decades before Hitler was even heard of,' George Orwell was to say shortly after the Second World War, 'the word "Prussian" had much the same significance in England as "Nazi" has today.' The British government therefore embarked on the First World War against Germany as a war of survival between ideas of civilisation: militarism versus liberalism, authoritarianism versus democracy – total ideas, justifying total commitment.[*]

All the men of Indian Expeditionary Force A to France went to liberate German-occupied territory in the name of democracy. Some 85,000 Indian soldiers and 50,000 non-combatants served with Force A on the western front. In the wider world the Indian Army served extensively to shut down the German colonial empire, partly as a natural adjunct of the British cause against Prussian militarism in Europe, and partly to secure British colonies. On 6 August 1914 the Cabinet at 10 Downing Street was already cooking up, wrote Asquith, 'with some gusto ... schemes for taking German ports & wireless stations in E & W Africa & the China Seas ... I had to remark we looked more like a gang of

---

[*] In going to war over these total ideas, the British assumed they did so for the benefit of all the peoples of their empire, while remaining rampant imperialists. As colonial rulers of India, they envisaged liberalism and democracy gradually developing there with British control (the so-called Pax Britannica) enduring far beyond the lifetime of any Indian living in 1914.

Elizabethan buccaneers than a meek collection of black-coated Liberal Ministers.' These extra-European anti-German schemes unfurled until the war's end, with some 40,000 Indian soldiers and 12,000 Indian non-combatants taking part, primarily with Indian Expeditionary Forces B and C in tropical Africa.

The greatest Indian numbers overseas, however, were involved in the war against the Ottoman Empire covering most of the Middle East. Approximately 430,000 Indian soldiers and 330,000 non-combatants invaded the region, making the Indian Army by 1918 the single largest Allied force on Ottoman soil. Turkey had been neutral until the end of October 1914, when it picked sides by sending warships over the Black Sea under a German admiral to bombard Tsarist Ukraine. 'The Turkish Empire has committed suicide, and dug with its own hands its grave,' Asquith proclaimed within days, as Russia, Serbia, Britain and France responded with declarations of war. 'It is the Ottoman Government that has drawn the sword, and which, I venture to predict, will perish by the sword. It is they and not we who have rung the death-knell of Ottoman dominion, not only in Europe, but in Asia.'

As Asquith heard that death-knell in early November 1914, he was distracted by the need for British notes of religious caution towards the Ottoman Empire as an Islamic state. At the time the global Muslim population stood at 270 million. Around 100 million Muslims were British subjects, 70 million of them living in the Indian Empire, which made Britain the greatest Muslim power of the day, as the French Empire in North Africa and the Russian in Central Asia had 20 million Muslims each, and the Ottomans 15 million. While most Indian Muslims' head of state was the King-Emperor, they generally revered his Ottoman counterpart, the Sultan of Turkey, as their highest religious leader. The overwhelming majority were Sunnis for whom the Sultan was Caliph, or the Prophet Muhammad's direct successor, in whose stewardship lay Islam's Holy Places including Mecca and Jerusalem. The British were anxious that Indian Muslims could see the war on Turkey as a war on Islam, stirring them into anti-British protest in sympathy with Ottoman co-religionists, and that Arabs under Ottoman rule could be equally alienated when they might otherwise turn on the Turks as Allied rebels. So Asquith was quick to reassure the King-Emperor and the Sultan's Muslim subjects alike. 'Nothing is further from our thoughts or intentions than to initiate or encourage a crusade against their belief,' he announced on 9 November. 'Their holy places we are prepared, if any such need should arise, to defend against all invaders and to maintain inviolate ... We have no quarrel with Mussulman subjects of the Sultan.'

In the earliest days of the war on Turkey, therefore, British sensitivity to Muslim opinion ruled out any large gathering of British Empire forces for an immediate strike on the Ottoman state. Instead the British government ordered only pinpricks on the Ottoman Empire's southern limits, reckoned to be the unavoidable minimum of military action at low risk of offending Muslims worldwide. They were all tasks in November 1914 for the Army in India. Thus Indian Expeditionary Force D of just one Indian brigade headed up the Persian Gulf. Its most obvious job was to guard from Turkish attack the Anglo-Persian Oil Company's refinery at Abadan, vital to the British government as Anglo-Persian's majority shareholder which depended on it to fuel the Royal Navy's warships, and lying on the coast of neutral Iran by the border of Ottoman Iraq (known to the British as Mesopotamia). But Force D's primary purpose was to put Indian and British boots on the ground in Iraq close to Abadan, just enough to give the local Arabs confidence of British support if they rebelled against the Turks.

Meanwhile Indian Expeditionary Forces E and F sailed to secure Egypt, a de facto part of the British Empire. Egypt's north-eastern border was the longest British imperial land frontier with the Ottoman Empire, and its main asset was another British government shareholding: the Suez Canal, the precious sea link between the Indian Ocean and the Mediterranean for Allied troopships and war materials.

From the second week of November 1914, however, the initial caution of the British war on Turkey receded as three pressures turned it into a tornado that over the next four years tore about the Middle East and European Turkey, carrying the Indian Army with it in all directions.

Firstly, the Sultan of Turkey made a dramatic intervention to wield his spiritual authority as Caliph as a force of Allied destruction. At Istanbul on 14 November 1914 he declared a holy war, or jihad, against the Allies, developing the world war into a collision between Christianity and Islam. In a joint effort with the Germans, the Turkish government orchestrated the Sultan's jihad to multiply anti-Allied fighters. It called on all Ottoman Muslims as obedient servants of Allah to defend their Islamic state against the Christian Allied invaders coming from the Persian Gulf and elsewhere, and on all Muslims of the wider world, especially in the British, French and Russian empires and Iran, to join the jihad to punish the Allies for conspiring to annihilate Islam. 'The rank of those who depart to the next world is martyrdom,' the Sultan's chief religious scholar, the Sheikh al-Islam, said of the holy warriors summoned by the official jihad proclamations that spread across Muslim Asia and Africa; 'those who sacrifice their lives to give life to the truth will have honour in this world, and their latter end in paradise.' For the sin of refusing to join the jihad, the Sheikh warned, the inevitable penalties were 'the wrath of God' and 'the fire of hell'. Within days, in the name of the jihad the Turkish Army was plotting attacks with German officers and desert-dwelling jihadists on British Empire troops, oil pipelines and other installations from Egypt to Aden, Iraq and Abadan – all places where Indian troops were targets.

Secondly, following a Russian request in New Year 1915 for new Allied operations to divert the Turkish Army from the Caucasus, the Allies kick-started coalition warfare out of the eastern Mediterranean towards Istanbul. This began in February 1915 with Anglo-French naval attacks launched from island bases in the Aegean Sea, before falling hardest with military landings on the Gallipoli Peninsula dangling from the Ottoman Empire's European fringe – where Indian Expeditionary Force G served.

Thirdly, the British kept bounding forward through the Middle East by following their imperialist noses to the war's end. They seized military opportunities on horizon after horizon from the edges of Egypt, Ottoman Iraq and the Indian Empire, all in British imperial security interests and eventually making Britain the dominant force in the Middle East with control over the Islamic Holy Places. There was no masterplan here; rather it happened almost by accident as the sum of grand strategic decisions taken in bursts to secure and expand the British Empire – broadly speaking, if the war on Germany was for democracy, the war on Turkey was for imperialism.

By November 1918, the British had a stranglehold over the Ottoman Empire resembling the grip of an enchanted giant squid, its master the Prime Minister in London, its main body the Indian Empire, and its two longest tentacles Indian Expeditionary Forces: one being Force D extending from British India 2000 miles up the Persian Gulf into Ottoman Iraq, the other Force E 2500 miles up the Red Sea to Syria.

'Forgotten heroes'?

In the 2014 media coverage of the First World War's centenary, from the *Guardian*, the *New York Times* and *Newsweek* to the BBC and the *Times of India*, Indian servicemen were most often described as 'forgotten heroes'. The underlying idea was that over the years the Indians had somehow slipped through the net of war memory which had tightly held on to Wilfred Owen, Siegfried Sassoon and other usual suspects, but that the Indians had shared the same heroic attributes – courage, determination, sacrifice, with the VCs to prove it – and well-deserved recognition was overdue. However, portraying the Indians as 'forgotten' was something of a deception. Since 1919 a great deal had been written and said about them, with controversies alive and kicking all along. However, portraying the Indians as 'forgotten' was something of a deception. Since 1919 a great deal had been written and said about them, with controversies alive and kicking all along.

From 1919 to the 1930s, the British celebrated the Indian soldiers as loyal heroes under the King-Emperor's banner to save democracy from Prussian militarism, bound in common cause with the British Empire's other troops. The shiny bronze Allied Victory Medal hanging on a rainbow-coloured ribbon handed to Indian veterans could not have been clearer about what they had fought for: 'THE GREAT WAR FOR CIVILISATION 1914–1919' it said on one side, with Nike, the ancient Athenian democrats' goddess of victory, standing tall on the other. Yet the British were wary of openly celebrating in parallel their cause against Turkey. This was taken for granted as supportive of the primary cause against Germany; its more awkward religious and imperialist aspects were left to the side.

In 1927 F. E. Smith, the Secretary of State at London's India Office, the British government department responsible for the Indian Empire, favourably compared the Indian infantry in France to the 300 Spartans at Thermopylae, 'those whose valour was immortal'. Smith had made his name as the legendarily flippant star London lawyer of his generation, but was entirely sincere in avowing that 'while all who fought suffered greatly and wrought nobly, the endurance of the Indians [in France] was specially to be remarked':

> they fought thousands of miles from their homes ... in a quarrel of which their understanding was less than perfect ... The special soldierly virtue of these troops [was] that they met with undefeated eyes the clash of a novel and horrible war,

certainly without the clear, perhaps without the discernible, stimulus of a danger to their own homes, or to their wives and children. Whence then came this spirit of endurance and of high endeavour? It came from the twin sources of an inborn and simple loyalty; of an instructed and very perfect discipline. Like the Roman legionary, they were faithful unto death. They had accepted a duty. They discharged it. More cannot be said: more need not be said.

Indeed, the British often commented that the Indian Muslim troops had been unruffled by the Sultan of Turkey's call to jihad. 'Time and again Muhammadan soldiers of the Indian Army have fought against their co-religionists … and have not exhibited any particular repugnance in so doing,' wrote George Barrow, a pre-war colonel of the 35th Scinde Horse who from 1914 to 1918 commanded Indian cavalry in France, Palestine and Syria:

During the Great War the Muhammadan sowar and sepoy neither showed nor expressed reluctance to shooting a Turk or running him through with a lance. Their conversation led one rather to believe they enjoyed doing these things. The fact is, as borne out by history, Muslim no more minds fighting Muslim than Christian minds fighting Christian.

An alternative view, espoused by some politicians of the Indian National Congress, the leading party of India's independence movement, saw the Indian soldiers as dishonourable mercenaries. In 1919 Mahatma Gandhi found the causes the Indian soldiers had served absolutely despicable. 'The Allies have proved themselves to be just as deceitful, cruel, greedy and selfish as Germany,' he said, while 'the British Empire, today, represents Satanism … repression and terrorism. [It] seems an evil thing [and] the height of tyranny. [For] its own imperial glory it will stoop to any atrocity.' Gandhi felt the war on Turkey had exposed British

democratic credentials as cavernously hollow. He saw little difference between the German conquest of Belgium and the British
conquest of Ottoman Iraq, or German troops who killed Belgian
civilians and Indian troops in Iraq who, he gathered, had 'cut
down inoffensive Turks or Arabs'.

As for Satanism, Gandhi had in mind the Indian Army's
actions in the Indian Empire to assert the colonial regime's
dominance. Most notoriously, in British India on 13 April 1919
in the Jallianwala Bagh, a public square in the Punjabi town of
Amritsar, Indian troops of two Indian regiments that had served
on the western front massacred a peaceful crowd the British
suspected of protesting against colonial rule. Gandhi scolded the
Indian soldiers of 1914 and after for taking up 'the sword of the
hireling', 'doing so merely for money', in the process shunning his
nationalist path of non-violence and peace. 'A loyalty that sells its
soul is worth nothing,' he wrote in disgust.

Other critics, meanwhile, disparaged the Indian soldiers' battlefield performance. The British private Frank Richards, in his
best-selling memoir *Old Soldiers Never Die* (1933), was one of
many British Army voices talking of low Indian fighting value on
the western front. 'Native infantry were no good in France,' he
wrote, 'a few enemy shells exploding round their trenches were
enough to demoralise the majority of them.' Richards averred
that to hold on to their trenches the Indians depended on help
from British troops, who 'the first night they went over found the
natives wailing and weeping ... The bloody niggers were no good
at fighting.' Many British writers of the 1920s and 1930s wrote
in the same vein, albeit in softer words of pity, seeing the Indian
soldier of 1914 as doomed to fare worse on the western front
than his European counterpart because he was unprepared. For
Rudyard Kipling, the Indians sent there were innocents abroad
peeping fearfully out of village India into the wider world for the
first time:

Have you ever thought what they endured on the spiritual side when they voyaged forth over oceans, whose existence they had never conceived, into lands which lay beyond the extremist limits of their imagination – into countries which, for aught they knew, were populated by devils and monsters? Columbus and his men did not confront half the dread possibilities which these men of India prepared themselves to meet.

Several of Kipling's illustrious contemporaries, including his fellow authors Arthur Conan Doyle and John Buchan and the politicians Herbert Asquith and David Lloyd George, had no doubt that the Indians were the unhappiest victims of the western front winter of 1914–15, suffering the sub-zero temperatures, rain and snow more painfully than hardier, naturally acclimatised Europeans. 'The Indians,' detected Conan Doyle, 'were fighting at an enormous disadvantage ... As well turn a tiger loose upon an ice-floe and expect that he will show all his fierceness and activity.' To Conan Doyle the Indian troops were in fact 'children of the sun, dependent on warmth for their vitality and numbed by the cold'. Buchan went further: 'the climate was their chief enemy ... They suffered terribly from the unfamiliar weather, and physical stamina gave way in many.'

Such criticisms developed by the 1990s into a clear-cut theory that the Indian troops on the western front had been military failures. Historians from the United States, Canada and elsewhere argued that the Indian Army had been a weak colonial fire-brigade of a force, ready only to douse meagre flames of local resistance in and around the Indian Empire. The American historian and Vietnam War veteran Jeffrey Greenhut described the pre-war Indian Army as trained for easy border scraps in the independent Pukhtun tribal areas between Afghanistan and British India against 'disorganized, ill-disciplined, and poorly equipped tribesmen'. The upshot, the argument goes, was that the Indian regiments sailed from India in 1914 oblivious of modern tactics as basic as taking cover in trenches. To make matters worse the Indian troops were 'a poor choice to fight a modern war', said Greenhut, digging into their psychology as villagers. He described them as uneducated peasants from a pre-industrial village culture, and therefore intuitively unready for the industrialised modern battlefield of Europe.

Greenhut and others charted an Indian Army collapse in western front battle, referred to as 'a history of failure'. They catalogued a deluge of battlefield breakdowns in 1914–15 by Indian infantrymen stunned by raking German shell fire, with their bewilderment fast leading to refusals to fight as they self-inflicted wounds at rates of up to 65 per cent a week to get on a ship home, or just scarpered from the front line. 'Indian unit after unit broke and fled the horror of the trenches' was the verdict of the American historian Pradeep Barua. 'What destroyed the Indians in France,' declared Greenhut, 'was the most severe imaginable form of culture shock.'

By the early 2000s the view of Indian Expeditionary Force A to France as a failure had become embedded in the narratives of the First World War's leading military historians. John Keegan's *First World War* (1999) summed things up with a series of asides that the Indian Army was 'scarcely suitable' for the western front, its men proving 'the only dissentients' from industrial battle. Indeed Keegan hinted that the Indians may have used knives to carry out war crimes of beheadings and mutilation, airily describing their 'barbaric flurries of slash and stab' in close-quarters trench combat as 'an introduction of tribal military practice into the "civilised" warfare of western armies'.

The perception that Indian troops failed in battle on the western front has often been the cue for gauging the political effect of European service on them. 'Village India saw Europe in its sordid wartime clothes and was not impressed with what it saw,' Percival Spear, a British historian living in India, wrote in 1965. Far from serving the British loyally to save civilisation in Europe, the contention here was that the Indians had been morally appalled by its bloodthirstiness while having their eyes opened by its democratic societies and liberal ideals. It followed that when they returned home, the British were now the enemy.

From this vantage point the pre-war Indian soldier had been a cowed colonial subordinate who had accepted British rule in ignorance of democratic alternatives, but post-war he was politically awakened and in the mood for revolution. For the American historian David J. Silbey in 2006, the post-war period was therefore abuzz with 'sepoy dreams of independence ... The veterans of the war returned to India and demanded something more than to be imperial subjects. In coming years, this would be fertile ground for the recruiting of the newly aggressive Indian National Congress led by Jawaharlal Nehru and Gandhi.' Quite how this squared with Gandhi's vehement rejection of the Indian troops went unsaid.

As for the Indian ranks' own views, they did not share in the western soldier's literary habit of putting down the gun to pick up the pen. Mainly illiterate, up to their last days in the 1980s they wrote no widely published war novels or memoirs such as Erich Maria Remarque, Ernst Jünger and other European veterans did, let alone war histories or plays. Equally there was not a single Indian war poet, in the classic western sense, telling of the trauma of the trenches. There were a few war memoirs by well-educated Indian non-combatants from Calcutta and other cities, but they were predominantly published in private on tiny print runs in Indian languages, and provided geographically limited snapshots from Indian hospitals or labour units in France and Ottoman Iraq. A rare Indian novel, Mulk Raj Anand's *Across the Black Waters*, appeared in 1939, about Hindu infantrymen on the western front in 1914–15; the author himself was a civilian and the son of an Indian Army non-combatant clerk who did not serve overseas.

In 1999, the British historian David Omissi momentously lifted a lid to release a chorus of Indian soldiers' own voices – the box was his *Indian Voices of the Great War*, an unprecedented anthology of hundreds of wartime letters by Indian servicemen and their families drawn from a collection of thousands, left in the London archives of the defunct India Office. The letters were not originals but wartime translations of the originals, which as a rule had been dictated by Indian combatants to scribes and hand-written. The originals had been intercepted in the Indian Army's mail system by a crack team of British censors gathered from Britain and the Indian Empire, who translated them into English before putting them back in the mail.

The letters, however, paint an incomplete picture, and a blurred one at that. They were collected exclusively from the mail of Indian Expeditionary Force A to France, and mostly between 1915 and 1917; the Indian troops on other fronts are represented only by a minority of censored incoming letters to France from British India, Ottoman Iraq, Iran, Somalia and East Africa. More problematic is that the letters come to us distorted and third-hand. The scribes who first wrote down the majority of them as dictations inserted many of their own preferred words or turns of phrase. Then in the British censors' hands some of the original letters' meaning must have been lost in translation, for instance where they guessed the meaning of Indian words they could not make out or did not know.

Furthermore, the Indian soldiers were keenly aware that their letters were being censored, severely restricting what they were prepared to say in them. A number of their letters were blatantly first written in code to hide thoughts, and they often decline to discuss female family members – subjects too personal for British eyes. In addition, the soldiers' letters were generally addressed to parents, wives, brothers, sisters and children at home, naturally leading them to lighten their messages about life on the western front to soothe family fears. For all that the India Office letters are a rich memory bank, then, their accounts can be only of limited value in terms of the global Indian experience.

As the First World War's centenary commemorations unfolded

in 2014, with Hindu, Muslim and Sikh communities around the globe taking part in renewed public interest in the Indian soldiers' story, a tendency emerged to tell it in binary terms of loyalty and disloyalty. By way of illustration, extensive attention was paid in newspapers, books, blogs and on Twitter to the stories of two Muslim brothers who fought with Indian Expeditionary Force A to France. The brothers were among the Indian recruits from outside the Indian Empire: they were Pukhtun of the Afridi tribe whose independent homeland, Tirah, was in the tribal areas between British India and Afghanistan. The older brother was none other than the Mir Dast who attended the Delhi Durbar in 1911 and won the Victoria Cross, for bravery under poison gas attack in Belgium in 1915. While convalescing that August from his wounds at the Brighton Pavilion – the former royal residence on the English south coast, converted into a wartime Indian Army hospital with its supposedly comforting Indo-Saracenic architecture – he received his medal at a special ceremony in the Pavilion gardens. 'By the great, great, great kindness of God, the King with his royal hand has given me the decoration of the Victoria Cross,' Mir Dast wrote in one of his much-quoted letters, preserved in the India Office collection, to regimental comrades in British India. 'The desire of my heart is accomplished ... Show great zeal in your duty, and be faithful.' The story went that shortly afterwards he returned to India as a loyal war hero, before being invalided out of the Indian Army in 1917. In Britain during the centenary Mir Dast was lionised as a Muslim hero. He was personally honoured in the national tradition by a blue plaque at the Brighton Pavilion, unveiled in 2016 for the Pavilion's 325,000 visitors a year to see.

Mir Dast VC's younger brother was portrayed quite differently. 'Mir Dast's fame and honour stand in stark contrast to the infamy and disgrace attained by his brother,' stated the Brighton Pavilion's official blog for Mir Dast's plaque. The brother's name was Mir Mast. According to British tradition, his story was a tale of pure disloyalty. Mir Mast had apparently deserted to the Germans in March 1915, switched into German service, been awarded the German Iron Cross for bravery – in some accounts by Kaiser Wilhelm himself – and then joined a Central Powers secret mission to Afghanistan to recruit Muslims to attack the British in the name of the Sultan of Turkey's jihad. His notebook from France was widely publicised during the centenary after it was found in India's national archives at Delhi, left behind by the British who had impounded it from his deserted trench. It begins with lists of basic vocabulary in two languages – one illegible, the other in English with neatly copied but occasionally misspelt words, such as 'testacles' and 'brests' – indicating a man trying to educate himself. Tantalisingly, there the notebook ends, so there are no personal thoughts on why he might have deserted or what he knew of the jihad. And there are no India Office letters from Mir Mast, so his story only went so far – typical, it seemed, of the generally illiterate million or so Indian servicemen who served overseas.

Rather than beams of loyalty or disloyalty, however, this book shines a more filtered light on the Indian soldiers, so that even the brothers Mir Dast and Mir Mast do not necessarily stand on opposite sides of a loyalty line. For Mir Mast was not the only deserter in his family: his VC brother also deserted. As one of this book's hitherto untold personal stories, the double family desertion is only surprising if Mir Dast is seen as a loyal hero. The real man behind the plaque was not so simple. Like his brother, he was first and foremost an Afridi with a highly individualistic tribal identity that shaped his worldview.

'Play fool, to catch wise'

In their regiments every Indian soldier had to cope daily with the painful disadvantages of being a colonial subject. In a world dominated by white men – where a seat in a railway carriage or a ship saloon could be off limits depending on the colour of your skin – they had to negotiate their subordinate position as best they could. In the presence of the British they were in a similar position to the British Empire's Jamaican slaves who said 'play fool, to catch wise' of their struggle to get by under their slave-owners, to whom speaking their minds could mean a flogging or worse. Or to African Americans of the Segregation Era, who when face to face with white privilege were described by the civil rights activist W. E. B. Du Bois as 'daily tempted to be silent and wary, politic and sly'; 'the young Negro of the South who would succeed . . . must flatter and be pleasant, endure petty insults with a smile, shut his eyes to wrong; in too many cases he sees positive personal advantage in deception and lying. His real thoughts, his real aspirations, must be guarded in whispers; he must not criticize, he must not complain.'

In searching for the Indian soldier's personal reality at war as a colonial subject, this book looks at the more familiar battlefields but also beyond them. The Indians' experiences in France have always received the most attention; their time in the forty-nine or so other countries in which they served needs to come into the picture more. Militarily, this book shows the Indian Army in a state of perpetual evolution, a phenomenon involving British, Indian and Allied politicians, General Staffs, British officers, recruitment drives, logistics, shipping and supply, all of which cannot be underestimated in how powerfully or directly they shaped the Indian troops' personal fates across all fronts. They determined when an Indian recruit joined the army and where he went, and they made the difference between life and death once he got there, depending on the quality of leadership, weapons, food and medical care. This makes the Indians' war story not just one of what they could see for themselves in front of them, but also one of policy, grand strategy and supreme command above their heads – right up to 10 Downing Street where their fates were ultimately controlled.

Politically, the fact that Indian troops looked down their rifle barrels and pulled their triggers over a thousand times at the Amritsar massacre of 1919 shows that their fighting to win the war ostensibly for democracy did not mean that afterwards they were suddenly its champions and lost to the British imperialists: at Amritsar they shot who the British told them to. Equally, the subsequent Indian nationalist disdain for the imperial Indian soldiers as mercenaries suggests that if they did back the nationalist cause in the 1920s and 1930s, they might have done so in a way that left a margin for the British to believe in them as loyal heroes of the empire. The great political riddle of the Indian soldiers of 1914–18 is whether they returned home from overseas minded to align themselves with either imperialism or nationalism, or both – perhaps wrestling with inner turmoil about their relationship with the British.

Socially and culturally, this book seeks to portray Indian soldiers as individuals of particular tribes, clans, faiths, castes and widely spread regions, rather than just generally as 'Indians' – something they would not necessarily have seen themselves as, given the primacy of their local identities. The Afridi brothers Mir Dast and Mir Mast and the other recruits of the independent Pukhtun tribal areas are an obvious case in point. Apart from the brothers, almost nothing was heard of the independent Pukhtun during the First World War's centenary commemorations compared to Punjabi and Sikh recruits. This was partly because in recent years their ancestral homes on the fringe of Pakistan have not been open for outsiders to visit and politely ask after them, Waziristan and their adjacent homelands having been among the most dangerous places in the world following the 11 September 2001 terrorist attacks on the United States. But the stories of the tribal areas' recruits, as much as those of the recruits from Afghanistan and elsewhere outside British India, need to be told alongside those of the Punjabis and Sikhs in order to understand how the war meant different things for Indian soldiers from different places. Not least, of course, for Muslims, whose feelings about the Sultan of Turkey's jihad naturally contrasted with Hindu or Sikh responses.

Beyond the thematic furniture, what sources does this book draw on to tell the Indian story anew? There are the India Office archive letters, of which many but by no means all have already been published. There are also some recently published Indian soldier diaries, especially those of the Hindu officer Thakur Amar Singh who attended the Delhi Durbar. His kept his diaries for forty-four years in eighty-nine hand-written volumes. They amount to possibly the longest continuous personal diary ever written, and cover 1914–18. He was from one of the princely States of the Indian Empire, Jaipur State in the north-western region of Rajputana, and was a well-educated rural nobleman whose home was the family estate; he lived there with his wife, Rasal, his parents, five brothers and one sister. His military education started at the age of ten, when he was sent away by his father to the neighbouring princely State of Jodhpur in Rajputana for tutelage under the most famous Indian soldier of the day – the Hindu prince and flamboyant socialite Sir Pratap Singh, well known to *Vanity Fair* and other western social bibles, and the strict commandant of the Jodhpur Lancers, widely regarded as the elite of all the princely States' Imperial Service Troops. Under Sir Pratap, Amar Singh joined the Jodhpur Lancers and became both multi-lingual and widely read, devouring classics by writers from Plato to Omar Khayyam and Victor Hugo. Having switched to the Indian Army by 1914, Amar Singh served with Indian Expeditionary Forces A to France and D to Ottoman Iraq and then in British India, often writing his reflections in his diary in the heat of the moment.

Needless to say, Amar Singh's privileged polymath perspective was far removed from the illiterate Indian servicemen's, but in three respects his diary is a crucial piece in the Indian Army puzzle. Firstly, like all the Indian troops he was still a colonial subject, so his views on being in that position can reflect how Indian troops in general may have felt. Secondly, his breadth of education allowed him to analyse Indians' common lot as colonial subjects in ways the illiterate majority could not, making his diary in places more revealing about the imperial world than the India Office letters. And thirdly, by 1918 he had risen to become the most senior Indian soldier in any Indian Army regiment, giving him a unique bird's-eye view of how the British treated the Indian ranks.

But above all, this book draws from overlooked interviews and conversations with Indian servicemen of 1914–18 written down by people they spoke with. Possibly the most significant of these interviews are the transcripts of an Indo-American interviewing team that in the 1970s and early 1980s travelled the countryside of northern India and southern Pakistan asking the last of the veterans for their thoughts with the wisdom of age on the world war of their youth. In Punjab they called it the *laam* or 'long war'. They talked of many things – such as what serving the British, life at the fronts and nationalist politics meant to them – and their children chipped in with their own thoughts on the war's impact on their fathers.

As for the other interviews and conversations with the Indians, they are mined from archives in Britain, Germany and India having been written down by soldiers and civilians of several nationalities. They come, for example, from British officers' private notes of Indian chatter, chiding and teasing in the trenches from France to East Africa; from reports of British India's domestic intelligence agency, the Department of Criminal Investigation, which spied on Indian troops; and from intelligence reports of the British Indian diplomatic corps whose agents in the independent Pukhtun tribal areas learned of the Afridi deserter Mir Mast's return overland from Germany in 1916, and overheard what he told his fellow tribesmen. Then there are US State Department reports on Indian prisoners of war in Germany and Turkey, and snippets of Indian soldiers' conversations preserved in wartime newspapers and post-war books, above all British and German memoirs. In addition, there is the investigative research of Indian and Pakistani journalists who for the 2014 centenary traced the families of Indian veterans of 1914–18 and listened to their war stories and songs of the home front, preserved by word of mouth down the generations.*

This book, therefore, is something of a detective history based on a wide range of fragmentary evidence. To start its story, it is essential to go back to the eve of the First World War to get the measure of the pre-war Indian Army. For this alone provided the Indian troops that served at the war's fronts into mid-1915 before the first wartime Indian recruits became available for overseas, and its officers and men formed the nucleus of the victorious Indian Army of 1918.

Too often the pre-war Indian Army has been assumed to be inferior to European armies, its men politically naïve and disconnected from the world beyond their villages. But such assumptions are fundamental miscalculations. When Indian Expeditionary Force A arrived in France in September 1914, one of its British officers who was an old hand with Indian troops posted a revealing remark to his wife: 'those who do not know them comment on their not evincing wonder at their novel surroundings'. The Frenchmen he had encountered since the Indians' arrival, he went on, imagined them to be strangers to foreign climes, yet the Indian soldier from pre-war experience was already, as the British officer put it, 'a man of the world'. The Indian soldiers were in fact seasoned professionals and cold-blooded killers, more travelled, politically aware and militarily skilled than they have been given credit for.

---

* From at least the 1970s, museums and archives across the UK carefully collected personal written and sound records or objects of the First World War, in particular documenting British soldiers' experiences. But there were not equivalent nationwide initiatives in India, Pakistan, Bangladesh or Nepal to preserve personal records of their servicemen of 1914–18. This likely left a considerable quantity of unknown First World War memories and material, including written reminiscences by a minority Indian Army veterans who could read and write, in homes across South Asia – despite the loss of much material during the upheavals of India's Partition in 1947.

One

THE ROAD
TO WORLD WAR

1

'THE PEASANT'S UNIVERSITY'

The men of the pre-First World War Indian Army were a tiny proportion of the Indian Empire's population, just 0.07 per cent of 310 million. In July 1914 there were 217,000 volunteer Indian servicemen. Around 150,000 of them were active professional soldiers, 35,000 reservist soldiers and 32,000 non-combatants; altogether roughly two fifths were Muslims, nearly as many were Hindus, and a fifth were Sikhs. They were not remotely representative of India's population as a whole. The combatant majority were members of an exclusive list of rural peasant farming communities to whom alone the British opened military service. These were the 'martial races', a mix of tribes, clans and castes mostly dotted about British India's northern provinces – in the plains and hills of Punjab, the valleys of the North-West Frontier Province, and the southern slopes of the Himalayas in the United Provinces of Agra and Oudh – or beyond British Indian borders in the independent Pukhtun tribal areas or in Nepal. The British selected them in the pseudo-scientific delusion that their offspring were genetically fitter for fighting than India's more numerous 'non-martial races'. As George MacMunn, the pre-eminent British buff on the subject, explained: 'In India we speak of the martial races as a thing apart because the mass of the people have neither martial aptitude nor physical courage, the courage that we should talk of colloquially as "guts".'

A dearth of sources on individual Indian soldiers' pre-war lives makes it difficult to fathom their personal motivations. But by generally following their journeys from their villages to the Indian Army between the 1890s and 1913, using snapshots from veteran interviews and also the viewpoints of British officers, it becomes clear that illiterate men of the martial races willingly joined up for a professional career with distinct benefits. The Indian Army for them was more than just an employer: it doubled as an educational institution that taught them many things, not least on overseas assignments prior to 1914. One British civil servant, as an administrator of numerous Punjabi martial race villages, judiciously summed it up with his nickname for the Indian Army: 'the peasant's university'.

From village to 'university'

If you walked into the pre-1914 village of an Indian soldier, you would see no obvious signs of the modernity of the day. In the Punjabi countryside the villages consisted mainly of small mud-plastered single-storey houses, windowless with low, flat roofs over a single room. In the Himalayas, the Garhwalis and Gurkhas had larger houses with upper storeys and balconies, often whitewashed all around, with thatched gable roofs. The soldiers' villages in general ran on old technology, with no paved roads but dusty mud or sand tracks along which unsprung bullock carts moved as slowly as they had for centuries, along with potter's wheels, leather buckets and the traditional toothbrush, the neem tree twig. Equally ancient was the use of honking geese as burglar alarms. In the absence of electricity, clocks or wristwatches, the time of day was commonly told in daylight by the length of shadows cast by houses or even by hairs on the back of the hand held up to the sun. Village sanitation was basic at best, with no plumbing, lavatories or pipes to bring in clean water.

Young villagers ordinarily did not venture far from their birth-places. The furthest most went was to a shrine or temple in their own district or province, or to religious festivals and markets in provincial towns. The wider Indian Empire, let alone the sea and the world beyond, was commonly a mystery to them. Meanwhile their villages were rarely visited by foreigners, in Punjab perhaps only by a British civil servant touring on horseback or a doctor offering a vaccination programme. There were no such visitors in the independent Pukhtun tribal areas, where outsiders were customarily forbidden, or in Nepal, which was officially closed to foreigners.

The foundation of village families' livelihoods as small farmers was their land. The fields surrounding a village were typically divided into smallholdings belonging to its families either outright or as tenants of rich regional landowners. The main crops were wheat and barley, farmed using wooden ploughs pulled by nimble bullocks. The villagers relied on farming so much because illiter-acy was widespread. In Punjab in 1901, for example, there were almost no village schools and 97 per cent of Punjabis could nei-ther read nor write. This lack of education perpetuated numerous customs and superstitions. For instance, to cure epidemic diseases including bubonic plague, malaria and smallpox that periodically ravaged the countryside, Punjabi villagers bought magic charms peddled by medicine men – there were potions for pouring on the ground in a circle around a patient's house, and concoctions of saliva sprinkled with pearl shavings. In the Gurkha valleys of Nepal, priests sacrificed birds in search of divine deliverance from disease.

Epidemic diseases and scarcity of modern medicine were just some of the many challenges of rural life. The villagers' land yielded low incomes because it was relatively unproductive: wheat yield per acre in 1911 averaged one third of Britain's and was ten times lower than the prairies of the American Midwest.

Any crop surplus they might have to sell could have a heartbreakingly low value depending on fluctuating prices on India's grain markets. The annual monsoon rains could be a blessing for the soil but a curse if they disintegrated the less robust mud houses, or if they flooded a whole village. Then again, poor rains led to drought and famine. To help tide over times of hardship, or to pay for important family events such as weddings with feasts and fireworks, villagers habitually turned to local moneylenders. Yet the rates of interest were often extravagant, plunging them deep into debt.

To cope with these kinds of challenge, village families tended to have many children and stick together – the family culture was for children to grow up feeling a total commitment to working and earning to guarantee the family's survival, rather than any free licence to put themselves first and choose a more individual path in life. 'My father and mother,' a wry Sikh said to them, 'you call those your sons and daughters who give you money. Those who do not, you refuse to look upon'.

A major problem for village families was supplementing their land income. They generally tried by looking beyond the village for money-making opportunities. Some of these were grasped locally; for instance Hindus in the eastern Punjab's Kangra Hills used nets to catch rare hawks for sale. Villagers also ventured further afield, emigrating to find agricultural, construction or police work anywhere from Australia and Singapore to the United States and Canada. Another option, of course, was soldiering in the Indian Army, which pre-1914 had 169 regiments, three quarters of them infantry with 750 men per battalion. Every year between 1900 and 1913, approximately 15,000 new recruits in their late teens came from the villages. They enlisted direct with a regiment at its depot in British India, usually placed in a town near its allocated martial race catchment areas, and they routinely signed on with a thumbprint because they could not write their name.

Villagers colloquially referred to military service as 'eating the Sirkar's salt', their way of referring to the military wage – 'Sirkar' was a word for the British as the governing authority, and salt signified money. Army pay by no means made a recruit a rich man, but it was a crucial part of his family's income. For an infantry private in 1914, the base rate of salt was 11 rupees a month, although there was a regulation that out of this each man had to make a small contribution towards the cost of his uniform and rations. A cavalry trooper could earn 34 rupees a month through paying a cash bond of around 250 rupees, known as an *assami*, which made him a shareholder in a regimental investment fund that paid for his equipment including his horse, either Indian-bred at the regimental stud or imported from Australia. For all Indian recruits there was a range of pay bonuses, such as for going on active service.

Long service was incentivised for all recruits by standard offers not only of a pension inheritable by family dependents, but also of a grant of up to 50 acres of canal-irrigated land next to retirement villages or 'canal colonies' veterans could move to in Punjab or the United Provinces of Agra and Oudh, the grant invaluably being protected by a British law prohibiting the transfer of grantee land to debt collectors. The carrot of irrigated land loomed especially large for recruits from areas of poor soil such as northern Punjab's hilly Salt Range, where agricultural productivity was hindered by heavy rock salt deposits. For a cavalryman retiring after long service who had bought a share in his regiment's investment fund, meanwhile, there was the added benefit of cashing it in for hundreds of rupees, depending on how much the fund had accrued in value.

When Indian recruits who had joined up before 1914 were asked in later life why they had volunteered for the Indian Army, they frequently said that the primary reason was *bhuk* – Punjabi for 'hunger', a way of saying 'money'. This was recognised across their communities, from Sikhs who enlisted looking for a pension to help them emigrate to the United States or Canada, to Gurkhas who in their poverty-stricken Nepalese valleys were traditionally known as *lāhures*. The moniker *lāhure* identified Gurkhas as migrant workers who since the nineteenth century had gone abroad, initially to the Punjabi city of Lahore, to enter foreign military service for a regular wage with which to feed their families and pay off their mortgages. The pay of the Indian Army's 35,500 Gurkha recruits between 1894 and 1913 was in fact Nepal's single largest source of foreign currency.

The secondary reason Indian recruits gave for joining up in the years before 1914 was *shauq*, meaning a keenness or zeal for soldiering. This was particularly significant for Hindus, Muslims and Sikhs from British India's provinces who had family or community traditions of military service, making it preferable to lowlier civilian labouring work, and simultaneously compatible with their *izzat* – a concept of honour or reputation that was absolutely fundamental to villagers' sensibilities of pride and shame, whether personally, for their family or their local community. 'To us there is a great hatred of coolie work,' said one Hindu Jat recruit of Punjab. 'Those who do that are not Jats.'* Most famously the Sikhs took pride in their reputation for military prowess going back to the pre-British years of the late 1700s and early 1800s when Sikh armies conquered much of northern India. 'We Sikhs are warriors by profession, so I decided to join the army to maintain the tradition,' recalled one Sikh veteran, Narain Singh, in old age of his decision to enlist in 1910. Similarly, there were Hindu Rajputs of the warrior caste known as Kshatriyas whose dharma (their righteous path through the universe) involved bearing arms, standing more physical hardship than other castes, and overpowering enemies. 'Every boy dreamt of being in the army,' said Mohan Nikam, the grandson of an Indian soldier of 1914 with Hindu Rajput

---

* 'Coolie', the derogatory term meaning unskilled labourer.

heritage, of his village in what is now India's western state of Maharashtra.

Certain Hindu, Muslim or Sikh village communities tended to provide recruits for particular Indian regiments, so that companies could be filled with fathers, sons, brothers, uncles and cousins serving together, or at least with local men of the same faith. This was another vital attraction of soldiering: the regiment was a home from home. The regimental British officers did much to make the regiment a comfortable professional environment where village religious or community customs were respected. They doggedly studied their men's languages, faiths and social ways, becoming quasi-anthropologists in order to ensure that the regimental kitchen turned out curries, dairy foods and other staples in keeping with company religious requirements; that daily prayers and annual holy festivals were accommodated in the regimental calendar; and that recruits were free to wear their hair as they liked according to their own community traditions, for example the Sikhs' waist-length uncut locks tied up under the turban, or the Waziristani style of curls about the shoulders. They also strove to make military service consistent with tending to village matters, allowing men generous home leave.

These things added up to the British officers' leadership ethos of 'kindly' (as they saw it) care. They did not just learn about their men, but could take a real personal interest. 'I think with me and with most of us the feeling was especially in the Indian Army that you were responsible for these chaps, these men under you, and that you had to see they got the best that could be given them,' said Claude Auchinleck, who joined the 62nd Punjabis in 1904. 'There was always that feeling that you belonged and that they belonged to you ... In the Indian Army you'd go to the home of your private soldier, not in uniform, and his father would greet you and give you a meal, and you'd talk to the boy as if you were a friend of his.' The Indian recruits certainly recognised the British officers' care as a benefit of military service.

'They had good relations with their men, and looked after them,' said a Sikh veteran, Suran Singh.

'I joined the army to learn more outside [the village] and see more things', added Suran Singh, touching on another benefit the British officers oversaw: the Indian recruits' basic army education. Its foundations were self-discipline, thinking ahead and time-keeping, instilled by rigid routines comprising drills, parades, route marches and kit inspections, an emphasis on hygiene, and bans on gambling and intoxicating drugs available in villages, such as homebrews loaded with *bhang* (a derivative of cannabis). At regimental schoolhouses recruits could enrol for primary education in their own languages and English, which one British officer of the Gurkhas, Eden Vansittart, gathered was of special interest among his men. 'It may seem strange but it is an undoubted fact that a number of recruits are yearly obtained who profess to enlist entirely for the sake of learning to read, write, and keep accounts,' he wrote. Many Gurkhas brought their wives from Nepal to live with their regiments in British India, and sent their sons to the schoolhouses. There were also music lessons to teach men to play in regimental bands with instruments ranging from Punjabi drums, wooden reed-pipes and sitars to brass trumpets, trombones, oboes, tubas and Scottish Highland bagpipes. Regimental sports coaching initiated men in European games, anything from soccer, cricket and hockey to rugby, fencing and athletics – swimming and roller-skating, too – all to bring on their physical fitness and feel for teamwork.

More importantly as professional soldiers, the Indian recruits became steeped in military knowledge. Their standard-issue weapons introduced them to factory-made technology: modern magazine rifles firing smokeless ammunition accurate up to a mile, Maxim machine guns firing 600 bullets a minute, and mountain artillery whose smokeless shells were accurate up to three miles. Marksmanship and individual fire were meticulously taught, with lessons in velocities, trajectories and range-finding.

The Indian recruits of the engineer regiments had the most varied technical education. The engineers of the Sappers and Miners learned about mathematics, electricity, explosive devices including land mines, reconnaissance balloons using processed gases, and telegraph and wireless signals systems. Others of the Pioneer regiments learned the arts of construction – for roads, railways, dams and docks – becoming skilled at manipulating rock, metal and wood with their specialist tools from dynamite to axes.

The highest plane of the Indian recruits' military knowledge, however, was their training in battlefield tactics. In the twenty years before 1914 Indian regiments were trained using not only the same manuals as the British Army, which increasingly focused on methods of European battle with the Germans as the enemy, but also their own mountain warfare manuals on how to fight the Russians, Afghans and independent Pukhtun tribes in the Indian Empire's Afghan and Iranian borderlands. The upshot was a varied annual diet of modern tactical training featuring common infantry themes such as digging trenches for protection from enemy fire, attacking by day or night in rushes of small, fast, flexible skirmishing groups of riflemen supported by artillery, and setting up machine gun posts. Some Indian cavalry regiments trained to fight dismounted against a European enemy whose firepower would limit mounted action, and learned how to cooperate with reconnaissance bi-planes.

Many Indian regiments had ambitious young British officers, obsessed with keeping their men schooled in the latest tactics. In the 5th Gurkhas, for example, William Villiers-Stuart was a dedicated moderniser whose scientific approach to training for his Gurkha company involved lectures using 144 graphic photographs of modern warfare from the Russo-Japanese War of 1904–5 – 'wonderful photos', he remembered grimly, 'in which actual battlefields, effects of bombardments, misery of wounded, and the dreadful state of the dead, were shown one at a time'.

Another of the 5th Gurkhas' young officers, Charles Bruce, a

Welshman, specialised in training his men in a different direction. Bruce was a boisterous man-child known for his bear-like stature, love of Punjabi-style wrestling – not as a spectator, but a contestant in a pit – and tendency to seduce the Nepalese wives of the regiment. His less light-hearted peers, like Villiers-Stuart, winced at Bruce's almost daily pranks, whether shaking hands with newcomers over the regimental dinner table only to yank them clean across it, or marching in reverse without warning to plough through the neat Gurkha ranks behind him.

But Bruce was deadly earnest when it came to mountain warfare training, in which he was one of the Indian Army's leading innovators. He helped to establish the Indian infantry's elite mountain troops known as 'Scouts', men he individually trained to make their own decisions as camouflaged snipers who could also move fast to reconnoitre over the most difficult ground. To teach such movement he invented a sport called *khud* racing, a cross-country endurance challenge on foot, run on courses zig-zagging up and down almost vertical hillsides. Bruce's Gurkha team usually won the great annual *khud* race, open to all the Army in India, because of their lower centre of gravity compared to troops from British India or Britain, helping them twist and turn better at pace. 'To see, from a distance, a batch of trained Gurkhas in a *khud* race coming down a really difficult bit can best be described as reminding one exactly of raindrops falling down a window-pane,' said Nigel Woodyatt, an admiring British officer of the 7th Gurkhas.

If an Indian recruit had not previously been on a British Indian steam-train, he would as a soldier. India had the world's fourth largest railway network, and the regiments used it constantly for regular postings about the Indian Empire, which inevitably took them into unknown lands. In the early 1900s the 40th Pathans (an Indian transliteration of Pukhtun, and pronounced Pat'haan) travelled 750 miles south-west of the independent Pukhtun tribal areas to the city of Jhansi in the United Provinces of Agra and

Oudh. This was farther than the 40th's Pukhtun recruits had ever travelled. On arriving at Jhansi railway station in the pouring rain they bumped into the 66th Punjabis whose recruits from British India's southern province of Madras were the first men they had seen from there, while the Pukhtun were the first men those from Madras had seen from the far north-west. 'It was a case of North meeting South, and Pathan and Madrassi eyed one another with the greatest curiosity,' remembered one of the 40th Pathans' British officers, Robert Waters. Next he heard loud Pukhtun laughter echoing through Jhansi station – the Pukhtun had seen elephants for the first time. Days later at Jhansi, the Pukhtun were enthralled by their first cinema visit. They suspiciously narrowed their eyes at moving people on screen in a film of Queen Victoria's 1901 funeral procession who seemed to appear from nowhere at the back of the screen before disappearing into thin air at the front. 'Certain sceptics among the men proceeded stealthily to circumvent the screen and then rushed back to see what had become of the marching columns,' Waters recalled.

The pre-war Indian recruits' education through the army, however, extended far beyond regimental training and sights within the Indian Empire – between 1900 and 1913 approximately 75,000 Indian servicemen travelled overseas too.

'The Great Wall was our daily view'

On joining his regiment, each Indian recruit swore an oath that he would serve the King-Emperor anywhere in the world. There was a real expectation that foreign service would materialise because the Indian Army had often served overseas from the 1700s to the late 1880s, initially in the Philippines then in Singapore, Ethiopia, Sudan, Egypt, Cyprus and Malta. But the Indian soldiers of 1914 were the most widely travelled generation yet, the older men across dozens of regiments having journeyed far and wide since the 1890s on trips as mountaineers, explorers, intelligence

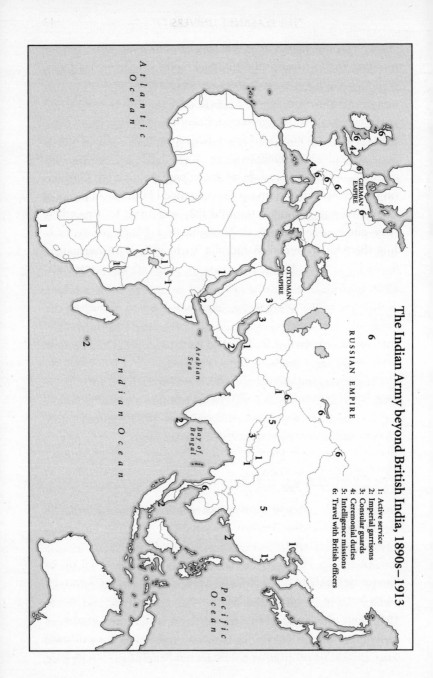

The Indian Army beyond British India, 1890s–1913

1: Active service
2: Imperial garrisons
3: Consular guards
4: Ceremonial duties
5: Intelligence missions
6: Travel with British officers

gatherers, bodyguards or archaeologists, alongside more routine missions to help secure the Indian Empire's outlying sea lanes, trade routes and telegraph communications.

The rambunctious Scout mastermind Charles Bruce of the 5th Gurkhas was behind the mountaineering trips. He shared his passion for this European sport with a number of his Gurkha Scouts who volunteered to learn Alpine-style snow- and ice-climbing with picks, crampons and ropes. He took the Gurkhas on dangerous expeditions up the unmapped Himalayan peaks of Nanga Parbat, Mount Trisul and K2, and on to Europe where they climbed mountains in Scotland and Wales before tackling the Alps from end to end, via Turin in Italy to Zermatt in Switzerland and Munich in Germany. 'When I heard that I was to travel with two Indians, I did not know what to expect,' said Jean Baptiste Aymonod, a Swiss guide handed two Gurkhas on an Alpine excursion. 'I feared they would be savages. But these men are charming to travel with, they are so friendly and intelligent.' Aymonod's Gurkhas were noticeably inquisitive about his home and family, and the Gurkha mountaineers in general were thoughtful about the Alpine sights. 'Here the grass climbs all the hills,' the Gurkha Amar Thapa said of Switzerland. 'It is not thus in our country. There the valleys are flat and green below, between walls of barren mountains.' As unusual Asian visitors, the Gurkhas attracted crowds of intrigued Italians and other European locals, at one village beneath Mont Blanc drawing out the whole population who gathered at the door of their inn, flattening their noses against the windows to catch glimpses of the men from Nepal.

Occasionally Bruce's Gurkha mountaineers wandered off by themselves. One of them, Parbir Thapa, took to the snowy streets of Zermatt in boredom on a December evening and began throwing snowballs at passers-by who were not nearly as amused as he was. 'The Zermatters in the winter by the evening are usually fairly pleased with things in general; the row penetrated into the hotel,' wrote Bruce. 'My friends and I ran out, and, seeing what had happened, joined in. We had a first-rate hour.' The same Gurkha disappeared from Bruce's rural home in Wales only to turn up three days later in the nearby mining town of Tonypandy, having befriended a local family of miners and stayed with them. Some of the other Gurkha mountaineers struck out into Germany alone when they got lost on the Bavarian rail network, catching the wrong train into the Rhineland.

Bruce's mountaineers were by no means the only Indian recruits who travelled in Europe. In 1909–10 a small party of the 39th Garhwals passed through Poland, Germany and the Netherlands on the final stretch of a 4000-mile overland journey of exploration, having set off from Kashmir into Central Asia's Altai Mountains, Mongolia, Siberia and European Russia, going by foot, horse, sled and Trans-Siberian rail. For this party's Garhwali Giyan Singh, the sights culminating in the Dutch port of Flushing on the North Sea and the final stop in London were 'a revelation', according to his British officer, Percy Etherton. 'He had never set eyes upon the sea, whilst the area of vast London, the wonders of tube railways, the ceaseless stream of people encountered in the streets, and numerous other astounding sights left upon him a profound and lasting impression.'

Around 2000 Indian troops visited London between 1897 and 1913 on official royal ceremonial duties. A few of the 4th and 5th Gurkhas travelled there with Maharajah Chandra Shum Shere Rana of Nepal in 1908, on a four-month trip from Kathmandu via Marseilles as they guarded his jewel boxes on the railway the length of France and at his private residence in Belgravia. But the majority came for Edward VII's coronation in 1902 and George V's in 1911. The India Office arranged their stays, keeping them entertained with tours of the London Underground, Whitehall, Westminster Abbey, Trafalgar Square and St Paul's Cathedral, and with outings to West End musicals, Windsor Castle, Ascot, rural agricultural shows and the Royal Navy dockyards at

Portsmouth and Southampton. They camped outside London by the River Thames at Hampton Court, where fascinated crowds flocked to see them, at times with unrestrained excitement, trampling into their tents.

In Asia, meanwhile, Indian soldiers travelled in countries bordering the Indian Empire. Some Gurkha and Pukhtun recruits went as bodyguards for their British officers travelling on leave, heading into the mountains of Afghanistan for instance, or through the jungles of Siam (Thailand) to Bangkok. Several Sikhs of the Sappers and Miners volunteered to join British Museum archaeological expeditions into the deserts of north-west China led by the world-famous archaeologist Aurel Stein in search of lost cities and Graeco-Buddhist relics. The Sikh troops worked as Stein's technical assistants for months at a time, gently scraping and blowing sand from the floors of trenches to uncover the city of Niya on the old Silk Road, photographing ancient sculptures and developing the negatives in improvised dark-rooms, or dexterously chiselling frescoes of Buddha off mud-plaster walls before storing them in padded packing cases they made out of dead-tree wood, tin and cotton wool. 'Again and again he expressed doubt whether his fellow-villagers far away in Punjab would believe him when he returned and told his tale,' Stein said of Ram Singh, one of his Sikh Sapper helpers.

Also in China, some Gurkhas travelled deep into the interior in disguise with their British officers on official intelligence gathering missions; one group sailed the entire length of the Yangtze River. But by far the largest group of Indian servicemen in China, some 33,000, travelled to Beijing, Shanghai and elsewhere in the east of the country in 1900–02. They went for the international intervention by a coalition force of the United States, German, French, Japanese and other major armies to suppress the Boxer Rising, the popular peasant movement that attacked foreign legations and business interests, shooting white diplomats and ripping up European-owned railway lines.

The Indian expedition to China for the Boxer Rising exemplified two significant features of pre-1914 overseas service for Indian recruits. The first was that the Army in India was the world's most experienced at shipping military expeditions. By tradition this was a British imperial speciality, involving troopships of the British merchant marine fitted out by the Sappers and Miners at the Indian Empire's great ports of Bombay, Karachi, Calcutta, Madras and Rangoon; the Royal Navy as the world's premier fleet, with command of the deep sea lanes and unrivalled experience of embarking and disembarking troops, supported by the Indian Empire's own navy, the Royal Indian Marine; and the Indian Army's British officer ethos of care, which helped to maintain, even enhance abroad the benefits of military service in British India to compensate for the absence from home.

Thus when Indian troops were sent from British India to east China in 1900 for the Boxer Rising they were taken away by sea with a confident British efficiency that ensured smooth, safe and sanitary travel. In China itself, the Indians garrisoned much of the eastern seaboard up to 1902 as part of the international coalition force of occupation while a diplomatic settlement was reached to compensate the foreign powers for Boxer damage to their interests. During the occupation the Indians were well cared for by the British. Specifically, their pay was boosted by a special allowance for active service, plus three months' pay in advance before departure from British India, and an extra two months' pay as a gratuity while in China. Their food continued to be served in keeping with their religions, but with a greater quantity and variety of meat, dairy products, vegetables and fruit. They could also, with help from scribes serving as non-combatants, exchange letters with their families through Indian field post offices which sold their own stationery and stamps at cheap army rates, and were linked to British India by regular mail ships.

As for their clothes, the Indians needed extra layers in abundance to cope with the severe Chinese winter of 1900–01, when amid heavy rain, hail and snow the temperature fell to –22°C, freezing beards, sweat and urine. They got them in the form of Canadian warm coats, sheepskin overcoats and lambskin vests, and Norwegian socks and fur gloves. The upshot was that the Indian sick rates were low, with just a few cases of frostbite and pneumonia. The same could not be said of the German Army contingent in China of 21,000 troops shipped direct from Europe. Their logistics were bungled for lack of experience deploying overseas, entailing inadequate food and clothing, and consequently German winter sick rates that rocketed ten times higher than the Indian Army's. 'The Germans are in an awful mess,' reflected James Grierson, one of the Indians' German-speaking British officers. 'I daresay they would be all right if they only had to cross the frontier into France, but this sort of thing is beyond their ken altogether and they are quite up a tree.'

The second significant feature of the Indians' pre-1914 overseas service shown in China was their engagement with foreign culture. The sources for this are few and far between, but the Hindu diarist Thakur Amar Singh was in China in 1900–01 attached to the Indian Army with the princely States unit the Jodhpur Lancers, and he wrote down his thoughts on Chinese culture which were likely typical of other Indian soldiers' reactions. Like them, he saw the great sights in and around Beijing – the Forbidden City and Temple of Heaven, the Summer Palace and Great Wall of China – and he was enthralled. 'The Great Wall was our daily view,' he wrote of one of his postings. 'I had walked for weeks continually on it, and was wondering what sort of man he must have been who started this enormous work.' Amar Singh then met Chinese families in whose homes Indian soldiers were housed. 'The inhabitants seem quite gentle and friendly and offer fruits, walnuts, chestnuts, tea, and liquor to all the troops. Their villages are most beautifully built and have separate rooms. Their houses are also clean and well built ... The most extraordinary thing is that they don't milk their cows. They don't know what milk is.

All their things are cooked by fat.' By the time the Indian Army evacuated China in 1902 after the Boxer Rising had subsided, a number of its men who had been there for two years had clearly been thinking in new ways like Amar Singh – they could now speak Mandarin.

Up to 1914 the Indian Army kept up constant foreign tours of duty, usually of two years a time for a regiment, and always with improved rates of pay and postal links with home. Gurkha, Pukhtun and Sikh battalions marched through the Himalayas into Tibet during the British invasion of 1903–4, enduring colder temperatures than in China yet with even more clothes, and noticing strange Tibetan habits such as sticking out the tongue as a sign of respect. At the Tibetan capital Lhasa they saw some of the world's least visited palaces and holy sites, wandering the inner sanctums of the Potala, the Dalai Lama's golden-roofed palace towering above the city, and the Jokhang Temple, the most sacred in Tibetan Buddhism.

Other Indian regiments in the early 1900s served widely in south Iran, an informal zone of the British Empire where they guarded British commercial interests and British Indian consulates. For instance, Punjabi Muslim troopers of the 18th Tiwana Lancers were assigned to the oil-field of Masjed Soleyman, operated by the British company D'Arcy Exploration's Canadian drillers and Iranian workers in temperatures of around 50°C in the shade. They grew accustomed to the sound at all hours of the monotonous pounding of the oil rigs imported from the United States, which before their own eyes in 1908 struck oil for the first time: a large black streak jetted 50 feet into the sky to a chorus of excited shouts in different languages. They also learned some Farsi, using it to haggle with Iranians at market stalls, and chat to nomadic tribesmen with whom they shared their goat curries.

Indian regiments provided British consular guards more widely in Asia, from Baghdad to Kathmandu and Beijing, and garrisoned imperial outposts around the Indian Ocean in Uganda, British

East and Central Africa, Zanzibar, Somalia, Sudan, Aden, Oman, Mauritius, Singapore and Hong Kong. For the Indian soldiers, the value of all their pre-war journeys was not just the extra pay and what they saw in so many different places, but how their travelling experiences shaped their family lives when they got back to their villages.

'Fools into wise men'

So many thousands of Indian recruits came home in the years prior to 1914 from a stint overseas that their arrival became almost an established ritual in their villages, which would come alive with anticipation at news of a regiment's return. The soldiers enjoyed a new status as worldly men held in higher esteem for their travels and accumulated pay packets. One Sikh back home in Punjab from London in 1911 was regarded 'with as much respect as if he had been a prophet', said his neighbour. As their fellow villagers excitedly crowded round in the street and on doorsteps, the soldiers told incredible stories of what they had seen in far-off lands, from European cities and the Alps to the great Chinese and Tibetan palaces with thousands of rooms. London was a particular point of fascination, and recruits back from there dwelled on what had impressed them most. For some Pukhtun it was the shops that sold guns; for some Gurkhas it was Tower Bridge – 'the bridge that breaks in two' – or the marvel that at London railway stations a man was able to make a living by taking pennies from people who needed to use public lavatories. The Hindu diarist Thakur Amar Singh no doubt spoke for many Indian soldiers back from the Boxer Rising by 1903 when he wrote, 'This going to China has made a man of me; now with my people, at any sort of meeting, I can talk on a subject that most men would be eager to hear.'

After the stories had been told, village elders from Punjab to the independent Pukhtun tribal areas and the Himalayas noticed something more profound that the soldiers had brought home with them through their education in the army: they walked tall with a new maturity. 'The service of the Sirkar,' reflected an Afridi elder, 'makes fools into wise men.' At early evening gatherings – the daily hub of village social life where hookahs were smoked, gossip swapped in hushed tones, and public matters discussed in the open – the Indian soldiers spoke more expansively and influentially than they had before enlistment, with self-confidence, reason and judgement. They now thought more broadly and questioned village habits, encouraging disciplined abstinence from cannabis and other popular drugs. They also improved village sanitation. 'One got as dirty in a minute as in a month in China,' a Punjabi recruit despaired of his village, where he insisted on cleaner houses and lanes in front of them such as the Chinese had.

But the benefits of military service were only one side of recruits' pre-First World War lives in the Indian Army. Overseas service itself could bring serious trouble at home, whether through straining personal relationships because of time spent away, or through shaming by local Hindu priests who thought the act of sea travel made a man spiritually impure – a problem greatest for Gurkhas whose tribes in remote Nepal clung to a traditional idea of sea travel as sinful. More importantly, each Indian recruit as a colonial subject had to face the fact that military service was also a daily trial of humiliation. Their varied reactions to this lay at the heart of how prepared they were to serve the British by 1914 – some recruits were clearly the most accepting of the benefits of military employment, while others were more prone to deserting, or even killing their British officers.

2

'INFERIORS IN THE SCALE OF HUMANITY'

The point of the Delhi Durbar of 1911 was to strengthen the Indian Empire's colonial social order by displaying the unshakeable primacy of British power, embodied by the King-Emperor to whom all India's soldiers were supposed to be loyal as their supreme commander. The King-Emperor, a constitutional monarch, was in fact the Indian Army's ceremonial commander-in-chief – supreme command actually lay in the hands of the Prime Minister at 10 Downing Street, who routinely delegated it to a long-distance double act, the senior and a junior partner of which daily kept in touch by secret telegram along the British Empire's undersea cables. The senior partner was the Secretary of State for India in London, only on whose say-so could the Indian Army deploy overseas; the junior was the Governor-General in British India, better known as the Viceroy, who headed the local Government of India and the Army in India. For the Hindu diarist Thakur Amar Singh, the spectacle of the Durbar was not so beguiling as simply to bind him as an unquestioning servant of the supreme command. His penetrating gaze saw past the pageantry at Delhi to pinpoint the ugly truth of how the Indian Army was run. 'The Indians,' he wrote, 'are looked upon as inferiors in the scale of humanity.'

Inferior treatment was the defining quality of the Indian recruits' military life up to 1914. They served at the lower end of an authoritarian colonial hierarchy, carefully constructed to manipulate and control their every move as racial underlings. The Indian troops were acutely aware of their status, and their readiness to serve was conditional on how prepared they were to put up with the British. Amar Singh's experiences in the pre-war Indian Army, and Indian veterans' interview comments in later life, reveal that the Indian soldiers who went to war in 1914 cannily handled their relationship with the British for their own ends. Pre-war their frustrations were legion, and the extent to which these boiled over largely depended on where a recruit was from. A Punjabi might bite his tongue at a racial insult from a white man, but a Pukhtun might murder.

'Keep the bleeding natives down'

As rulers of the Indian Empire, the British regarded themselves as supermen. They carried, they were sure, special Anglo-Saxon genes that granted them the physical and mental powers to be the human race's natural leaders. Yet to ensure their primacy over Indians as their racial inferiors, they relentlessly projected an aura of ascendancy they called their 'prestige'. The British Army private Frank Richards, who served in India in the early 1900s, explained 'prestige' as the need to 'keep the bleeding natives down ... the more you are down on them the better they will respect you'. This crude psychology demanded that the Indian Army had to be dominated by white men. For the Indian recruits, it meant their constant subjection to belittling British treatment to disadvantage them compared to the Army in India's British soldiers.

In British India's military bases, known as cantonments (pronounced 'cantoonments') and shared by the Indian and British armies, there was segregation between Indian and British zones with patent differences designed to uphold prestige. The Indian troops' cantonment housing generally consisted of huts described by a British officer of the 129th Baluchis as 'hovels ... insanitary, dangerous to life and disgraceful to Government. I have no words to describe the filthy and dilapidated condition of some of them. [They] were so badly built and so fragile that many of them usually fell down on the first shower of rain. The soldiers then, after much loss of kit and some danger to life, had to patch them up in the best way they could; they were really quite unfit for human habitation.' The British troops had their own airy and well-lit modern barracks with swimming pools, gyms, coffee houses, billiard rooms and libraries. The Indians' British officers, meanwhile, had cosy bungalows and clubhouses with dining, smoking and games rooms, some decorated with ancient Indian art, hunting trophies and tartan carpets.

Although the Indian regimental hospitals in the cantonments were run by well-qualified British or Indian doctors of the government's Indian Medical Service, they were comfortless and badly equipped in the extreme; they had no chairs, clothes or bedding for patients, no rooms for separating infectious cases, and no operating theatres. The British regiments had fully equipped modern general hospitals with spacious wards. British troops received more than double the wage of Indian recruits, and higher pensions too. And they were exempt from corporal punishment for military crimes – deemed too inhumane for white men – whereas the Indian troops could still be flogged with the cat-o'-nine-tails of nine knotted 24-inch whip-cord lashes secured to a wooden handle in a white hand. Prestige's final insult in the cantonments was that Indian troops were forbidden from talking to, let alone touching, white women, usually present as British officers' wives.

Prestige upheld an Indian promotion ceiling that applied to all Indian regiments, denying Indian recruits equality of command with their white officers. The Indian Army's pyramid of regimental command had a British peak and an Indian base. Each Indian battalion was led by twelve British officers who held the standard western ranks from lieutenant to colonel and had a right of command over Indian and British troops – the King's Commission. Beneath the British officers were the Indian officers; sixteen per battalion and all of inferior status because they had only the Viceroy's Commission, a lesser right of command that extended over Indian troops only.

The three Indian officer ranks of the Viceroy's Commission were peculiar to the Indian Army and without any real British Army parallel. They ran in the infantry from the most junior, called a 'jemadar', up to 'subadar', the middle rung, and the most senior, 'subadar-major'. The Indian infantry had its own names for non-commissioned officers, or NCOs, as did the cavalry for both Indian officers and NCOs. Indian officers were customarily promoted from the ranks after long service for their charisma and proven influence over their village peers; a few local headmen were commissioned directly from their village for their pre-existing influence. The British trick with Indian officers was to try to enforce prestige while making leaders of them. 'Our endeavour,' counselled George Younghusband in 1908 as commandant of the Indian Army's most famous regiment, the Queen Victoria's Own Corps of Guides, 'is to train the Native officers to be excellent company and troop leaders, and yet ... to keep alive the absolute faith and confidence in the faith and superiority of the British officer, however young, for the higher leading. The task is a difficult one and requires infinite tact and quiet but never failing self-confidence on the part of the British officers.'

Prestige also dictated that the Indian officers be denied army career prospects beyond their regiments. Above regimental level, the pre-war Army in India had some sixty-five generals. They were posted to its ten divisions and forty brigades, its higher Northern and Southern Army Commands, and its highest level,

Army Headquarters, the seat of India's Commander-in-Chief which shuttled between the Himalayan hill-town of Simla in the hot weather and Calcutta or Delhi in the cold. All the positions of high command were reserved exclusively for British officers, of both the Indian and British armies. The same applied to the Army in India's staff officers assisting each commander, from staff captains at brigade level upwards. Indian recruits were barred from enrolling at the Army in India's Staff College, opened permanently in 1907 in British India's north-western province of Baluchistan, just as they were from the Home Army's older Staff College at Camberley in southern England. A sprinkling of staff posts were traditionally handed to maharajahs or Indian landed nobles, but they were purely honorary. To be a serving Indian soldier, therefore, was to join a regiment, never to leave it, and never to be treated as the equal of a white man.

To nurture the Indian recruits' acquiescence to all the strictures of prestige, the British isolated the Indian regiments as incubators of loyalty – the idea being to keep their men comfortable enough with all the benefits of military service while cutting them off from teachers of nationalist or subversive thinking who might encourage them to reject their treatment as racial inferiors. Much of the British attraction to the martial races lay in their rural isolation from the urban mainstream of British India's nationalist politics in the early 1900s. The nationalist politicians were almost uniformly well-educated civilians from rich and officially non-martial families of Calcutta, Bombay and Madras, and their politics, channelled through the major parties such as the Indian National Congress, were typically moderate. Rather than seek a popular following or national independence as their immediate goal, they patiently negotiated with the Government of India for torturously incremental improvements to Indians' political status. By 1914, the British had allowed them a modicum of political representation in British-controlled public bodies. Above all they had seats in legislatures such as the central Imperial Legislative

Council, at Delhi, which passed laws for all British India, and in advisory bodies up to the Viceroy's Executive Council, the equivalent of the British Prime Minister's Cabinet.

The villagers of the martial races were far removed from the Indian political elite as they lacked social connections with them, and had no vote in the elections for the legislatures. Accordingly, they took no part in the nationalist politicians' polite conversations at Delhi or other cities with the Viceroy and his provincial governors. In the absence of any Indian National Congress or other nationalist call to the countryside for mass support, the villagers, and in turn Indian recruits, generally did not identify themselves nationalistically as Indians, but in local terms, of clan, caste or tribe, as Hindu Rajputs, Sikhs and so on. The British therefore recruited the martial races as men who would see military service in narrow local terms, as materially advantageous for their rural communities, rather than as an affront to any common nationalist destiny; by extension, the British calculated, the Indian recruits would be more inclined to accept prestige than otherwise. To keep the Indian troops thinking locally, the British planted the cantonments outside urban limits, and barred entry to nationalist agitators.

A further shield of prestige was a British pre-war policy, 'the colour bar principle', whereby the Indian Army was banned from fighting white armies. The imperial thinking here was that if the Indian troops went into battle against white men and had moments of superiority, however fleeting, prestige would be punctured and they might start spurning white authority and even look to overturn it. The colour bar principle was invoked in the British Empire's 1899–1902 war against the white, Afrikaans-speaking Boers in South Africa; Indian cavalry joined the British forces there, but did not fight.

There was, however, a pre-1914 link between the nationalist politicians and the Indian Army as they pressed the Government of India into modest alleviations of prestige, spoken of as political concessions. While the politicians achieved such concessions in the Indian Civil Service and the legal and medical professions via the opening of senior posts to Indians, they tried to do the same for the Indian soldier by calling for King's Commissions for Indians. In response the British opened the door, but as slightly as possible to leave British officers' prestige unaffected. The move was made by Lord Curzon as the Viceroy in 1903. He inaugurated the Imperial Cadet Corps, a King's Commissions training academy open only to a handful of young cadets from Indian royal and aristocratic families, mainly from the princely States of India. The insincerity behind the Imperial Cadet Corps as a vehicle for racial equality was reflected in its sorry story up to 1913.

The Imperial Cadet Corps' academy reading list included Robert Louis Stevenson's *Treasure Island*, and eleven of its graduates from 1905 received a specially watered-down King's Commission, becoming lieutenants with a right to wear the same uniform as British officers, but with no power of command over British troops. The new Indian officers with King's Commissions were assigned to a peculiar compartment of command created to marginalise them, called the Native Indian Land Forces. This dangled somewhere between the Indian Army's British officers and its Indian officers with Viceroy's Commissions, the British never quite bothered to specify. Some of the Indian officers with King's Commissions were posted to the Indian Army, not to its regiments but to the Indian divisions, as aides-de-camp to British generals. A similar concession towards racial equality was made in 1911 when Indian troops became eligible for the Victoria Cross. Formerly they had in their own Indian Army medals system a VC parallel, the Indian Order of Merit, 1st Class. But the opening of the VC to them was really a cynical ploy to apply a veneer of racial respect that would be publicly noticed.

The lie to Victoria Cross eligibility as any mark of true racial equality was given by the Army in India's hidden British safety mechanisms to guarantee that the Indian regiments would remain unequal imperial subjects at all costs. The total number of British Army troops in British India – 75,000, entailing a 1:2 ratio of British to Indian troops – was a pseudo-scientific calculation to safeguard the British regime. The ratio was officially deemed the minimum balance required for genetically superior British soldiers to defeat their racially inferior counterparts in the event of a widespread and violent Indian mutiny. To guarantee an Indian defeat, the British Army was more heavily armed, not with rifles and machine guns, which were issued to Indian and British troops alike in the Army in India from 1900, but with artillery. While the Indian artillery had mountain guns, the British had heavier field guns and howitzers with which to obliterate rebels if necessary.

Indeed the Indian regiments were organised to kill each other should the British desire it. Despite their titles such as the 62nd Punjabis or 129th Baluchis that pointed to a particular regional or ethnic composition, they were a mix of 'class' regiments, with a full complement of eight companies all recruited from the same martial race, and 'class company' regiments, which were recruited from a range of martial races, and whose companies were like a ship's watertight compartments holding men of different religions and provinces. The purpose of the mix was to exploit the Indian troops' lack of a pervasive national identity: the British relied on the troops' local identities from one regiment or company to the next to predispose them not to unite in an anti-British cause, rather to turn on one another on British orders. 'If one regiment mutinies, I should like to have the next so alien that it would be ready to fire into it,' said a Secretary of State for India, Charles Wood, 'so that Sikh might fire into Hindu, Gurkha into either, without any scruple in case of need.'

Such, then, was the British design of the pre-war Indian Army in order to maintain prestige and keep control of it as a body of racial inferiors. Yet how did all this make the Indian recruits feel, and how willing were they to serve the British in spite of it?

'Two-facey'

'After a quarter of a century or so of service we most of us come home and do not leave behind us a single close Indian friend,' remarked Leopold Jones, a British officer of the 86th Carnatics. 'Our friendships with Indians are never "intimate" in the usual sense of that word. Those of them with whom I became friendly exhibited a strange reluctance to talk about themselves.' What Jones perceived was how carefully the Indian recruits chose their words in front of their British officers, hiding thoughts they realised were not in their interests to say out loud – an approach to authority described by one Punjabi Muslim veteran as 'two-facey'.

Behind their British officers' backs, the Indian recruits had their own secret world where they aired things not for British ears. They mimicked their British officers' dodgier Indian accents, discussed their own womenfolk and families, and dropped obscenities such as the Punjabi *madarchod*. And they complained to each other of the unfairness of their unequal treatment compared to British troops. Many resented their lower wage and thought they should be paid the same. Many wanted better pensions, larger land grants and comfortable modern barracks. They also fumed at the promotion ceiling. 'It is a general British complaint that Indian officers are not fit for higher responsibilities,' said Laxman Singh, a subadar-major of the 15th Ludhiana Sikhs, 'but the thing is, no trial is given to that and no chances afforded.' Some Viceroy's Commissioned Indian officers objected to the opening only to royalty and aristocrats of the pre-1914 King's Commissions for Indians, and were jealous of those they came across as aides-de-camp in their divisions. 'If a commission of this class is to be given, why not give it to us?' said a Viceroy's Commissioned officer in 1910, describing the Indians with a King's Commission as 'nothing more in the village than we are'.

The Hindu diarist Thakur Amar Singh was one of the first

King's Commissioned Indian officers in 1905. In 1913 he was then
the first to be promoted to captain, making him the Indian Army's
most senior Indian officer. Amar Singh had grasped the chance
of a King's Commission as 'a real good thing for the Indians of
good family who wish to get honourable service', but he had many
frustrations of his own as an aide-de-camp up to 1914, with the
5th Indian Division at Mhow in central British India. 'I was full of
hopes,' he wrote of sharing at least some of the responsibilities of
British officers of his rank, 'but I was destined to disappointment.'
Amar Singh was habitually demeaned by token tasks that bored
him, such as putting up Chinese lanterns and moving carpets at
one British general's house, shopping for pillows for another's
wife, or finding shady spots for British officers' chairs and tents
at training exercises. 'I had no worries but at the same time I did
not appreciate the work,' he reflected, concluding that 'native
officers ... means nothing worth bothering'.

Amar Singh's pre-1914 frustrations at British treatment easily
ran into hot anger. 'God only knows what is going to be our
dignity in a few years' time,' he wrote in one moment of ire. 'I
wish God would show a day to me when we Indians would be a
free nation moving about at our own free will and ranked as a
nationality on the same footing as England ... I fear I shall never
see it ... I wonder if ever a day will come when an Indian will be
a Commander-in-Chief.'

It should not be assumed that in having these thoughts before
1914 Amar Singh was a literate and well-educated oddity alongside a wider mass of illiterate and politically ignorant Indian
soldiers. Some recruits from the villages of Punjab had a sense of
such anti-imperial ideas, albeit not developed or harnessed by the
mainstream Indian nationalist politicians. In 1913, for example,
an Indian officer of the 82nd Punjabis was sent a letter from a
Sikh immigrant in California of a kind mailed to a number of
Sikh troops. The immigrant wrote that he was a member of a
revolutionary group formed of Punjabis living in the United

States and Canada named Ghadar, meaning 'Mutiny'. Ghadar's ultimate aim was the violent overthrow of the Government of India, the initial objective being to shake it by acts of terrorism with the help of mutinous Indian regiments. 'The condition of Mother India is worse than that of any other country, as we cannot open our mouths to talk. All become terror stricken even at seeing one white man,' the letter from California proclaimed. It went on:

> All Indians living in America and Canada are prepared to kill and die. No one wishes to see these evil Englishmen. The only remedy against these tyrants is that the troops should mutiny ... You should write to me what is going on in India at the present time. Also write whether anything is talked about the Government in the regiments or not, and whether men are still giving their heads for eleven rupees as of old ... Do not let the white men know what I have written. Remember, lest you get into trouble; but understand and inform your friends.

Such letters in the years up to 1914 contributed to intense debate among Sikh recruits on their subjugation under colonial rule, and how they should best maintain their warrior tradition and community pride. Their British officers detected in them an elevated self-esteem associated with revolutionary ideas of Sikh revival, including restoring Sikh control of Punjab as had been achieved by Maharajah Ranjit Singh, the great Sikh leader of the late 1700s and early 1800s. 'Undoubtedly there are movements among the Sikhs which are weakening their loyalty to the British Raj', said Alfred Bingley of the 7th Rajputs in 1912, 'From a military point of view the Sikhs are suffering from "swelled head".'

Nonetheless, when in front of their British officers, most Indian recruits routinely adopted a cautious, courteous attitude of subservience. They did so partly because prestige achieved some of its intended effect, stifling their potential for more confident self-assertion. And they had a social respect for the British officers as a ruling class they recognised as the *sahib log* – a term differentiating them as a cut above white people in general, the *gora log* – and whose King-Emperor, judging by his tour of the Indian Empire in 1911, clearly represented a governing authority to be reckoned with. 'They had been rulers of our country for a hundred years,' said one Sikh veteran, Harbaksh Singh, of the Indian troops' pre-1914 view of the British, 'and somehow, in the villages ... they were looked upon as superior.'

Yet the Indian recruits' subservience was more a means to personal profit. This was a tendency Jawaharlal Nehru diagnosed as common to the Government of India's poorer Indian employees 'whose sole objective is to get on in life'. They were motivated, he wrote, by a 'desire to cringe and please the bosses ... the haunting fear of unemployment and consequent starvation pursues them, and their chief concern is to hold on to their jobs and get other jobs for their relatives and friends'.

The material benefits the Indian recruits primarily enlisted for had a common denominator: they all increased with the favour of British officers. British officer discretion was the decision-making power behind promotions, which took the base rate of monthly pay up to 150 rupees in the infantry and 300 rupees a month in the cavalry, with corresponding pension rises. Furthermore, land grants were handed out strictly on British officers' letters of recommendation to provincial authorities.

So despite the Indian troops' frustrations at being treated as racial inferiors, and their awareness to some extent of anti-imperial political ideas, they were in the habit of swallowing both when the British were around. Complaining or showing disrespect could turn down the tap of army benefits to a trickle when they wanted a full flow. On the contrary, they went out of their way to please their British officers, for instance playing sports they did not enjoy, or sending obsequious letters to those away from the regiment, telling them how they were missed with messages like 'your place is empty', seeking favour for when they returned.

Indian officers had the closest relationships with the British officers. In the pyramid of Indian regimental command they knitted a battalion together as the British officers' trusted eyes and ears among the men. And they smoothed their path through the working day with a knack for saying what their British officers wanted to hear. 'All senior Indian officers do not tell the facts in their true light without colouring them, and some even say "all is well" when "all is not well",' observed Subadar-Major Laxman Singh of the 15th Ludhiana Sikhs. 'Officers commanding units get only that information which their senior Indian officer tells.'

When Indian officers did decide to speak candidly to British superiors, they were usually shrewd judges of how to do so nicely. To describe one well-intentioned but gaffe-prone commandant, an Indian officer gently said, 'The Colonel, since the day he got command of the Regiment, has spent all his time trying to thread a needle at the wrong end.' The Hindu diarist Thakur Amar Singh was well aware of the game Indian recruits were playing. 'An Indian as a rule,' he wrote, 'does things either when his own interest warrants it or his superior is watching.' Laxman Singh was also wise to the politicking of his juniors in conversation with British officers as they jockeyed for promotion. 'Jemadars are always trying to bad mouth subadars so that they may go and get promotion in their place,' he said.

If Indian recruits were especially unhappy about some regimental matter in the years up to 1914 – a problem with their food, for example – they occasionally made collective representations. These were planned in secret, invariably non-violent, and carried off in good order; a company might appear at dawn outside their British officer's bungalow, with an Indian officer spokesman ready to make their representation with a minimum of fuss in the hope of improving a term of service by regimental arrangement. They were not mutinies or open expressions of anti-imperial ideas to reject British authority – the recruits were extremely loath to enter into these, there was far too much for them to lose.

The representations in fact showed how pre-war Indian troops and Indian nationalist politicians had parallel but unconnected conversations with the British, in order to negotiate improvements to their positions as collaborators with the empire. While Indian politicians addressed the Viceroy to improve their lot in the high political sphere, the troops spoke with their British officers to improve theirs in the regiment.

Pre-war Indian troops, therefore, widely kept good discipline in a way that allowed the British to say they were loyal. In February 1914 Charles Cleveland, the director of British India's domestic intelligence agency, the Department of Criminal Investigation, reported as much having monitored the cantonments for signs of sympathy with the revolutionary group Ghadar, following its letters to Sikh troops. He had gathered from British officers that 'the Sikhs are suffering from "swollen head"', yet wrote 'Nothing has transpired to make [my Department] think that the Indian Army has been touched by the blandishments or incitements of the revolutionaries.'

But the Indians' willingness to serve was dependent on their pay, pensions and land being worth it. The material inspiration for their loyalty was accordingly disparaged by Nehru, who felt that it 'does not bring out the mentality of real service, the devotion to public service or to ideals'. Instead, he said, 'it picks out the least public-spirited persons ... They drift to government service ... because of lack of opportunity elsewhere, and gradually they tone down and become just parts of the big machine, their minds imprisoned.'

There was, however, a class of Indian recruits whose minds were conspicuously free, prompting them to care less than the rest for British rewards, and to commit more serious acts of indiscipline. They were the men from the independent Pukhtun tribal areas between British India and Afghanistan, which were some

400 miles long and dozens deep, a rugged mass of mountains, pine forests, deep ravines, rushing rivers, boulder-strewn hills and valleys, without roads or railways. The mentality of the Pukhtun recruits was quite different from that of Punjabi or other recruits from British India exactly because their tribal areas were independent, empowering them as individuals in ways unseen in the villages under British rule. As one British officer of independent Pukhtun, Colin Enriquez of the 21st Punjabis, put it, 'there is more of the wolf in him'.

'We are very untrustworthy people'

The Indian Army by 1914 had approximately 7500 independent Pukhtun soldiers, serving across forty regiments. They saw the world through their own passionately tribal eyes – as Afridi, the tribe of Tirah in the north of the tribal areas which provided a third of the Indian Army's independent Pukhtun; as Mahsud, a major tribe of Waziristan in the south yielding 1300 recruits; or as Mohmand, Orakzai and others of territories which like Tirah and Waziristan were in the exclusive possession of their particular tribe. So self-assertive were these tribesmen that each man was a law unto himself, rendering their value as imperial soldiers highly ambiguous. As the Mahsud would say in their soft Pushtu dialect with a knowing shrug and a smile, 'we are very untrustworthy people'.

All the independent Pukhtun tribes lived by their ancient and egalitarian tribal code 'Pukhtunwali', meaning the way of the Pukhtun. Each individual closely observed its mores of honour, hospitality, rivalry, revenge and courage, giving rise to feuds in which retribution for insults was exacted personally to maintain pride. The feuds were typically between families of the same tribe over *zar*, *zan* or *zamin* – gold, women or land – and they were often settled in cold blood by both men and women. Feuding was exceptionally dangerous by the early 1900s because around

100,000 Pukhtun men had become the proud owners of their own European modern rifle. The tribal areas had no ban on owning guns as British India did, and many tribesmen bought their rifles on the local arms market from cartels operating out of Europe that smuggled the weapons through Oman, Iran and the Afghan province of Helmand; others bought their rifles from Australia, or stole them from the Army in India. Murder by rifle was so common a feuding fate for men, women and children that the tribesmen who feuded the most, above all the Afridi, had come to live not in Punjabi-style villages but in spread-out homestead-forts topped with multi-storey towers, their gun-slits rising above gardens of roses and apricot trees.

The tribal areas were a smouldering bed of resistance to the bordering Indian Empire. Their mullahs, the literate holy men learned in the Koran who commanded great respect as the author-ities on the tribes' rough and ready brand of Islam, continually preached against the British. They spoke of them as an existential Christian threat to Pukhtun independence, warning of imperial intentions to annex the tribal areas and impose western-style laws that would spell the end for Pukhtunwali as they knew it, collapsing their tribal universe. From time to time the mullahs called for jihad against the Christian imperialists at their door, stoking anti-British tribal feelings into flame in order to gather *lashkar*s (war parties of between 20 and 300 men) to serve Islam as mujahideen, or holy warriors. The *lashkar*s then broke into British India's adjacent North-West Frontier Province to raid towns and villages, or ambush Army in India camps and patrols.

Tensions between the independent Pukhtun and the Indian Empire led to no fewer than sixty-six separate Army in India inva-sions of the tribal areas between 1849 and 1908. The invasions were known as small wars, and lasted weeks or months until a truce was brokered and the Indian forces withdrew. The invasions were never to conquer or annex, but to punish particular tribes for jihadist incursions into British India. The tribes bitterly opposed the invasions, fighting back with an absolute refusal to accept defeat – a tenet of Pukhtunwali, whose defence was their highest honour and motivation.

By the early 1900s, the Afridi and the Mahsud had fought the British the most and were particularly adept defenders of their homelands of Tirah and Waziristan with their modern rifles. In one Anglo-Afridi small war of 1897–8, deep in Tirah's mountains and ravines, tireless Afridi *lashkar*s inflicted a series of minor tactical disasters on the British Army. They outmanoeuvred and annihilated detachments of the Northamptonshire Regiment and Yorkshire Light Infantry, taking no mercy on some of the wounded Tommies. They stripped them naked and mutilated them as marks not just of their rage at the invaders, whom they utterly rejected as outsiders with no place in their tribal world, but of Pukhtunwali's permanence too. 'The Hague Convention,' wrote the British officer Hugh Nevill in 1912, referring to the international law of the day on humane treatment of enemy wounded and surrendered, 'is to them not even a name.'

In the Anglo-Afridi war of 1897–8, over 500 British soldiers fell to rifle fire – a third of them were killed and a few had limbs blown off by large-calibre sniper bullets. Indeed, some British battalions had to be withdrawn early from Tirah, exhausted by the intensity of the mountain fighting and flummoxed by the Afridi *lashkar*s. To Winston Churchill, serving with the Tirah Expeditionary Force in 1898 as a young British Army officer, the campaign amounted to a 'fruitless errand ... To enter the mountains and attack an Afridi is to jump into water to catch a fish.'

The Indian Army's Afridi, Mahsud and other independent Pukhtun recruits joined up mainly for money, like the rest of the martial races, although they alone looked to earn enough to buy a modern rifle as a prized status symbol at home, at a cost of up to four years' basic infantry pay. In the cantonments, the independent Pukhtun soldiers liked to carry themselves somewhat differently to the recruits from British India. They walked with a

swagger as free men who had chosen to descend from their uncon-
quered mountains, and they looked down their noses at Punjabis
as lesser men whose people were under the British thumb. They
also spoke to their British officers differently. They took pleasure
in self-confidently speaking their minds more freely than recruits
from British India would normally dare, looking their white
officers square in the eyes, asking mischievous questions and earning a well-deserved reputation for impertinence. 'Do you wish us
to tell you what would please you, or to tell you the truth?' asked
one grinning Mahsud. 'What is going to happen when the British
leave India?' an Afridi stirred.

'An outsider may learn a good deal about [independent Pukhtun
recruits'] character by watching the way they play games,' thought
Edmund Candler, a British journalist who spoke several Indian
languages and covered the Indian Army for the British and Indian
press in Tibet and elsewhere for over a decade before 1914. On the
regimental sports ground, Candler saw how independent Pukhtun
took the least trouble to please their British officers by playing
games by the rules, preferring to amuse themselves. 'Directly the
elements of a man-to-man duel were recognized cricket became
popular,' he wrote of one regiment's Afridi company. 'They were
out to hurt one another. They did not care to bat, they said, but
wished to bowl ... Needless to say the batsman was the mark
and not the wicket.' The Afridi players' own game was to see who
could bowl or throw the ball the hardest at the batsmen, aiming
for the most painful consequences.

All the while, the independent Pukhtun had three volatile
characteristics that set them apart from other troops as potential
military criminals. First, they brought Pukhtunwali into Indian
regiments as a tribal code of behaviour vital and alive in its
traditional form, relatively undiluted by British influences – in
contrast to recruits from the non-independent Pukhtun tribes of
British India, whose harder edges of Pukhtunwali had softened
through their assimilation into the North-West Frontier Province's

imperial order. This primed the independent Pukhtun more than other Indian soldiers to stand up for themselves, as they so often did at home in order to revenge challenges to their honour.

Second, independent Pukhtun recruits grappled with the moral quandary of how to be true servants of their tribe and Islam – resisters of the British as their mullahs preached – while also serving the Christian imperialists who in their tribal areas were the enemy. The tension was so acute that some of the independent Pukhtun tribes' clans, such as the Afridi Zakkas, spurned Indian Army service, declaring themselves morally superior to it. Muslim recruits from British India, of course, might also feel a tension as Muslims serving the Christian British, but their tribes or clans did not sustain the same levels of active anti-colonial resistance as the independent Pukhtun.

Third, the British psychology of prestige did not wash with the independent Pukhtun. Their freedom at home and cultural pride made a nonsense in their minds of any British mystique as a superior white race. Besides, the colour bar principle had effectively been lifted for them by the British invasions of their tribal areas: the tribes had fresh memories of out-thinking and annihilating British platoons; their *lashkar*s had seen hundreds of white men bleed or die at their mercy.

The elders of the Afridi clans that provided the majority of the Indian Army's independent Pukhtun recruits had seen enough of small wars in the tribal areas by the early 1900s, and they encouraged enlistment. They saw army employment, as the British did, as a path to peace in promoting diplomatic relations between the tribal areas and British India, and advised young Afridi recruits of the economic wisdom of a steady army career. They also told them that to benefit from British favour, army discipline should be kept despite provocations to their honour that might come their way, and that feuding or the more extreme ways of upholding Pukhtunwali were best left at home. Many of the Afridi recruits followed the elders' advice to build a long army career. But their tribal culture was too strong for this approach simply to prevail, as was the case for Mahsud and other recruits from independent Pukhtun tribes. Whether young and impetuous or older and wiser, the independent Pukhtun recruits' tenets of Pukhtunwali or Islam could push them to commit the most serious military crimes – desertion and murder – more than any other class of Indian recruit.

If a Punjabi or some other recruit from British India deserted, the consequences were dire. He would need to emigrate outside the British Empire, probably abandoning his family, to avoid the British catching him to mete out the standard punishment: trial by court martial and a sentence of penal servitude for life, or death by hanging. Yet an independent Pukhtun recruit who deserted could slip back into the tribal areas to escape prosecution forever more, for the British had no jurisdiction there, and handing them in was against the tribal code.

So independent Pukhtun recruits who found Indian Army service unbearable before 1914, as a number did either for some episode of wounded tribal pride or in search of peace of mind for anti-British Islamic feeling, deserted relatively freely. In 1913, for example, all the 127th Baluchis' Mahsud recruited from the Giddi clan deserted overnight from British India to Waziristan after one of their own had been overlooked for promotion in favour of a junior of the rival Mahsud Palli clan. The passing over of their man for a junior rival was an insult to their honour the enormity of which their commandant had not realised, and guided by Pukhtunwali they refused to stomach it. Independent Pukhtun also had a tendency to desert with their army rifles instead of saving up to buy one.

It was not unheard of for Indian recruits from British India to murder one another in the cantonments, usually out of jealousy over promotions they saw as unfair, an overlooked and enraged soldier shooting the promoted man. But it was only independent Pukhtun recruits who had a track record of murdering white men. In China in 1900–02, the white troops stationed there from continental Europe for the Boxer Rising had a nasty habit of insulting the Indian troops as racial inferiors. At Beijing, Shanghai and elsewhere they shoved them out of the way in streets, railway stations and office entrances, shook their fists in their faces, and shouted jibes like 'Indian coolie, Indian coolie', to mean they were only fit to pick tea or wave a fan for a white man. These humiliations infuriated all the Indian troops. The Punjabis and Gurkhas mostly kept their cool, shouting back 'German coolie, German coolie' and at worst flashing a fist or a bayonet to cut French or Russian goaders. But the independent Pukhtun killed. Afridi troops told their British officers they might have to do this for the sake of their honour, and one of them, of the 57th Wilde's Rifles, actually did it when he stole into a German camp with his magazine rifle and shot five German soldiers, three of them dead.

Then in British India between 1904 and 1914, Mahsud recruits murdered six British officers, the assassins being impressionable young men who on leave in Waziristan had been persuaded to kill by their mullahs as acts of jihadist resistance. One of these killings was a triple murder in the North-West Frontier Province in April 1914, outside a British officer's bungalow during early evening drinks. The Mahsud murderer was a sepoy named Sarfaraz and an unlikely assassin, having previously appeared devoted to one of his British officer victims, who had done everything a British officer was supposed to do to build a personal bond with his Indian recruit. It showed how life for a British officer leading independent Pukhtun was a form of Russian roulette: they might be gone in the morning, or you might be. In some Indian regiments, it was a matter of course to post Hindu or Sikh troops to guard the independent Pukhtun guards outside rooms British officers were in. 'We always had mixed guards,' wrote Lionel Dunsterville, a British officer of Afridi in the 20th Punjabis. 'Anyone with a grain of sense would naturally do this.'

As it was common knowledge among the Indian Army's British officers that, compared to the other Indian troops, the independent Pukhtun were unpredictable to the point of being totally untrustworthy, some British officers wanted nothing to do with them. But some were magnetically attracted. One of the latter in early 1914 was Lieutenant Harold Lewis, a twenty-six-year-old bachelor devoted to his career. Lewis had applied to the 129th Baluchis despite its all-Muslim companies being 75 per cent independent Pukhtun – a mix of Afridi, Mahsud and Mohmand, alongside a British Indian minority of Punjabi Muslims (there was no Baluchi company). From Oxford, Lewis was one of the finest recent cadets at the Royal Military Academy in England at Sandhurst, the centre for initial training of all British officers, where he had won the Sword of Honour for best cadet. He had joined the 129th Baluchis in 1910, within a year gaining the Indian Army's higher standard qualifications in Urdu and Pushtu, plus popularity among his British officer peers for his generous spirit, natural charm and thoughtfulness. Lewis also impressed his senior officers, who were almost lyrical in praise of him. 'He was exactly the right type of man for the job,' waxed one. 'A gentleman, a good soldier, a sportsman, and an officer who realised the supreme importance of making friends with the men, and safe-guarding their interests at all times.'

The men of Lewis' company were young Mahsud of under three years' service. 'I suppose our regiment is a more difficult one to run than any other in the country,' he casually wrote to his mother in May 1914 because of its independent Pukhtun. 'If they feel that one of them has cause for grievance, one never quite knows what they may do. It makes life very interesting, but also very busy, as officers have to spend a great deal of time in the lines trying to probe the eastern mind and to get to know the men.'

Lewis wanted to work with the 129th Baluchis' Pukhtun because he was attracted by the challenge, and he was deeply curious about their tribal mentality, so different to western points of view. He was charmed by their free-thinking questioning of him in Pushtu as much as he questioned them, and by their world-view through Pukhtunwali whose twists and turns he learned as best he could, enabling him to say the right things and talk easily with them. Some British Army officers who understood the tricky task taken on by Lewis and the Indian service's other officers of independent Pukhtun were more than a little impressed. 'The British officer who can control, lead and inspire trans-border men,' wrote George MacMunn, 'must be something more than a man among men.'

Yet how ready were Lewis' Mahsud and the rest of the pre-1914 Indian recruits to follow their British officers when the order came to fire their guns on human targets picked by the British? What commitment had they shown when asked to lay down their lives for the empire, and how skilled were they at fighting? In the pre-1914 era, the Indian Army was in fact one of the world's most active forces in the line of fire, including modern shell fire, with experiences in Asia and Africa that showed it to be much tougher, more professional and pitiless than might be imagined.

3

'HE MERELY OBEYS ORDERS'

By 1914 the Hindu diarist Thakur Amar Singh felt he had the Indian soldier's measure as a fighting tool of British imperial power. 'The Indian fights because his officers want him to,' he reckoned. 'If the officers want him to shoot at the French tomorrow, he would do so & never bother his head about it. He merely obeys orders.' This was precisely what the Indian regiments were paid and trained for. Ultimately, each was supposed to have that magical spirit of military togetherness known as esprit de corps, making their men bands of brothers – ready to fight for each other and their officers through thick and thin without pausing to ponder moral qualms.

From 1897 to 1913 approximately eighty Indian regiments saw active service in Asia and Africa, with the younger Indian recruits and British officers at the turn of the twentieth century going on to become the senior ones of 1914, including the future Afridi Victoria Cross recipient Mir Dast of centenary fame. Before 1914, the Indian troops were just as ready to follow orders as Amar Singh suspected, as they killed civilians, defended trenches under fire, attacked men of their own religion, and advanced against shells from artillery made in Germany.

These aspects of the Indian Army's pre-1914 service have

curiously been ignored by its critics, who have seen its men as without much of a military clue and predestined to fail on the world stage from 1914; but the Indian soldier scarcely deserves such pity.

'It was not necessary for my heart to be moved'

The Indian Army had two types of operations between 1897 and 1913 that made clear its formidable military qualities. The first was terrorising local populations in and around the Indian Empire, which the Indian troops did repeatedly with ice-cold professional efficiency. They were the hell let loose to instil a fearful British lesson that to defy imperial power was to be crushed by it, and in this they proved terribly ready to follow their officers' orders. In China in 1900–02, the Indian recruits sent against the Boxer Rising were brutal. They ransacked and burned villages, executed Chinese civilians out of hand with their rifles, and blew up parts of towns with explosive mines while distraught inhabitants watched on. 'Even hearts of stone would have melted and felt compassion,' said one Hindu soldier of the 7th Rajputs who took part, Gadhadhar Singh. But he soon snapped out of this to put his professional duty first. 'It was not necessary for my heart to be moved by pity because I had come to fight against the Chinese.' The Indian troops' suppression of the Chinese was made complete by their looting of Chinese valuables to take back to British India as campaign dividends. By themselves they stole silver from Chinese houses and businesses; in organised parties under British officers they made off not only with two enormous golden bells from Beijing's Temple of Heaven for melting down and selling off, but also with a large block of the Great Wall of China.

In 1903–04 the Indian troops treated the people of Tibet much as they had the Chinese, killing numerous fleeing, hiding or surrendering Tibetans. In one incident men of the 8th Gurkhas hauled six Tibetans from a mountain cave and threw them to their deaths off a 300-foot cliff; in another a Gurkha beheaded a captured Tibetan with the man's own sword. In 1911, on the shores of the Persian Gulf, Hindu troops of the 104th Wellesley's Rifles destroyed Iranian villages, burning them along with their date palm groves and crops – all to deter local gun-runners in the supply chain of rifles from Europe to the independent Pukhtun. Sikh and Gurkha troops were equally severe in 1911–12 in the jungles of the Indian Empire's far north-east, where they took on Abor tribesmen armed with rocks and arrows, opening fire on their villages with machine guns and mountain artillery, ostensibly as punishment for the murder of a British civil servant. Then Hindu troops killed Hindu civilians. This happened on the other side of the Indian Empire in 1913, at Mangadh Hill in what is now Rajasthan State in north-western India. Hindu Rajputs of the 7th Rajputs, 104th Wellesley's Rifles and other Indian units with machine guns massacred a large hillside gathering of unarmed Hindu men, women and children of the Bhil people, who were with their guru preaching against the dominance of the British and their Indian princely allies. In local oral memory the Hindu troops shot around 1500 of the guru's Hindu followers. 'The relentless firing,' the granddaughter of one of the slaughter's Hindu victims later said, 'was halted by a British officer only after he saw a Bhil child trying to suckle his dead mother.'

The second type of pre-1914 Indian operations was against tribal warriors or professional soldiers who had modern weapons. There were hints in combat around the Indian Ocean periphery in the early 1900s that the Indian regiments' modern tactical training had given them a steely resilience to pressure. In the bush of central Somalia in 1903, a fifty-strong detachment of the 52nd Sikhs was surrounded and killed to a man by a force of several thousand Somali and Arab jihadists with rifles who opposed western influence in the Horn of Africa. The British official investigation into the affair indicated a desperate struggle, with the Sikhs not giving in as the jihadists attacked from all directions; the Sikhs appeared to have shot many jihadists with rapid individual fire until in the final moments, all their ammunition gone, their last men standing charged with bayonets fixed to fight to the death.

But the true range of the pre-1914 Indian regiments' tactical strength was shown where they fought the most: the independent Pukhtun tribal areas, in the Army in India's sixty-second small war there (against the Afridi *lashkar*s in Tirah in 1897–8), up to its sixty-sixth (in 1908 against the *lashkar*s of the Mohmand in their territory of the same name).

Since its first small war in the tribal areas in 1849, the Indian Army had been locked in a cycle of tactical one-upmanship in mountain warfare with the independent Pukhtun. The friction between them brimmed with innovation from one campaign to another, on what was effectively a static front between British India and the tribal areas. Each side continually learned from the other to improve their fighting skills in the valleys, ridges, forests and mountains up to 8575 feet. The *lashkar*s of the independent Pukhtun took the lead as masters of mountain warfare, and in response the Indian troops had to become masters of it themselves – no mean feat of arms, a fact admiringly recognised by the British Army's most renowned expert of the day on small wars, Charles Callwell. He described fighting in the tribal areas as 'a special branch of the military art. It is fighting in guerrilla fashion ... in campaigns almost the most trying which disciplined soldiers can be called upon to undertake.'

The *lashkar*s fought in scattered parts, moving speedily and all but imperceptibly in light shoes made out of dried grass, and wearing their everyday loose yellow-grey cotton clothes which doubled as camouflage. Carrying just their modern rifles, ammunition, a knife or a small sword and some food, they used boulders, crags and crevices for cover, hiding, watching and waiting for their moment of attack. This could come at any hour, and most frequently in the form of sniping – an independent Pukhtun speciality. But there were also fusillades of combined rifle fire by thousands of tribesmen at a time to send a lead wind of bullets. And there were surprise group assaults when *lashkar*s appeared in swarms, firing and moving rapidly, often charging in for the kill with their loose clothes billowing behind them, knives or swords drawn. 'We must remember,' a seasoned Scottish general of the Indian Army, William Lockhart, warned some Tommies during the Anglo-Afridi small war of 1897–8, 'that we are opposed to perhaps the best skirmishers, and the best natural rifle shots, in the world, and that the country they inhabit is the most difficult on the face of the globe.'

This, then, was what the Indian regiments had to respond to, and their tactical training in mountain warfare brought them by the early 1900s to a high pitch of readiness. They entered the tribal areas in divisions, which fragmented into brigades and many smaller parts. At night the Indian units took permanent cover in deep trenches and outposts fortified with loopholes, machine guns and barbed wire. In 1908's Mohmand small war, which lasted a month, the 59th Scinde Rifles in their trenches came under nightly fire from thousands of Mohmand rifles. 'The fact that in all the many night attacks nobody of the Regiment was hit in the trenches speaks for itself,' noted the Scinde Rifles' regimental history. When the Indian troops failed to dig their trenches or build their outposts properly, they were punished. In Mohmand one night during a thunderstorm, the 22nd Punjabis' poor cover was spotted by Mohmand snipers who used the illumination of lightning flashes to shoot dead nine of the regiment's exposed Sikhs and Punjabi Muslims through the head, and wound another nine in the neck or upper chest.

To deal with the *lashkar*s' snipers at night – 'the perfect pest' in the words of the 5th Gurkhas' mountaineering man-child Charles Bruce – the Indian regiments sent out their elite mountain troops individually trained as Scouts. These were often supervised by Bruce himself. His Gurkha Scout protégés who had run his cross-country *khud* races and climbed the Himalayas and the Alps were more than ready to ghost up and down the tribal areas' mountainsides in the hours of darkness. 'The men became very good at ruses of all kinds and especially at taking advantage of every description of ground, in which they were almost as good as the extremely clever and active enemy himself,' wrote Bruce. Another British officer, Thomas Holdich, said the Scouts could move 'with all the agility of mountain cats (or Afridis)', and they certainly did. They tracked some tribal snipers to learn their sleeping habits, before silently descending on them at rest in ridge-top nests or caves to kill at close quarters. Some of the *lashkars*' snipers in Waziristan met particularly grisly ends at the hands of Gurkha Scouts who decapitated them with *khukuris*. This horror was seemingly encouraged by Bruce in reprisal for the tribesmen's tendency to mutilate imperial troops, and carried out by Gurkha Scouts in order to prove their sniper kills, which they would brag about afterwards, personally dumping the heads in triumph before Bruce.

By day in the tribal areas, in temperatures up to 47°C in the shade, the Indian regiments went after entire *lashkars*, frequently locating them on Scout intelligence. Indian companies, in their khaki uniforms turned black with sweat, pushed down valleys and up ridges. They always looked to wrest control from the *lashkars* of the high ground controlling mountain passes, attacking in rushes from cover to cover in scattered, rifle-firing groups using their own initiative. As they did so, Indian machine gunners often fired in support, while Indian mountain artillery shrapnel shells streamed over their heads, timed to burst in the air ahead of them.

The modern firepower on both sides could be devastating. One Indian division's attack in 1897, on a pass on the edge of Tirah, was stopped in its tracks by heavy rifle fire from Orakzai *lashkars* holding the heights who in just a few minutes inflicted Gurkha and other casualties of thirty-one killed and ninety-seven wounded; a fresh Indian attack only succeeded with mass artillery support from twenty-four mountain guns firing rapidly together. Then in Tirah in 1908, in a small war against the Afridi Zakka clan, an Indian division fired 100,687 bullets and 1034 shells in one week to kill and wound 350 Afridi of Zakka *lashkar*s. That week yet more Zakkas fell maimed or killed from land mines of 14 kilograms of explosive, hidden and detonated by Sappers and Miners. In 1908's month-long Mohmand small war, Indian fire-power inflicted a total of 1500 Mohmand casualties.

The Afridi and Mohmand themselves in 1908 shot down 300 Indian troops killed or wounded, the Mohmand capturing and mutilating a small number of others. The Indian units' rate of loss was so much lower than the *lashkar*s' because they had grown used to taking cover in trenches, and to moving about with covering fire from machine guns and artillery on the mountainsides, protection that scythed down *lashkar*s making occasional massed attacks.

Strange as it may seem, some of the Indian Army's best-performing troops in the tribal areas were its own independent Pukhtun. There was no question of them as Pukhtun fighting for the British mutilating their Pukhtun opposition; this could never be motivated by Indian regimental service under Christian leadership, mutilation being a ritual of tribesmen acting for a purely Pukhtun purpose, such as expressing defiance as a tribal warrior. Killing for the British was another matter. In a professional capacity working for the empire, the independent Pukhtun recruits proved willing enough to use their homegrown talent for mountain warfare to kill their brother Muslims.

A number of Afridi companies served in Mohmand in 1908. They were tight-knit groups of long-serving troops from particular clans. For instance, the 57th Wilde's Rifles had an Afridi company of the Malik Din clan. The company's senior Afridi officer was a lion of a man, Subadar Arsala Khan, known for his action above words and for carrying his own Mauser pistol in his belt. His father, Umar, had been the regiment's subadar-major, with a practical wisdom to make the most of his British connection beyond the means of promotion, doing diplomatic work for them in the tribal areas in return for cash. Umar recruited Arsala for the 57th Wilde's Rifles Malik Din company in 1890. He taught him, it seems, to prize British employment: when the Anglo-Afridi small war of 1897–8 erupted, many Afridi troops deserted with their rifles to fight with their tribe, yet Umar and Arsala stayed put at their cantonment, abiding by the British order to all Afridi servicemen to remain neutral. With his professional dedication and natural charisma, Arsala quickly rose to a Viceroy's Commission, and went to China with Wilde's Rifles in 1900–02 for the Boxer Rising; it was in fact an Afridi of his company who killed German troops there for racial insults.

Arsala proved a jewel among Indian officers in Mohmand in 1908, leading men of his Malik Din company with remarkable determination. One morning he led them into a deep ravine complex in small groups that used alternating short rushes to drive out a Mohmand *lashkar* in a hot rifle firefight. Later the same day he led them into some rocks near their trenches to silence some Mohmand riflemen in a hand-to-hand fight, two of whom Arsala shot dead with his Mauser pistol – in the process earning himself the Indian Army's second highest medal for bravery, the Indian Order of Merit, 2nd Class.

The future Afridi VC Mir Dast also fought in Mohmand. In 1908 he was an NCO of the 55th Coke's Rifles, in their Afridi company recruited from his Qambar clan. Mir Dast had enlisted in 1894. Shortly afterwards he had marked himself in his British officers' eyes as a particularly loyal type in an unpleasant cantonment incident. A Punjabi civilian had surreptitiously approached Mir Dast and other Afridi of his Qambar company to talk of Indian revolution, and had reproached them as slaves in British service; he was probably oblivious that this was the last thing a Punjabi should say to independent Pukhtun. Mir Dast and the other Afridi took serious offence and beat him to a pulp, dumping his blood-spattered but breathing body in a nearby river. Mir Dast and his Qambar company were many times more forceful in the Mohmand small war of 1908, his third campaign with the 55th Coke's Rifles in the tribal areas. They fought as hard as Arsala Khan's Malik Din. Mir Dast himself earned the Indian Order of Merit, 2nd Class, for shooting two Mohmand and bayoneting another, all dead, having spotted them hiding in some bushes by a village and attacked on his own initiative, even fighting on against them after he was badly wounded.

Arsala Khan and Mir Dast left no record of their feelings about receiving medals for killing their Muslim brethren on behalf of the Christian imperialists. But they most likely did not wear the medals about Tirah on leave. They might well have felt shame in them as other Pukhtun recruits felt shame in Mohmand, for fighting for the British against their own. During one shoot-out at a Mohmand village, a British officer, William Birdwood, overheard the regrets of a non-independent Pukhtun recruit of the Yusufzai tribe. 'He was a fine shot, and as he picked off man after man he kept muttering that it was a dreadful thing to be firing at his brother Muhammedans,' Birdwood remembered. Birdwood then saw an Indian Muslim soldier in Mohmand tending mournfully to the dead of a Mohmand *lashkar*, the Muslim recruit laying their motionless bodies straight on their backs, crossing their arms and placing their turbans on their heads – the man was an Afridi who had just killed them with his regiment.

A group of six Afridi of the Indian Army deserted in Mohmand in heed of enemy calls to their trenches for them to join the *lashkar*s, and turn their rifles on their Christian officers. The Afridi, however, had been tricked. The Mohmand did not want them, they wanted their rifles and ammunition, of which the Afridi deserters were promptly relieved along with all their clothes. They were abandoned naked to find their own way back to Tirah, and there was little sympathy for them when they got home. Their elders said they had 'defiled the ground where they had been fed' – an Afridi way of saying they had thrown away a good job they would have done better to keep.

The British Army, meanwhile, despite its substantial presence in British India, was much less seen in the independent Pukhtun tribal areas. After its minor disasters against Afridi *lashkar*s in the Anglo-Afridi small war of 1897–8, it was deliberately held back in the early 1900s. In Waziristan small wars of 1901–2, twenty-one Indian battalions were deployed and not a single British; in Mohmand in 1908 the imperial battalions were 90 per cent Indian. 'No one in his senses would send British soldiers,' said an unusually outspoken British Army officer, Ian Hamilton. 'They might lose their way; they might require to be extricated, or form the text for a regrettable despatch by getting cut up completely.'

The truth was that Indian Army regiments had developed special skills in mountain warfare through long experience, whereas British regiments had not built up the same expertise because their postings to India were temporary. In this sense the Indian Army was unquestionably superior – but the British kept that quiet for the good of prestige. The Indian Army's best of the best in fact had a famous name: they were the Frontier Force, a collection of a dozen elite regiments that since the 1850s had served continually against the independent Pukhtun in the small wars and in patrolling the British border – including Charles Bruce's 5th Gurkhas, Mir Dast's 55th Coke's Rifles and Arsala Khan's 57th Wilde's Rifles.

The commandant of another Frontier Force regiment, Walter Venour of the 58th Vaughan's Rifles, declared in 1913 that the Indian Army's mountain warfare skills were 'a useful fighting asset to any unit under any conditions'. Venour spoke with confidence based partly on the Indian Army's experience against modern shell fire. This had come in August 1900, when three Indian regiments were at the forefront of a wide advance on Beijing by the international coalition force in China for the Boxer Rising. The Indian troops encountered the Chinese Army's

Guards division, trained by German Army instructors and armed with German modern rifles and field artillery. 'We were being shelled the whole time,' recalled Alfred Bingley, a captain of the 7th Rajputs, in an Indian attack on the Chinese Guards' trenches led by the 51st Sikhs of the Frontier Force. At 2000 yards from the trenches the Sikhs adopted their company attack formation for the independent Pukhtun tribal areas, pressing forward at pace in small and scattered rifle-firing groups. As they went, twelve of the Chinese Guards' field guns dropped shrapnel shells among them, killing or wounding twenty-six who fell with severe haemorrhages and fractured bones. But the Sikhs kept going, using inclines in the ground and other natural cover to carry the Guards' position.

The Sikhs' casualties were minimised because of their scattered attack formation, designed to reduce losses against independent Pukhtun rifle fire by not presenting an overly concentrated target, yet achieving the same purpose under Chinese artillery fire. To the Sikhs' right as they had been shelled, a battalion of the United States Army had advanced in closer formation and suffered the consequences: triple the casualties. 'The Indian Army here made a good show and as far as I can see was never behind any other foreigners,' considered Thakur Amar Singh. The military correspondent of *The Times* in China reported the Indian troops' own thoughts at Beijing after their experience of Chinese shell fire. 'They are themselves satisfied – and not without reason – that they could give a good account of themselves if they were ever called upon to meet some of their present allies in the field.' 'Our gallant Indian soldiers,' he concluded, 'are fitted to stand face to face with Continental troops.'

Any view of the pre-war Indian troops' readiness for world war, however, would be incomplete without including the British preserve of Indian high command. This too had its own readiness. The pre-war Indian Army had a modern brain in the form of the Indian General Staff, a vital asset prepared by the British

Empire's visionary rising star of high command, the Scotsman Douglas Haig.

'Let us be <u>quite prepared</u>'

Douglas Haig sailed from England for Bombay in 1909 at the age of forty-eight to be the first Chief of the Indian General Staff. The son of a wealthy whisky baron, he had grown up in Edinburgh, and studied politics, ancient history and French at Oxford. After falling in with the University's drinking clubs the Bullingdon and the Vampyre, Haig had left a term early without a degree, intent on getting on with his ambition in life: making it to the top of the British Army. Haig had joined the 7th Hussars, one of the smarter British cavalry regiments, and gone on to shine at the British Staff College, bagging the more cerebral soldier's laurel of 'passed staff college' or 'p.s.c.'.

A steady rise had ensued as one of the British Army's harder-working officers and outstanding modernisers. A general by 1909, Haig was also welcome in royal circles at Balmoral Castle, Sandringham and Ascot as an old friend of Edward VII. He was a quiet and unusually staccato speaker; notoriously he got stuck for words on the spur of the moment, the joke going that he was as fluent in French as he was in English. Yet he had enormous inner certainty and the confidence to take big decisions quickly. His wife Doris knew that – they had first met in 1905 at Windsor Castle on a Thursday, played golf on the Friday, got engaged on the Saturday, and married a month later at Buckingham Palace.

Haig initially winced at the idea of serving as Chief of the Indian General Staff. For a start, his two daughters were too young to go to India with him, and as a doting father he would miss them. And, like most British Army officers, he had no love or even like for the country. Rather he looked down on it, partly as a parochial backwater with its Indian princes instead of English kings, and partly for its distance from Europe, which he preferred as the heartbeat of modern military affairs with its concentration of the world's largest armies and navies. Haig took up the opening of Chief of the Indian General Staff only as short-term pain for long-term gain – he wanted to ready the Indian Army for a coming world war with Germany, his professional obsession, on which he was in no two minds. 'The Germans will catch us when we are least expecting it,' he wrote, 'so let us be quite prepared.'

Haig saw Germany as the greatest danger to the British Empire, whose downfall as the pre-eminent world power was unthinkable to his imperialist generation. The Germans, he was convinced, would soon make a bid to supersede the British by invading France to dominate continental Europe, then by allying with the Ottoman Empire to expand German influence in the Middle East, probably towards India, exploiting railways between Berlin, Aleppo and Baghdad. 'To hold our own against Germany in Europe or Asia or Egypt we must have an Army,' Haig avowed.

By 'must have an Army', Haig meant that the British Empire's survival depended on its disjointed and locally controlled military parts around the globe, from the Home Army to the Army in India, the Canadian and Australian armies and so on, combining into 'a homogenous Imperial Army controlled from one centre – which must be London'. He was sure that only then, building on the British Army's pre-1914 total of 247,000 active regulars, could this Imperial Army match the German Army, which had 3.8 million men. Further, Haig felt his Imperial Army must be globally mobile with the Royal Navy's help. 'It ought to be con-centrated at the decisive point (wherever that may be) to help defeat the Enemy's main force,' he wrote. Haig did however have a most likely decisive point in mind: France. 'France is in a most difficult position vis-à-vis Germany,' he stated. 'Yet we cannot allow her to go under because our turn would come next, and it seems obviously better to fight with an ally than alone ... We must be able in our own interests to support the French on land.'

In 1910, Haig seriously doubted what role the Indian Army was ready to play in the global conflagration he saw on the horizon. It was particularly weak in artillery. The Indian Mountain Artillery had just seventy-two guns and the British artillery in India 336 field guns and howitzers, but the German artillery had around twenty times as many guns, almost all of them heavier. Another weakness was in numbers of men: the German Army outnumbered the Indian Army 18:1, and the Indian reserve was small at 35,000 men, geared to replenish relatively low losses from rifle fire in the Pukhtun mountains, not large losses from German shelling in Europe.

Haig grudgingly accepted that the politics of colonial government meant the Government of India's coffers were double-locked against paying for any Indian Army expansion in artillery or men. It was the Liberal Prime Minister Herbert Asquith in London who held the keys, and in effect he had thrown them away. Asquith dictated not only that the Government of India adopt a policy of military economy to increase Indian budgets for education, famine relief and other areas of Liberal welfare, but also that the colour bar principle be kept firmly in place, leaving no margin for expensive preparation of the Indian Army to fight the Germans. Asquith was in fact explicit on this point after talk of Haig's idea of Indians fighting in France had reached his ears at 10 Downing Street in 1911. 'I would never in any circumstances agree to such a use of Indian troops,' he told his Secretary of State for India, Lord Crewe.

So to prepare the Indian Army to join his Imperial Army of the future, Haig had to deal in initiatives of no extra cost. He paid special attention to teaching India's British generals about leadership in a German war, hoping to wean them off their traditional diet of high command in the independent Pukhtun tribal areas. Haig's principal tutee in 1910–11 was the fifty-two-year-old British Army general James Willcocks, who as India's Northern Army Commander was its most senior field commander. Willcocks was gregarious and compared to Haig sparkled socially, but without the polish of Oxford and the royal orbit. He came from a substantially poorer background, his father having been a penniless teenage runaway from England who wound up in British India; in fact, Willcocks had been born and grew up outside Delhi. He counted Indian villagers among his friends from childhood, and had spent two years in his teens as a merchant sailor on tramp steamers working trade lanes from Arabia to Italy, ending up in England almost as penniless as his father had left it. He twice failed the officer cadet entrance exam into Sandhurst before scraping in at his third attempt.

Willcocks had gone on to join the British Army, but served exclusively with the Army in India and never in Britain. He started out in the late 1870s with an unfashionable Irish battalion in Punjab, proving an unruly junior officer with a quick temper, a warm heart and habits of writing poetry, gambling, drinking and smoking cigars. Without the family money or the intellectual leanings to apply to the British Staff College, and lacking any social connections to ease his way to promotion, Willcocks had discerned the only way for him to make a successful career was a strong record of field service. So he built one, pursuing Indian appointments and wider imperial secondments with an almost desperate determination.

By 1908 Willcocks had served in thirteen British campaigns in deserts, mountains and jungles from Afghanistan to West Africa, earning him the singular distinction of being the British Army's most decorated soldier for active service. Along the way he had picked up a deep tan, a knighthood for rescuing a beleaguered British garrison in what is now Ghana, and a nasty leg wound in the Burmese jungle – from a spiked bamboo booby-trap and aggravated by swamp leech bites – that left him with a lifelong light limp and daily recourse to a steel leg-brace. 'A nomad I was born and have lived,' Willcocks reflected, as his long-suffering wife Winifred was all too aware. 'The love of adventure must be partly hereditary ... The Army has been my home. War has been for me one long inspiration, and the bugle-call is still the best music I know.'

In January 1908 Willcocks had been handed command of the 1st Indian Division, based at the city of Peshawar in the North-West Frontier Province. 'I have always been a very poor man, but had I been offered a choice between a fortune and command of this particular Division,' he wrote, 'I would unhesitatingly have chosen the latter. It was just the one thing I had dreamed of for years, the fulfilment of my highest hopes.' He had been so delighted because the 1st Division's Peshawar station was by the jaws of danger that were the independent Pukhtun tribal areas, into which Willcocks led the last two British invasions of the pre-1914 era – the small wars of 1908 against the Afridi Zakka clan and the Mohmand. In both these wars Willcocks had led Indian regiments in classic mountain warfare fashion, on horseback at the head of their brigades, and in classic Willcocks fashion, with a Union Jack raised at his side on the move. He had personally issued battle orders by word of mouth for mountainside assaults hastily arranged on the spot. There had been no need for writing detailed battle orders as the Indian regiments were so highly trained in mountain tactics; besides, there had been no time, as the independent Pukhtun *lashkar*s' movements were so fluid their holy warriors had to be caught on the hop.

Willcocks' main task of command in the tribal areas, therefore, had been to inspire, talking daily with the troops to encourage them and pick up their spirits after any sharp reverse. In the fading light one evening in Mohmand, for instance, he had consoled the Punjabi Muslim and Sikh companies of the 22nd Punjabis who had lost eighteen men dead or wounded to Mohmand snipers the night before. He spoke fluently in colloquial Punjabi, having known it since he was a boy, using characteristically kind words while throwing in spontaneous turns of homely phrase, and referring individually to the fallen. Some of the Indian Army's British officers listened in, mightily impressed: 'I have heard no other British service officer – and indeed, few of the Indian army – who could address Indian troops as he did,' William Birdwood reckoned. Willcocks' press corps in Mohmand were also in awe. 'He is the soldier's friend,' commented the *Punjab Times* correspondent in Mohmand. 'Soldiers love him, and will go anywhere with him.'

Willcocks, then, was the archetype of the British general in India whom Haig wanted to prepare for European war, wary that their style of personal leadership in the tribal areas would not do against the Germans in France. For Haig, the American Civil War of 1861–5, the Franco-Prussian War of 1870–1 and the Russo-Japanese War of 1904–5 were the guides for the British Empire's European battlefields of tomorrow. On these, he could see millions of men in open countryside, or in city sieges, arranged in divisions within army corps, army corps within armies, and armies within army groups – and orchestrated by generals not as the soldier's friend in the trenches but in office-building headquarters far behind, as the soldier's remote controller. The headquarters needed to be at a remove so the generals could be bureaucratic master-brains. They had to see their men as numbers on paper in order to achieve the perspective to wield the forces involved, issuing strict timetables for their infantry, artillery and air forces to bring off great attacks in concert. The problem for Haig was that Willcocks and India's other British generals had paid little thought to how to do such things to win battles in Europe – by habit they had focused on the Pukhtun as their most likely enemy.

So in 1910–11 Haig gathered India's generals at command conferences to mould them in his image as students of European warfare. He schooled them in Carl von Clausewitz's *On War* (1832), quoting it reverentially as 'the most profound book on the subject and still the best guide on general principles'. He told them his list of moral qualities essential for leading large forces bound to suffer heavy losses from German shell fire: 'courage, energy, determination, endurance, perseverance, and unselfishness'. He threw in some of his uncompromising dictums, for example 'any decision – even a bad one – is better than indecision'. He then handed out tests in the form of dossiers with questions on planning attacks by multiple divisions in European battle, giving generals a few days to provide him with answers on paper. Some of the generals took the correct scientific approach, using their initiative to work out missing details, and returned meticulous answers. Others did not make such good stabs, scarcely taking interest in the exercise as too remote from their Indian military world – Haig's views on war with Germany were far from common. Willcocks was the worst. He did the opposite of what Haig wanted. 'He does not even make a try but asks for more information,' Haig tutted. 'I think he is quite beyond his depth as an "Army Commander".'

Haig's censure was unalleviated by any social warmth between the two. Willcocks declared that Haig was 'a man with whom, and not withstanding every possible endeavour, I could not hit it off'. They had no mutual friends, Willcocks being a complete stranger to Haig's social haunts in London clubs, British palaces and castles; he even described himself as much the less sophisticated social animal: 'a soldier who has lived in khaki it is true, but worn it in far-away portions of the Empire, and seldom been seen in the purlieus of Pall Mall'. For his part, Haig was immune to the charms of Willcocks' colonial chat and stories of boyhood in British India, sharp scraps in Africa and Burmese booby-traps. He chuckled at him in private as an eccentric adventurer who belonged in imperial outposts with his second-rate senses of social grace and how to dress, nicknaming him 'Sir Willbuck'.

Another avenue for Haig to ready the Indian Army for world war was to develop the Indian General Staff itself. It was a fledgling institution that had emerged from Indian military reforms of the early 1900s under Lord Kitchener, the six-foot, bushy-moustached British Army hero who had led the British forces to victory against the Boers in South Africa in 1902. Kitchener had then been the Indian Commander-in-Chief up to 1909, zealously modernising the Army in India by creating its structure of brigades and divisions, sending senior officers to report back from the Russo-Japanese War, and founding the Indian Staff College in Baluchistan. He also reorganised the staff officers assisting the Commander-in-Chief at Army Headquarters in specialised departments, broadly divided between those organising the fighting formations, which became the Indian General Staff, and those organising the logistical or non-combatant support units, which became the second-string Administrative Staff.

Kitchener's successor as Commander-in-Chief, Garrett O'Moore Creagh, a Victoria Cross-holding Irishman formerly of the 129th Baluchis, had begged Haig to become the Indian General Staff's first Chief – Creagh was shy of office work and saw Haig as his ideal right-hand man at Army Headquarters. Haig therefore had a free hand from Creagh to make what he could of the Indian General Staff, and he modernised it by inspiring new levels of professionalism by his own ferocious example. He demanded longer working hours, more rigorous paperwork and more capable officers, assembling the Army in India's most intellectually disciplined and adaptable staff brains, whether p.s.c. or not. Willcocks looked on unenthused, taking relatively early finishes to his working day to spend time with 'my best friend', his wife Winifred. 'Most of my senior friends were slaves to work,' he said of the change of gear Haig had brought about among the staff. 'From early forenoon to late evening they appeared to live in the midst of office files, and after getting home they generally had piles of papers to look over. No eight-hour days for them; a twelve-hour day better describes what they uncomplainingly endured.'

To help lay foundations for his proposed Imperial Army, Haig rearranged the Indian General Staff's departments into new directorates that mirrored the modern management structure of the British General Staff at the War Office, London's equivalent of Army Headquarters. That way the staff in India and London could cooperate more easily should they be brought together under London's direct control one day, as he hoped. Haig also set the Indian General Staff, and their Administrative Staff peers, working on mobilisation plans to get the Army in India out to France as efficiently as possible, matching the British General Staff's planning in London to do the same for the Home Army.

Haig's plans for an Indian Expeditionary Force to France sharpened the Army in India's traditional speciality in shipping military expeditions, exemplified by the deployment to China in 1900 for the Boxer Rising. They provided for three Indian infantry divisions and four Indian cavalry brigades to embark at Bombay and Karachi for shipping to Egypt and on to France, and featured painstaking minutiae from railway timetables to the weights of regimental baggage allowed on troopships. Indeed Haig prepared a sister scheme to ship an Indian Expeditionary Force up the Persian Gulf to Basra, in case the Ottoman Empire allied with Germany.

Meanwhile Haig held himself aloof from the Indian troops. As an elite British Army officer he had no personal interest in them as the ranks of a colonial service separate to his own, and remained content to view them from a distance. However, he was positively impressed by their professional appearance, for example in 1911 at Delhi where 33,000 Indian soldiers turned out for inspections by George V as their new King-Emperor. Haig noted that at one parade they were 'perfect ... the men stood like rocks', and on a ceremonial march-past on specially laid grass they 'looked splendid, I have never seen troops march better', including the Afridi officer Arsala Khan with the 57th Wilde's Rifles, who were chosen as the march's lead Indian regiment to represent the Frontier Force.

This praise of Haig's was hard-earned because his view of the Indian recruits was not sugared by sentiment. He frequently referred to them as money-men, writing of the Indian service in 1911 as 'a mercenary army, its loyalty must be bought & cannot be presumed'. With European war in mind for them, Haig considered increasing their pay, pensions and land grants as 'very necessary ... to give them a greater interest', but there was not the money for this under the Liberal policy of Indian military economy.

When Haig left British India in 1912 for a new post with the Home Army, the Indian Army's high command, staff officers and mobilising capacity to fight the Germans in Europe were undoubtedly readier than when he had arrived two years earlier. This, in addition to their active service experience, made the Indian Army of 1914 a globalised, worldly-wise weapon. It was something of a rapier, with the Indian General Staff its handle and the Frontier Force its point.

However, the Indian Army's preparedness for world war in 1914 should not be overstated. As Haig knew, it was far from complete, especially in comparison with the great armies of continental Europe that were primed to fight there: the French, German and Russian armies were relative broadswords with their millions of men and extensive artillery. James Willcocks knew well another flaw, that a minority of the Indian regiments had low standards of professionalism, far cries from the Frontier Force. They had not seen active service for twenty years or more, stationed continuously in central or southern India where they had stagnated under unambitious officers. Willcocks had inspected one of them, the 88th Carnatics, at Calcutta in 1910 and seethed at their scruffiness – on sentry duty sitting on the ground, boots off, smoking cigarettes. 'You are the worst regiment I have ever seen anywhere,' an apoplectic Willcocks had thundered.

Still, when the Indian Army's summons arrived in 1914, it was ready to go. How willing its men would be to see things through, given their frustrations at unequal racial treatment, and those thoughts hidden from the British – or not, in the case of the independent Pukhtun – remained to be seen.

Two

1914

4

'VIVENT LES HINDOUS!'

'Vive Angleterre!', 'Vivent les Hindous!', 'Vivent les Alliés!' the delirious French crowds shouted on the streets of Marseilles in the early afternoon sunshine, men and women waving their hats and cheering at the roadside, standing on café tables and chairs, all welcoming the Indian troops marching in from the port. The crowds lined the streets for five miles through the city as the troops made their way to camp, on a racecourse by the coast road to the Côte d'Azur. It was 26 September 1914, Indian Expeditionary Force A to France had arrived that morning, and the people of the city that day adored them as heroic liberators from German oppression. 'These strangers from a distant land,' said the novelist Maurice Barrès, 'astound us by standing shoulder to shoulder with us in the defence of French soil.'

The first Indian regiment to land was the 129th Baluchis, with their majority of independent Pukhtun and young British officer Harold Lewis. The 129th's regimental band returned the rapturous welcome on their Indian drums and pipes by striking up the French national anthem, the Marseillaise, sending the crowds even wilder. Many people were so excited they broke in among the marching Pukhtun, Punjabi Muslims and Sikhs, women running up to kiss them, pin roses to their tunics and hand them French flags, while children jumped up to hang around their necks and swing between them. The Frontier Force's 57th Wilde's Rifles, with the Afridi officer Arsala Khan and his company of Malik Din clansmen, marched behind the 129th Baluchis, their turbans bobbing in a sea of smiling French faces. 'Never have troops had a more hearty welcome in a foreign city than the Indians received here,' a British reporter of the *Daily Mirror* breathlessly wired home.

Indian Expeditionary Force A had covered the 6000 miles from British India to France in just fifty-one days since the Cabinet's original call, including a week's stopover at Cairo. And these were momentous days: Douglas Haig's pre-war Indian General Staff plans enabled Force A to mobilise more swiftly than any previous major Indian deployment, and its progress attracted global press attention and electrified Indian politics as the colour bar principle for the Indian Army was scrapped. All the while Harold Lewis, Arsala Khan and the others of Force A's Indian regiments – packed with well-trained veterans of China, the independent Pukhtun tribal areas and other pre-1914 campaigns – moved with a calm professionalism, never knowing their destination until they were far from British India.

'Thrown into the scale'

'If we are entering into the struggle,' the Prime Minister Herbert Asquith told Parliament on 6 August, 'let us now make sure that all the resources, not only of this United Kingdom, but of the vast Empire of which it is the centre, shall be thrown into the scale.' Asquith went on that the British Army needed 500,000 new recruits, India was ready to send two divisions to Europe alongside forces from Canada, Australia and New Zealand, and an initial £100 million from the British taxpayer was required to help pay for them all. He gave the rationale for these measures only vaguely, indicating that his new Secretary of State for War,

India's former Commander-in-Chief Lord Kitchener, had given him a 'sense of the gravity and the necessities of the case', and that 'the Mother Country must set the example'. Asquith left unsaid exactly what Kitchener had advised and what the example was – these were in fact government secrets of the Cabinet Room at 10 Downing Street that had only become known to Asquith himself in the last twenty-four hours, involving the confidential lifting of the colour bar principle.

In the Cabinet Room Asquith had chaired an impromptu war council of senior ministers and armed services advisers including Haig and Kitchener. They had discussed Britain's grand strategy against Germany, and quickly come to grave conclusions. Haig repeated much of his pre-war thinking on the need for an Imperial Army at the decisive point to defeat the Germans, telling Asquith that the British Empire must gather a force in France as strong and as soon as possible. 'Great Britain and Germany would be fighting for their existence,' read Haig's note on what he said. 'Therefore the war was to be a long war ... I held we must organise our resources for *a war of several years*. Great Britain must at once take in hand the creation of an Army. I mentioned one million as the number to aim at immediately.' Kitchener agreed with Haig on the need for at least a million men, and put a number on the war's length: a minimum of three years.

It was on this basis that Asquith's war council mobilised Britain's naval and military forces around the world, sending the British Expeditionary Force to France – the BEF, initially 100,000 men of the Home Army – and reeling in support from all corners of the empire. Haig and Kitchener took it for granted that the Indian Army would come to Europe part of this scheme, with the colour bar principle automatically abandoned out of strategic necessity. The Mother Country's example Asquith told Parliament of, therefore, was intensive and expensive mobilisation to underwrite a war of several years, to be waged by the British Empire as a whole.

The war council's sole dissenter on lifting the colour bar principle was an old India hand, Frederick Roberts, a Victorian Commander-in-Chief in India who could still smell the gunsmoke at Delhi from the Great Rebellion of 1857, which as a young soldier he had fought to put down. 'He strongly deprecated the sending of Indian troops to Europe, to the horror of K. and all the other Generals,' Asquith recalled. More than anyone else in the Cabinet Room, Roberts was a purist when it came to prestige, and he shuddered at the prospect of allowing Indian troops to fight the Germans; he had seen enough of them killing white men half a century earlier.

The lead balloon of his colonial preoccupations was ignored even as it fell. Haig, knowing that India had his mobilisation plans for an Indian Expeditionary Force to France, endorsed the war council's decision to call for two Indian infantry divisions and a cavalry brigade for the BEF as a start. Kitchener relayed the decision to the India Office, where the Secretary of State, Lord Crewe, made no quibble about lifting the colour bar principle and wired the Government of India to request the Indian units for Egypt, on standby for France.

The Viceroy in 1914, who was to be India's war leader until 1916, was Charles Hardinge. A former diplomat of the British Foreign Office who had served from St Petersburg to Tehran and Istanbul, he had been the Viceroy since 1910. Intellectually vain and a little clipped and cold in public, he was a warm family man in private. He had married the love of his life, Bena, in 1890 and had three children, two of them now young men in the British Army and the third the apple of his eye, his daughter Diamond, aged fourteen. Hardinge had always been inseparable from Bena, depending on her behind the scenes, above all in 1912 after a Hindu terrorist bombing at Delhi nearly killed him on an elephant. The explosion had been heard six miles away, and Hardinge had suffered deep cuts from metal bomb fragments in his neck and back. Bena had nursed him back to health following several operations to remove the metal, but he had been on edge ever since, and had removed all independent Pukhtun from his Indian Army guard for fear of assassination.

In March 1914 Bena had gone back to England to see their two boys. Hardinge had seen her off at Bombay, watching as her ship faded into the evening gloom on the horizon. 'It was a sad moment for me, but I did not know then how sad,' he said. In July an unexpected telegram arrived for Hardinge at Simla with tragic news: in London, unexpectedly, Bena had died after an emergency operation. Hardinge was inconsolable. 'I was entirely knocked out by this blow, and was only saved from collapse by the untiring kindness and sympathy of Diamond.'

Hardinge had barely slept for three weeks by the time the First World War broke out, when he received the India Office's request for the two Indian divisions and a cavalry brigade to be put on standby for France. He was still getting hand-written letters from Bena delivered by sea-mail, and the war came as a jolt to distract him. 'I am extremely busy with the details of the military preparations,' he confided in a friend. 'I have absolutely no time for anything else, and I am very glad of it.'

Hardinge worked closely at Simla with India's new Scottish Commander-in-Chief Beauchamp Duff, an Indian Army officer appointed in 1913 for his bureaucratic credentials. Duff had only a brief regimental career with the 9th Gurkhas in the 1880s before gaining his p.s.c. at the British Staff College, and renown as one of India's outstanding staff minds with a string of appointments at Army Headquarters. For mobilisation in 1914, Duff had the more than capable help of two Canadians recently brought in to continue the Indian General Staff's pre-war modernisation. Firstly Percy Lake, whose family was from Quebec, and who was a former Chief of the Canadian General Staff, now the Chief of the Indian General Staff; and secondly George Kirkpatrick from Ontario, Lake's Director of Military Operations, who had wide staff experience in Nova Scotia,

London, South Africa and most recently in Australia as the military Inspector-General.

From 7 August, on shifts twenty-four hours a day, Duff, Lake and Kirkpatrick clicked Army Headquarters at Simla into war mode, regularly reporting to Hardinge. They used Haig's pre-war plans to mobilise as Indian Expeditionary Force A the Indian units requested by London. They picked the 3rd and 7th Indian Divisions based in Punjab and the 9th Cavalry Brigade at Secunderabad to the south, containing Frontier Force and other high-quality Indian battalions for the European test. From the political point of view, they were instructed by Hardinge to give the two divisions six British battalions, for the good of prestige to remind the Indian troops they were colonial subjects.

Duff, Lake and Kirkpatrick then swiftly followed the procedures laid down by Haig for gathering Indian Expeditionary Force A at British India's western ports of Bombay and Karachi, equipping and shipping them to Egypt. They blocked out railway lines for troop trains; they allocated British batteries of field artillery, discounting the Indian Mountain Artillery for France as too low calibre against heavier German guns; they organised Indian Medical Service stretcher bearer companies, horse-drawn ambulances and field hospitals, along with animal transport units including pack mule corps; and they requisitioned merchant ships from around the coast of India for the Sappers and Miners to convert into troopships complete with access ramps, rifle racks, baggage containers and animal stalls.

'The order to mobilize could not have come at a worse time,' observed Kenneth Henderson, a young Glaswegian officer of the 39th Garhwals. His regiment was at Lansdowne, a Himalayan hill-station, when on 8 August the fateful yellow envelope arrived for war service overseas, destination unknown. A third of the regiment's Garhwalis selected for Indian Expeditionary Force A were on summer leave in their villages in the Garhwal mountains. 'Some of our men's homes were from 15 to 20 days' road journey distant,' wrote Henderson. 'In some cases men could not come, or even be summoned owing to interruption of the precarious Himalayan communications by landslips, flooded rivers and the like in the height of the monsoon.'

Other Indian regiments of Force A had similar difficulties once they had their yellow envelopes. They were stationed on an arc spanning 2500 miles from an Afghan border post in British India's north-western province of Baluchistan to the North-West Frontier Province down to Hyderabad, south-east of Bombay. They also had a third of their men on summer leave, British officers too – anywhere from hunting on the Indian Empire's Tibetan border to trips to Australia and fishing in the west of Ireland. But they had to get ready for their trains to port in just two weeks.

The response of the Indian troops on leave was resoundingly professional. They came in as quickly as they could, whether called through Punjabi post offices or by Afridi runners sent into the independent Pukhtun tribal areas where the post did not go. Some even came back of their own accord. 'The esprit de corps of the Regiment was so fine,' the 59th Scinde Rifles' regimental history recorded, 'that in many cases men on leave and furlough, hearing bazaar rumours as to mobilization, returned of their own accord without waiting for any official notification.'

Only tiny scraps of Indian conversation survive from the hour of Force A's mobilisation. But it seems clear its Indian troops, like the Afridi officer Arsala Khan of the 57th Wilde's Rifles, had no understanding of the cause of their mobilisation as a showdown between democracy and Prussian militarism. Rather they assumed they were needed for China, Somalia or some other previous destination around the Indian Ocean to put down another anti-imperial rising. At the 129th Baluchis' cantonment at Firozpur in Punjab, their British officer Harold Lewis noticed how his independent Pukhtun troops from Tirah and Waziristan made a point of distancing themselves from whatever the cause was. 'Heaps of men when talking about the war always talked about your troops, your ships,' he wrote.

A few men did decline to come in on mobilisation. Predictably they were independent Pukhtun on leave in their tribal areas, where their mullahs, who had heard news of war in Europe, took the opportunity to predict painful deaths for Pukhtun recruits of the British there. The mullahs seem to have known a little of the horrors of European war, apparently including poison gas after tales of its use in the Italo-Turkish War of 1911–12 had reached them on the Islamic world's grapevine. 'All our women were mad with terror at these stories,' said a Pukhtun elder, 'and hung round the necks of reservists and recruits, imploring them not to go to certain death in an unknown country where they would not even have a grave.' In Waziristan, one Mahsud soldier was even stopped from rejoining by his womenfolk tying him up at home. Nonetheless, most of Force A's Indian regiments managed to regroup in two weeks to catch their trains on time, in the case of its six Gurkha battalions by drawing on other Gurkha units to fill the places of men on leave in Nepal who would take weeks longer to come in.

Sir Pratap Singh, meanwhile, the socialite and Hindu Rajput commandant of the princely States regiment the Jodhpur Lancers, had at the grand age for an active soldier of seventy rushed to Army Headquarters at Simla. He was on a charm offensive for his Lancers and their titular Commander-in-Chief the Maharajah of Jodhpur, aged seventeen, to get them attached to Indian Expeditionary Force A as the princely States' representatives. In Jodhpur State, he had been known in private when there were no British about for his sharp tongue against them, for instance for social slights he had endured from haughty British civil servants. But now he pulled out all the stops to secure European service for his regiment as befitting his social status among the princes and his undimmed military ambition, having served in Britain's wars in Afghanistan, China and elsewhere since the 1870s. Sir Pratap was granted his wish in mid-August, when the Commander-in-Chief Beauchamp Duff judged the Jodhpur Lancers well trained and reliable enough to face the Germans.

Sir Pratap did not stop there, however, next fishing for an honorary staff appointment in France with the BEF's General Headquarters. 'Ever looking to Your Majesty as my second God,' read Sir Pratap's toadying telegram to Buckingham Palace in hope of a good word from George V,

> I consider it my sacred duty to serve Your Majesty personally at this time. I will deem it a special mark of royal favour and a great honour if allowed to serve on Your Majesty's Staff. Your Majesty's old Rajput soldier eagerly awaits royal commands to be present at your gracious feet.

The Hindu diarist Thakur Amar Singh, as the Indian Army's most senior Indian officer with a King's Commission, was also given a slot with Indian Expeditionary Force A. He was at home on his family estate in Jaipur State on 17 August when he got his mobilisation order, to join the 3rd Indian Division at the port of Karachi in a continuation of his pre-war role as an aide-de-camp. Amar Singh's family, like every other Indian soldier's, had no idea where he was going. His wife and mother were 'too much upset by the news of my being ordered for active service', he wrote, in large part because he was leaving behind his one-year-old baby girl, adored all the more after he and his wife Rasal had previously lost three girls and a boy to infant deaths from smallpox and other diseases. Unfortunately Amar Singh's diary for the subsequent mobilisation period disappeared in 1915 aboard a mail-ship sunk by a German submarine, but most likely he – along with his fellow Hindu Rajputs of Force A such as those of the 41st Dogras – shared something of Sir Pratap Singh's Rajput view of foreign service:

Wars and strifes, being painful and horrifying, are looked upon as uncivilized and detestable, but to us Kshatriyas such chances of upholding our Dharma [righteous path] are rare, and so naturally, on the commencement of this Great War, my innate feeling of serving . . . was roused. Religiously, for a Rajput, war is an open door to heaven.

Amar Singh took his astrologer's advice on the most auspicious time to depart for the war on 18 August, waving farewell to his family at precisely 7.09 p.m. He then visited his Hindu priest for a travel blessing, taking away a *Rudrakash* (holy beads for chanting mantras) no doubt praying for his little girl to live until he returned, before crossing the border out of Jaipur State into British India.

The troop trains of Indian Expeditionary Force A steamed into the ports of Bombay and Karachi from the third week of August. For those coming into Karachi from Punjab, the summer heat in the Sind Desert had been so extreme it caused Force A's first casualties, some British troops of the Connaught Rangers from Galway in the west of Ireland, who died of heat stroke. The regiments of Force A spilled off their trains on to the quaysides at both ports to wait their turn to board ship over the following days. Most of the younger Gurkha recruits saw the sea for the first time, going down to the beaches at Bombay to investigate. Having never encountered saltwater before, they were surprised by its strange taste and its lack of lather with their soap; some of the Gurkhas reasoned they had chanced upon a dirty patch of water and ran down the beach looking for a cleaner spot.

Force A's regiments embarked slickly, guided by experienced officers and men such as the 57th Wilde's Rifles' Afridi officer Arsala Khan who had served overseas at one time or another since the 1890s, and also using Indian General Staff guidance notes. Some battalions were so practised they embarked in forty-five minutes flat. The only real trouble was given by Force A's four-legged friends – the stubborn mules of the pack transport on the gangways at Bombay. 'There was one animal which had evidently made up its mind that it would not take a sea voyage, but after kicking half a dozen men and scattering the crowd it yielded to the inevitable and stood upon the gangway,' recalled Heber Alexander, a British officer of the 9th Mule Corps. 'There was not then room enough to kick, so some of the men hoisted the beast on their shoulders and bore it triumphantly up the gangway and into the hold: that mule literally smiled over the trouble he was giving.'

The Force A convoys sailed from 22 August, with Royal Navy escorts, essential given that German cruisers were on the prowl for Allied shipping. The Gurkhas' attentions turned to how their ships found the way. Their common conclusion was that these vessels must work like trains and be attached to rails under the water.

'Bengal Lancers fluttering down the streets of Berlin'

'For my part, I venture to hope that our Indian troops coming to Europe will be in at the death,' the former Viceroy Lord Curzon told a boisterous crowd at a packed concert hall in Glasgow on 11 September. 'I should like to see the lances of the Bengal Lancers fluttering down the streets of Berlin, and I should like to see the dark-skinned Gurkha making himself at ease in the gardens of Potsdam.' Curzon's speech tapped into the British public's excitement following Lord Kitchener's announcement on 28 August that Indian Expeditionary Force A was bound for France. Kitchener had confirmed it to Parliament, rubber-stamping the war council's previously secret decision of 5–6 August to lift the colour bar principle. The timing was down to the BEF's heavy losses in late August, on its desperate 200-mile retreat under German attack from Mons in Belgium back into north-eastern France on the left of the French Army; Kitchener needed to show that BEF casualties could be replaced by ready reinforcements, and Indian Expeditionary Force A was part of the answer. Internationally, Kitchener's announcement aroused instant praise and condemnation, turning Force A's passage to Europe into a major news story in the world's press.

The Secretary of State for India Lord Crewe set the tone of the British public response to the news. He preferred not to draw attention to the bleak strategic causes of lifting the colour bar, but to push a positive message that doing so was a generous British gift to the Indian people. Crewe told Parliament that raising the colour bar was a token of newfound British government fairness and respect for Indian subjects, opening a new channel of equal opportunity:

> It is well known in India that the African troops of the French Army [who] have been assisting the troops in France are of native origin ... It would have been a disappointment to our loyal Indian fellow-subjects if they had found themselves debarred for any reason from taking part in the campaign on the continent of Europe. We shall find our Army there reinforced by [Indian] soldiers, high-souled men of first-rate training ... and we feel certain that if they are called upon they will give the best possible account of themselves side by side with our British troops in encountering the enemy.

Crewe's speech was widely reported in the British press which revelled euphorically in the lifting of the colour bar: it took the war to a new pitch of global drama while reinforcing the moral worth of the British cause for democracy. *The Times* talked of the bar's raising as 'momentous ... for the world', 'turning the first page of a new history of civilization', and 'manifest proof and sign of new developments in the relations of East and West'. It added that 'no incident in this world-wide struggle has made a deeper impression upon the Imperial mind than the swift and successful transportation of the picked legions of India', calling Indian Expeditionary Force A 'India's glorious answer to the Kaiser ... Asia has joined in the battle against brutal lust for power, and her weapons are turned against him.'

The German press naturally saw no glory in the colour bar story, portraying the French African and Indian troops as racial inferiors who had no place on Europe's battlefields against their cultural betters. The German sociologist Max Weber captured the national mood by decrying the gathering Allied forces of Africa and India in France as 'an army of niggers, Gurkhas and all the barbarians of the world'. In the cafés of Berlin, a journalist of the *New York Times* noticed 'an interesting tendency to make fun of the fighting value of the native Indian troops, whose landing at Marseilles received much publicity in the German press'. Meanwhile Karl Götz, the Bavarian artist, designed some popular bronze medallions mocking the Indian Army at Marseilles as nothing more than a travelling circus, with the Indian troops as the elephant handlers.

In British India the colour bar issue was seized upon by the mainstream Indian nationalist politicians as a lever for British concessions towards self-government. A British war for democracy was one the Indian politicians could sincerely support, but with the trade-off that they would receive democratic benefits once it was won. They took this approach in line with their moderate pre-war politics of cooperating with the British for improved status as imperial subjects, in the process garnering increased Indian press support, but still not cultivating a mass popular following. 'We can put a wall of Indians in the field against which the Germans will hurl themselves in vain,' avowed Bhupendra Nath Bose, the President of the Indian National Congress, in a typical display of the Indian politicians' loyalty. 'In the melting pot of destiny, race, creed and colour are disappearing. Let us be ready for the future ... I see my country occupying an honourable and proud place in the comity of nations.'

The grieving Viceroy, Charles Hardinge, took real satisfaction in the Indian politicians' support for the war. It seemed a reward for his 'progressive' relationship with them since he had taken office in 1910, striving for a relatively liberal partnership in which he championed the incremental concessions to improve Indians' status within the empire, but under ongoing British control rather than any self-government like the empire's self-governing 'Dominions', such as Australia or Canada. The lifting of the colour bar was the latest concession, and he was content it had secured the partnership for now. 'Let us display to the world an attitude of unity, and of unswerving confidence under all circumstances in the justice of our cause and in the assurance that God will defend the right,' he said in a speech of 8 September reminding the Indian politicians what he expected of them.

The colour bar news reached the ships of Indian Expeditionary Force A by radio on 31 August, in the sweltering heat of the Arabian Sea. For Harold Lewis of the 129th Baluchis, his immediate response was sheer excitement. 'I never dreamed that we could actually get into a European war, in the Indian Army,' he jotted excitedly. 'It is too good to be true.' But then his thoughts turned to the political implications for prestige, and he agreed with other British officers on what these would be: 'The general opinion was that an Indian victory over white troops would have a bad effect in India.'

Lewis asked his independent Pukhtun troops how they saw the prospect of fighting the Germans. 'The men are very keen though the chief desire is to be allowed to keep any German rifles they capture.' He wondered whether his younger recruits' home lives, peppered with killings by modern guns in feuds, might be some preparation for the European war. 'Our men go in risk of their lives daily at home, but they have never had to lie in the open under shell fire,' he thought. 'Still, I think they will do it well. They are fatalists absolutely. Man can only die once, they say, and war is a worthy place to die in.'

However, almost nothing is known of other Indian troops' thoughts at sea when they heard of their deployment to France to fight white men. Back in British India, Hardinge was sure 'there is not a single sepoy that has gone to France that does not realise ... he is on trial with European troops', adding the Indians would be 'determined ... not [to] be found wanting.' Conversational snippets to show whether the sepoys recruited from British India really thought this themselves aboard their troopships have yet to come to light. As for Indian recruits from elsewhere, the young Gurkhas appeared most absorbed by their surroundings as they headed up the Suez Canal, captivated by their glimpses of sea life, gaping in particular at porpoises and flying fish.

Force A's leading troopships arrived in Egypt on 9 September, and it paused there for a week to provide garrison troops at London's request. Its 3rd Indian Division disembarked at Suez with customary expeditionary efficiency, and a few days later marched through the streets of Cairo. The object was a show of force to intimidate the city's people, a top-up to the prestige of local British control after Egypt's British Army garrison had left for France.

By 23 September Force A had re-embarked at Alexandria to cross the Mediterranean, to reach Marseilles on the 26th. The British press was on hand to greet it, *The Times* covering its disembarkation in glowing terms, spotting 'the perfection of the transport and commissariat of the various detachments – their endless trains of carts and lorries, mountainously piled with fodder and foodstuffs, with ammunition and camp-gear of every description, all moving from ship to camp with clockwork preci-sion'. The younger Gurkhas again marvelled, struck by the sight of their first Western metropolis. 'The 101 new wonders of a European town,' wrote Edward Tuite-Dalton, a major of the 3rd Gurkhas, 'combined to complete the bewilderment of the Gurkha ranks, whose feelings may well be compared to those of Alice in Wonderland.' At their camp outside Marseilles, the Indian troops then awaited their senior commander whom they had not seen yet. Many of them knew him, though: it was James Willcocks.

'Give them my salaams'

James Willcocks landed at Marseilles on 30 September. He had come straight from Punjab to lead Indian Expeditionary Force A's main infantry battle formation on the western front – the newly created Indian Army Corps, containing the 3rd and 7th Indian Divisions. This was known as the Indian Corps for short, while its divisions, for their time with the BEF, were renamed the Lahore and the Meerut respectively in order to avoid confusion with the 3rd and 7th British divisions. With Willcocks were Indian General Staff officers for his corps headquarters staff, carefully picked from among India's best as nurtured by Douglas Haig before the war.

Willcocks' first thought at Marseilles was to visit his Indian soldiers in camp, where he enjoyed many a reunion. 'I was personally acquainted with every officer and a great many of the N.C.O.s and men,' he wrote. 'I was in the happy position of having with me troops all of whom I had helped to train at one or other of the numerous military stations of north India.' With several Indian officers such as the Afridi Arsala Khan, Willcocks reminisced about the Mohmand small war of 1908, and with others about regimental guest nights in India when they had dined, smoked and sung together. 'The condition and spirit of the troops so far arrived in France is excellent,' Willcocks wrote to Kitchener. 'Nothing could be better.' Kitchener soon replied, 'I am glad to hear that the Indian troops are *razi* (happy), give them my salaams and tell them I feel sure they will maintain their records of the past when they meet the Germans.'

Up to mid-October the Indian regiments headed north from Marseilles, by rail into the rich countryside of Languedoc and Aquitaine. They passed medieval castles, mile after mile of vineyards, and high viaducts with rivers far below. 'Our men are immensely struck with the country,' Harold Lewis remarked having heard his independent Pukhtun comment on how green France was. One of Lewis's Mahsud leaned out of the train for a closer look only to fall off, and had to make his way back to the last station. He rejoined easily enough by another train, no doubt well entertained in the meantime by the women and children of the countryside who at every station cheered the Indian troops as liberators, giving them coffee, baguettes, apples, pears and bunches of grapes, and even personal trinkets such as puff-powder boxes. The locals asked for the Indians' uniform buttons and regimental badges as mementos, and threw so many flowers through the carriage windows that floors were soon covered in stalks and petals.

On the trains the British officers generally tried to appear cheerful and relaxed about what lay ahead, but there were some who could not hide their fear. 'I remember noticing with something of a shock one early morning on our rail journey,' said the 39th Garhwals' Kenneth Henderson of a brother British officer of the regiment, Major Pelham Home,

> that he took out a flask and had a nip of brandy 'to steady himself'. And he never was without a lighted cigarette between his fingers, except when actually asleep. What we feared most was the effect on the men. [My Garhwali orderly] asked me what had happened to Home Sahib; and when I explained that it was an illness, he smiled queerly and said the men were saying he was afraid.

The British troops from India with Willcocks' Indian Corps drank much harder. At Toulouse railway station in the early evening of 1 October, the Connaught Rangers raucously celebrated their regiment's part in the siege of the town a hundred years earlier, each man downing a litre of red wine.

The Indian trains came to a halt west of Paris in the Loire valley. Here the Indian Corps camped for two weeks in mid-October, on the banks of the River Loire, as a staging post in order to add motor lorries and other vehicles to its mule pack transport from India. 'The motor lorries were new to them,' wrote Willcocks, noting the curiosity of his Indian troops. 'They simply took it for granted that in a European war everything was going to be new.' Many of the Indians took day trips into the local town, Orléans. 'The men from camp are allowed to make use of the lorries when visiting the town, where a great deal of shopping is done,' said a British transport officer. 'One frequently sees a cheerful crowd of 50 or so Sikhs, Pathans and others thundering along the road.' Looking out from the lorries they were intrigued by the roadside crucifixes of rural Catholic France, assuming these represented tortured criminals as a public warning against crime.

The Afridi officer Arsala Khan and his Malik Din company of the 57th Wilde's Rifles focused on professional matters. Not only fitness training and route-marching through fields – from which they returned with gifts of fruit from friendly farmers – but also spending hours a day at a French Army shooting range to practise with new rifles issued at Marseilles to all Indian Expeditionary Force A. The rifles were a slightly different pattern from those Force A had sailed with; its men now had Home Army Lee-Enfield Mark IIIs instead of Army in India Mark IIs (the change allowed them to use the same Mark III ammunition as the original BEF). The rifle swap has often been highlighted by historians as putting the Indians at a distinct disadvantage, as if they were exchanging Victorian weaponry for something modern and uncomfortably unfamiliar, which all British troops had before the war and they did not. But the swap amounted only to a slight change to the same type of modern rifle that they and British troops had been trained with in India. Still, the Afridi of the Frontier Force's 58th Vaughan's Rifles were taken aback by the change in rifles. 'The remarks of the Afridis as they were ordered to throw their [pre-war Mark II] rifle worth at least 800 rupees in Tirah on to a heap of other rifles, and take a new one, were worth hearing,' recollected their British officer, Captain Alexander Lind. 'They had never imagined there were so many rifles in the world.'

Thakur Amar Singh, meanwhile, arrived at the Indian Corps' camp on the Loire on 8 October. As ever without any real work to do as an aide-de-camp, he greeted the Hindu, Sikh and Muslim maharajahs or aristocrats who had been given honorary staff positions, and rode off alone into the Loire valley to explore. In the vineyards, he slipped off his horse to touch the neat rows of vines. 'These people know how to make a place beautiful,' he wrote. 'I am going to try and grow in this system in Jaipur when I get there.' He also found the great Loire châteaux, going inside the Château de Fontainebleau for a guided tour. 'I have no command of language sufficient to describe it, I never thought anything could be so superb and magnificent.' Sitting outside a café by the Château de Blois, Amar Singh became the centre of attention. 'There was a whole crowd of boys and girls and young and old men and women round me. I was a new object to them.'

Back in the Indian camp, Arsala Khan was freshly promoted as the 57th Wilde's Rifles' acting subadar-major, the pinnacle of his career so far. This was almost certainly a responsibility he was set on living up to, like his father Umar before him; any fear he might show in front of his Malik Din clansmen could be the shameful talk of Tirah for years to come. Arsala Khan and his Afridi had of course long known of the German Army, given that one of their own Malik Din company in China had shot and killed German soldiers for insulting them during the Boxer Rising. It was no doubt a point of mirth among them that the incident had indeed panicked the entire German camp, with hundreds of German troops rushing from their tents all because of one man of their tribe.

James Willcocks did his best to stir the Indian troops on the

Loire ahead of battle. 'You will be helping to make history,' declared his Order of the Day for 10 October:

> You will be the first Indian soldiers of the King-Emperor who will have the honour of showing in Europe that the sons of India have lost none of their ancient martial instincts and are worthy of the confidence reposed in them. In battle you will remember that your religions enjoin on you that to give your life doing your duty is your highest reward ... You will fight for your King-Emperor and your faith, so that history will record the doings of India's sons, and your children will proudly tell of the deeds of their fathers.

The impact of this rhetoric on the Indian troops themselves can only be guessed at. Perhaps some felt inspired, or perhaps it went in one ear and out the other, something to shrug at – just fine British words.

The 57th Wilde's Rifles with Arsala Khan, the 129th Baluchis with Harold Lewis and the hard-drinking Connaught Rangers were the Indian Corps' first regiments to leave the Loire for the front, in the third week of October. Willcocks had wanted the whole Indian Corps to have more time to collect itself with further equipment from Home Army stocks, including a few new machine guns, signalling apparatus and field telephone systems, besides heavy British artillery to augment their British field guns from India. Kitchener had just given such time to the Canadian Expeditionary Force arriving in England – six months' training on Salisbury Plain – but he refused in the case of Indian Expeditionary Force A. Knowing well the Indian battalions' pre-war training and battle experience as their ex-Commander-in-Chief, he gave them no leeway, judging them, unlike the Canadians, ready to go straight into battle.

Since the BEF's retreat from Belgium in August it had fought with the French in September at the Battle of the Marne, blocking the German onslaught on Paris. The Germans had then taken the defensive east of the capital and gone in search of decisive victory by encircling the Allied forces of Belgians, French and British from the north. Finding no way through against the French in the Somme valley in late September, by October they were looking to smash past the Allies in Flanders – the low-lying farming plain by the North Sea, dotted with villages, manure heaps and woods, and criss-crossed by canals, irrigation ditches and hedgerows. The Germans gathered a large force there for a fresh offensive, and the Allies prepared their own line. The BEF took up a large swathe of it, around 35 miles hinging on the medieval town of Ypres, to the right of the French and Belgians who held the line up to the North Sea.

The Indians reached their railheads in Flanders from 19 October, some going through Calais. 'The men had been told that the coast of "Vilayet" (England) could be seen from Calais, and they were greatly excited about this,' wrote the 9th Mule Corps' officer Heber Alexander, 'but unfortunately it was raining hard; there was a thick mist, and no white cliffs were visible.' Inland, as the Indians turned out of the Flemish railway stations, British and French reconnaissance aeroplanes flew back and forth overhead, and desperate refugees escaping the Germans to the east streamed along the roads pulling carts laden with household possessions. Amid all this the Indians had little sense of where they were. 'Do just tell me, which is Belgium and which is France: in which direction is London: and where are the enemy now?', one Muslim of the 129th Baluchis asked near his railhead on encountering Philip Howell, a British officer of the 4th Hussars (who spoke Pushtu as an ex-officer of the Indian Army's Guides). Then, as it got dark, the Indians began to see multiple flashes on the horizon, followed by sharp muffled sounds like distant slamming doors. The German artillery was launching Berlin's final bid to win the war in the west in 1914 – the First Battle of Ypres – attacking the length of the Allied line.

The Indian regiments' part in First Ypres was to be widespread. John French, the BEF's Commander-in-Chief, directed them to reinforce the BEF line at both ends, some on the left in Belgium by Ypres and some on the right in France by the village of Neuve Chapelle. The Indian vanguard, sent to the Belgian end of the BEF line, was the 57th Wilde's Rifles with their Afridi officer Arsala Khan. To get up to the British trenches on the morning of 22 October they were collected from near their railhead by red London buses freshly brought over the English Channel as troop carriers, still emblazoned with their pre-war London advertisements for Buchanan's Black & White Scotch whisky, Carter's Little Liver Pills and Glaxo baby food. 'This was of course lost on the men,' recorded Wilde's Rifles' regimental history, 'but produced much amusement among the Connaught Rangers, [and] a certain longing for a glimpse of England among the officers.' Wilde's Rifles stepped off their buses at the Belgian village of Wulverghem, where British Army officers were waiting to show them to their trenches.

As it happened, the first men of the Indian Army to go into the front line in the First World War were not from India: they were Arsala Khan's Afridi company of Malik Din clansmen. With them was their British officer of many years Ronald Gordon, a Scotsman in his late thirties who had led them to China in 1900 and into Mohmand in 1908, and who had in fact just got married, in Melbourne, Australia on 6 August, getting his ship the next day to rejoin his Afridi. With Gordon and Arsala Khan at their head, the men of Tirah marched into the unknown.

5

'IN THE NICK OF TIME'

'The Indian Expeditionary Force arrived in the nick of time,' proclaimed the former Viceroy Lord Curzon in 1917, as a senior British Cabinet minister looking back on First Ypres. 'That it helped to save the cause both of the Allies and of civilization, after the sanguinary tumult of the opening weeks of the War, has been openly acknowledged by the highest in the land, from the Sovereign downwards. I recall that it was emphatically stated to me by Lord French himself.' John French did say such things not only to his political and royal superiors, but also to his fellow British generals, declaring of the Indian reinforcements 'each man was worth his weight in gold'. F. E. Smith, the future Secretary of State for India writing as the wartime Attorney-General, added his emphatic judgement, also in 1917: 'the Indian Corps saved the Empire. The proposition to those who know the facts is almost self-evident.'

All these British grandees had a global nightmare in mind. The consequences of Allied defeat at First Ypres, they thought, would have been a German breakthrough to capture all of Belgium, the northern French seaboard and Paris, guaranteeing Allied defeat in western Europe – and shortly afterwards in eastern Europe too, where the Russian Army could not have coped alone against the

Germans combined with the Austrians. By extension, it seemed to them, Prussian militarism would have triumphed over democracy in Europe, and the Allies' African and Asian empires would have been exposed to a German takeover. Yet the world, they were saying, never woke up to this nightmare because of Indian Expeditionary Force A.

After more than a hundred years, it can safely be said the idea that Indian Expeditionary Force A averted an Allied apocalypse has hardly made it into the history books. Rather, the Indian part in First Ypres has predominantly been seen in terms of failure because of self-inflicted wounds and running away from shell fire. The reality, however, was even more remarkable.

The Indians at First Ypres did indeed save the BEF, some did shoot themselves, and some did run away, but they were also skilled professionals who showed themselves ready to kill, dig trenches and suffer shell fire for the British as they had been before 1914 in Africa and Asia. And this was no one-off – the Indians simultaneously did similar things on the far side of the world with the Japanese Army, at the siege of the most intricate German trench system anywhere, in north China.

'The Pathans are getting to work already'

As First Ypres started on 19 October, the British and French high commands had ambitions to take the offensive, envisaging an Allied advance towards Brussels. But once the German 4th Army began attacking the northern half of the Allied line and the 6th Army the southern, aiming to concentrate superior numbers against weak points for a breakthrough, the Allies quickly realised that their task was one of desperate defence. Up to 22 October, the Germans pushed back the Belgians and French near the North Sea coast, the BEF's left in front of Ypres and its right in France. 'It has been a ticklish time,' Archibald Home, a British Army cavalry officer of the original BEF drawn from the Home

Army, wrote on the 22nd in the Ypres sector. 'We always fight on a thin line with no reserves ... It is a game of pure bluff, that is all.' In reinforcing the BEF, the Indian regiments – totalling approximately 17,000 men – were split up into numerous parts as small as half-companies, frequently moving here and there in response to the latest German attacks.

The Afridi officer Arsala Khan and his Malik Din company of the Frontier Force's 57th Wilde's Rifles, with their newly-wed British officer Ronald Gordon, became the first Indian troops to enter the trenches of the First World War in the fading light of 22 October, on Belgian farmland south of Ypres. They marched not into any well-established trench system but across open countryside right up to the BEF front line as it then was, no more than a string of waist-high, boggy farming ditches. They were shown the way by some of the BEF's dismounted Scottish and English cavalrymen, veterans of the retreat from Mons and the Marne including Home, whom they were relieving. Soon after, the cavalrymen passed the war's opening comments on Indians in battle, saying how struck they were by the nerve of the Afridi for filing into their trenches in silence and steadily digging them deeper before asking a particular question. 'All they wanted to know,' noted Home, 'was why they were not going forward – a fine spirit.' Ronald Gordon, Arsala Khan and their Malik Din company were familiar enough with trenches, of course, having dug and slept in them for a month during the Mohmand small war of 1908; and the Afridi may even have had a sense of a grudge to settle for those old German insults in China.

The Afridi of the 57th Wilde's Rifles suffered the first Indian casualties of the war on the night of 22–23 October, as they repelled a small German assault. The most seriously wounded was an Afridi sepoy named Usman Khan, whose reaction seemed to show the Malik Din company's determination to fight together. He was hit by two German bullets in the upper body but insisted on remaining in the Afridi firing line, and he left it only after a

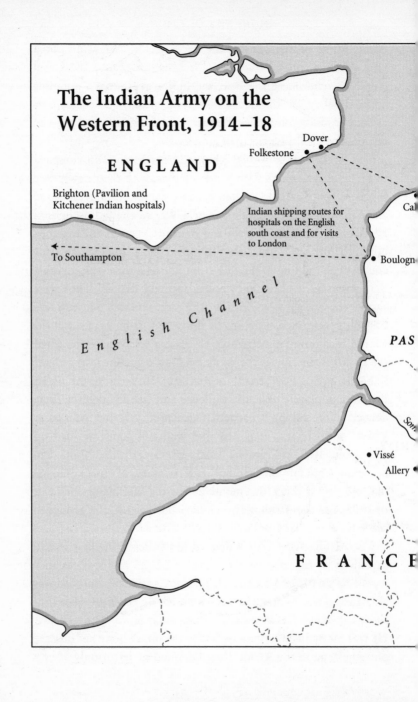

The Indian Army on the
Western Front, 1914–18

ENGLAND

Dover

Folkestone

Brighton (Pavilion and
Kitchener Indian hospitals)

Cal

Indian shipping routes for
hospitals on the English
south coast and for visits
to London

To Southampton

Boulogn

English Channel

PAS

Som

Vissé
Allery

FRANCE

shell splinter tore into both his thighs; he protested feebly as he was carried away, muttering that he could still fire his rifle.

In the BEF line several miles to the south, meanwhile, the Afridi of the Frontier Force's 58th Vaughan's Rifles were also taking a professional approach to trench warfare. They appeared more alert to its hazards than even their own commandant, Walter Venour, the man who in 1913 had described the Indian Army's mountain fighting skills as 'a useful fighting asset to any unit under any conditions'. Venour made a point at first light of showing no fear, but he took it too far for the regiment's strapping Afridi NCO, as Captain Alexander Lind of the 58th recalled:

> Venour looked out over the top, when he was thrown flat on his back in the mud by Havildar Lashkarai, an Afridi in charge of the signallers, who realised the danger. Colonel Venour's comments in the most virulent Pushtu, of which he was a past-master, left Lashkarai unmoved and ready to repeat the performance. He immediately looked over again and unfortunately Lashkarai was not quick enough. Colonel Venour fell back into his arms, shot through the head ...

As these troops of Tirah showed their professional nous in the first Indian experiences under fire at First Ypres, their fellow independent Pukhtun from Waziristan exceeded them by going straight after the Germans. The 129th Baluchis' Mahsud companies spent their initial days at the battle in Belgium near Ypres. Up to 29 October their area was little shelled, but it was crawling with German snipers. 'They don't seem to mind the rifle fire (which is much the most dangerous) in the least,' the Pushtu-speaking British cavalry officer Philip Howell observed of the Mahsud on 24 October, confirming their own officer Harold Lewis's thought on their voyage to France that their constant in-fighting with modern rifles at home was some preparation for European war. 'The Pathans are getting to work already,' Howell went on. 'A

German sniper worried us all day from a hidden position about 800 yards away. So we sent out a wild young Mahsud to stalk him – and he came back in less than an hour with the German sniper's rifle!' That week other Mahsud of the 129th Baluchis made up their own minds to hunt down German snipers. Lewis watched one of them, Hakim Khan, set off. 'Without a word,' he wrote, 'Hakim started walking off alone across an open field towards the advancing enemy. I ordered him to come back but I might as well have saved my breath.'

Near Ypres on the night of 31 October, Lewis's Mahsud joined together to put their pre-war training in fire and movement to devastating use. They attacked a German-occupied Belgian farmhouse, moving quickly from two directions. 'The Germans rushed out and fired into us at about ten yards,' Lewis remembered, but the Mahsud shot down several. Outside the farmhouse's back door, Lewis paused side-on to blaze off his revolver at a German firing at him from the doorway. Miraculously Lewis's life was saved by the steel frame of his field binoculars hanging from his neck, as two of the German's bullets deflected off it; the German was the unlucky one, shot dead by Lewis through the heart. Inside the farmhouse Lewis and the Mahsud took on dozens more Germans. 'Much of the fight was a room-to-room hunt, which was greatly to the liking of the men,' observed the 129th Baluchis' regimental history. Before long the Mahsud had taken the farmhouse, killing nine Germans, wounding thirteen and capturing fourteen, the remaining Germans running away. 'It was a very good game,' the visibly exhilarated Mahsud told Lewis as they marched their prisoners off. For Lewis himself, the fight had been a 'burst of intense excitement . . . marvellous . . . Our men are very cool under fire, don't seem to mind a bit'.

To the south at First Ypres, Indian regiments on the right of the BEF's line in France used their pre-war training in fire and movement to capture a whole village, Neuve Chapelle, if only briefly. Two companies apiece of the 47th Sikhs and the Bombay

Sappers and Miners stormed the village on the morning of 28 October. They crouched in their trenches in front of it during an impromptu preliminary bombardment by British artillery lasting half an hour – much like the Indian Army had cooperated with artillery for years in the independent Pukhtun tribal areas. The Sikhs and Sappers then attacked at the appointed hour of eleven o'clock, covering the 700 yards to the German trench screening Neuve Chapelle in short rushes by Sikh and Sapper sections, overlapping one another to give alternate cover fire. 'The ground between us and the village was dead flat plough, devoid of cover, but the advance continued with parade-ground precision in spite of some casualties,' recalled Francis Nosworthy, a young British officer from Kingston, Jamaica, who was leading a Sapper company. In the final yards before the German line, the Sikhs charged with bayonets lowered as they let out their war cry 'Waheguru Ji Ka Khalsa, Waheguru Ji Ki Fateh!',* bayoneting the few Germans in the front trench who had not retreated into the village.

The Sikhs and Sappers rolled into the village's streets under fire from the houses and rooftops. Old Indian comrades of the pre-war years fell all around. 'Muhammad Khan rushed up to me, trying to speak,' wrote Nosworthy, 'but he could not do so as he had been shot through the throat and was bleeding. I persuaded him to go back, but his wound proved mortal and so I lost a particular friend.' The Sikhs and Sappers broke into several houses, each a fortress and only won at the cost of dozens of casualties on both sides among the stairs, landings and bedrooms. Some of the German troops in the houses were in terror of the Indians, believing German Army rumours that they were barbarians hellbent on mutilating their prisoners – when in fact Indian pre-war training had made a point of taking prisoners humanely, searching them for papers and taking them away for interrogation. A young German soldier taken prisoner by the Sikhs in one house

* The cry is a call to purity of faith and victory belonging to God.

broke down in tears in fear of torture as his captors searched him, prompting a Sikh officer to reassure him, 'Daro mat, jawan, daro mat' ('Don't be afraid, lad, don't be afraid').

The Sikhs and Sappers fought in the streets of Neuve Chapelle into the afternoon. On the main street, German riflemen popped up and down in windows to shoot the Sappers' British officers. In one instance a Punjabi Muslim Sapper calmly knelt in the street, waited for the German to pop up for another shot, and shot him dead the moment he did. The Sikhs and Sappers pushed the Germans out on the far side of the village to capture it, but only for a matter of minutes before German reinforcements drove them back. Nosworthy and his Sappers held on to the main street by seizing furniture from houses and building a road block, with Sappers giving covering fire from windows above. They defended their road block tenaciously, holding off a number of German counter-attacks. By four o'clock Nosworthy was the last British officer standing in Neuve Chapelle, isolated with only one Indian officer and thirteen Sappers left. He abandoned the village with them and the remaining Sikhs, taking as many of the wounded as they could, looking back over their shoulders to see those left behind being taken prisoner.

'The Indians fought in a manner which at once established their reputation as first-class fighting men,' James Willcocks said of the Sikhs and Sappers' six-hour fight, which had cost them a total of 564 casualties. 'I have never met a man who saw it, or who was on that part of the Front at that time, who has not owned that it was as brave a show as could be.' Willcocks had been six miles back, moving into his new Indian Corps headquarters at a château in the village of Hinges. The Indian Corps was concentrating in the area in order to take over the right of the BEF's line, a 10-mile stretch – one third – in the French Pas-de-Calais department.

'As I leaned over the banisters,' Willcocks wrote of settling in at Hinges château on 29 October, looking down into the hall where Indian, British and French officers, electricians, telephone operators, orderlies and cooks buzzed about talking in Punjabi, Pushtu, English and French, and German prisoners stood under guard at the front door, 'I felt a stern joy that it was my good fortune to be entrusted for the first time in war with so varied a task as the control of such divergent elements of humanity, in the heart of a great European country.' But though reports of the Sikhs and Sappers at Neuve Chapelle came in to warm Willcocks' heart, within days others arrived of a quite different nature, swinging his mood into one of blind panic.

Some of these reports concerned the 15th Ludhiana Sikhs. On the night of 24 October, the regiment had gone into the BEF's front line north of Neuve Chapelle, next to some French troops. Their initial mistake had been to attack them. 'I regret to say that the first people we shot in the Great War were undoubtedly French,' one of the Sikhs' British officers, John Smyth, then aged twenty-one, later admitted. 'It was dark and there was a bit of a mix-up going on, so there was some excuse.' In the morning, the 15th Sikhs made their second mistake. This was to walk about their shallow front trench and the surrounding field chatting, instead of digging their trench deeper to avoid offering a target. They were in fact one of the weaker Indian regiments in France, their training having gone stale recently in widely scattered desert stations in British India's north-western province of Baluchistan. The Sikhs soon saw German aeroplanes with black crosses on their underwings circling in the sky above, and dropping bright flare lights behind them. If the Sikhs wondered why, the answer lay in the plumes of smoke rising from the flares: call signs to far-off German heavy artillery, alerting them to a fresh target.

Shells began to rain down on the Sikhs – enormous 90lb howitzer shells, packed with high explosive and shrapnel that detonated on impact, blowing earth, metal and bodies 60 feet up in the air and giving off black and yellow fumes. Dozens of Sikhs were blown away at a time, often wounded in the arm or upper body because their shallow trenches covered only their legs. Then the

Sikhs began shooting themselves. They were in shock, disoriented by the dreadful power of the howitzer shells dropping from the skies. Soldiering in the Sikh warrior tradition was all very well, but their deal in the Indian Army had suddenly gone bad. 'This sort of war is not what we were out for,' said one of the Sikhs. They felt that staying alive and well for their families easily outweighed taking on German firepower for the British, in a war they did not see as their own (they referred to it as 'the Sahibs' war'). If they wounded themselves when their British officers were not looking, the unharmed Sikhs calculated, they could mix with those wounded by the Germans, and exercise a traditional Indian Army right of the wounded on active service of choosing to go home. Many of the 15th Sikhs therefore shot themselves in the hand, as did men of a few other Indian regiments such as the 47th Sikhs, similarly shelled in exposed positions. Up to 3 November, there were a total of 1049 Indian hand wounds at First Ypres – by no means all self-inflicted, though in hundreds of instances they were.

As news of these self-inflicted wounds trickled in to Indian headquarters at Hinges château in the last days of October, Willcocks grew increasingly alarmed. Then things got worse. He heard that men of several Indian companies in Belgium and France were running away from their trenches, seeking refuge in drains, ditches, houses or woods. They belonged to four regiments – the 2nd Gurkhas, 8th Gurkhas, 9th Bhopals and 129th Baluchis – and they did it between 28 October and 2 November. The general pattern here was that isolated companies got caught with little or no trench protection by heavy concentrations of shelling, in some cases by the biggest German siege guns, recent destroyers of concrete Belgian forts. Some were hit in their primitive ditch-trenches, which were obliterated, and some in the open. The bombardments wore down their company cohesion in anything from hours to minutes amid showers of autumn rain, usually after most of their British and Indian officers had been killed or wounded, and their men had seen their fellow villagers scythed down by shrapnel, disappear beneath collapsed trench walls, or blown wounded into water-filled shell holes to drown. All these things sooner or later pushed the Indians involved beyond the limit of their endurance, and they took flight. The Indians' own words do not survive, but they were described by British observers who saw them as 'terrified by the shrapnel', 'very shaken', and 'insane from the horror of the bombardment'.

Back at Hinges château by 2 November, incoming reports of Indian flights under fire had turned Willcocks' anxiety at self-inflicted wounds into a dread that the Indian line might give way for a German breakthrough. With the Indian Corps thinly spread on its 10-mile front with no reinforcements, Willcocks sent his Chief of Staff – Havelock Hudson, one of Haig's pre-war favourites on the Indian General Staff – to deliver a desperate message to John French at the BEF's General Headquarters in the nearby French town of Bailleul. Hudson personally told French that the Indian Corps 'might go at any moment' and must be reinforced. But French angrily dismissed this, 'If they must go, they can go – into the sea or to hell,' he shouted at Hudson. French had no men to help the Indian Army: he was desperate himself to use what further reinforcements he had – mainly dismounted French cavalry – to patch up the left of the BEF line in Belgium before the ramparts of Ypres, where on 29 October the heaviest German attacks had begun to fall. By 3 November, however, Willcocks was regaining his composure, realising that he had misread the security of the Indian line. The majority of his Indian units were not running away; the more common Indian reaction to German pressure was company togetherness and resilience, instilled by their training and fighting experience, as had been seen before 1914 in the midst of Chinese shell fire, under mass attack in Somalia and in the independent Pukhtun tribal areas.

One of the most resilient Indian regiments under attack at First Ypres was the 57th Wilde's Rifles. On 30–31 October, in rain-soaked Belgian fields in front of Ypres, they were part of a general retreat of the BEF's left under heavy attack as shells dropped every second ahead of advancing Germans, with blinding flashes of high explosive and whirring shrapnel. The 57th's Afridi Malik Din company's fighting retreat was initially organised by Ronald Gordon. 'He did the most gallant thing I have ever seen,' a watching British Army officer wrote to Gordon's wife in Australia. 'He took a platoon and went forward to check the advance of the Germans to cover the retirement of the rest of his company, though he must have known it was certain death. While advancing he was shot through the head and died instantaneously.' The Afridi officer Arsala Khan stepped in to lead in Gordon's place, as Willcocks gleaned from speaking to men who saw it. 'The occasion generally discovers the man, and he was there,' Willcocks said of Arsala Khan. 'Leading a counter-attack with the bayonet he gained sufficient time to pull his men together, and then, although vastly outnumbered, skilfully withdrew [them] to Messines.' In this village, Arsala Khan and his Malik Din showed their feelings at losing Gordon having served with him in China, Mohmand and elsewhere since 1900. 'He was extraordinarily popular with the men, and I have never seen them so cut up about anything as they were when they came in,' wrote another of their British officers.

As for the 57th Wilde's Rifles' remaining companies in Belgium near Messines, the Punjabi Muslims had stubbornly held on to their ground for too long, been surrounded and lost heavily at close quarters. Of their Hindu Rajputs, one section had been immovable, firing rapidly from under a hedge-line while lying on their stomachs until all were killed or wounded but for one, an Indian officer named Kapur Singh; he was seen committing suicide with his last cartridge, apparently to join his men in the afterlife rather than surrender. Then the Sikh company fell back to a farm in the short, swift bounds of their mountain warfare training, pausing for bursts of rifle and machine gun fire to stop oncoming bugle-blowing Germans in their tracks.

Fighting spirit also breathed through the machine gunners of the 129th Baluchis on the BEF's left in Belgium on 30–31 October, similarly under attack in the retreating line in the Ypres area. They fired their two Maxim guns to the very last, clinging to patches of otherwise abandoned front line. One of their Maxims was only silenced by a direct shell hit, and the six-man crew of the other – a mix of an Afridi, a Mahsud, a Mohmand and Punjabi Muslims – took turns to fire theirs for as long as they could. 'Alas,' said Harold Lewis of this crew, watching them from behind by a farm ablaze from incendiary shell fire, 'only one survived the storm of lead and steel in the shattered fragments of but waist-high trenches. I cherish the reflected glory of having been in their vicinity.' The crew's sole survivor was the Punjabi Muslim Khudadad Khan. He had been severely wounded, knocked unconscious and left for dead after the Germans had shot or bayoneted the five others with him. For this action he became the first Indian soldier Victoria Cross holder, seen by the regiment as on behalf of the whole crew.

In France during those last days of October and into early November, other Indian regiments at First Ypres held together under fire in the Indian sector on the right of the BEF line. The 59th Scinde Rifles endured a whole day under fire in their front trench without budging for a hundred casualties, earning a hand-written note from Willcocks: 'I was very pleased to hear how well you are doing your duty. I know the 59th will add to its high reputation.' The 39th Garhwals were shelled on their first days in the trenches, but they held on too. 'One thing struck us,' wrote their British officer Kenneth Henderson, 'and that was the steadiness of our men under artillery fire. It was marvellous how well they stood it and how steady they were.' It was in fact not the Garhwalis but Henderson's brother officer, the cigarette-smoking and brandy-nipping Major Pelham Home, who went because of the shell fire. Home, wrote Henderson, 'had gone off his head' from nervous strain on the regiment's first day under fire, 'generally carrying on in a way seriously to unsettle the men'. Home sleep-walked in the front line that night, blurting out 'no more ammunition', 'surrender', and other snapshots from his nightmares. 'The result,' wrote Henderson, 'was that was the last we saw of poor Home', who left for a psychiatric hospital in England.

Willcocks, meanwhile, saw to it that the outbreak of self-inflicted wounds was stamped out by the first week of November. His remedy was rapid punishment. To make an example of Indians who had deliberately wounded themselves, he held courts martial under Indian Army law and sentenced two of the accused to death by firing squad, and several others to prison sentences of fourteen years. As a further deterrent, he suspended the tra-ditional Indian soldier's right to choose to go home if wounded, ruling that men with hand wounds must return to duty in the trenches once passed fit (their injuries usually taking five weeks to heal). The Indian self-infliction of wounds suddenly stopped. 'The question of self-maiming I hope is settled,' Willcocks reported to Lord Kitchener:

> It was a source of very great anxiety to me for some days; but the men fight <u>well</u> ... The Doctors are so nervous of giving evidence & I myself naturally <u>loathe</u> hearing it. Still duty is duty & I will not slacken my efforts but keep my eyes open. I have this matter well in hand & I have many people watching the laggards. As a whole the men are splendid I know. I had to shoot two men – I hope no more.

The Indian regiments' active part in First Ypres was over by 5 November. Their dispersed companies had concentrated in France in the Indian sector on the BEF's right, while the German attacks up to the end of the battle in the third week of November targeted the Allied line in Belgium, grinding to a halt once mutual exhaus-tion set in. All round, the Indian troops' experiences at First Ypres show how problematic it is to typecast the Indian soldier as loyal, heroic or a failure. Those who shot themselves in order to go home were of course neither loyal nor heroic in the traditional military sense. As for the Afridi officer Arsala Khan and others who fought hard in keeping with their training and experience since the 1890s, they proved ready enough for the European battlefield; indeed, Arsala Khan's leadership displayed that the Indians could lead themselves without their British officers.

Furthermore, on the matter of how suited or prepared the Indian troops were for a European war, it is important to recognise that they were not alone on the western front in 1914 when it came to self-inflicting wounds and fleeing from shell fire: numerous British, French, French African and German troops did the same. Asians, Europeans and Africans alike were pushed beyond the limit of human endurance by shell fire. Douglas Haig, commanding the BEF's I Corps at First Ypres whose trenches were outside Ypres itself, had seen something of this on the roads east of the town during the battle. He shared his experiences with George V over dinner in early December as they discussed the British Army's performance, as Haig recorded in his diary:

The King seemed ... inclined to think that all our troops are by nature brave and is ignorant of all the efforts which Commanders must make to keep up the 'morale' of their men in war, and of all the training which is necessary in peace in order to enable a company for instance to go forward as an organised unit in the face of almost certain death. I told him of the crowds of fugitives [of British regiments] who came back down the Menin road from time to time during the Ypres battle having thrown everything they could, including their rifles and packs, in order to escape, with a look of absolute terror on their faces, such as I have never before seen on any human being ...

Then the Prime Minister, Herbert Asquith, having reviewed the BEF's courts martial statistics following First Ypres, disabused himself of the notion that Indian rather than British soldiers self-inflicted wounds. 'There have been quite a number of cases lately of privates being tried and sentenced for mutilating their left hands, so as to make them incapable of handling a rifle,' he stated in December. 'I knew this had happened with the Indians; that it should have spread to our men shows what a shattering thing the trenches must be.' James Willcocks came round to this view at the same time. 'The Indians naturally do not like shell fire,' he wrote. 'Who does?'

'Like a Crystal Palace firework display'

The Indian troops at First Ypres were not the only ones to come under German shell fire in trenches in late October and early November 1914 – Indians also faced German artillery on the other side of the world. The 36th Sikhs were stationed in China at the war's outbreak, at Beijing and on the east coast as consular guards. In October they joined a British Empire contingent at the Japanese Army's siege of a German seaport in north-east China, Qingdao (also transliterated as Kiaochow or Tsingtao). Qingdao lay on the tip of a peninsula in German colonial possession which was covered in hills, ravines and streams, interspersed with Chinese farmers' fields of sweet potato and peanuts. The Japanese had invaded neutral China to attack Qingdao, prompting Kaiser Wilhelm to tell the seaport's German governor that the honour of their country was at stake against Asian opposition he saw as racially inferior: 'it would shame me more to surrender Kiaochow to the Japanese than Berlin to the Russians'.

On its landward approaches through the hills and fields, Qingdao certainly had the defences for resolute resistance, manned by German infantry and marines. They consisted of miles of interlocking trenches with concrete redoubts, bristling with machine guns and topped by powerful long-distance searchlights. In addition they were fronted by barbed wire entanglements and booby-trapped land mines, and backed by artillery guided by aeroplanes and giant sausage-shaped grey observation balloons. All this amounted to a level of German trench construction as yet unseen in the fields of France and Flanders.

The 36th Sikhs arrived opposite the German lines at Qingdao during a typhoon on 28 October. They took over trenches in heavy rains and high winds from a Welsh regiment, in the hills at the centre of the Japanese position which ran right across the peninsula. To avoid any mishaps similar to the 15th Ludhiana Sikhs' shooting of French troops in France, the 36th Sikhs wore bands of white linen on their turbans, identifying them as allies to Japanese troops. Trained in trench digging before the war, the 36th Sikhs started digging forward to help the Japanese develop the siege, camouflaging their parapets – much as Indian regiments had in fact done on pre-1914 active service in Somalia and the independent Pukhtun tribal areas – using sweet potato vines pulled from the hillsides.

'Work on the trenches was done only at night,' noted the Sikhs' British officer Ernest Knox, 'and throughout the time it was carried on, the Tsing-Tao defences were like a Crystal Palace firework display.' As the Sikhs dug in the darkness, German searchlight beams from the concrete redoubts ahead raked back and forth across the Allied lines, and German star shells and flare rockets illuminated the night sky. 'If a rocket burst over the trench everybody at once threw themselves flat on the ground till the light had died out,' wrote Knox. 'For the first night or two ... among the Indian troops it was difficult to get much work out of the men, as they were so taken up with watching the various lights. Low suppressed murmurs of admiration could be heard when a particularly brilliant rocket would turn night temporarily into day.'

The Japanese artillery began bombarding Qingdao in earnest on 31 October, continuing for days as towers of thick black smoke went up from the seaport's burning Standard Oil storage tanks. The Germans replied with sporadic bursts of machine gun and high explosive shell fire. 'The local, or perhaps capricious, effect of these shells was very noticeable,' Knox observed. 'Two sepoys of the 36th were lying asleep in a shelter and a shell burst inside it. One man's head was blown off, but the other man was totally uninjured.' Like many of the Indian regiments under German shell fire at First Ypres, the well-trained Sikhs stuck together and held to their trenches.

On the morning of 7 November, the Sikhs saw white flags waving above the redoubts of Qingdao, signalling its surrender before the main Allied infantry assault materialised. The Sikhs marched triumphantly with the Japanese into the seaport, through the trenches the German governor had decided to give up as his artillery began to run out of shells. As a tiny proportion of the Allied forces at Qingdao – the Japanese had 60,000 men – the Sikhs had no real claim to shaping the events of its fall. But what of the idea that Indian Expeditionary Force A to France had an incalculably bigger impact at First Ypres, arriving in the nick of time to save the situation on the western front?

'We had no other troops to put in'

Indian Expeditionary Force A really did save the BEF at First Ypres – but indirectly. By 1 November, the BEF's eighty-four original British battalions of the Home Army that had sailed from England since August were very tired. They had fought virtually without rest, and were down to around 30 per cent of their original numbers. Almost all had fewer than 300 men, eighteen had fewer than 100 men, while the British cavalry was similarly reduced from fighting dismounted like infantry. All in all, the original BEF's British Army units had an estimated 30,000 men. 'If we want any more men in the front line,' quipped one British cavalry officer, 'we had better go across and see if the Germans would lend us some.' The Germans not only outnumbered the British 2:1, but also had much more artillery.

In the last week of October, the BEF's commanders of its British corps from the Home Army admitted the tight spot they were in. Douglas Haig wrote that his I Corps, holding part of the left of the BEF line before Ypres, was 'exhausted . . . 2 Brigadiers assure me that if the Enemy makes a push at any point, they doubt our men being able to hold on'. Also on the BEF left, Haig's neighbouring British IV Corps commander Henry Rawlinson confessed, 'We are hanging on only by our eyelids; we want men, and always more men.' On the BEF right, the II Corps commander Horace Smith-Dorrien wrote 'My poor troops are simply worn out.' The BEF's fundamental dilemma was one of averting fatal over-stretch – how to hold its 35-mile line into November with so few men who were so tired when the German attacks kept coming until mid-month.

The BEF was able to cling on because the Indian Corps arrived with around 22,000 Indian and British troops to hold a total of 12 miles, or about a third, of its line, principally on the right in France. In early November on the BEF's left by Ypres, where the German onslaught fell heaviest, its original British corps avoided defeat on the narrowest of margins with French assistance and a few British Territorial home defence troops who had volunteered for France. For the BEF's Home Army corps to have also held the right of its line without the Indian Corps' assistance would have been too much for them: their British troops would have been spread too thinly to keep the Germans from breaking through. After First Ypres, Haig talked in private of how the Indian Corps had 'saved the situation by filling a gap', while his intelligence staff officer John Charteris acknowledged it had been 'invaluable . . . when we had no other troops to put in'. And if the Indian Corps saved the BEF's line from collapsing, it also saved the whole Allied line at First Ypres – of which the BEF held half – and therefore probably the Allied cause in the west in 1914.

Why, then, has Indian Expeditionary Force A's part in the Allied story of survival in 1914 not loomed larger in the history of the First World War? One reason is that it was not general public knowledge at the time. By First Ypres the British press had moved on from celebrating the lifting of the colour bar – which was already yesterday's news, there was only so far it could be celebrated when British African troops remained prohibited from fighting in Europe under their own colour bar. Rather, the press was eager for Indian battle stories, but British government censorship prevented much battle information on the Indians getting out. The story-starved British press generally turned to fantasy, inventing reports from First Ypres of Sikhs as superhuman slayers of 20,000 German troops in an afternoon, Gurkhas throwing *khukuri*s through the air with deadly accuracy, and Indians shooting down aeroplanes with their rifles. Grains of truth were few and far between, some appearing in *The Times*, which described the BEF's Indian troops at First Ypres as 'long-service professional soldiers ... fighting as steadily as the rest of the Army'. So little reliable news of Indian Expeditionary Force A reached India in November that the Viceroy, Charles Hardinge, said 'people in India are wondering what has happened to the troops and where they have gone'. He was compelled to write to James Willcocks asking for private updates.

In British national memory, First Ypres came to be seen as the British Army's ultimate moment of sacrifice of 1914, scarcely mentioning Indian Expeditionary Force A as the BEF's lifeline. But the Indian factor should be included to recognise that the Indian Army was ready before the war to deploy fast to France, and to fight when it got there. The achievements of Force A at First Ypres become all the clearer in light of its sister Indian Expeditionary Forces' experiences against the Germans in 1914 – Forces B and C to East Africa. These cooperated in an ambitious attempt to capture German East Africa largely by themselves, yet unlike the Indian part in First Ypres, it was an utter fiasco.

6

'THE RIFF-RAFF'

Among the major European powers in 1914, Germany's colonial empire was both the newest and the smallest. Acquired since the 1880s for purposes of international prestige as befitting a world power, it encompassed, besides Qingdao, a handful of Pacific islands from the Marshalls and Marianas to Samoa and the Solomons, and the African territories of Togoland, Cameroon, German South-West Africa (now Namibia) and German East Africa (now Tanzania). The majority of the German colonies' active involvement in the First World War was short-lived as they were seized in 1914–15: the Pacific islands by the Japanese, Australians and New Zealanders, and much of the African lands by Allied colonial African forces.

The notable exception was German East Africa. It was one and a half times the size of Germany, with an African population of 7.5 million, an Indian diaspora of 14,000 and some 5000 white German settlers. Its pre-war defence force, the Schütztruppen, was minimal with a total strength of 2400 locally recruited African troops under white German officers. But their companies were highly trained in bush fighting, and they were commanded by a resourceful Prussian General Staff officer, Paul von Lettow-Vorbeck. They were to expand from 1914 to 16,000 officers and men, a quarter of them white Germans, and to last longer in the field than any other German colonial force by following Lettow-Vorbeck's indefatigable example.

German East Africa's northern neighbour was British East Africa (now Kenya), whose security depended ultimately on the Royal Navy's command of the western Indian Ocean. Its pre-war defence force on land was the King's African Rifles, who were as diminutive as the Schütztruppen and also manned by local Africans and white officers. In terms of size alone at the war's outbreak, the King's African Rifles could not guarantee the British colony's protection from German invasion over its southern border, stretching 450 miles from the sea to Lake Victoria. The Army in India, therefore, being Britain's traditional military reserve for East African emergencies, was called on by the Cabinet in August 1914 to help secure British East Africa – giving rise to Indian Expeditionary Forces B and C.

The original objective for Force B was fairly limited. It was to capture Dar es Salaam, the capital of German East Africa and the only major German seaport on the Indian Ocean. Force C, meanwhile, was set for British East Africa. Its task was to land at Mombasa to join the King's African Rifles on the defensive, on the colony's southern border. In September, however, London wildly expanded Force B and C's missions. The two were now to make a synchronised attack on German East Africa by sea and land to bring the whole territory under British authority.

This extravagant joint enterprise naturally called for dynamic leadership in the field, and for regiments of sufficient quantity and quality to match the Schütztruppen. But Forces B and C were not so fortunate. Force B's waspish Deputy Chief of Intelligence, Captain Richard Meinertzhagen, got an inkling of this as it gathered for embarkation at the port of Bombay in early October. Meinertzhagen was an eccentric British Army officer whose German surname came from his London merchant banking family; known before the war as an amateur zoologist who introduced the

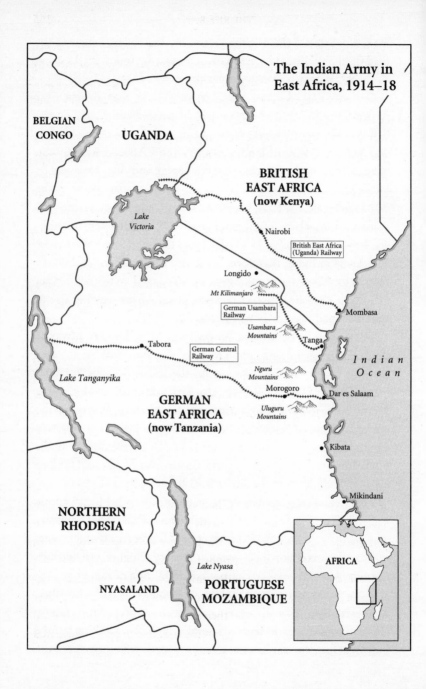

The Indian Army in East Africa, 1914–18

BELGIAN CONGO

UGANDA

BRITISH EAST AFRICA (now Kenya)

Lake Victoria

Nairobi

British East Africa (Uganda) Railway

Longido

Mt Kilimanjaro

German Usambara Railway

Usambara Mountains

Mombasa

Tanga

Tabora

German Central Railway

Indian Ocean

Nguru Mountains

Lake Tanganyika

Morogoro

Dar es Salaam

GERMAN EAST AFRICA (now Tanzania)

Uluguru Mountains

Kibata

NORTHERN RHODESIA

Mikindani

AFRICA

Lake Nyasa

NYASALAND

PORTUGUESE MOZAMBIQUE

African giant forest hog (*Hylochoerus meinertzhageni*) to western science, he was fresh from the Indian Staff College. On meeting Force B's Indian troops on the Bombay quays, he not only questioned their total number of just 5000 plus a British battalion, but also their military value. 'Our troops, sad to relate, are rotten ... all the riff-raff of the Indian Army,' he wrote in his diary. 'They constitute the worst in India, and I tremble to think what may happen if we meet with serious opposition.' He recognised some of them from peacetime, for example the 13th Rajputs, whom he had come across at Delhi in 1912. 'From what I saw of them then they were hopeless ... They were considered inefficient and had been reported on as unfit for active service.'

Also gathering at Bombay to set sail alongside Force B was Indian Expeditionary Force D to Ottoman Iraq, but it had different problems. Its original regiments were among the Indian Army's best. But they had Muslim companies with independent Pukhtun, who just days after embarking for Iraq would start objecting to fighting the Turks as fellow Muslims. Then in November, when the 130th Baluchis were set to follow them from Bombay to Iraq, the regiment's independent Pukhtun would go further to show their own feelings, attempting the war's first Indian mutiny and British officer murder.

'Dispirited and disgruntled'

Indian Expeditionary Force C had sailed from Karachi for British East Africa in August 1914, with 2200 Indian troops. On 16 October it was followed into the Indian Ocean by Forces B and D in convoy – B heading straight for Mombasa to liaise with C, while D branched off to the Persian Gulf. Meinertzhagen's misgivings about Force B's Indian troops only intensified on their voyage. He wearily described their sea journey as 'hell on crowded ships in tropical heat', leaving 'all the Indian troops ... dispirited and disgruntled'.

Meinertzhagen was almost as concerned about Force B's senior British officers, deriding them as 'nearer to fossils than active, energetic leaders of men'. Its commander was Arthur Aitken, aged fifty-three and one of the Indian Army's least illustrious generals in the pre-war years. Aitken had neither staff college training nor any campaign experience since 1888 in Sudan, marks of an unambitious and average officer. He was no modern commander in the mould of Douglas Haig with a scientific interest in the art of war. On the contrary, he was a nonchalant presence on Force B's troopships, reading novels on deck and assuming Force B would defeat the Schütztruppen as racial inferiors. 'The Indian Army will make short work of a lot of niggers,' he confided in Meinertzhagen.

Indian Expeditionary Force B's greatest weakness, however, lay in its supreme command. When the Cabinet had embarked on the war and called for the British Empire's resources, to coordinate them it had no efficient system of global supreme command in place from peacetime, centralised in London – something Douglas Haig, of course, had thought essential in his pre-war hopes for a combined British 'Imperial Army'. Instead, the Prime Minister Herbert Asquith improvised by setting up various Cabinet committees and sub-committees to oversee different campaigns, generally delegating the day-to-day management of the empire's forces to British government departments or to local imperial governments.

As a result, from August to October 1914 the plans for Indian Expeditionary Forces B and C to East Africa were developed haphazardly, being a joint concoction by London's Colonial Office (responsible for tropical African colonies), the India Office and the Admiralty. The proposal for Forces B and C's capture of all of German East Africa came from the India Office's military secretariat, a small pre-war collection of military advisers to the Secretary of State led by a bullish and over-confident Indian Army general, Edmund Barrow, and quite separate from the Indian

General Staff in India. Barrow used the India Office's power over the Army in India for overseas deployments to demand both Forces B and C for East Africa while cutting out the Indian General Staff from the planning of their operations, keeping this largely for himself. 'We were told to mind our own business', recalled India's Canadian Director of Military Operations George Kirkpatrick of Barrow's approach.

The upshot was that the attacks of Forces B and C on German East Africa were planned partly by British government sub-committees in London, and partly by the British East African government in Nairobi, in both cases without General Staff advice. This created a vacuum of the proper military planning that had benefited Indian Expeditionary Force A to France, and indeed the Indian troops in China, where the siege of Qingdao was tightly controlled by the Japanese General Staff. Accordingly, the London and Nairobi planners for Forces B and C cooked up an ill-considered masterplan by the end of October that bungled the things a General Staff was supposed to help them to do. They failed to assess the high quality of the Schütztruppen, Barrow picking low-quality Indian regiments as good enough to face them in order to save better Indian regiments for Europe or Ottoman Iraq. In the process, Barrow brought Aitken into the picture as some of the chosen Indian regiments' pre-war brigade commander. Further, Force B was to invade German East Africa from the Indian Ocean in cooperation with the Royal Navy, but the planners failed to earmark a suitable landing place; nor did they carefully select a time for Force C's contribution, a diversionary attack inland over the border from British East Africa, intended to draw-off the Schütztruppen from defending the coast against Force B.

Aitken could have pushed to fix these things as he finalised the plan of attack at Mombasa on 31 October, in conference with the British East African authorities, naval officers, Force C's commander and Meinertzhagen. He missed his chance, agreeing only to a vague plan that identified general points of attack on a small-scale map without local particulars of time or place. His Force B was to make its amphibious assault on Tanga, the closest German port to British territory, while Force C's diversionary effort was to go in 250 miles inland at Longido, in the mountains on the far side of Mount Kilimanjaro.

At dawn on 2 November, Force B's troopships arrived off the German East African coast, slightly north of Tanga. 'The battle of Tanga,' Meinertzhagen later commented, 'is the best example I know of how a battle should not be fought, not only in the events leading up to the fight but in its conduct from the General Officer Commanding to the rank and file who suffered.' Force B's disembarkation was the polar opposite to Indian Expeditionary Force A's slick landing at Marseilles, shambolic in every way. Aitken did not insist on reconnaissance of a landing beach, plumping instead for one he could not see clearly from his distant ship. It turned out to be very bad. The waters before it hid high coral reef, and the beach itself was a mangrove swamp beneath awkward cliffs and surrounded by dense undergrowth. After several Indian regiments disembarking from their troopships on rowing boats got stuck on the reef, at the beach their men became so bogged down in the swamp they had to re-embark. Aitken then switched to new beaches for Force B, so it took an unnecessary fifty-six hours to land – forfeiting the element of surprise, and giving Lettow-Vorbeck crucial time to rush the Schütztruppen by railway from inland to Tanga, which had been virtually undefended. There is no record from the Indian troops themselves, mostly Hindus, of what they felt during Force B's landings. As far as Meinertzhagen could tell among those he rowed ashore with, there was no silent steadiness as with the first Afridi to enter the trenches in France. The Indian troops' agitated talk gave him the impression that 'before they ever landed they were overcome with fear ... with jumpy troops I fear the worst'.

Aitken had Indian mountain artillery at his disposal, but he declined to land it to combine closely with his infantry. Instead he rushed the 13th Rajputs, 61st Pioneers, 63rd Palamcottahs and other battalions into the attack from dawn on 3 November, advancing from their landing beaches towards Tanga in wide lines through dense bush in air thick with humidity. Ahead were entrenched Schütztruppen, but unlike the Sikhs and Sappers in France at Neuve Chapelle a few days earlier, the Indian units at Tanga were generally untrained to fire and move in determined rushes. The moment they came under enemy rifle and machine gun fire, they panicked and fled in terror for the beaches. 'I saw the whole ghastly business,' wrote Meinertzhagen of the first Indian attack:

> No amount of heroic example on behalf of the British officers prevailed. Officer after officer was shot down trying to rally the men and stem the tide of flight ... Our men behaved disgracefully, showing no military spirit or grit ... Our British officers behaved like heroes, but none of them had a chance with their men running like rabbits and jibbering like monkeys ... These are jolly fellows to fight the Germans with.

The second Indian attack in the afternoon of 4 November seemed more promising, with artillery support from Force B's Royal Navy escort, HMS *Fox*, and from its Indian mountain guns wedged among coal bags on a troopship deck. Yet Meinertzhagen saw another Indian collapse. 'We only heard a few shots in front of us and were within 600 yards of the town when the enemy opened a heavy fire and bullets came thick, men falling in all directions,' he recalled. 'Half the 13th Rajputs turned at once, broke into a rabble and bolted, carrying more of the 61st Pioneers with them. I could not believe my eyes when I saw it.' Meinertzhagen flew into a blind rage, chasing through the bush after the fleeing Indians to make them fight. He shot not only a Hindu officer of the Rajputs who refused, but also an unwilling

Rajput sepoy who was 'half-crazy with fear' and had pointed his rifle at him.

Then there were the bees. The Schütztruppen shot some large African bee hives in the upper reaches of palm trees that were dotted about the bush, bringing out angry swarms which swooped to sting many of the Indians repeatedly, sending them back all the faster. At this point Meinertzhagen saw something even more surprising: Indian troops in the rear deliberately firing at Force B's British battalion, of the Loyal North Lancashire Regiment, as it pressed ahead. Quite why they might have done this is unknown. 'We don't mind the German fire,' one of the British privates told Meinertzhagen, 'but with most of our officers and N.C.O.s down and a bloody crowd of niggers firing into our backs and bees stinging our backsides, things are a bit 'ard.'

The Hindus of the Kashmir Rifles, a princely States unit, were among the few sepoys who managed to keep their presence of mind amid the bees, wrapping their turbans around their faces for protection. The Kashmir Rifles were in Force B's minority who had been well trained before the war, giving them the wherewithal to sustain the attack. They broke into the streets of Tanga with the Lancashires, skirmishing up to the market and the Kaiser Hotel as shells from the *Fox* and the Indian mountain guns at sea slammed into the upper storeys about them. But they had too little support to remain in Tanga for long, and the Schütztruppen drove them out.

Aitken gave up and ordered Force B to re-embark the following day. Many of the Indian troops showed every intent of getting away as fast as they could. 'Rifles were thrown away and men rushed into the sea up to their necks, many swimming out towards the transports,' Meinertzhagen observed of the general confusion after the evacuation order. 'To see whole battalions standing in deep water with only their heads showing was too dreadful.' By 6 November, Indian Army machine guns, ammunition boxes and stores were strewn across the abandoned white sands of Tanga, and Force B was gone. 'Here we are now, out of sight of land and steaming for Mombasa, a beaten and broken force,' Meinertzhagen cursed.

Indian Expeditionary Force C had made its diversionary attack east of Kilimanjaro at Longido on 3 November with 1500 troops, attacking a Schütztruppen camp in a volcano crater. The 29th Punjabis hinted at what might have been achieved at Tanga with higher-quality Indian battalions. Well trained in mountain warfare, they advanced up the volcano in evaporating morning mist, rushing from dense undergrowth with Indian mountain artillery firing alongside to capture a rocky spur above the German camp, and then German trenches on a ridge below. The attack was eventually driven back by Schütztruppen machine guns to the side. In any event, Force C's diversion proved too small, too far away and too late to be of any help at Tanga.

At the War Office in London, after news had come in of Indian Expeditionary Forces B and C's botched attempt at capturing German East Africa, Lord Kitchener was 'savage and spoke angrily of the East African affair', a visiting friend remembered. Kitchener promptly rectified the fundamental weakness of the East African campaign, ending its divided control and dearth of General Staff direction. He stripped the India Office and Colonial Office of the management of Forces B and C, and put both Forces under the War Office's direct control. Thereby the British direction of the war in East Africa was centralised and made subject to British General Staff advice – an early step towards an effective global British supreme command in London. Kitchener also recalled Aitken, banished him from active duty, and left both Forces B and C wallowing in British East Africa, strictly on the defensive.

In the Indian Ocean, meanwhile, the Indian Army played a part against the German navy. This belonged to a section of twenty-five independent Pukhtun recruits of the Orakzai tribe, although only a little is known of them. They were serving with the 40th Pathans at Hong Kong when the war broke out, and volunteered within days under their Orakzai officer Gul Zaman for secondment to the Royal Navy as marines on the *Empress of Asia*, an auxiliary British cruiser working with other Allied navies to contain the Germans on the oceans. It seems Gul Zaman and his men volunteered because they had pre-war experience serving at sea for their regiment, as rifle-bearing guards on British merchant steamers in the South China Sea against Chinese pirates. Aboard the *Empress of Asia* from August to October 1914, they sailed in Chinese waters alongside British, French and Chinese sailors up to Qingdao, where offshore they watched the artillery flashes and flares of the siege from within the Allied naval blockade of the port.

By early November the Orakzai marines had sailed on with the *Empress* in pursuit of one of the most elusive German cruisers, the *Emden*, which had bombarded Madras as it caused havoc in the Indian Ocean. On 10 November, the *Empress* arrived at North Keeling Island, an uninhabited coral atoll a thousand miles west of Indonesia, covered in coconut palms and within the Cocos Islands. The *Emden* had beached here the previous day in battle with the Australian navy, and Gul Zaman and his Orakzai were charged with boarding her to help carry off the prisoners of war, many of them badly wounded. They stepped on to a twisted, burnt-out wreck of first-rate German engineering, its funnels blown off and the decks smeared with the blood of over a hundred dead Germans who had put up a fiercer fight than their compatriots at Qingdao. The Orakzai helped take 211 prisoners before they set sail with the *Empress* once more, this time for Aden. What the Orakzai marines felt about life at sea is unknown, as indeed is whether they had much geographical sense of where they went or where the Germans were from. What is known, however, is that while they chose to serve against the Germans, there were other independent

Pukhtun troops who said they wanted to do the same – instead of fighting the Turks.

'Why could we not be sent to fight Germans?'

On 23 October 1914, the troopships of Indian Expeditionary Force D were in the sweltering heat of the Persian Gulf. They were anchored off Bahrain, on standby to move up the Gulf if war with Turkey broke out. At this point Force D had a total of five Indian regiments, all high-quality, which initially Army Headquarters in India had chosen to join Force A to France. Their switch to Force D had apparently come as a disappointment to them. 'Their hearts had been set on fighting in Europe,' a British officer of the 20th Punjabis wrote of the regiment's Hindu, Sikh and Muslim troops at Bahrain. 'They said openly they had little enthusiasm for the operations in which we were likely to take part.'

The men of the 20th Punjabis may well have had a professional feeling of being left out, knowing that other top Indian regiments had been sent to France as worthy of fighting the German Army, and that they had been allotted lesser local duties familiar from pre-war service in the Persian Gulf and Iran. Yet the 20th Punjabis' most outspoken men – independent Pukhtun – stated a different reason for their lack of enthusiasm: it was because they were Muslims. 'They objected strongly to being employed against their co-religionists, Suni Mohammedans. The Sultan was head of their religion, and as such to be venerated,' recalled their British officer. 'Why could we not be sent to fight Germans?' his Afridi asked. 'Why could some of the many Indian regiments recruited from Dogras, Sikhs, Rajputs, Gurkhas, etc., whose religious susceptibilities would in no way be affected, not be detailed to carry on the campaign with Turkey?'

Indian Expeditionary Force D invaded Ottoman Iraq on 6 November. Unlike its unfortunate sister Force B to German East Africa, Force D had not only strong regiments but also an

The Indian Army in Iraq,
Iran and Central Asia,
1914–18

TURKEY

OTTOMAN
IRAQ
(Mesopotamia)

ARABIA

Euphrates

Mosul

Tigris

Tikrit

Ramadi   Fallujah
Nasiriyah   Baghdad
          Kut al Amara
Quma
Basra   Shu'ayba
      Khafajiya
      Abadan

Persian Gulf

Bushire

Hamadan

Enzeli

Baku

Caspian Sea

Krasnovodsk

RUSSIAN EMPIRE
(Soviet Central
Asia after 1917)

Tehran

IRAN
(Persia)

Arabian Sea

Mashhad

Helvun

Herat

AFGHANISTAN

Kabul

Trans-Caspian Railway

Dushakh

Bairam Ali

Tashkent

Kashgar

CHINA

INDIAN EMPIRE

MOHMAND
TIRAH
WAZIRISTAN

Independent Pukhtun
tribal areas

outstanding Indian Army commander in Walter Delamain. He was experienced in amphibious operations in the Persian Gulf having led the pre-war Indian attacks in Iran on Gulf gun runners, involving quick beach landings from a troopship. Since Force D's anchorage at Bahrain he had carefully planned with Royal Navy officers for its disembarkation in Iraq, and made sure to reconnoitre for the best available landing sites on the muddy Iraqi coastline at the mouth of the Shatt al-Arab, the waterway leading from the head of the Persian Gulf to Basra. Force D's landings accordingly went well compared to Force B's at Tanga, with generally efficient drop-offs by rowing boats at different spots in the shallow and difficult tidal waters.

Even better, Force D had a shrewd plan of attack meticulously prepared by the Indian General Staff's Canadian Director of Military Operations, George Kirkpatrick, providing for its advance to Basra 60 miles up the Shatt al-Arab in careful steps. Force D pushed up to Basra in just three weeks, its troops cooperating closely on the muddy banks of the Shatt with Indian mountain artillery, Royal Navy gunboats and armed yachts as they fired and moved through date palms and Turkish trenches, killing and wounding 2300 Turkish troops. They captured Basra unopposed on 23 November, after the Turkish garrison had fled. The Indian troops were soon patrolling the streets as military police, occasionally slapping their necks to squash mosquitoes so much larger than those at home that they nicknamed them 'the elephants'.

Just before Force D had arrived at Basra, it found itself short of six Afridi. They were all of the 20th Punjabis and had taken off with their Lee-Enfield rifles during the night of 19 November, to desert to the Turks. Their British officers were saddened but unsurprised. 'The previously expressed reluctance on the part of all Mohammedans against fighting in Iraq, and the well-known intensity of the religious prejudices of the Afridis in particular, explained the occurrence,' according to the 20th's regimental history. 'It was later ascertained from the Turks that the deserters refused to fight against the British, and gave as their reason for desertion the desire to get up to Baghdad to do reverence to their saint's tomb.'

The very next day at Bombay, the 130th Baluchis – an all-Muslim regiment, over half independent Pukhtun with Afridi and Mahsud – were preparing to embark to join Force D in Iraq. But the Afridi desertions there had prompted the Indian Commander-in-Chief Beauchamp Duff to lose trust in the 130th Baluchis to fight the Turks, so he changed their destination at the last minute from Basra to Mombasa. The regiment never made it on board, however, as its independent Pukhtun discipline imploded all the same.

On the Bombay quayside, a young Mahsud of the 130th named Mamakhan Khan leapt without warning on the closest British officer, Major Norman Anderson, killing him in seconds with a detached bayonet. The murder had been brewing for months among the 130th's Mahsud after one of their own was rejected for promotion to subadar-major in favour of an Afridi, to them a grievous slight. Mamakhan's revenge in cold blood was on behalf of them and their tribe; it was probably of no consequence in Mahsud eyes that Anderson was personally blameless in the promotion decision – he likely represented a British system they felt bound to resist in reprisal. Mamakhan was swiftly sentenced to death by court martial and executed. Beauchamp Duff was unsure what the rest of the 130th Baluchis' men were thinking, so he whisked the lot of them off to Burma, for special confinement and a discreet investigation into their complicity in the murder.

There was no indication that Mamakhan had been motivated by the Sultan of Turkey's jihad proclaimed at Istanbul six days earlier – news of this had yet to spread around British India. But at least some independent Pukhtun recruits were aware of the jihad. In France on the same day as the Mahsud murder in Bombay, from German aeroplanes in the sky above snow-covered Indian trenches showers of green leaflets fluttered down, into Indian hands. The leaflets were written in Indian languages that a few of the Indians, if they had been to the cantonment schools before the war, were able to read. 'TRUE INFORMATION', read one leaflet: 'The Sheikh al-Islam has proclaimed a Jihad on the Id at Mecca against the British, Russians and the French. The Sultan of Turkey has started a war against the same oppressive people.' The leaflets described the Allies as Christian powers of darkness in whose service Muslims sinned against Islam by opposing the Sultan Caliph, and entreated the Indian troops to rise up against the British. They also held out Kaiser Wilhelm as a sympathetic benefactor who would reward deserters to German lines with sanctuary in Germany and double pay, or a free passage home should they so desire.

The call to jihad was in fact just one of several tests of the Indian troops' commitment to the British during what was their toughest assignment of 1914, far more challenging than Tanga, Longido or Basra: the western front winter.

7

'THAT GOD-FORSAKEN GROUND'

In November 1914 after First Ypres, the Germans switched to the strategic defensive on the western front, to prioritise their offensives in Poland against the Russians (a strategy that would last until 1916). Having conquered almost all of Belgium and much of north-eastern France, the German Army consolidated its gains by entrenching as close as 25 yards from the Allied line. That November and December the Indian Corps under James Willcocks continued to hold the same sector on the BEF's right in France as it had during First Ypres, spanning 10 miles in the Pas-de-Calais. 'If any one had thought how best to dishearten good soldiers, they could not have chosen a better method,' Willcocks said of the countryside allocated to his corps. 'That God-forsaken ground,' he went on, 'was enough to turn sour the cheeriest mortal that ever shouldered a rifle ... It was the most dismal, swampy and disgusting region on the whole British front; not a hillock or a mound to relieve the terrible monotony, nothing but fetid bogs on every side.'

Later in the war, it would become standard for BEF units to rotate for spells of six days in the front line, often in the drier, chalky ground of the Somme valley where they held well-constructed trenches with dug-outs, drainage and high parapets.

But for the Indian regiments in the winter of 1914, before the BEF moved down to the Somme or British wartime recruits boosted BEF numbers to allow for regular rotation, more was demanded – they had to hold their trenches for spells of up to three weeks or more.

In the BEF line to the Indians' left, running into Belgium, the remnants of the first British units in France suffered similarly long periods. British and Indian soldiers alike who lived to see further western front winters were to remember the one of 1914 as the worst. It was not just the weather – by early November heavy rains, frost and snow set in as the temperature at night plummeted to –10°C – but the state of the trenches.

As First Ypres wound down, the Indian trenches were still little more than boggy farming ditches. Deeper for the Indians' digging since October, they often filled with freezing water or liquid mud up to the knee or higher. They had walls of soft clay that would suddenly collapse, crushing anyone leaning against them. Then there were the daily explosions from German shells, grenades and mortar bombs, nicknamed *patakas* by Indian troops after the firecrackers used at home in festivals; their terrible shrapnel or bomb fragments could rip along a trench with only bodies to stop them. Furthermore, at night German flare rockets and search-lights meant that the cover of darkness could never be relied on.

The Indians, along with the rest of the BEF, had little means of reply to all the German *patakas*. The BEF's shell stocks were very low after First Ypres (its field guns were restricted to firing just ten rounds a day, or fewer), and it had no pre-war supplies of trench weaponry, searchlights and flares like the German Army. 'Those who experienced the feelings of depression and anger at the failure of our nation to have prepared its armies, and saw their men suffering under every disadvantage and unable adequately to retaliate, know how bitter that experience was,' the 58th Vaughan's Rifles' Captain Alexander Lind said of the winter of 1914. As for the Indian troops' own feelings that winter in the

Pas-de-Calais, the sources are scanty, not least because the censors' translation of their western front letters had barely started. But such second-hand scraps of their conversation as survive from the period leave little doubt about how they felt.

'We are not fish'

'The war is not like war in old times,' the Indian soldiers in France frequently commented of their frightful twist of fate. 'We are not fish,' remarked one in deep gloom at the numbingly cold, metal-infested waters of their trenches. 'We have to deal with a terrible and powerful enemy, who is completely equipped with every sort of contrivance,' commented Subadar Azim Khan, a Punjabi Muslim of the 57th Wilde's Rifles. An Afridi was equally admiring of the Germans' equipment: 'If the Germans allied themselves with us Afridi we could lick the world,' he said. 'We have been hit but have never seen a German,' remarked many others, frustrated at their helplessness to fight back in kind against the German Army's grenades and trench mortars.

Meanwhile the Indians grieved for those regimental friends of their villages, sea voyages and former campaigns in China, Tibet and Mohmand who fell under German fire in 1914. Between October and Christmas, there were approximately 7000 Indian casualties on the western front, 30 per cent of them killed or missing presumed dead, reducing the Indian regiments from their full complement of 750 men each to an average of 450. 'It is very hard to endure the bombs, father,' wrote a Garhwali in one of the very first censored Indian soldiers' letters. 'It will be difficult for anyone to survive and come back safe and sound from the war. The son who is very lucky will see his father and mother, otherwise who can do this? There is no confidence of survival. The bullets and cannon-balls come down like snow.'

The Indian troops also felt resentment towards the British for deliberately – or so they thought – sacrificing them to save white troops. On their journey from Marseilles to the front they had seen few French or British troops, and in some places more French African troops from Senegal and Morocco. This surprised them since they had been told on their voyage they were going to a white man's war. 'We did not know any black troops were taking part in this war,' one Indian officer had said to James Willcocks. 'Where are the white men?'

At First Ypres, after the Indians had relieved British troops and made local attacks alone, such as their storming of Neuve Chapelle on 28 October, they came to the conclusion they were being put into the most dangerous positions ahead of British troops. This seemed only to be confirmed in the Indian sector on the right of the BEF line into December, where the British battalions were the minority who had sailed with them from India. 'The red pepper is little used and the black more,' a Hindu soldier wrote home, using the Indians' common code on the matter.

In truth the Indian soldiers had not been deliberately sacrificed ahead of white troops, rather they were ignorant of what they could not see, and they did not have a sense of proportion for their own losses. The British Army's figures in France and Belgium in 1914 totalled some 70,000 killed or wounded, ten times the Indian losses, while white French troops held most of the 400-mile Allied front line that stretched to the Swiss Alps.

Still, the Indians' perception of their overuse was all, and they constantly talked of it. They felt – like the Sikhs who had self-inflicted wounds at First Ypres – that 'the Sahibs' war' was more than they had bargained for, and they wanted to go home. If they were going to stay to fight in France, many protested (it appears Sikhs more vocally than others), they should get a pay rise of at least double their 11 rupees per month, up towards what British troops earned.

So when German aeroplanes began to drop jihad leaflets over the Indian trenches in November, it was overt encouragement to the Indians to act on their grievances and reject the British. As if the leaflets' messages were not clear enough, the Germans also hoisted large notice boards above their own trenches with more of the same. 'Indian Soldiers. The Holy War has begun, Death to the accursed English' read one of them; 'Holy War. Indians fight on our Side' another. And through loud-hailers from the German trenches came mysterious Urdu voices (Indian prisoners of war in Germany would later find out who they were) calling them to jihad and revolution. On the western front in winter 1914, then, the Indian troops had the temptations to give up as imperial soldiers, or the low spirits to do a bare minimum on duty to help their chances of getting out of France alive.

James Willcocks was well aware of this. As the Indians' commander in the mountain warfare tradition, his first concern was to stay in touch with them to inspire them. He often spent his whole day out from Indian headquarters at Hinges château, riding as far forward as he could and then walking up to the trenches to speak with his men, dragging his steel-bound leg behind him through the mud. 'There alone,' Willcocks said of the trenches, 'could one understand the real life the men lived, and appreciate what they were doing.' In December 1914, when Willcocks began writing confidential reports for the Viceroy, Charles Hardinge, he described the Indians' fighting spirit as he saw it: 'taken as a whole they do extraordinarily well ... Here life is held cheap and victory can only be won with heavy losses. The Indian soldiers serve for a very small remuneration, they are serving in a strange foreign land; they are the most patient soldiers in the world ... ready to lay down their lives for the Government they serve.'

But were the Indians really ready to lay down their lives that grimmest of winters, despite all the grievances, casualties and calls to defect? Part of the answer lies in the British care they received in parallel as an antidote. The demands of military service may have risen much higher than before the war, but so did what the British offered in return.

'Money is being poured out like water everywhere'

'In recent years the soldiers of all overseas expeditions from India have been amply supplied with all necessaries, warm clothing etc.,' the lately retired Indian Commander-in-Chief Garrett O'Moore Creagh wrote to *The Times* in October 1914 as Indian Expeditionary Force A gathered in France. 'I have no reason to believe that the same is not the case with regard to the present expedition. I therefore believe that the men on service have all they require.' Creagh had in fact commanded the largest pre-war Indian expeditionary force (to China in 1900–02), so he spoke as an authority on how the material benefits of military service for Indians were customarily kept up or improved overseas. Force A was no exception. In 1914 it received unprecedented day-to-day British care and 'comforts', both official and charitable, to compensate its men for the demands they faced. 'The question of comforts for Indians is being rather overdone,' George Allen, a well-connected London publisher, observed in December. 'People are all so anxious to help that money is being poured out like water everywhere.'

Force A received some supplies direct from British India such as Indian cooking pots, and opium – a ration for Sikhs carried over from pre-war days and disguised in BEF supply logs as 'Indian treacle'; it was taken daily by some Sikhs who were addicted, and kept handy in the trenches as a painkiller with magical restorative effects (the 15th Ludhiana Sikhs indeed shared their opium with badly wounded British troops). Yet in deploying to France, Force A exited the Government of India's sphere of control and entered the British government's. And in joining the BEF, whose supply base was Britain, Force A plugged into the Home Army's network of transport, medical and other logistical support just as the British Army contingent in India plugged into the Army in India. Thus from Marseilles onwards, Indian Expeditionary Force A became an appendage of the Home Army, and was in the hands of the War Office and Kitchener, who proved to be its guardian angel.

By September 1914, in order to supply the entire BEF for the long war he had foreseen from the start, Kitchener was vigorously placing large orders with military suppliers in Britain and the United States. In the process the British government threw off its Liberal pre-war policy of military economy, with Parliament from August consistently voting for large increases to British military expenditure to provide for the BEF. Kitchener paid close attention to the supply of Indian Expeditionary Force A, feeling a residual duty of care to the Indian Army as its ex-Commander-in-Chief. He appointed British civil servants as his special inspectors of the Indian troops in France, directing them to ensure that British government logistical care reached the Indians as quickly and thoroughly as possible through existing Home Army channels, for example its medical service the Royal Army Medical Corps.

Meanwhile in London a British charity for the Indian troops in France was set up, called the Indian Soldiers Fund. Its founders were largely retired senior British figures of the Indian Empire, from the ex-Viceroy Lord Curzon and old governors of British Indian provinces who now sat on company boards in the City of London to the retired Indian Commanders-in-Chief Lord Roberts and O'Moore Creagh. 'Our duty towards our Indian troops has but only begun with their arrival on European soil,' announced one of the charity's public appeals, in *The Times* in October 1914:

> It ought to be a matter of our first solicitude to see that our Indian soldiers lack nothing that lies in our power to give them. Little reflection should bring home to us how much their efficiency as fighting units, as adventurers on a foreign soil and under a foreign sky, depends on their being liberally and amply equipped with warm clothing and hygienic appliances ... Our appreciation of their valour and our sympathy with them in

their hour of trial should at once become manifest in the most practical way.

The founders of the Indian Soldiers Fund launched a spectacular fundraising effort by calling on their impeccable contacts all over the British Empire – merchant bankers, insurers, industrialists and colonial planters; the Indian Shi'a Muslim leader the Aga Khan; current imperial governors; wives of former Viceroys, the Duchess of Bedford, the Duke of Westminster and the British royal family. They pulled in donations from all corners of the globe, from American, British, Chinese and Egyptian banks; from the English-speaking world's great electricity, oil, steam navigation, insurance, sugar, food manufacturing and motor car companies; and from public collections in Australia, Fiji, Hong Kong, Burma, British West Africa, Jamaica, Barbados and Scotland. Altogether, the Fund raised £250,000, equivalent to 1.3 per cent of the Army in India's total budget in 1913–14, a colossal sum for comforts for a few Indian regiments. The department store owner Harry Gordon Selfridge then provided one of his warehouses in London for storage of the Fund's donations and purchases in transit to France. Further charity aid for Indian Expeditionary Force A came from the Red Cross, the St John Ambulance Association and the Young Men's Christian Association (or YMCA), and from the rulers of India's princely States. The Maharajah of Gwalior single-handedly paid for forty-one motor ambulances and a fleet of motor lorries, while thirty-three other princes donated a £400,000 Indian hospital ship.

Kitchener and his special inspectors of Indian troops brought together all these strands of British government and charity aid from November 1914, by which time the Indian Soldiers Fund had spent over £50,000. The result was a profusion of logistical support of a kind the Indians had never seen before. In the trenches, under James Willcocks' watch, the Indian Corps' experienced Administrative Staff officers distributed unprecedented quantities of food. The Indians got as much fresh meat as they could eat, mainly goats imported from Algeria and slaughtered behind the Indian front line, with Indian company representatives monitoring their proper religious preparation. Alongside the goat meat the Indians got an array of food from both France and Britain, from vegetables, eggs, milk, cereals and jams to sweets, spices, chutneys and chocolate.

'It was extraordinary with what regularity the men were fed,' Willcocks wrote of his staff's food deliveries by motor lorry, Indian mule pack and cart to Indian regimental field kitchens in hedgerows, woods and barns behind the front line, the cooks being Indian non-combatants who had travelled with Force A. 'By hook or crook,' Willcocks continued, 'the company cooks would manage to send up excellent viands, frequently preparing them under conditions anything but conducive to good cookery.' All the indications are that the Indian troops were highly appreciative. 'So good are the arrangements that rations of every kind of thing to eat are brought right up to the trenches,' said Amir Khan, a Punjabi Muslim of the 129th Baluchis. 'It is a perpetual wedding feast,' remarked another. The 39th Garhwals' British officer Kenneth Henderson soon saw a change in his regiment's appearance: 'The men got noticeably fat on the liberal and good rations.'

The other supplies crammed into the Indian trenches included rum, large tea urns with Indian tea leaves, millions of cigarettes, and charcoal braziers. Then there were hundreds of thousands of clothes, largely public donations to the Indian Soldiers Fund, from waterproof turban covers, plastic capes, Wellington and knee-length rubber boots to balaclavas, scarves, gloves, mittens, shirts, wool jumpers and thick socks. 'Clothes we have in such abundance showered on us we do not know what to do with them,' wrote Charles Tribe, the 41st Dogras' colonel, in early December. His counterpart of the 2nd Gurkhas, Charles Norie, was similarly placed: 'I have so much warm clothing that if we move I must leave several cart-loads behind if it is not taken from me.' 'Since the real cold set in it is a case of being over-clothed,' Willcocks reported to the Indian Soldiers Fund on 10 December after hearing rumours from England that the Indians had only their thin tropical uniforms. 'I have seen every unit and corps of every sort, and no one takes more trouble than I do to see they have enough. It is <u>absolutely untrue</u> for anyone to say the Indian troops now in France are underclad.' The Indians' British officers in fact had to keep an eye on their men's packs to stop them overloading with clothes they wanted to take home.

More important was Indian Expeditionary Force A's medical care provided by Kitchener and the War Office. Force A had arrived in France with its Indian Medical Service stretcher bearers, horse-drawn ambulances and field hospitals, but these were too small and sparsely equipped to cope with the Indian casualties at First Ypres. By December, Kitchener had largely relieved the Indian Medical Service of caring for the Indian wounded in France, spreading the strain onto new, War Office-managed and state-of-the-art medical facilities. These extended from motor ambulances and casualty clearing stations near the trenches, to hospitals in French schools, hotels and mental asylums made available by local mayors as far as Marseilles, to hospital ships in the English Channel, and hospitals in Brighton and elsewhere in southern England – all dedicated to the Indians alone, and set up with the help of the India Office which fished out retired doctors of the Indian Medical Service to advise on religious requirements.

In the last week of November, one of Kitchener's inspectors who monitored the Indian troops' logistical care saw for himself the quality of the new medical attention. At the French town of Rouen near the front, the inspector saw a depot for British Army troops recovering from light wounds that was so overcrowded and ill-equipped most of the men were sleeping on the ground. In the nearby Indian Convalescent Depot, however, 'the conditions were strikingly better':

All the tents had bottom boards, trestle-beds, bolsters, and braziers. In consequence the Indian convalescents were vastly more comfortable than their British comrades across the road and seemed very happy and satisfied ... I have observed the tendency to concentrate a disproportionate amount of attention upon providing sick or wounded Indians with comforts to which he has never been accustomed ... whilst the British have been left out in the cold.

Kitchener's chief inspector of the Indian troops' medical care in France was Walter Lawrence, a convivial, multi-lingual member of the Indian Civil Service who had passed first in its open entry competition, notorious as the British Empire's hardest examination. On 15 December Lawrence assured Kitchener that 'conditions on the whole are excellent; the arrangements are of course very superior to those obtaining in Military Hospitals in India for Indian troops'. At one Indian hospital that day, behind the Indian line at St Omer, Lawrence heard from the patients themselves what they thought. 'I have satisfied myself by long talks with the Indians that they are comfortable, contented and grateful.'

At the same time in the trenches, the Indian troops' level of sickness was a revelation: they stood the climate better than the British. The BEF's doctors found throughout the winter of 1914 that their sickness rate was half that of the Tommies. The nub of this medical phenomenon was that the Indians took better care of their calves and feet. British troops, excepting a minority of Scotsmen in kilts, wore close-fitting boots with puttees (the cloth strips wrapped between ankle and calf to hold a soldier's boots and breeches together). Together their boots and puttees constricted blood circulation in the lower leg. Combined with prolonged exposure to cold water on the sodden trench floor, this frequently caused their feet to swell and turn blue with blisters and sores – a condition known as 'trench foot', distinguishable from frostbite caused simply by low temperatures. The Indian troops suffered less from both trench foot and frostbite. The major reason was the traditional Indian Army practice of wearing oversized boots that allowed room for good blood circulation and two pairs of socks, which kept the Indians' feet healthier and warmer than they would have been in tighter British boots and puttees. Almost as important was Indian regimental doctors' insistence that the Indians keep their feet as warm and dry as possible, using their freely available socks and foot ointments from the Indian Soldiers Fund. And, of course, all the Indians' food and warm clothes was good for their health.

Although a few Indian regiments such as the 41st Dogras still suffered high rates of frostbitten feet, the average Indian daily sick rate in France was very low at 2 per 1000, several times lower than in peacetime India. The few Indian cases of disease were mostly viral, either malaria which Garhwalis and Gurkhas had caught as they passed through Himalayan lowlands on mobilisation, or mumps, a European virus the Indian troops had no childhood immunity to.

The Indians' coping with the western front winter was no surprise after they had dealt with temperatures twice as cold on their pre-war expeditions in China and Tibet. Indeed, home for some 45 per cent of the Indian Corps' original Indian troops from Afridi to Garhwalis and Gurkhas was mountainous regions where sub-zero temperatures, rain, frost and snow were commonplaces. The Indians certainly complained daily about the wet and the dampness of their trenches, but so did British troops. 'I am at a loss to account for the impression prevalent in some quarters that the Indians were specially tried by the climate,' the 39th Garhwals' British officer Kenneth Henderson was to say after the war, once Arthur Conan Doyle and other writers had spread the idea. 'The majority of Indians kept in excellent health the whole time they were in France.'

Alongside their material and medical care, the Indians received regular visits during the winter of 1914 from British leaders to boost their spirits. Willcocks was their most frequent senior caller in the trenches, where he was known as Wil Kak Sahib. In late November, for instance, he visited a Sikh regiment which had been soaked, shelled and bombed in the trenches continuously for three weeks, but they gave him a rousing welcome. 'When we turned up the Sikhs burst into their martial full-throated war-song,' wrote F. E. Smith, the future Attorney-General and Secretary of State for India who was accompanying Willcocks as the Indian Corps' press officer. 'It brought the tears into one's eyes.'

Willcocks liked to amuse the men by handing out some of the more garish clothes from the Indian Soldiers Fund which he picked out himself from the shipments from London, for instance a waistcoat he described as 'an extraordinary garment ... made up of patches of every hue under the sun ... and trimmed with gold lace'. He gave it to a Sikh, selecting him as a 'sulky-looking fellow' who needed cheering up, after another Sikh of his company had told Willcocks, 'Oh, he is a pessimist; he thinks the war will never end; of what use is anything to him?' Willcocks went with the waistcoat up to the man, and, he recalled, 'in his own language asked him, as a favour, to accept it at the hands of his General':

> The sepoy took it in a rather surly manner and opened it, but even his torpor gave way when he saw the gorgeous coat. All the others roared with laughter, in which he joined heartily, and putting it on said, 'General Sahib, you have altered my ideas of the war, for this proves that people must still be full of humour in England ... I will send it home to my village, and attach a card to it: "Taken by me Singh in single combat with the German Emperor ... ".'

Willcocks tried to put the Indians at their ease on his trench visits with talk of what was on their minds. A common topic was the Germans' superior trench weaponry, and Willcocks sought to hearten the men with hope of better fighting days to come. 'I often said to the Indian officers and men that although England had been sadly behind in providing us with the means of paying back the enemy in his own coin, she would assuredly make up way, and then would come our turn.' During these conversations the Indian troops felt comfortable enough to joke in front of Willcocks. 'They gradually became sarcastic,' he remembered. 'One Jawan (young fellow) ... declared that if the Germans would exchange weapons the war would be over in a week. "Not if we kept them as clean as you do," remarked a comrade, and all laughed. I discovered our recruit had been reprimanded that morning for having a dirty rifle on parade.'

Some of the Indian troops even joked with Willcocks about the German leaflets proclaiming jihad. Willcocks read out the leaflets in the trenches to show the men he did not take them seriously, and they responded in kind. One Punjabi Muslim joker shouted out to his company's laughter, 'We now understand what "Made in Germany" means!' Other Punjabis used the leaflets to wipe their bottoms. Among the Punjabis, at least, the leaflets' overtures to desert seem to have fallen flat that winter. No doubt they saw the Germans as an enemy who meant them harm – they had enough reasons in those 7000 Indian casualties. Indeed, one of the very first Indian censored letters in France, by a Muslim officer from British India to his brother at home, suggests how many Muslim troops might have seen the jihad. His letter hinted that the holy war was altogether too remote from his priority of earning as much money and land as he could from British employment for his family. 'What better occasion can I find than this to prove the loyalty of my family to the British Government?' he wrote of his western front service. 'Turkey, it is true, is a Muslim power, but what has it to do with us? Turkey is nothing at all with us.'

The highest-ranking Indian Army general to visit the Indian troops in France that winter was its former Commander-in-Chief Lord Roberts. Aged eighty-two, he was still energetic and full of charisma as a veteran of thirty battles going back to the 1850s, being best known to Indians for leading the Indian Army to victory in the Second Anglo-Afghan War of 1878–80. His first stop, on 10 November, was an Indian hospital at Boulogne; he left it with tears streaming down his face after meeting severely wounded Indians who weakly tried to rise from their beds to salute him. Then at two parades in his honour on 11–12 November, at the Indian Corps' Hinges château headquarters and the nearby town square of Locon, Roberts met men of several Indian regiments including some whose fathers had fought with him in Afghanistan. He made a gallant gesture of solidarity on both occasions by removing his overcoat because the men did not wear coats to meet him. He spoke to them personally, shaking their hands and taking the time to hear their family stories as he tried not to shiver. His farewell speech at Locon forgot his objection at the war's outbreak to the Indians fighting the Germans; instead he encouraged them to do it well:

> I have fought with [Indian troops] too often in every kind of climate, and against every kind of enemy, not to be sure that there are no conditions so hard that [you] will not do [your] duty as soldiers. How well you are doing it I have heard from your Commanding Officer, General Sir James Willcocks, and the account he has given me has filled me with emotion. You are suffering much, but you are fighting in loyalty to your Empire and King ... You will then fight on as long as may be necessary. And it may be long ... Let every man then do his utmost until the enemy is defeated. In this way you will do your duty to the Empire to which you belong, and the glory of your deed will live for ever in India.

Roberts was driven away from Locon by motor car along a road that Willcocks had lined in his honour with representatives from every battalion of the Indian Corps. Roberts insisted on stopping again and again to get out of his car and meet the men, still without his coat. This is thought to have cost him his life after he caught a bad cold and died two days later in bed at a house in St Omer. Willcocks sent Indian troops to the house to escort Roberts' coffin, on a gun carriage draped with a Union Jack, his sword and cap on top, to the town hall for a funeral service. 'It is sad, what parting with one like him is not?' said a Punjabi Muslim soldier Roberts had met. 'But, thank God, we saw him here at the last, and I, if I live, will be able to tell my children in the Punjab that he shook hands with me and spoke to me in my own language.'

In December the Indians in France had their most exalted visitor: the King-Emperor. George V visited an Indian hospital, spending forty minutes with an interpreter among the wounded men, one an amputee who broke into tears when George spoke to him. Then he met Indian troops at Locon square and elsewhere near the front, which seems to have made a great impression. His visit, according to the 41st Dogras' Major Henry Barstow, 'had a marked effect on the spirits of the men, who talked of little else for some time'.

As the icing on the cake of British care in the French winter of 1914, the King-Emperor's visit likely made the Indians feel in some measure valued and respected parts of the British war effort, enough to help keep them going while not dispelling their sadnesses and grievances. They strongly felt they were overworked and underpaid for western front service, but it was significant that they said they wanted a British pay rise, not no British work. For the British, the proof of the Indians' ongoing commitment to imperial service, however fragile it may have been, was in their fighting performance. The Indian infantry in France in late 1914 remained professional with their own pride and honour: if the Germans killed their comrades, they were not going to take it without fighting back.

8

'ENTERPRISES AND SURPRISES'

In holding their trenches on the western front in late 1914, James Willcocks wanted his Indian troops to be aggressive. Convinced that inactivity and passivity under daily German fire would only lower their spirits, he spurred them to retaliate. In a memorandum of early November 1914 to British officers of the Indian Corps, he was emphatic that the Indians' mountain warfare skills bestowed a flair for 'enterprises and surprises in which the Indian Troops do and must excel. I, therefore, desire that constant enterprise be shown, and that every ruse and device which the ingenuity of officers and men can bring into useful play, should be employed to harass the enemy, disturb his rest, and inspire in him a wholesale respect for, and awe of, the Indian Corps.'

But beyond their pre-war skills something more was needed. Just as the Indian Army before 1914 had competed with the independent Pukhtun *lashkar*s in a cycle of tactical imitations and innovations, to survive in France it needed to compete in the same way with the Germans. By the time of the Christmas Truce of 1914, which the Indian infantry played their part in, they were no longer novices at trench warfare but learning and steadily gaining expertise. 'The men, now that they understand the game, are doing marvellously well,' Willcocks reported to the Viceroy, Charles Hardinge. 'The sepoy is a very adaptable soldier.'

'They could outwit the Hun'

The 39th Garhwals were the first Indian regiment to live up to Willcocks' directive for enterprises and surprises. They used their mountain warfare training to deliver the BEF's first trench raid of the war, after dark on 9 November. 'The Germans were found to have established themselves on a short frontage within 50 yards of our line, and were evidently digging like beavers, judging by the earth thrown up,' wrote the Garhwals' British officer Kenneth Henderson. 'It was decided to rush the work and after despatching the occupants, to fill it in.' A fifty-strong party of Garhwals crawled quietly on their stomachs through unharvested turnips and cabbages across no man's land, which was yet to be cluttered with the dense barbed wire entanglements of later in the war. The Garhwals got to the German parapet unnoticed, lay quite still, and then suddenly leapt over at the signal of a British officer firing his revolver, shouting as they went. 'No German in that trench escaped,' recalled Henderson. 'I believe it to be one of the few occasions when the famous kukri was effectively used. The trench was deep and narrow and the men could not use their bayonets, so they used their kukris; and only two prisoners were brought back.' Willcocks was delighted with their night's work: 'They had learned that if they kept low and used their own tactics they could outwit the Hun.'

The Indian regimental Scouts then used their particular skills as they had for years in the independent Pukhtun tribal areas. They rooted out German snipers, a number of whom had sneaked through gaps in the BEF line during First Ypres to hide in houses or farms behind. The Scouts of the 59th Scinde Rifles and other Indian units hunted them down, working in small teams to identify their hiding spots and approach them in silence. They killed several, including one whose nest they discovered in a haystack complete with air-holes, food and water.

Indian Scouts also gathered intelligence in no man's land, creeping with their British officers up to the German parapet to identify German battalions or sketch the trench layout. Some Scouts went out by themselves, including Muslims still showing no inclination to take up the German leaflets' offer of sanctuary. On a dawn sortie in December, the Afridi officer Arsala Khan of the 57th Wilde's Rifles with two of his Malik Din Scouts peeped into a German trench and found it to be occupied by a few napping men, whom they shot dead. Other Muslim Scouts in no man's land even scrawled obscene messages on the jihad notice boards. Meanwhile there were Indian recruits who sniped expertly, not simply because they were Scouts, but because they were independent Pukhtun. 'An Afridi who had been some days in the trenches was most reluctant to leave his trench,' one Indian regiment's British doctor ascertained. 'He said that lying sniping all day reminded him so much of home.'

The Indian Sappers made the most of their pre-war training, above all in explosives. In early November, as they watched German troops dig numerous forward trench bays known as 'saps' close to the Indian line, they noticed that these were occasionally left unoccupied – a chance to plant land mines in them, just as they had against the Afridi Zakkas in 1908. They detonated land mines in the saps to deadly and disgusting effect, in one instance blowing German body parts into an Indian trench. Demolition was next. Overnight on 11–12 November, a Bengal Sapper company stole into a stretch of no man's land 300 yards deep, heading into six houses used as German machine gun posts. They drove the Germans out of one house before laying charges to blow all six high into the night sky.

The Sappers' crowning achievement that winter, however, was improvising to compensate for the BEF's lack of trench weapons compared with the Germans. It started in November with a Canadian from Ottawa named Oliver Wheeler. He was a young British officer of the Bengal Sappers, known in the Indian Army as its leading climber of North American mountains. Wheeler was in an abandoned German sap with some of his Muslim men, taking a break from filling it in with the clay mud. 'I was sitting on a nice square seat, smoking a cigarette, when Jemadar Abdul Aziz Khan asked me whether I knew what I was sitting on,' Wheeler remembered. 'Examination showed the seat to be a stack of several hundreds of German "hairbrush" bombs, fitted with detonators and ready for throwing. We carried them from the enemy's sap to our trench, and copied them, using gun-cotton.'

Besides these German copies, otherwise known as 'stick grenades', the Sappers made hand grenades in November of their own design. They did so at their impromptu arms factory in France, a commandeered iron works behind the Indian line in the village of Béthune. Before the war, in 1911–12, the Sappers had designed hand grenades at their workshops in British India and thrown them in action in the Indian Empire's north-eastern jungles against the Abor tribesmen. At Béthune they used this pre-war knowledge to make an Indian pattern of hand grenade nicknamed, after its casing, the 'jam tin bomb'. They trawled the Indian regimental field kitchens and French villages for jam tins which they packed with explosive and metal fragments such as nails. Then they put in a detonator with a short naked fuse poking through the lid, a smearing of clay. At Béthune they also manufactured trench mortars with a range of 200 yards. Again these were based on the Sappers' own pre-war design, substantially copied from the Japanese Army and used since 1905 in Indian trench training exercises. They made the mortar barrels out of iron piping or wood wrapped in metal wire, and the bombs from sawn-off artillery shell cases, each filled with three and a half pounds of explosive and a timed detonator.

By late November the Sapper factory at Béthune was producing hundreds of hand grenades a day, mostly jam tin bombs (the simplest to make), along with numerous trench mortar barrels and bombs. The Indian regiments were taught to work with these new weapons – no easy matter as the jam tin bomb fuses, lit with matches or cigarettes, were tricky in the wet weather, and the mortar bombs were prone to premature explosion as they left the barrel. It seems the Indian troops welcomed the jam tin bombs in particular, which finally empowered them to reply in kind to the stream of German hand grenades they had had to put up with in their first three weeks in the trenches. The 129th Baluchis' British officer Harold Lewis noticed how his Mahsud were always at the front of the queue for the jam tin bombs, desperate to get their own back on the Germans. They lost no time in no man's land at night to raid occupied German saps, bombing the men digging them into retreat. 'They love these expeditions,' Lewis observed of the Mahsud, 'it suits them to the ground.'

The Indian regiments' most inventive use of the jam tin bombs, however, was in the improvising of their own tactics to capture German trenches. On the frosty morning of 23 November, the Germans attacked from saps to capture the central section of the Indian front line, by the village of Festubert. But the Indians took back the entire lost line through combining their pre-war skills of fire and movement with jam tin bomb throwing. By hasty regimental arrangement, scattered parties of Afridi, Garhwalis and Gurkhas first helped to contain the German incursion by blocking it on either side with rifle fire and jam tin bombs. Then overnight, from opposite ends of the captured line, they attacked towards each other to clear out the Germans in between. They went in rushes on the trench floor, using their bombs and bayonets in hand-to-hand fights, with rifle fire support coming down from runners on the ground above. By dawn on 24 November they had recovered their line at Festubert, at a cost of 1150 Indian casualties.

James Willcocks had watched the fight from dusk till dawn. He had stood vigil in the freezing night air at the top of a tower in the garden of his Hinges château headquarters, glued to binoculars to make out his men's progress by rifle and jam tin bomb flashes. 'I can remember no occasion in my life when I felt more acutely the desire to succeed, for where my Corps was in the grips of death was my entire world,' he wrote.

Some of the Garhwali survivors emerged from the trenches covered in blood from head to foot. One of them whose name is not known made the only recorded Indian comment on the fight. He said the Germans were hard to strangle because their necks were fat: 'They are not bony men.' Darwán Singh Negi, a Garhwali NCO, became the second Indian Victoria Cross winner for his part in leading the bayonet rushes. Also decorated was a long-serving Afridi officer of the Frontier Force's 58th Vaughan's Rifles – 'thoroughly reliable', said his British officer Alexander Lind – for his tenacity in throwing jam tin bombs against Germans at close range. He was the future deserter Jemadar Mir Mast, as yet giving no hint to his British officers of any subversive sentiment or jihad on his mind; his award was the Indian Distinguished Service Medal, the Indian Army's third tier of recognition for bravery (after the Victoria Cross and the Indian Order of Merit).

'At first we spoke with contempt of the Indians,' a German soldier wrote home hours after retreating from Darwán Singh Negi, Mir Mast and the rest:

Today we learned to look at them in a different light ... the devil knows what the English had put into those fellows. Anyhow, those who stormed our lines seemed either drunk or possessed with an evil spirit. With fearful shouting, in comparison with which our hurrahs are like the whining of a baby, thousands of those brown forms rushed upon us as suddenly as if they were shot out of a fog, so that at first we were completely taken by surprise ... truly these brown enemies were not to be despised.

With butt ends, bayonets, swords and daggers we fought each
other, and we had bitter hard work.

During the Festubert fight, the Indians' jam tin bombs had
run out when they still needed more. This happened all too frequently that winter as the BEF waited on British factory-made
grenades with ring-pulls, which Lord Kitchener had ordered.
On 16 December, Harold Lewis saw the Mahsud of the 129th
Baluchis driven to their own awful solution to running out of jam
tin bombs. The Mahsud had captured a German sap using jam
tin bombs in the early morning darkness, only to be trapped in
the sap after dawn as German machine gunners covered no man's
land all the way back to the 129th's trenches. 'Every single man
who tried to cross those fatal 30 yards was shot, it was sickening,'
wrote Lewis, peeking at the action from the Indian line. Lewis
with some Bombay Sappers and Sikh Pioneers did all they could
to rescue the remaining Mahsud by digging a new trench towards
the sap 'like maniacs . . . raising cheers to keep up their spirits and
to make the Germans less cock-a-hoop.'

While the Mahsud in the sap had their rifles and bayonets to
hold off the Germans coming at them up the trench linking it
with the main German line – their NCO Sahib Jan 'on several
occasions relieved the situation by charging single-handed with
fixed bayonet,' said Lewis – their jam tin bombs quickly ran out in
reply to German grenades. 'I saw bomb after bomb fall amongst
them,' Lewis went on:

> and our men picked them up and threw them back. Many
> burst before this could be done and our poor men were blown
> to pieces . . . They were absolutely fearless and have gained the
> admiration of everyone who saw or heard of them. But so many
> of the men I liked and some I almost loved, have died, that it
> is rather difficult to bear up, it was such a slaughter . . . When
> night fell they crept back, those who remained. We lost 120.

The Indian Army on one of its pre-1914 missions, to China in August 1900. Indian cavalrymen ride into Beijing's Forbidden City for a victory parade, shortly after the city's capture by an international coalition force of the Indian, United States, Japanese and other armies.

The Delhi Durbar of 1911 with the King-Emperor's canopy at the centre of the great Durbar amphitheatre, guarded by the thousands of Indian and British troops in front of the public stands, unified – supposedly – in loyalty to the British Empire.

A rare photograph of Indian soldiers in action before 1914 – here in the Abor lands of the Indian Empire's north-east in 1911, after torching a frequent target seen in the background: civilian homes.

The Viceroy who mobilised the Indian Army for world war in 1914 as its civilian head in British India, photographed at the start of his viceroyalty in 1910: Charles Hardinge, with his wife Bena and children (left to right) Edd, Diamond and Alec.

Experiences shared by the 1 million Indian servicemen sent overseas in the First World War – gathering at port in British India, here at Bombay in 1914 (top); passing the time on deck at sea, here in the Persian Gulf in lifejackets in 1916 (middle); and disembarking in foreign lands, as here in East Africa, packed onto a landing craft at the port of Dar es Salaam in 1917 (bottom).

The Indians landed at Marseilles on 26 September 1914 to help liberate German-occupied France – a Sikh regiment marches into the city flying the French tricolor, a gift from locals who welcomed them off their ships with cheers, hugs and kisses.

An Indian Hindu soldier on his way to hospital on the western front during the Indian Army's first days there in autumn 1914; he may well have been one of hundreds who shot at themselves rather than at the Germans – self-inflicting wounds, they thought, was the quickest way to get back home.

Training in France in the winter of 1914–15, when the Indian Army on the western front learned many new ways of European warfare, adapting in response to the German Army.

Halbmondlager – or Camp Crescent Moon – in Germany, south of Berlin, where Allied Muslim, Hindu and Sikh prisoners of war captured in Europe were held. The camp was a secret school of revolution with an anti-Allied propaganda programme for the Indians and other prisoners; central to the scheme was Germany's first mosque, built in 1915 complete with its minaret 80 feet high.

An Indian washes his foot at his own leisure inside Camp Crescent Moon in 1915 as a German guard looks on affably, with the prisoners' heated barracks behind – a comfortable kind of captivity compared with the Indian soldiers' treatment in their horrific prisoner of war camps in Syria and East Africa.

Indian Muslim soldiers of the Afridi tribe who deserted in France in March 1915, seen here that May in Ottoman Iraq at Baghdad with their ringleader, Jemadar Mir Mast (far left). They were bound for Afghanistan on a secret German mission they had volunteered for at Camp Crescent Moon.

In action at Gallipoli in 1915 – Indian artillerymen haul their mountain gun up one of the peninsula's steep ridges.

For 16,000 Indian troops, being wounded in France or Belgium in 1914–15 meant evacuation to hospital in England; these men recovered at the Brighton Pavilion Indian hospital under the gaze of the local painter Charles H. H. Burleigh.

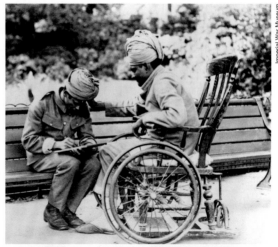

Contact with home from the Indian hospitals in England was by letter. The Indian patients sent and received thousands of letters a month, often dictating theirs to scribes – here in the Brighton Pavilion garden in summer 1915 – if they were illiterate.

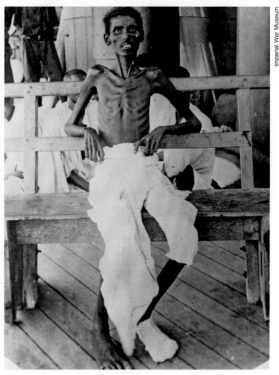

A French girl with a new friend – Indian troops were billeted on northern French village families from 1914 to 1918, and were known for their kindness.

An Indian soldier in May 1916 captured at the Iraqi town of Kut, after the five-month Turkish siege that had starved him and the rest of the 6th Indian Division into surrender.

The Indian Army's supreme commanders in London (from left to right) – in theory the King-Emperor George V; in practice, his wartime prime ministers H. H. Asquith and David Lloyd George.

Three British generals rarely seen by the Indian troops, but who in London or Delhi took some of the big decisions about where they went or how they were cared for day to day. From left to right: Lord Kitchener who called the Indians to France in 1914; William Robertson, the British Cabinet's senior military adviser on global strategy between 1915 and 1918; and Charles Monro, the Commander-in-Chief in India from 1916.

The Indian Army had eighteen Victoria Cross winners in 1914–18; these three, wearing their VCs, are Gobind Singh of the 2nd Gardner's Lancers (left) photographed in 1917; Khudadad Khan of the 129th Baluchis (centre) painted in 1935; and John Smyth of the 15th Ludhiana Sikhs (right) at a reunion for all VC holders in London in 1956.

'We have learnt a good many lessons'

After First Ypres, the Indian trenches began to acquire their own names, such as Baluchi Road or Ludhiana Lane. This reflected the Indians' place by mid-December 1914 as founding fathers of what became the western front's 10,000 miles of trenches. The construction and maintenance of these day to day was a life-saving art, and the Indians were among the BEF's first to master it.

'We have learnt a good many lessons,' Harold Lewis wrote of the 129th Baluchis' progress in late November. Their first lesson was never stop digging. Each Indian regiment constantly needed to build and repair its trenches to maximise concealment from German fire, besides keeping the water down with drainage channels. 'Everywhere one goes one digs and digs and digs,' Lewis said. 'We live like rabbits, dug into the very bowels of the earth.' They installed dug-outs as British officers' quarters with sleeping bunks, desks and fireplaces, to which the Sappers added electric lights and radiators. Many Indian troops went out of their way to help make their British officers' dug-outs as comfortable as possible, for example in the 39th Garhwals by paving the floors with bricks. Outside the dug-outs, some Gurkhas made their trenches more homely by building thatched shelters to sleep under.

The Indian regiments learned that the most efficient way to hold their trenches was to spread out to minimise casualties, keeping the front line lightly held and the majority of the men in reserve trenches behind. Then each trench needed 'traverses' – vertical barriers built of mud from the trench floor to the parapet – at intervals of 10 yards, book-ending trench sections to contain exploding German projectiles. The Indian troops learned when to dart round a traverse from one trench section to the next by listening out for the different incoming shells or mortar bombs, whose sound varied depending on their weight and proximity. 'You can tell the shell which is going to burst near you by the bass note as it whistles through the air,' observed Lewis.

Another Indian lesson learned in the trenches was to install loopholes, the slits in parapets for watching and firing into no man's land without exposing the head, with fire-steps up to them. 'By day you can hunt and snap shoot any German head unduly exposed. And the horrid exultation when you hit one!' Lewis wrote. The Sappers put electric searchlights next to some of the loopholes; a few were motor car headlights wired up to a local generator. The Indians also learned to stop shooting at the daily sights of German aeroplanes and zeppelins (usually too far away for there to be any realistic chance of damage), and, grimly, to live with the dead. 'Really our susceptibilities become very dull,' Lewis thought. 'One sees so many dead that the sight of one more means absolutely nothing. I walked this very day over what I took to be a sack, but was really a man's stomach. His head was buried, but the toes gave away what it really was.' Lewis's brother officer of the 129th Baluchis, Captain Ronald Davies, found that their Mahsud deliberately trod on their dead in trenches where there had been heavy German fire. 'As I went along I remember the advice given me by the sepoys I met: "You can walk on him, Sahib, he is dead. No, not on that one, he is terribly wounded but not dead yet."

The 129th's British officers noticed how some Indian troops took to their routine trench duties with a professional pride while others showed little interest. The most intent on high standards seemed to be their Mahsud. On a November afternoon, for instance, one Mahsud was riled by a Punjabi in an adjacent trench sitting on the trench floor, lazily pointing his rifle in the air and firing without taking aim. The Mahsud strode over to berate the Punjabi, as the 129th's commandant, William Southey, saw. '"That is not the way to fire; look at me." He deliberately stood up and fired over the parapet, taking careful aim; then reloaded, aimed and had another shot. Then he turned round to the man and said, "That is the correct way."'

Behind the Indian trenches, Indian Expeditionary Force A's

Indian princes and aristocrats in honorary staff positions took varying degrees of interest in trench life. The older maharajahs kept to their cottages at a safe distance behind the Indian sector, attending to their State business with civil servants. The younger ones tended to explore the countryside more in their motor cars, for example the teenage Maharajah of Jodhpur who sped around the rural lanes drunk. But a few ventured up to the front line in December, tempted by the improved state of the Indian trenches. The Maharajah of Tikari spent a night in line with the 15th Ludhiana Sikhs. In the morning, he emerged from his dug-out in blue silk pyjamas carrying a gun case and asking for a free loop-hole. 'Shortly afterwards I heard some dull clangs followed by roars of rage from the German trench,' recalled the Sikhs' young officer John Smyth. 'I suddenly thought of the Maharajah and went along to see what he was at. There he was in his lovely pyjamas with a 500 Express Elephant rifle ... chortling with joy and methodically knocking out every Boche loophole within range.'

The Hindu diarist Thakur Amar Singh was another trench tourist. Having moved up to the front from Orléans in early December to join his brigade staff of the Indian Corps' Lahore Division, he still had no meaningful duties and plenty of spare time. On 17 December he visited the 1st and 4th Gurkhas' trenches near the village of Givenchy. 'They were very narrow and slippery,' he wrote in his diary. 'It was quite an experience being there. About a couple of feet above your head the bullets fly and some come and plant themselves in the parapet.' Amar Singh was especially impressed by the British officers. 'I think the British officer is a wonderful man,' he wrote of them that day:

> They are fellows who have always lived more or less quite comfortably and their point is to remain clean. Here they were plastered in mud, wet through up to their knees and unshaved ... sleeping with their clothes on in this cold in the damp trenches but in spite of all this quite cheerful and setting

a good example to the men ... They take a lot of trouble to do
their duty.

Amar Singh found the Gurkhas equally muddy, and busy firing
through the loopholes, but without the bonhomie of the British
officers. They asked Amar Singh when the war would end, and
despaired at his guess of four to five months. 'I told them to
cheer up as no one dies before his proper time.' Amar Singh tried
throwing some jam tin bombs from the Gurkha line at a German
sap just 15 yards away, but their fuses were too wet and none of
them went off. Still, he wrote, 'I was very glad I went out to the
trenches today. I have seen something of real modern warfare.'

Unknown to Amar Singh and the Gurkhas in the Indian
trenches by Givenchy, the miners of the German VII Corps were
tunnelling beneath their feet, preparing the western front's first
explosive mine attack from underground shafts. This came on 20
December, and it shattered the Indian Corps, which had almost
nothing left to give after eight continuous weeks in the front
line. At 9 a.m., the Germans detonated ten explosive mines, each
weighing 50 kilograms and laid at 100-yard intervals under the
centre of the Indian position. The trench floors where Gurkhas,
Hindus and other Indian troops stood quivered, then cracked
apart with an ear-splitting explosion, punching high into the sky.
Mud slopped back down on to stunned Indians wobbling with
blurred vision and hearing loss, their parapets, fire-steps and
dug-outs now levelled into a liquid brown expanse. Many of the
Indians were missing, lost to the ground beneath, either killed or
buried alive.

As German infantry pressed forward throwing grenades,
there was a general retreat at the Indian centre. Several Indian
and British companies went immediately, giving up on the fight
when mud came up to men's thighs, pulling off boots, swallowing
ammunition boxes and jamming rifles. The exceptions included a
few Gurkhas who fought hand-to-hand with their *khukuris*, some

to be taken prisoner, and Harold Lewis with the 129th Baluchis' Afridi. Lewis and his men fired at the onrushing Germans right up to close quarters. 'The Germans were all drugged and grinning like jackals,' Lewis wrote. 'I saw them at 5 yards range so I ought to know. Apparently they give them spirits of ether before a charge.' After Lewis looked up to see a German rifle pointed at his head and heard a click because its chamber was empty, he decided it was time to retreat. But his Afridi did not want to give in. 'Why should we go?' one Afridi, Sattar Khan, shouted at Lewis in Pukhtu (their variant of Pushtu). 'We have no ammunition, but there are twenty of us and we have bayonets.' Nonetheless Lewis ordered the Afridi to fall back with him, on the way continuing to deny Sattar Khan who clutched his arm, imploring, 'Let us go back.'

'The state of the wounded beggars all description,' wrote Roly Grimshaw, a British officer of the 34th Poona Horse, of the Indian centre's retreat during the day of 20 December, which he saw behind the Indian line on the road up to Givenchy:

> Little Gurkhas slopping through the freezing mud barefooted; Tommies with no caps and plastered in mud and blood from head to foot; Sikhs with their hair all down and looking more wild and weird than I have ever seen them; Pathans more dirty and untidy than usual – all limping or reeling along like drunken men, some helping an almost foundered comrade, in most cases misery depicted on their faces.

There were several Indian counter-attacks at Givenchy from 20 to 22 December, regaining a little ground, such as when the Afridi officer Arsala Khan led his Malik Din company with their rifles against seventy Germans in a captured Indian trench, killing and wounding half of them as the rest fled. But the Indian counter-attacks were doomed to fail with the BEF still so low on grenades and shells, and the Indian Corps dug a new front line a few hundred yards back. The British Army's I Corps under Douglas Haig, in reserve since First Ypres, relieved the Indian Corps from the night of 22 December, taking over its whole sector.

By Christmas Eve, the 39th Garhwals were the last Indian unit in line waiting to hand over to a British battalion of I Corps; their trenches were on the Indian line's far left outside the area of the German mine attack. That night the Garhwalis saw some strange flickering lights appear – lighted candles on small Christmas trees the Germans put up all along their front trench. 'Our men were astonished,' wrote the Garhwalis' colonel, David Drake-Brockman, 'as it looked, they said, like their own "Dewali" festival in India.'

On Christmas morning the Garhwalis heard the Germans singing Christmas carols, before seeing them appear at 3 p.m. in no man's land without weapons, walking towards them over the snowy ground. The Germans came to sit on the Garhwalis' parapet, beckoning their Himalayan enemy into no man's land to give them Christmas presents, as Drake-Brockman saw:

They were trying to converse with our men and giving them cigarettes, biscuits and boxes of cigars. As I could speak German I conversed with them. They all belonged to the 16th [3rd Westphalian] Regiment, and ... seemed very jolly, as if they had had a good feed with plenty to drink. In fact, they told me that they had had a good dinner. One of them said to me that there must be 'Friede auf der Erde' ['Peace on Earth'] on this day, being Christmas Day ... The truce was well kept for all that night. Not a shot was fired. The silence, so different to the usual crack of rifles and spluttering of machine guns, was almost uncanny.

Douglas Haig had Christmas lunch miles back with the BEF's Commander-in-Chief John French at its General Headquarters. French told him he was to command a new formation for launching the BEF's first offensives in the west: its First Army, containing the British IV Corps and the Indian Corps. Of all the BEF's corps commanders, Haig already thought that the Indian Corps had comfortably the worst. He had not been impressed by James Willcocks before the war, of course, but had seen enough of him in France to confirm his low opinion.

As Haig's I Corps had taken over the Indian line near Givenchy on 22 December, Willcocks, for all his rapport with his men, seemed to have no grip on modern generalship. Haig had thought Willcocks' headquarters at Hinges château reeked of lax staff standards, with Indian staff officers casually taking their after- noon tea into the early evening, and leaving the building in a dirty state. Then Willcocks had handed over the Indian line to Haig without any useful analysis of Indian and German positions; rather he had panicked and made a frantic appeal. 'Reports on the situation in these parts were not satisfactory,' Haig had noted. 'Willcocks said the Indians were done: they would not fight any more and they simply ran away. And he begged me to relieve his Corps at once.'

Haig in fact thought Willcocks should be dismissed from the BEF, yet the two would have to work together closely in 1915. The Indian Corps was set for a primary role in Haig's First Army offensives, which would demand more of the Indian troops even than they had suffered in 1914, and ultimately bring out in Willcocks an unusual approach to battle for a western front gen- eral: trying to save his men from the slaughter.

Three

1915

'AN ANTI-BRITISH CRUSADE'

By January 1915, Germany held around 650,000 prisoners of war in camps across the country. The majority were Russians captured on the eastern front, in what is now Poland, as the German Army advanced towards Warsaw. But a small minority, 300 or so rising to 800 by the end of 1915, were Indian soldiers taken on the western front. The British government and the charities caring for the Indian troops in France, above all the Indian Soldiers Fund, were anxious to ensure that Indian prisoners in Germany were well looked after, and were poised to redirect clothes, food and other supplies to them. But there was a problem. The German Foreign Office, responsible for communicating with Allied governments on prisoners of war in Germany, was little answering British requests for information on the Indian prisoners, declining to say where they were.

On 7 January, a British diplomat in the Netherlands, Ernest Maxse, advised London on why the Germans were being so reluctant. He gathered from his sources in Germany that its prisoners captured in Europe from the Allied imperial forces of Africa and Asia – from French Moroccans and Russian Koreans to the Indians – were being gathered at secret propaganda camps outside Zossen, a small town south of Berlin in the province of

Brandenburg. Here, Maxse reported, 'a special mosque is to be built', which was in fact Germany's first. 'In my opinion ... the German Authorities are trying to start an anti-British crusade amongst the native officers and men of the Indian Army now in captivity.'

He was spot on. The flipside of Germany's overt military strategy in Europe was a secret revolutionary one concerned with the wider world. If the subject peoples of the Allies' empires were roused to insurrection against their colonial rulers, the Germans hoped, the Allies could be compelled to devote precious resources away from Europe, thus reducing those available to encircle Germany. Provoking revolutionary disorder from Morocco to the Caucasus and India was therefore the Germans' goal, and the Allied colonial prisoners of war were going to help them do it.

The principal bridge between Germany's revolutionary strategy and the Indian Army was the Sultan of Turkey's jihad, which the Germans intended to exploit as a propaganda tool to whip up anti-Allied subversion across the Islamic world. The jihad leaflets dropped on the Indian troops in France were only one spoke in a great wheel of anti-Allied jihadist initiatives backed by the Germans and the Turks which extended in 1915 from Germany to Egypt, Iraq, Iran and Afghanistan. The year would bring the Indian troops opposing calls, from the Central Powers to join jihadist forces and from the British to fight them. The Muslim troops would naturally be the most directly affected, especially those held prisoner in the secret German propaganda camps. But far and wide they would have to decide whether to help make or break the jihad.

'The mouth of hell opened'

In January 1915, there were 70,000 British Empire troops in Egypt, their largest gathering in the Islamic world. The Egyptian garrison had the Australian and New Zealand Army Corps – the

Anzacs – in training outside Cairo with a majority of raw war-time volunteers, but its backbone was Indian. In late 1914 Indian Expeditionary Forces E and F to Egypt had sailed there direct from India. Force E was a mixed lot of Indian Army and mounted princely States units such as the Bikaner Camel Corps and Hyderabad Lancers, while F had three first-rate Indian Army brigades. These included the strongest Indian brigade anywhere: the 28th Frontier Force Brigade, of four Frontier Force battalions, created for France but diverted to Egypt after Turkey joined the war. As the best trained troops in Egypt, the Indians took the main military role in its defence and held trenches on the Suez Canal.

Among Force F's many long-service professionals was the Scoutmaster Charles Bruce, now a commandant in the 6th Gurkhas, and several of his well-travelled pre-war Gurkha mountaineers. Most of their time in January 1915 was spent with the other Indian troops on the sandy Canal banks digging trenches between the Red Sea and the Mediterranean; the main frustration of the task was not the ground being too wet, as on the western front, but too dry, with sand easily blown into the trenches on the wind. The Indians' trenches were mainly on the west bank, and the few on the east bank were outposts on the Sinai Desert's edge. Day to day the Indians took breathers from digging to watch Allied shipping pass, from warships and submarines to troopships and passenger liners. Gurkha Scouts trained by Bruce went patrolling in the Sinai, on the alert for small parties of Turkish Army saboteurs out to block the Canal by laying naval mines. They had some success, for instance a night patrol under Subadar-Major Harkabir Thapa – of long pre-war mountaineering experience with Bruce – drove off some Turks, shooting one and capturing discarded explosives as the rest ran away. Meanwhile the Bikaner Camel Corps and Allied aeroplanes reconnoitred over long distances about the Sinai, looking for any approaching Turkish forces.

With none in sight, Bruce and his men had free time for climbing a new peak together: the Great Pyramid of Giza. 'I was

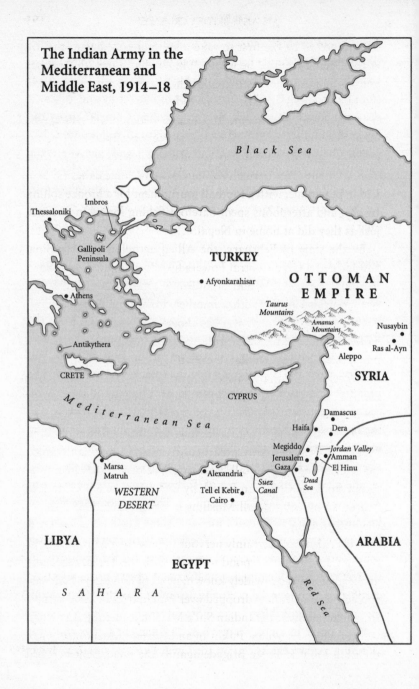

The Indian Army in the
Mediterranean and
Middle East, 1914–18

Black Sea

Thessaloniki

Imbros

Gallipoli
Peninsula

Athens

Antikythera

CRETE

TURKEY

• Afyonkarahisar

*Taurus
Mountains*

*Amanus
Mountains*

**OTTOMAN
EMPIRE**

Nusaybin

Ras al-Ayn

Aleppo •

SYRIA

CYPRUS

Mediterranean Sea

Damascus •

Haifa •   • Dera

Megiddo •

Jerusalem •   *Jordan Valley*

Gaza •   • Amman

*Dead
Sea*   • El Hinu

Marsa
Matruh •

• Alexandria

*WESTERN
DESERT*

Tell el Kebir •
Cairo •

*Suez
Canal*

LIBYA

EGYPT

S A H A R A

*Red
Sea*

ARABIA

determined to be the first to take a gang of Gurkhas to the top of the Great Pyramid,' he wrote. 'I knew that if the 5th Gurkhas got word of this they, knowing my habits, would most certainly forestall me, and that the rascals did, for as we got near the top of the Pyramid down came Turner and Beddy of the 5th with a lot of their own people, delighted to have got the better of us, and jeering at us in what they called a suitable manner!' At their camps by the Canal, much of the Gurkhas' life carried on as it had in peacetime, with a football tournament for a bronze sphinx trophy, and afternoons spent barefoot fishing for eel in streams, just as they did at home in Nepal.

By the start of February, the Allied aeroplanes in the Sinai had located a large Central Powers force heading for the Canal, marching by night. It had 20,000 men, mostly Muslim troops of the Turkish Army, with a number of German Army officers, engineers and doctors. It also had thousands of transport animals such as camels carrying or pulling artillery, shells and machine guns, as well as rectangular, German-made aluminium pontoons for crossing the Canal. Raised in Syria, this Turko-German force came in the name of the Sultan's jihad, carefully composed by the Turkish government to symbolise Islamic solidarity against the Allies. It travelled with a large green jihadist standard from Mecca, clerics who daily preached jihad to the men, and whirling Mevlevî dancers in tall hats. Its grand design was liberating Egypt from the Christian British by capturing the Suez Canal to inspire an uprising by all Muslims in Egypt, including those of the Indian Army.

The British were certainly nervous of how their Muslim troops on the Canal would respond to battle with the Turks, especially as the jihad was now widely known; news of it in Egypt had been spread by more leaflets dropped over Indian trenches and camps. In January at Suez, the Indian Shi'a Muslim leader the Aga Khan warned the independent Pukhtun and Punjabi Muslim troops of the 28th Frontier Force Brigade against the jihad. Sent by Lord

Kitchener as an agent of Allied propaganda, he told them on parade that the jihad was driven by German exploitation and was not truly holy, and that the Turks were the aggressors when the British were no threat to Islam's Holy Places; therefore, he declared, their loyalty should remain to the British, who were defending themselves in the moral right. There were signs of concern among the Indian Muslim troops in Egypt about fighting the Turks: from December 1914 to the start of February 1915, around two dozen, mainly independent Pukhtun, deserted with their rifles into the Sinai to join the Turks; a few other Punjabi Muslims tried to follow them but were caught, and executed or sentenced to penal servitude for life. Yet others seemed uninterested in joining the jihad, some of the 62nd Punjabis on the Suez Canal paying more attention to their latest member, found wandering behind their trenches – a chocolate-brown Sudanese sheep with long, flat ears they tenderly adopted as their mascot.

The Turkish attack on the Canal came out of the Sinai in the early hours of 3 February, falling heavily on the 62nd Punjabis' sector. At first the Punjabi sentries on the west bank could not see across the Canal because of a stinging sandstorm. But this calmed, allowing the moonlight to light up Turkish troops sliding down the east bank to lay their aluminium pontoons on the water and row across, under sporadic red and white rocket signals guiding their artillery. 'I was in charge of a pontoon,' a captured junior Syrian officer said afterwards. 'We got halfway across the Canal in perfect silence when the mouth of hell opened, and the pontoon was sinking in a swirl of stricken men amid a hail of projectiles.'

The 62nd Punjabis – including their Muslims – took the first shots as the battle burst out on the Canal, with widespread and heavy firing from Indian infantry, Egyptian artillery, Allied warships and torpedo boats. The captured Syrian officer was in fact taken by the 62nd Punjabis after he and a few other men on pontoons swam to the west bank; the Punjabis and some Sikhs of the 128th Pioneers raced down from their trenches, shot and bayoneted those who resisted, and took the rest prisoner. The Syrian officer said the 62nd's Muslims reproached him for fighting for the wrong side, while other Turkish prisoners asked a rhetorical question which may well go some way towards explaining Punjabi scepticism about the jihad: 'If the Holy Places are really in danger, what are we doing down this way?'

By mid-morning on 3 February the Turko-German force was in retreat, decisively defeated and abandoning their bullet-riddled pontoons beside hundreds of their dead floating on the water or slumped on the Sinai sands. Indian Muslims therefore shot the jihadist hand they were supposed to shake at Suez, to the admiration of their British officers on the Canal. 'It was very wonderful,' wrote Charles Bruce, 'to see how little the Mohammedan troops in the Indian Army allowed their feelings for the Turks as co-religionists to interfere with their duty.'

Up to August 1915, Gurkha and other units of Indian Expeditionary Forces E and F in Egypt further secured the Suez Canal with periodic anti-jihadist operations around its southern sea approaches. On Allied cruisers they steamed down into the Gulf of Suez for strikes against Turkish Army agents and groups of local Muslim tribesmen who together espoused the jihad and threatened to disrupt sea traffic, for instance by attacking Sinai ports under British protection. The 7th Gurkhas made one of these attacks in February, landing at night to annihilate a jihadist camp in the desert. They moved inland in rushes, firing over 5,000 bullets to kill dozens of Bedouin. Indian troops from Egypt also protected the Suez Canal right down the Red Sea to Aden, where in July the 28th Frontier Force Brigade drove back invading Turkish troops and jihadist Yemeni tribesmen who had attacked the port's fresh water supply. Sikh Pioneers, meanwhile, occupied Red Sea islands to deny the Turks artillery bases to fire on British shipping, and to help dampen local support on the Arabian coast for the jihad. The most persistent jihadist opposition, however, was faced by Indian Expeditionary Force D to Ottoman Iraq.

'Make every effort to repel the Infidels'

When Force D had seized Basra in November 1914, its chief diplomatic representative of the Government of India, Percy Cox,
proclaimed the occupation a British blessing in exchange for
Turkish rule. 'We have no enmity or ill-will against the populace,
to whom we hope to prove good friends and protectors,' he told a
public gathering of Basrans in Arabic. 'The British flag has been
established, under which you will enjoy the benefits of liberty and
justice.' The Government of India's unofficial intention was in fact
to annex Basra province. The Viceroy Charles Hardinge, Cox and
his deputies at Basra envisaged it as a new colony for the Indian
Empire and Indian emigrants, Hardinge himself seeing it as 'a
vista of endless opportunity and wealth in the not too far future'.
The Iraqis were not told this, but in any event did not welcome
Force D's foothold in their country, being rightly wary of British
intentions and wanting to rule themselves.

The southern Iraqis were predominantly Shi'a Muslims, and
so did not recognise the Sunni Sultan of Turkey as a spiritual
authority as Sunnis did. But their own Shi'a religious leaders of
Iraq's holy cities of Karbala and Najaf, with encouragement and
funding from visiting German and Turkish agents, nonetheless
called them to the Sultan's jihad in late 1914 as a means to resist
the Christian-led invasion of their country. 'In the Name of God,
the Compassionate, the Merciful,' the Grand Mujtahid, the most
senior Shi'a cleric of Iraq, announced in one of his summons to
jihad, 'it is forbidden for any Muslim to assist the Infidels ... their
support must be for the Muslim war effort. We trust in your zeal
and sense of honour to make every effort to repel the Infidels.'
The call to jihad also went out into Iranian areas bordering Iraq,
again with German and Turkish agents as local facilitators.

Into early 1915 beyond the British-occupied bubble around
Basra, far up Iraq's two great rivers the Tigris and Euphrates, and
across its deserts into Iran, Iraqis and Iranians therefore rallied

under the banner of jihad to drive the British and their Indian troops back down the Persian Gulf. They were ready to do so alongside the Turkish Army, which many disdained as an enforcer of foreign rule from Istanbul, but cooperation was legitimised by common Muslim duty.

By April 1915, Indian Expeditionary Force D had expanded to two Indian divisions, and had consolidated its occupation of Basra by seizing a Turkish outpost 60 miles to the north, at Qurna by the Tigris. In the desert of the Euphrates region west of Basra, meanwhile, an Iraqi jihadist army of 17,000 holy warriors had gathered, mainly of the Muntafiq tribal confederation, armed with rifles, lances and spears. They had travelled from up to 200 miles away, sailing down the Euphrates towards Basra in a flotilla of wooden and reed rivercraft, waving green and gold flags of jihad, their numbers swelling as they went. They agreed with the Turks to attack Basra with 7000 Turkish troops, the plan being for a single offensive to throw out the British for good.

The jihadists and the Turks made their move on 12 April in the flooded desert at Shu'ayba, some 15 miles west of Basra, against Indian Expeditionary Force D's entrenched position on a ridge shielding the town. This was the decisive battle for Basra and the Sultan's jihad in Iraq, and it was won in the desert mud largely by nine high-quality pre-war Indian regiments, some with Muslim troops who had also served on the Suez Canal in February. They fought almost continuously for seventy-two hours, initially from their trenches shooting to pieces several all-out frontal assaults by thousands of jihadists and Turks. They then pressed straight ahead in wide lines under fire towards the Turkish trenches a mile off, capturing them and some of the jihadists' flags as hundreds of their own men were killed or wounded. The jihadists and Turks retreated in disarray to confirm Force D's victory, the jihadists' losses of an estimated 3000 holy warriors breaking their will to attack the British in such large numbers for the rest of the war.

Force D then fought jihadists east of Basra, encroaching over the border into Iran. Here in early 1915 the Bani Turuf and other local tribes joined in the jihad, alongside Turkish regiments based nearby in Iraq and roving German officers, to sabotage British government property on Iranian soil and attack Indian units. In February they blew up sections of Anglo-Persian Oil's 138-mile pipeline connecting the Masjed Soleyman oil-field and the Abadan refinery, lighting up the desert night sky with jets of flame; in March they routed a small punitive column of Force D sent in response, killing dozens of the 7th Rajputs, including some Hindu sepoy prisoners whom they beheaded. Force D retaliated in greater strength in May, sending the 12th Indian Division from Basra over the Iranian border on a meandering march of destruction in dry, roasting heat through marshes, creeks and pink flamingo colonies.

The 12th Division sought out in particular the Bani Turuf as the tribe most active with the Turks and Germans in the local jihadist movement, making an example of their largest village Khafajiya, of marsh-reed and mud houses. Its British field artillery bombarded the place, the gun-sound reverberating for miles around as women and children fled and the shells set the houses ablaze, burning alive shrieking horses that were still tethered. Indian machine gunners fired at defiant jihadist riflemen clinging to their homes, before men of the 76th Punjabis – a band of Muslims, led by Subadar-Major Ajab Khan from Punjab – volunteered to go in for the kill. They surrounded the jihadists' last refuge, a large house with mud walls thick enough to withstand the shells, and burst in. They came out a short while later, uniforms black with sweat and bayonets dripping red, having killed thirty-three jihadists from room to room, and taken eleven prisoners.

As the jihadist captives sat on the ground under the Muslim sepoys' guard outside the smouldering village, one of them recognised the Indians' British officer, Arnold Wilson – a pre-war professional of the 32nd Sikh Pioneers who was fluent in Arabic and Farsi. In early 1914, Wilson had travelled through the Bani

Turuf's lands as the guest of their sheikhs, courteously befriending them as he made maps for the Government of India. The captured jihadist who recognised Wilson was one sheikh's coffee maker, or *qahwaji*, and had served Wilson at his master's house.

'Wilson, why have you brought this on us?' said the *qahwaji*. 'It is you who have led these men here. Was it for this that you ate our bread and wandered in our marshes and made maps? ... Now the blood of our brothers is on your head. May God pardon you.' Wilson stood in silence. 'It was useless to argue,' he later wrote. 'It was not without inward misery that I saw the blazing village and the dead bodies.' Perhaps Subadar-Major Ajab Khan and his Indian Muslims felt the same about the sacking of Khafajiya and killing their co-religionists for the British. More certain is that once again the Indian Army's Muslims had fought Muslims to achieve British ends. Khafajiya and smaller, similarly brutal operations by the 12th Indian Division that May in neighbouring Iranian and Iraqi locales deterred their tribesmen from pursuing the jihad, and Anglo-Persian's oil infrastructure was left untouched for the war's duration to produce millions of barrels' worth of oil for British warships.

In 1915, however, some 2000 Muslim troops in Indian regiments mutinied or deserted in British India, Singapore, Aden and France, showing how strong their feelings against British service could be. The first mutiny of the year was in Burma by the 130th Baluchis, in January at Rangoon where they were confined for investigation following the murder of their British officer by a Mahsud at Bombay in November 1914. The court of inquiry at Rangoon into that murder found all three of the regiment's Mahsud companies complicit and untrustworthy, and they were immediately dismissed from the army. But they were not released, instead being treated as hostile aliens on British Indian soil, and locked up until the end of the war at a remote prison in central Burma by the Irrawaddy River. As for the January 1915 mutiny by their regiment, it happened when the remainder were ordered to embark at Rangoon to join Indian Expeditionary Force B in East Africa. The Punjabi Muslim companies accepted the order, but the three Afridi companies did not, mutinying to avoid boarding their ship to Mombasa, without violence. So what made them do it?

As independent Pukhtun, it seems the Afridi were relatively outspoken and honest at their court martial. They gave no hint that they had mutinied because of the Sultan's jihad. A few said their grievance was the possibility of having to fight the Turks as their co-religionists. 'This was however generally ridiculed by their comrades who pointed out that they daily fought against their co-religionists,' remembered Herbert Raitt, one of the presiding military judges. Rather, Raitt said, the real Afridi grievance was 'inequality' – meaning 'difference of treatment between British and Indian ranks ... [They said] the poorly paid Indian soldiers should get the same things equally with the highly paid British soldier.'

So it appears these Afridi refused to serve overseas for the British on racially discriminatory terms, deeming the pay not worth the risk of never returning to their families, who depended on them. For saying these things in non-violent protest, two of the Afridi were executed, 202 of them were sentenced to prison in the Andaman Islands in the Bay of Bengal, and three Afridi officers were dishonourably discharged.

Elsewhere in British India, approximately 1500 Muslims deserted their Indian regiments between August 1914 and July 1915. They were practically all independent Pukhtun who made off for their tribal areas, usually after they had been called for overseas duty. The prevailing British wisdom was that their religious consciences forbade them serving Britain as Turkey's enemy, but the case of the Afridi mutineers of the 130th Baluchis suggests they rejected overseas service as too heavy a burden in return for unequal treatment compared to British soldiers. Indian recruits from British India had of course resented their unequal conditions of service in pre-war days, and their grievance of unequal pay had surfaced on the western front in the winter of 1914. Yet the independent Pukhtun were in a league of their own in how stridently they acted on such grudges, able as they were to desert to their free homelands where the British could not catch them for a court martial.

The other Indian Muslim mutinies of 1915 were threefold: at Singapore among the 5th Light Infantry in February, at Aden among the 126th Baluchis in May, and at Jhansi in northern British India among the 8th Cavalry in June. They were all violent. At Singapore, Muslim Rajput companies murdered two of their British officers and thirty-two European civilians, including women; they released German prisoners of war taken from the blown-out wreck of the *Emden*, but were soon captured (a crowd of thousands witnessed a British firing squad publicly execute forty-seven of the Muslim mutineers). At Aden, eight Brahui Muslims from British India's north-western province of Baluchistan attempted to murder their British officers. Then at Jhansi, two Muslim recruits from British India achieved it, shooting four with their rifles. The motives of all three mutinies remain mysteries. The mutineers may have objected to or feared overseas service if they had heard news of the casualties on the western front; they may have had regimental grievances against unpopular British officers, or been inspired by the Sultan's jihad or another revolutionary call to arms.

There was one Indian Muslim soldier, however, whose motives for deserting the British in France are much clearer: the Afridi Jemadar Mir Mast of the 58th Vaughan's Rifles, recently decorated for bravery with jam tin bombs against the Germans. In 1915 he set out on a journey that would take him from the trenches of the western front to the German propaganda camps south of Berlin, and on to Kabul as a German agent on secret jihadist service.

10

'I COULD NOT BEAR THE NEWS'

In August 1914, the Germans did not imagine they alone could plot the schemes for their revolutionary strategy for the Allied empires. To help them, they invited to Berlin from around the world leading intellectuals and revolutionaries of peoples under Allied rule, to form advisory national independence committees. By September, alongside Irish, Moroccan, Tunisian and other committees, the Berlin Indian Committee had emerged. According to its member Har Dayal, a pre-war founder of the Punjabi revolutionary group Ghadar in North America, the Berlin Indian Committee was a jumble of 'sincere but misguided patriots, unprincipled adventurers, self-indulgent parasites, scheming notoriety hunters, simple-minded students, and some victims of circumstance'. They were mostly Hindu and Muslim advocates of extremist or violent Indian nationalism who in consequence lived in exile from the Indian Empire as outlaws, and who answered Berlin's call to revolution anywhere from German universities to Switzerland, California and Brazil.

They came to Berlin with ideas for assassinations, railway sabotage and gun-smuggling in the cause of Indian independence, but their main sponsor in German government – the Nachrichtenstelle für den Orient, or New Intelligence Bureau for the East – directed them to focus on Islamic revolutionary propaganda for the Sultan of Turkey's jihad. It was the Berlin Indian Committee, therefore, that authored the jihad leaflets showered on the Indian trenches in France in late 1914. And for all that Punjabi Muslims joked about those leaflets, Jemadar Mir Mast and at least twenty-two Afridi of the 58th Vaughan's Rifles took them very seriously indeed. 'When the war broke out with Turkey, I could not bear the news,' Mir Mast later said, the leaflets having carried it to him, prompting his desertion with the twenty-two as the first step in his defection to the Germans.

'A Mauser pistol and a good German rifle'

On the western front on 3 March 1915, at around 1 a.m., a British officer of the 58th Vaughan's Rifles named John Tancred was doing a routine round of his Afridi company's trenches. In the moonlight he crawled into no man's land, to check on the 'island' ahead – an isolated forward post held by seven Afridi, dug into no man's land where the Indian line behind was too flooded and boggy to man. But none of the seven were there. He had not heard a sound from their direction, they had just disappeared. Tancred scrambled back, immediately calling for Jemadar Mir Mast. He told him to gather Afridi volunteers, double the number who had gone, and occupy the island as soon as possible; the missing men might be deserting but still be nearby, and Mir Mast's order was to get them back. If there was one man who could talk them into returning, Tancred thought, it was Mir Mast, the charismatic leader of the Afridi company 'who had distinguished himself greatly in every action ... and had at all times shown excellent example and reliability'.

Through the day of 3 March Tancred left Mir Mast and his thirteen men alone on the island, it being too dangerous to crawl out to it in daylight. Once darkness had fallen, Tancred sent two more Afridi to fetch him an update from Mir Mast. But after an hour he had no word from them, so he sent out more men to check on them. The message soon came back that the island was empty – a total of twenty-three Afridi sent there since the previous night, all of the same clan of Tirah, the Qambar, had disappeared, as had their Lee-Enfield rifles. Tancred and the regiment's other British officers realised they had deserted, 'an event which will never be forgotten nor forgiven in this Battalion,' wrote Captain Alexander Lind. 'The discovery of this desertion was a terrible blow, especially the treachery of Jemadar Mir Mast, whose courage, devotion to duty and reliability had hitherto been unquestioned.'

The British officers assumed the vanishing of the Afridi was down to independent Pukhtun pique. One of the twenty-three was an arrogant NCO named Guli Jan who days earlier had been overlooked for promotion to a Viceroy's Commission he wanted badly. The commandant had let him down gently in a personal interview, Guli Jan replying that he would strive to show a better example to the men and win promotion next time. Now it appeared he was the ringleader of twenty-three deserters, with the others taking off with him in solidarity on a point of clan pride. Things were not what they seemed, however. The ringleader was not Guli Jan, it was Mir Mast.

Like all Indian officers wanting promotion and better pay, for years Mir Mast had thought many things he had never said to his British officers (even non-violent defiance, as the Afridi mutineers of the 130th Baluchis had found at Rangoon only two months earlier, could lead to execution or a spell in the Andamans). Mir Mast certainly resented the unequal treatment of the Indian soldier. 'Commanding your own regiment is an honour and privilege you can never get in British service,' he would say when explaining his feelings at the time. What actually triggered his desertion was the leaflets in the Indian trenches about the Sultan's jihad. Having learned basic literacy before the war at the cantonment schoolhouse, he could read them, and they struck a chord in him as a Muslim and an independent Pukhtun. His heart was on Turkey's side, he decided he would prefer not to continue fighting the Germans, and he was prepared to find a way out.

His fellow Qambar deserters felt similarly, and looked to Mir Mast as the most powerful character in their company. He said afterwards they had been planning to desert with him for weeks, so long before the NCO Guli Jan was denied his promotion, although this was no doubt a spur. They had been attracted by the jihad leaflets' offer of good German treatment, and had only hesitated to take it up because they were unsure whether to believe it. But by the beginning of March they had agreed that when the Germans next attacked the Indian line they would sling their rifles over their shoulders, hold up their hands in surrender and go over to the German side. Then their chance came to desert in groups while on island duty, and Mir Mast improvised a new plan. Each group took the leaflets with them to the island, and sent one of their Afridi ahead to show a leaflet to the Germans, to verify that deserters really were welcome. When this was confirmed (German front line troops were under orders to treat Indian prisoners with special courtesy as potential allies), the Afridi verifier gave the agreed signal – three short whistles – for the others to follow. Once Mir Mast's own group had gone over in this way, he told the Germans that fifty more Afridi of his company wanted to come too.

When the desertions were discovered, however, the remainder of Mir Mast's Afridi company were disarmed, withdrawn from the front line and locked in an empty factory. James Willcocks then presided over a month-long court of inquiry into the matter, following which he kicked nine men out of the Indian Corps as the most blatantly in sympathy with the deserters, including some of their family. He put them on a ship at Marseilles for Egypt, where they were punished with non-combatant labouring work. The rest of the Afridi company expressed mixed feelings, some saying they approved of the desertions, others that they were disgusted by them and had every intention of 'continuing to serve loyally if given the chance to wipe out the disgrace'. Willcocks put them all back on duty as if nothing had happened. 'I decided to deal with the regiment softly,' he explained. 'I appreciate they are Afridis, tribesmen who are very individual, brave and deserving of respect. And I happen to like them.'

Jemadar Mir Mast and his fellow deserters, meanwhile, were being interrogated by the Germans at Lille in occupied France. Asking the questions was Paul Walter, from Berlin's Foreign Office. He quickly found that the Afridi had understood the jihad leaflets' offer of sanctuary to include keeping hold of their Lee-Enfield rifles, which they hoped to take home to Tirah. They were not at all happy they had been relieved of them on the way to Lille, and repeatedly demanded that Walter give their rifles back to them. But they also told Walter many things he wanted to hear, with Mir Mast as their chief spokesman. They hoped to return via Istanbul to the independent Pukhtun tribal areas, and from there to fight the British alongside the Turks, preferably using German grenades and other weapons they had seen in France. If the Germans wanted more Afridi to desert from his regiment, Mir Mast added, there was one way they could improve the jihad leaflets. 'Write, "We'll give you a Mauser pistol and a good German rifle",' he advised. 'That's enough. Then they will all come.' Walter was left with the distinct impression that the Afridi deserters' chief concern was acquiring modern weapons to take home. But he summed up his general impression of how they felt as anti-British by commenting that they had an underlying pride in their faith, as if they were saying together: 'We have sold our military duty for 11 rupees a month but we haven't sold our religion.'

The Germans took Mir Mast and his fellow Afridi east from Lille by railway, 500 miles through Belgium into the heart of Germany. Their journey's end was among low hills and a secluded pine forest south of Berlin, at the gates of a camp surrounded by high barbed wire fences, with German troops in sentry boxes and watchtowers. They had arrived at one of the propaganda camps at Zossen for captive colonial subjects of the Allied empires: Halbmondlager, or Camp Crescent Moon, a secret school of revolution for Indian prisoners of war.

Here the truth of the jihad leaflets' promise of good treatment in Germany was revealed. In the words of Daniel J. McCarthy, a US State Department inspector of British Empire prisoners of war in Germany, Camp Crescent Moon was no ordinary camp, it was 'the model camp of Germany'. The Allies' European or white prisoners of war had their own camps elsewhere about Germany, from the Rhineland in the west to Saxony in the east. In some of these, German neglect and mistreatment were rife: there were Russians starved with little more to eat than potato peelings; Canadians beaten with rifle butts and wire whips; and British forced into slave labour, for instance up to twenty hours a day at a chemicals factory without protective gloves, burning the skin off their hands. The Indians' experience at Camp Crescent Moon, however, was quite different.

Inside the camp, Mir Mast and the Afridi deserters found their quarters a dramatic change from the trenches and their old cantonment housing in British India. They had large, well-built wooden cabins with ten windows down each side, arranged in blocks by religion for the men of the Indian Army, and without any German guards. Inside their cabin Mir Mast and the Afridi were welcomed with crackling stove fires in spotless rooms, insulated by double walls and porches with double doors. They had comfortable beds with several blankets each and straw mattresses, on bunks for the sepoys in communal rooms, and on an iron bedstead for Mir Mast, who like all Indian officers in the camp had his own room.

Alongside the cabins, the Afridi and other Indian prisoners had wash-houses with modern bathrooms, and rooms for washing and drying clothes. They also had their own cookhouses.

They were fed mutton, rice, potatoes and chapattis – some of the ingredients coming from parcels freshly received from the Indian Soldiers Fund in London – with every facility given to their religious rites for food preparation. Their freedom of religion in the camp was in fact almost complete, with observance of daily prayer and religious festivals fully allowed. There was even an ornate mosque under construction as a gift from Kaiser Wilhelm, modelled on the Dome of the Rock in Jerusalem and featuring a multi-coloured exterior, a minaret and a white-tiled foot-washing area by the main entrance. Meanwhile they were excused from any labour, and free to exercise every day on the camp's sports grounds with football pitches.

'We left this camp with the general impression that this was indeed an ideal camp where the men were treated in a humane and kindly way,' wrote McCarthy of a visit in mid-1915. The supervising German officers, he added, 'were men who had seen service in India and the East, who spoke and understood the language of their prison groups and whose attitude of sympathy and understanding was very touching for a German camp'.

Yet McCarthy did not see behind the scenes at Camp Crescent Moon. As one of its German officers, Captain von Hardenberg, said in a secret memorandum of 1915 entitled 'Enlisting for the Holy War', the Indians and other inmates were candidates for revolution: 'Their treatment must always aim at weaning them from the interests of our enemies, and turning them to us. They must ... be impressed with Germany's greatness by every means suited to their mental capacity ... The gravest matter is trying to enlist them for the holy war ... For us it is inciting oppressed nationals to rise against their oppressors.'

All the while at Camp Crescent Moon there was a propaganda programme to indoctrinate the prisoners in violent nationalism. The lessons were given by men of the national independence committees including the Berlin Indian Committee, alongside radical Islamic clerics brought in to preach from North Africa and Turkey – some of whom had called out from the German trenches in France through loud-hailers to the Indians. Mir Mast, his fellow Afridi deserters and the other Indian prisoners attended morning classes where their Indian revolutionary and clerical teachers passionately denounced Britain as a cruel and exploitative colonial power. They appealed in particular to the Muslim prisoners to join the Sultan's jihad, avowing the moral duty to save Islam from Christian tyranny. The Germans' incongruous status as Christians themselves sponsoring the jihad was explained away with the argument that Germany alone among the European nations was Islam's true friend, backed by tall tales of its Islamic credentials, such as Kaiser Wilhelm's conversion.

After their lectures, the teachers tried to persuade the Indian prisoners with various photograph books showing German military power in the ascendant, for example snapshots of the German Army's great strides towards Warsaw into mid-1915 against the Russians, and with anti-Allied newspapers such as *El Jihad*, which were also used in reading and writing classes. To stress Germany's close links with the Sultan himself, visiting Ottoman dignitaries gave speeches to thousands of the Allied Muslim prisoners, Indians, French North Africans, and Russian Tatars of Central Asia, all on special parade together. The Turks bore greetings from the Sultan Caliph, led prayers of Muslim strength through unity against the Allies, and presided over ritual slaughters of oxen and sheep decorated in red and white ribbons, before leading chants of 'Long live our Sultan!' as they departed.

When Mir Mast and the Afridi deserters began attending the propaganda classes at Camp Crescent Moon from mid-March 1915, their most flamboyant lecturer from the Berlin Indian Committee was Raja Mahendra Pratap. A Hindu in his late twenties, Pratap came from an ancient line of north Indian princes disenfranchised by the British in the early 1800s for opposing the burgeoning Indian Empire. Wealthy, well educated and whimsical, he was a cosmopolitan creature of comfort who liked to dress elaborately in Asian and European costume. He had been on a round-the-world honeymoon with his Sikh wife in 1907, travelling from British India to France, the United States and China. On the way he had bought furniture in Venice, a St Bernard puppy in Berlin and Japanese pugs in Yokohama, and been wide-eyed at St Peter's Basilica in the Vatican City, the Parliament Building in Budapest and the White House in Washington DC.

Pratap's breadth of outlook and taste for the immediate shot through his politics, which rejected the mainstream of the Indian National Congress. He had dipped his toe in its debates at the annual meetings of 1906 and 1910, yet found the Congressmen too prudent and patient, while they saw him as temperamentally unsuited to their moderate path. 'A delightful optimist, living completely in the air and refusing to have anything to do with realities,' said one Congressman of him. 'He seemed to be a character out of medieval romance, a Don Quixote who had strayed into the twentieth century.'

Rather, Pratap had his eye on some radical fast-track to Indian independence, ideally with him as the architect and then first president of a great Indian republic with equality for all religions. But living in British India before 1914 he had no connections with like-minded Indian revolutionaries in exile, and was short on ideas for exactly how to bring down the British. When the war broke out, he was at his summer home in the Himalayan city of Dehradun with his wife, Venetian furniture and dogs, and it inspired in him a dream of toppling the Government of India with German help. 'I began to feel decisive sympathy for the Germans who were fighting this dirty British empire,' he wrote. He was prepared to give up everything for India's freedom – as he told his wife when he abruptly left for Germany one night in late summer 1914, leaving her in tears, never to see her again, and turning his back on his sleeping children, a girl aged five and a baby boy. 'I happened to leave my wife and children at the age of 28,' he later said, coldly. 'One can give up one's family relations should one so desire.'

By February 1915 Pratap was in Berlin. He quickly went far with bold bluff, posing as a prominent and well-connected revolutionary leader. Within days he talked his way into not only a personal twenty-minute audience with Kaiser Wilhelm, but also an official guided tour of the eastern front in Poland. As an honoured guest of the Kaiser, he flew in a German Air Force bi-plane over the trenches, watched from the German line with high-power field binoculars a specially laid-on artillery barrage that pummelled Russian parapets, and dined with one of the Prussian elite, the German 9th Army's commander, August von Mackensen.

All this helped Pratap's rapid rise as the Berlin Indian Committee's biggest cheese, advising the German Foreign Office on how to start a revolution in British India. Recognising the Sultan's jihad as the button to push, he proposed a German diplomatic mission to Afghanistan's Emir Habibullah at Kabul. Habibullah was the world's leading neutral Muslim monarch, and if he allied with Germany, Pratap said, he would join the Afghan people and army in the Sultan's jihad and invade British India. Pratap forecast a domino effect of this: it would raise *lashkar*s in the independent Pukhtun tribal areas to assist the Afghan invasion, and then encourage the people and princes of India to rebel. To help ensure his Hindu countrymen would cooperate with the Afghan jihad to demolish British rule, Pratap suggested he should go with his proposed mission to Kabul, and embed himself in the Afghan forces as a champion of Hindu cooperation with Muslims. He suggested taking with him Hindu and Muslim Indian prisoners of war from Camp Crescent Moon, to fight in the Afghan ranks. The German government quickly accepted Pratap's plan as a means to revive its previous scheme along the same lines. A German military mission had left Berlin for Kabul in 1914, only to lose momentum for lack of Turkish cooperation; it was now languishing in the Middle East short of men, money and supplies.

Pratap offered his mission to Afghanistan to the Indian prisoners at Camp Crescent Moon, asking for volunteers to fight with the Afghans for India's freedom. He had originally hoped to take significant numbers of Indian prisoners to form the nucleus of an Indian national army, but the mission's diplomatic nature, as well as the need for secrecy and mobility on the overland journey to Kabul, meant he could only take a few. He found not a single volunteer among the Hindu prisoners, largely of the 9th Bhopals captured at First Ypres, who told him of their fears for their families if they joined a rebellion against the British. 'Some of them dared to tell me that should they work with us for freedom, their children at home would be massacred,' wrote Pratap, cursing their unwillingness to put freedom struggle before family as he did (in talking of massacre, they no doubt recalled British reprisals against Indian rebels in the Great Rebellion of 1857).

The one group of Indian prisoners who did step forward were the independent Pukhtun, including all the Afridi who had deserted with Jemadar Mir Mast. They were not interested in fighting for India's freedom, but in the opportunity of getting home on the mission's back, besides being in sympathy with a potential extension of the Sultan's jihad by the Emir of Afghanistan, whom they respected as the Pukhtun world's Prince of Islam. Pratap picked Mir Mast to join the mission as the obvious Afridi leader, and four other Afridi on Mir Mast's recommendation. He then took them out of Camp Crescent Moon and onto the train to Berlin.

'Long faces when I roll up with my three brown ones'

In Berlin in the first week of April 1915, Mir Mast and the other four Afridi formally entered German service with regular pay – not military service but diplomatic, for the German Foreign Office. Their mission head was Werner Otto von Hentig, a young German Army officer recalled from the trenches of Poland in light of his pre-war diplomatic experience in China and Iran.

Hentig and the mission's handful of German officers under him, similarly recruited for their pre-war experiences in Asia, spoke Farsi, a language so close to Pushtu they could communicate easily enough with the Afridi. To cement their place in German service, the Afridi agreed to parade in public in Berlin in the Königsplatz, the square in front of the Reichstag building. The occasion was the centenary commemoration of the birth of Otto von Bismarck, the first Chancellor of unified Germany. The Afridi presented arms to the Kaiser's representative on the day, his grandson Prince Wilhelm of Prussia, second in line to the German throne, as if they had never felt much allegiance to the British King-Emperor George.

Mahendra Pratap, meanwhile, turned to advising Hentig on suitable diplomatic gifts for Afghanistan. The mission's baggage duly included powerful field binoculars, a cinema projector and cameras; gold fountain pens, gold watches and radio alarm clocks; and gold-plated rifles, with telescopic sights, and Mauser pistols. There was also a set of twenty-seven letters of introduction, from the German government and for Pratap to deliver. These were on thick parchment, embossed with sharp-clawed Teutonic eagles, and had grandiose tidings of goodwill and revolution from Kaiser Wilhelm and the German Chancellor, Theobald von Bethman-Hollweg, written in immaculate calligraphy in various languages. The letters were addressed to Emir Habibullah and other royalty Pratap had said were likely candidates for revolution, from the Maharajah of Nepal to Indian princes. To protect the baggage and the rest of the mission, Mir Mast and his Afridi were armed with Mauser rifles, for now under lock and key in a strong-box in Hentig's charge.

The Afridi also met the final members of the mission, swelling its number to fifteen. They were mainly Indian Muslims from the Berlin Indian Committee, notably Abdul Hafiz Mohamed Barakatullah, a bespectacled fifty-year-old with a kindly exterior that hid a life devoted to jihad. Before the war, under cover as a professor of Indian languages at the University of Tokyo, he had been one of the world's leading exponents of jihad against the European empires, publishing anonymous pamphlets and papers, one of them demanding 'the rising of all Islam as soon as she is ready and willing to open her gates for believers to fight under the Green Banner of the Prophet'. On university vacations he had travelled to Cairo, Istanbul and New York to develop a jihadist network, and in 1914 had rushed for Berlin. The mission also welcomed another Pukhtun soldier from Camp Crescent Moon, suggested by the Afridi as a cook. He was not an independent tribesman like them, but a Yusufzai from British India's North-West Frontier Province. Named Said Ahmed, he had been with the 129th Baluchis in France in 1914 and captured after the German mine blasts of 20 December. 'I gladly agreed to join the mission,' he later said. 'I saw an opportunity of returning to India.'

The mission to Kabul under Hentig left Berlin on 9 April, its Afridi and Said Ahmed travelling with fake identities in German East African passports. For the first leg of their journey by rail to Istanbul, they split into three groups under German officers to avoid Allied detection, taking different routes through Austria-Hungary and neutral Romania and Bulgaria. Along the way the Pukhtun saw sights of great cities, gazing at Vienna, Bucharest and Sofia's tall buildings, boulevards and tram systems. Mir Mast's group, of three Afridi including him and the mission's German doctor, Karl Becker, were arrested at Bucharest's Gara de Nord railway station by the Romanian police for looking suspicious, but Becker bribed them out of it. The Afridi discovered that eastern Europeans in general seemed ill disposed to them as racial outsiders. 'Long faces when I roll up with my three brown ones,' Becker noted in his diary of the receptionists' welcome at Bucharest's Grand Hotel Trajan.

The mission arrived at Istanbul's Sirkeci railway station in the third week of April. Mir Mast and the Afridi waited at a hotel as Hentig and Pratap went about the city preparing for their onward journey. Hentig withdrew gold from Deutsche Bank, and with Pratap had audiences with the Sultan of Turkey and the Minister of War, Ismail Enver, securing more grandiloquent letters of introduction from both for the mission's collection. At the end of April, the mission took on a Turkish Army attaché, Kazim Bey, and left Istanbul on the Baghdad Railway into the fertile valleys of Turkey's Anatolian heartland. In the harsher terrain of eastern Syria and northern Iraq, where the railway line was incomplete, they took open carts and river boats, exposing them to swarms of locusts that bit them all. They reached Baghdad in late May to a warm welcome at an official Turkish banquet, and took on three more Afridi volunteers, all deserters from the 20th Punjabis near Basra in November 1914.

They crossed the Ottoman border into Iran on 2 June. Hentig's plan was to cut across the rugged centre of the country to Afghanistan, linking up on the way with the previous, stalled German military mission to Kabul. In Iran, Mir Mast and the Afridi finally got their hands on their Mauser rifles to guard the mission from tribal bandits or Allied forces. The latter were a real threat, the Italian consul at Baghdad having tipped off the British about the mission's passage through the city for Afghanistan. In response, the Viceroy Charles Hardinge sent two Indian regiments, the 19th Punjabis and 28th Light Cavalry, over the border from British India's north-western province of Baluchistan into Iran. Under his orders to annihilate Hentig's mission, they scrambled to form a screen in front of the Iranian-Afghan border by linking with Russian cavalry coming down from northern Iran.

In the absence of rail or motor transport, Hentig and his men could make only laborious progress across Iran over weeks using meagre animal transport, bought locally with his gold. They usually rode bare-back on camels or gaunt, slow horses, and had a horse-drawn cart that proved even less comfortable. 'The conveyance containing the soldiers is in a miserable condition,' wrote Doctor Becker of the clanking contraption carrying Mir

Mast and other Afridi on 27 June. 'The wheels are always rolling off, and one at the back goes absolutely to pieces this afternoon.' Most nights the mission slept in remote villages, seeing out the day hunched exhausted in the moonlight around camp fires, smoking local opium-pipes.

By mid-July, they were deep in central Iran's Salt Desert, one of the driest places on earth. 'Great heat, burning wind,' Becker jotted down in the company of the Afridi as his thermometer rose to 49°C. 'Too hot to sleep. No tree, no bush, no bird, no fly to be seen; only a few solitary locusts and lizards. Our water supply is pretty low ... one's mouth so parched, speech is almost impossible.' What little water they could find at wells or oases was saline or worm-infested. 'Almost all of us are out of sorts,' Becker wrote on 20 July of German, Afridi and Indian alike. 'Our faces are pale and yellow; one suffers from indigestion, the other's down with fever.' Some days the mission struggled to move, verging on collapse from dehydration, sleeping on empty stomachs made all the worse by what came out of the sand: poisonous snakes, giant scorpions and endless small insects.

Tempers began to fray with rifts emerging between the Afridi and Indians. The Afridi steadily lost respect for Mahendra Pratap as the going got tougher. He had visibly wilted, to them behaving like a scared and spoilt child. He broke down in tears and sobbed as they tried to go to sleep; he hogged or hid food from them to eat it alone; and he insulted them in tired rants as interested only in money, and out to murder the mission to steal its gold. One of the Afridi almost snapped with Pratap over some unshared fruit, raising his rifle to shoot him as they rode on camels, only to restrain himself at the last moment. Mir Mast then had heated arguments with the mission's cook from British India, Said Ahmed. It seems Mir Mast talked ardently of the jihad and condemned the British as sinful Christian oppressors, and Said Ahmed talked back, giving a better account of the British as imposers of law and order in his home district.

As the desert heat rose to 52°C from July into August, Hentig's band amalgamated with the previous military mission to Kabul. With the latter's leader, a Bavarian officer by the name of Oskar von Niedermeyer, he plotted their final few weeks up to the Afghan border. They learned from desert-dwellers that Indian and Russian army detachment had been sent to block their path into Afghanistan, and decided their best chance of getting past them was to split into three groups. They preferred to take their chances against the Russians to the north more than the Indian regiments coming up from the south, who would likely have better intelligence on their whereabouts from numerous Iranian spies in British pay on the lookout at desert wells. So two groups with Hentig, Niedermeyer, Mir Mast and Pratap carried on eastwards towards the Afghan border hoping to find a gap in the Russian screen, while the third group, under the German doctor Becker with three of the Afridi – a mix of those from Camp Crescent Moon and Baghdad – struck off to the north-west as a decoy to attract Russian forces and help create a gap.

Becker's group did its job, diverting a Russian cavalry patrol and fighting it at the mud-walled village of Helvun by an oasis. His three Afridi earned their pay in a drawn-out afternoon skirmish, firing their Mauser rifles from the village's towers, the Russians replying from behind the oasis palm trees. At sundown, after one Afridi had been shot dead, Becker ran away into the desert, leaving the remaining two Afridi to fight down to their last cartridge. The Russians surrounded and captured them, before torturing Sepoy Haidar Khan, who had deserted in France with Mir Mast. They cut off half of one of his ears and all of the other, and so ended his world war, presumed dead from loss of blood, having travelled 11,000 miles in twelve months from British India to France, Germany and Iran, fighting for both the Allies and the Central Powers. The Russians spared the remaining Afridi. He had gunshot wounds to the forehead and stomach, and staggered off into the desert.

The German mission's other two groups found their gap between the Russian patrols and made it over the border into Afghanistan on 19 August. Their surviving the Salt Desert had been a remarkable feat of organisation, endurance and evasion. Some of their Indian Army pursuers of the 19th Punjabis had discovered for themselves quite how dangerous the Salt Desert could be. These had included thirty-nine Afridi who after deployment to southern Iran for the chase had been stood down, distrusted to carry out their orders to kill Mir Mast and the mission's other Afridi. They felt this an insult, and had deserted with their Lee-Enfield rifles, attempting to walk home to Tirah through the Salt Desert. Almost all of them did not make it. Thirty-seven were found at the end of a trail on the sand of clothes and rifles they had discarded as they became fatally heat-stricken and dehydrated. They lay face-down, dead, their hands in holes they had dug desperately for water in their last minutes. Two had survived by reaching the nearby Helmand River by the Afghan border, and lived to tell the tale in Tirah.

In western Afghanistan in late August, the German mission contacted the governor of Herat, the oasis city near the Iranian frontier. 'People who have not travelled through a desert can not understand the joy of arriving at an oasis,' Mahendra Pratap wrote of their arrival. Mir Mast went into Herat first, chosen because unlike his German officers or Pratap he had a local Pukhtun touch for announcing their appearance as foreigners. The governor of Herat invited the mission stay at his palace as he awaited instructions from Kabul on allowing it to proceed. Hentig, Niedermeyer, Mir Mast and the others were free to wander the palace's green gardens, water pools and orchards. 'With the intoxicating scents from the garden,' Niedermeyer recalled, 'it was like a fairy tale.' They ate Afghan pilaf and slept long hours, met with the governor's tailor to replace their tattered clothes and toured the city's ancient mosques.

Just as the German mission sought to carry the Sultan's jihad to

Afghanistan and British India, however, the jihad's very continuation was threatened at the Ottoman centre as the Allies opened a new front to go for the Ottoman regime's jugular, with the Indian Army there from the first day: the Gallipoli campaign.

11

'JUST LIKE THE PHOTOS'

'This is really the critical month of the war,' the Prime Minister Herbert Asquith noted on 30 March 1915 of the coming April, 'so much depending upon whether the coin turns up Heads or Tails at the Dardanelles ... the war ought to be over in three months.' Asquith anticipated the British Empire's military landings from 25 April on the Gallipoli Peninsula with naval, French and Senegalese support. They promised fabulous strategic profits if successful in capturing the peninsula and the Dardanelles, the adjacent waterway leading up to Istanbul from the Aegean Sea. The Turkish government would be rocked, even knocked over to take Turkey out of the war, denying Germany its overland access to Asia, effectively ending the Sultan's jihad, and swelling British prestige in the Islamic world. The Russian war effort would be boosted too, not least by a new Dardanelles supply route between the Mediterranean and Ukraine. Furthermore, neutral Bulgaria, Romania and Greece might well be persuaded to join the Allies, tipping the balance of forces in Europe against the Central Powers.

The British Empire forces on Gallipoli totalled 410,000 men of the Mediterranean Expeditionary Force. They were largely British, Australian and New Zealander, but also included 16,000 Indian servicemen. These were a mix of Indian Mountain

Artillery gunners, Gurkha, Muslim and Sikh infantry, maharajahs' States troops and non-combatants such as Indian muleteers. They all arrived on Gallipoli with their pre-war British officers, including Charles Bruce, and formed Indian Expeditionary Force G. For many of them, Gallipoli would be their introduction to European battle under heavy fire. In Force G's ranks were the 5th Gurkhas' companies whose pre-war training had involved lectures with photographs of the Russo-Japanese War. On their first sight of Turkish shelling's bloody harvest on Gallipoli, some Gurkhas spoke of flashbacks to the lectures, telling their British officer Kenneth Erskine, 'it is just like the photos' and appearing 'quite unmoved'. The Gurkhas' training, as they would soon show as a sight themselves on Gallipoli's European battlefields, had readied them for much more.

'Absolutely the boys for this class of country'

The Gallipoli Peninsula stretched 40 miles from the south-eastern corner of continental Europe down into the Aegean Sea, shaped like the neck and head of a diving duck, and edged by thin beaches of sand and pebble, giving on to precipitous cliffs and ravines, on to higher ridges inland covered in green scrub. At dawn on 25 April 1915, a British Empire fleet set ashore British and Anzac forces on the peninsula's southern tip and its western beaches, along with the first of the Indian troops – mountain artillerymen of the 26th Jacob's Battery, around half Muslim, the rest Hindus and Sikhs. Their mountain guns were hurried ashore on the western Anzac beaches on mule-back, Turkish shrapnel shells bursting above their heads. By noon they were in action as the only artillery on land to help establish the Anzac beachheads and support the initial Australian attacks. More Indian mountain gunners of the Frontier Force's 21st Kohat Battery also landed on the 25th, bringing the total of Indian artillery guns on Gallipoli to twelve. They would remain there for the following eight months of trench warfare, fighting almost every day and firing some 20,000 shells at the Turks.

The Indian mountain gunners used their pre-war training for the independent Pukhtun tribal areas to rush their guns on mule-back about the Anzac, British and Indian lines on Gallipoli, shooting from front trenches, ridges, and galleries dug into hillsides. 'Whenever the guns were located by the enemy's shrapnel they simply dismounted, packed on the mules, and in a few minutes were blazing away as good as ever in a new position,' observed a New Zealander, Raymond Baker. The first Indians wounded or killed on Gallipoli were Muslim artillerymen, in the last week of April. Throughout the campaign into 1916, the Muslim gunners yielded no deserters to the Turks, exhibiting a relentless dedication to their gun crews rather than any overriding religious sympathy for the enemy. On the contrary, among Gallipoli's beaches, bivouacs and hill tracks, they turned warmly to the Australians and New Zealanders as new Christian friends.

Respecting the Indian gunners' professionalism from the outset, the Anzacs developed a comradeship with them. 'They were always hanging around chatting to our fellows,' a British officer of the 21st Kohat Battery, Arthur Fergusson, said of the Anzacs, 'though how they communicated was a marvel. They were a nuisance at times, sitting in the open when the guns were firing and giving the show away, and we had on occasion to have armed sentries to keep them out.' The Anzacs learned to greet the Muslim gunners with 'salaam', and more practical phrases in Urdu – 'enough to yell at them to take cover when there was concentrated fire on the beach,' said one New Zealander, Frank Cooper, who added 'they will very seldom run away from shell fire'. In the beach areas some of the mountain artillery's longer-serving Indian officers exuded a natural authority and exerted an informal command over younger Australians, who deferred to them to make way or form queues at their word. Sergeant Fred Aspinall, an Australian signaller, was so impressed by the Kohat

Battery's Sikh Subadar-Major Pakta Singh that he asked for his signature, gladly scribbled in Urdu (and it seems the only surviving hand-writing by an Indian soldier on Gallipoli).

The first Indian infantry on the peninsula were a brigade extracted from Indian Expeditionary Force F in Egypt. They landed on 30 April at its southern tip, on the Cape Helles beaches, where the British and French armies were concentrated beneath the Turkish-held heights of Achi Baba overlooking the Dardanelles behind. They had four Indian battalions: the 6th Gurkhas under Charles Bruce, the 14th Sikhs, and the 69th and 89th Punjabis. 'I shall never forget,' wrote Bruce of the 6th Gurkhas' view on arrival, 'steaming into Helles in the early morning of a glorious spring day, and watching the bombardment of Achi Baba and the neighbouring hills by our fleet – the gorgeous colouring and tranquillity of the sea and the masses of shipping and the great warships in action. Even as we steamed in we could see the earth rising from the sides of the hills where the shells broke.'

The 69th and 89th Punjabis, however, were sent to France just two weeks later, ostensibly to pre-empt trouble among their four Punjabi Muslim companies over fighting their Turkish co-religionists. Yet by their mid-May departure, these Punjabi Muslims and their machine gun crews had shown professional commitment much like the Indian Muslim mountain gunners on Gallipoli, having fought the Turks three times since November 1914 – initially on the Yemeni coast to help secure the Suez Canal's southern approaches, then during the Turkish attack on the Canal, and in the Gallipoli front line itself. Any British fear that they would refuse to face the Turks was likely a convenient pretext for their withdrawal, the actual reason being that they were from British India. The guiding hand here was Ian Hamilton, the British Army commander of the British Empire forces at Gallipoli, who wanted more troops from Nepal.

'I am very anxious to get a Brigade of Gurkhas,' Hamilton had told Lord Kitchener in late March as the War Office began directing the military side of the Gallipoli campaign, 'a type of man who will, I am certain, be most valuable on the Gallipoli Peninsula. The scrubby hillsides on the south-west faces of the plateau are just the sort of terrain where these little fellows are at their brilliant best ... each little "Gurkh" might be worth his full weight in gold at Gallipoli.' After Hamilton had got the mixed Indian brigade of Gurkhas, Sikhs and Punjabis instead, it seems he slyly took matters into his own hands, using the Islamic argument to switch the 69th and 89th Punjabis for two Gurkha battalions from Egypt. He requested the Frontier Force's 5th Gurkhas and the 10th Gurkhas, leaving him with almost what he wanted: an Indian brigade on Gallipoli with 75 per cent Nepalese troops, well trained in mountain warfare.

Charles Bruce's 6th Gurkhas quickly lived up to Hamilton's hopes. 'We found the terrain quite suitable, which was a relief to us,' Bruce wrote of Cape Helles. 'Most of our work was over broken and accented ground with a good deal of scrub. This suited our men perfectly.' On 12 May, at Hamilton's bidding, they carried out a surprise night assault Bruce described as 'a little duty that exactly suited the genius of the Gurkha'. Their objective was to seize the Turkish-occupied crest of a headland directly above the Aegean on the left of the British line at Helles, and known as the Bluff Redoubt. At night Bruce's Scouts reconnoitred the headland's jagged 300-foot cliffs, climbing up from the beach below to identify a steep cliff-face not covered by the Turkish guns. The following night, Bruce organised the Gurkhas' hushed ascent of this cliff without the Turks noticing. They rushed the Turkish trenches at the top, in time with British field and naval artillery dropping a curtain of shell fire inland to deter Turkish reinforcements. The Gurkhas shot the startled Turks on the cliff-top, capturing their machine guns and digging new trenches to join up with the British line on lower ground to the right. Hamilton was exuberant. 'The Gurkhas have stalked the Bluff Redoubt and have carried it with a rush! They are absolutely the boys for this class of country.' In their honour, he renamed the headland on British maps as 'Gurkha Bluff'.

The 6th Gurkhas then spent sixty-five consecutive days in the Cape Helles trenches. They gradually learned the ways of trench warfare much as the Indian troops in France had done in 1914, acquiring an ear to differentiate between types of incoming shell, and the skills to construct traverses. They also answered numerous factory-made Turkish grenades with their own meagre supply of inferior jam tin bombs, locally made by the British Army. Bruce sent out his Scouts as he had in the independent Pukhtun tribal areas since the 1890s. They slipped into no man's land at night, reconnoitring, sniping and attacking Turkish outposts, then making rapid getaways running in zig-zags as they had practised in the pre-war cross-country *khud* races. It seems Bruce continued to encourage the horror of decapitating their sniper quarry. A few of his Scouts were seen returning to Indian lines at Cape Helles with Turkish heads, for instance by Joe Clement, a Royal Marine on night watch next to Bruce's Gurkhas. 'Out of the dark came this voice to warn us not to shoot,' Clement remembered, '"All right, Tommy, all right." Then I saw this smiling face coming in and it wasn't till he'd got in the trench that I realised he was carrying the head of a Turk! He had used his kukri.'

At the start of June, the 5th and 10th Gurkhas arrived from Egypt to replace the 69th and 89th Punjabis. At Helles Bruce cheerfully welcomed his old regiment the 5th. 'Naturally I knew all the officers intimately and a very large number of the men into the bargain,' he wrote, counting among them several of his pre-war Gurkha mountaineers such as Subadar-Major Harkabir Thapa. Yet on the afternoon of 4 June Bruce's good cheer faded as he guided the 5th Gurkhas along the beach by Gurkha Bluff to some knife-edged spurs. The 5th were to attack up the spurs as the sun went down behind them in the first of the Allied summer offensives on Gallipoli, known as the Third Battle of Krithia, intended to capture the heights of Achi Baba. 'I don't think I ever had a more unpleasant task given me in the whole of my life,' Bruce said of his walk on the beach with the 5th Gurkhas, 'knowing full well the most hazardous nature of their task … and the practical certainty that I was saying goodbye to my best friends.' For Bruce, the whole offensive, which extended for miles inland to the regiment's right, was 'to attempt the impossible with quite inadequate means':

> The amount of artillery and ammunition available, not only for keeping up a pretty continuous daily bombardment but for providing an intensive effort such as was required for the advance of the army on 4th June, was entirely and absolutely ludicrous. For ordinary purposes the amounts were down to two rounds per gun of ammunition a day, and even the amount saved to prepare for the battle of the 4th was hopelessly inadequate. Considering the amount of artillery at the disposal of our troops it appears, too, that the bombardment was spread over far too large a front.

The British preliminary bombardment on 4 June was indeed a product of Ian Hamilton's optimism over his better judgement, and it failed, leaving the Turkish trenches, machine guns and artillery virtually intact. When the 5th Gurkhas' companies attacked that afternoon in rushes up their spurs, they faced streams of Turkish bullets and shells from above with little more than their rifles to return fire. 'Naturally the attack was a complete failure,' Bruce wrote miserably, having heard it from the 6th Gurkhas' trenches nearby. The 5th Gurkhas lost 130 wounded or killed, including Subadar-Major Harkabir Thapa. Of the Gurkhas taken prisoner, at least one managed to escape. He was Dhan Sing Gurung, who wrestled himself free, ran off as the Turks chased him, and jumped off a cliff into the sea. He ducked and dived in the water to dodge Turkish rifle fire from the cliff-top, and safely swam back to the Indian beaches.

The 14th Sikhs suffered worse than the 5th Gurkhas that day, attacking up Gully Ravine to the right. They suffered 410 casualties as their men stuck together through a blizzard of Turkish rifle and machine gun fire to reach the Turkish front line. With their bare hands they tore through barbed wire untouched by the British artillery to capture a trench, only to withdraw without the numbers to cling on to it against counter-attack. 'So bang goes one of the finest regiments of the Indian Army,' rued their wounded Lieutenant Reginald Savory.

Bruce's time came on the night of 30 June when a Turkish hand grenade explosion in the 6th Gurkhas' trenches broke one of his legs and badly damaged the other. 'My little present which took me off the Peninsula and sent me to England to hospital for a year,' he said. 'For two days I felt a shocking traitor, but ... the real feeling I had was relief – relief from the continual noise and relief from the continual strain and rest at last, for we had been virtually two months in the firing line ... from start to finish the whole thing was one long nightmare.'

As for the feelings of the Nepalese men Bruce left behind in the 6th Gurkhas' trenches, they are barely documented. One of them, Kulbahadur Gurung, who was captured on 4 June at the Third Battle of Krithia and held prisoner in Turkey for three years, gave glimpses in a post-war interview. Kulbahadur Gurung was a father aged twenty-eight who had enlisted in 1905. He had arrived on Gallipoli in April 1915 self-admittedly indifferent about the Turks as an enemy, saying 'it was all the same with us'. When he left the peninsula in June, he believed it to be an island and was proud of his regiment compared to the 14th Sikhs, boasting 'Gurkhas are better soldiers than the Sheiks'. Another Gurkha of his regiment, Gulab Bahadur, also taken prisoner on 4 June, subsequently said 'all the Indian troops were in terrible condition'. He was probably referring to their worn-out uniforms and widespread dysentery. Both were symptomatic of the deficient British logistical support on Gallipoli, whose dependence on long distance sea links contributed to shortages of clothing, food, clean water and medical supplies. Some Gurkhas self-inflicted wounds, hoping for evacuation to hospital in Malta, Egypt or Bombay. Nonetheless, by late June the Gurkhas' fighting spirit on Gallipoli was generally intact, as they would soon show.

'Up to this time,' remarked the regimental history of the 5th Gurkhas, who were temporarily amalgamated with the 6th Gurkhas, 'there existed a feeling among the men that in their encounters with the Turk, through no fault of their own, they had had by no means the best of it, and all were anxiously awaiting the occasion to do as they had been done by ... chances of getting even.' While Gallipoli's Turkish defenders had shot down Gurkha attacks, thrown grenades and fired shells from afar, they had not yet exposed themselves in the open, attacking the Indian line. They finally did so against the Gurkhas at Cape Helles between 2 and 5 July, in mass night-time attacks down the slopes of Achi Baba. They came on at a jog-trot chanting 'Allah, Allah' in full voice, illuminated by flare rockets bursting above and a Royal Navy searchlight at sea. The Gurkhas' firing line got congested as they jostled for a place to shoot, leaving no standing room at the parapet; several Gurkhas forced their way to a clear shot, clambering up others to fire over their heads. The Nepalese certainly appeared to have a point to prove – they shot dead an estimated 2500 Turks in no man's land as they held their line and stopped the attacks, their rifles becoming so hot that they charred.

A few days later, the Gurkha and Sikh infantry were shipped off the peninsula for a break, having been in their trenches at Cape Helles for ten consecutive weeks. They sailed to the Aegean island of Imbros, an Allied naval and air base, resting there for three weeks. They camped on the coast, swam in the clear Aegean waters and watched German bombers flying over the sea towards Gallipoli; they sat about in the sun with Anzacs, picking up new words like 'Asstrely' ('Australia'), and played football with British recruits. They also received replacement uniforms, and walked to the local town, Panaghea, looking for bars and beer. 'One feels so free,' Philip Palin, the 14th Sikhs' colonel, reflected on Imbros, 'not having to dodge bullets and shells and being able to live decently above ground instead of having to grovel in dug-outs and trenches.' The Indian troops no doubt agreed with him, and with the Sikhs' young officer Reginald Savory who wrote home of Gallipoli, 'we don't want to go back'. But back they went in early August, not to Cape Helles but to the Anzac beaches on Gallipoli's western side – straight into the most ambitious Indian operation yet on the peninsula.

The latest Allied offensive on Gallipoli pivoted on the 5th, 6th and 10th Gurkhas attacking inland from the west coast, within a wider British imperial assault line of Sikhs, New South Welshmen, Wellingtons, Maoris, Gloucesters, Lancastrians and other infantry. The Gurkhas had been chosen as the lead troops for their pre-war mountain fighting skills, which they had relatively intact with around 50 per cent of their original men. They were to march six miles from the Anzac beaches to capture the lightly defended heights of the Sari Bair range, which ran down the centre of Gallipoli and overlooked most of the Turkish position on the peninsula, the Dardanelles and their Asian shore. The opening attack went in between 6 and 9 August over a tangle of ravines, precipices, cornfields, and hills thick with prickly scrub up to six feet high. During the day, Turkish reconnaissance aeroplanes flew back and forth over the higher slopes of Sari Bair, and at night British searchlights offshore lit up the landscape.

'We fought as on manoeuvres in India,' thought Major Cecil Allanson, Charles Bruce's replacement in command of the 6th Gurkhas. Allanson and the 6th Gurkhas battled for over seventy-two hours from the beaches to the summit of the Sari Bair range, their Scouts tracking down and killing Turkish snipers up the hillsides, wiping their blood-stained *khukuri*s clean on green bushes. They encountered Turkish trenches only on the summit itself, which they assaulted to timetable at first light on 9 August after it had been battered by naval artillery. 'For about ten minutes, we fought hand to hand, we bit and fisted, and used rifles and pistols as clubs; blood was flying about like spray from a hairwash bottle,' wrote Allanson. 'And then the Turks turned and fled, and I felt a very proud man; the key of the whole peninsula was ours, and our losses had not been so very great for such a result.'

Allanson led the 6th Gurkhas in pursuit down the far side of the summit, with a clear view of Turkish supply roads down to the Dardanelles. But then they were hit by their own guns, New Zealander howitzers on the Allied side of the summit sending shells plunging on to them. 'It was an appalling sight,' remembered Allanson. 'The first hit a Gurkha in the face; the place was a mass of blood and limbs and screams, and we all flew back to the summit to hold our old position just below.'

This was the turning of the tide. The wider British imperial infantry line provided no support for the Gurkhas, rather going into reverse. It had struggled to get as far as them, some units wandering in the wrong direction, lost in the difficult terrain without maps, while others collapsed exhausted in the heat of the day among the shrubs with dehydration, diarrhoea or wounds; none had enough artillery support. So Allanson's Gurkhas were called back to the lower hills above the Anzac beaches. 'It was a sad moment,' he wrote. 'Victory had slipped us ... we gave up the key to the Gallipoli Peninsula.'

Allanson's word is all there is for his men's feelings on their retreat from the summit of Sari Bair. 'The men were utterly worn out, suffering from want of sleep, hunger and thirst,' he noted. 'Throughout these four days no man ever disobeyed or showed any inclination to disobey any order I gave.'

By September, the Allied forces at Gallipoli were back on the defensive. That month the Indian infantry there was joined by the 4th Gurkhas from France, raising its proportion of Gurkha to Sikh battalions to 4:1. On the Indian home front, however, public attention on Gallipoli overwhelmingly focused on the Sikh minority, narrowing in on the 14th Sikhs' near annihilation on

4 June at Gully Ravine. This event figured prominently in the local politics of the primary Indian recruitment ground – Punjab – as Punjabi members of the revolutionary group Ghadar returned to India from the United States and Canada. They were back to engineer a great Punjabi uprising, and their plans depended on the Indian soldiers stationed in British India fighting for their cause.

'Bled absolutely white'

The Viceroy, Charles Hardinge, had begun 1915 at Delhi newly overwhelmed with grief. In late December his eldest son Edd, an officer of the 15th Hussars, had died of wounds in France. 'He was such a splendid boy in every way,' Hardinge wrote. 'Nothing could console me for the loss of my wife and eldest son during the short space of six months.' He depended yet more on his teenage daughter Diamond, and arranged for his surviving son, Alec, to move from the British Army in England to join him in India. Outwardly, Hardinge summoned the strength to keep up a pretence of serenity. Appearances were critical for prestige – he felt duty bound to appear unruffled in public, setting a tone for all British administrators in India that nothing should disturb their poise; they were to project an air of certainty of victory over the Central Powers, and of British rule continuing as an ordinary fact of life.

But in private Hardinge questioned whether he could keep control of the country. His underlying concern was a matter of colonial principle: the need to keep military forces in hand to guarantee the regime against rebellion. Pre-war pseudo-science dictated of course that the Army in India required 75,000 British and 150,000 Indian troops to secure the Government of India, the ratio of 1:2 calculated to be the minimum to ensure a defeat of rebellious Indian troops. These figures were uppermost in Hardinge's mind from August 1914 when he began to sanction the depletion of the Army in India's British and Indian numbers at London's behest for service against the Germans and Turks. 'We are indeed most anxious to do all in our power to help,' he had advised the Secretary of State for India, Lord Crewe, at the war's outset, 'but we as a Government have a very serious responsibility for the maintenance of order in India.'

By February 1915, Hardinge felt London had asked him for too many troops. He complained to a friend in private of 'the evil tendency at Whitehall to regard India as a milch cow', the country having released approximately 150,000 soldiers since the start of the war, including Indian Expeditionary Forces A to F and four fifths of India's pre-war British Army garrison, mainly shipped back to the Home Army to make new British divisions for the western front. 'Here we have been bled absolutely white, and have practically nothing more to give,' wrote Hardinge, describing his domestic military position as 'a gamble' and 'a serious danger'. To fill the gap of India's departed pre-war British troops, London sent British Territorial or home defence volunteers. Yet these were virtually untrained and on their arrival by mid-1915 the Indian General Staff deemed them unfit for active service.

To make matters worse, the Indian Army's pre-war reserve of 35,000 men had proved a poor replenisher of Indian battalions' casualties overseas. The reservists were generally too old, physically unfit (some even had no teeth) and under-trained. They had widely joined the reserve up to 1914 to qualify for pensions, and been kept on as village elders likely to support the British in order to make sure they got them. Without an effective army reserve to call on in late 1914, India's Commander-in-Chief Beauchamp Duff had had no choice but to cream off pre-war companies from battalions still in India, to slot into others with the Indian Expeditionary Forces. This significantly weakened India's garrison not just in quantity but also in quality – Lord Kitchener insisted that only the very best regiments be drawn on for replacing casualties on the costly western front.

Hardinge, therefore, was wary in early 1915 that his Indian garrison was so weak it could be embarrassed or even ruinously exposed by unrest it could not contain. The gravest threat on this count was Afghanistan, if Emir Habibullah at Kabul joined the Sultan's jihad and attacked British India with the independent Pukhtun tribes at its side. Yet within British India a more immediate revolutionary threat flared up from Ghadar, involving a mutiny scare over Sikh regiments that stretched Hardinge's government to desperate measures to keep control.

Around one thousand Punjabi revolutionaries of Ghadar, the majority Sikh, had returned to India from North America by late 1914. Their masterplan for an uprising was to win over the countryside with promises of a new democratic republic of India to be won by bloody revolution, firing its way to victory by turning the Army in India's guns on the British. The scheme hinged on Punjabi villagers attacking cantonments while mutinying Indian regiments seized the arsenals to arm them. To get Indian soldiers to join their plot, Ghadar agents visited virtually every cantonment in northern India up to February 1915, targeting Sikhs above all, while also seeking out soldiers on home leave. 'You go and fight for the sake of the whites,' read one Ghadar newspaper they distributed to Indian troops. 'You always attack other countries. Why do you not take your own country into your charge? Have you vowed to live as slaves of the English?'

Many of the Sikh soldiers approached were stung by these taunts, and were sympathetic to the Ghadar agents' appeals to Sikh patriotism and visions of revolutionary momentum among villagers. Several in Indian regiments stationed in Punjab and the United Provinces of Agra and Oudh said they would throw in their lot with Ghadar, for example men of the 23rd Cavalry at Lahore, the 26th Punjabis at Ferozepore and the 128th Pioneers at Meerut. The Ghadar agents set 21 February 1915 as the great day to launch their uprising. In anticipation of the date, some of their Sikh soldier accomplices deserted beforehand; others stayed with their regiments to await villagers' attacks on their cantonments as the signal for them to mutiny and seize the arsenals.

The Sikh troops involved tended to be long-service profession-als and committed freedom fighters, looking to release years of frustration with the British. For instance, there was Lachman Singh, a charismatic Sikh NCO turned Ghadarite of the 23rd Cavalry. He gave his sword to his Ghadar contact as a token of his sincerity and honour as a soldier, pledging that he would muster all the support he could at his cantonment.

Lachman Singh and the other Ghadar conspirators' plans never got off the ground, however. British India's domestic intelligence agency the Department of Criminal Investigation had secured Lachman Singh's cousin as an informant and spy, and he had infiltrated Ghadar and attended leadership meetings. The cousin identified to his British handlers the Ghadar ringleaders and their Indian Army accomplices, and gave details of their next moves. Meanwhile in the 12th Cavalry, some Pukhtun troopers had got wind of their Sikh squadron's intention to mutiny in league with Ghadar, and informed on them in return for Viceroy's Commissions. Informers within other Indian regiments also chose British rewards over revolution. Ghadar was roundly betrayed, and the Department of Criminal Investigation smashed it with a series of arrests before 21 February.

In the following weeks, some undetected Ghadarite Sikh soldiers of the 23rd Cavalry plotted to assassinate their British officers with chemical bombs of Ghadar design, but they bungled. As their regiment was moving by railway in Punjab, they hid their bombs in the regimental baggage. One of their bags with a bomb in it was accidentally knocked about at a station, and the bomb went off, wounding five cavalrymen and blowing their plot.

Lachman Singh was one of sixteen Ghadarite Indian soldier conspirators of the 12th Cavalry, 23rd Cavalry and other Indian regiments who were sentenced to death by court martial and executed for leading mutiny or murder plans, or for withholding these from their British officers. 'If I had to live more lives than one,' said one of the unrepentant conspirators, Kartar Singh

Sarabha, in his dying words, 'I would sacrifice each of them for my country's sake.'

There were further prosecutions and punishments of Ghadarite Indian soldiers of the 23rd Cavalry and 26th Punjabis, not by traditional court martial but by special tribunal under the Defence of India Act of 1915. This was a repressive Indian security law promoted by Hardinge and approved by London. It gave the Government of India powers to detain without proof suspects of terrorism and political crimes, including inciting hatred and mutiny, and to try them forthwith by special tribunal with no right of appeal to sentences, including the death sentence. 'I am not prepared to be at all particular about the liberty of the subject or about the need for legal proof before suspected persons are interned for such time as may be necessary,' the Secretary of State for India, Lord Crewe, admitted of the powers under the Act, exposing the limits of British Liberalism when it came to making sure of colonial control.

The Act's passing into law in March for the duration of the war was a measure of how very alarmed the British were by Ghadar. The Indian General Staff in fact strongly advised Hardinge of the need for it as a means to keep the Army in India's domestic duties to a minimum when trained troops were in such short supply. Furthermore, the Act's inception demonstrated how the mainstream Indian nationalist politicians remained cooperative with the British and India's war effort. Those sitting in the Imperial Legislative Council at Delhi unanimously voted the Act through, their moderate politics of concession-seeking justifying a blind eye to its anti-democratic essence.

In the Sikh villages of Punjab that provided Indian Army recruits, meanwhile, Ghadar revealed fault lines in their support for the British. In January 1915, Ghadar agents preaching in Sikh villages had deterred many young men from joining the army, causing a sharp fall in Sikh recruitment. By August, however, Sikh recruitment had recovered as the agents' influence waned. This was partly in consequence of the British using their Defence of India Act powers to clamp down on the agents' activities, through prison sentences or orders of confinement at home. But the more pervasive factor was the encouragement of military service by the Sikh elders, a collection of long-established religious and rural landed leaders. They were inclined towards moderate politics of cooperation with the British to underwrite their Indian Army connection: military service was the Sikhs' most lucrative avenue of employment. This made the elders unwilling to promote Ghadar's radical republicanism, and they saw its acceptance among serving soldiers or potential army recruits as conflicting with their community's well-being. In the spring they fretted that Ghadar had spoiled their relationship with the British and wanted to repair it. Then came news of the 14th Sikhs' heavy losses on Gallipoli on 4 June at Gully Ravine, and it took centre stage.

'In the highest sense of the word extreme gallantry has been shown by this fine Battalion,' the Gallipoli commander Ian Hamilton stated in his report on the 14th Sikhs at Gully Ravine, which was widely published in the Indian press shortly after the action. His report described no man's land after the Sikhs' attack as 'thickly dotted with the bodies of these fine soldiers all lying on their faces as they fell in their steady advance on the enemy', and concluded emphatically:

The history of the Sikhs affords many instances of their value as soldiers, but it may be safely asserted that nothing finer than the grim valour and steady discipline displayed by them on the 4th June has ever been done by soldiers of the Khalsa.* Their devotion to duty and their splendid loyalty to their orders and to their leaders make a record their nation should look back upon with pride for many generations.

---

* *Khalsa*, a Punjabi word for 'pure', means the community of the Sikh faith.

The Sikh elders seized on the story as one they could use for business with the British. They made a spate of public pronouncements on how it was the 14th Sikhs at Gully Ravine, not Ghadar, who exemplified the true Sikh spirit in harmony with the colonial power. In July at the Golden Temple at Amritsar in Punjab, the holiest *gurdwara* or place of worship in Sikhism, there was a meeting of thousands to pray for the men of the 14th Sikhs as martyrs of their faith, with a declaration that 'the Sikhs would always continue to fight for the Government as bravely as ever'. In August, at a Sikh public meeting at the Punjabi city of Rawalpindi to mark the anniversary of the war's outbreak, a sermon extolled the duty of 'every Sikh to place everything ... at the disposal of the benign British government which has shown so many favours', followed by shouts from the congregation of 'Sat Sri Akal!' ('Victory to the faithful!'). Then the Sikh elders paid courteous visits to Charles Hardinge and Michael O'Dwyer, the Irish governor of Punjab. Their message, according to O'Dwyer, was that Ghadar had brought 'the Sikhs as a whole into discredit, and their interests as well as their honour were involved'. They looked, he wrote, on the 14th Sikhs' sacrifice at Gully Ravine 'not with sorrow but with a feeling of pride'.

Hardinge and O'Dwyer noticed that the recovery from the Ghadar-induced dip in Sikh recruitment started in earnest with the news of the 14th Sikhs at Gully Ravine. They drew the conclusion, as O'Dwyer put it, that 'the Sikh spirit, instead of being daunted by that terrible sacrifice of Gallipoli, was roused thereby to a higher pitch of martial ardour ... from that day the Sikh eagerness for recruiting received its strongest impetus'. Indeed, Hardinge gathered on British India's military grapevine that post-Gully Ravine the Sikh recruits at regimental depots in Punjab were suddenly enthusiastic compared to earlier in the year, saying to their British officers 'they really want to serve in the war, not just for land and money, which astonishes us'.

However, such Sikh recruits were likely overcompensating to

ease British suspicions of them related to Ghadar. Rather than Gully Ravine simply reviving Sikh recruitment by inspiring their martial spirit and natural taste for war, the Sikh elders had probably nurtured a political appearance of this to the British. It seems they encouraged their young men to enlist in greater numbers to help mend the Sikh relationship with officialdom, and to take personal responsibility for upholding their community's material livelihood through martial values and shows of loyalty. The hidden feelings of the Sikh recruits themselves can be guessed from what they were saying away from British ears. A telling soundbite survives from a Sikh veteran of the immediate aftermath of the 14th Sikhs' Gully Ravine attack, as the survivors were counting their numbers and recovering the wounded. One Sikh asked his comrades what had become of their British officer 'Savory Sahib' (Reginald Savory), who was lying unconscious in no man's land with a bayonet wound to the head; the others replied, 'Leave him to his fate' – implying, of course, a distance from the British and a limit to their loyalty. Equally, in the 12th Cavalry there were outwardly loyal Sikhs of the regiment who were not court-martialled like several of their Ghadarite comrades but who privately sympathised with them. They despised their regiment's two Pukhtun troopers who had turned informers for Viceroy's Commissions, denouncing them as shameful to Sikhs and Muslims of other regiments, who publicly shunned them as a result.

Among the Sikh prisoners of war in Germany at Camp Crescent Moon, two factions emerged with different views on the British in response to the camp's revolutionary propaganda. One faction politely declined the German offer of volunteering for revolutionary schemes, saying that they wanted no part in German-backed revolution in British India, preferring to continue to receive the benefits of British service. Yet the other faction called themselves 'the patriots', embraced the nationalist propaganda and did volunteer for German schemes, including the diplomatic mission to Kabul joined by Afridi.

Clearly, then, Sikh soldiers' willingness to serve the British was not so straightforward as a Ghadarite blip in early 1915 followed by an abrupt reconnection with martial ardour in British service because of Gully Ravine. This is what the British liked to see, but then there was much they did not hear.

It is striking that throughout the First World War, the British awarded no Sikh the Victoria Cross. It may be that following their pre-war diagnosis of Sikh 'swollen head' and wartime findings of Sikh recruits' sympathy for Ghadar, they withheld the VC from any Sikh as a means of colonial control. Perhaps the British official mind up to 1918 considered that to decorate a Sikh with the VC was to risk inspiring in Sikh troops too much boldness which could turn into anti-British action.

During the downturn in Sikh recruitment in the early months of 1915, Hardinge had been concerned about how recruitment in general might be affected by word of the front line on the lips of the first badly wounded Indian troops back home – men maimed for life or amputees with artificial legs made of wood and cork. In March, however, Hardinge heard from the Chief-Commissioner of British India's North-West Frontier Province that 'many men are returning from the front and boasting of their bravery and the number of Germans they have killed, each being in his own village a Rustam'.*

In any event, the Indian Army's overall recruitment figures in British India from August 1914 to June 1915 were buoyant, the martial race communities providing 65,000 volunteers, five times the pre-war rate. Behind this climb was the Indian Army's pre-war recruitment system intensifying its efforts in the old manner, with Indian regimental depots calling on their pre-war village recruitment networks, depending in particular on serving or pensioned Indian officers to bring in the numbers in return for bonuses. The 19th Punjabis, for instance, had enrolled 900 Punjabi Muslim and

---

* A hero; Rustam was a famous warrior of ancient mythology.

Sikh wartime recruits by summer 1915. The guiding spirit was their Muslim Subadar-Major Fateh Khan, who was well rewarded with a bonus of 300 rupees and a sword of honour, presented to him personally by Hardinge.

The Indian Commander-in-Chief Beauchamp Duff prescribed the new recruits a minimum of eight months' basic training at their regimental depots, so that from June 1915 around 8,000 recruits a month became available for active service. Many set sail immediately for the Indian Expeditionary Forces, with those entering the Mediterranean encountering a new threat: German U-boats. A U-boat attack in fact caused the greatest loss of Indian life in a single day of the Gallipoli campaign, on 19 September. *U-35*, out hunting from its base in Croatia, sank the troopship *Ramazan* carrying Indian wartime drafts from Alexandria to Gallipoli for the 10th Gurkhas and 14th Sikhs. Some 300 Gurkhas and Sikhs were drowned, sucked into the depths while clinging to the railings on the *Ramazan*'s bow as she went down. 'Poor chaps, all gone,' wrote Neville Irwin, a British officer of the 10th Gurkhas, who having jumped into the sea watched them disappear. 'A terrible experience, the worst strain I have ever had.'

Ninety Gurkhas and Sikhs had also jumped off the *Ramazan*, in life-jackets, and were picked up with Irwin by lifeboats. The boats found their way to the remote Greek island of Antikythera, where for a week local farmers kindly looked after the Indian Army castaways, giving them black bread, goat stew and red wine, and cow sheds to sleep in. The Greek Navy eventually took them off the island to Athens, before they returned to British care in Malta, going on from there to Egypt.

While wartime Indian recruits were badly needed at Gallipoli to replace the Indian regiments' casualties, the greatest need for them in 1915 was elsewhere: in France, where the demands on the Indian infantry went far beyond those of 1914, leading the Indian troops to question their commitment to the British more than ever before.

12

'KESKERSAY'

'Who are these Jermun people?' a Mahsud with the 129th Baluchis asked. He was talking in Pushtu to his British officer, Charlie Campbell, at a village behind the Allied line in France in January 1915. Campbell was a twenty-eight-year-old pre-war professional of the 40th Pathans, a diligent speaker of Urdu and Russian besides Pushtu. He had been on leave in England in summer 1914 when the War Office had drafted him into the British Army, to fill a gap in a battalion of Dubliners with the original BEF. He had served with the Dubliners continuously in a British corps' trenches in France up to Christmas 1914, growing an unkempt beard he still wore. And now he had switched to the Indian Corps, temporarily attached to the 129th Baluchis as a casualty replacement.

'We have heard of the French and knew of the power of the King Emperor and the Russ,' Campbell's Mahsud inquisitor went on, 'but these Jermuns have sprung from where? We do not know them.' The Mahsud had only just met Campbell. He was also a replacement from another regiment – a pre-war sepoy fresh up from Marseilles, sent from the 127th Baluchis in British India. Some other Mahsud of the 127th who had sailed with him for the 129th sauntered over to join the conversation, darting their own questions at Campbell. 'How long would it take to go to Hindustan in an air boat?' said one. Another went for a more impudent line: 'Would it not be sound to trim your beard?'

Their chat with Campbell was part of a typical experience for Indian infantrymen in France in 1915: meeting new faces as casualty replacements constantly joined the Indian Corps. The replacements came from far and wide. From January, the Indian Corps' original twenty battalions of 1914 received intermittent injections of pre-war professional officers and men of at least forty Indian regiments stationed elsewhere, from Aden and British India to the princely Indian States and Ceylon, including many veterans of the Indian Army's pre-1914 campaigns. Among these replacements in New Year 1915 was the Afridi Jemadar Mir Dast, veteran of the Mohmand small war in 1908 and older brother of the deserter Jemadar Mir Mast. Now aged forty, in late 1914 Mir Dast had been with his regiment the 55th Coke's Rifles in British India's North-West Frontier Province, and had sailed to France for the 57th Wilde's Rifles, to join their Afridi company. From April, the Indian Corps' other casualty replacements included whole pre-war Indian battalions from Hong Kong, Egypt and Gallipoli; then from June came thousands of young wartime recruits from British India and Nepal.

The Indian Corps spent most of 1915 on the defensive in France under James Willcocks, holding the same sector of the BEF line in the Pas-de-Calais as it had in winter 1914. The Indians' defensive duties over 1915 would bring them new experiences both terrifying as they encountered poison gas for the first time, and exhilarating as they not only took reconnaissance and sniping to new levels in no man's land, but also spied behind enemy lines. Meanwhile, the BEF expanded with more units coming in from Britain, so that the Indian battalions increasingly rotated in the front line, spending shorter spells there than they had in 1914. This gave them more time at rest among the French villages, for periods of up to a month or more.

'You will scarcely believe it,' Charlie Campbell with the 129th Baluchis wrote to his mother on 2 February after his men had had five weeks' rest, 'but I heard a Pathan ask a Sikh who was crawling along the road today "Keskersay." The Sikh smiling said "Pied, Mal."'* The Indian troops were starting to talk French to each other if they had no home language in common – just one strand of their revealing conversations behind the trenches that the British paid close attention to, most of all in the Indian Army hospitals in southern England where they came together to reflect on their European service and share their feelings about it.

'The men have worked extraordinarily well'

'One section was held by Pathans, and some of them were singing to a sitar,' James Willcocks recalled of his visit to his Indian Corps' front line near Neuve Chapelle on the afternoon of 2 September. 'I had years ago learned their favourite song, "Zakhmi Dil" (The Wounded Heart), so I joined in and gave them a verse. Men from other parts of the trenches came running over, and presently to dance and music we were having an improvised concert.' That evening Willcocks wrote to the Viceroy, Charles Hardinge, about how different the Indians' trenches of 1915 were compared with the winter of 1914. 'The men have worked extraordinarily well in the trenches and our defences are worth seeing,' he stated. 'No more hastily dug trenches full of slime and water, but model breastworks, drained and defended with skill and care.'

Since January, the Indian infantry in France had received new trench fighting equipment as British factories delivered on Lord Kitchener's orders to help the BEF match the Germans: uniforms of British Army-style cloth thicker than their pre-war khaki; duckboards, trench wall rivets, dug-out frames, picks, spades,

---

* 'Keskersay', phonetic French for 'What is it?' ('Qu'est que c'est?'); and the reply: 'Foot, bad.'

shovels, sandbags and barbed wire; telephone systems to connect front trenches with battalion headquarters behind; Vickers heavy machine guns, 'Mills bomb' hand grenades with ring pulls, and Stokes mortars firing 1lb bombs 800 yards; trench periscopes and telescopic rifle sights. With their improved trenches, equipment and regular trench warfare training in back areas for newly arrived drafts, the Indian troops' wherewithal to occupy the front line kicked on considerably from their lessons of 1914.

Some sepoys began writing home from France about how adapted they had become with months of experience behind them. 'Do not concern yourself too much about me,' Jemadar Muhammad Azim Khan, a pre-war professional Punjabi Muslim of the 57th Wilde's Rifles, wrote to his father in June 1915. 'I do not think of myself at all now. Fighting is now to me nothing more than an ordinary game. I am never put out.' 'There was a little fear at first, but essentially it wasn't too bad,' said the equally phlegmatic Sikh veteran, Suran Singh, of his time in the improved Indian trenches. '[My men] were and felt themselves to be veterans,' thought a British officer of the 47th Sikhs, 'whose business it was to adapt themselves to circumstances in war, and to teach others to do the like.'

All the while the Indians grew accustomed to the variety of small animal life in their trenches, from flies and frogs to itchy parasites. 'Our people have many lice in their clothes', an Afridi of the 129th Baluchis, Ghufran Khan, wrote home in a letter of April. 'But there are no mosquitoes or other creatures which bite mankind, and no snakes or scorpions at all.'

There were no Indian flights under shell fire on the western front in 1915 such as there had been in late 1914 – partly because there was not a single German offensive against the Indian sector in 1915, making for less intense shell fire on the Indian line, and partly because the Indian trenches afforded better protection. Up to the summer, Willcocks had most confidence in his Frontier Force regiments as steadfast in the front line, with their accumulation of well-trained pre-war professionals as casualty replacements from other Frontier Force units in British India. He felt some of his Gurkha battalions were shakier. Many of their Gurkha reinforcements in early 1915 were rural policemen who, as migrant workers, had been patrolling the hills of British India's north-eastern provinces of Assam and Burma. They had been sent to France for lack of trained Gurkha army units in India and on their own agreement for increased pay, but they had barely any military training. In July, three Gurkhas, possibly police drafts who did not have the ingrained discipline of long-serving regular Gurkha soldiers, abandoned their posts in the Indian Corps' front line. At their court martial Willcocks passed the death sentence. 'I hate doing it but it is absolutely necessary as an example,' he confided in Charles Hardinge, 'and so I had them shot on a parade of Indian troops. This is a really big struggle and one has to harden our heart when it comes to battle discipline.'

Day to day in 1915 the Indian troops in France were still a menace to the German line. In January, Sikh miners of the Bengal Sappers followed the German example of the previous December and dug their own underground gallery beneath the German trenches, detonating it successfully and inflicting a number of casualties. The independent Pukhtun continued to take the lead among the Indian snipers, patiently locating their German counterparts who were firing from camouflaged hideouts in no man's land, for instance among the summer leaves in trees. Often lying in long grass and using their new telescopic sights, the Indian snipers spent hours watching and waiting for German snipers to show themselves, and took full advantage when they did. Some even went to fetch equipment from the dead as trophies; one British officer saw an Afridi sniper return with a German rifle and 'the Hun's helmet, a grisly sight, as his bullet had crashed through the man's brain'. Sikh Scouts reconnoitring in no man's land also brought back trophies. In August, two of the 47th Sikhs stole a five-foot square sign on a German parapet bragging about the recent capture of Warsaw ('Warschau gefallen!').

The consensus among the Indian Corps' British battalions alongside the Indians was that the independent Pukhtun were the masters of reconnaissance in no man's land. 'Patrolling far in advance of our lines ... the Pathans were unequalled in ... gaining an enemy trench unseen,' said Major Arthur Wauchope of the Black Watch, who sent some of his Highlanders to learn from the Afridi of the 58th Vaughan's Rifles. Norman Ellison, a British private from Liverpool, remembered seeing Pukhtun Scouts in summer 1915:

> dressed in overalls, camouflaged with yellow and green paint splashes, with faces and hands likewise disguised and an upstanding fringe of rushes as headgear ... they became part of the undergrowth, through which they could creep without snapping a twig ... sometimes as one of our scouts was creeping along with elaborate caution, his ankle would be seized by a hand, and looking down in alarm he would see the laughing face of a Pathan silently enjoying the success of his little joke.

It had in fact struck the independent Pukhtun of several Indian regiments in France that the German jihad leaflets presented an opportunity to enter enemy lines under false pretences in order to spy – an old Pukhtun trick played on British camps during small wars in their tribal areas. In early 1915 some Afridi and Mahsud asked their British officers for permission to attempt the ruse in the German trenches, but were turned down on account of the dangers of being shot at any stage of trying it. One of the men denied permission was a young pre-war Mahsud NCO named Ayub Khan. In December 1914 he had been stationed in British India near Waziristan with his regiment the 124th Baluchis, and his Mahsud company had been ordered to sail for France as casualty replacements for the 129th Baluchis. Twenty-two of his company's Mahsud had straightaway deserted to dodge the overseas draft, but Ayub Khan had declined to go with them, in itself an indication of professional commitment. Indeed, once his British officers had discovered the desertions, Ayub Khan had sworn to them, according to the 124th Baluchis' regimental history, 'he would either die in France or return an Indian officer'. In France in early 1915, Ayub Khan joined the 129th under the command of their pre-war officer Harold Lewis. The two got on well as Ayub Khan tried to impress for a promotion, although Lewis had drawn a line at his request to desert to spy. But Ayub Khan made up his own mind to do so, vanishing from the 129th's trenches in the early morning darkness of 22 June. At midnight that day he dropped back in over the parapet, very tired, and refusing to give Lewis any account of his escapade until he had got some sleep.

On waking he told Lewis where he had been. 'I went up to the German wire, lay down, and slept,' Ayub Khan began. 'As dawn broke I stood up, raised my hands and called out "Musalman".' He was welcomed into the German line, assumed to be a deserter; 'I was treated well, and the men in the trenches gave me cigarettes.' He was then taken four miles to the rear on a light railway, to the German-occupied French town of Marquillies. 'I waited outside a big office. At length I was called inside and interrogated by a Staff Officer through the medium of an officer who spoke very bad Hindustani.' Following questions about the BEF, the interrogating staff officer – the Prussian Generalleutnant Kurt von dem Borne – told Ayub Khan 'how wrong it was for Mussalmans to fight against the allies of Turkey', and asked why he had deserted. 'I am of an independent race,' Ayub Khan replied, 'I am not an Indian. I do not see why I should daily risk my life.' He added there were twenty more Mahsud of the 129th Baluchis who felt the same. 'We all want to desert, but we dared not come over together lest we should be mistaken for a raiding party and be fired on and killed. We decided that I should come alone and arrange matters.' Von dem Borne offered Ayub Khan 20 marks for each of the other twenty Mahsud, equivalent to 300 rupees in total, if he returned to the Indian trenches and brought them over to the Germans. Ayub Khan struck the deal, agreeing a time and place for the mass desertion, and was taken by motor car to the German front line to crawl back to the 129th Baluchis.

The morning of his return to the regiment, Ayub Khan showed no inclination of sticking to his side of the bargain with von dem Borne. Rather, he poured out to Lewis every scrap of military intelligence he could. He had spent his time with the Germans making a mental note of all he saw, so he was able to report a range of information, of a kind considered valuable on the western front: German regimental numbers he had seen on epaulettes; the technical details of German trench construction down to the design of parapets, machine gun nests and dug-outs; and the layout behind the German trenches, including ammunition dumps and the whereabouts of von dem Borne's headquarters.

Word of Ayub Khan's story soon reached James Willcocks and he went up to the 129th's trenches to hear it from the man himself. 'Ayub Khan carried his life in his hand,' Willcocks reflected, 'for had his actions caused one doubt of any kind among his captors he would assuredly have been shot.' Yet Willcocks still tested the young Mahsud NCO's word by directing the Indian Corps' artillery to fire on one of the spots he had identified as an ammunition dump. Willcocks took the ensuing 'very considerable explosion' as the proof he needed, and spontaneously gave Ayub Khan 300 rupees to match von dem Borne's offer, along with a special promotion in the field to a higher grade of NCO. He also directed that a large sign be put up above the 129th Baluchis' trenches saying 'The Traitor Has Been Shot'. This was a ruse 'to notify the Hun that the treachery had been discovered', and therefore to pre-empt any shelling of the regiment's line by the Germans 'in a fit of pique if they felt tricked'.

Lewis felt that Ayub Khan's solo spying surpassed the bravery even of the 129th's Punjabi Muslim machine gunner Khudadad Khan, the first Indian soldier to win the Victoria Cross. For

Lewis, Ayub Khan's devotion to duty in the presence of the enemy was unique. John Hannyngton, the 129th Baluchis' commanding officer, and Willcocks agreed: they recommended Ayub Khan for a VC. The BEF authorities, however, rejected the recommendation and forbade Ayub Khan's story from going public under a censorship ban. Their concern was that self-appointment as a spy was no example to the British soldier, who should not be encouraged to do the same; it was too individual an action, too dangerous. Hannyngton and Willcocks compensated by arranging for Ayub Khan not only the highest medal for Indians alone, the Indian Order of Merit, but also a Viceroy's Commission. Lewis was always to feel that Ayub Khan had been hard done by. 'The I.O.M. and the promotion to Jemadar that he earned were hardly sufficient reward,' he thought.

In his interrogation by von dem Borne, Ayub Khan had been asked if the British fed the Indian troops well. He replied 'Yes, excellently'. He would hardly have been justified in saying otherwise. Into 1915, the Indians' culinary arrangements at the front only improved on the abundance of the winter of 1914, with additional foodstuffs from the Indian Soldiers Fund such as apples, oranges and other fruits, some specially ordered from the Caribbean and exported on refrigerated ships. The Fund also continued to funnel comforts into the Indian trench sector. Indeed Willcocks presided over a new system of personal requests from the Indian troops to the Fund; so now there were towels, soaps and neem tree toothbrushes; Aspirin tablets, Horlicks Malted Milk and Johnson & Johnson plasters; electric torches, bottles of hair dye and footballs; coffee, cigars, smoking jackets and playing cards; a portable organ, harmonicas and a flute; gramophones with hundreds of records including readings of the Koran; and phrase books with French translations of Indian languages. The YMCA, meanwhile, carried on caring for the Indian troops in France, for example by providing Indian recruits newly arrived at Marseilles with a cinema showing the French comedy films of Max Linder, and with lectures on the war and European geography.

A few of the Indians understood that such care for them was charitable, but their prevailing impression was that it all came from the Sirkar. 'The Government gives us every possible thing that we can want,' a Hindu Jat NCO, Ramji Lal, wrote home to Punjab in late 1915, 'the arrangements are perfect ... Nowadays we Jats are treated with such respect by the Government that it is beyond words.'

'It brought water from my eyes and nose'

In April 1915, several Indian battalions – including the 57th Wilde's Rifles with the Afridi officers Arsala Khan and Mir Dast – discovered all too late that there was one piece of trench warfare equipment they desperately needed but did not have: gas masks.

The Second Battle of Ypres started in Belgium on 22 April. Like First Ypres, the battle was German-initiated, yet it had no comparable offensive strategy for a breakthrough; it was a limited local attack as the eastern front remained the German priority. The Allies did not know this, instead treating the attack as an emergency requiring rushed counter-attacks to save their position in the west. Arsala Khan, Mir Dast and the rest of Wilde's Rifles were summoned with the Indian Corps' Lahore Division from the Indian sector in France to reinforce the far left of the BEF line, north of Ypres. They marched over the Franco-Belgian border on the night of 24–25 April in pouring rain along slippery cobbled roads. They took their place, footsore, in the wide Indian line that counter-attacked outside Ypres in broad daylight at two o'clock on the 26th, over rolling farmland and before their British artillery had had time to locate either the new German front line or any of the artillery they were up against.

Arsala Khan, Mir Dast and the Afridi of Wilde's Rifles, along with Indian companies to their sides of the Queen Victoria's Own

Corps of Guides, the 40th Pathans, the 47th Sikhs and the 129th Baluchis, never reached the German line. They went forwards in rushes only to be mown down by Germans who had been missed by their preliminary bombardment, either machine gunners or artillery batteries behind, whose exploding shells tossed some Hindus and Pukhtun 70 feet into the air. 'The Lahore Division had failed – to do the impossible,' as the 129th Baluchis' regimental history put it. By three o'clock hundreds of Indian casualties lay strewn across no man's land, mixed up with the Lahore Division's British troops who had attacked with them, the survivors lying low or crawling back to their trenches. One of the first wounded Indians to get back was the Afridi Arsala Khan, finally found by a German bullet after six months on the western front, while Mir Dast lay out unharmed ahead of the Indian trenches.

It was then that the air above the German line began to turn yellow-green. Jets of vapour streamed up from the parapet at intervals along hundreds of yards, forming a thick cloud that gently rolled on the breeze low over no man's land. This was chlorine poison gas. Its effect was to over-stimulate lung fluids to prevent oxygen intake – death by drowning.

The Indians' British officers had warned them of poison gas on their march into Belgium, after the Germans had opened Second Ypres using it against French and Algerian units. 'Precautionary orders were issued that should gas be used against us a moist handkerchief or flannel should be placed over the mouth. Soaking the handkerchief in urine was recommended,' a British officer of the 47th Sikhs recalled. Indeed, Arsala Khan, Mir Dast and the other independent Pukhtun troops might have heard of poison gas from the reports of the Italo-Turkish War of 1911–12 that had reached their tribal areas before 1914.

But all this was of little use when the BEF had no gas masks. 'The most they could do was to cover their noses and mouths with wet handkerchiefs or pagris [turbans],' remembered the 129th Baluchis' commanding officer John Hannyngton, looking out from the Indian trenches at the men still in no man's land. 'In a few minutes the ground was strewn with the bodies of men writhing in unspeakable torture, while the enemy seized the opportunity to pour in a redoubled fire.'

As the Indian and British troops who could walk began bolting back from no man's land in mass panic, Mir Dast out with the remnants of Wilde's Rifles kept his calm. His first reaction to the gas was to stay still, holding his breath and pressing his face into the muddy farmland, hoping it would blow over. It kept coming, however, and Mir Dast breathed it in. 'I inhaled the gas, say, for eight or ten seconds,' he later estimated, 'and that was enough for me. It brought water from my eyes and nose. There was a choke in the throat, and I felt giddy.'

Mir Dast scuttled back to the Indian trenches, where he sat down and told another Afridi to pour water over his head. He sat for several minutes gathering himself in this way with his eyes shut. Then, on his own initiative, he returned to no man's land amid the thinly lingering gas to help men who could not get back by themselves. 'I found that all the British officers and the Indian officers superior in rank to myself on the spot had either been killed or wounded,' Mir Dast said. 'I saw soldiers belonging to different units aimlessly running about here and there.' In the dying light he organised some of them to keep up a covering fire as he led others forward to bring bodies in, risking his life again and again under fire.

'With a party of men, I removed the bodies of the officers who had been killed, and took eight British and Indian wounded officers to a place of safety. We worked the whole night.' These were Mir Dast's actions at Second Ypres (on a day his deserter brother Mir Mast rested at an Istanbul hotel) for which he was awarded the Victoria Cross, the second Indian Muslim recipient after Khudadad Khan at First Ypres.

Mir Dast was pulled out of Belgium with the Lahore Division on 1 May. 'This gas gives me no rest,' he told another Afridi, 'it gives me great pain.' But it seems despite his gas wounds he chose to stay on duty to march around 40 miles back to the Indian sector in France, stumbling and slipping with the remnants of Wilde's Rifles along the wet cobbled roads under fire from German howitzers. 'It was a toilsome march,' wrote Captain Stewart Blacker, temporarily with the 57th from the Queen Victoria's Own Corps of Guides. 'Shells burst ... and the stricken countryside reeked with their smoke and fumes ... The men had not yet recovered from the exhaustion of fighting, many were in some degree still gassed'. Once Blacker, Mir Dast and the rest had returned to the Indian sector on 2 May, they had marched a total of eighty-five miles since 24 April and come, Blacker said, 'to the limit, so we thought, of human endurance'.

It appears that Mir Dast remained on duty in the Indian Corps' trenches in France until June, when he received a nasty shell wound to the left hand. He was evacuated to the English south coast as one of the 14,000 Indians from the western front treated there in the Indian Army hospitals. These were the main gathering places for men of Indian Expeditionary Force A across regimental boundaries, where they daily discussed what western front service meant to them – in Mir Dast's case, as a Victoria Cross recipient, with the King-Emperor himself.

'Here the ladies tend to us as a mother tends her child'

Mir Dast was taken to the Brighton Pavilion. Like the other Indian Army hospitals in England, it was still under War Office management with Indian government and charitable support. The hospitals' care had improved even on that for the Indian troops in France in late 1914. They had everything from spotless wards, modern operating theatres, X-ray machines and leg muscle electro-therapy rooms to orthopaedic departments, laboratories and well-stocked kitchens, all with the customary regard for the Indians' religious and social customs. They had indoor gardens with divans and outdoor gardens with benches, as well as their own influx of Indian Soldiers Fund gifts at the Indian troops' request, whether illustrated magazines, the board game halma (the best-selling American variation of checkers), cricket bats and balls, or sets of dominoes. In addition, shows were put on with Indian actors, dancers, pianists and other musicians, and with screenings of Charlie Chaplin films.

'I received the kindest of treatment, and we have full liberty and every facility in respect of observing our prayer times,' said Mir Dast of the Brighton Pavilion, where he had his own room and a wheelchair for when his gas wounds made him too tired to walk. 'We are very well looked after,' agreed Isar Singh, a wounded Sikh of the 59th Scinde Rifles writing home to Punjab from Brighton. 'Do not be anxious about me,' he added, 'men in hospital are treated like flowers.' Another Sikh wrote to his father about the multi-lingual nurses, both British and Indian. 'Here the ladies tend to us, who have been wounded, as a mother tends her child. They pour milk into our mouths, and our own parents, brothers and sisters, were we ill, would only give us water in a pot ... The ladies even carry off our *excreta*, so kind are they ... They wash our bed clothes every week and massage our backs when they ache from lying in bed.'

The Indian nurses at the Indian Army hospitals in England in fact included Mahatma Gandhi's wife, Kasturba. She was one of the hospitals' auxiliary care workers, having volunteered from Britain's Indian diaspora at the war's outbreak. 'Mrs. Gandhi was particularly anxious to see that no Indian patient suffered or felt embarrassed on those delicate questions of caste distinctions,' recalled Daya Ram Thapar, a twenty-year-old Indian medical student at Edinburgh University who worked alongside her, as the same kind of volunteer. 'She undertook to look after the feeding of seriously ill orthodox patients and often used to clean their utensils if they objected to being fed by non-Hindus.' Thapar also worked next to the Bengali poet Sarojini Naidu, renowned as the 'Nightingale of India'. Among the wounded Indians, he noticed, 'Mrs. Naidu was hankered after as she had a pleasant smile for all and spent her time reading and writing their letters to the homefolk'.

The quality of the medical care at the Indian hospitals in England ensured that mortality rates were minimal, at around 1 per cent or lower. Meanwhile the British government arranged for full observance of funeral and burial rites for the hospitals' Indian dead, with Hindu cremation pyres on Patcham Downs, five miles from Brighton, and to the west in the New Forest by the coast; the ashes were cast into the English Channel. Muslim soldiers' burials took place at the Shah Jahan Mosque at Woking, south of London, in a specially created cemetery approved by its senior Muslim cleric.

The hospital care for the Indian patients in England was of course substantially intended to help maintain British prestige through favourable reports. 'This kindness shown to our soldiers in England is of priceless value', Charles Hardinge presumed in April 1915 with Punjab and India's other recruitment grounds in mind, 'for it is all retold at length, and possibly with exaggeration, in the villages, and only tends to increase our prestige in this country, and also the attachment that the lower classes have to the Sirkar.' The hospitals in England were the stuff of imperial propaganda. The British brought in a throng of writers, painters, photographers and cinematographers to record the medical care as a clean spectacle of comfortable beds, smiling patients and relaxed recovery. They promptly publicised this veneer in numerous newspapers, picture postcards, commemorative booklets and cinema newsreels, all to help persuade the world how ready they were to act in their gallant colonial subjects' best interests. But the propaganda papered over the hospitals' underlying truth: prestige dictated strict British control of the Indian patients as racial inferiors, much like in the cantonments of pre-war British India. Above all, the Indians were forbidden from sexual contact with white English women. British Army sentries and police therefore secured the gates of the Brighton Pavilion and nearby Indian hospitals, and rolled out barbed wire along the tops of their perimeter walls. The Indian patients were allowed out only under official supervision, for a stroll on Brighton beach or sight-seeing tours to London.

There was bitter resentment. 'This place is a very large prison,' Ram Kirshan Thapa, a wounded Gurkha, wrote in July 1915 at Brighton's Kitchener Indian Hospital. In October another Gurkha patient, at an Indian convalescent depot by the New Forest, felt the British treated him like an animal. 'For exercise, we get about as much as a little pig does in the yard in which he is kept. We are not allowed to say even a single word to the English people. We are permitted to walk 100 yards to the sea, but neither to the right hand nor to the left. If anyone is seen talking to a woman, young or old, he is severely punished.' 'Has not God given the individual a right to go about and talk to others as he likes?' protested one Indian sub-assistant surgeon at Brighton, Jagu Godbole; his boiling anger at the racial discrimination led him to attempt murdering his British hospital commandant, only for his pistol shot across the commandant's office to miss.

To Walter Lawrence, Kitchener's chief inspector of Indian troops' medical care in France, whose remit included those hospitalised in England, it was clear that discontent among them was rife. He heard how wide-ranging their grievances were over the months of 1915 on his tours of the Indian wards in England. He found that the false rumour of the Indians' sacrifice ahead of white troops at First Ypres persisted, while gripes very much of 1915 related to the Indian regiments' casualties in France wrecking their pre-war equilibrium, with the majority of fellow villagers and familiar British officers out, and outsiders in. 'The Sepoys have been accustomed to look upon their regiment as a family,' Lawrence reported to Kitchener in summer 1915 of patients who were original members of the Indian Corps:

they have lost the officers whom they knew, and the regiment, which formerly was made up of well-defined and exclusive castes and tribes, is now composed of dissimilar elements. The 15th Sikhs is now composed of men taken from nine different units ... In many Battalions, when a Sepoy is asked whether he wishes to go back to his regiment, he knows that it is a regiment commanded by officers whom he does not know and composed of men with whom he has no caste or tribal affinity ... The further the Sepoy gets away from his adopted family the regiment, the more he longs to get back to his own family.

As pre-war personal bonds were broken in a battalion, sepoy patients had particular anguish over new British officers they did not know and had not built up favour with, who might hand promotions to casualty replacements from other regiments. 'The officers are strangers and will not listen,' said one sepoy of the isolation he had felt in France without 'my own Commanding Officer ... before whom I might complain.'

The deepest grievance Lawrence heard among the Indian patients in England in 1915, however, was the fact of having to go back to the front in France. This concerned the rule imposed at First Ypres suspending the pre-war right for Indian wounded to go home if they chose, and compelling all lightly wounded to return to their battalion once they had recovered in hospital. Having originated of course to deter self-inflicted wounds at First Ypres, the rule had continued in 1915 to boost the Indian Corps' fighting numbers, with only the badly wounded allowed to go home at British discretion.

The Indian patients' vehement objection to the rule was simply that a man honourably wounded had discharged his duty to the Sirkar and therefore should be free to choose to go home, as of old. They commonly spoke of the denial of this pre-war right as *zulm* in Punjabi or *zālém* in Pushtu, meaning something unfair, cruel or oppressive. 'I cannot do the double' was their expression when they told Lawrence with a shake of the head that going back to the front line was too much for those already wounded. Behind this charge of *zulm*, naturally, was their desire to go home. 'The chief characteristic of all the Indians who have come to Europe,' Lawrence was sure, 'is their intense love for their homes. They are a very domestic people, and it is clear to me that they are not suited for long campaigns at any great distance from India ... The one over-ruling influence on the morale of the Indian Sepoy is the intense longing to get back to his family.'

Their longing for home could be all the more fraught depending on the nature of their letters in hospital in England from their families. 'The Sepoys await these letters with great anxiety,' Lawrence saw, 'and unfortunately these letters have brought news of plague, cholera, famine, of disputes about land, and of domestic worries connected with marriage and infidelity.' To make matters worse for the Indian patients, he added, 'prices in India have been very high, bullocks have died owing to the drought, and many of them have sustained heavy losses at home. All this affects their spirits.' As Lawrence noted of one Indian soldier's own words of despair at his domestic misfortunes: 'That enemy plague has laid low my whole family and I am out of my mind ... Well, no man can fight against our merciful God ... there is nothing for it but patience.' Cruelly, in 1915 the Indian troops had no home leave from France, India being deemed too far away for it; only their officers with King's Commissions could take periodic leave from France to England, like British Army officers.

Aside from the Indian patients' service grievances and painful family worries, there was one subject they talked more happily of to Lawrence: the people of France. 'They have a very strong liking for the French, who have treated them very kindly, and have shown them that they regard them as their equals,' Lawrence gathered throughout 1915. In the villages in France where the Indians had been billeted on local families during rests from the trenches, their hosts had welcomed them as liberators from the

Germans much like the people of Marseilles had in September 1914. These French families had invited them into their kitchens for drinks by the stove, cooked and washed for them, and given them money as parting gifts. 'The people freely opened their doors to us,' Mir Dast said of the 57th Wilde's Rifles' billets. 'They simply loved us ... They treated us as if we were so many members of their families.' 'The French people regarded Indian soldiers as their own brothers,' a veteran of the 15th Ludhiana Sikhs, Mitt Singh, remembered in old age. 'They had a great respect for us,' thought another Sikh veteran, Dukh Bhanjan Singh. 'They were our best friends.'

The Indians had reciprocated in their billets with kindnesses of their own. Some regimental bands gave concerts with their Punjabi drums, wooden reed-pipes or Scottish Highland bagpipes, while other men helped out around the home or farm, for example swinging axes to chop wood or sickles to harvest wheat. It was with the French families that the Indian troops learned most of their spoken French, picking up enough by mid-1915 for French to be a language of command in some Indian companies where new British officers did not speak their men's own language.

The most significant thing the Indians learned in their billets, however, was that the French were not ruled by foreigners like they were. As a result of feeling treated as equals to white men by French families – contrasting sharply with the British way in pre-war India – many had fresh thoughts about their status as British subjects. 'We felt that the French people were so lucky and enjoying their freedom,' said Mitt Singh of the 15th Sikhs after the war. 'So we also felt that India should be free.'

Such thoughts, however, did not translate into any Indian mutiny in France or England. Rather, they encouraged the Indian troops to seek a better deal with the British. Their priority remained keeping their job to maximum advantage, which increasingly meant on improved, more equal terms – not least of pay. 'The Sepoy, especially the Sikh, is frankly a mercenary,'

Lawrence concluded. In all his conversations with the Indian patients, the Sikhs were the most insistent on better pay as a fair return for their sacrifices while on European service; it was only the Gurkhas who did not push the point. Lawrence alerted Charles Hardinge to this in early 1915, and the Viceroy set the cogs of Indian bureaucracy in motion to approve by August for all Indian troops on European service (meaning both in France and at Gallipoli) not only a 25 per cent pay rise and 50 per cent pension rise effective from the date of landing in theatre, but also a bonus of 100 rupees handed in cash to every wounded soldier disembarking at Bombay.

'I am perfectly certain that this is a very wise precaution,' Hardinge said of the improved financial package, 'for it is essential at the end of the war to have a contented army returning to our shores.' Moreover, to help soothe the domestic worries of the Indian troops in France, Hardinge secured a new Indian law in 1915 that barred civil legal proceedings from going ahead against soldiers serving overseas in their absence. Lawrence kept the Indian troops in hospital in England informed of these financial and legal developments, which he told Hardinge were 'very useful to me in my conversations with the men' and were 'greatly appreciated' by them.

In order to restore their term of service allowing the wounded the right to choose to go home, the Indian patients in England took matters into their own hands. They decided the best means was collective representation by petitions to the King-Emperor. At the Brighton Pavilion, Mir Dast personally submitted one of the petitions, his opportunity coming with George V's visit to the Pavilion to bestow his Victoria Cross medal.

Before the medal-giving ceremony on 25 August in the Pavilion garden sunshine, Mir Dast was asked by the India Office to write a petition for anything he wanted as an extra reward for his bravery, and to present to the King when they shook hands at the ceremony. The expectation was that he would ask for money, a promotion or land, but Mir Dast decided to stand up for what he knew the Indian patients in general wanted. 'I have no son that you might give him a jemadari,' Mir Dast wrote in his petition. 'But this is my request, that when a man has once been wounded, it is not well to take him back again to the trenches. For no good work will be done by his hand, and he will spoil others' also.' The British, however, would not budge. Their national need for as many men in the field as possible was too great, and the right to choose to go home remained suspended for the Indians.

'Just as fish are caught in a net'

By summer 1915, there was no indication of how long the Indian infantry in France and England would be kept for the western front, and they felt trapped. In the Indian hospitals, there were a few Gurkhas and other Indian soldiers who in total despair and depression committed suicide – Walter Lawrence reported their bodies being found, but said no more (the British in fact did not provide 'shell-shocked' Indian soldiers with any psychiatric hospital care as they did for British, such as Craiglockhart hospital in Scotland which Wilfred Owen and Siegfried attended). A significant minority of sepoys who lacked the will to fight on malingered for a ticket home or an extended stay in hospital. There were Sikhs who fabricated knee injuries, lung problems and losses of hearing; others, including Dogras and Garhwalis, used toxic seeds and berries to induce inflammations or turn their urine red. But malingering was a dangerous game because those caught were imprisoned.

Indian self-inflicted wounds briefly reappeared in Belgium at Second Ypres among a few hundred fresh drafts from India, who shot themselves in hand, calf or foot. They had not felt the deterrent effect of the Indian executions and imprisonments at First Ypres, and there was a false rumour among them that lightly wounded Indian troops could once again choose to go home. James Willcocks sternly taught them otherwise, imposing hefty prison sentences so that the practice ceased as quickly as it had in 1914.

As for desertions in France, the numbers were negligible. Around thirty Indian troops are known to have deserted to the Germans in 1915 beyond the Afridi who went over in March with Mir Mast; no Indians are known to have deserted into free France or England as British soldiers did. So far as the official list relates, of the Indian deserters in total on the western front in 1915, 95 per cent were independent Pukhtun, indicating that desertion among troops from British-ruled territory remained unattractive because of the consequences at home. The 5 per cent of known Indian deserters in France from British India were Sikhs and Hindus. They included in February a Hindu NCO of the 41st Dogras named Hardas Singh, in an extremely rare case of physical attack on a British officer. Hardas Singh shot and severely wounded his officer Major Henry Barstow before making off over no man's land. His and Barstow's accounts of the incident suggest that his immediate motive was revenge. Barstow had recently given evidence against him at a court martial in France for indiscipline, resulting in his demotion to a lower grade of NCO.

The majority of the Indian infantry in France, however, served with low rates of indiscipline. Indeed, from October 1914 to September 1915, a higher proportion of the Indian Corps' British troops were convicted at courts-martial than Indian. In March, for instance, 0.5 per cent of the corps' British troops were convicted, as opposed to 0.05 per cent of the Indians. 'Dissensions might well be expected,' Willcocks wrote in July in a confidential report on his Indian troops to Buckingham Palace for George V, 'but it is extraordinary how little there has been.'

What, then, was sustaining the Indians' will to serve obediently? It was primarily their pursuit of pay – many sent regular remittances home and saved up their extra earnings in Europe – while their food, medical care and charity comforts were of course appreciated. Furthermore, they took solace in daily prayer, and profoundly felt obligations of *izzat* or honour on behalf of King-Emperor, Sirkar, caste, clan or family to carry out their military duties. 'Show great zeal in your duty,' Mir Dast VC at the Brighton Pavilion told a fellow Afridi, 'be faithful, and eat the salt of the Government with loyalty.' 'I now expect to return to the front at any moment, as I am quite recovered,' Subadar Muhammad Azim Khan of the 57th Wilde's Rifles wrote to his father in June from Brighton's Kitchener Indian Hospital. 'Everything is in the hands of God. As He has kept me in safety so far, so I hope He will continue to do so ... I will fight to the end for my King, and will have no hesitation in sacrificing my life.' For another Punjabi Muslim, Jemadar Sultan Shah writing home from France, 'our caste has got to win a name by serving Government ... We get our livelihood here all right, but what about our *izzat*? The whole object of military service is to raise the reputation of one's caste, and that is what we have to do.' 'It is necessary for men not to behave like jackals,' a Hindu Rajput also wrote home thinking of his caste, 'the son of a Kshatriya does not show his back on the field of battle.'

In the eyes of one Gurkha writing home in October 1915, the Indian troops' grim predicament on the western front ultimately involved an acceptance of their inability to go home combined with a persistent professionalism. 'We have been caught just as fish are caught in a net,' he pondered. 'Now what I hope is that since I have eaten the Sirkar's salt for so many years and have cheerfully fought so many fights and have come here to conquer land for the Sirkar, I shall not be beaten. The government will be victorious and I shall gain reputation and my parents too will become famous, and if I am killed my name will go down in posterity.'

It was precisely these kinds of commitment that were needed for the Indians on the western front to persevere through their toughest twelve days of 1915 – in the Anglo-French offensives.

'AS WHEN THE LEAVES
FALL OFF A TREE'

The western front's great tactical conundrum was how to break through the enemy's trenches. Breaking into the first line was one thing, but it was quite another for attacking troops to push on and capture a strategically meaningful zone of the enemy front miles wide and deep against defensive fire coming from several sides, let alone secure it and then break through into the countryside beyond for victory. In 1915 the BEF made its first attempts to break through, launching four offensives in France on the right of the BEF's line: the battles of Neuve Chapelle in March (the same village the Indians had briefly captured at First Ypres), Aubers Ridge and Festubert in May, and Loos in September. They were all fought by Douglas Haig's First Army, as part of wider Anglo-French offensives to liberate German-occupied territory.

The Indian Corps took part in each one of these First Army offensives, going on the attack for a total of twelve days to become one of the BEF's most experienced army corps of 1915. In the process it evolved a new attacking capability for European warfare, an achievement amounting to a tactical revolution as the Indian Army moved far beyond its traditional mountain fighting knacks against independent Pukhtun *lashkar*s. For the Indian troops, their experience of the First Army offensives came down to advancing under heavy German fire or shooting down German counter-attacks. 'Such a scene has been enacted as when the leaves fall off a tree and not a space is left bare on the ground, so here the earth is covered with dead men and there is no place to put one's foot,' a Garhwali, Amar Singh Rawat, wrote home after the Battle of Neuve Chapelle:

So many men were killed and wounded that they could not be counted, and of the Germans the number of casualties is beyond calculation. When we reached their trenches we used the bayonet and the kukri, and blood was shed so freely that we could not recognize each other's faces; the whole ground was covered in blood. There were heaps of men's heads, and some soldiers were without legs, others had been cut in two, some without hands and others without eyes. The scene was indescribable ... Now I have not any sure confidence that I will see you people again; there is nothing but hopelessness.

The Indian troops' medical inspector Walter Lawrence spoke with those wounded in the First Army offensives shortly after they came into the Indian hospitals. Their common impression, he gathered, was that 'they have been in the greatest war that the world has ever known ... They say that all that has been written in the Mahabharat and in the Ramayan is altogether true.'* Lawrence recognised that they had 'gone through great strain and have often suffered severe shock,' and found that their 'tired and bewildered brains' had only 'the vaguest idea ... as to what the war was about'. They told him 'they were fighting against three

---

* The two great epics of Hindu mythology – of royal warrior-gods leading armies of millions and avenging evil – whose stories the Indian recruits had heard at home as children.

Kings, and they often confused Australia with Austria. They had no sense whatever of geography: they had a kind of idea that the Germans were on the East, and they knew that India also lay in the East.'

The Indian infantrymen's personal senses of the First Army's offensives and the war in general were uppermost in James Willcocks' mind as the Indian Corps' commander. In November 1914, when Lord Roberts, the former Indian Commander-in-Chief, had visited the Indian troops in France, he had discussed with Willcocks the question of what could be expected of the Indians at war in Europe. He and Willcocks of course assumed that the Indian troops were physically and mentally inferior to British. But they were equally if not more concerned about the Indians' comparative lack of patriotic commitment to the British cause, and how this gave them less motivation to fight the Germans than more nationalistically driven British soldiers.

Roberts, with his experience of Indian soldiers going back sixty years in Afghanistan and elsewhere, advised Willcocks that given the Indians' lower stake in fighting the Germans, there was ultimately only one way to maintain their willingness to do it: they must be exposed to battle less than British troops. 'No one has a higher regard for them than I have,' Roberts told him, 'but they have their limits. Up to that they will do anything and face anyone; beyond it they cannot go.' Willcocks' duty, Roberts said, was to keep this view of the Indians before the higher command because 'if they were to be employed without discrimination it would end in failure'.

Willcocks entirely agreed with Roberts. From his almost daily talks with the Indian troops into 1915, he felt more deeply than any other British general their feelings on western front service. 'Blood is thicker than water,' he said of British compared to Indian commitment to the cause in Europe, the Indians fighting out of their own particular 'sense of duty to an alien race'. 'The Indians cannot be treated as pure machines,' he thought. 'You will not get from them their best, unless they recognise that they are understood ... you cannot expect a ship to keep up full steam when the engineers and stokers are lying shattered in the hold.'

Willcocks therefore made it his mission to do what he could to make his superior commander for the First Army's offensives – Haig – use the Indian infantry sparingly. The lower the Indian casualties, he believed, the better the Indians would feel and the more willingly they would carry on serving. 'Allowance must be made for their ways of thought and feelings,' Willcocks insisted. His approach, however, was seriously out of kilter with Haig's, so much so that in September it would cost him his command.

'The air seemed to be one huge scream'

The BEF's inaugural offensive strike by Haig's First Army went in on 10 March. The Indian Corps provided half the assault troops to the right of the British IV Corps, and attacked out of its own sector it had held since 1914 in the Pas-de-Calais. Haig's hope was to breach a 1.5-mile-wide stretch of German trenches in front of Neuve Chapelle village, before pushing on to capture the high ground three miles ahead, the Aubers Ridge, which overlooked German Army railways and the occupied French city of Lille.

Preparations for the attack were much as Haig had envisaged before 1914 for European battle, with high commanders and staff needing to develop complex battle plans on paper at headquarters far from the front line. Willcocks, however, took a relatively slim part in the Indian Corps' planning for 10 March, disinclined by nature to engage in such cerebral soldiering and unprepared for it by staff training or experience. During the fortnight leading up to the battle, he went on leave in London to see Winston Churchill and other acquaintances. In the days after his return to France on 4 March, he tended to head out from Indian headquarters at Hinges château to talk with his troops as usual. He therefore

delegated the Indian planning for the Neuve Chapelle offensive
almost entirely to his well-trained Indian General Staff officers.
The master-brain among them was his Chief of Staff, Havelock
Hudson, the old favourite of Haig's in pre-war India. In 1911
Haig had in fact described Hudson as 'a first rate fellow, absolutely trustworthy and keen for the good of the show. He is not
p.s.c. but is first rate notwithstanding'.

Under Haig's close guidance, the main emphasis of Hudson's
planning for the Indian Corps' half of the Neuve Chapelle attack
was destroying German front trenches by preliminary bombardment. The Indian Corps had British artillery totalling 150 field
guns and heavy howitzers for the job, mostly its pre-war guns
from India. They had tens of thousands of shrapnel and high
explosive shells made in British factories on Kitchener's orders
since the war's outbreak. It was a conglomeration of gunnery over
twenty-five times as powerful as any seen in the Indian Army's
pre-1914 small wars against Pukhtun *lashkar*s. As for the assaulting Indian troops, they received intensive instruction so that each
one had a definite responsibility either in quick-moving, rifle-
firing, grenade-throwing skirmishing groups to win ground, or in
trench digging parties to secure it. They also had clearly defined
objectives, which were pointed out to them on accurate maps
of the German positions made from a new British intelligence
source – aerial photographs taken by state-of-the-art cameras on
reconnaissance bi-planes.

Willcocks' most significant part in the Neuve Chapelle planning, meanwhile, was very nearly to pull the Indians out of the
battle. He had been greeted on his return from leave in London
with the news of the twenty-three Afridi deserters of the 58th
Vaughan's Rifles led by Jemadar Mir Mast, and it made him
panic. It seemed like a sign to Willcocks that the Indian troops'
limits Roberts had warned of might have been reached, meaning
they might be so tired of trench fighting they would not advance
in the imminent offensive. Willcocks shared his doubts with Haig

in person on 4 March, suggesting emotionally that the Indian regiments should not be used. After listening impassively, Haig calmly advised Willcocks 'it would mean the end of the Indian Army if their officers said they could not undertake an offensive strike', and gave him twenty-four hours to think it over. In his characteristically cool turn of diary phrase, Haig put it mildly in writing that Willcocks spoke in a 'strain which displeased me' – 'the keynote of all the work is *offensive action*'.

The next day Willcocks' mood had swung the other way: he now told Haig 'the Native Regiments will fight well'. This change of tune followed his discussion with Havelock Hudson on the Indian preparations for the Neuve Chapelle offensive, whose thoroughness gave him a new confidence in the part the Indian troops were prepared to play. 'Hudson had worked out all plans and orders with such scrupulous care that when the battle commenced I felt it was already half over, for each and all knew what was to be their share in it,' Willcocks later wrote.

In the early morning light of 10 March, the Indian Corps' preliminary bombardment hit the German trenches before the village of Neuve Chapelle as planned, for thirty-five minutes without a second's pause. 'Most dreadful sound, the air seemed to be one huge scream,' wrote James Barnett, the doctor of the 34th Sikh Pioneers in the Indian front line as the shells smashed down ahead, blasting German barbed wire, parapets and bodies high into the air. Another British officer of the 3rd Gurkhas said it was 'an indescribable din' like 'standing under an enormous railway bridge, over which thousands of express trains were passing at lightning speed'. The Gurkhas were the lead Indian assault troops alongside Garhwalis. Together their companies used their initiative during the bombardment to move up and out of their trenches, crawling forward on their bellies to reach their objectives all the quicker. They had to keep so low because many of the shells flew flat above them. When one Gurkha raised his head, it was swept off by a passing British shell.

Once the bombardment lifted, the Gurkha and Garhwali skirmishers rushed forward without hesitation, leaping into the obliterated German trenches to bayonet and grenade the shell-shocked survivors. They then knocked out some untouched German machine gun posts in a brewery on the outskirts of Neuve Chapelle, the guns inside having been concealed from the reconnaissance bi-planes and British artillery, but now silenced after a Gurkha charge led by Arthur Tillard, a wily veteran of the Anglo-Afridi small war of 1897–8 and the senior Indian regimental officer on the spot. The Gurkhas and Garhwalis went on to storm the village, fighting from house to house, entering through broken windows or shell holes in the walls, firing through doors and lobbing grenades up the stairs. By late morning they had captured Neuve Chapelle as planned by linking with the British IV Corps, whose men cheered the Gurkhas marching German prisoners through the streets and handed them cigarettes. In the early afternoon the Indians secured the village by digging a trench on its far side in farmland, over half a mile from the original Indian line, and the second wave of Indian assault troops came up behind them.

Seven miles back at Indian Corps headquarters at Hinges château, Willcocks had been waiting anxiously by his telephone connected with the front trenches for the first news of the Indian assault. When it rang, 'it was one of the moments I often live again,' he wrote:

'Practically all our first objectives captured.' 'Hurrah!' I shouted, and with such energy that, as the French women at the back of the house afterwards told me, they thought a bomb had burst inside. And so it had! The bomb was ... the story that the cables would bear throughout the world, viz. that the Indians, led by British officers, could drive Germans from their own deliberately selected entrenchments.

At that point, however, the offensive began to break down. In the late afternoon of 10 March, the leading Indian second wave units were ordered by their brigadier, the former commandant of the 106th Hazaras Claud Jacob, to wait for the British IV Corps' troops to come up on their left. Yet these were delayed into 11 March, largely by communications problems as their telephones connecting the front line with headquarters in the rear had been cut off by German shells landing on the wires. All day on the 11th, therefore, Indian reserves including the 15th Ludhiana Sikhs and 47th Sikhs waited in Neuve Chapelle village or behind it for orders to go forward which never came, leaving them exposed to German shelling. They sought cover in the semi-destroyed dug-outs of captured German trenches, ruined houses or new trenches they dug for themselves.

The Hindu diarist Thakur Amar Singh saw the Sikhs as he stood out of the way on a street corner. He had no active part in the battle, his odd-jobbing duties as an aide-de-camp remaining almost professionally pointless as ever; in fact much of his time in 1915 was free for him to go to London with the Indian princely staff officers, to drive about the West End in the Maharajah of Rutlam's Rolls-Royce or drop by the Savoy Grill. Yet he had ridden up to Neuve Chapelle village to see something of the battle, arriving on 11 March just as the Sikh battalions' wounded from the German shelling were heading back through the streets, bound for hospital. 'I watched them empty their magazines and throw all the ammunition in the ditch,' Amar Singh remembered. 'Some even took their bandoliers full of ammunition and threw them with a sigh of relief.' By nightfall the German shells had reduced to rubble much of the village, which was still held by Indian troops. They saw its ruins overnight in the flickering light of buildings set ablaze by the shells. The church burned the brightest, illuminating skeletons in the graveyard whose churned-up coffins had been thrown open.

The First Army's advance had still not resumed by first light on 12 March, when a Bavarian division counter-attacked in an attempt to throw the Indian Corps back across the half-mile of ground it had won. The Bavarians appeared out of a wood in mist in grey greatcoats and *pickelhauben*, the Prussian-style spiked helmet, charging straight at the new Indian front trench before Neuve Chapelle. 'The Indian troops had a real taste of killing,' wrote Willcocks of Gurkha and other Indian machine gun and rifle fire that stopped the Bavarians at 60 yards, much like the Indians had shot down the Turkish attacks at Suez in February and Gallipoli in July. 'It was like a hot-weather dust storm in India that looked as if it must pass over us; but at the very moment of reaching us, it was as if a fierce rain had suddenly extinguished it,' one Indian soldier told Willcocks. The Indians shot around 5000 Bavarians, over double their own casualties in the entire battle. 'Nothing was to be seen but heaps of dead and wounded Germans,' recorded *The Indian Corps in France* (1919), an official history written by the corps' press officers, of the scene in front of the Indians after the Bavarian attack. 'Piles of wriggling, heaving bodies lay on the ground, and the air resounded with shrieks, groans, and curses ... For hours afterwards wounded Germans continued to crawl into our line.'

During the day of 12 March the First Army's advance finally resumed. But Indian and British troops alike could not get across no man's land in the face of multiple German machine gunners who had come up as reinforcements, improvising new posts the British artillery failed to target accurately at short notice. By dark, Willcocks had heard enough of Indian charges failing against these, and of Indian reserves marching to the front line only to be shelled on the way by German batteries the British artillery had also missed. 'The wearied troops,' he wrote, 'were getting done up after their trials of two whole days without rest.'

To save Indian casualties, Willcocks cancelled any more Indian assaults to continue the offensive – a bold step against the express wishes of Haig, who had repeatedly ordered Willcocks to keep trying regardless of loss. With the Indian Corps exempting itself, Haig was forced to call off the battle, icily remarking afterwards, 'Willcocks is no support whatever when operations are in progress.' Willcocks, however, appeared to Haig 'as pleased and proud as can be!' following the battle, positively glowing at the Gurkhas and Garhwalis' success on the morning of 10 March and the slaughter of the Bavarians on the 12th. 'If we did not get as far as we had hoped to do, we taught the Huns a very sharp lesson,' wrote Willcocks. 'As far as the Corps was concerned we had shown that Indians will face any enemy.'

The Indian wounded at Neuve Chapelle between 10 and 12 March totalled some 1500, around a fifth of the British total after the British IV Corps had attacked in larger numbers against stronger German defences and reinforcements. Once the wounded Indians had reached their hospitals in England, Walter Lawrence was taken aback by their spirits. 'I have never seen a greater change in my life,' he thought. 'The men are cheery and smiling ... bright and confident. This change has struck everyone. In many cases men who were obviously disinclined to return to the front, now express a wish to get back as soon as possible. They have seen the German dead, and they all seem anxious to have another go at them.'

'The purring of a multitude of gigantic cats'

Haig's next First Army offensive strike came on 9 May at the Battle of Aubers Ridge. It was full of Haig-inspired innovations to improve on Neuve Chapelle. He decided to attack on a wider front, 10 miles from end to end, with the Indian Corps in the middle (attacking a little south of Neuve Chapelle village, and on the right of its usual sector) and the British I and IV Corps on either side. This was partly to probe more widely for German weak points, and partly to dilute the effect of German reinforcements who would have to spread out more. Then the British artillery was to focus less on the German front trenches, giving more attention to targeting strong-points deeper in the German position, to help assaulting units keep up their momentum. To the same end, the assaulting companies were to attack with more firepower in their hands than the rifles and grenades they had had at Neuve Chapelle, from mortars and machine guns to new portable French-made light artillery Haig called 'bomb-guns'. Furthermore, the assault troops were not to wait for units held up at their sides to develop the attack – something Haig especially regretted about Neuve Chapelle after the second wave of Indian infantry had done so on 10 March, gifting the Germans more time to gather reinforcements – but to push on rapidly.

Again Willcocks' Chief of Staff Havelock Hudson was the Indian Corps' lead planner, under Haig's gaze. Hudson ensured that the assaulting Indian troops were meticulously prepared, including Garhwali and Gurkha crews with the new French bomb-guns. The Indian Corps' British artillery also had more firepower, up from 150 to 180 guns with more heavy howitzers.

But when it came to the preliminary bombardment on 9 May, short at forty minutes at first light on what was a bright spring day, the Indian units in the front line did not hear 'one huge scream' as they had two months earlier. The bombardment this time was audibly weaker and stop-start. The British artillery in fact achieved just a quarter of the accuracy and intensity of Neuve Chapelle, a catastrophe caused by a number of unforeseen technical problems. Its gun barrels had become worn from intensive use at Neuve Chapelle, reducing accuracy. To make matters worse, its batteries had many dud shells due to manufacturing defects from the primitive stages of mass production; their target-finding up to 9 May had been hampered by visibility constraints in cloudy and wet weather; and their new fire-plan, trialling more widespread shelling of the German position, took too much fire away from the German front line. Meanwhile the Germans had strengthened their front trenches in light of their Neuve Chapelle experience, re-designing them to be more shell-resistant. They were now deeper with loopholes moved right down to the bottom of the parapet, for machine gun muzzles to poke out at ground level.

Therefore when the Indian assault troops – men of the Meerut Division's Dehra Dun Brigade – began creeping ahead into no man's land during the preliminary bombardment, they could barely do so for their own shells falling short. Then on rushing forward at zero hour at 5.40 a.m., they saw a very different sight to the opening minutes of Neuve Chapelle: the German front line was almost completely intact.

'There could never before in war have been a more perfect target than this solid wall of khaki men, British and Indian side by side,' as the diary of the German 57th (Duke Ferdinand of Brunswick's) Infantry Regiment described its machine gunners' ground level view. 'There was only one possible order to give – "Fire until the barrels burst."' The Dehra Dun Brigade fell in heaps, 'cut down as if by an invisible reaping machine,' wrote F. E. Smith, the Indian Corps' press officer at the time, 'the sound of the fire from a distance resembling the purring of a multitude of gigantic cats'. The only troops of the Dehra Dun Brigade to reach the German line were a few Gurkhas who discarded their rifles and darted from shell hole to shell hole up to the enemy wire, sprinting along it until they found a gap, then charging through with their *khukuri*s drawn, the last that was seen of them.

Willcocks met Haig for a First Army corps commanders' progress report over lunch at a village three miles back. He reported that the Indian Corps could attempt a second assault but not a third if the high casualties continued, at which Haig left the room in silence. Haig suspended the entire offensive at six o'clock, left with no other choice as it became clear that all three of his attacking corps could make no advance with their generally defective artillery. The pause was only temporary, though, as Haig put his First Army's Indian, British I and IV Corps back on the offensive six days later at the Battle of Festubert, starting on 15 May, the

Indian Corps attacking slightly further south than on the 9th. Again Haig innovated, trying to improve on experience. This time he opted for a longer preliminary bombardment of forty-eight hours, to allow for gradual corrections for better accuracy, and he concentrated the bombardment on a narrower front to increase its effect. He tweaked the infantry plan of attack by switching to a night assault; the cover of darkness might help the Indian and British troops get forward under fire.

Havelock Hudson prepared the Indian striking units as before, innovating himself by adding more mortars and machine guns to them. But the bombardment and infantry assaults failed all the same. The British artillery from 13 May still had problems with sighting in bad weather, besides running low on high explosive shells for parapet-blasting. Then the cover of darkness did nothing for the Indian assault troops early on 15 May as the Germans turned night into day with flare lights, shooting the Indians down as soon as they moved into the open.

The Battle of Festubert wound down by 25 May, after none of the First Army's corps had made any appreciable progress for want of effective artillery. Since January the Indian Corps had lost a total of 1500 Indian soldiers killed and 6400 wounded, a casualty rate whose effects among his Indian units were obvious to Willcocks. 'Those who came first plainly show they have had enough and personally I know they <u>have</u>,' he wrote to the Viceroy, Charles Hardinge. Through June, Willcocks reflected on his Indian troops' offensive performance, before reporting confidentially to Buckingham Palace: 'Homesick beyond words, cut off from their friends and relations; with no personal bias in the quarrel, they have freely given their lives, health, and most cherished ideas for England. Can man do more?' The 'marvel' of their western front experience, he went on, was 'how much they have done and how willingly they have done it ... His Majesty knows well ... how our numbers have been reduced, and in my opinion the work of the Indian soldiers has been beyond praise.'

In early July Willcocks resolved to give his Indians a summer rest from the trenches. He wanted in particular to allow the Muslims to fast in peace over the month of Ramadan. 'They will appreciate it beyond words,' he reported to the Palace, 'it will be a signal mark to them that even in the midst of war we appreciate their Religion, so dear to them. It is such a good opportunity of doing them a good turn.'

Willcocks gained the Indian infantry's release from the trenches for Ramadan by sombrely telling Haig they were too tired to resist a determined German attack. Although two weeks later, on 25 July, Haig was surprised by Willcocks' change in mood after Indian wartime recruits had started arriving in significant numbers. 'Now Willcocks is in the highest spirits and says that he now has the finest force that ever left India for a campaign!!' Haig noted. 'I wonder how long he will retain these good spirits.'

'In Flanders ... for better or for worse'

Lord Kitchener was determined in 1915 to keep the Indian infantry in France indefinitely. He wanted them to share in the BEF's eventual victory, to maximise it as an achievement of a united British Empire, thereby strengthening post-war imperial unity. 'Even if only two men are left, one shall be the Lahore and the other the Meerut Division,' he said at the War Office. In August the Government of India agreed. The Viceroy Charles Hardinge and his Commander-in-Chief Beauchamp Duff viewed an early withdrawal of the Indian infantry as likely to be interpreted as the Indian Army failing in Europe, creating a politically undesirable impression of defeat in British India. 'We ought to regard the Indian troops in Flanders as there for better or worse,' Hardinge wrote. Indeed, he ruled out the Indian Corps' return home until the end of the war. As he was struggling to maintain India's traditional pre-war internal security ratio of two Indian soldiers to one British, he refused to have the Indian infantry back from

France in the absence of his pre-war British garrison; doing so, he thought, would raise the number of Indian troops domestically to an unsafe level.

Duff, meanwhile, told Kitchener he had the Indian wartime recruits to replace Indian Corps casualties on the western front for months to come, having enough by September to lift the Indian battalions' official strength up from their pre-war standard of 750 men each to 1000. 'The Indian Army must see to a finish their role of supporting the British Army in the field in France,' Duff affirmed. He had in fact by the end of August found a total of 30,000 casualty replacements for the Indian Corps, double its battle casualties since 1914.

On 1 September, therefore, Kitchener ordered the Indian Corps to spend a second winter on the western front. Willcocks was equally satisfied that his Indian troops should go nowhere. 'I am dead against their leaving France at all,' he wrote on the 2nd. Willcocks was persuaded by Kitchener's approval of exchanging his poorest-performing Indian battalions for fresh units from Egypt. He singled out the 15th Ludhiana Sikhs, for example, as a 'disappointment' for their relatively high rates of self-inflicted wounds in 1914 and malingerers in 1915. Furthermore, Willcocks agreed with Kitchener and Hardinge that there was no need to remove the Indian infantry from the western front on account of the coming winter weather, given that they had withstood the winter of 1914 better than British troops. As Hardinge put it, 'they can stand the cold of Europe as well as we can resist the heat of India,' adding, 'the idea that the Indian troops should not be exposed to another winter of trench warfare [is] absolutely wrong'.

Kitchener did not consult the Indian troops themselves over his decision to keep them on the western front for a second winter. On making it, he was reassured by Willcocks' view that they were in 'fine fettle' and 'going well' after their summer rest over Ramadan. By September, the Indian Corps' Indian battalions had anything from a few dozen to a few hundred Indian ranks who had landed in France in 1914, the rest being drafts of 1915. They also each had a dozen or so of their pre-war British and Indian officers with experience of trench warfare since 1914 – such as the 40th Pathans' Charlie Campbell, the 57th Wilde's Rifles' Arsala Khan and the 129th Baluchis' Harold Lewis – who held their companies together as regimental memory men, founts of trench craft to guide the uninitiated. The Head Indian Censor in France, Evelyn Howell, a pre-war Government of India diplomat assigned to Waziristan and a leading translator of Pushtu poetry, was sanguine in autumn 1915 about the Indian troops' mood having read more of their letters than anyone else. 'Never since the days of Hannibal,' he reflected, 'has any body of mercenaries suffered so much and complained so little as some of the regiments of Indian infantry now in France.'

'A thousand and more reasons for doing nothing'

In August Douglas Haig earmarked the Indian Corps to take part in his First Army's fourth offensive strike. This would start on 25 September and focus on the Loos coal mining area several miles south of the Indian sector, which was still in the Pas-de-Calais by Neuve Chapelle. Haig allotted the Indian infantry a diversionary role for the battle's first day. They were to attack the German trenches from their line to the right of Neuve Chapelle village, over flat farmland at Moulin de Piètre, and well to the left of the main attack by British Army corps among the slag heaps of Loos.

Haig asked Willcocks to prepare by choosing a specific area of German front for the Indian Corps' assault, and writing a paper on why it was preferable to other local options. Willcocks, however, was still minded to avoid Indian casualties if he could. He handed Haig a paper objecting to an attack anywhere on the Indian Corps' front, citing insufficient artillery, a conclusion based on Indian experience during the First Army offensives in May. 'A most discouraging document,' Haig bristled. 'He had a thousand and more reasons for doing nothing.'

The paper proved Willcocks' undoing. It prompted Haig on 3 September to lose patience with him at a First Army corps commanders' conference with other generals. He snapped that Willcocks had 'no initiative and tactical skill ... anyone who wrote that appreciation is unfit to command'. 'He personally insulted me,' Willcocks said of Haig's sharp words, 'and I asked him if he no longer trusted me to relieve me of my command.' Haig did just that. 'I had gone to the Conference in high spirits,' Willcocks wrote. 'I was leaving it, little caring whither I went. I should have to depart before even I could shake the hand of many brave Indians, officers and men, my lifelong friends. I felt I must perforce go without saying a word, lest any spark of ill-feeling should be revealed.'

Willcocks exited to London in shock that his command had ended 'with a greater suddenness than I had imagined possible'. A few days later he wrote to Hardinge to explain what had happened. 'The man who has served under Sir Douglas Haig's command and who has any opinions of his own,' Willcocks told him, 'will know as I now do how <u>impossible</u> a thing he had undertaken. For 37 years I have laboured to do my duty and it is really in defence of my brave Indian soldiers that I have fallen at last.' Ultimately, Willcocks felt, 'in a war like this the individual is nothing', and he had paid the price for deciding for himself 'how much can or cannot be demanded from the Indian soldiers ... Personally it is a terrible blow to me, as a soldier financially but I am glad I had the moral courage to go.'

Haig replaced Willcocks with Charles Anderson, a British Army officer of whom he had a higher opinion. Anderson was a pre-war Army in India general of the Royal Artillery, aged fifty-eight and slightly older than Willcocks. He had been one of Willcocks' brigadiers in the Mohmand small of war of 1908, and had arrived in France in 1914 in command of the Meerut Division, which he had led through the offensives of Neuve Chapelle, Aubers Ridge and Festubert. He had adapted better than Willcocks to European battle, grasping the combining of infantry and artillery with a more scientific approach and aggressive attitude.

Once installed at Indian Corps headquarters to plan for the Loos offensive, Anderson did not have Havelock Hudson, who was freshly promoted by Haig to command a BEF British division. Instead Anderson's Chief of Staff was the younger and more energetic Ronald Charles, a thirty-nine-year-old officer of the Bengal Sappers and Miners who before the war had graduated from the Indian Staff College, and from 1914 had served on the Indian General Staff in France. Charles was an efficient officer typical of the Indian Corps headquarters by September 1915. It had developed – as had its two subordinate Indian divisional staffs – into a smooth-running machine packed with competent, relatively young Indian and British service officers with pre-war staff training and a year's learning on the western front.

The Indian Corps' plan for Loos was its most sophisticated yet, showing how much it had evolved for European warfare. Anderson and Charles worked closely with the Meerut Division's new commander Claud Jacob, the former commandant of the 106th Hazaras who had led the second wave of Indian assault units during the Neuve Chapelle offensive; Jacob had indeed turned into the Indian Army's outstanding senior officer in France, simply 'excellent' Haig thought. On the Indian Corps' front nearly a mile wide, Anderson, Charles and Jacob, with Royal Artillery advisers, tried to correct the errors of the earlier Indian offensives' preliminary bombardments. Conforming to a wider First Army fire-plan, the Indian bombardment was extended over four days from 21 September (twice the duration of the bombardment at Festubert in May) to achieve a better spread of fire both on the German front line and on positions behind. And the barrage – from the Indian Corps' largest yet collection of artillery pieces, some 200 guns with tens of thousands of improved shells in from

British factories over the summer – was not only of increased intensity, but also of increased accuracy. This was down to a new system of BEF target-finding involving British Royal Flying Corps spotter bi-planes with light radios, which relayed the map coordinates of where shells fell. In addition, the Indian General Staff innovated by slotting field guns into the Indian front line to blast the German parapets at point-blank range. The Bengal Sappers and Miners prepared preliminary firepower of their own, digging a gallery beneath the German trenches to lay a one-ton explosive mine.

The Indian assault units of Gurkhas, Punjabis and others, meanwhile, were readied with an unprecedented array of modern equipment for an Indian operation, all provided by Kitchener. They had more Vickers heavy machine guns, Stokes mortars and ring-pull grenades than before, plus new French-made light machine guns, all of which they used to support the preliminary bombardment. In the process they waved turbaned Indian dummies above their trenches, to trick the Germans into coming out from cover too early and into the fire. To help the Indians' assault, they had new phosphorus smoke bombs to throw to cover their movements, and special coloured flags to wave signals to Royal Flying Corps spotters with radios in bi-planes directly above, the quickest means available to pass back messages from the infantry to the artillery.

Moreover, the Indian Corps was to use British chlorine poison gas for the first time. The gas was brought in long cylinders into the trenches by British technicians, for release on the wind towards the German line alongside the Indian assault troops. To protect the Indians themselves against it as much as any more German gas, they had new BEF gas masks, primitive by the war's later standards of respirator masks. They were just cloth head-bags with large, round glass eye-pieces and a short protruding beak. 'I believe the British have been converted to our religion and are trying to imitate our many Gods,' a sepoy joked as his company tried them on. 'I have already seen many "Hunumans", and "Ganesh" will shortly follow.'*

Much as for the earlier offensives of March and May, the Indian companies had specific instructions to win ground in skirmishing groups or to secure it with trench digging parties, once again using detailed maps of the German trenches made from aerial photography. But there was a fundamental change to their tactics: they were told to take full advantage of any gap they found. 'Assaulting troops are not to delay in the enemy's front line trenches, but will push on and capture the supporting line,' read Jacob's order to the Meerut Division on the point. 'Bodies of infantry are not to halt if portions of the line are held up but will press on.' Jacob was teaching a lesson he had learned at Neuve Chapelle on 10 March when late in the day his second-wave Indian assault troops had waited for the British IV Corps held up at their side, and lost their chance to win more ground before German reinforcements closed in.

By zero hour at 6 a.m. on 25 September, the Indian Corps' preliminary bombardment had largely wrecked its target front trenches. At the British officers' whistles, the Indian assault units raced forward in their gas masks under phosphorus smoke cover, throwing grenades and firing heavy and light machine guns, while the Bengal Sappers blew up their mine to obliterate the trenches above, and the chlorine gas was released. The Indians captured much of their targeted first and second German trench lines, and the 8th Gurkhas some of the third. Here, however, the Gurkhas encountered a new attacking hitch.

Through the earlier Neuve Chapelle, Aubers Ridge and

---

* As told to James Willcocks, and seemingly charting the Indians' take on the development of the British gas mask, from the original 'Hanumans' or basic cloth-hood gas masks of mid-1915 (referring to the Hindu deity Hanuman, who took the form of a monkey) to the predicted 'Ganesh' gas mask. This anticipated the next step in British design, surely a longer mouth-piece (Ganesh, of course, being the Hindu god with the face of an elephant).

Festubert offensives, the Indian Corps had solved the problems of breaking into the German trench system, but now at Loos, having broken in deeper than before, it faced a new problem: how to keep gains made by units that had got ahead of others and lost touch with them (the problem experienced in August by the 6th Gurkhas at Gallipoli on the summit of Sari Bair overlooking the Dardanelles). As the most successful Indian assault troops, the 8th Gurkhas became the most isolated. Alone in the third German line without any close fire support from other battalions, the Gurkhas were forced back or taken prisoner, suffering 481 casualties. 'So strongly had a continued offensive been insisted upon that it is not surprising that troops who already were so full of offensive spirit should have been misled into going forward too fast and too far,' Charles Norie, an Indian brigade commander at Loos, remarked of the 8th Gurkhas. 'In doing so, they omitted to examine thoroughly the enemy's trenches for lurking Germans [and] did not sufficiently deal with possible approaches for counter-attacks.'

The Indian Corps' diversionary role at Loos did not go beyond the first day. The battle itself lasted into October among the coal heaps to the right of the Indian sector. It petered out with marginal gains by British divisions, mostly of wartime recruits, many of whom ran back in panic on their first exposure to German fire.

At the Indian hospitals in England, meanwhile, Walter Lawrence noticed an upturn in Indian spirits as he had in March after the Neuve Chapelle offensive. 'The Indian wounded who come into hospital are very pleased with themselves,' he reported to Kitchener in October. 'The Indians did very well in this last business,' adding, 'they did too well and went too far' – a reading of the battle he had gleaned from the Indians themselves, hinting at their understanding of western front tactics. The Indian Corps had in fact pierced the German defences at Loos further than any British corps in the year's earlier offensives. This was a hard-earned achievement through experience, with every indication that the Indian infantry would improve further in the BEF's offensives to come in 1916.

But this never came to pass. Developments in the Islamic world meant that within weeks of Loos the Indian Corps ceased to exist, asset-stripped of its British and Indian components, soon to be scattered across three continents.

Four

1916

14

'THE PASHA OF BAGHDAD'

'General Nixon's Force is now within measurable distance of Baghdad,' the Prime Minister Herbert Asquith announced to Parliament on 2 November 1915 in his regular war update, referring to Indian Expeditionary Force D in Ottoman Iraq and its commander John Nixon, formerly of the 18th Tiwana Lancers. 'I do not think that in the whole course of the war there has been a series of operations more carefully contrived, more brilliantly conducted, and with a better prospect of final success.'

Asquith's omens were born of how spectacularly Force D had burst out of the Basra area since May. As Asquith told Parliament, it had pulled off 'a brilliant series of land and river operations' in mid-1915, 'both on the Upper Euphrates and the Tigris'. On the one hand, Force D had advanced 100 miles up the Euphrates west of Basra. Its 12th Indian Division had gone on an improvised amphibious adventure on the river's brown waters and surrounding marshes to capture the Turkish garrison town of Nasiriyah. This was no easy victory but a triumph of grit and guts, largely by well-trained pre-war battalions of Gurkhas, Pukhtun and Punjabis. In oppressive humidity under the beating sun, the thermometer rising to 43°C, they had made steady progress in a flotilla of Royal Navy gunboats, river steamers, barges and bellums (the flat-bottomed, narrow local wooden craft). At times they had dragged the craft by rope through shallows as the troops waded ahead on foot, mosquitoes whining about their ears and Nixon barking instructions through a megaphone from his steamer's crow's nest. By night to a cacophony of croaking frogs they had held trenches dug outwards from the river banks, and, after days of sporadic fire from Turkish outposts and Iraqi tribal marauders, on 24 July had stormed Nasiriyah town's stubbornly defended Turkish trenches. On the other hand, on the Tigris north of Basra, Force D's 6th Indian Division had gone over 300 miles by October, also by flotilla with resilient pre-war battalions. Making deft tactical manoeuvres in the desert combining frontal and flank attacks, they had captured a series of Turkish garrison towns up to the river town of Kut.

Force D's advances up the Euphrates and Tigris alike had ostensibly been a means of securing Basra. This justification had been argued by the Government of India, and waved through at each step by the India Office, yet with a lurking, ever-growing ambition to take Baghdad to bejewel the British Occupied Territories in Iraq and strengthen the case for post-war annexation. The guiding official mind was the Viceroy, Charles Hardinge. His viceroyalty was set to expire in March 1916, and he was increasingly attracted to rounding it off with a famous victory, sealing his place in the sun of the British Empire's annals – as he confided in a friend, 'I hope to be the Pasha of Baghdad before I leave India!'

In August 1915, therefore, Hardinge began floating before the British government the idea of a strike on Baghdad. At the time, Force D had around 30,000 mainly Indian troops based at Basra and stretched up the Euphrates and Tigris, but Nixon advised Hardinge that these were too few to press on from Kut another 200 miles up the Tigris to attack and hold Baghdad. Hardinge was loath to reinforce Force D from British India on account of his domestic security concerns, above all a possible declaration of war by Afghanistan as the German mission from Berlin approached Kabul. So he asked London to release the necessary reinforcements for the Tigris, from either Egypt or France. Lord Kitchener blocked Hardinge's request into September, preferring to concentrate the British Empire's forces in the west, and of course ordering the Indian infantry in France to spend a second winter there. However, following the BEF's disappointments at the Battle of Loos, Kitchener's star as a strategist was on the wane, and with it his influence in the Cabinet. And the eyes of Asquith and other Cabinet colleagues who were more attracted to eastern ventures as alternatives to the western front began to fix on Baghdad as just what they were looking for.

By October 1915, the Cabinet was fretting that the Allied war effort looked distinctly lacklustre. That year, while the Allied offensives both on the western front and at Gallipoli had failed, the Central Powers' thrusts into Poland, Ukraine and Serbia had dramatically furthered their conquest of Europe. Furthermore, the Central Powers had been strengthened in September by Bulgaria joining them, opening up a direct rail link between Germany and Turkey; whether or not Afghanistan would follow suit, no one quite knew. To offset the Allied setbacks in Europe, and to bolster British prestige in Afghan opinion, Asquith and the majority of his Cabinet wanted a success to make headlines and appeal to imaginations around the world – Baghdad, to them the ancient city of *Arabian Nights*, seemed the answer. They therefore reviewed Kitchener's refusal of reinforcements from the west for a strike on it, and reversed the decision against his advice. The reinforcements they selected, at Hardinge's suggestion, were on the western front: the Indian Corps' Lahore and Meerut Divisions, seen as the natural choice to join Indian Expeditionary Force D ahead of British divisions. Thus the order came through to the Indian Corps in France on 31 October to withdraw from the trenches and disband for its two divisions to transfer overseas, although their destination was a secret kept in government.

The consequences for the Indian troops on their way out of

France would prove more extreme than they or the Cabinet could have imagined. If there were places in the world worse than the western front, they were headed straight for them.

'Shall we live to return to India? That I cannot say'

On pulling out of their BEF trenches in November 1915, the Lahore and Meerut Divisions sent representatives from all their Indian regiments to Château Mazinghem in France, near Dunkirk, for a royal farewell parade. 'In a warfare waged under new conditions and in peculiarly trying circumstances you have worthily upheld the honour of the Empire and the great traditions of my Army in India,' the Prince of Wales and future King Edward VIII told them, reading out a personal message from his father, George V:

> I mourn with you the loss of many gallant officers and men ... I shall ever hold their sacrifice in grateful remembrance. You leave France with a just pride in memorable deeds already achieved and with my assured confidence that your proved value and experience will contribute to further victories in the new fields of action to which you go. I pray God to bless and guard you and to bring you back safely, when the final victory is won, each to his own home – there to be welcomed with honour among his own people.

The feelings of the Indians themselves at their order to leave France for an unknown destination are virtually undocumented. According to the 47th Sikhs' regimental history, their men felt reluctant to go, with the words of Subadar Harnam Singh supposedly capturing their view: 'We came to defeat the King's enemies. They are not yet defeated.' But the Indians' general mood was probably that anywhere would be better than the western front. For the 3rd Gurkhas, a sense of how they looked back on the land they were leaving is given by a Nepali song of theirs later in the war. 'For fifteen months we fought in France, eating much mud,' they sang,

> The sea-wind blew away the hats from our heads ...
> When I reach Marseilles I cannot count the ships
>   on the sea.
> Shall we live to return to India? That I cannot say ...
> Falling in battle my brothers died by the curse of
>   Kali* ...
> Carrying my friend and brother my body has been
>   wetted with drops of blood.
> In France thus daily they were killed by the guns of the
>   enemy ...
> In the houses of France I found no refuge from the
>   perils of the bullets ...
> The shells of the guns come quickly: where shall I hide?

From early December 1915 at Marseilles, the Lahore and Meerut Divisions boarded their troopships to steam eastwards. They went without their most capable senior commanders and Indian General Staff officers because Douglas Haig – now the BEF's Commander-in-Chief, replacing John French – kept them in France for the British Army as trusted old hands, including Charles Anderson, Ronald Charles, Claud Jacob and Havelock Hudson. By Boxing Day, the last of the Indian infantry's troopships had left France, and the Indian Corps had officially ceased to exist (accordingly the Lahore and Meerut Divisions lost their BEF monikers, becoming known once again by their Army in India numbering as the 3rd and 7th Indian Divisions).

The Indians' troopships from Marseilles stuck close to the coast past Monaco and the snow-topped Alps before heading south

---

* The Hindu goddess, and referring to a fated hour of death.

with views of Genoa and other Italian ports. The Hindu diarist Thakur Amar Singh, with the 3rd Indian Division's staff on the SS *Erinpura*, enjoyed the change of scene. Like everyone else, he passed time by guessing where they were going; was it Gallipoli, Egypt, East Africa, Iraq, India or elsewhere? On another ship, the 40th Pathans' officer Charlie Campbell felt a curious longing for the western front, which was not uncommon among men of long service there who had grown so used to daily trench routines they could think of little else. 'I swear I'd like to be back in those filthy, sodden, freezing trenches,' he wrote to his mother.

As Corsica and Sardinia went by, Amar Singh joined the lookouts on deck, both Indian troops with machine guns pressed against the railings and Royal Marines with heavier mounted guns. They were watching for U-boats, which finally came after them in the Mediterranean south of Italy. The first attack was on the 9th Gurkhas' transport the *Cawdor Castle*, by shell fire from a U-boat's deck gun as the Royal Marines shot back. The Gurkhas leaned over the railings next to the marines, watching the German shells drop short into the sea. 'Their main comment was that there was nothing to fear from such small shells, and that they had experienced very much worse in France,' their British officer Frederick Poynder overheard. The *Cawdor Castle* got away by zig-zagging at full speed, as did Amar Singh's ship. 'Thank God we have escaped,' he jotted in his diary.

On 29 December, however, another U-boat off Crete torpedoed the SS *Persia* carrying several British officers of Garhwali and Gurkha regiments who had been through the Indian Corps' battles from First Ypres to Loos. The torpedo struck at lunchtime, giving them and hundreds of British, American and Portuguese civilian passengers five minutes before the ship sank. Survivors remembered seeing the Indian Army officers on deck desperately fighting to help women and children get away first in the lifeboats as the *Persia* went down, leaning to port. Some of the officers pushed the boats on the starboard side with all their might to hang right over the side for lowering, but to no avail against the lean of the doomed ship. So there was a rush for the lifeboats on the port side, where John Lodwick of the 3rd Gurkhas was last seen furiously pulling up a cricket net that had been arranged on deck for play after lunch, only to droop over the ship's side, tangling with one lifeboat's release mechanism to jam it. Within minutes, hundreds of the *Persia*'s passengers, including Lodwick and several of the other Indian Army officers, among them a lieutenant of the 9th Gurkhas with his wife and youngest child, had drowned.

Meanwhile, the regiments of the 3rd and 7th Indian Divisions, stopping over in Egypt, found out where they were going. Their guesses on their voyage were almost all right as a complicated reorganisation was taking place. The two divisions themselves were going to Iraq, but half of their Indian battalions from France were extracted for postings in Egypt, Aden or East Africa, and replaced by others already in Egypt which had fighting experience since 1914 in France, Suez, Gallipoli, Yemen or Aden. As reconstituted, therefore, the 3rd and 7th Indian Divisions had a new mix of war experience, the majority knowing the western front the best. Their most significant constitutional change was the removal of their several regiments with independent Pukhtun companies, which were not trusted to fight the Turks. Accordingly, the 57th Wilde's Rifles with the Afridi officer Arsala Khan and the 129th Baluchis with Harold Lewis and his Mahsud were among those earmarked for East Africa.

From the last week of December, the 3rd and 7th Indian Divisions' troopships sailed for Iraq down the Suez Canal, to cheers from Australians waving their slouch hats in the trenches alongside. The Indian veterans of France on board had mixed feelings about their redeployment. While longing to return to India, they were very disappointed to learn that their 25 per cent pay increase for European service was discontinued for service in Iraq. Still, they took it for granted that the fighting in Iraq would be easier, of lower intensity and less trench-bound. 'In France, if one fights on the ground one is killed,' commented one Punjabi Muslim, 'but in Iraq, I am told, war is carried on according to the old methods.' The Indians' British officers were not overly enthused by their switch to Iraq, a little miffed that this subsidiary Turkish theatre was something of a relegation from the main German front. On New Year's Eve, in the silence of the Arabian Sea, they kept up their spirits to the strains of 'Auld Lang Syne', toasting in 1916 with champagne.

'Sahib, the blood will not stop running, I am growing faint'

When the bulk of the 3rd and 7th Indian Divisions arrived at the head of the Persian Gulf in early January 1916, one of their first impressions was how shoddy Basra port was. Unlike Bombay, Marseilles, Alexandria and other ports they had passed through since 1914, it had no modern facilities for ocean-going ships – not a single wharf, jetty or pier for unloading, just *mahaila*s, the small local barges, to ferry men and materiel from anchorages in the middle of the Shatt al-Arab to makeshift landing spots among the palm groves. 'Things are in a hopeless muddle,' thought Thakur Amar Singh.

After disembarking to no welcome, the two divisions were presented with a quite different task to supporting the capture of Baghdad. They were too late because by November 1915 the 6th Indian Division had moved up the Tigris on Baghdad alone. It had gone in haste to keep up its momentum since the summer, with its regiments led primarily by battle-hardened British and Indian officers who had been with Indian Expeditionary Force D since 1914, while a large proportion of their sepoys were young Indian wartime recruits. On the 22nd, by the great ancient arch of Ctesiphon on the banks of the Tigris some 15 miles south of Baghdad, the 6th Division had come upon the city's outer defences, a river blockade and extensive Turkish trenches in the desert. Its Indian and British units had captured the first Turkish trench line, but at such heavy cost under machine gun and shell fire they were forced to retreat for lack of reserves. They had tumbled back down the Tigris nearly 200 miles under Turkish pursuit by early December to the town of Kut, where the Turks trapped them by blockading the river and entrenching 30 miles downstream. The 6th Indian Division was therefore under siege, and the new, Cabinet-approved mission of the 3rd and 7th Indian Divisions from France was to rescue it at all costs. Should the 6th surrender at Kut, the Cabinet feared a humiliation the British could ill afford for their prestige in the Muslim world, for they had just decided to give up at Gallipoli and evacuate the entire peninsula, confirming a Turkish defensive victory.

The 6th Division's commander at Kut was Charles Townshend, whose curious career since the 1880s, hopping between the Royal Marines and four regiments of the British, Indian and Egyptian armies, as well as attaché or staff posts in Paris, South Africa and India, reeked to his British peers of a man out for himself. Townshend had compared himself to Napoleon, his idol, as he led the advance up the Tigris to Ctesiphon, and once under siege at Kut, he cursorily took stock of the town's food supplies to estimate that his men would start to starve if not relieved by February 1916. Taking Townshend at his word by field radio, Indian Expeditionary Force D's commander John Nixon had little option but to rush the two Indian divisions from France up the Tigris as soon as possible as the relief force.

'The first thing I noticed,' Thakur Amar Singh, with the 3rd Indian Division, wrote of the desert north of Basra, 'was the awful condition of the country.' Having grown used over the past year to the green fields of the Loire, the Pas-de-Calais and England on leave, he was struck by the lack of Iraqi cultivation, and the monotony of the level, treeless, white-grey sandscape. 'I had hoped we had seen the last of mud in Flanders,' he went on, 'but not a bit of it.' This was surely a repeated thought among the Indians from the western front, most of whom had to march the 200 miles from Basra to the front at Kut, slogging through driving rain that soaked them to the skin and turned the ground into sticky ankle- or knee-deep mud that sucked boots off.

'We are absolutely tied down to the river,' Amar Singh wrote of their march up the Tigris. 'Why we have not got a light railway running from Basra, I cannot understand with all the resources of India behind us.' Southern Iraq in fact had neither railways nor modern roads, and Force D had hardly any of the flat-bottomed river steamers needed to navigate the Tigris. Furthermore, the Indian regiments from France and Egypt had been shipped to Iraq almost entirely without their horse, mule and cart transport. So their baggage was commonly carried behind them on river barges, dragged by ropes in the hands of Iraqi labourers. Lacking tents, night after night the Indian troops slept in the open shivering on the mud, dreaming of their billets in French villages or hospital beds in Brighton.

In the Kut area from January 1916, the 3rd and 7th Indian Divisions formed Force D's new Tigris Corps, yet this bore only a passing resemblance to the old Indian Corps at the Battle of Loos. On leaving France, the Indian infantry had handed in most of their BEF trench fighting equipment as provided by Lord Kitchener: their ring-pull grenades, phosphorus smoke bombs, trench mortars, French-made light machine guns and bomb guns, all and more were gone. So too, of course, was their old Indian Corps commander Charles Anderson with its best senior commanders and staff. Nixon therefore appointed himself as the Tigris Corps commander, and under him were improvised divisional and brigade headquarters, largely filled with a mixed lot of senior British officers from Egypt, Iraq and British India, none of whom Haig wanted in France. Worse, the Tigris Corps had just a quarter of the artillery pieces that had backed the Indian Corps at Loos, with a tenth of the power because it had no heavy guns. Indeed, its artillery was incapable of much accuracy for want of western front-style target-finding systems, such as up-to-date air reconnaissance with radio relays.

Then the Tigris flooded by Kut in early 1916. This limited the Tigris Corps' options for attacking the Turkish trenches below the town to advancing straight along particular avenues of desert that were the least flooded, dispelling possibilities of more imaginative manoeuvres to achieve surprise.

From January to March, Nixon rushed the Tigris Corps' two Indian divisions from France into repeated frontal assaults to relieve Kut before its food ran out – in the midst of which Townshend reported he had more food than originally thought, having overlooked the townspeople's grain reserves, thus buying more time. For the Tigris Corps, the scenes on the battlefields before Kut resembled the worst Indian days on the western front in spring 1915 at Second Ypres, Aubers Ridge or Festubert. The sepoys charged in wide lines over the open, flat, muddy desert at trenches that had barely been bombarded by their weak artillery, and against which the main weapon they held was the rifle. They were shot down in their thousands by Turkish machine gunners in a series of failed actions known as the Battles of Sheikh Sa'ad, Wadi, Hanna and Dujaila. By the end of March on the Tigris, the Indian battalions' knowledge of trench warfare from France had been substantially wiped. Their few intact pre-war Punjabi Muslim and Sikh companies of the Frontier Force, who had not served in France and had come to Iraq with their old mountain warfare skills, were destroyed as a result of charging the most persistently. There had been little the Indians' senior commanders and staff could achieve with the firepower available. Yet what fleeting opportunities they had for taking Turkish positions of strategic significance, they threw away because of their poor coordination of brigades to exploit weak points.

Many of the Tigris Corps' Indian casualties had seen the best of the front line medical care in France at the Battle of Loos, where the Indian trenches had been linked to motor ambulances by a light railway in order to evacuate the wounded rapidly. The Tigris Corps had nothing of the kind. Its Indian Medical Service units had hardly any stretcher-bearers, doctors or field ambulances, so that from January to March most of the Indian wounded were left out in the open for days in the cold and wet, some to be robbed and murdered by local Iraqis of the Bani Lam tribe. To evacuate the wounded, there was only a small number of army transport carts from India, horse- or mule-drawn and without suspension springs. These carts inevitably gave a rough ride, agonising for men with broken limbs, and deadly for those with untended stomach wounds, haemorrhages or spinal injuries. Some of the Indian wounded found the carts so unbearable they clawed their way to the sides and flopped themselves out, choosing the alternative agony of crawling to the only field hospitals five miles back. The hospitals had beds for 250 wounded men in the early months of 1916, but had to deal with 4000. Maimed soldiers lay outside them untreated, slumped in gluey mud. They had little or no first aid, at best dressings that went unchanged for up to ten days, bringing on gangrene and maggots.

The field hospitals would not have become so choked had there been enough hospital boats on the Tigris, but there were none. Into March, therefore, the Tigris Corps' wounded from the Kut battlefields were taken away slowly downstream on Indian Expeditionary Force D's few river steamers, or dragged on barges behind – not that it made much difference: both were devoid of medical facilities. On board the steamers, British insult was added to Turkish injury by doctors of the Indian Medical Service. They were so hidebound by pre-war customs of prestige that they gave the British wounded priority in the cabins and covered areas. This left many Indians crammed on bare decks, laid in rows often without shelter, drenched in winter rain that sent pools of their excrement washing down the decks from patient to patient. On one of the barges with similar conditions, the supervising British doctor, Andrew Cook Young, said he felt 'ashamed of himself as a man, ashamed of himself as a doctor, and ashamed to look the miserable dying men in the face'. As Cook Young saw, a number of the Indian wounded died of neglect on their Tigris boats before they reached Basra, where the survivors were transferred on to ships bound for Bombay hospitals.

'The Indians did not understand the change of conditions after France,' wrote the Tigris Corps' official war correspondent, the pre-war Indian military reporter Edmund Candler, who from January walked the banks of the Tigris near the Kut battlefields. 'It was as if the Sirkar had forgotten them,' he sensed of the Indians' feelings about their change in medical fortunes:

> In France the Sirkar had never failed, and they thought now that appeals would bring some kind of god out of the machine. They clutched at one's feet imploring small services it was impossible to render ... 'Sahib, I am cold; cannot I have a blanket or a coat?' 'Sahib, the blood will not stop running, I am growing faint.' To hear them imploring ... crying out ... was pitiful.

Word of the shocking medical care quickly spread up to the front line so that the walking wounded frequently chose to stay there rather than risk the field hospitals. One Muslim NCO of the 125th Napier's Rifles, Sher Khan, stayed in the front trenches for a week after being shot through both jaws, an arm, a lung and a knee; only then did he finally limp away in search of first aid. A wounded Indian officer of the 9th Bhopals spoke the minds of many in saying to his British officer, 'With the regiment I have a chance, but in hospital I should certainly die.'

During pauses in the Tigris Corps' attacks between January and March, the Turks made a succession of tactical retreats over 10 miles back up the Tigris towards Kut, to stronger and drier trench lines 20 miles from the town. The Tigris Corps crept after them in equal measure, its Indian regiments digging trenches as they went. This meant arduous trench holding work, all too familiar to those with western front or Gallipoli experience. Once again they constructed parapets, traverses, dug-outs and fire-steps, they patrolled no man's land, and they hunted for snipers, who were often concealed under brown Turkish Army blankets in the desert. Many of the Indians were well qualified to judge the daily Turkish shelling of their trenches, reckoning it to be as accurate as the Germans' in France, yet less frequent and with lighter shells. Some days the veterans of Second Ypres called poison gas alarms, but these were false: their noses were full of the stench of putrefying corpses in no man's land.

All the while the supplies sent up to the Tigris Corps' front line were a trickle compared to the torrent the Indians had known in France. The men lost weight with their meagre rations of hard, stale biscuits and rotten *atta* (wheat flour), half-cooked with sodden firewood and the red-brown Tigris water. In any event, their rations were often thieved by the roving Bani Lam. Some British officers and Indian troops turned to scavenging blood-soaked scraps from the haversacks of the dead, and even ate desert weeds. Needless to say, practically none of the Indians' food and comforts from the Indian Soldiers Fund and other charities on the western front had followed them to Iraq. And worst of all, they lost touch with home. In France the Indians had received their mail every week without fail, but now it was once a month if they were lucky, so poorly was the Kut front integrated into the Indian Army's postal network.

For the few Indian letters sent home from the Tigris Corps in early 1916, there were no censor-translators in Iraq as in France to preserve them. The war correspondent Edmund Candler, however, heard something of what the men would have written. One Hindu Jat sepoy, Candler wrote, 'lamented in his sad fatalistic way, in his far-away voice, that he had ever been taken away from France'. As another sepoy veteran of France put it, 'the misery we are enduring here is as great as the comfort we enjoyed in France'. The common refrain Candler heard from Indian lips was 'In France, Sahib ...' before praise of the western front flowed. Indeed, in comparison to France the Indian troops reviled the desert plains of Iraq they now fought for. Having loved the French, they came to hate Iraqis when they saw the Bani Lam dig up Indian graves to steal the clothes of the dead. 'It passes my understanding why the Sirkar should desire this Satanlike land,' a Muslim soldier remarked to Candler. 'In France men were glad to be out of the trenches for a turn in billets,' wrote Candler, 'but here there were no resources to fall back on ... I heard a regiment that was going to be relieved by another, grumble at having to pack up.'

Thakur Amar Singh remained behind the Tigris Corps' trenches with the staff in camp supervising regimental baggage, but he still saw how the conditions at the front sapped Indian spirits. 'A young soldier of the 47th Sikhs shot himself in the arm when he came to get water but the Gurkha patrol caught him,' he wrote in his diary at the end of February. 'We took evidence and the fellow was sent for trial. I felt for the fellow as he was quite young – about eighteen.' By March in the Tigris Corps' front line, the Indian troops were showing a disinclination to carry on attacking in ways James Willcocks had feared might happen in France but which had barely materialised there. That month hundreds of the younger Indian wartime recruits who now filled the ranks stopped following orders for assaults, staying in their trenches as their British officers charged. Many sought to escape the trenches altogether, taking opportunities in droves to assist the wounded to the rear.

As for the besieged 6th Indian Division in Kut, it fought its own battles. Its men dug 30 miles of trenches, mainly on the north side of town not bounded by the Tigris, and suffered 2200 casualties in keeping the Turks out. Their commander Charles Townshend did not spend time with them as Willcocks had with the Indian troops in France. Instead he remained relatively aloof in a house he chose as his headquarters, from time to time emerging for walks with his terrier Spot. Although Kut had the food for his men to hold out into April, they nonetheless began to starve before then.

Gurkhas apart, the Indians in Kut generally refused on religious grounds to eat what little meat was available – mule, horse and camel – so that the town's grain began to run out sooner than it would otherwise have done. As severe malnutrition and disease set in by mid-April, most of the Indians began meat-eating under duress, with Indian officers leading the way under threat of demotion if they did not set the example. Some Hindus still refused to break caste by eating meat and chose to pre-empt their death by starvation, walking down to the Tigris to stand in plain sight with their arms folded for a Turkish sniper to take them.

In Kut's military hospital, meanwhile, its doctors of the Indian Medical Service worked tirelessly through Turkish shelling and air raids. One of them was Kalyan Mukherji, from a wealthy Calcutta family, who had trained as a junior doctor at Cambridge University. 'The mortality rate in the hospital has soared,' he wrote in despair on 16 April. 'In the last 15 days many have died for lack of food. Of what use is medicine now? There's nothing to eat. People are coming to the hospital because starvation has made them weak. With nothing to give them, how can we help? Apart from that, there are no medicines left either.'

The Tigris Corps' relief attacks resumed in April, culminating in the actions at Sannaiyat against riverside Turkish trenches 15 miles downstream from Kut. Although the corps was boosted by the British 13th Division, evacuated from Gallipoli and in from Egypt, its assaults continued to grind to a halt with heavy casualties in the open desert. It still lacked the artillery to overcome the Turkish defenders, and was hampered by rains and floods. The Indian trenches filled with slimy water up to the troops' armpits; some of the wounded drowned after slipping into the depths, never to be seen again. The weather turned in mid-April, bringing exhausting heat and flies.

Under-supplied and increasingly disease-ridden, the Tigris Corps was coming to the end of its tether. Both Indian and British troops were now running away from Turkish counter-attacks. 'The troops have done all that was possible and are now dead beat,' Thakur Amar Singh could tell. By 25 April, the Tigris Corps had nothing more to give and its attacks were called off. The Cabinet's decision of October 1915 to advance on Baghdad had cost Indian Expeditionary Force D a total of 30,000 mostly Indian battle casualties, 8000 of whom were dead. There were some final relief efforts by alternative means – from a gunboat ram-raid by the Royal Navy through the Turkish blockade on the Tigris near Kut, food supply air-drops into the town by the British Royal Flying Corps, and a secret Cabinet offer of a £2 million bribe for the Ottoman Minister of War Ismail Enver to allow the 6th Indian Division freedom on parole – but they were too little too late. The Turks wanted the unconditional surrender of Kut, and they got it on 29 April, capturing the whole 6th Division in the process, some 10,500 Indian and 2600 British prisoners.

The Turks released 1130 of the Kut military hospital's worst cases, mostly Indian, for return to Indian Expeditionary Force D by river steamer. Thakur Amar Singh encountered them on their way down the Tigris to Basra, and spoke with one Rajput soldier named Virbhan who had a badly broken arm. 'He was literally nothing but skin and bones,' wrote Amar Singh. 'His eyes were bulging out and as I talked to him sympathetically the poor fellow actually cried. He was not strong enough even to talk.'

Amar Singh did his best to comfort others who had been released with Virbhan. 'I assured them all that they would now soon be back in India and with their families, people would look upon them as heroes who have performed great deeds and no one would ever dare to say anything against them.' For the remaining 9000 or so Indians who surrendered at Kut, however, already starved, raddled with dysentery and dispirited, the worst was yet to come as prisoners of war in Turkish hands.

'Inferno'

In the last days of April and into early May in the desert outside Kut, the Turks gathered the 6th Indian Division's prisoners for transportation into captivity. They separated all the British and Indian officers to travel ahead to camps in western Turkey. The officers' journey northwards in the coming weeks was uncomfortable, by river boat, railway, mule cart, donkey and German motor lorry. Along the way they saw many dead Armenians strewn at the roadside or thrown down wells, grim signs of the Turkish government's mass killings. The officers were treated respectfully by their Turkish guards and tolerably fed. But their Indian and British men had a very different experience from May to August. They underwent a horrific 600-mile death march from Kut through the Iraqi desert to labour camps in Ottoman Syria outside Aleppo and in the nearby Amanus and Taurus mountain ranges, which stretched into Turkey up the Mediterranean coast. 'It was like one thing only,' said an Austrian officer who encountered the prisoners of Kut on a mountain road at the end of their march as an army of walking skeletons driven on by Turkish rifle butts, 'a scene from Dante's *Inferno*.'

The march came about because the Turkish authorities did not have enough transport for the captive Hindu, Muslim, Sikh and Christian ranks of the 6th Indian Division, having allocated what little was available to their officers. From Kut, day after day in searing heat and choking dust, the Indian and British ranks suffered horrific maltreatment from Turkish guards, both soldiers and policemen, and from local Iraqi civilians, who appeared from the villages they passed. They were beaten, whipped, knifed, stoned and shot, while their boots, clothes and water bottles were ripped off them. Some were also raped and infected with sexually transmitted diseases.

The prisoners were too weak to resist all the abuse, a consequence not just of their privations under siege but also of how poorly they were fed on the march. They initially had a small boatload of food sent upriver from Indian Expeditionary Force D, which they soon gobbled up outside Kut, the desperate Indian troops fighting each other for it. Thereon they had what the Turkish Army could spare them, chiefly old stocks of its staple biscuit ration – a rock-hard slab five inches long and three quarters of an inch thick, made of coarse flour and husks, sometimes with earth mixed in and often green with mould. Paltry rations of black bread and flour were also available. The Indian prisoners used the flour to make chapattis, which they heated over tiny fires fuelled by dried dung they picked off the desert floor or reeds they pulled from the Tigris. Otherwise they had to barter for food at high prices from their Turkish guards or Iraqis, usually in return for what few pieces of uniform they had left. To drink they had only gulps of the muddy Tigris water, or what they could scoop up in their hands from open village drains flowing with excrement.

The Indians' diet on the march aggravated their existing intestinal infections from the months spent inside Kut. Many of them with gastro-enteritis passed bloody diarrhoea before dropping unconscious to die on the sand, filthy and emaciated. Others who collapsed in the desert crawled into the streets of villages to slump fly-covered in fetid corners, begging for scraps and slowly starving to death. Only a lucky few got any medical care, either from Turkish doctors or from a handful of convalescent Indian Medical Service officers who travelled up from Baghdad behind the main officer group.

The Indians who survived the march the best were regimental groups of old professionals who stuck together as teams to protect one another, bringing on the slowest and feeding the weakest. The men of the 7th Gurkhas did this, their pre-war NCOs filling the place of their officers, and refusing to let their companies break down. The youngest Punjabi wartime recruits fared the worst, lacking the pre-war professionals' levels of training to work for each other. Their groups disintegrated more easily, stumbling on in isolated fragments that much reduced their chances. By August, across the desert between Kut and Aleppo, around 2000 of the marching Indian prisoners lay dead, along with a larger proportion of the British ranks. Some of their corpses were buried by regimental comrades in shallow graves excavated by hand, only to be dug up by jackals at night. Iraqi civilians cleared up a few other dead prisoners from around their villages by slinging them into ravines. But most of them remained where they had fallen in the desert.

From September, the Turks forced the surviving ranks of the 6th Indian Division into hard labour. Their task was to help construct the Ottoman Empire's unfinished masterpiece of pre-war infrastructure, the Istanbul to Baghdad railway. Under the supervision of the railway's German and Austrian engineers, the Hindu and Sikh prisoners were concentrated along the line in the Syrian desert east of Aleppo, in the locales of Ras al-Ayn and Nusaybin. 'Their conditions were truly pitiful,' wrote Percy Walter Long, an Urdu-speaking British sergeant of the Royal Artillery, who was put with them. He saw them daily on the construction sites, labouring from 4.30 a.m. to 6.30 p.m. in gangs, breaking and carrying stone to build embankments and lay track ballast:

They resembled animated skeletons hung about with filthy rags. No tents or other shelter had been provided, and they were living in holes in the ground like pariah dogs ... Scores of them were too sick to move from their holes, and I saw many who were obviously dying, yet I was told that they received no medical attention whatever. I chatted to a few of those men, and as we talked the tears streamed down their faces. These were loyal soldiers of the British Empire, and it was awful to think that this was the end of their service ...

The Muslim, Gurkha and most of the British prisoners from Kut laboured further west on the railway, in the Amanus Mountains in north-west Syria and the Taurus range in southern Turkey. They were the skeleton army the Austrian officer had seen as incarnations of hell on earth. 'We were set to work at blasting and tunnelling,' recalled Muhammad Qadir Khan, a Punjabi Muslim prisoner of the 120th Rajputana Infantry. 'I was weak and not fit for much work, so I was beaten and told to work harder. Nearly all who were on the work were beaten and ill-treated.'

Throughout the winter of 1916–17, the labouring Indian prisoners of Kut were fed just enough to keep them working – bread, beans, meat now and then, and water they had to fetch from desert wells or mountain streams. Yet hundreds died of exposure, malnutrition and typhus. On newly completed sections of the railway, they occasionally saw what the Cabinet's decision to capture Baghdad had ultimately led to for them: a part in strengthening enemy supply lines, plain to see as German rail trucks rattled by carrying artillery, machine guns and other weaponry for the Turkish Army in Iraq.

'This terrible business has been conducted with criminal negligence'

For the Cabinet, the immediate result of the failed push for Baghdad and the surrender at Kut was a public backlash in London against its management of the Indian war effort in Iraq. Indian Expeditionary Force D's dire logistical conditions on the Tigris in late 1915 and early 1916 first became known in British political circles through private contact from its British officers, some of whom had returned to England wounded, enraged and set on bringing to account whoever in government was to blame. Their leading spokesman in Parliament in summer 1916 was Aubrey Herbert, the Member for South Somerset, who had served on the western front and Gallipoli before transferring to Iraq as a Turkish-speaking intelligence officer. Herbert well remembered the Prime Minister's talk to Parliament in November 1915 of

Force D's operations as the war's most 'carefully contrived' and 'brilliantly conducted', with 'a better prospect of final success' than any other. Herbert felt Asquith had been more than economical with the truth, and on behalf of the troops he had seen suffer on the Tigris he was determined to uncover it.

'The storm burst so unexpectedly that the Prime Minister was clearly taken aback by this straight hitting,' *The Times* reported of the questions Herbert hurled in the House of Commons in July. 'Mr Asquith denied that there was a desire to keep anything back. Several Members laughed at this and he shot an angry glance in their direction.' In his climactic Parliamentary assault on Asquith that summer, Herbert demanded an independent inquiry into the war in Iraq. He wanted a categorical report on what had happened to Indian Expeditionary Force D, describing this as 'what we owe to the loyalty of the Indian troops'. Herbert even hinted that if an Indian soldier could be shot by firing squad for not fulfilling his duty, then those most answerable for Force D deserved a similar fate. 'Admiral Byng was condemned and executed on the ground that he had not done as much as he could to damage the enemy,' said Herbert, referring to the Royal Navy officer's famous punishment in 1757 for incompetence at war with Spain. 'I think that judgment on Admiral Byng is an indictment I should like to see fall on responsible people in India.' Edward Carson, the former Attorney-General famed for his cross-examination of Oscar Wilde and now Leader of the Opposition, was a good deal blunter. 'This terrible business has been conducted with criminal negligence,' he told Asquith across the despatch boxes.

Under intense pressure, Asquith agreed to an independent Parliamentary inquiry into Iraq. This was the Mesopotamia Commission, set up in August 1916 to investigate 'the origin, inception, and conduct of operations of war in Mesopotamia, including ... the responsibility of those departments of Government whose duty it has been to minister to the wants of the forces employed'. It was to report in 1917, and would have to answer the question that was on the minds of many Indian troops: if the British had cared for them so well on the western front, why not in Iraq too?

Herbert had in fact spoken in Parliament of 'a great many men in high position now trembling in their shoes' on this very issue. He was thinking of one man in particular at the head of the Indian Army, the man who had said 'I hope to be the Pasha of Baghdad'. Charles Hardinge had a lot of explaining to do.

15

'A TIN FULL OF KEROSENE'

If there was a neutral political centre of Islam in 1915 primed to back a jihad against the British, it was Kabul. The court of Emir Habibullah was the global hub of pan-Islam, a loose movement endorsing the solidarity of the Ummah, or worldwide Islamic community, to rebuff Christian domination of Muslim lands from Morocco to the Dutch East Indies, and save Islam from western corruption. Among the leading radical pan-Islamists at Kabul were the Emir's younger brother Sardar Nasrullah, not merely the Commander-in-Chief of the regular Afghan Army but a *hafiz* (one who has memorised the entire Koran), and influential Afghan mullahs. Nasrullah and the radicals were disgusted by British interference in Afghan affairs, especially a treaty imposed in 1879 subjecting Afghan foreign policy to British approval. To them, the best way to purge their country of British abuses was clear: an Afghan jihad rousing combined army and tribal attacks on British India to trigger a third Anglo-Afghan war, which could force the British into giving up their treaty rights over Afghanistan's foreign policy.

But the authority to call an Afghan jihad rested with Habibullah. Whether he saw eye to eye with his brother and the radicals on jihad had been an open question for years. In 1907 the Afghan court and clergy had been outraged by the Anglo-Russian Convention, a bilateral concord over Central Asia that had restated British control of Afghan foreign policy without consulting Kabul. In response, in 1908 Habibullah had gone to the brink of calling a jihad to take Afghanistan to war with Britain, only to pull back at the last moment. Up to 1914, Habibullah had been outwardly receptive of the radicals' hopes for a jihad yet he had never taken the plunge. As the First World War broke out, rumour had it at Kabul that the radicals' patience with him was wearing thin; plots were afoot, it was murmured, for a coup to replace him with Nasrullah. 'His Majesty ... is sitting on a volcano which may burst out at any moment,' reported the British Agent at Kabul, Malik Talib Mehdi Khan. 'It is a foregone conclusion that someone will ... put an end to his life ... The Mullas are still the leaders of the people and they are bound to fan the fire of fanaticism. Unfortunately a large number of them are residing on our border.'

On 26 September 1915, therefore, when the German mission on behalf of the Sultan of Turkey's jihad – with the Afridi Jemadar Mir Mast and other Indian prisoners of war from Germany's Camp Crescent Moon – arrived at Kabul on horseback from Herat, it had come to the right place. The plan of its diplomatic leader Werner Otto von Hentig, endorsed by his Indian nationalist accomplices including the cosmopolitan revolutionary Raja Mahendra Pratap and the ex-Tokyo University professor Abdul Hafiz Mohamed Barakatullah, was to ally with Nasrullah and the pan-Islamist radicals, adding weight to their ready-made cause for a national jihad to persuade Habibullah to declare one. The chances seemed promising enough as Habibullah had allowed the mission to proceed from Herat with his blessing, and welcomed all its members at Kabul as honoured guests, putting them up in his suburban palace in the walled Gardens of Babur.

The independent Pukhtun tribal areas, meanwhile, were electrified by the news of the German mission. Rumour ran wild; it was said German officers leading a force of 400,000 German and Turkish troops were marching to Afghanistan to invade British India. The tribes were waiting on Habibullah's call to jihad as their Prince of Islam to decide on what their part in the invasion might be. 'Germany is a man running about the world with a tin full of kerosene, throwing the kerosene on everything he comes to and setting it alight,' mulled one Afridi elder. Mir Mast had every intention of returning to Tirah to call the Afridi to arms against the British, which he would indeed do in 1916, finding an audience not just in over a thousand Indian Army deserters who had returned home from British India since the war's outbreak, but also in his brother Mir Dast, back from Brighton bearing his Victoria Cross to continue recuperating from his gas wounds.

In the wider Islamic world as much as in Afghanistan and the independent tribal areas, 1916 was crunch time for the Sultan's jihad. In addition to the German mission to Kabul there were numerous other Berlin-backed jihadist schemes hatching from Iran to the Sahara with German or Turkish agents involved. The men of the Indian Army were drawn into the jihad's chaotic compass more than ever, whether fighting jihadists for their regiments, or entering German service in unprecedented numbers as prisoners of war at Camp Crescent Moon. By the year's end, the Indian troops had played a decisive role in the jihad's fate, the Muslims among them torn between their simultaneous duties to their Christian colonial masters and to their faith.

'Spread out your wares before me'

At Kabul in mid-October 1915, the German mission was driven in a royal motorcade from its quarters in the Gardens of Babur to the royal mountain retreat at Paghman, outside the city, to open talks with Emir Habibullah. Mahendra Pratap began the proceedings at Paghman by presenting the mission's letters of introduction from Kaiser Wilhelm, the German Chancellor and the Sultan. 'I look upon you as merchants,' Habibullah responded. 'You should spread out your wares before me so I can choose whatever I like and leave whatever I do not need.' Out came the Germans' radio alarm clocks and other gifts of goodwill, before negotiations began in earnest. These lasted on and off for weeks as the mission's diplomatic front men Hentig, Pratap, Barakatullah and its Turkish Army attaché Kazim Bey offered money and military assistance from Berlin and Istanbul in return for Afghanistan joining the Central Powers, following the Sultan's jihad and declaring a national jihad against British India. Into December Habibullah did not give any definite answer, leaving the mission guessing; one day he gave positive assurances, the next he backed out of them. The mission also made contact with Nasrullah and the radical pan-Islamists, who told the Germans that public opinion was in favour of jihad and expected it.

Mir Mast was too junior to address Habibullah on behalf of the mission. Instead he worked as Hentig's secret agent on the streets of Kabul, taking instructions personally in the morning at the Gardens of Babur and during the day blending into the bazaars. He helped to rouse anti-British public opinion by handing out a Kabuli pro-German newspaper, *The Lamp of the News* (*Sirāj al-Akhbār*), guest-edited by Barakatullah and with fiery articles by Pratap. He also acted as Hentig's go-between with Nasrullah and the radical pan-Islamists behind Habibullah's back, and engaged in counter-espionage by seeking out the British Agent's informers and bribing them to pass on British intelligence to the Germans. Mir Mast, Hentig wrote, was 'invaluably helpful' in all this, having 'natural talent and astounding cunning'. The mission's Yusufzai from British India of the 129th Baluchis, the cook Said Ahmed, did not go out as Mir Mast did, remaining at the Gardens of Babur to guard Hentig's luggage.

Pratap was otherwise busy laying the foundations for an Indian republic. On 1 December 1915 he announced himself

Life President of a new Provisional Government of India, with Barakatullah as his Prime Minister. Pratap claimed as its adherents several young Indian revolutionaries lately fled to Kabul from Punjab, and incongruously also Mir Mast and the other Afridi with the German mission – it appears not with their consent, because as independent Pukhtun they would scarcely have given it.

Over Christmas, Habibullah seemed to be warming to the German mission, giving Hentig a fine present of vintage red wine and cognac. Then in the New Year he negotiated a treaty with Germany on the understanding that he would join the Central Powers and declare the Afghan jihad they were looking for, subject to 20,000 to 100,000 German or Turkish soldiers arriving in Afghanistan to support it. But on 29 January 1916 he revealed the game he had been playing. At a grand assembly of tribal leaders from all over Afghanistan (the Loya Jirga, only summoned in times of national emergency) Habibullah confounded public expectation that he would declare jihad at last. Instead he passionately argued that in the Afghan people's interests he must remain neutral. He had in fact strung along the German mission to appease Nasrullah and the radical pan-Islamists, always resolute in himself that war with the Allies carried too high a risk of ruin for himself and Afghanistan. His father had been put in power by the British in 1880 to resolve an Afghan civil war, and he was apprehensive that if he spurned them as his family's patrons, they and the Russians might bring the world war to his country and depose him. 'Convey my assurances,' he now charged the British Agent at Kabul, 'in plain and repeated terms that I am a true friend of the British Government.'

For the Viceroy, Charles Hardinge, Habibullah's declaration of neutrality at Kabul came as a profound relief because of the dire implications had Afghanistan joined the Central Powers. Hardinge described British India's border with the independent Pukhtun tribal areas from May to November 1915 as 'in a state of incessant war', referring to the parts north of Tirah where the Mohmand and other independent tribes made no fewer than six attacks into the North-West Frontier Province, inspired by their mullahs supporting the Sultan's jihad. The Army in India's few remaining regiments well trained for mountain warfare had repelled the attacks, but only just. They had been so stretched that the Indian General Staff advised Hardinge that an Afghan invasion in addition would be uncontainable without reinforcements from abroad. Thus did the Indian General Staff's Canadian Director of Military Operations, George Kirkpatrick, say that for the military authorities 'the period of the war during which there was the greatest strain felt in India' was late 1915 while Habibullah bided his time.

By May 1916 the German mission to Kabul had broken up to go its separate ways. According to Hentig, Mir Mast and his other Afridi were 'deeply stirred' when bidding him farewell having gone through so much together since Berlin, adding 'one had come after the other to strengthen his arsenal' by requesting to keep their German rifles. On settling their pay, Hentig awarded medals for 'outstanding performance' to Mir Mast and an Afridi NCO who in France in March 1915 had been the very first of their band to go over to the Germans bearing a jihad leaflet. They got not the Iron Cross for military service, but minor classes of the Prussian chivalric orders of the Crown and the Red Eagle for diplomatic service. Hentig held Mir Mast in such high esteem that as he left Kabul for neutral China to return to Germany via Hawaii, he named his horse for the Chinese leg of the journey 'Mirmast'.

Hentig in fact took with him into China Said Ahmed of the 129th Baluchis, who journeyed on in German pay in favour of returning home to British India where he would be tried for aiding the enemy. They travelled together as far as north-east China, where Hentig negotiated with the British ambassador at Beijing for Said Ahmed's repatriation on condition of immunity from prosecution. The Government of India agreed, preferring to recover Said Ahmed than leave him in German service, a potential source of embarrassment if the Germans made a news story of it. Hentig paid off Said Ahmed, leaving him in British custody in October at the port of Tianjin. Here Said Ahmed boarded a ship for the first time since he had landed at Marseilles with Indian Expeditionary Force A in September 1914, and sailed home.

Back at Kabul, Mahendra Pratap stayed on as Life President of his Provisional Government of India, in mid-1916 scheming a phantom Hindu-Muslim 'Army of God' to invade British India in lieu of the Afghan Army. Mir Mast, meanwhile, had his own plans. For him, the Sultan's jihad was not over. If Habibullah would not fight in its name, he thought, his tribe would have to do it for themselves.

'The Turks will enlist the Afridi'

Before leaving Kabul for Tirah at the end of May 1916, Mir Mast cut a secret deal with Nasrullah. He promised to prepare the Afridi for holy war, while Nasrullah pledged to send him a large sum of money for the purpose, assuring him that the radical pan-Islamists would soon arrange for an Afghan jihad after all. Nasrullah was indeed making similar arrangements with men of other independent Pukhtun tribes. He agreed with Mir Mast that the Indian Army deserters in Tirah were likely recruits for jihad, and the intended funds were largely to pay and equip them once Mir Mast had gathered them in readiness to invade British territory at the forefront of an Afghan jihad. All this was against Habibullah's policy towards the independent Pukhtun tribes, however. To him they were an obstacle to a British invasion, not a first line of attack. As Habibullah put it as an avid reader of war news from Europe, they were 'the trenches and wire entanglements of the fortress of Afghanistan'. In dabbling with Nasrullah, therefore, Mir Mast added the Emir of Afghanistan to the British as an authority he would freely defy.

Mir Mast got home to Tirah in June. He brought as his guests two Turkish officers plucked by Nasrullah from their advisory roles in the Afghan Army to lend credence to him as a messenger of the Sultan of Turkey's jihad. In July, after prayers one Friday at central Tirah's Bagh mosque, the two Turks appeared with Mir Mast holding up behind him a large red flag with the Turkish crescent, as he appealed to an assembly of 5000 Afridi representing most of their clans. He explained that in France, on hearing of the Sultan's jihad, he had deserted to join the Germans as friends of Muslims. He then boasted with a touch of trickery of personal dealings on his travels with Kaiser Wilhelm, the Sultan and Habibullah. 'If I wish it I can have any amount of money,' he stated in light of his connections, 'but all I want and have in view is the welfare of my poor tribe.' He went on to set out his vision of a bright Afridi future in alliance with Turkey. 'It is promised by the Sultan that colleges, schools and arms factories should be opened in the Afridi country, and throughout our borderland our people must be taught the arts of providing their own arms and ammunition and all necessaries of life.' More immediately, he said military employment was now open to the Afridi under the Turkish officers' sponsorship in a new Tirah regiment led by him; its duty was to await a call from Kabul to follow the Sultan's jihad and attack British India. This Tirah regiment was naturally preferable to serving in the Indian Army, he said, because it would have no promotion ceiling for Afridi as was the case in the Indian regiments under British officers. 'The Turks will enlist the Afridi and grant them the ranks of Colonels, Majors and Captains to command their own.'

Many of the listening Afridi were impressed by Mir Mast's agenda of orienting their tribe's external relations towards Turkey. A number showed it over the next few days by bringing gifts of sheep to his house. Then 400 volunteered for his new Tirah regiment, almost all of them Indian Army deserters from British India since 1914, no doubt in sympathy with Turkey but also needing gainful employment. Some of them had just come back from Kabul themselves, having gone in search of work as unemployed Indian deserters to ask Habibullah for special permission to join the Afghan Army. They had left in short order, angrily rebuked by Habibullah. He treated them, said one Afridi, 'to some very plain speaking, saying that men who had behaved so treacherously in one service would do the same in another and that the Afghan Army did not want men of that stamp'.

In creating a job for these men and the other volunteers in his Tirah regiment, Mir Mast provided them with a wage of 16 rupees a month, modern rifles and billets near his home. He paid for the regiment through a large loan from a Tirah moneylender, secured on his word of Sardar Nasrullah's promise of funds, and he drilled his recruits with the two Turkish officers on an improvised parade ground outside his house. In the summer evenings his men followed him about Tirah's valleys, announcing his arrival at public gatherings with volleys of rifle fire up into the air before he gave jihadist speeches to drum up more volunteers.

As for Mir Dast VC, who was convalescing at Mir Mast's house, he had landed at Bombay in November 1915, welcomed as a hero with a public reception and an interview with the *Times of India*. 'His Gracious Majesty with his own hand pinned the Victoria Cross on me, shook hands with me and congratulated me,' he told the newspaper. 'My heart was filled with joy and gratitude.' On his arrival in Tirah, some men of his regiment who had deserted when he departed for France formed a welcoming party, but he refused to speak to them, cursing them for leaving him and other pre-war comrades to fight the Germans alone. Once reunited with Mir Mast, all the indications are that Mir Dast looked with dismay on his brother's jihadist path. For Mir Dast sided with their tribe's anti-jihad faction, led by a majority of the elders. They saw no German, Turkish or Afghan material support for the Afridi, and costly British reprisals as the most likely result of their tribe taking up jihad. They sniffed reckless foreign self-interest behind Mir Mast's proposed Turkish alliance, and wanted no part in it.

By September, Mir Mast's pro-Turkish movement was causing such tension among rival Afridi factions that it had become intolerable to the anti-jihad elders, compelling them to restore tribal harmony the hard way. They ruthlessly dismantled it, issuing death threats to the two Turkish officers, which sent them scurrying into hiding, before raising a *lashkar* to throw them out into Afghanistan and forcibly disband the Tirah regiment. They then set the *lashkar* on Mir Mast himself for giving refuge to the Turks as unwelcome outsiders and meddlers with the tribal peace. His punishment was by fire – his house, with Mir Dast VC safely removed, was sent up in flames and burned to the ground.

Disillusioned and homeless, Mir Mast was left in poverty. Nasrullah refused to stump up any cash for the Tirah regiment, too wary of punishment from Habibullah if he did. This consigned Mir Mast to a life of crippling debt to his moneylender, unalleviated of course by his Indian Army pension, lost to him when he deserted in France.

As Mir Mast's jihadist journey ended in ashes and cashless, ten of his Afridi co-deserters of the 58th Vaughan's Rifles whom he had left behind in Germany were in a tight spot themselves. They and thirty-two other Afridi prisoners of war at Camp Crescent Moon had volunteered in mid-1915 for the largest jihadist scheme on offer there: an international Jihadist Legion made up of battalions of African and Asian Muslim prisoners. The idea was for them to join the Turkish Army in Syria and Ottoman Iraq to fight for the Sultan's jihad, with their story as champions of Islam making good propaganda.

At the camp's mosque, the Jihadist Legion's Afridi volunteers had sworn an oath of allegiance to the Sultan's jihad with a hand on the Koran, thereby accepting German pay, uniform and officers. After months of training at the camp with their German officers, who had treated them with courtesy to earn their trust, in

March 1916 they had journeyed by rail together through Bulgaria to Istanbul, along with the Legion's 2000 French Moroccans, Algerians, Tunisians and Russian Tatars. They had made a strong impression in the Turkish capital, parading smartly for the approving War Minister Ismail Enver.

The Legion's companies had then been divided between the Ottoman fronts, with the Afridi going to the Turkish Sixth Army in Iraq to the north of Baghdad. By May, however, all the companies began to unravel. Their respectful German officers were replaced with condescending, openly mistrustful Turkish officers who substituted favourable German terms of service with lower Turkish standards. This meant slashing their pay, reducing their rations, imposing harsher discipline and giving them less comfortable washing and sleeping arrangements, in the process goading them that they had been over-pampered in Germany.

The Legion's Afridi promptly deserted, their jihadist zeal as professed at Camp Crescent Moon evaporating as their deeper purpose dictated their next moves. They wanted to go home. The Legion had carried them much of the way, and they took their chances in different directions. Some struck out southwards for Indian Expeditionary Force D's lines below Kut, hoping to spin a story of forced relocation from Germany, and others eastwards into the Iranian desert, making straight for Tirah.

In Tirah by late 1916, Mir Dast VC had sufficiently recovered from his gas wounds to return to British India for Indian Army duty, rejoining the 55th Coke's Rifles. He was warmly received and continued to be celebrated. In September, at a special reception at Simla's Viceregal Lodge for 192 Indian soldiers decorated for bravery in France, Gallipoli and Iraq, he was filmed by an official cinematographer for a cinema newsreel, and in the *Times of India* report on the occasion he was the only attendee given individual attention. The Afridi VC, however, was more like his brother Mir Mast than their respective British and German medals suggested.

Soon after Mir Dast's return to the 55th Coke's Rifles, the senior regimental post of subadar-major fell vacant. As a long-serving VC, Mir Dast was the star candidate. Yet his commandant overlooked him on grounds of seniority, favouring an older Punjabi Muslim who had no awards for bravery and had not served overseas. Slighted and hotly pride-pricked that such a Punjabi was deemed his better, Mir Dast saw no honour for him in the regiment now. So he deserted. Only a few details are known, coming from a letter by John Villiers-Stuart, his long-standing British officer of Coke's Rifles. It appears either Mir Dast made off from his regimental station in the North-West Frontier Province to complete the short journey to his independent homeland, or he took home leave with the secret intention of not returning. At any rate, he joined his brother and the other deserters of Tirah – in the end they were all Afridi who could only take so much of the British. 'I don't blame him,' thought Villiers-Stuart. 'Whose fault was it really?'

Mir Dast naturally fell from official grace. He was dropped from government guest lists, cut out from media coverage, and the bureaucratic wheels began turning to deny him his pension like any other deserter. However, Villiers-Stuart happened to be at Simla the day Army Headquarters was processing Mir Dast's pension disqualification. He heard of it by chance, and rushed to find the senior Indian General Staff officer who could stop it. As Villiers-Stuart put it, the officer 'played the game . . . M. D. was allowed his pension. But, well, the Regiment lost something.'

'Strong religious scruples against service'

After Emir Habibullah confirmed Afghan neutrality in January 1916, Charles Hardinge turned his mind to Muslim feeling within the Indian Army. The Viceroy was most concerned about the several thousand remaining independent Pukhtun recruits, partly in light of Mir Mast's example, but also because since mid-1915 the ongoing trickle of Indian deserters in France, Iraq and British India had consisted almost entirely of independent Pukhtun. For Hardinge, the prime trigger of Pukhtun desertions was 'strong religious scruples against service in the war', leading him to take a series of extraordinary measures in February and March to minimise them. On the home front, he opened an offer to independent Pukhtun troops of voluntary honourable discharge if they objected to Britain's war with their Turkish co-religionists, which around a third took up, and he suspended all recruitment of independent Pukhtun. Then, he not only barred independent Pukhtun from serving in Iraq, but also transferred all those who were there to East Africa – now the Indian Army's official overseas depository for independent Pukhtun as a theatre so hard for them to get home from as deserters they would not even try.

There were no such measures for the Indian Army's Muslim recruits from British India, who according to conventional colonial wisdom were less concerned by the war with the Turks. Into early 1916, many Indian regiments in Egypt and Iraq had Punjabi Muslim or Pukhtun recruits from British territory, and these did indeed appear consistently loyal, with desertions exceptionally rare. They included the 89th Punjabis' Punjabi Muslim companies which had been withdrawn from Gallipoli allegedly for their religious disinclination to fight the Turks, but fought relentlessly against them in the Kut relief attacks, with Shahamad Khan, a machine gunner who had joined up in 1904, winning the Victoria Cross. Furthermore, reports got back to the British of Punjabi Muslim officers in captivity epitomising the straightforward spirit of Indian loyalty they liked to see. At Camp Crescent Moon, the 129th Baluchis' Punjabi Muslim Subadar-Major Mala Khan was reportedly so resistant to German overtures he kept a black book of the Indian prisoners who accepted them, which he would hand to the British.

Equally, there were stories that among the Muslim officers from British India captured at Kut in April 1916 with the 6th Indian Division, some were conspicuously pro-British in captivity. They were separated from the officers of other faiths taken at Kut, and taken to Istanbul for favourable treatment as potential recruits for the Sultan's jihad. In July, the Sultan himself received them at his Topkapi Palace by the Bosphorus, and personally handed them swords of honour with an appeal to join the jihad. According to their own accounts, the first two Indian officers in line, from Punjab, only had contempt for the idea of breaking their oath to the British. Subadar-Majors Khitab Gul of the 120th Rajputana Infantry and Hasan Muhammad of the 104th Wellesley's Rifles in succession threw their swords on the palace floor at the Sultan's feet, in Hasan Muhammad's case with the flourish of a foot stamp. Their stunt led to three weeks' solitary confinement each with no bread or sunlight.

But there was a real crisis of conscience among the Punjabi Muslim recruits over the war's spiritual significance. By 1916 they were widely debating, partly by letter between the fronts, whether serving the British made them truly moral servants of Islam. They had one chain letter, dubbed 'Snowball' by the British, describing a dream with a message from the Prophet Muhammad that questioned the meaning of sin. Through discussion of the letter, Punjabi Muslim troops expressed their worries that fighting for a Christian power was unholy for them as Muslims. 'God is holy,' wrote Haq Nawaz, a Punjabi Muslim serving in France, 'and the Prophet also is holy, should not the Authority placed over us also be holy? ... We do not serve the Authority from our hearts; but on the surface we show more than loyalty. So without doubt we greatly err.'

Moreover, it was not just independent Pukhtun who strongly objected to fighting the Turks. In Iraq in February 1916, the all-Muslim 15th Cureton's Lancers recruited from Punjab mutinied at Basra. They had just been transferred from the western front, and they rejected not British service but fighting their co-religionists. 'For true Muslims,' said one of the mutiny's convicted Indian officer ringleaders, 'it is better to disobey ... than to go to the front and fight against one's Islamic brothers.'

'The small craft behaved like bucking broncos'

In 1916 the Indian Army still had to fight jihadist forces in Asia and Africa, and its Muslim recruits did so as much as any others. Twenty Indian regiments with Muslim troops were active in anti-jihadist operations throughout the year in Iran, which although neutral was dotted with German agents encouraging Iranian tribesmen, not least with cash, to wage the Sultan's jihad against British consuls, commercial interests and military targets. The Indian Army's Afghan regiment, the 106th Hazara Pioneers (recruited from Shi'a Muslim Hazaras of central Afghanistan who lived in British India as refugees from Afghan Sunni persecution), was the terror of nomadic Muslim communities in southern Iran that produced jihadist raiding parties. These had attacked Indian Army overland supply convoys out of north-west British India, heading for the Indian troops in east Iran who were screening the Afghan border to catch German agents. In response, the 106th Hazaras collectively punished above all their co-religionists the Muhammad Shahi tribe, destroying or seizing the tribe's material wealth in July, including its flocks of 10,000 sheep and goats. By the time the Hazaras quit Muhammad Shahi country in November, its people were refugees with barely the resources to live, let alone fight, absolutely desperate and dependent on the charity of neighbouring tribes to survive.

Simultaneously on the Iranian coast of the Persian Gulf, Indian regiments operated against the jihad from their base at Bushire, Iran's biggest seaport and a centre of British commerce. They had either landed there from Royal Navy ships as detachments from Indian Expeditionary Force D in Iraq or had marched up from British India, and they dug trenches along Bushire's desert limits to keep out jihadist raiders in German pay, of the local Tangestani tribes. These Indian units had Muslim and Sikh troops with western front experience who at night kept watch by shining powerful searchlights on their parapets over the desert. By day they ventured beyond their barbed wire entanglements to assault desert villages or forts suspected of harbouring jihadists, crushing any opposition by combining their machine gun fire with heavy naval artillery in the Gulf waters. Inland in central Iran from July, a column of 500 mostly Muslim troops of the 124th Baluchis alongside Indian cavalry marched 1500 miles on a four-month operation; they countered German agents and jihadists who were attacking British consular posts and banks. By the end of 1916, therefore, Indian regiments and their Muslim soldiers had been seen across half of Iran, and were all too familiar to the local people as Britain's brutal answer to the Sultan's jihad.

It was by no means just the Indian Army's Muslim troops, however, who served against the jihad into 1916. The 15th Ludhiana Sikhs fought the most wide-ranging anti-jihadist operations. In November 1915 they had been stationed in Egypt at Alexandria after their year on the western front. At the time, the Senussi, a puritanical Islamic order, was making jihadist attacks out of the Libyan Sahara into Egypt's Western Desert, backed by German and Turkish officers with money and guns delivered by submarine. The Sikhs were selected to spearhead the garrison of Egypt's response in the form of the Western Frontier Force – a mix of the Sikhs and less experienced British, Australian, New Zealand and South African units – all gathered at short notice to push the Senussi back into Libya.

The 15th Sikhs rushed westwards along the Mediterranean coast in late November in fishing trawlers. 'The men were packed on board like sardines,' recalled their young officer John Smyth. 'It was frightfully rough and the small craft behaved like bucking broncos. The men were terribly seasick – and so were some of the officers.' Smyth had been through not only First Ypres and the French winter of 1914, but also the Indian Corps' offensives in France up to spring 1915, and in fact wore the Victoria Cross for leading a Sikh party with grenade boxes over no man's land under heavy German fire that May.

Smyth and the Sikhs landed at Marsa Matruh, in the Western Desert near the Libyan frontier. 'We did not have any special landing craft and there were no ports or quays,' he wrote. 'So we ran our transport ship up on to the beach and slid the men ashore on planks. There were a number of splintered bottoms ... and one broken leg – but we were in action in a matter of hours.' The Sikhs' desert war against the Senussi in the Saharan winter sunshine lasted until February 1916 with 'plenty of hard fighting', said Smyth, as they led a series of wide assaults on Senussi trenches among the dunes and oases. The Senussi were testing opposition. They had European training, machine guns and light artillery, in addition to their desert craft, mobility by camel and tactical retreats. They killed or wounded a total of 200 Sikhs, shooting some in the back after playing dead in the sand, which the Sikhs punished by throwing the tricksters on to blazing tents to burn them alive. The Sikhs left the campaign having inflicted casualties ten times as many as their own, helping to drive the Senussi into Libya and shut down the Saharan jihadist front.

Next the 15th Sikhs took part in the Indian Army's greatest single anti-jihadist operation of 1916, in the independent Pukhtun tribal areas. That autumn the mullahs of Mohmand preaching the Sultan's jihad raised *lashkar*s of 6000 Mohmand to invade British territory. They did this with two jihadist agents of the Central Powers, both Indian Muslim revolutionaries and pre-war emigrants to the United States who had joined the Berlin Indian Committee in 1914, and gone with the German mission to Kabul in 1915; now they were sponsored by the Emir of Afghanistan's brother Nasrullah. The 15th Sikhs were part of the Army in India's pre-emptive attack on the *lashkar*s. It was delivered on

15 November by the 1st Indian Division, and used a fresh combination of global fighting experience and expansive firepower
previously unseen on the Pukhtun frontier.

With the Queen Victoria's Own Corps of Guides, 15th Sikhs
and 36th Sikhs on the ground, the 1st Indian Division had officers
and men who knew mountain, trench and desert warfare from
France to China. In support the Indian General Staff provided
new fighting means on land and in the air that it had been building up since 1915 to cover for the Indian garrison's depletion of
well-trained pre-war regiments. There were Rolls-Royce Indian
armoured cars with heavy machine guns; twelve of India's inaugural fighter planes of the British Royal Flying Corps carrying
bombs and light machine guns; and British howitzers and other
field artillery guided by target-finders on the planes, communicating by radio.

The Mohmand *lashkar*s made the mistake of concentrating
in the open on the British border, and the Indian force seized on
it to throw them back in a tightly coordinated advance with all
guns blazing, the aircraft going on to bomb and machine-gun
their retreat. The 15th Sikhs and other Indian regiments then
drew on their trench warfare experience to perfect a trench system
17 miles wide along the Mohmand border, with high parapets,
searchlights, machine gun blockhouses and continuous electrified
barbed wire, charged at a deadly 4200 volts. The Mohmand were
therefore blockaded from British territory, ensuring that there
was no way forward for their jihad. 'All sorts of wild animals
used to get electrocuted on the wire every night,' John Smyth
wrote of the 15th Sikhs' trenches, 'and, to start with, one or two
humans as well.'

The Indian Army had spent two years fighting disparate armed
forces supporting the Sultan of Turkey's jihad from North Africa
to the Middle East and the independent Pukhtun tribal areas.
The Russians and the French had also fought jihadist forces, in
north Iran, the Caucasus and French North Africa. By the end

of 1916, the jihad's failure was generally admitted, having not raised or sustained enough local resistance to the Allied colonial empires to divert significant resources from Europe. This made for a considerable Allied success, in which the Indian troops had been instrumental, hammering many a military nail into the jihad's coffin by crushing insurrectionist hopes across the British imperial sphere. The jihad's appeal to the Indian Muslim troops had not fallen on entirely deaf ears given their widespread concerns about fighting Turkey. But it was only a few renegades, above all the Afridi officer Mir Mast, who were prepared to cut their British ties. For the vast majority, pay, pensions and land grants meant more than holy war.

16

'LOOKING FOR GERMANS'

At dawn on 13 September 1916 in the western Indian Ocean, a flotilla of motor boats powered at speed towards a white beach with palm trees as seaplanes circled above. The motor boats had ropes stretched taut behind them, dragging several lifeboats packed with a thousand assault troops, covered from behind by the guns of a battleship 130 metres long and cruisers, gunboats and troopships. Many of the troops on the lifeboats were veterans of the western front, including the 129th Baluchis' British officer Harold Lewis and their Mahsud Ayub Khan who had spied in German-occupied France. They belonged to Indian Expeditionary Force B to German East Africa, backed by the Royal Navy. Force B was now making its second attempt at amphibious attack on one of the German colony's ports, following its disastrous effort at Tanga in November 1914. This time the objective was Mikindani, 400 miles south of Tanga near the border of Portuguese Mozambique, an area targeted because vital seaborne supplies for the German commander Paul von Lettow-Vorbeck's Schütztruppen had recently landed there from Germany.

Unlike Tanga, the attack on Mikindani went to plan. As Harold Lewis, Ayub Khan and the rest of the troops splashed out of their lifeboats and ran on to the beach, they were expecting German machine gunners concealed in the palms to open fire. But nothing happened. It turned out the Germans were gone, and the Indians occupied Mikindani unopposed.

Securing German East Africa's south coast was the latest move in the sweeping Allied offensives of 1916 down from British East Africa to conquer the colony, and the absence of the Schütztruppen at Mikindani was typical. For the 40th Pathans' British officer Charlie Campbell, with Force B direct from the western front, these offensives in East Africa's vast expanses of coast, bush, jungle and mountains came down to one thing: 'Looking for Germans', as he wrote home to his mother. 'It seems droll doesn't it after France, having to look for them,' he added.

The Schütztruppen were hard to find because they were so widely dispersed. In taking up the challenge of looking for them, Force B had improved on its low-quality Indian units of 1914 which had crumpled under pressure at Tanga. By early 1916 it had a preponderance of the independent Pukhtun barred from the Turkish theatres as untrusted Muslims and sent to East Africa, the theatre of no escape. With desertion not a real option, Ayub Khan and the other Pukhtun took a full share in the Allied East African offensives of 1916, finding not just Germans and the Indian Army's atonement for Tanga, but also unfamiliar African culture, languages and animals.

'Here you say Jombo'

After skulking back to Mombasa from Tanga in November 1914, Indian Expeditionary Force B had absorbed its sister Force C in British East Africa, C being scrapped as a separate entity. Force B had then spent all of 1915 guarding the British colony's 450-mile southern frontier with German East Africa, running from the Indian Ocean through the savannahs of Tsavo and

Serengeti, past the snow-capped Mount Kilimanjaro, and on to Lake Victoria.

Day to day Force B's Indian regiments had held isolated outposts at stations and bridges on the Uganda Railway, roughly parallel to the German border. They had not distinguished themselves, however. They had been largely the same poorly trained units sent from India to East Africa in 1914, and their low standards had fallen even lower with stale British and Indian officers, slack discipline and sapped spirit. 'The posts are quite useless,' Force B's acerbic Deputy Chief of Intelligence and Tanga veteran Richard Meinertzhagen had railed in April. 'When one passes them the men are lounging about, often without a sentry, and in many cases there is no attempt to dig a trench or build up head-cover [and their] barbed wire [is] still in coil, unrolled and thrown into some long grass ... Heavens, what a lot of trash we have out here.'

At one of these Indian posts, the jittery Kapurthala Infantry, a Punjabi princely States battalion, had embarrassed themselves by reporting a non-existent Schütztruppen night raid – they had been ruffled by a march-past of wandering baboons. The Indian Army regiments did little better, allowing bridge-blowing attacks by Schütztruppen to succeed unopposed. A bridge guard of the 98th Infantry, for example, had been 'rushed in broad daylight, not a shot being fired in defence,' wrote Meinertzhagen, 'the men merely gaped with astonishment'. The men of the 98th had then done nothing as the Schütztruppen removed their rifles, destroyed the bridge at leisure and walked off. 'Another most disgraceful incident due to rotten soldiering and gutless soldiers,' Meinertzhagen thundered. 'What a contempt the Germans must have for our men!'

Regardless of Indian Expeditionary Force B's quality in garrisoning British East Africa in 1915, it did not have the quantity to resume the offensive. Force B made up the bulk of the British colony's 15,000 troops alongside the King's African Rifles, which were altogether too few. But by early 1916 troop numbers in British East Africa had more than doubled, London having agreed to build them up with the South African government to invade German territory, in pursuit of shared interests of imperial security and aggrandisement. Accordingly, most of the fresh troops were white South African infantry and cavalry, available having conquered German South-West Africa in 1914–15.

The Indian reinforcements, meanwhile, were mainly its Muslim misfits banned from Turkish theatres. The 40th Pathans arrived from Marseilles at Mombasa in January, their British officer Charlie Campbell with the Afridi company. The 40th may in fact have been the strongest battalion in East Africa because they had a high proportion of fully trained, experienced pre-war regulars, both officers and men. Some were their wounded from Belgium and France who had returned from hospital. Among the others were their twenty-five Orakzai marines, rejoined from Aden having been at sea since 1914 with the Royal Navy on their voyage to the wreck of the *Emden* in the Cocos Islands and beyond. Then the 40th had over 300 seasoned independent Pukhtun drafts, complete with pre-war Pushtu-speaking British officers, who had fought with other regiments in Ottoman Iraq since 1914 and been ejected from the theatre under the ban on their facing the Turks. The 129th Baluchis with Harold Lewis came like the 40th Pathans direct from France, strengthened by a recent influx of pre-war Mahsud drafts from well-trained sister Baluchi battalions.

Indian Expeditionary Force B's disreputable roll of reinforcements extended to the 130th Baluchis and 5th Light Infantry. They were posted to East Africa so that their disgraced names, widely reported in the world's press for their total of three mutinies at Bombay, Rangoon and Singapore in 1914–15, could be quietly forgotten. The 130th Baluchis had been reconstituted with a blend of well-trained pre-war drafts, a few of their own but most of other units. The 5th Light Infantry came from

German Cameroon, having been shunted there in 1915 as the sole Indian regiment to participate in the Allied capture of German West Africa. The 5th's experiences in Cameroon had centred on long marches through grasslands, swamps and jungle; it had barely been under fire, and had no battle experience to match the men from France and Iraq.

After landing at Mombasa, the Indian reinforcements moved inland on the Uganda Railway as far as Kilimanjaro up to March. On the way they had new encounters with a variety of Africans. Most of these were porters, indispensable for carrying regimental equipment and supplies in East African warfare as the rugged region's roads and railways accessed only a tiny proportion of it. The 40th Pathans were joined by porters from the Winam Gulf area of Lake Victoria who had bamboo poles to carry their Vickers heavy machine guns from the western front. Their Afridi were taken aback at how these porters, men and women alike, freely went about by day stark naked after the custom in their Lake Victoria villages; they frowned harshly on the immodesty, which was unthinkable in Tirah.

On meeting the black African soldiers of the King's African Rifles, the Afridi were soon swapping smiles and easy phrases. They began picking up Swahili, their second new language of the war after French. 'Our men are quite pleased with the salutation Jombo,' noticed Charlie Campbell. 'They have remarked how droll it is in France you say Bomjo and here you say Jombo.' The white South Africans, however, were not remotely friendly to the Afridi. Abrasive and with an arrogant sense of their own toughness, they were openly disgusted at the prospect of fighting alongside the Indian Army. They came out with the old insult of 'coolie' for the Afridi as racially weaker soldiers, just as the Germans had in China before the war. Campbell shook his head at their conceit. 'The S. Africans,' he wrote, 'have yet to learn that the Indian soldier may be a fool but he is a man.'

'It is more nervy than in France I think'

The Allied offensives of 1916 into German East Africa were underway by late March. The invading imperial forces from British East Africa cooperated with Belgian advances from the west out of Belgian Congo and Rwanda, and British African forces attacking from the south-west, out of the corners of the British Empire that are now Zimbabwe and Malawi. The supreme commander of the forces advancing from British East Africa was the forty-five-year-old South African Jan Smuts. With a firm eye on his public image back home, his priority was avoiding large battle casualties; he wanted no talk, as he put it, of 'Butcher Smuts'. As a commander in the recent South African conquest of German South-West Africa, he had fought a war of rapid manoeuvre and encirclement, dividing his forces and making substantial use of cavalry to trap the enemy. His strategy for German East Africa was the same, with multiple columns marching in different but converging directions, initially out of the Kilimanjaro border area. Thereby Smuts hoped to round up Lettow-Vorbeck's Schütztruppen, who by early 1916 had a total of 2700 German and 11,400 African soldiers, in forty companies spread between the Indian Ocean coast and Rwanda.

Indian Expeditionary Force B contributed the 40th Pathans, 129th Baluchis and other Indian units to Smuts' infantry columns starting out east of Kilimanjaro, attacking south-eastwards on foot towards the Indian Ocean coast 300 miles away. This, then, was their general direction on the offensive from March to September as they struck into the heart of German East Africa.

The Indians' marching conditions were not easy under the tropical sun, against which their mainly Muslim troops wore their turbans loosely to let a strip dangle over their necks and backs. It rained a great deal, turning the ground into a muddy morass much as they had experienced in France or Iraq. Yet in other respects

German East Africa proved a theatre very different to anything they had seen before.

'Two people could be holding hands,' Charlie Campbell observed of the 40th Pathans' progress at one point, 'and yet see absolutely nothing of each other.' As they marched down plains and valleys great and small, across rivers and around hills, the landscape was a relentless tangle of bushland. It could be so thick with shrubs, thorn bushes, branches, leaves and flowers, pressing close against the face, that visibility was restricted to just an inch or two. Both the 40th Pathans and 129th Baluchis habitually hacked their way through with machetes, sometimes emerging into woodland or forest with acacia and baobab trees, or into more open areas where thick grass in red soil grew up to the height of a man, or higher. It was, of course, a world away from Flanders fields or the Iraqi desert.

As they went the Indian regiments had sudden brushes with animals of strange shapes, sizes and colours, peeping over, popping out or scampering away – from giraffes, gorillas and ostriches to hippos, wildebeest and crocodiles. One of Charlie Campbell's Afridi, in a way Campbell felt was typical of an independent Pukhtun instinct for self-possession, was pointedly nonchalant about such sights. 'Mehrab Din refuses to be struck with the wonders of other lands and always has one better at home,' wrote Campbell. 'Out on safari the other day I asked him what the Coy would think and do if suddenly charged by a rhino. "Nothing," he said "we have them at home."'

When the 129th Baluchis were actually charged by two rhinos, Harold Lewis watched his Mahsud stand their ground and shoot them down. Both the Afridi and Mahsud saw men wounded or killed in big cat attacks out of the long grass, not that it stopped them sloping off by themselves to go on lion and panther hunts, keen to face the dangers. Without their own words in Pushtu for most of the African animals, the Afridi variously labelled them with Indian military ranks (subadar-major for the biggest specimens) or used joke names after their own men where they saw a resemblance.

The tactics in East Africa were not primarily a question of artillery winning ground for infantry, as on the western front or the banks of the Tigris. Rather artillery mobility and target-finding were so difficult, given the terrain, that neither side could rely on it much. Indeed, Smuts' entire forces on the offensive in German East Africa had just half the number of artillery pieces the Tigris Corps had during the attacks to relieve Kut. Fighting in East Africa was more a matter of marching on the designated line of advance, and patrolling with rifles deep into the surrounding bush to see if there were any Schütztruppen about.

'This kind of warfare is very nervy,' Harold Lewis scribbled on his way through the bush with the 129th Baluchis' Mahsud. 'It is more nervy than in France I think.' In the trenches of the western front he had experienced the strain of being in an enclosed space that could be fired on from long range by the enemy straight ahead, on a routine day with a few seconds' warning from the sound of incoming shells. In German East Africa, Lewis found the stress lay in almost never knowing where the enemy was, and only finding out through rare close-range fire that could come at any moment, from any direction. Day after repetitive day on the exhausting offensive march in the bush, Lewis' Mahsud and the 40th Pathans would go mile upon mile without a Schütztruppe in sight, passing hours in silence, occasionally broken by a gentle bush breeze, a screeching bird or a screaming monkey. Then suddenly a German machine gun in the long grass would open fire. Pukhtun patrols would hurriedly have to locate German trenches nearby that usually defended a red mud road or a bush track; they would then have to outflank the German position by tearing their way through the surrounding bush. But the Schütztruppen almost always melted away in time to escape encirclement and capture.

Before Smuts' offensives had started in March, Lewis' Mahsud had had brief training near Kilimanjaro in bush fighting and tracking from the locally experienced King's African Rifles. They made the most of it in German territory up to August, adapting to the new conditions with a twist of their own skirmishing flair bred in Waziristan, priding themselves on mastering bush fighting where the emphasis lay on the individual's wits, his feel for the ground, and how he handled his rifle. Lewis in fact discovered that his Mahsud took to bush warfare as they had the trenches in France, as an opportunity to show they were not daunted by anything. 'My Mahsuds are having the time of their lives in this bush,' he wrote, 'putting the wind up the Huns with their patrols.'

One of Lewis' Mahsud named Qalaband formed a patrol he called his *jangian*, or warriors. With faces painted and turbans stuffed with grass and leaves, Qalaband's *jangian* regularly dissolved into the bush. They made a habit of bringing Lewis evidence of their tracing and trouncing of German outposts, for example on 1 April delivering him a German officer's revolver, an African officer's shoulder stripes, a sentry's rifle and a bugler's bugle, each taken from men they had shot dead from the long grass at a Schütztruppen railway outpost eight miles away. As for the Mahsud Ayub Khan, the 129th Baluchis' self-appointed spy in German-occupied France, he equally revelled in bush patrolling. During one patrol he overpowered a German officer and manhandled him by the scruff of the neck all the way back to the regiment, throwing him in front of Harold Lewis and the other British officers, announcing 'Here is a Hun.'

'Most of them did not know what fear was,' Lewis wrote of his Mahsud on patrol in the bush. Lewis's brother officer of the Baluchis William Thatcher shared his admiration: 'To see these troops is to see real soldiers ... they used less ammunition than anyone else and produced more corpses.' In their view the Mahsud outclassed the Schütztruppen, not just as fighting men, but as men. Lewis in particular felt this with his high pre-war regard for the Mahsud and their Pukhtunwali, whereas he disdained the

Schütztruppen as 'animals'. They tortured and mutilated some of his men; one was found in April 'cut about badly and stuck like a pincushion with bayonets'.

'Do not any longer refer to our sepoys as coolies'

In July, Indian Expeditionary Force B's independent Pukhtun contingent increased with the arrival at Mombasa of more western front veterans: the 57th Wilde's Rifles, with their Afridi officer Arsala Khan and his Malik Din company, who had been resting in Egypt. They joined Smuts' offensive not in the same bush columns as the 40th Pathans and 129th Baluchis heading south from Kilimanjaro, but with other columns sent up into the mountain ranges of eastern German East Africa.

Initially they went into the Usambara Mountains (today in Tanzania) to capture the high-altitude German scientific research laboratories at Amani, before marching south to attack the Schütztruppen holding the Nguru Mountains. In the Ngurus on 9 August, outside the village of Matamondo, Arsala Khan's Malik Din company re-engaged in trench warfare not much different to some of their western front experiences. Assaulting German trenches defended by six machine guns, they rushed up rainforest-covered slopes in a wide line with the King's African Rifles. While Arsala Khan was shot down wounded on open ground, one of his men, Salim Khan, led a platoon to capture a machine gun, killing the crew and turning the gun to fire on the Schütztruppen behind. As usual, however, the enemy disappeared before they were encircled, leaving twenty-eight Afridi casualties in their wake.

A hundred miles to the east of Matamondo that August, the 40th Pathans and 129th Baluchis emerged out of the bush onto the Indian Ocean coast, at the town of Bagamoyo. They spent the last week of the month on the beach there recovering from their six months' offensive trek from Kilimanjaro, feasting on fresh fish and mangos, bathing in the sea, and sleeping under coconut trees. They moved a few miles south on 4 September to the capital Dar es Salaam, which they entered unopposed after the German colonial government had cleared out. The 40th Pathans marched through the crowded streets and bazaars as triumphant conquerors, to the tunes of their regimental Scottish Highland bagpipes and drums. Their independent Pukhtun, Punjabi Muslims and Hindu Dogras jubilantly shouted 'Ki jai!' ('Victory!') again and again, indeed parading twenty-seven captured white German soldiers in front of them, with the way ahead cleared by dancing African scouts.

Yet Smuts' offensive from Kilimanjaro since March had only met partial success. Its sweeping column movements – carried out mainly by the South Africans, a large proportion of them cavalry – had conquered the north-east quarter of German East Africa down to the German Central Railway, while the accompanying Belgian and British offensives into the west of the colony had made similar gains. The Schütztruppen, however, had given up ground but not the fight. Their resolute commander Lettow-Vorbeck had decided on tactical retreats to the south of Dar es Salaam and the Central Railway, where they remained undefeated and unbowed.

The performance of Indian Expeditionary Force B in Smuts' offensive up to the capture of Dar es Salaam had done much to salvage the Indian Army's reputation in East Africa since Tanga in 1914. Even in the eyes of Force B's most exacting critic, its intelligence officer Richard Meinertzhagen, the better-trained and more experienced Indian troops in from France, Iraq and British India by early 1916 had brought about a dramatic improvement. For him, the pick of the lot was the 129th Baluchis with Harold Lewis and their Mahsud, who 'have proved themselves to be the best of the Indian regular battalions and have fought well and hard when engaged. On occasions they have done brilliantly.' Lewis and the 129th's British officers, Meinertzhagen added, were 'excellent ... keen and know their work'.

At times the South African troops had stuttered by comparison. On their arrival in British East Africa in early 1916, despite their posturing they had lacked professional officers and training like the 129th Baluchis, and their experiences in German South-West Africa of mobile warfare had little prepared them for tackling German trenches in East Africa. Near Kilimanjaro in February, when the South Africans had made their opening attack on Schütztruppen in trenches at Salaita Hill, one of their raw units fled in panic as soon as they came under fire, ignominiously losing their machine guns as they ran away. It fell to the pre-war Indian companies of the 130th Baluchis alongside to hold the South Africans' ground and retrieve the machine guns under the same fire, which they did with conspicuous discipline. The 130th made a point of returning the South African machine guns to their owners with a word to the wise. 'With the compliments of the 130th Baluchis,' said a note they left with the weapons. 'May we request that you do not any longer refer to our sepoys as coolies.'

'He is the bravest man I ever knew'

From Dar es Salaam in early September, the British imperial forces in German East Africa quickly pushed on by sea to secure the south coast – entailing the 129th Baluchis' part mid-month in the well-organised but unopposed amphibious attack by motor boat on Mikindani near Portuguese Mozambique. Smuts continued the advance inland into October, again with multiple columns manoeuvring widely in order to trap the Schütztruppen, but this time planned in cooperation with forces of Portugal, an Allied power since March, who were to head north from Mozambique.

By the start of December, the 129th Baluchis had Harold Lewis in command of the regiment, and Ayub Khan still among the Mahsud. They had marched inland with the King's African Rifles to central German East Africa's remote Mtumbi Hills. Here they occupied the stone hill fortress of Kibata and its surrounding hills, which had been abandoned by the Schütztruppen on another tactical retreat under Lettow-Vorbeck.

Yet Lettow-Vorbeck could not resist making a conventional counter-attack to besiege Kibata. His tactical retreats so far had been born not of any true guerrilla strategy, but of pragmatism to avoid capture. In Kibata he saw a rare position he could attack in traditional German style, as he had been trained as a young Prussian officer, concentrating his forces on a vital point to anni- hilate the enemy. So he gathered Schütztruppen outside Kibata with all the artillery and shells he could muster, including two mountain guns, a howitzer and a more powerful heavy naval gun salvaged from the German cruiser *Königsberg*, which the Royal Navy had sunk in a nearby river delta in 1915.

Lettow-Vorbeck opened his bombardment of Kibata on 7 December, focusing on the stone fortress and the 129th Baluchis' trench on the next hilltop. 'Except for the size of the shells, I have never experienced such a hot one, even in France,' commented Harold Lewis in the 129th's trench with a mixed company of Mahsud, Mohmand and Punjabi Muslims. Lettow-Vorbeck's guns may have been few, but so were their targets, and their shell- ing was relentless. Lewis and his Muslim troops were bombarded the most in Kibata because they held the highest ground: their trench was hit in one fifty-minute spell by 120 shells.

As Lewis and a significant number of his men, including Ayub Khan, were western front veterans (some, like Lewis from the days of First Ypres), they could use their experience to cope with the barrage and its supporting machine gun fire. They kept dig- ging, mending and improving their trenches and clung on under the cover of their parapets and traverses, rescuing one another from repeated burials in the earth after shell blasts. The 129th's officer William Thatcher even said that their sense of security from their trenches at Kibata, after months of bush patrols, had 'a friendly feel for those who had been in Flanders'.

The 129th Baluchis had a full week of static trench warfare, resisting numerous attacks by Schütztruppe companies across the no man's land between Indian and German lines. The battle for Kibata culminated on 15 December with a Mahsud night raid on the nearest Schütztruppe trenches, using the first ring-pull Mills grenades the 129th had received since France. Ayub Khan led the Mahsud assault troops in the dark across no man's land, wriggling on their stomachs up to the German parapet, timing their attack to coincide with the reappearance of the moonlight from behind clouds.

Ayub Khan threw the first grenade, signalling the moment for the Mahsud to attack. 'Nothing but the impossible would have stopped them, and once in the trenches nothing could live,' wrote Lewis, who watched the Mahsud as he followed up with reserves. 'They were like a crowd of furies, and I have never seen anything to equal their dash.' Ayub Khan was shot in the face but fought on as the Schütztruppen were killed, captured or driven out, and their position taken. 'He is the bravest man I ever knew,' reckoned Lewis, 'and I know there is no braver in the world.'

The Mahsud night assault was decisive because the fighting since 7 December had worn down both sides, the 129th Baluchis suffering 70 per cent casualties in total. By Christmas 1916, Lettow-Vorbeck had withdrawn into the bush of central German East Africa, much weakened yet still undefeated. The 129th's fellow defenders of Kibata – Africans and other Indians – had played their part on the hills around, but it was the 129th who were awarded the garrison's flag for the pivotal Mahsud attack, a tattered Union Jack Lettow-Vorbeck had fired 500 shells at. 'The 129th Baluchis,' Lettow-Vorbeck later wrote, 'were without a doubt very good.'

In France, meanwhile, the Indian Army had continued to go on the attack – not Indian infantry, but cavalry, in the BEF's greatest offensive yet and Douglas Haig's first as its Commander-in-Chief: the Battle of the Somme.

'Many new techniques of war'

At the end of 1915, while Indian Expeditionary Force A in France had released its two Indian infantry divisions to Force D in Iraq, it had remained on the western front with thirteen Indian cavalry regiments. These along with some British regiments filled two Indian cavalry divisions, of the BEF's Indian Cavalry Corps. Almost all the Indian cavalry in France had sailed there in 1914. Before the war they had been trained to help infantry mainly through mounted reconnaissance or charges over flat ground with lances lowered or sabres drawn to rout a retreating enemy, things they had occasionally done in small wars in the independent Pukhtun tribal areas. Pre-1914 they had had rifles and machine guns, but unlike the Indian infantry no widespread trench warfare training.

By 1916, however, the Indian cavalry in France had transformed into some of the BEF's best-trained and most experienced fighting units. In old age in Punjab, Indian cavalry veterans would look back on this transformation as the defining feature of their fighting experience against the Germans. As one of them, Mansa Singh, said in 1972 of his service on the western front with the 6th King Edward's Own Cavalry, 'we came to know many new techniques of war'.

From winter 1914 to spring 1916 the Indian cavalry units in France learned to fight like modern infantry, through both tours of dismounted trench duty in quiet sectors and training courses behind the lines. They learned skills of trench construction and holding, with new equipment from spades, picks, Stokes trench mortars and ring-pull Mills grenades to gas masks, steel helmets, French light machine guns and heavier Vickers guns. Their horsemanship was by no means neglected, rather it was reinvigorated by the British General Staff to focus on rapid offensive movements on the trench landscape. Training in this began in earnest in early 1916, with exercises in the French countryside to prepare the

Indian cavalry as mounted infantry, ready to secure limited areas of open ground behind German front trenches once British battalions on foot had broken in. The Indian cavalrymen therefore practised moving up the battlefield from reserve positions along tracks specially marked out with flags by the British General Staff, and crossing captured trenches on portable bridges, before charging ahead 1000 yards to dismount, dig in and wait for the infantry to reinforce.

In 1914–15, the Indian cavalry's casualties in France had been relatively light because of their limited use compared to the infantry. They had been held back during the BEF First Army's offensives from Neuve Chapelle to Loos, waiting with their horses from India in fields behind the trenches for chances to exploit any Indian or British infantry break-ins to open country – chances that never came. The upshot was that their tight-knit pre-war squadrons had been left substantially intact, and ever-improving. 'They had ... become extraordinarily self-reliant,' William Watson, a British officer of the 38th Central India Horse, said of them by mid-1916, 'and whether digging or drilling, whether mounted or dismounted, or merely polishing their accoutrements, were working very well indeed.'

Alongside their new military know-how by 1916, the Indian cavalrymen made their great cultural discovery of the war so far: Paris. On 14 July that year, several represented the Indian Army at the Bastille Day parade at the Élysée Palace, where President Raymond Poincaré inspected them alongside Algerian, Russian and other Allied troops. 'Paris is a fairyland, if there is any place on earth that approaches heaven it is Paris,' wrote home one of them, Ali Khan, a Punjabi Muslim. He had explored Paris after Bastille Day with two friends of his regiment, bumping into a group of kind-hearted Parisians who unlocked the city for them. 'We were asked by some people whether we spoke French,' he recounted:

I have acquired a lot of French and can speak and understand it well ... the others with me also knew French, more or less. We therefore told the people that we understood French, at which they were much delighted. They begged that, if we desired to go sight-seeing, we would accompany them, and said that we would be conferring a great honour on them. We went with them gladly and they conveyed us in their own motor car ... We were taken to all the famous places, and were treated more graciously than it is possible for me to describe.

Ali Khan and his friends were shown dance and music halls, museums and a zoo, and the Palace of Versailles, all paid for by their French hosts who also took them to restaurants. 'Their intelligence and affection and sympathy and politeness are beyond description,' he felt.

'Kamerad!'

On the same day as 1916's Bastille Day parade, the Indian cavalry in France went into battle for the first time using their new attacking skills as mounted infantry. They did so at the Battle of the Somme, which started on 1 July in Picardy, around 60 miles to the right of the Indian infantry's old trenches in the Pas-de-Calais. The BEF fought the battle under Douglas Haig on a 20-mile Anglo-French front as a piece of concerted Allied grand strategy – the offensive had originally been planned to put maximum pressure on Germany through going in simultaneously with a Russian offensive in eastern Europe and an Italian one in the Alps.

The Indian Army's part at the Somme was always going to be small: the Indian cavalry were a tiny fraction of the BEF, just 0.75 per cent of its total of 1.35 million troops. Since the last British offensive, in the autumn of 1915 at Loos, the BEF had moved on considerably as a mass army. For the Somme attack it had 1437 artillery pieces – over double its guns at Loos – with millions of shells, which Haig hoped would be enough to break through the German lines. Yet British gunnery on that scale was in its infancy and there were problems in terms of aim, accuracy and how best to use it to help infantry get forward. When the British infantry attacks started on 1 July, therefore, the artillery only made way for limited, isolated break-ins, which remained the case as the battle continued up to November.

The Indian cavalry's role in Haig's plan was reinforcing infantry success, so they stayed in reserve for most of the battle. They became a common sight for British troops in the rear areas, as they waited with their horses heavily packed with guns, waterproof coats, water bottles and blankets, besides bags of dried raisins, nuts and cereals for them and their mounts. Some of the waiting Indian cavalry had the time on their hands to ride back into the untouched fields and forests of Picardy, where they organised their own jumping meets, and went on boar hunts in the summer heat. But when there was a measure of British infantry success, the call came for the Indian cavalry to go on the attack themselves.

The first Indian cavalry charge on the Somme was through cornfields at sunset on 14 July, at the centre of the British front line near a German-held wood, the Bois des Fourcaux. The 20th Deccan Horse was the lead unit, with its Sikh squadron chosen for the assault. The Sikhs rode up their special cavalry tracks, past blasted tree stumps, over their bridges across captured trenches and into an open cornfield at the front of the battlefield to charge on, as they had been trained. The Sikhs galloped in a wide line with their lances lowered, straight at teenage German troops who fled in terror. The Sikhs speared some of the teenagers to death and took prisoner others, who flung their arms around the horses' necks shouting 'Kamerad!' ('Comrade!', their cry of surrender) and begging for mercy. A little further on in front of the Bois des Fourcaux, the Sikhs dismounted under fire to hold a new front line, setting up their French light machine guns to hold off counter-attacks as British infantry came up in support.

In September the Indian cavalry at the Somme made another mounted attack to nudge forward the British line, by the village of Gueudecourt. Here, just as the Sikhs had in July, the 19th Fane's Horse charged under fire to dismount and hold a new line. This was the second and final Indian cavalry charge at the battle, which was something of a disappointment to one of the galloping British officers of Fane's Horse at Gueudecourt. 'Infantry officers should have made more use of the horses,' he said adamantly. 'The experience of the regiment goes to prove that a man on a horse stands a better chance of getting through a hostile barrage than a man on foot.' This was a common conclusion, based on mounted speed over short distances decreasing the time of exposure under fire in the open, before dismounting to find cover. 'At the same time,' added the British officer, 'one feels extraordinarily naked and vulnerable when mounted and heavy shelling is going on, but that is only when standing still!'

The Indian cavalry's experienced machine gun crews, meanwhile, were spread dismounted around the British front trenches at the Somme. 'The battle is raging violently,' wrote Daya Ram, a Hindu Jat machine gunner of the 2nd Gardner's Horse, after a twenty-one-day stretch in the front line in August. 'At some places corpses are found of men killed in 1914, with uniform and accoutrements still on. Large flies, which have become poisonous through feasting on dead bodies, infest the trenches, and huge fat rats run about.' Still, he said, 'after two years' experience, we have grown used to all these troubles and think lightly of them'. They had grown used to the comforts, too, for the Indians' logistical support in France was as good as ever, as Hemayat Ullah Khan, a Muslim of the 6th King Edward's Own Cavalry, explained in a letter of 6 August to his imam in British India. 'However heavy may be the firing,' he wrote, 'fresh goat's flesh, and dal [dried pulses] and cakes of various kinds with gur [cane sugar] and tea reach the trenches of the Indians without fail. The entire force is very pleased with these arrangements. If we have to make a journey by road of fifty miles, we find, when we reach our destination, that our rations are already there, having been sent on by motor cars.'

When the Somme offensive ground to a halt in November, the BEF had advanced up to six miles at a cost of 420,000 British, Australian, Canadian and South African casualties. By comparison the Indian cavalry's entire losses in the four-month battle had been just 200 men, mostly wounded, and each of them had the ongoing benefit of the Indian medical arrangements set up in France by Lord Kitchener in 1914. 'If anyone should become suddenly ill, or be wounded,' Hemayat Ullah Khan of the 6th Cavalry wrote to his imam, 'he is straight away conveyed on a stretcher to the motor ambulance and in a few minutes he finds himself in a hospital. The hospital is a place of greatest comfort, and there so much attention is shown to him, as he has never in his life experienced before, even in his own home.'

The question lingered, of course, why the men of Indian Expeditionary Force A in France for almost two years had had the quality of care Hemayat Ullah Khan described, yet things had been so different for the men of Indian Expeditionary Force D to Iraq. The public answer was soon to be given by the independent Parliamentary inquiry into Force D's failings on the Tigris. It would reveal the great systemic failings of the Indian Army's war effort and indicate how they should be fixed, making all the difference for Indian servicemen and their families.

Five

1917

17

'A CEMETERY OF REPUTATIONS'

His viceroyalty timed out, Charles Hardinge had sailed home from British India in April 1916. At night through the Mediterranean he had watched over his daughter Diamond asleep on the ship's deck with the other children by the lifeboats, a precaution for a quick getaway in case of U-boat attack. Soon after landing at Dover on 23 April, he had taken up his old job at the Foreign Office in London as its senior civil servant. He had worked at the heart of the British government for over a year, seeing German air raids and the downfall of Herbert Asquith as Prime Minister in December 1916, replaced by the younger, more dynamic and decisive Welshman David Lloyd George.

Then on 27 June 1917, Hardinge was suddenly thrown into the public eye when the Parliamentary inquiry into the Indian campaign in Ottoman Iraq published its Mesopotamia Report. The report caused a scandal, the single greatest episode of public scrutiny of the Indian Army in the First World War. The Indian military contribution to the war effort was witheringly brought under the microscope, with unprecedented naming, blaming and blasting of those responsible for the disasters on the Tigris in 1915–16 up to the surrender of Kut. 'The Report is simply a cemetery of reputations,' F. E. Smith, the old Indian Corps' press officer and now the Attorney-General, told a packed House of Commons. Hardinge was among those whose reputation was buried in the report's pages, which told of the tragedy on the Tigris as substantially his blunder.

'The men who left them thriftily to die'

On 11 July, on the heels of the Mesopotamia Report's publication, Rudyard Kipling released his protest poem for Indian troops in London's *Morning Post* and the *New York Times*. 'They shall not return to us, the resolute, the young, / The eager and whole-hearted whom we gave' his *Mesopotamia* mourned for the dead of Indian Expeditionary Force D on the Tigris. 'But the men who left them thriftily to die in their own dung, / Shall they come with years and honour to the grave?'

In recalling Force D's wounded who suffered so in their own excrement on Tigris barges, the thrifty men Kipling had most in mind were Charles Hardinge and his Commander-in-Chief in India, Beauchamp Duff. Kipling went further in *Mesopotamia*, accusing the pair of 'the slothfulness that wasted and the arrogance that slew'. His criticisms captured the emotion in the explosion of outrage in the British and Indian press at the report's findings. For the *Morning Post*, Hardinge 'failed not merely as a viceroy but as a man'. The *Daily Mail* said of Duff, 'Nothing less than dismissal from the Army would fit his mani-fold incompetence', and the *Times of India*, 'nothing can excuse his complete failure'.

The report in fact named an order of responsibility for the events leading to Kut's surrender. Force D's commander John Nixon was first, for his misplaced optimism in advising that he could open the road to Baghdad with the 6th Indian Division alone in late 1915, gambling that by accelerating its advance he could overwhelm the city's Turkish defenders before they were reinforced. Second and third place went to Hardinge and Duff, partly for accepting Nixon's advice, but more for their overall roles as the Indian Army's civilian and military principals who had directly managed the campaign in Iraq.

The report faulted Hardinge and Duff for presiding over Force D's expansion – in terms not only of distance by sending it some 500 miles up the Tigris beyond its original objective, Basra, but also of troops by adding to it two Indian divisions from France, doubling its previous number – without increasing its logistical support in proportion. The pair's toughest critic in the report was Josiah Wedgwood, a Member of Parliament for Newcastle, who shamed them for showing 'little desire to help and some desire actually to obstruct the successful prosecution of the war'. 'Turkey has done more for Germany than India has done for England,' Wedgwood concluded of Hardinge and Duff's leadership. 'Had they thrown themselves heart and soul in to getting India to do all that was humanly possible both in men and material, the whole course of the war might have been altered.'

On 12 and 13 July Parliament debated whether the culprits named in the report should face punitive action. 'There was undoubted mismanagement, thousands of gallant lives were lost under conditions of unspeakable torture,' Lloyd George told the House of Commons while introducing the British government's position. 'There was suffering which is indescribable. Someone or something is to blame. It is either the system or the individuals working the system, or perhaps both.' He did not care to judge the balance, instead urging Parliament to rise above the report and drop the idea of individual punishments. 'There are 20 millions of men at this hour interlocked in deadly conflict for the future of the world,' he reminded Members. 'I do beg the House ... to say to the Government, "Get on with the War!"'

But there was a strong mood in the Commons for retribution. John Nixon's name nonetheless receded from the ring of censure, as he was generally admitted to have been rash but bold in a way a soldier must be. Rather it was Hardinge and Duff who were pilloried. Josiah Wedgwood reappeared to critique their management of the Indian Army with a 'niggling and mean spirit which will lose us every war in which we enter', while Aubrey Herbert, the report's main instigator, stooped lower in saying that Duff 'did not play the part you might expect from an English soldier or an Englishman'.

Herbert, like everyone else who spoke in the debate, was scrupulously respectful of the Indian troops of the 3rd, 6th and 7th Indian Divisions who had fought on the Tigris for months despite their lack of equipment, food and medicine. For Herbert they had:

> answered the call of their Empire in the finest possible manner ... I suppose it would be invidious to discriminate in the courage of our various Armies where all have behaved so magnificently, but, if one did try to discriminate, and if one were anxious to put the courage and devotion of one Army above those of others, I believe you would have the same verdict from every front. They would say that the men who fought at Kut and finally were captured at Kut, that the troops ... who went to the relief of Kut ... have accomplished the greatest achievements in this War of any force we have had.

As the debate continued, Hardinge's defenders spoke up for him. They counselled compassion on personal grounds. 'Immediately on this war breaking out remember what he was going through as a man,' said Mark Sykes, a Cabinet special adviser on the Middle East. 'I say this because he never can say it ... His wife was cruelly taken from him in a most tragic way, and then immediately afterwards his son fell in the war in Flanders. But Lord Hardinge went on with his duty.' In the event, after the two days of debate Parliament dropped the idea of punitive action. The Attorney-General F. E. Smith explained at length that any court proceedings would probably last for years, deflating the interest in them.

It has commonly been thought that following the poetic, press and Parliamentary vilification, Beauchamp Duff committed suicide. In 2006, for instance, the national newspaper of the land of his birth, *The Scotsman*, reported under the headline 'First World War disaster general's medals go under the hammer' that he 'killed himself after being blamed for one of the worst military disasters of the First World War'. A number of British and American military historians such as Kristian Coates-Ulrichsen subsequently said the same, as did the Wikipedia entry for Duff. The story goes that on the Mesopotamia Report's publication he suffered in silence the stains on his honour, making no public statement while turning to the bottle, before the shame became too much for him and he committed suicide on 20 January 1918 by overdosing on sleeping pills.

The reality was a little different. The Cabinet had recalled Duff to England in ignominy in 1916 after Kut's fall, but privately he protested he had done his duty in difficult circumstances. 'I have had a pretty hard time these last two years,' he told a friend shortly before his recall. 'Until they have tried it, no one could realise what it is not merely to send from India – for that is comparatively easy – but to maintain Indian forces in the field in every quarter of the globe.' Duff felt that John Nixon had not kept him fully informed of Indian Expeditionary Force D's medical shortages, and that he had done his best to provide Force D with extra river craft and supplies. In 1915 Duff had in fact sent river steamers to Iraq requisitioned from the Indian Empire's great rivers only for many to sink at sea, and in early 1916 he had been waiting on delayed orders for more river boats for Iraq from Britain and elsewhere. 'I have had to buy all over the world, and then cannot get enough ships,' he rued.

But Duff almost certainly did not commit suicide. In the summer of the Parliamentary debate on the Mesopotamia Report, he began unobtrusively preparing his written rebuttal, working with a formidable lawyer, the former Attorney-General and Lord

Chief Justice Charles Russell. It was that winter, while Duff was hard at work with Russell at his London club, the Caledonian in St James's, that he was found dead in his bed one morning, sitting up, head bowed with his glasses on his nose, a novel fallen from his hands. His determination to clear his name and the coroner's report suggest no suicide, rather a man who took sleeping pills in a normally safe dosage, but one that was too much for his weak sixty-three-year-old heart given the enormous strain he had been under.

Unlike Duff, Hardinge spoke publicly in his own defence when the Mesopotamia Report was published, forcefully rejecting the accusations against him as grossly unfair. 'I objected to anything that might imply censure where I could admit none,' he later wrote in his memoir, *My Indian Years*. Indeed, he was publicly unrepentant until the end of his life in 1944, and arranged for the memoir's posthumous release so that he did not have to answer for it. In *My Indian Years* he claimed that he had a noble record as the Indian Army's civilian head. His main argument was that he had released almost all of the Army in India's well-trained pre-war units for overseas service, despite the domestic security threats he faced from Ghadar, the independent Pukhtun and Afghanistan, whose seriousness he always maintained was scarcely realised abroad. As for Indian Expeditionary Force D's calamitous advance on Baghdad, he openly blamed it on his military advisers, scorning Duff as the Indian high command's weakest link; 'never was there so great a failure,' the Viceroy said of his Commander-in-Chief.

Who, then, was responsible for the Indian suffering and deaths on the Tigris between Basra and Baghdad in late 1915 and early 1916, and the failure of the 3rd and 7th Indian Divisions from France to save the 6th at Kut?

'To occupy Baghdad with our present forces would be most unwise'

If there was one man most at fault, it was Charles Hardinge. Kipling had the measure of why in his line 'the men who left them thriftily to die'. Over the three financial years of 1913–14 to 1915–16, the Government of India's net annual military expenditure under Hardinge rose from £19.9 million to £22.3 million. In contrast, while the British government's war expenditure had risen by £100 million within two days of the war's outbreak by vote of Parliamentary credit, a further twelve such credit votes up to 1916 had raised it by £3.1 billion. In November 1914, meanwhile, Parliament had voted for the British taxpayer to pay for the Indian Army's overseas expenses above its normal costs in British India. Under Hardinge, therefore, British India's military expenditure from 1914 barely rose to support its expanding overseas expeditionary forces, even though Parliament had made the British government's vastly increased war budget available for the purpose. The consequences were experienced by the Indian troops on the Tigris who were left, as Kipling said, to 'die in their own dung'.

In London, Lord Kitchener had of course in 1914 inspired an energetic, far-sighted government response to the war. His preparations and procurement for a long conflict underpinned the numbers of the British Empire troops in France multiplying by a factor of fourteen between 1914 and 1916, up to 1.4 million men, with the transport, food and medical supplies to match, as the Indian troops on the western front experienced. Yet from the war's very start, Kitchener had detected in the Government of India a somewhat different grasp of the global situation, telling Duff in September 1914 that Hardinge's military leadership was 'a great disappointment . . . I do not think you yet realize in India what the war is going to be'.

Kitchener had sensed that Hardinge was running the Indian Army for the world war as economically as possible, reacting to the war's needs by using what military resources India already had, rather than proactively increasing them for overseas commitments. Hardinge had indeed not cut himself free from India's peacetime culture of military administration, which was one of strict thrift and tight red tape to keep taxes low and increase social spending. From August 1914 he carried on pursuing military economy as he adopted a business-as-usual approach on the Indian home front, maintaining the pre-war balance of government expenditure in favour of the social budget, in large part to nurture the war support of the Indian nationalist politicians. But in doing so he neglected to make sure the Indian soldier on the Tigris was provided for as in France. Hardinge could justifiably point to India's continuing pre-war policy of military economy as breathing originally from his Liberal superiors in London; he, though, was the man in power on the spot and he failed to see the need to move on from it.

It is telling that in Iraq from 1914 up to the surrender of Kut, there were no British photographers, cinematographers and others copiously documenting British treatment of Indian soldiers like at Brighton and other hospitals in England. Contemporary photos of Indian Expeditionary Force D between Basra and Baghdad are in fact exceptionally rare up to April 1916, and for some months non-existent. While Hardinge spoke in 1915 of the hospital care in England for wounded Indians as 'priceless' for its propaganda value, the simultaneous British neglect of the Indian troops in Iraq reflected something they wanted to keep out of the news: where the British chose not to produce imperial propaganda, their care for the colonial subject could be callously cheap.

As for the decision to advance on Baghdad in 1915, Hardinge had been its most consistent promoter in power with his ambition to be 'the Pasha of Baghdad' before he left office. His veto would have stopped it, along with the Indian troops' suffering that ensued, but he pushed for it, suppressing his Indian General Staff advice on the risks. In October 1915, for example, Beauchamp

Duff handed Hardinge a memorandum by the Indian General Staff's Director of Military Operations, the Canadian George Kirkpatrick, warning that 'to occupy Baghdad with our present forces would be most unwise', and expressing 'doubts whether ... with our present insufficient number of light-draught steamers, we could adequately supply our troops'. Hardinge ignored such advice, reflecting his vanity. He had a certain intellectual self-satisfaction, boosted by his high-flying civilian career; he felt he knew better than his military advisers, and rarely sought their counsel. Indeed, before 1914 Douglas Haig as Chief of the Indian General Staff had warned Hardinge that low expenditure left the Indian Army poorly prepared for an overseas war against Germany or Turkey. But at the time Hardinge had not merely disagreed, but been contemptuous. In private up to 1914 he wrote that Haig was 'hare-brained', 'extraordinarily tiresome to deal with', and could 'see no further than the end of his nose'. And he went further: Haig was 'strangely ignorant of foreign affairs', his ideas of war with Germany and Turkey being 'fantastic and ... in complete opposition to the international politics of the day'.

Nevertheless, the most fundamental problem behind Indian Expeditionary Force D's failures on the Tigris – and what needed to change the most for the well-being of the Indian troops – was the structure of the British Empire's supreme command from 1914 to early 1916. Its critical flaw was not being unified. Asquith, as Prime Minister, had embarked on the world war by following peacetime precedents for London's control over imperial defence. For the Indian Army in Iraq, this meant it had a split structure of supreme command. The Cabinet in London had final say on grand strategic decisions such as advancing on Baghdad, while the Viceroy in India had control of local operations and logistics. But crucially, there was no effective bridge for sound decision-making between the two power centres in 1914–15, because they had no common General Staff.

On the one hand, the Cabinet was advised by the British

General Staff at the War Office. This had practically no information on Force D up to the end of 1915, as it was not responsible for operations in the Indian sphere including Iraq, and was banned from communicating with India. On the other hand, at the same time the Indian General Staff had no official presence in London, where the India Office's Secretary of State advised the Cabinet on Indian strategy without any organised professional military advice. Then Hardinge made matters worse as India's military link with the India Office via private telegram. He stopped Indian General Staff advice he did not like from getting to London, such as the memorandum of October 1915 cautioning that 'to occupy Baghdad with our present forces would be most unwise'.

Adding to all the confusion, John Nixon in command of Indian Expeditionary Force D was himself in direct telegram touch with the India Office. Yet he was a man of blistering willpower and aggressive impatience, demanding that his logistics simply stretch to serve his battles. Nixon's characteristic reports up to October 1915 heralded operational leaps up the Euphrates and the Tigris in so dazzling a way that their dearth of measured assessment of Force D's increasingly overstretched transport, medical and supply units was overlooked. He was in the business of winning Force D's war on the Turks, and by nature he did not trouble his civilian superiors with the full danger of his logistical gambling.

The upshot was that London approved the advance on Baghdad in October 1915 with a broken and bad supply chain of General Staff advice right up to 10 Downing Street, and therefore without realising the risks of failure and the suffering to which it was condemning the Indian troops. Still, even with London's decision to go for Baghdad, the city's fall instead of Kut's might well have been achieved if Indian Expeditionary Force D's resources earmarked for the operation had been better used – had they been concentrated for a decisive offensive. But the sorry General Staff structure in place missed the opportunity of arranging this. Extraordinarily, the 6th Indian Division lunged for Baghdad in

November while the 3rd and the 7th Divisions remained in France, when these divisions in France were the very reinforcements the Cabinet had sanctioned as indispensable for the operation's success. And when the 3rd and the 7th got to Iraq in early 1916, they were rushed up the Tigris without being concentrated for a decisive relief offensive. They were frittered away piece by piece, going into action as soon as possible, because Kut's food (at the estimate of its miscalculating commander Charles Townshend) was thought to be running out quicker than was the case.

In the final analysis, the Indian Army from 1914 up to the fall of Kut had in Charles Hardinge a war leader of shallow military wisdom, who tragically for many Indian soldiers in Iraq treated global war as business as usual when it demanded drastic changes to India's pre-war capacity to provide for them in the field. What was really needed to bring about such changes was a new Viceroy, a new Indian Commander-in-Chief, a new commander of Indian Expeditionary Force D, and above all a new structure of imperial supreme command to conduct unified grand strategy. To coordinate all this, someone else was needed: a master of grand strategy, one mind to guide them all and the Indian Army. The man for the job was in London. The son of a Lincolnshire village postman, he had left school at the age of thirteen in 1873 to work as a domestic servant, and his name was William Robertson.

'AN AMBULATING REFRIGERATOR'

At Christmas 1915, William Robertson became the Chief of the Imperial General Staff (as the British General Staff was formally called), aged fifty-six. Having left domestic service in his teens – 'I was a damned bad footman,' he is reputed to have said – he had enlisted as a British Army private, embarking on an unprecedented rise up the ranks to Chief. On the way he served in India, the independent Pukhtun tribal areas and South Africa, married the daughter of an Indian Army officer, got his p.s.c., and qualified in eight languages – Urdu, Hindi, Farsi, Pushtu, Punjabi, Gurkhali, French and German. His rural working-class background was very unusual for a British officer, and his peers knew him for his unpolished accent and gait; 'aitchless when excited, and flat-footed', wrote Edward Spears, an urbane war-time British General Staff liaison officer between London and Paris, 'he lurched down Whitehall, an ambulating refrigerator'.

Robertson was quiet but witty, qualities that helped him fit in with his richer, public-school-educated brother officers. His higher promotions had come through the opportunities of staff work, which was perfectly suited for his capacious, clear and plainspoken mind. With invaluable western front experience as the BEF's Chief of Staff in 1914–15, his place as Chief of the

Imperial General Staff in New Year 1916 was in London as the Cabinet's senior military adviser, bypassing Lord Kitchener whose fall from influence his appointment had sealed.

In Cabinet, Robertson was surrounded by some of the British Empire's fleetest thinkers and most brilliant arguers, men such as David Lloyd George and Winston Churchill. Their quick conversational twists and turns were beyond him – he once wondered out loud whether he was 'attending a Cabinet or a committee of lunatics' – and he did not try to compete with them. His style of advice, he wrote, was 'to keep on a straight and unbiased road'. He would say simply what he meant to say, even if the politicians did not want to hear it. As he himself described his talk in Cabinet, having grasped a geranium, 'When the politician says, "It looks to me like a camellia" or "I think it's a carnation", or "It smells like a rose", or "It might be a hibiscus", you don't try to prove that it is not a camellia, or a carnation, or a rose, or hibiscus; you simply repeat "It's a geranium."'

Once Robertson's uncompromising eye had fixed on Ottoman Iraq in early 1916 during the Tigris Corps' attempts to relieve Kut, he reckoned the campaign conditions of Indian Expeditionary Force D were 'so utterly bad as to be incredible to anyone not on the spot'. He quickly diagnosed the root problem, identifying 'that a sound system of command is a requisite condition of success, and that no worse system could have been devised than that of dividing the control of the military forces of the Empire between two separate departments (India Office and War Office) and two separate army headquarters (Simla and London)'.

Robertson, therefore, over a year before the Mesopotamia Report was published, set about rearranging the machinery of the Indian Army's supreme command. He continued a process of centralisation that Kitchener had started in East Africa after the Tanga disaster in 1914 by taking control of Indian Expeditionary Forces B and C away from the Colonial Office and India Office. By mid-1916, Robertson had put Force D under the direct control of London too. This meant that the British General Staff at the War Office, in effect himself, directed British strategy in Iraq. It took over from the India Office to supervise Force D's operations and logistics, and began communicating daily with India's Commander-in-Chief, now Robertson's direct subordinate.* For the first time, there was unity of supreme command in London over all the Indian Expeditionary Forces, and it was to bring about a stunning reversal of the Indian Army's fortunes in Iraq.

'I am very sorry for Willcocks'

An immediate priority for Robertson in order to improve Indian Expeditionary Force D was appointing new high commanders. He wanted to brush aside weaker Indian Army senior commanders and replace them with some of the British Army's best – those well qualified and experienced in staff work before the war, who since 1914 had shown themselves rich in common sense and adaptability to manage complex forces against the Germans or Turks.

When Kut surrendered in April 1916, John Nixon had already been replaced as Force D's commander by the former Chief of the Canadian and Indian General Staffs, Percy Lake. That July, the sixty-one-year-old Lake's health failed him at the front. Robertson replaced him with an outstanding and broad-minded British Army commander nine years younger, Stanley Maude, a Coldstream Guardsman and British General Staff officer. Before the war, Maude had served in Egypt, South Africa and Canada, and been an avid battlefield tourist in the United States; during it, his service had spanned the western front, Gallipoli, Egypt and the Kut relief attacks. Maude was a devout Christian with monastic self-discipline. A teetotaller and non-smoker, he denied himself

---

* Once under War Office control, Indian Expeditionary Force D became known in England as the Mesopotamia Expeditionary Force. From the Army in India point of view, it was nonetheless still Force D.

anything that he felt would impair his psychical and mental fitness, and kept up vigorous daily exercise including jogging and boxing. Indeed he was so discipline-obsessed that in peacetime at home he had drilled his three young children, a boy and two girls, for a quarter of an hour every morning outside before breakfast as if they were Coldstream Guards. At war Maude's work ethic was so unstoppable that he rejected home leave as frivolous. As a staff officer, he had a detail-hoarding mind with such powers of recall and analysis that even some of his most analytical seniors not given to hyperbole called him a genius.

To replace Beauchamp Duff as India's Commander-in-Chief in mid-1916, Robertson chose wisely. He appointed Charles Monro, of Scottish family and a contemporary of Douglas Haig's at the British Staff College. Rotund, jovial and charismatic, Monro radiated warmth, and unlike Maude or Haig had a personal touch with the British ranks. With a scientific mind and reputation for training and bringing on his juniors, his steady wartime ascent from a divisional command came courtesy of Haig's thorough approval of his ability up to 1916 on the western front, where he had followed in Haig's footsteps to command I Corps and the First Army. Monro was however best known for his brief stint as Commander-in-Chief in the Mediterranean. In late 1915 he had advised the Cabinet to withdraw from Gallipoli, prompting Winston Churchill's quip 'he came, he saw, he capitulated'.

For one British general, the news of Maude's appointment to Iraq and Monro's to India came as painful signs that for him the war, and with it any chance of future military employment, was over. Since leaving the Indian Corps in France in September 1915, James Willcocks had languished in England, drifting forlornly between his suburban house in Essex and London for lunches at clubs, where he would spend afternoons telling old stories of the Indian Empire to journalists. As an Englishman born and raised in British India who had spent almost all his working life there, England never felt quite like home to Willcocks. He had few

friends in the imperial motherland, as he had found while commanding the Indian infantry in France, having been treated as a
social inferior for his modest British Indian family background.
Indeed, in France most of the British Army commanders of the
original BEF from England had been distinctly unfriendly towards
Willcocks, sniffily treating him, he said, as 'a rough Indian-bred
soldier', 'a bushman from Asia, as something which must perforce
be tolerated but not encouraged ... I was a stranger.'

On his exit from France, Willcocks, for whom the Army in
India was his real home, had been hopeful of another command.
But in England his only friend in a high place was Kitchener, from
pre-war Indian days, who by late 1915 had lost the clout to make
senior appointments. Furthermore, Willcocks had no friends of
influence to help from France, least of all Douglas Haig. In early
1916, Willcocks unsuccessfully turned to Robertson for a command, writing letters with new ideas for postings in response to
each reply stating no vacancy – first in India, then Cameroon,
East Africa, Arabia and Russia. He next asked Robertson for permission to quit the British service, to go to Albania or Romania
to enlist as a private soldier; Robertson did not bother to reply.
In fact when Robertson had replied to Willcocks, it was by hasty
dictation without much care, sometimes addressed to 'Willcox'.
'If I had not been severely handicapped by lameness from my old
wound,' Willcocks said, cursing his leech-bitten leg, 'I should have
joined the French Foreign Legion.'

Willcocks' isolation seemed complete in June 1916 when
Kitchener disappeared in the North Sea, presumed drowned after
his ship, on a diplomatic mission to Archangel in Russia, was
sunk by a German naval mine. To Willcocks' dismay, he was not
invited to his old friend's memorial service at St Paul's Cathedral
as no one at the War Office had bothered to think of him for the
guest list. 'It is very difficult for me to understand my position,' he
wrote to Robertson. 'I honestly do not know why the War Office
has cast me aside ... What then General is the unpardonable fault

I have committed, which keeps me from all employment in this great war, after a life spent mostly on active service in the Field in all parts of the Empire?'

Robertson never gave Willcocks the answer, but it was that he had seen and heard enough of Willcocks in France as the BEF's Chief of Staff in 1914–15. The British military world had moved on from Willcocks' speciality of pre-1914 mountain warfare and personally caring for his Indian troops, talking with them every day: it was now a place for cool scientific minds commanding men from afar, and efficient, aggressive young staff officers on the up and trying to impress them. Willcocks was on the scrap heap, and Robertson did not have the heart to tell him. By 1917 the reality had dawned on Willcocks that his military career was finished. Needing money, he was forced to accept a job he did not want – the governorship of Bermuda, one of the slimmer pickings among even the more undesired outposts of the empire. 'I have simply been driven from a proud position to degradation,' he wrote.

In April, Willcocks sailed off sadly into the North Atlantic for a holiday in New York, before going on to Bermuda. 'I felt utterly depressed,' he said of his arrival in the colony as the new governor, 'it certainly did not suit me ... when the world was in arms'. He would spend up to ten days at a time by himself offshore in a hut on a tiny island, in low spirits drinking whisky and watching hurricanes. Willcocks did at least have the sympathy of his old Viceroy. 'I must say I am very sorry for Willcocks, he is heart-broken,' Charles Hardinge commented. 'Whatever may be his faults, he is devoted to his Indian troops who also have confidence in him, and it is a sad ending to a fine military career.'

As Willcocks' Indian Army career ended unwillingly, Charles Monro's as India's Commander-in-Chief started in the same vein. 'I hate the prospect of going to India most heartily,' he wrote on sailing from England, arriving to take up his post in October 1916. 'Still, it cannot be helped as soldiers have to go where they are told.' Without any family connections with India to inspire a sense of personal fondness, Monro's focus was entirely professional. He was essentially Robertson's British General Staff agent. His purpose on Robertson's instructions was to realise India's potential as Britain's second centre of global military power. He was to help overturn the Hardinge–Duff era's reluctance to develop Indian resources for the war, and extract as many as he could to help win it. Crucially, this new approach was endorsed by Hardinge's replacement as Viceroy, Frederic Thesiger, known by his inherited title of Lord Chelmsford. In contrast to Hardinge, the new Viceroy was intellectually modest and had a milder taste for his own opinion, making him more open to the advice of others. With administrative experience as a former governor of two Australian states, he had been selected as a steady hand at the Indian tiller for an intensified war effort.

Monro and Chelmsford chimed personally to build a close working rapport, becoming a dynamic duo untrammelled by the pre-war rhythms of Indian bureaucracy – a break, of course, from the approach of Hardinge's administration. They agreed that for British India's war contribution to multiply, its leadership needed to incorporate the latest trends in managerial thinking. In London from December 1916, David Lloyd George as the Prime Minister led a new, streamlined War Cabinet with a core of just four members to advise him. The War Cabinet was designed as a more efficient vehicle of supreme command than Asquith's approach of consulting in regular Cabinet, with interminable sub-committees to consider different areas of policy. In imitation of Lloyd George's executive model, Chelmsford set up the Indian Defence Committee, a body of four advisers for him on all military matters. The four included Monro as Commander-in-Chief and George Kirkpatrick, formerly the Indian General Staff's Director of Military Operations and now its Chief. Significantly, Monro's and Kirkpatrick's regular military advice for Chelmsford was discussed openly in the Indian Defence Committee, where alternatives to viceregal suggestions were welcome, a far cry from Hardinge's more unilateral, isolated ways.

Then Monro breathed a fire of the highest professionalism through Army Headquarters. He discerned that under Duff a full sense of being at world war had never quite taken hold of its departments, with a slight slackness having set in, staff officers still wearing their peacetime dress with white shirts. Monro's first action was to put a stop to this; only khaki field service dress would do. To lead the logistics departments, Monro brought in new senior staff, appointing only those tried, trusted and in tune with him. Their main qualification was not a p.s.c. but practical experience of staff work on the western front or at Gallipoli that made them authorities on modern requirements in the field. One of them was Havelock Hudson, James Willcocks' old Chief of Staff in the Indian Corps and subsequently a British divisional commander in France. After two and a half years there, he was now India's new Adjutant-General, responsible for recruitment, pay and other such matters.

Alongside the logistics departments, Kirkpatrick as the Indian General Staff's Chief was assisted by a fresh batch of senior officers. He chose these partly for their relative youth, most being in their early forties, but more, as Monro wished, for their staff experience at the fronts. They included some of the best brains in the Indian and British armies. There was Andrew Skeen, a pre-war teacher at the Indian Staff College who had served on the Indian Corps' staff under Havelock Hudson in France, before learning some hard lessons on the Australian and New Zealand Army Corps' staff at Gallipoli. Another was Hubert Isacke, a staff officer in pre-war London and India who had gone to France in 1914 with the 7th Indian Division's headquarters. He had stayed on the western front up to 1916 with the British General Staff, earning a high reputation for his intelligence and organisational skills, for which Robertson sent him to India to help Monro.

In contrast to the first two years of the war, therefore, by 1917

British India had a carefully coordinated and highly capable military leadership. Just as Robertson had intended, its senior officers pulled together with the new Viceroy to debate and deliver the essential groundwork for reviving Indian Expeditionary Force D in Iraq as a force based in India: a sweeping reorganisation of war effort on the home front.

'Here you wear worn-out shoes, there you'll wear boots'

To expand the Indian war effort, Chelmsford and Monro inevitably had to spend more money. Thus from 1916 the Government of India's annual military expenditure went up by roughly 25 per cent. They invested much of the extra funding in initiatives to increase India's output of supplies for the Indian Army, and indeed for other Allied armies. They created numerous Indian boards of supply run by senior staff officers alongside British civilian specialists in industry and trade, some sent specially from Britain. The boards rapidly proliferated government contracts with Indian manufacturers and distributors of war materials, such as the Tata Steel and Iron Company. Indian factories were soon pouring out millions of articles: uniforms, rough-tanned cowhides for boots, water bottles, tents, lanterns, jute sandbags, entrenching tools, rifles, cartridges, artillery pieces and shells. Indian suppliers also provided large quantities of mechanical transport for land and water – from railway tracks and rolling stock to river craft, motor lorries and Ford vans – and tens of thousands of horses, mules, ponies, bullocks and camels for cart and pack transport. Equally there was a boom in new medical equipment for well-stocked hospital vessels (for sea and river), field hospitals, motor ambulances and laboratories.

Such output was vital for Monro's parallel increase of the Indian Army's size, doubling the number of Indian battalions. He began in earnest in December 1916, not only adding second or third battalions to the pre-war Indian regiments, but also creating new regiments. Seeking to fill their ranks, he found that the army's pre-war recruitment system, kept in place by Hardinge and Duff so that recruiting officers still ventured out from their regimental depots to find their own volunteers, was unworkable. While the pre-war system had provided replacements for the Indian Army's overseas casualties of 1914–15, its returns had steadily diminished by mid-1916 as the particular villages it depended on were almost sucked dry. Monro therefore scrapped it in favour of his innovative 'territorial' recruitment system.

The territorial system meant that recruitment was no longer organised locally per regiment, but overseen by a new central recruiting directorate. This identified various territorial zones for recruitment in British India's provinces, and handed quotas of recruits needed per province to provincial sub-directorates, which were then responsible for allocating quotas of their own to recruiters at district level. The territorial system continued to cast the Indian Army's net over rural rather than urban areas, villages rather than towns and cities, but it did so more widely than the old system. The districts previously untapped by the army were mostly in the north, in Punjab and the United Provinces of Agra and Oudh, with the others around British India from Bombay, Baluchistan and Bengal to Burma and Madras. In addition, the princely States were asked to provide more recruits for the Indian Army as well as their own forces. In doing all this, Monro looked beyond the pre-war list of martial races, and expanded eligibility for military service to seventy-five communities.

The results of the territorial system were remarkable. Whereas in the war's first two years under Beauchamp Duff approximately 190,000 Indian volunteer combatant recruits had stepped forward, the figure for the third and fourth years under Monro was 420,000. By the end of 1917, Monro had formed fifty-five Indian battalions with new classes of recruits including Himalayan Kumaonis, Bengali Muslims and Burmese Kachin hill tribesmen, besides Punjabi Christians, Mahars from east of Bombay and

Coorgs of Madras. Monro found the British officers for the new Indian units primarily by enlarging the Indian Army's British officer reserve, a process Duff had started from the pre-war base of just forty officers. Under Monro, the reserve swelled to 5300 officers, many passing through new training colleges in India from Baluchistan in the north-west to the Nilgiri Hills in the deep south. The preferred British officer cadets came from India's white community – civil servants, tea planters, account-ants, stockbrokers, lawyers and engineers – who usually had at least a grounding in the Indian languages of command. 'Anglo-Indians', however, who had one white European parent and one Indian parent or grandparent, were barred from joining up too for combat leadership, on the racial grounds that they did not have pure Anglo-Saxon genes and were inferior natural leaders. From abroad, Monro took in permanent Indian Army white officers from England and Canada, and volunteers temporarily transferred from the British Army's reserve and Territorial home defence force in the British Isles. All round, he lifted the Indian Army's British officer corps to a total of 9500, nearly four times the pre-war number.

Monro simultaneously increased the recruitment of Indian non-combatants for the Indian Army's logistical services. He drew on communities from around the Indian Empire of Pukhtun, Punjabi Muslims and Parsis, Mahrattas, Rajputs and Sikhs, Madrassis, Tamils and Telugus. From 1914 to 1916, Indian non-combatants had served everywhere the Indian troops had gone, supporting them in all sorts of capacities: as cooks, bakers, kneaders, vegetable gardeners or laundrymen; tin-smiths, packer-men, horse-drawn cart supply drivers, muleteers or sweepers; carpenters, coopers, stretcher bearers, doctors or ward orderlies, veterinarians or grooms. Indeed, Indian children aged as young as ten had taken on some of the most menial roles on the western front. They had been recruited by unscrupulous Indian civilian contractors who lined their own pockets by signing up almost anyone they could for non-combatant work overseas, in return for their government fee per person. Indian non-combatants had also served in Greece, on Europe's south-eastern front, opened by the British and French armies in late 1915 at the Mediterranean city of Thessaloniki on the Aegean coast, as a springboard to liberate Serbia.

From late 1916, Monro's Indian non-combatant recruitment drive had fresh emphases on clerks and other literate administrative assistants to help with the expanded army's bureaucracy, and on skilled transport and medical personnel for Iraq. Overall, he pushed the total number of Indian non-combatant recruits between 1914 and 1918 to 445,000 volunteers. Over half of them were from Punjab and the United Provinces of Agra and Oudh. They generally served with the Indian Army's traditional logistical branches whose units Monro also expanded, but a significant minority from 1917 joined 'Labour Corps'. These were initially called for by London's new Directorate of Labour at the War Office, created by Robertson to coordinate military labour from around the British Empire to support Allied forces in Europe and Asia. Monro formed fifty-four Indian Labour Corps for France, and a further nineteen for Iraq.

The sheer numbers Monro achieved in enlisting Indian combatants and non-combatants in the recruitment years of 1916 and 1917 are intriguing when there were very good reasons for men not to join up from their villages. The letters home from Indian troops on the western front had been full of dire warnings after the BEF's offensives had started in 1915. 'For God's sake don't come, don't come, don't come, don't come to this war in Europe,' Abdul Rahman, a Punjabi Muslim NCO of the 59th Scinde Rifles, had written that May, 'machine guns, rifles ánd bombs are going day and night, just like the rains in the month of Sawan [the monsoon]. Those who have escaped so far are like the few grains left uncooked in the pot.' Many other letters similarly related the physical dangers at the front in 1915–16, describing the wounded writhing like live fish thrown on the ground, or the dead lying about like plums shaken from a tree. By 1917, enough villages had received such letters – and men returned wounded – for the risks of overseas service to be widely known. There were mothers, wives and children across Punjab and other provinces who did not want their menfolk to hazard life and limb in battle for the British, let alone suffer themselves the anguish and fear of separation. It was common to see mothers arguing with their sons on the way to the recruitment to station to stop them. How, then, did Monro succeed in getting quite so many villagers to volunteer?

Having widened the Indian Army's recruitment areas to cover many new districts and villages in British India, Monro innovated by involving the provincial civil authorities in exploiting them. Provincial governors down to local district officers had their own rural social networks of Indian civil servants, tax collectors, police, landowners, village headmen and holy men who could work as brokers in the villages to fulfil the recruitment boards' quotas. These brokers could trade off their local connections and influence, spreading the call to arms by talking Indian to Indian in the local dialect, persuading families to part with volunteers. Getting them to do it promptly and energetically was vital to supply the Indian Expeditionary Forces, so they were encouraged by a range of British incentives to get a sizeable catch wherever they cast their net. In Punjab, for example, the Irish governor Michael O'Dwyer oversaw a rewards system for Indian brokers who hit or exceeded their quotas. They could get promotions and pay rises; cash bonuses and land grants of up to 400 acres each; and flattery in the form of honorific robes, swords and titles bestowed in public ceremonies. Equally, there were harsh penalties for those who failed to net enough recruits, such as demotion in their civil employment, or even dismissal.

Monro spoke of potential recruits in the villages as his customers, aware that they would need attractive inducements to volunteer. He therefore upgraded the army employment benefits for the Indian brokers to peddle. While maintaining the pay rise granted under Hardinge in 1915 for Indian soldiers fighting in Europe, Monro scrapped the parallel bonus of 100 rupees for wounded men returning home, replacing it with a revamped pay structure for all combatants. This had multi-tiered cash incentives to attract volunteers with short-service ambitions (the minimum period of service being the duration of the war) as well as those who wanted a full professional career. Now a recruit got a cash gift of 50 rupees on enlistment, an extra 15 rupees on completion of basic training or posting overseas, and infantrymen no longer had to contribute, as they had since pre-war days, to the cost of their uniform and rations. Recruits then got extra field service allowances, which if earned in full through exemplary behaviour could double their standard monthly wage of 11 rupees. On top of all this, Monro brought in a rolling bonus of up to 60 rupees for every six months' service completed, and he raised non-commissioned officers and Indian officers' basic pay by up to 20 per cent.*

As for pensions, Monro increased them too, and he made it easier to get one. He adjusted the pre-war qualification regulations that had remained under Hardinge. He reduced the long-service qualification from eighteen years to fifteen. He allowed not just the honourably retired or badly wounded to qualify, but also those invalided out of the army with medical conditions made worse by field duty, even if their condition was pre-existing and aggravated by their duty rather than caused by it. In addition, he relaxed the restrictions on dependents who could inherit a soldier's pension – for instance allowing war widows to do so after remarriage, which previously had lost them their first husband's pension.

Alongside Monro's pay and pensions improvements, the

---

* Indian recruits' basic pay and pension still remained lower than British soldiers'; as before 1914, prestige demanded it.

provincial governments arranged for yet more material benefits. In Punjab, the governor Michael O'Dwyer granted tax breaks for villages that provided recruits, such as tax credits for families of the wounded, or land tax relief for locales giving up high proportions of men. Most attractive of all, O'Dwyer earmarked 180,000 acres of canal-irrigated land for Indian officers and men with distinguished service records overseas, the worthy to be assessed on their return home.

Monro then made sure that once an Indian recruit had joined up, the day-to-day army care in British India made him more comfortable than before. Instead of the decrepit pre-war cantonment housing for Indian troops, he initiated standard modern barracks with kitchens, wash-houses and latrines, as well as new Indian officers' quarters with verandas and private rooms to accommodate their wives. He opened up cantonment warehouses and storerooms as special Indian Army shops, at which recruits could buy cut-price clothes, food or almost any stock except weaponry and drugs, so long as it was for their families and not for resale. To replace the inadequate pre-war Indian regimental hospitals, Monro opened new, well-equipped general hospitals, with offshoot convalescence centres and psychiatric units, providing a total of 53,000 beds; these medical facilities sprouted in particular at Bombay and in the city's surrounding hills for men passing through the port. Furthermore, for the long train journeys around the Indian Empire that were so often the Indian soldier's lot, Monro made carriages more comfortable with new bunks, fans and water coolers. And he did not forget refreshments at railway station stops, installing new Indian Army tea rooms on the platforms.

Monro also improved Indian recruits' education as a service benefit. He provided the cantonment schoolhouses with more teachers and learning materials for a novel range of courses, albeit primarily aimed at better preparing soldiers for overseas fronts, for example through lessons on unfamiliar modern equipment.

For the Indian non-combatant recruits of the expanding trans-port, supply and medical units, he set up new technical training schools that turned out drivers for locomotives, Ford vans and tractors, and mechanics for railways, motor boats and ice-machines. And to incentivise non-combatant volunteers to attend these training schools, Monro improved their pay if they acquired new skills at them.

With all of these inducements to trumpet about the coun-tryside, the provincial authorities' recruitment brokers visited villages far and wide to sell military service. They waxed lyrical about army life as an opportunity to explore the world while getting handsomely paid, clothed and fed, besides the chance to earn the honour of the brave in battle. In some Punjabi districts the brokers brought poets, musicians and singers to perform at early evening recruitment parades. 'Here you eat dried bread, there you'll eat fruit' rang out one of their ditties on the Indian Army's bounty. 'Here you are in tatters, there you'll wear a suit. Here you wear worn-out shoes, there you'll wear boots.' After the songs, Indian officer veterans back from France often made inspiring speeches, playing strongly on kind British care at the front before asking young men to form a queue to enlist.

British speakers also addressed such gatherings, spinning the higher causes at issue. 'If anyone asks what are the men wanted for, let this be your reply,' Michael O'Dwyer said in August 1917 on a public speaking tour of Punjab's recruitment grounds. 'They are wanted not only to defend the British Empire but to defend your own hearths and homes. Those would be menaced by a German success in Europe or Asia'. Always in the broadest of terms never much explained, O'Dwyer's speeches claimed that the Germans threatened to invade the Indian countryside, bringing atrocity, plunder and slavery; so it was villagers' duty, he declared, to prove their mettle and fight to protect their country.

The boom in Indian recruits under Monro by 1917, however, was born not of any true faith in speeches such as O'Dwyer's, but of poverty, pay and pensions. Village families accepted military service much as they had before 1914: the material rewards were too tempting to turn down. Some villages gave up to two thirds of their able-bodied men, getting all the money they bargained for. The soldier families of Punjab's Gurgaon district, for example, pocketed 1.6 million rupees in 1917 for military service. 'My loyalty to the British is reasoned, not blind,' Tassaduk Husain, a Punjabi Muslim policeman, said of his family in the province's Rawalpindi district where one in every eight men volunteered, including his nephew, killed in France, and his two cousins who were serving in Iraq. 'We are considered by the public among those who are ultra-loyalists,' he went on. 'No sacrifice to serve my masters the British would be too great for me. My family has tasted their salt and if we have gentle blood running in us we will be true to it.'

In Iraq, meanwhile, what the British got for all the men and materials they bought on the Indian home front was the means for Indian Expeditionary Force D under Stanley Maude to go from strength to strength – all the way to Baghdad and beyond.

19

'NO LONGER A CINDERELLA'

O nce the Battle of the Somme had come to a close by December 1916, its significance for the Indian Army in Ottoman Iraq was twofold. Firstly, such success as the Allies had at the Somme – no breakthrough, but they had weakened the German Army, which would help wear it down over the longer term – confirmed the ultimate logic of the British Empire's war effort on land, namely concentration of force at the decisive point, the western front. This meant Iraq remained a theatre of secondary importance to winning the war, warranting fewer resources. Secondly, at 10 Downing Street the Prime Minister David Lloyd George felt that the public mood following the BEF's enormous losses at the Somme could be lifted by gains in Iraq, in other words by a good news story. 'You must give us Baghdad if you possibly can,' he urged William Robertson as his Chief of the Imperial General Staff, much as Asquith's Cabinet in October 1915 had looked to capture the city when faced with earlier western front disappointments.

Robertson himself was by no means averse to the idea, seeing utility in making headway on the Iraq front as a check on the Central Powers' potential expansion towards Iran, Afghanistan and the Indian Empire. Yet he was only prepared for Indian

Expeditionary Force D to go again for Baghdad if this time it was primed to achieve the objective. He knew that the prerequisite was Force D's logistical renaissance, and that in Stanley Maude he had the ideal man to bring it about.

Robertson would not countenance for Indian Expeditionary Force D anything like the British investment in men and money for the BEF. But he still sanctioned such quantities of both that by late 1916 Force D, as one of his British General Staff colleagues recognised, was 'no longer a Cinderella, apparently looked upon with comparative indifference by Government Departments in Simla and in Whitehall'. On the contrary, Maude made sure that into 1917 Force D became the British beast of the Middle East, a war machine so well organised that the Indian Army would flatten the Turkish trenches up the Tigris where before it had failed, in what Robertson, no mean judge of military achievement, called 'one of the most brilliant chapters in the history of the Great War'.

'Not only good but very good'

From March 1916 there was a surge of troops in Iraq in Indian Expeditionary Force D from 50,000 to 200,000 by autumn 1917. Some were British but most were Indian, and under Maude from mid-1916 their life as Gurkhas, Punjabi Muslims, Sikhs or otherwise became very different from the days of John Nixon and Kut's surrender. They were well fed at numerous field canteens serving meat from frozen stores, fresh vegetables, fruit, iced sodas and much else. In the evenings they were entertained in the desert at open-air theatres by Indian actors, concerts with Indian bands, and cinema screenings of American and British films. Then there were sports, from fishing with rods and nets on the Tigris to football tournaments. Maude swooped in by bi-plane to present football cups to Indian regimental teams, speaking with them easily enough in Hindustani, by mid-1917 having learned the language since his appointment to command Force D. 'I was in close touch with the Troops,' he wrote. 'I could see them and feel their pulse.'

The British care reflected that under Maude Force D was deluged with new supplies and equipment. Most came from Charles Monro in India and William Robertson in England, and some from the British administration of Iraq's Occupied Territories. 'The troops are getting plenty of everything and are very happy,' Maude was sure in March 1917, 'the last thing to come being the mackintoshes for the Indian troops which only arrived recently from England.' Compared to the Indian troops' nightmare on the Tigris in early 1916, Iraq had become a logistical theatre of dreams.

The standard of logistical care Robertson had set for the Indian Army in Iraq was, as he put it, 'not only good but very good' – or close to western front levels. The upgrade had started in early 1916 when Beauchamp Duff, in some of his better decisions as India's Commander-in-Chief before the fall of Kut, selected a few British officers of global experience for the Indian staff in Iraq. For instance Duff sent George Buchanan, a civil engineer renowned for his pre-war work on ports and rivers in Burma, and George MacMunn of the British Army, who as a pre-war p.s.c. and logistics specialist had done wartime staff work in London, France, Egypt and at Gallipoli. Robertson then added many of his own staff choices from mid-1916. He sent a steady flow of more civil consultants and professional British staff officers, several from England and France, and all expert in riverine logistics or other areas of need. One of Robertson's most important picks was the leading British Army doctor Francis Treherne, who as a BEF medical director in France in 1915 had managed the Indian infantry's formidable front line medical care.

'There were to be no mistakes this time,' noted MacMunn of his work under Maude on Force D's logistics staff. By 1917, Basra had become a modern port with dredged channels, docks, wharfs and floating workshops. It was linked to the interior up the Tigris and Euphrates by Force D's river fleet, now so enhanced it was the world's largest with over 1000 steamers, barges, tugs and motor launches, plying up and down river lanes neatly marked out with buoys. Whereas in March 1916 Force D's diminutive river fleet had carried 300 tons a day upriver, in the last quarter of 1917 the daily average was 5000 tons, of food, mail bags, munitions and other supplies. Railways of Tata steel were then laid down alongside the Tigris and Euphrates, and mechanised transport such as Ford vans became ubiquitous on new, British-built Iraqi roads, as did animal transport from load-bearing camels to bullock and mule carts. There were also modern hospital facilities in abundance, from field ambulances on the roads to hospital boats on the rivers, with scrupulous sanitation, plentiful beds, doctors and nurses, and the latest equipment including electric fans, X-ray sets and bacteriological laboratories.

Force D's logistical improvements were made possible by its increase in non-combatant workers, up to 225,000 by mid-1917. They were mostly Indians – for example of the Madras Gardeners' Corps, sent to Iraq to grow vegetables – with minorities of Jamaican, Scottish, Egyptian and Chinese workers provided by London, as well as Iraqis and Somalis employed by the local British administrators of Iraq's Occupied Territories.

While many of Maude's Indian battalions had a sprinkling of long-serving British and Indian officers who kept alive their old regimental spirit and memories of former fronts including France, their men were generally new drafts. In the Iraqi desert from summer 1916 he oversaw training camps for them to impart not the individual initiative and self-reliance of the Indian Army's pre-war mountain warfare training, but the more basic skills of a modern mass army for trench fighting. They were taught to follow strict instructions on when and where to move, advancing in company waves over ground won largely by artillery, firing at close range with not just rifles but also new Lewis light machine guns, ring-pull grenades and Stokes mortars from British factories, and bayoneting to finish off the enemy in one trench before moving on to another.

In autumn 1916, Maude organised the higher Indian battle formations in Iraq for the first time with the attention to detail typical of European operations. In constant touch with Robertson and Monro for approval and advice, he created two new Indian army corps: I Corps and III Corps. He chose their senior commanders and staff officers on merit, for visible vim and experience of major battles and General Staff work on the western front, Gallipoli and elsewhere. After his daily early morning swim in the Tigris, in October and November Maude proved a domineering dynamo in supervising his subordinates' preparations to resume the offensive on the Turkish trenches below Kut, in the direction of Baghdad. He paid obsessive attention to their planning for assault troops, making sure they applied their lessons of trench warfare, and kept up to speed with British General Staff tactical circulars from France. Equally he worked with his logistics staff to arrange unprecedented transport, supply and medical support for the Indian front line on the Tigris, sticking to the principle that logistical capacity must equal operational ambition.

From mid-December 1916 to March 1917, Indian Expeditionary Force D was let loose by London to avenge the fall of Kut and steamroll the Turkish Army for 200 miles up the Tigris to Baghdad. Maude's two army corps burst through the stoutly defended Turkish trench systems around Kut to recapture the town by February and seize Baghdad in March, and then pushed on in multiple directions to secure Baghdad province in desert heat of up to 48°C. His operations were later described by Robertson as 'a masterpiece', being well planned and relentless on both banks of the Tigris.

All round, Maude had combatant units double the strength of the Kut relief efforts in early 1916, with 50,000 mostly Indian troops cooperating with artillery batteries of 174 field and heavy guns. His style of attack up to Baghdad in March was to target (or bite) limited patches of Turkish-held ground one after another, consolidating his hold of each by trench-digging before moving on. His battalions struck according to meticulous timetables allowing for preliminary artillery barrages that slaughtered and scattered the Turkish defenders, and they advanced in wide lines of companies with Lewis light machine guns and other small arms, just as they had been instructed to do in their desert training camps.

At Maude's insistence his assault troops avoided the Indian Army's offensive mistakes of 1915 at Gallipoli on the Sari Bair ridge or in France at Loos of going too far ahead in isolation from other units, instead remaining compact in their forward momentum. For flexibility and surprise, they had the help of 'bridging trains' – columns of British engineers and Indian Sappers that bridged the Tigris using portable pontoons – so they could switch quickly from one side of the river to the other to get around a Turkish position. They had further support from Royal Navy gunboats and British Royal Flying Corps bombers. Meanwhile frequent British reconnaissance flights fed back intelligence on Turkish movements to Maude, which he acted on in his forward headquarters by communicating with his corps commanders by field radio.

When it came to fanning out his forces 100 miles beyond Baghdad to Fallujah, Ramadi and Tikrit between April and November 1917, Maude's offensive approach was much the same as before. Yet I Corps and III Corps were increasingly widely dispersed, making his continuing tight grip of his subordinates' staff work all the more a marvel of operational control. 'The campaign has been an intensely interesting experience to me,' he wrote to Robertson in October, touching on how he had continually improved his management of his army corps, 'and I have loved every minute of it'.

It is doubtful that Maude's Indian troops felt the same enthusiasm. There were a few raw Indian companies with no will to finish trench assaults, the Punjabis of one agreeing that on arriving at their target trench they would all throw down their weapons, put up their hands and give up as they meant the Turks no harm. They went ahead with this, foolishly – the Turks returned the sentiment by butchering them out of hand. 'Served them all right,' said Maude without a shred of sympathy. But many of his sepoys, well prepared by their desert camp training, were tenacious in repeated hand-to-hand trench fights against Anatolian Turk units whom Maude described as 'tough customers', 'stubborn' as he had seen at Gallipoli. The Turkish defenders clung on to their ground most doggedly until February 1917, when south of Baghdad they began surrendering and retreating in large numbers.

'I cannot tell you how magnificent has been the work of the whole force,' Maude wrote at Baghdad in April to a friend in London of his gains upriver from Kut:

> It is a real pleasure to command such an Army. The troops have fought like tigers, and with a dash and determination worthy of our highest traditions, but although all this has been superb we should have been doomed to failure if it had not been for the splendid work done behind the Army. The communications were magnificent throughout, river and rail transport running without a hitch, and my every need was met with the utmost promptitude ... The troops were practically on full operations scale of rations throughout ... Our river transport is excellent now, and gets stronger day by day with the arrival of new ships and barges ... Our medical arrangements, too, are most satis-factory now, and in all stores we are indeed well found.

The Iraqi tribesmen of the Tigris carried on plundering and murdering on the Indian supply lines, mutilating some Indians who fell into their hands. Maude's approach to them was unfor-giving. 'If they interfere with our operations in any way,' he declared, 'they must expect no mercy, but that we shall destroy and burn everything that they have got and kill and hang.' Thus again and again Maude sent Gurkha, Punjabi and other Indian units with British artillery to do just that. They freely burned, shelled and killed, leaving behind dozens of dead Iraqis in a given village and taking away thousands of livestock. When the Cabinet provided Maude with a proclamation for the people of Baghdad on his capture of the city, his troops and the Iraqis knew its finest words – 'Our armies do not come into your cities and lands as conquerors or enemies, but as liberators' – would have been more accurate the other way round. By the end of 1917, the British Occupied Territories of Iraq covered 100,000 square miles, and Indian Expeditionary Force D had grown to 420,000 men subjugating some 2.25 million Iraqis.

'We knew he was talking to his mother'

Maude's Indian troops in Iraq took around 10,000 Turkish prisoners of war in 1916–17, at times treating them no better than they did hostile Iraqi villagers. It seems a vicious cycle developed, whereby some Indian and Turkish troops reciprocated prisoner torture or killing on the battlefield. There were men of the 47th Sikhs, for instance, who resolved to take no mercy on their next Turkish prisoners after one of their NCOs had his eyes taken out by needles in Turkish hands. 'A couple of days later we captured or surrounded a large group of Turks,' remembered the Sikh veteran Suran Singh in a post-war interview, 'and we killed them all with vengeance, very bloody. I participated in this.'

Yet ordinarily the Indian troops humanely treated their Turkish prisoners, escorting them to Basra for transfer into captivity in British India, mostly in Burma. These Turks were in fact exceptionally well treated, as international observers testified. 'Bad treatment is unknown,' the Red Cross reported in April 1917 of the Turkish camps in British India, noting not only the absence of compulsory work, the profusion of good food, and medical care as had traditionally been provided in India for British troops, but also opportunities for painting and long walks at leisure, and sports including horse riding, boxing, football and athletics, with prize money to make the contests more interesting. 'Turkish prisoners, on returning to their country,' the Red Cross concluded, 'will testify that England had treated them with all the humanity they could wish for.'

The Indian prisoners of the Turks, meanwhile, experienced gradually improved conditions of captivity in Syria and Turkey in 1917. At the Indian ranks' prisoner labour camps on the Istanbul–Baghdad railway, their supervising German engineers organised them more systematically than before, for instance with tents to sleep in. This had resulted partly from the efforts of the 6th Indian Division's doctors of the Indian Medical Service, who had been taken prisoner with the men at Kut. They had become their advocates before the Turkish camp commandants and German engineers, pleading for better working conditions.

Among the Indian prisoners labouring in the Syrian desert at Nusaybin, a young Hindu doctor named M. L. Puri, a western-educated Punjabi, took charge of relief parcels that were arriving by early 1917. These came from the Indian Soldiers Fund in London, the Red Cross and the Government of India, and were packed with cooking utensils, rice, sugar, tea and other essentials that the prisoners barely received from the Turks. Puri conscientiously collected all the parcels in a central store in order to distribute their contents equally, but in doing so his darker side came out. There were Indian non-combatant prisoners – ambulance orderlies and others of the 6th Division's medical and supply units – who pilfered parcels from his central store. In anger Puri took drastic measures to stop them, personally seizing them to brand them with marks of shame. Some he smeared with black soot across their foreheads, cheeks and down their noses, others he burned with a red hot poker, forcing it on to their hands and permanently scarring the flesh. 'Thieves were encouraged by the Turkish soldiers and sentries, who bought the stolen articles from them on nominal prices,' said Puri after the war, defending himself during a British inquiry into his inhumane treatment of his own countrymen. 'Whatever I did, was all done openly and with the best of intentions in the world. My actions were watched by about 4000 non-commissioned officers and men ... All were disgusted with the thieving, and they were puzzled how to deal with this matter, and check the evil.'

Throughout the Indian prisoners' labouring on the Istanbul–Baghdad railway in 1917, they had hardly any news from home. At most they received two or three letters each, and sometimes, as Puri saw, these could only tip them into despair. His best friend in captivity was Kalyan Mukherji, the Bengali doctor from Calcutta. Mukherji received a letter from home telling him that his daughter, his only child, had died, and then shortly afterwards another letter with news of his mother's death. 'After that he lost interest in everything,' wrote Puri:

> He ate much less and couldn't sleep at night ... he became delirious. But his enunciation was quite clear even in his delirium; he spoke in Bengali – words poured out of him. Even though I and the other doctors could not understand exactly what he was saying we knew he was talking to his mother. His grief was so great that there was no mistaking it. After six days, on March 18, his delirium ceased. And later that night it was all over.

As for the several hundred Indian officer prisoners of the 6th Division held at camps in Turkey, they were treated more along the lines of the Turkish prisoners in British India. Many Hindu and Sikh officers lived comfortably at the town of Konya south of Ankara, sleeping in requisitioned houses, receiving a British officer's rate of pay*, and free to wander Konya with a Turkish

---

* Officers' pay was an entitlement under international law for prisoners of war, which the Turks paid on the same scale to Indian Army regimental officers without distinguishing between King's Commissions and Viceroy's Commissions.

sentry and buy their own food. Some of them passed their days learning Turkish, and by late 1917 could read Turkish newspapers at cafés and talk with shopkeepers. Their good fortune was to have a benign Turkish commandant, but their fellow Hindu and Sikh officer prisoners held at the town of Afyonkarahisar nearer Istanbul were not so lucky. Here the commandant was by all accounts a drunken sadist who with his assistant-commandant criminally maltreated both Indian and British prisoners. They stole the prisoners' clothes and relief parcels to sell in the local market; they flogged them with a cow-hide whip and caned the soles of their feet; and they allegedly raped some.

It was, however, not the Indian soldiers on the battlefields of Ottoman Iraq or even in the prisoner of war camps in Syria and Turkey who suffered the most cruelly into 1917: that fate befell the Indian Army in East Africa.

'WHY DID I LEAVE MY LITTLE TRENCH IN FRANCE?'

Indian Expeditionary Force B continued to serve in East Africa throughout 1917. It remained integral to the British Empire forces in German territory as they kept up their swirling offensives across great distances, to encircle the Schütztruppen of Paul von Lettow-Vorbeck. Force B's contingent of Indian battalions of western front experience was increased in May 1917 with the arrival from Aden of the 33rd Punjabis, who had fought at the Battle of Loos. Then more independent Pukhtun drafts came in who were surplus to requirements on Turkish fronts, as did further Indian regiments from British India. All the Indian units in East Africa depended heavily on their minority of pre-war professional British and Indian officers – such as Charlie Campbell of the 40th Pathans, Arsala Khan of the 57th Wilde's Rifles and Harold Lewis of the 129th Baluchis – to pass on their long, hard-won fighting knowledge, most importantly in the specifics of bush warfare against the Schütztruppen.

By 1917 bush fighting skills had become ingrained in Force B's Indian units in German East Africa, with Lewis and others of local experience teaching bush warfare training courses to new

arrivals from India. In parallel, the Indian battalions' bush prac-
tices of 1916 had evolved. For instance, they fought in cooperation
with artillery more frequently than before; their patrols now crept
up to Schütztruppen trenches while unrolling long metal wires
behind them, so that artillery batteries could wind in the wires
to find the range of indirect fire support (where a battery takes
aim without a direct line of sight to its target). Equally, the patrols
themselves were stronger on account of new British-made small
arms that began to reach the East African front line in significant quantities, including light machine guns and mortars which
became standard issue as they already were in France and Iraq.

The Indian and other Allied attacking columns in German East
Africa in 1917 succeeded by the end of the year not in encircling
Lettow-Vorbeck's Schütztruppen, but in driving them out of
German territory, south into Portuguese Mozambique. This was
a victory of sorts through conquest if not enemy surrender. In
London William Robertson was satisfied that the Schütztruppen
had been trounced, 'worn threadbare' and 'broken up into detach-
ments without cohesion'.

But the Indian troops involved by late 1917 were not in a
much better state. 'They are not too well done out here,' Charlie
Campbell wrote of the 40th Pathans' independent Pukhtun who
were wise to field service conditions elsewhere, 'they miss France.'
Campbell felt the same himself. 'Why did I leave my little trench
in France?' he wrote. In fact, so consistently awful were Indian
Expeditionary Force B's logistical conditions – even more painful
than Force D's on the Tigris up to the surrender of Kut – that
German East Africa more than any other theatre was the Indian
Army's chamber of horrors.

'I want to die a strong man, not a half-starved weakling'

In 1916 and 1917, the British Empire forces in East Africa experienced virtually insoluble problems of supply. The crux was not

so much provision – since the War Office had taken control of the British campaign in the theatre in November 1914, Lord Kitchener and Robertson had overseen increasing quantities of supplies – but distribution. The British imperial troops in German East Africa from early 1916 never held fixed front lines for months or years as on the western front, or at Suez or Gallipoli. As pursuers of small, widely dispersed forces that darted about unpredictably and withdrew deep into wilderness, they themselves were always on the move in fragments. To stay fed, clothed and otherwise supplied, they needed their transport services to keep up with them. However, East Africa's landscape and under-developed pre-war transport infrastructure made this logistical challenge very difficult from the outset.

Both of East Africa's pre-war region-wide railway lines were in British hands by 1917 (in British East Africa near the southern frontier from Mombasa to Lake Victoria, and in German territory from Dar es Salaam to Lake Tanganyika). But because they ran west to east, in 1916–17 they were of limited use for supplying the British imperial forces that generally attacked north to south. Although new railway lines built to follow troop movements were of some help, they were no real solution; they could never be built fast enough given the construction problems posed by the bush, mountain and jungle terrain. East Africa had many rivers, but not one followed a predictable line of advance over a long distance to a consistently occupied enemy position, like the Tigris from Basra to Baghdad. Motor lorry or van transport was of little use for lack of suitable roads, and the available air transport – relatively weak bi-planes – could only carry low weights of cargo such as cigarettes air-dropped to Indian posts. Horses, mules and donkeys with cart- or pack-loads were constantly used on the ground, yet their mortality rates from equine disease were up to 100 per cent a month. The main mode of supply in East Africa, therefore, was human. For the campaign the British recruited over a million African porters from the

Congo, Rwanda and elsewhere to work in human chains, stretching for thousands of miles on countless tracks. Still, these porters created supply problems themselves: they often ate the food they carried for the troops. Furthermore, they were vulnerable to strains of disease they had not built up an immunity to outside their home areas; they had their own fallen, from disease at a death rate of 20 per cent.

For the Indian troops in the ever-shifting East African front lines into 1917, the upshot was partial and patchy supply at best. They had poor rations for months on end, at times receiving only sacks of stale flour that had hardened like cement during portage. They nearly starved, and had to find their own food. Some Afridi wandered into the bush to hunt antelope; Dogras dug up edible cassava roots; Kashmiris fished the rivers. It was all the more remarkable, then, that some of the independent Pukhtun troops insisted on observing the fast of Ramadan, 'in spite of the dispensations allowed on active service and every effort being made to dissuade the men,' wrote the 40th Pathans' British officer Robert Waters. During Ramadan, he added, these devout Muslims 'kept to the strict letter of the law through all the heat, heavy fatigues, and long marching' – an all but unendurable test of their faith.

Clean water, meanwhile, could rarely be carried to the Indian troops in the field. They usually drew their drinking water from contaminated rivers and pools thick with mud or slime, so dysentery was rife. Then their boots were frequently worn out and their cotton uniforms torn to rags even by just a day of passing through thorn bush. Without a regular supply of replacement clothing, the Indians took to wearing captured German kit. The rainy season of early 1917 was German East Africa's worst for ten years, yet they had no waterproofs. 'What one wouldn't give for the food alone in France, for the clothing and the equipment!' wrote Reginald Thornton, one of the 40th Pathans' veterans of Second Ypres. 'I am perfectly ready to be killed, but if that is to happen, please, I want to die a strong man, with all my faculties intact, not a half-starved weakling.'

To make matters worse, the Indian infantry's daily duties in German East Africa in 1917 were doubly trying compared to the western front or Iraq. They had not only to fight – patrolling the bush remained exhausting and nerve-racking – but also to carry out engineering tasks usually performed by specialists. On the march they met natural obstacles far too numerous for Indian Expeditionary Force B's Sappers and Miners to tackle for them. In April, for example, the Afridi company of the 129th Baluchis had to build by themselves a bridge with piers over a ten-foot-deep jungle river, using trees they felled and ropes they fashioned from tree creepers. 'The men, who had never done such a thing before,' recalled their British officer Arnold Gover, a pre-1914 Indian Army regular attached from the 121st Pioneers, 'were simply bored with the whole business ... The first pier I built almost entirely with my own hands, when suddenly a hawk-faced Afridi Indian officer realised that there was something in it after all and plunged into the water at my side to help; then the men began to get interested; at first they had all denied that they could swim, now several of them remembered that they could.'

The end of a day's march through the bush was barely a chance to rest as the Indian troops had to build their own camps for the night. They slept in huts they improvised out of tree branches and grass, and protected with thorn bush fences or perimeter trenches. While rats crawled over the sleeping Indians, the enemy at least chose to stay away. In April 1916 the Schütztruppen had tried a night attack on an Indian camp south of Kilimanjaro held by the Mahsud of the 129th Baluchis, and had learned a lesson to leave them alone. 'Poor fools! They must have been very badly informed as to our strength or the quality of the troops they had to deal with,' Harold Lewis wrote to his parents:

They came on with bugles blowing and men shouting, and firing heavily ... We were soon thick as peas on our perimeter, with plenty of M. guns, and we fairly laid them out. Some of them got to within 30 yards and a few to five yards, and they came on again and again and kept us awake nearly all night, though a lot of our fellows slept very soundly a yard or two behind the firing line. Their France experiences stood them in good stead, and they were very cool and collected. One of my Mahsuds got six bullets in him round and about the left arm and shoulder, but I could not get him to hospital ... he said he was still quite capable of using a revolver with his right hand. The attack finally finished, and the Huns retired.

The Schütztruppen were in fact of less concern than attackers of another kind the Indian troops faced day and night: insects. 'The first time he got me through a thick flannel shirt in the small of the back, I really thought I had been shot,' wrote the 40th Pathans' Charlie Campbell of being bitten by the tsetse fly, a frequent Indian Army experience. Then Indian troops brushing against grass or leaves in the bush often picked up African ticks, which bit them causing inflammations, headaches and occasionally bad infections. Worse was the jigger or chigoe flea, a South American parasite inadvertently brought to East Africa a few years earlier. The jigger flea burrowed under Indian troops' toenails to lay eggs in the skin; these turned into infestations of larvae and maggots, eating away at toes and feet and leading to black swellings and pus-filled sores. The worst sepoy jigger flea cases could no longer walk, and lost their toes and even their feet.

But most devastating of all to the Indian troops was the female Anopheles mosquito, transmitting malaria, which incapacitated more than it killed. Malaria so ravaged British officers and Indian ranks alike that regiments could be reduced to nearly no fit fighting men – in May 1917, the 129th Baluchis were down to just eleven. The British medical authorities in East Africa provided the

Indian troops with a quinine prophylactic and mosquito nets, yet the problems of transporting supplies prevented these from being distributed around the theatre, and where they were received their application was inconsistent. In any event, avoiding mosquito bites on the move in the field was practically impossible.

What ultimately confirmed East Africa as the toughest Indian front, however, was probably the greatest misfortune an Indian soldier could have in the First World War: being taken prisoner by the Schütztruppen.

'He looks as if he would never smile again'

Among the Turkish prisoners of war held in British India, the death rate was between 1 and 2 per cent. For the Indian prisoners in Germany it was 20 per cent (caused largely by tuberculosis), while for those in Turkish captivity it was 30 per cent. But in German East Africa the Indian prisoner death rate was 65 per cent. A total of around 600 Indian soldiers were captured there from the Battle of Tanga in 1914, mostly Hindu and Muslim pre-war professional soldiers with service records going back to 1900 or so. The majority of them were initially held in the Morogoro region at the centre of the German colony, before the British imperial forces' advance from the north in mid-1916 prompted their relocation westwards to Tabora, south of Lake Victoria. The Indian experience of German East African captivity is largely known from conversations and interviews with Indian veterans, recorded after their liberation by November 1917 as Allied forces overran German territory. 'He gave the most horrible accounts,' wrote Harold Lewis of the 129th Baluchis after speaking with a Muslim Indian officer freed at Tabora. 'He said he was quite sure he had gone through his time of purgatory in this world, and that he had nothing more to fear. He looks as if he would never smile again.'

On capture, the Schütztruppen routinely stripped the Indian

soldiers of their clothes and belongings – always their boots, socks, puttees, haversacks and water bottles, often their breeches too, and sometimes more, leaving some Indians wearing only loin cloths made of their turbans or strips of bark they tore off trees. The instant theft was because the Schütztruppen, fighting on the run and making the most of any resource on Lettow-Vorbeck's orders, needed all the supplies they could get; to them, for instance, puttees were bandages. From the point of capture, the Indian prisoners were force-marched, even if wounded, long distances from the front lines to their camps, 'driven like cattle' as several Indian veterans put it. Relieved of their boots, they had no option but to go barefoot, which allowed mosquitoes to feast on the tops of their feet, and the jigger flea to start feeding under their toenails.

At night in their camps at Morogoro and Tabora, the Indian prisoners slept in filthy, overcrowded thatched huts they had to build for themselves. They had no washing facilities or latrines inside, and were not allowed out before morning; they were left in the dark to clean up their own excrement on the earth floor with their hands. Each morning the Indian prisoners, officers included, were forced into virtual slave labour from dawn till dusk for white German contractors. They chopped wood in forests, cut grass, made bricks and quarried; they pounded grain in flour mills, worked spinning machines in cotton factories, and carried loads as porters; they also cleaned their Schütztruppe and African police guards' latrine pits. The Indians habitually laboured shackled together in gangs of ten to fifteen men, shuffling about with chains choking their throats and scraping into their ankle-bones. Their feet, often writhing with jigger flea maggots, sometimes became so bloody that they left long red trails behind them.

The prisoners were poorly fed with meagre and irregular rations of maize, millet, lentils, beans, rice, peanuts or cassava shrub roots. 'We had a very hard time of it and were treated far worse than coolies,' recalled Sar Baz, an Afridi NCO of the 57th

Wilde's Rifles. He had served in France in 1914–15 and then
Egypt, before his capture in the Uluguru Mountains of central
German East Africa in September 1916. 'Sometimes we were
allowed to gnaw the bones of animals our guards shot in the
jungle, but were never given any meat,' said the Afridi. 'We had to
go and drink water scooping it from the sandy bed of the stream.
We had no drinking vessels to collect it in and couldn't bring it
away, and often went thirsty.'

Some of the Indians found extra food for themselves while
working in the jungle, for example chomping leaves from tama-
rind trees. If they tried to ask their African guards for any extra
food or drink, they could be brutally punished. One Hindu
prisoner, Sripati Bandal, a twenty-five-year-old Mahratta from a
village south-east of Bombay who had been captured at Tanga in
1914, learned this to his appalling cost when he asked for water
at Morogoro. He lodged his request with an Indian translator
named Mirza Umar Beg, a Punjabi Muslim immigrant of German
East Africa's pre-war Indian diaspora, and paid by the Germans
to communicate between the Indian prisoners and their African
guards. In response to Bandal's request, Umar Beg tortured
him by urinating into his mouth and all over his face, which he
repeated on other Indian prisoners who also asked for water.

Their lack of sustenance left the Indian prisoners terribly
weakened and prone to tiring early in the day at their labour.
When they complained about their unrelenting work or blood-
covered chains, paused out of exhaustion or broke down, they
were beaten. Their white German supervisors, African guards
and the Punjabi translator Mirza Umar Beg slapped, punched and
kicked them, smashed them with rifle butts or lashed them with
kibokos, a local rhino-hide whip. 'We were beaten at their sweet
will without any fault,' said Dewan Ali, a Hindu of the princely
States unit the Kashmir Rifles. Kadam Khan of the 130th Baluchis
recalled repeated floggings with the kiboko, 'just as if we were
bullocks.' The beatings killed a number of Indian prisoners, some

on their morning march to their worksites; they were dumped at the roadside, battered and crumpled, to die alone. There are no records of African civilian kindness for them in this state, rather the Indian veterans remembered local African women spitting at them. And all the while the Indian prisoners had no mail and no contact with home.

A captured regimental doctor of the Kashmir Rifles, Sub-Assistant Surgeon Muhammad Din, did all he could for the prisoners, but not much was within his power. Malaria, dysentery and diarrhoea were endemic among them, and there were almost no medical supplies, leaving jigger flea infestations to get as bad as possible. At Tabora in late 1916, one Punjabi Muslim officer prisoner, Lal Khan, saw men die of medical neglect. 'A havildar [NCO] of the 108th Infantry had suffered badly from jiggers for some time without treatment,' Lal Khan said. 'Eventually he was brought to hospital and his feet were immersed in a pot of what looked like hot water. When they were taken out about 15 minutes later, I saw that all the flesh had fallen away from the feet. He died the same day.'

By mid-1917, the Indian prisoners' plight in German East Africa had marginally improved as a result of relief parcels of clothes and first aid. These came from Indian Expeditionary Force B's supply depots in British-occupied German territory, and in a few cases from donors in the Indian Empire such as the Maharajah of Kashmir. Yet the parcels often did not reach the men. 'The Germans showed the parcels of clothes to us jeeringly and then appropriated them,' recalled Haweli Khan, a Muslim prisoner from Kashmir. 'I eventually became mere skin and bones.'

The handful of British officers of the Indian Army captured in German East Africa were held separately from the Indians and not forced to work. They were occasionally granted requests to visit the Indian camps, where in August 1917 one of them, Charlton Palin, a German-speaker of the 129th Baluchis, found that 'unless several of the sepoys were given more food they would only live for another three weeks.' He protested in writing to Lettow-Vorbeck, yet the German commander replied matter-of-factly 'I regret that a certain number of Indian men will die within three weeks unless they are given extra rations,' according to Palin's translation. 'Food is scarce with the whole of the German Army in East Africa,' Lettow-Vorbeck went on, 'so extra will not be issued to prisoners of war.'

Around a hundred Indian prisoners attempted escape from their camps in German East Africa. In some instances Afridi, Hindus or Muslim Dogras distracted African guards at night while the escapees made their exit from their huts in the opposite direction, crawling out and then running off. Many wandered through bush and jungle for weeks, eating leaves and drinking rain water as they searched for Allied lines. Dozens made it, but many died on the way of privation, and those recaptured were severely beaten.

When Allied forces liberated the surviving Indian prisoners in German East Africa in late 1917, the doctors of Indian Expeditionary Force B were shocked at their low numbers in proportion to men captured and their appearance. 'All were suffering from extreme emaciation,' wrote Doctor James Husband of the Indian Medical Service. 'All complained of the callousness and . . . cruelty of their captors.' The Punjabi translator Mirza Umar Beg was caught and promptly tried as a war criminal at a British military court in Dar es Salaam. He was found guilty and sentenced to death by firing squad. His executioners knew him – they were men of the Kashmir Rifles he had tortured.

At the end of 1917, the Indian infantry in East Africa were so weakened by malaria they were withdrawn, bound for British India. They had lasted longer than the South African forces, who had previously departed for the same reason. The campaign was therefore left mainly to British imperial African troops from East and West Africa. The Indian Army fought on with them in the form of mountain artillery batteries, who joined in their pursuit

Men of the 15th Ludhiana Sikhs in the Sahara Desert in early 1916 guarding captured Libyan fighters of the Senussi, the Islamic sect they fought in the Allies' war against the Sultan of Turkey's jihad.

An Indian column on the march in the East African (now Tanzanian) bush, 1916.

Indian cavalrymen representing the Indian Army in Paris at the Bastille Day celebrations on 14 July 1916; by then many of them had learned to speak French.

Indian cavalry moving up to the front line at the Battle of the Somme in July 1916, where they would gallop at German infantry with their lances lowered.

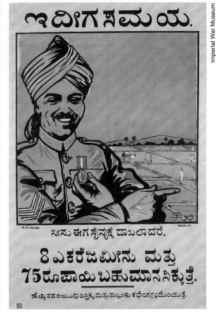

Wartime recruitment posters of British India, calling men to arms to defend their country as part of the British Empire, and pointing clearly at the tangible rewards: money, promotions, medals and land grants.

An Indian carpenter takes a break on the Greek front at Thessaloniki in 1916. He was one of the Indian Army's approximately 500,000 non-combatants of 1914–18, officially not soldiers but 'followers' or 'labourers'.

Sir Pratap Singh, the oldest serving Indian soldier who, in his seventies, fought with the Jodhpur Lancers in France and Palestine between 1914 and 1918. Seen here at Douglas Haig's British General Headquarters on the western front in June 1916, being introduced to the French Commander-in-Chief, Joseph Joffre.

An unknown Indian cavalryman lying dead in France in 1917 next to Ernst Jünger, the German author. Jünger's platoon had dragged his body as a trophy from no man's land to behind German lines for the photo opportunity.

As invaders of Ottoman Iraq, one Indian soldier (top) helps build a trench to secure British-occupied territory near Baghdad in 1917, and another (bottom) shares his food with a local woman.

Indians serving in Asia in 1917–18: at evening prayer in the Iraqi desert (top); riding yaks on secret service in the Himalayas heading for Soviet Central Asia (middle); and bathing in the Yarkon River, now in Israel (bottom).

Indian cavalry in October 1918, occupying Haifa in Syria.

Ganga Singh, the Maharajah of Bikaner, standing behind the US President Woodrow Wilson and others at the Paris Peace Conference in the Irish painter William Orpen's 'The Signing of the Peace in the Hall of Mirrors' (1919). Bikaner, representing the Indian Empire's autonomous 'princely' States, wears the British uniform of a general by virtue of his honorary King's Commission.

The Indian victory parade in London, August 1919, marching up The Mall from Admiralty Arch towards Buckingham Palace.

A Mahsud tribesman (possibly a war veteran) in his homeland of Waziristan in 1919–20, where men of his tribe who had served the Indian Army in France and East Africa now fought against it.

The Indian servicemen brought back many war mementos and trophies from overseas – this German helmet from France was prized among the Naga tribesmen of India's north-east, who added the bison horns and hair as marks of their bravery in victory.

Indian veterans at home in 1925 in the Punjabi village of Dulmial, now in Pakistan, posing proudly with their own cannon given to the village at their request (and still there today). The cannon was a special British reward for providing more recruits than any other village in the Indian Empire.

of Lettow-Vorbeck and the last of his Schütztruppen hiding out in Portuguese Mozambique.

Hundreds of the Indian troops pulled out of East Africa in late 1917 never did get home. They died of African diseases as they sailed back across the Indian Ocean, their bodies being tossed overboard by the ships' merchant seamen without any ceremony, not even listing their names. Soon Arthur Conan Doyle, John Buchan and other British writers would of course pity the Indian infantrymen on the western front as those especially debilitated by a foreign climate. They would even misleadingly explain the Indian Corps' disbandment in France in 1915 in terms of sepoy problems with the European cold weather. But the hot, malarial, jigger-flea-ridden climate of East Africa was surely the worst for the sepoys, and the one they were the most desperate to depart, if such a distinction can be made between the fronts.

As for Indian Expeditionary Force A to France in 1917, it had 10,000 Indian cavalrymen mostly entering their third year of western front service. Some of them, however, had started to write home quite unlike many sepoys there in 1915 whose messages had been so desperate. As if taking leave of their senses, these men of three years' experience of the mud and blood of Europe appeared willing to stay on. 'I do not wish the war to end soon,' a Sikh, Natha Singh, wrote from France to a friend in Punjab. 'I have no intention of returning to India ... May the Holy Guru save me from India.' Their time on the western front, it seemed, was transforming their world view.

21

'BONJOUR PETITE FILLE LOUISE'

'Madame, moi bien content village Visse, bonne santé, beaucoup bonjour petite fille Louise, petit garçon Louis,' a Muslim Indian cavalryman named Amir wrote in November 1916 on a postcard he sent from the French hamlet of Vissé, in the Somme department, to a local family in the nearby village of Allery. 'Madame dire beaucoup bonjour Mlle Germaine Darras et Cécile Niquet de la part du Soldat Amir." Like many of the 10,000 Indian cavalrymen then on the western front with Indian Expeditionary Force A, he was increasingly able to use French, and had become firm friends with a village family he had been billeted on behind the trenches of the Somme, staying in touch once his regiment had moved to another back area. By 1917, their third year on the western front, the Indian cavalrymen had grown intimate with French culture in a way the Indian infantrymen who left the country in 1915 had not had the time for. Many had come to feel France was a home from home where they gained new perspectives, and with these new ideas on how they would

---

* 'Madame, Me very happy village Visse, good health, much hallo little girl Louise, little boy Louis. Madame, say much hallo Miss Germaine Darras and Cécile Niquet on behalf of Soldier Amir.'

change things for their families when they returned to them. As one Pukhtun sowar wrote home, 'there are thousands of lessons here for a man to learn.'

By the end of 1917, however, the Indian cavalrymen were the Indian Army's minority in France, following the arrival of 28,000 Indian non-combatants of the Indian Labour Corps. Compared to the sowars, the labourers came from a wider range of Indian communities, including aboriginal tribes of the Indian Empire's far north-east; all of them were on a journey of cultural discovery of their own. Indeed, in 1917 the men of the Indian Army in Europe would travel much further afield on the continent, encountering its cities and peoples from Italy and Switzerland to the Netherlands and Romania.

'Insects which have crawled out of a black wall'

'They are very curious and ask and talk a lot. They would walk for half an hour to get some milk [and] stand around watching your every move as you serve them,' a priest in Belgian Flanders, Father Achiel van Walleghem, wrote of Indian troops passing through his village of Dikkebus in 1915. 'By and large they are friendly and polite, yet their curiosity often gets the upper hand. They take you in from head to toe and they especially like to take a peek through the windows of our homes.' By 1917, the Indian cavalrymen's observation of Belgian and French rural life had given them so many new thoughts they saw the world afresh. 'We are worms in a dung-hill,' one Sikh said to describe the limits of his village community's outlook, now that he was familiar with French society. 'I think we more nearly approach insects which have crawled out of a black wall,' said a Hindu soldier. 'You talk about heaven and the city of Indra, they are nothing at all.'*

---

* As in Indra the deity in Hinduism, seen in some ancient mythology as the King of the Gods.

By 1917 in their French billets, the Indian cavalrymen had grown used to their host families treating them gratefully as liberators and more as equals than their British officers did. They had become friends with families in the Somme valley in particular, having stayed there the most and been invited to birthday celebrations and other family occasions. 'I found in France the love, respect, beauty and honesty of those people,' recalled Ranjodh Singh, a Sikh veteran, in a post-war interview. 'They regarded us as their own relatives ... We could mix with them because they loved the Indians very much.'

The cavalrymen became known for spending time in billets looking after children whose fathers were away with the French Army. They played games with them, carried them on their shoulders, tied little turbans around their heads and cooked for them. The children's politeness made a great impression. 'There is a custom here which children are taught from the day of their birth, the custom of returning thanks,' a Punjabi Muslim cavalryman wrote to his wife. 'If a child receives anything from anyone it promptly says the word "Merci" ... My wish is that our children should immediately be taught to use this word "Merci" so that they may have become used to it by the time I return. All the other people at home should also learn to use the word.'

French farming culture was a revelation to the Indian cavalrymen, full of wonders foreign to their own fields. They marvelled at the French countryside's greenness, its dependable rains, its fertile soil with a yield twice that of India's, and its sheer variety of crops from barley, flax and apples to beetroot, radishes and turnips. They admired the durability and efficiency of French metal ploughs, harvesting machines and other factory-made farming tools, the handling of cows for milking several times a day, and the use of dogs to pull carts, churn butter and herd sheep. At the farm and village houses, they noted approvingly the contrasts with their own traditional mud-plastered houses; here there were sturdy brick walls, tiled roofs and drainpipes, and arrays of crockery, dressers, mirrors and clocks. 'Their houses were very beautiful and well decorated,' said the Sikh veteran Ranjodh Singh, 'their standard of living was very high.' The cavalrymen also acquired a taste for French food and drink, especially enjoying cider and red wine.

They were greatly struck by how French villagers carried themselves in public. 'I have seen such examples of fortitude and bravery among the French that I can hardly express myself,' wrote Sher Bahadur, a Punjabi Muslim of the 34th Poona Horse, in January 1917:

> I saw one day a peasant ploughing, and a bicycle orderly came up to him and gave him a telegram and went off. I asked the orderly what he had given him, and he said it was a telegram telling him his son had been killed. The old man read the telegram and waited two or three minutes and then went on ploughing. I have seen many cases in which old people have lost three or four sons, and yet have remained unshaken by the blow. There is no wild lamentation as with us in the Punjab, nor do they get into the same state as we do ...

Some cavalrymen wished their own families would show such stoicism. 'It is very wrong of you to work yourself up into a state of illness through anxiety for me,' wrote Jiven Singh, a Sikh cavalry NCO, to his wife in Punjab. 'Just look at the people here. The women have their husbands killed and yet they go on working as hard as ever. It does one's heart good to see them. May God teach our women to behave like them!'

France's marriage customs seemed remarkable compared to India's traditions of arranged marriages for early teens. The cavalrymen supposed that marriage in India, with dowries and loans to pay for weddings, was more costly than in rural Catholic France, and that wife-beating, which was common in Punjab's domestic culture, was happily absent from French households. 'There is affection first between the two parties, who are never less than eighteen years of age,' pondered Teja Singh, a Sikh of the 9th Hodson's Horse. 'After marriage there is never any discord between husband and wife. No man has the authority here to beat his wife. Such injustice occurs in India only. Husband and wife dwell together here in unity.'

Furthermore, the sowars thought the French people were profoundly honest in their dealings in cafés, shops and markets, where the advertising of fixed prices and selling at them contrasted with the bartering and more variable prices of Indian rural life. Added to the French villages' crime rate being so low that many cavalrymen assumed there was none – 'There is no sign of theft. Grain, potatoes and such like things lie in the fields unguarded,' reflected Bakhshish Singh, a Sikh cavalryman – and the apparent social equality of Frenchmen in the absence of a religious caste system, the French appeared to be extraordinary. 'The people are like angels,' wrote another Sikh. 'All they lack is wings.'

The cavalrymen's conclusion was that all the French farming nous, wealth and social order they admired stemmed from something they had been denied: education. They identified the French village schools as a basis of society that India did not have. 'I have seen in this country that no person is uneducated,' wrote a Punjabi Muslim, Firoz Khan. 'No doubt they think that we are very stupid since we can't read. Truly they are right. What is a man without education? Nothing.' The cavalrymen noticed in particular the education of French girls, and French women's relative freedom to use their knowledge as adults. 'In the smallest villages there are schools in which girls and boys are taught,' commented Teja Singh of the 9th Hodson's Horse. 'Women work in just the same way as men. One may be a stationmaster, another a schoolmaster – the difference is simply this, that God made them women.'

Some were so taken with France they thought of immigrating. 'When the victory comes I intend to live in this country,' wrote a Sikh sowar. 'I never even dream of India. My heart is quite estranged from it ' Others were thinking of making India more like France. 'I swear to you I am disgusted with life in India,' avowed Sayed Habib, a Pukhtun. 'If I had my way, I would put every man and woman in India on board a ship and, after bringing them here, showing them over the country, would return them to India, so that they might learn how to use their lives to best advantage.' 'What we have to do,' wrote Bishan Singh of the 6th King Edward's Own Cavalry, 'is to educate our children, and if we do not we are fools, and our children will be fools also.'

By 1917 there were several Indian cavalrymen who had French children of their own, the result of relationships with local women they had met in their billets. One Punjabi Muslim, Mahomed Khan, married a young local woman in April who was pregnant with their baby, born to them in October. Mahomed Khan's marriage, like others between both Muslim and Hindu cavalrymen and local French women, was vehemently disapproved of by many regimental comrades and by family in India, principally as a union with a Christian and therefore outside their religion. Such was Mahomed Khan's family's opposition, carried in blistering letters from home, that he tried to appease them by pretending he had been entrapped and ordered to marry. He wrote to his family in Punjab's Rohtak district saying that his French wife had twice of her own accord petitioned the King-Emperor in London for permission for him to marry her, and the King-Emperor had twice said it was his wish. 'According to His Majesty's order, the wedding came off,' Mahomed Khan claimed. 'There was a General Sahib and a Muslim jemadar as witnesses. But I swear to God that I did not want to marry, but after the King's order I should have got into grave trouble if I had refused.' Mahomed Khan subsequently took frequent short leave from his regiment stationed on the Somme to see his French family and baby girl, Margueritte. Yet he received so many more letters from home disapproving of his marriage that he began to curse his child in his replies. Margueritte, he wrote bitterly, 'is the daughter of a Kafir from whose hands it is unlawful even to drink water.'

Indian cavalrymen also had children with unmarried French girls after liaisons in local villages and barns, or with married women they had affairs with for up to two years or more while the husbands were away with the French Army. Little is known of local responses to these relationships. So strong was the Catholic taboo on sex outside marriage in rural society that they would have been widely disapproved of, and talked about little or not at all in the villages for the shame. In three known cases of the French-Indian babies born outside marriage, they were accepted within their French families as children of the village, but stigma was still attached to them in the eyes of other locals. The prejudices at play here were not simply social, but also racial – for all that the Indian soldiers felt treated as equals in rural France, the locals themselves were not entirely free of the European racial prejudices of their time.

From the British point of view, the Indian soldiers' marriages to French women were of course a slap in the face of their prestige, as indeed were Indian visits to white French prostitutes at Rouen and elsewhere near the front. 'In every village there are four or five hotels,' a Punjabi Muslim cavalryman, Fateh Muhammad Khan, had boasted in January 1916 of the local brothels in a letter home to a friend, 'and each of these today is an ample realisation of the paradise of which we have read in books and heard from the Mullahs ... I send you a picture of a girl. When you see it, you will realise what beauty there is in France.' However, many cavalrymen disdained comrades who visited brothels as straying from their religion with Christian prostitutes, and they shunned those who came back to the regiment with sexually transmitted diseases. 'If a man gets venereal disease,' wrote Ajab Khan of the 38th Central India Horse in October 1917, 'each and everyone perpetually looks askance at him.'

All the while, the Indian cavalry in France had among them India's oldest serving soldier at the age of seventy-three, who was probably also the oldest soldier on the western front: the Hindu socialite and commandant of the premier princely States' unit – Sir Pratap Singh of the Jodhpur Lancers.

'Remember you are only little Gobind Singh'

Sir Pratap Singh had served in France and Flanders since October 1914 with the Jodhpur Lancers, who included his teenage sons Hanut and Sagat, both officers from whom he demanded strict professionalism. True to his pre-war social form, Sir Pratap habitually took leave of his Lancers to mix on high, making the most of his honorary staff appointment at the BEF's General Headquarters. He met with Douglas Haig for private chats as an old acquaintance from India, sitting in Haig's office 'happy, purring like an old tiger', said one onlooker from the War Office. Sir Pratap lunched at French villages or in Paris with European leaders – the French President Raymond Poincaré, the French Army's Commander-in-Chief Joseph Joffre and King Albert I of Belgium. He also assiduously kept up his warm pre-war friendship with the British Royal family, dining with George V at Buckingham Palace, and sending him and the Queen-Empress Christmas presents of *phulgar*s or traditional dressing gowns from Jodhpur State. Indeed, he received gifts in return such as ginger and other things the King and Queen knew he liked. The Prince of Wales (the future Edward VIII) would deliver these on behalf of his parents, visiting Sir Pratap's rented house in France near General Headquarters.

To Haig, George V and almost anyone else who would listen, Sir Pratap declared in his wilfully idiosyncratic English that his heart's desire was fighting to the death for the British. 'I going knocking over one German, dying for my King-Emperor!' he once exclaimed in his quick talk. He was at pains to set himself above the maharajahs and nobles of princely India who also filled honorary staff positions on the western front, but unlike him did no regimental soldiering. In 1915 when most of them went home, he stayed on in the hope of mounted action. 'Me not liking propaganda, me fighting man,' he would say to the British, 'me thinking charging time coming soon'.

Sir Pratap was often in the trenches with the Jodhpur Lancers as the Indian cavalry regiments rotated dismounted in the BEF's front line in France to keep their infantry skills sharp. They held quiet trench sectors in 1917, much as they had in 1915–16, in the Somme and Aisne valleys. In March, after the Germans had abandoned 1000 square miles in the Somme valley to retreat to a new defensive line with a shorter front, the Siegfried Position, the Indian cavalry followed up on horseback. They rode through the wasteland left by the departed Germans. It was covered in slaughtered cattle, felled fruit trees, poisoned wells, land mines, booby traps and burning villages, in bleak contrast to the French countryside they knew behind the Allied trenches. The Indians were distraught, and seem to have taken the scorched earth personally as a crime against a people and country they had taken to heart, writing a number of stridently anti-German letters. 'The evil deeds of the German have excited universal indignation,' wrote Dayal Singh, a Sikh officer of the 6th King Edward's Own Cavalry. Another Sikh of the regiment, Man Singh, said 'we feel miserable to see the shattered houses all round.' For Kartar Singh of the 38th Central India Horse, the Indian cavalry's business with the Germans was unfinished:

> We will not return till we have penetrated into Germany ... Our lust for battle is not yet satisfied. For three years we have experienced many trials and fought in various ways; but the real fighting will commence when we begin to burn their houses and break open their doors and despoil their goods ... even if the war lasts ten years, we shall have our mark here.

The Indian cavalry showed such commitment in the BEF's next offensive, the Battle of Cambrai from late November to early December 1917. As they had done at the Somme, they galloped ahead of British infantry to make rapid local gains. In one charge the 2nd Gardner's Horse jumped rows of German barbed wire, a trick they had specially trained their horses for. 'Thanks be to God, the attack was made with the utmost bravery and it achieved splendid results,' wrote Jowan Singh of the regiment's leading Sikh squadron. 'The fury of our charge and the ardour of our war cries so alarmed the enemy that he left his trenches and fled ... We speared many of the routed enemy on our lances, and brought back many prisoners.'

A Rajput of the 2nd Gardner's Horse, Gobind Singh, won the Victoria Cross at Cambrai on 1 December for riding with messages through a long stretch of no man's land from one Indian dug-out to another. Three times he galloped between the dug-outs, and each time his horse was blown from beneath him by German bullets and shells, but he made it home by sprinting at one moment and crawling the next. Sir Pratap Singh, meanwhile, was in reserve behind waiting by a canal with his Jodhpur Lancers, agitating to lead his men in a mounted charge of their own. 'Whenever I met the Generals, I used to ask them when the cavalry charge will take place,' he wrote, 'but it never came about as I wished.'

At Cambrai the 18th Tiwana Lancers and other Indian cavalry attacked as infantry alongside one of the latest western front weapons: British tanks. In the early morning mist, they advanced on foot next to tanks which were peppered by German bullets, sending sparks flying off like blows to an anvil. Some of the tanks then opened fire on the Indians by mistake, killing a few. But the dismounted sowars kept going, pressing into a wood under German artillery and aeroplane fire. 'I must say I was delighted to see your fine fellows and everyone admired your advance as you came up that ridge towards the wood, because the Hun was throwing a good deal of stuff at you,' a British officer of the Grenadier Guards wrote to the Tiwana Lancers afterwards. 'But your fellows came on without turning a hair, and more than one of our men remarked on it.'

The 18th Tiwana Lancers' casualties at Cambrai were low by western front standards, totalling seven men killed and thirty-two wounded, with seventeen horse casualties. The other Indian cavalry regiments suffered similar or lower losses, which drew them closer together as bands of long-serving brothers. Jowan Singh of the 2nd Gardner's Lancers described his friend Kartar Singh, killed by shell fire, as 'a hero who has given his life for his King. He is not dead; he lives forever. He has gone straight to Paradise, because that is the reward of death in the field of battle in the service of the King.'

There were some isolated instances of crime among the Indian cavalry in France, such as the rape of a nineteen-year-old French woman by two Sikhs, and the murder of a bullying Hindu NCO by one of his men who was then executed by a Hindu firing squad of their regiment. But the vast majority stuck to their duties. 'Our men are quite happy as they are making money hand over fist,' thought Robert Manderson, a British officer of the 3rd Skinner's Horse, as his men saved up their earnings at the 25 per cent extra pay rate for Europe.

Sir Pratap Singh often went round the Indian cavalry regiments in their French billets to give morale boosting talks on serving the British honourably. 'I always exhorted them to keep up the name of India,' he said. He spoke longest with the Hindu troopers who were Rajputs like himself, and accompanied the Rajput VC of Cambrai, the message-rider Gobind Singh, to his VC investiture at Buckingham Palace. Gobind Singh was unassuming and known for his modesty, but Sir Pratap still felt he needed a reminder of how to behave after George V had pinned the VC to his chest with kind words of congratulation in Hindustani. Sir Pratap ushered him into a Palace side room, grabbed him by the ears and shook his head so hard his turban fell off. 'You think you are a *bahadur* (brave hero) don't you?', Sir Pratap shouted. 'But don't let it go to your head. Remember you are only little Gobind Singh, little Gobind Singh, little Gobind Singh. Just remember to get on with your duties as before.'

While the Indian cavalrymen on the western front felt senses of duty, obligation and honour to serve the British as Gobind Singh VC and the others did at Cambrai, and of course were enamoured of many things French, they still sent letters home ruing their lot in Europe. 'I am always praying to God that He will grant us to come back and see our dear ones who will receive us with open arms,' Sobha Ram, a Hindu Jat sowar, wrote in January 1917 to his family in Punjab. 'How true,' he went on, 'were the words of the poet "Oh bee, how often I have warned you against sipping the honey of the flowers, because one day or other you will get caught and yield up your life writhing in agony". This is the situation in which we find ourselves.'

Home leave had in fact been opened to the Indian cavalry in France in November 1916. But the odds were against many getting leave soon. It applied only for 5 per cent of each regiment at a time, with the longest serving or those with special compassionate grounds going first, all chosen by their British commandant. 'If thirty men from each regiment are granted leave at intervals of three months, 120 men per regiment will have leave per annum,' calculated the 34th Poona Horse's Jemadar Shamsher Ali Khan, a Punjabi Muslim. 'Thus very few men will reap the benefit ... Anyhow, the orders as they stand must be accepted as a great concession.' Others simply felt dismay if they did not qualify first for home leave. 'Only those are going who have done two years. I am not in the running at all, as I have only been out a year and a half,' lamented a Hindu of the 2nd Gardner's Lancers named Bhagirath. 'I have not the slightest hope of returning before the end of the war ... I have come to the conclusion that we are Government donkeys who always get a full load. I only want life and health, and that is all I think of.'

However, the Indian cavalrymen in France received letters in

1917 counselling them to be careful what they wished for. 'It was our fate to leave the fine climate of France and to go to a horrible country where climate and weather was our most deadly foes,' wrote a Sikh NCO whose regiment were back in British India. 'The first week of our arrival plague broke out, and we lost 15 men in three squadrons ... You may think us lucky having got back to our own country, but I can assure you that every one of our regiment thinks field service a hundred times better than this.' One Hindu redeployed to India even described leaving France as being 'cast out of Paradise ... If the opportunity were to come again for me to return to France I should consider myself to be fortunate.' There were indeed some Indian infantrymen wounded on the western front in 1914–15 who were given just such a chance to return – and they took it, going back not to fight, but with the Indian Labour Corps.

'German helmets have taken a hold on their fancy'

In north-east Italy in the summer of 1917, a group of Indian Catholic tribesmen built a tennis court near Bologna, at the town of Faenza in the Piazza d'Armi. They were aboriginal Santhals from the remote forested uplands of the Chota Nagpur Plateau, in the Indian Empire's north-east. They built the court, Faenza's first, for their British officers and dug ditches nearby to drain the site of a new camp. This was one of several camps set up on a 2000-mile overland Indian trail the length of continental Europe. It stretched from the port of Taranto in Italy's far south, up to Faenza, west to the Auvergne of central France, then north to near the French shore of the English Channel. The camps were staging posts for the Indian Army's latest contingent for the western front: the 28,000 non-combatants of the Indian Labour Corps. They were to travel on trains through Allied Italy instead of sailing direct to France in order to save on British shipping, which was in increasingly short supply in 1917 as Germany waged unrestricted submarine warfare in the Mediterranean, Atlantic and North Sea.

Once London's Directorate of Labour had requested the Indian Labour Corps for France, the tentacles of the Indian Army's reformed territorial recruitment system under its Commander-in-Chief Charles Monro spread in early 1917 to suck in the villagers required. India's local civil authorities carried the offer of Labour Corps employment to some rural regions that had provided pre-war Indian soldiers, above all in the North-West Frontier Province, Punjab, and the Himalayan foothills of the United Provinces of Agra and Oudh. Yet they focused more on remoter communities without traditions of military service. These were predominantly isolated tribes of the forests and jungles of north-east India in the provinces of Bihar and Orissa, Assam and Burma, including those future tennis-court builders the aboriginal Santhals, who had been converted to Catholicism by Belgian Jesuit missionaries. Then there were some other recruits from further south – Bengali Christians, and Jews, Parsis and Hindus of the Bombay area.

Some of the Indian Labour Corps volunteers from the Himalayan foothills of the United Provinces stepped warily down to its small town recruitment stations, making it clear to the recruiters where they wanted to go. They asked for 'Phranch' not 'Bachchra' (France not Basra) having heard the balance of opinion on the rural grapevine about which of the two the soldiers preferred. They and the other Indian Labour Corps recruits entered into contracts to work on the western front, mostly for a fixed term of one year, and governed by Indian Army law, making them a part of the army. Each of them joined a particular labour company named after their home region or town near it, such as the 31st Bihar, the 42nd Ranchi or the 51st Santhal companies. Like the Indian soldiers, the labourers' driving motivation was economic: a regular wage with three months' advanced pay was a windfall for their generally impoverished agriculturalist families. Some from the Lushai Hills of Assam in north-east India were enticed in particular by the prospect of saving enough money in France to return home more eligible for marriage. Still more attractive for the Lushais and others from Assam and the Himalayas was a lifetime local tax exemption, guaranteed by certificates handed out by the local civil authorities.

The Indian Labour Corps' companies were given a military veneer with khaki uniforms and company officers. Although several of the officers were Belgian Jesuit missionaries familiar with their men, some were British strangers who did not speak their languages. A few others were the wounded Indian soldiers who chose to return to the western front. They were pensioned Garhwalis, Gurkhas and Punjabis who had fought there in 1914–15, presumably had a fondness for France, and elected to go back to make money without the dangers of regular infantry work. One Labour Corps company almost fell apart on meeting their officers for the first time, at the routine medical inspection when they were asked to strip naked. This was a shaming experience, and they objected especially to the inspection of their genitals for signs of sexually transmitted disease. 'The men were shocked and horrified, because exposing themselves was only to give point to an intended mortal insult,' William Alderson, a British captain of the 42nd Ranchi Company, remembered of hill-men from the Indian far north-east. 'A great cry of "Nai!" went up … and it took some time to sort out … without them all heading for home.'

On the sea lanes from British India across the Indian Ocean and Mediterranean to Italy from April 1917, the Indian Labour Corps sweltered in hot, cramped quarters below deck. These conditions killed a few who had embarked with cholera, and their bodies were dropped into the sea. More died of cholera in southern Italy at Taranto, where they were buried, while others were held in quarantine for a month. As the Indian labourers travelled the length of Italy by railway passing medieval stone towns on hill-tops and much else they had not seen before, the unrestricted

German submarine warfare they had just escaped at sea shaped the work that lay ahead for them in France. Significantly increased sinking of Allied shipping meant war materials were scarcer, and therefore the Indian Labour Corps would have more salvage work to do than otherwise, looking for metal, wood and other debris – a dangerous task that would take them to the trenches.

When the Indian labourers started work on the western front in June, they cleared up parts of the Somme battlefield which the Germans had abandoned in their retreat to the Siegfried Position. They stripped bare disused trenches or dug-outs, and lugged rusty barbed wire and other front line debris onto motor trucks for disposal or recycling. Father Frans Ory, one of the Indian Labour Corps' Belgian Jesuit missionary officers, wandered about the derelict trenches with his company of tribal labourers from British India's north-eastern province of Bihar and Orissa, many of them former pupils at his missionary school at Ranchi. He saw how shocked his men were by what they found. 'Every five yards we come across bones still wrapped up in their puttees, arms and legs blown off by shell-fire,' he wrote at Thiepval on 26 September. 'One of our old Ranchi boys had his heart full and stood by weeping.'

Father Ory warned his men never to handle the smaller battle-field debris, but some did not listen, the sound of their screams revealing accidental self-inflicted wounds. One labourer fiddled with a tubular detonator for a shell he picked up to make a cigarette-holder, only for it to explode in his hands and shred them. Another man spotted what looked like a flask with a stopper where the drink inside should pour out, but it was a tear gas canister, which he opened only to gas himself. 'It is in their nature to take lessons from experience alone,' shrugged Father Ory. His men took to collecting stray bits of German uniform, putting them on with their own twists. 'German helmets have taken a hold on their fancy,' he observed. 'When the steel pike has been knocked off, they stick field flowers in the hole.'

The Indian Labour Corps did many other jobs around north-eastern France in support of the Allied forces. Its companies worked looms to make mattresses, cut stone in quarries, chopped down trees in forests, and made charcoal, an ingredient for gas masks. They also made trench duckboards, built an aerodrome, burned limestone in industrial kilns, and laid roads and railway tracks. They worked around nine hours a day, day after day. Indeed, they rested so little that exhaustion set in among several companies, and British supervisors administered opium to keep the men going.

The labourers had an uneasy relationship with their Indian officers who had chosen to return to the western front having fought there in 1914–15. These veterans kept aloof and liked to assert their superior status as old combatants. As the winter of 1917–18 drew in, they preferred to go cold rather than wear the warm coats made available to the labourers. Some in fact looked on the labourers with contempt as their social inferiors. 'The men are utterly filthy and take no care of their health,' said one of the old soldiers, a Punjabi Muslim, who disapproved of his men's lack of the hygiene and discipline he had known in his regiment.

Each evening the Indian labourers trudged back to their camps, which were isolated and scattered about the countryside up to five miles from the nearest village. They were confined to their camps when not at work, which afforded them very little interaction with the local people. Their camps were initially so dreary and devoid of almost anything but tents that a company of Lushai tribesmen from India's north-eastern hills of Assam decided to improve theirs. 'We looked around and collected corrugated iron sheets and other things, and we built a big rec-reation hall,' explained Sainghinga Sailo, the Lushais' company clerk. 'The other room was made into a canteen. We pooled our money to buy and sell all kinds of things. The canteen began to make a profit. We bought a bioscope. Since many of us had not seen "moving pictures" it brought us much joy.' Occasionally the labourers encountered servicemen from other countries for the first time, for instance Australian troops camped nearby. As well as exchanging cigarettes and eating together, the Indians and Australians played football. There was frequent laughter during these games as the Indians shouted out English phrases the Australians used, like 'Come here, you bloody fool', 'Stick to it, Johnny', and 'Hang on, man'.

Army contractors soon set up shop in the Indian Labour Corps' camps. The labourers' officers discouraged them from buying much, better to save money for home. Still, there was a shopping craze for things the labourers did not have back in their villages, such as tinned sardines, soap and safety razors, and above all cheap watches, most prized for having glow-in-the-dark hands. The watches helped the labourers develop new understandings of time, including adapting to the seasonal timings of sunrise and sunset, more variable than at home nearer the equator. The labourers were openly disappointed not to see more of France beyond their camps and worksites, a Lushai company from India's north-east agreeing that they hoped in coming to Europe they would 'see the world'. The India Office eventually granted them their request to visit London, organising week-long entertainment tours of the city for parties of ten labourers with their officers – as it had in fact also done for Indian infantrymen in November 1915 and subsequently for Indian cavalrymen. Elsewhere around Europe, meanwhile, the range of new countries, cities and people encountered by Indian servicemen had expanded dramatically.

'The Italian prisoners were very very good to us'

In Germany by 1916, parties of the Indian prisoners from France held south of Berlin at Camp Crescent Moon had been taken to see the sights of the city. German officers had guided the tours, intent on impressing them for the camp's propaganda purposes with Germany's wealth and modernity. At the camp late that year and into early 1917, the 500 or so Indian prisoners had then met an eclectic delegation of German and Austrian academic researchers: anthropologists, ethnologists, linguists, musicologists, cinematographers and photographers. The German authorities allowed the researchers in as the camp's propaganda programme wound down with the ebb of the Sultan of Turkey's jihad, and they studied the Indian prisoners as exotic specimens for pseudo-scientific and cultural reasons. Getting up close for weeks, the researchers took facial portraits, plaster casts and cranial measurements, filmed the Indians performing religious rituals and dances, and recorded their folk songs and fairy tales.

One of the German linguists, Wilhelm Doegen, introduced the Indian prisoners to modern sound recording technology. He preserved their spoken word on Edison phonograph gramophone discs, asking them to talk about their religions or just themselves. Some of the Indians seemed to enjoy meeting him and helping, laughing at each other's village dialects. Yet for Mall Singh, a twenty-four-year-old Sikh soldier who had sailed to France in 1914 and was recorded by Doegen in December 1916, there was only sadness to tell of. 'There once was a man. He was drawn into the European war. Germany made this man a prisoner,' Mall Singh said mournfully. 'He wants to return to India. If God has mercy, He will soon bring peace. Then this man will go away from here.'

Some of the Gurkha prisoners captured in France in 1914 had been transferred from Germany to Switzerland, to stay at an Alpine chalet near Lake Geneva. They had moved in May 1916 under a compassionate Anglo-German agreement for British Empire prisoners incapacitated by wounds or sickness to be interned in Switzerland under Red Cross care. The Gurkhas were eligible having contracted tuberculosis. They had travelled out of Germany by train through the border city of Konstanz with hundreds of British and Canadian internees. In Switzerland they had stopped at Lake Geneva's Montreux railway station, where thousands of cheering townspeople met them waving hats, handkerchiefs and flags as a band played the Swiss national anthem. This eruption of Swiss goodwill was followed by a public gala breakfast on the lake shore, at which all the internees were the guests of honour. The Gurkhas then settled in at their chalet nearby, cared for by Swiss doctors.

Back in Germany, in spring 1917 the government transferred the majority of the Indian prisoners left at Camp Crescent Moon (some 450) to Romania, recently conquered by the Central Powers and now German-occupied. The move was meant to be of mutual benefit. The warmer climate would help the Indian prisoners shake off their tuberculosis and other respiratory infections, which had been a constant problem for them in Germany; and now that the revolutionary propaganda programme for them had come to a halt, their exemption from labouring work was lifted, and they could help exploit Romania as a new source for German supplies.

By the summer the Indian prisoners had been relocated to a German agricultural colony in south-east Romania, where they were well treated. Their work was relatively gentle, cultivating fruit gardens and harvesting crops in fields, for which they received regular pay. They had free time for prayers, football, and swimming in the Ialomita River, and slept in snug farm building dormitories arranged by religion, with electricity, bunks and blankets. Their parcels from the Indian Soldiers Fund kept coming, including clothes for the coming Romanian winter of 1917–18. Their health improved, and their death rate went down from 20 per cent to 8.5 per cent. The hundred or so Indian soldiers still held prisoner in Germany, almost all of them cavalrymen captured in France over 1917, were also put to work, on German farms, giving them a close look at German rural life to add to their experiences in France.

Indian prisoner movements elsewhere in Europe took the total number interned on compassionate grounds of ill health in neutral countries to around a hundred, with more going from Germany to Switzerland and also to the Netherlands. The internees in Dutch care included the 4th Gurkhas' Subadar-Major Sher Singh Rana, at The Hague as a psychiatric patient. At Camp Crescent Moon he had warned the Gurkha prisoners against the propagandists' invitation to revolution as against their Indian Army oath, dishonourable and inviting British penalties. The Germans had punished him with solitary confinement, as a result of which he appears to have had a mental breakdown.

Under compassionate agreements with the Turkish government, meanwhile, around 1000 severely wounded or sick Indian soldiers were released from captivity in Turkey and Syria for repatriation. Some of them left in November 1917 by way of Istanbul on a hospital train that headed west into Europe. They spent the winter of 1917–18 in northern Austria, at the Mauthausen prisoner of war camp. Here they made new friends among the Italian prisoners from the Alpine front. 'In Mauthausen there was hardly anything to eat,' recalled Yakhatu Shivdi, an NCO of the 110th Mahrattas who had been captured near Baghdad in November 1915. 'The Italian prisoners were very very good to us and saved our lives, giving us their own things; they gave us half their bread.'

In February 1918, Shivdi and his group from Istanbul moved on through Switzerland. 'We were very well received by the Swiss, the women and children cheering and giving us cigarettes,' he said of their reception at Zurich and other railway stations. They were joined on their train towards the French border by the British ambassador to Switzerland and his military attaché, Henry Picot, formerly of the Indian Army, with his wife and daughter. 'On visiting the cot cases,' wrote Picot, 'I came across two Indian soldiers, one of whom, a man of low caste, who had served as a transport driver, appeared to be very cheery, and to all outward appearance in good health':

I spoke to him in his own language, and asked why he was in bed. In reply, he turned aside the bed covers, disclosing the stumps of both legs amputated high above the knee. I was much taken aback, and could only ejaculate, 'You have done well by the Sirkar', a remark which met with the response, 'Oh, that is of no consequence, I would have done better if I could.' The other, a high caste man ... seemed to be ill at heart rather than of body. I tried to cheer him by speaking of his early return to India, and of the sunshine of his own country, but nothing I could say gave him any comfort.

On Europe's south-eastern front by the end of 1917, in Greece at the Aegean port of Thessaloniki where the British and French forces were blocked in by the Bulgarian Army, an Indian non-combatant contingent of mule corps of approximately 5000 men had been there for almost two years. Some had previously served with their mules with Indian Expeditionary Force A to France and Force G to Gallipoli, making them the Indian Army's only men to have served against the Germans, Turks and Bulgarians. As they loaded their carts at camps outside Thessaloniki with supplies for the troops, rattled along the stone and dirt roads up to the Allied trenches and brought back wounded or malaria-stricken British and French soldiers, they were known for talking to their mules in soft, caring tones, and for grooming them tenderly. They had home leave only for limited numbers like the Indian cavalrymen in France. They therefore came to know well Thessaloniki's ancient streets, which from their camps they saw bombed by German air raids, and burn in the enormous fire of August 1917 that ruined two thirds of the city.

Records of Indian interactions with European culture on the Greek front do not survive as they do for the western front. It seems the Punjabi muleteers at least thought over local agricultural techniques compared with those at home. They helped to farm crops for Allied supply, initially with Punjabi-style wooden ploughs of their own making harnessed to their mules, before they switched to more dependable Greek iron ploughs. The Indian who ventured farthest inland from Thessaloniki seems to have been Santa Singh of the 3rd Mule Corps, who was captured by the Bulgarians in the summer of 1917 while chasing an errant mule. He was held prisoner some 60 miles north-east of the port at Fort Rupel (today in Greece's Central Macedonia Region), where he worked as a cook for an Indian pilot of the Bulgarian Flying Corps; the pilot had in fact emigrated from Calcutta to northern Greece in 1912, married a local girl, settled in the Macedonian mountains and enlisted with the Bulgarians in 1915. Santa Singh escaped back to the Allied lines after a month's captivity, however, seemingly having had little contact with the Bulgarians himself.

As the Indian Army continued serving in Europe into 1918 from the Somme valley to Thessaloniki, back in British India there had been great political developments. The burning question of Indian politics in the First World War was what political concessions would the British give in return for India's contribution to the imperial war effort? The question had of course arisen in 1914–15 in parallel with the moderate Indian nationalist politicians' backing for the war, and its answer by 1918 would show where the Indian soldiers fitted into the now rapidly developing mainstream nationalist cause.

Six

1918

22

'THE POLITICAL SELF-DEVELOPMENT OF THE PEOPLE'

During Charles Hardinge's viceroyalty up to 1916, he had given only vague hints to the Indian nationalist politicians as to what political concessions the war might entail for British India. 'England has instilled to this country the culture and civilization of the west with all its ideals of liberty and self-respect,' he declared in a much publicised speech of 1915 on the future of the imperial mission, reasoning that the inevitable consequence of those ideals must be some divestment of British governing powers. This, he said, was a 'glorious task' which must elevate British purpose in India to a higher plain of 'encouraging and guiding the political self-development of the people'. He went a little further in his viceregal farewell speech in March 1916, describing Indian self-government as 'a perfectly legitimate aspiration', yet still did not elaborate on how or when it might be realised.

The truth was that Hardinge did not know, and he and the British government were publicly silent on the matter – neither Delhi nor London was inclined to dwell on proposals for Indian political reform when their focus was winning the war. But in December 1916, the Indian politicians brought strong pressure on the British to chart a course towards self-government. Members of the Indian National Congress and its counterpart the All-India Muslim League petitioned for India to have self-governing Dominion status within the British Empire equal to Australia, New Zealand, South Africa and Canada, including a widened electoral system beyond the existing meagre representation for Indians in legislatures such as the Imperial Legislative Council. Their justification for this kind of progress was supercharged in early 1917 by a sudden international energising of pro-democracy movements. In March, Russia's Tsarist autocracy fell to be replaced by a liberal socialist interim regime, the Provisional Government, promising universal suffrage; and in April the United States joined the Allies, prompted by Germany's submarine warfare in the Atlantic which had sunk neutral American ships and taken American lives. The American entry into the war was especially significant, with President Woodrow Wilson re-articulating the Allied cause to a joint session of Congress in Washington DC. 'Prussian autocracy was not and could never be our friend,' he declared. 'The world must be made safe for democracy ... We are but one of the champions of the rights of mankind.'

By mid-1917, therefore, both domestically and internationally, the British silence on political progress in India was becoming embarrassingly uncomfortable. The Indian politicians had got something in the spring in the form of representation in London on the Imperial War Cabinet. This was an inflated version of the Prime Minister David Lloyd George's ordinary War Cabinet, and it sat temporarily at 10 Downing Street as a British Empire council on defence policy; it had an Indian Congressman along-side Australian and other white politicians of the British imperial world. Then on 20 August the British finally stated their polit-ical intentions in India. This was the momentous Montagu Declaration on constitutional reform, read out in Parliament by the Secretary of State for India, Edwin Montagu, a Jewish Liberal:

The policy of His Majesty's Government, with which the Government of India are in complete accord, is that of the increasing association of Indians in every branch of the administration, and the gradual development of self-governing institutions, with a view to the progressive realisation of responsible government in India as an integral part of the British Empire ... I would add that progress in this policy can only be achieved by successive stages. The British Government and the Government of India, on whom the responsibility lies for the welfare and advancement of the Indian peoples, must be judges of the time and measure of each advance ...

In the days leading up to the Montagu Declaration, Lloyd George's War Cabinet had felt compelled to make it by the Allied cause rather than any overriding enthusiasm for Indian self-government. 'We are really making concessions to India because of the free talk about liberty, democracy, nationality, and self-government, which have become the common shibboleths of the Allies,' explained the War Cabinet's former Viceroy Lord Curzon, whose pen produced the Declaration's final wording, 'and because we are expected to translate into practice in our own domestic household the sentiments which we have so enthusiastically preached to others.' Montagu himself interpreted his Declaration as a relatively small step for India. For him, 'the gradual development of self-governing institutions' meant no great leaps towards Indian independence or India as a single, self-governing political unit with its own parliament free of British control, but at least 500 years more of British rule with Indian cooperation.

Further, to Montagu and the War Cabinet his Declaration was explicitly not a reward for the Indian Army's war service. In their minds, its constitutional concessions were to mollify the Indian politicians, who, said Curzon, 'have no right to claim them on the ground of war service, for they have rendered no such service'. Curzon was referring to the fact that the Indian politicians and their families had not fought in the Indian Army, whose villager ranks, in British eyes at least, remained sequestered from nationalist politics as an exalted preserve of the highly educated. But the Declaration had two immediate implications for Indian recruits. First, if it was not aimed at them, what political reward did they get for offering up their lives to the fight against the Central Powers? And second, what did it mean for their relationship with the nationalist politicians?

In both respects by mid-1918, the answers were painful for the villagers of the Indian Army's recruitment grounds. As the political reward for the Indian troops, the British would open the door to equality of command with white men more widely, but prove extremely selective about who they allowed through. Meanwhile the Indian politicians – including Mahatma Gandhi – related most closely to Indian recruits by actively encouraging them to serve the British. In doing so they subscribed wholeheartedly to the Allies' democratic ideals that had propelled the Montagu Declaration, but it is far from clear that the Indian recruits shared in these too.

'He may control the destinies of Englishmen'

Even though in August 1917 Edwin Montagu and the War Cabinet did not see his Declaration as a political reward for Indian troops' war sacrifices, they agreed that such a reward was necessary in parallel with the Declaration. They were mindful that by 1914 Indian lawyers and civil servants (known as 'civilians') could rise to senior posts with authority over British individuals in the courts or government departments, whereas the Indian Army had kept intact the absolute superiority of the British officer. The Hindu diarist Thakur Amar Singh had of course found this as one of the tiny minority of serving Indian soldiers granted a pre-war King's Commission with no right of command over white men. Yet Montagu felt that the Indian Army as an institution of state now must move with the times, and no longer remain such an exclusive enclave of white privilege. 'It is absolutely impossible,' he advised the War Cabinet, 'to tell an Indian that he may control the destinies of Englishmen if he becomes a judge or an Indian civilian, that to the talking people and to the politicians all avenues are open, but that if he fights for the Empire he can never expect to hold a position of authority.'

Simultaneous with his Declaration, therefore, Montagu announced as the political reward for the Indian troops the lifting of the racial bar denying them equality of command. The mechanism for this was a new right for any Indian soldier to receive a King's Commission in the Indian Army the same way a British officer did, with equal pay and pension. In theory, an Indian soldier could now exercise power of command over white soldiers of inferior rank, and rise as high as his ability deserved in the Indian General Staff or Indian high command, right up to Commander-in-Chief.

Yet the new right's potential to compromise British prestige, and the limited British intentions of the Montagu Declaration it accompanied, ensured that its practical effects in the Indian Army's command structure were tightly constrained in the colonial interest. Its true nature as a half-hearted political gesture was reflected in its announcement without any plan for its day-to-day workings. Almost all the details were up in the air – how many candidates to allow; how to prepare or examine them for entry to officer cadet training; how to pay for their cadet training if they were from a poor village family; whether to train them in India by themselves or in England with their British peers; whether to place them in command of Indians of other religions or castes who might reject their authority; or how to fit them and their wives into British cantonment society, when they had their own dietary requirements and non-western social traditions such as purdah.

In short, for the British granting equality of command was easier said than done. The only faintly practical step for the time being was taken to lend a public appearance of change. In August 1917 the War Cabinet bestowed not a single King's Commission on the mass of Indian soldiers who had fought with the Indian regiments in the trenches since 1914, the very men who were supposed to be rewarded. Rather it turned to the aide-de-camp Indian officers from royal and aristocratic families who had pre-1914 King's Commissions, handing nine of them upgraded regular King's Commissions in the Indian Army. The majority of the nine were not even from British India, and they included Thakur Amar Singh.

Having been with Indian Expeditionary Force D in Iraq in April 1916, that summer Amar Singh had taken home leave to Jaipur State, which was specially available to him on account of his inessential staff duties and non-fighting role. He had been extremely anxious to get home having just heard in the Iraqi desert by letter from his wife Rasal that their young daughter and only child, whom he had last seen at home as a one-year-old in August 1914, had died of smallpox – their fifth baby taken from them by disease. 'I really don't know why God is so cruel to me and my wife,' he wrote of their tragic losses. 'What I am most afraid of now is my wife's feelings and health.' After his two months' home leave, Amar Singh's next Indian Army posting in late 1916 had been another as an aide-de-camp with light duties. This time he was on the Indian logistical staff at the port of Bombay, where into 1917 he monitored the complaints of Indian troops sailing away or coming home, for instance about butter rations at the port being adulterated with coconut oil by fraudulent suppliers. That spring, Amar Singh's wife gave birth to their sixth child, a girl named Ratan (meaning 'Jewel'). Then in August, when his pre-war King's Commission was upgraded with the new right of equal command, he remained, as a thirty-nine-year-old captain, the most senior Indian officer serving in the Indian Army.

In many respects Amar Singh had been longing for equality of command. Since 1914 he had thought through the idea of political concessions for India in return for cooperating with the British, and been set on the exchange as worth it. On the western front in September 1915, his views on whether the Indian infantry should be spared a second French winter and sent home were unequivocal in terms of improving Indians' status among white men. He described their potential departure from Europe as 'the worst thing that could possibly happen':

> in the future when some one would like to insult us he would fling it in our teeth that we were not considered good enough to fight the Germans & so had to be sent back ... I would much rather that every one of the Indians in France were killed than sent back ... They must see it through whatever happens. It is on them that the honour of India rests. India will get tremendous concessions after the war which she would not have gained otherwise – at least not for several years to come.

Up to late 1916, whether in France, at sea on troopships, in Iraq or British India, Amar Singh had been exasperated by the lack of respect that British privates showed to him and other Indian officers. For example, he resented their habit of not saluting him. 'There are very few Tommies indeed who take any notice of me,' he wrote. 'There is no getting away from the fact that this is not right.' When Amar Singh finally got equality of command, therefore, he was proud of his improved status; it was something of a personal release from years of racial disrespect. Yet his satisfaction was overshadowed within days by a financial slight. The Indian officers with upgraded King's Commissions learned that their improved pay and pensions on the British officers' scale were to be pegged from the date of the upgrade in 1917, rather than backdated to the grant of their original King's Commissions from 1905. They protested with threats of resignation over the issue, and succeeded in getting the starting date of their original King's Commissions as effective for the payments.

Even then, equality of command had come too late for Amar Singh to mean much for his career. He had no real ambition to rise a rung higher in the Indian Army to become a major, which according to the ordinary promotion regulations would take him sixteen years. He wanted to quit both the Indian Army and British India, in order to return home to serve in the Jaipur State forces; then he could spend more time at home with his wife and their baby girl, Ratan. His main reason for staying in British service was his improved pay and pension, which he accumulated into 1918 on the logistical staff at Bombay. He led an easy life there, living at the Taj Mahal Hotel with time on his hands for driving about the city with his princely and aristocratic friends in their Buicks and Dodges, taking trips to the cinema to see Charlie Chaplin films and the British documentary feature *The Battle of the Somme*, or going on tours of local Buddhist caves.

So when in June 1918 the call came to Amar Singh at Bombay to join an Indian regiment – all nine of the Indian officers with upgraded King's Commissions were being moved into regular Indian regimental service to put the privilege of their new power of command into practice next to British officers – he recoiled from the opportunity. 'This was rather a bombshell,' he wrote of his posting to the 16th Cavalry on internal security duty at Delhi. 'It was with a wrench that I left Bombay ... I did not want to change my present appointment where I was perfectly happy ... I wanted to stick to odd jobs where there is less to do & more pay to get.'

Amar Singh joined the 16th Cavalry in July with not so much a spring in his step as discomfort at the prospect of hard work as a regimental officer. After arriving at the regiment's cantonment outside Delhi he turned down the command of a squadron, choosing the easier option of a half-squadron to avoid any embarrassing mistakes, unfamiliar as he was with the latest training routines with French-made heavy machine guns and other modern weapons. He had a relatively gentle time with the 16th Cavalry over the summer of 1918, learning the regimental ropes as he oversaw new Indian recruits as young as fifteen at the riding school and rifle range. He got to know his British peers when off-duty by driving them in his motor car into Delhi, or riding with them in the countryside to hunt boar and porcupine. 'I do not try to mix too much amongst them & still I do not try to hold off,' he wrote of this process of assimilation.

Little is known of the reaction among the mass of the Indian ranks in Europe, Africa and Asia to the August 1917 opening to them in principle of equality of command. The indications are that they welcomed the ostensible boost to their status that so many had wanted before 1914. 'It is a matter for much congratulation that our Government has conceded this right to us,' thought Jeswant Singh, a Sikh of the 19th Fane's Horse, in a letter home from France.

The chances for most Indian troops of taking advantage of the concession remained low in 1918. The Government of India acted that year to show a greater commitment to equality of command than raising up Amar Singh and his fellow privileged pre-war officers. However, it looked not to the seasoned Indian regulars from the villages with the most distinguished service records, but to a young generation of Indians under the age of twenty-five who could exercise the new right more meaningfully in the long term, with a whole career ahead of them as King's Commissioned officers. To train them, the Government of India opened a new Indian officer cadet college at Indore in central India, with an initial class of forty-two. Not one of these cadets was in fact from Punjab or other rural regions traditionally tapped for the Indian ranks, as the British deemed young villagers uneducated and thus unfit to enter the officer course. Instead, the Indore cadets were either Indian royalty or from well-educated families who lived in towns and cities. There was Kodandera Cariappa, a Hindu aged seventeen, the son of a civil servant in the southern province of Madras and fresh from high school. Then there was the twenty-two-year-old Ajit Rudra, a Christian from Delhi who had been educated at leading public schools in British India and Ceylon before studying at Cambridge University. He had indeed enrolled in the British Army in England in the summer of 1914, and served with it on the western front, including at the Battle of the Somme.

Partly as the Indore cadets would not graduate to receive their King's Commissions until 1919, the Government of India made more of equality of command in 1918 by handing out a number of special automatic King's Commissions for Indian regimental officers. Again well-educated Indians were favoured, with several of the automatic King's Commissions going to Indian civil servants lately recruited as temporary officers for the remainder of the war. The best the British did for the villager Indian troops who had borne the brunt of the Indian Army's fighting since 1914 was honorary King's Commissions carrying no power of command but an enhanced pension. They granted these mostly to long-serving Viceroy's Commissioned Officers considered unsuitable for full King's Commissions on the grounds of being over-aged and under-educated. The recipients' feelings are not recorded, but no doubt were mixed. Their frustrations would surely have included still being bound by old norms of prestige, such as remaining, despite their long careers, junior to the freshest British officers aged as young as nineteen. Yet their King's Commissions were at least marks of respect for their war records, and they were keen enough to exercise their right to wear the British officer-style uniform that would make them stand out as higher status in their regiment or the village. Among the honorary recipients was the first Viceroy's Commissioned Officer to enter battle on the western front in 1914, the Afridi officer Arsala Khan of the 57th Wilde's Rifles. There was no honorary King's Commission for his fellow Afridi Mir Dast VC of the 55th Coke's Rifles, however: he had disqualified himself by deserting.

By 1918, therefore, the Indian soldiers' wartime political reward of equality of command amounted to little for villagers who had fought on the western front and elsewhere. It might mean more as an opening for their children, if in the future they could get them the education to follow in the footsteps of the Indore cadets such as Kodandera Cariappa or Ajit Rudra – a post-war dream some would in time pursue. But what of the Indian nationalist politicians' relationship with the Indian troops in 1918? They collaborated with the Government of India to drive military recruitment to new heights after a direct appeal from London in response to a new crisis in the west. Yet so detached were the villagers from the nationalists' ways of thinking about the war that some even forcibly resisted enlistment, and instead of serving the Indian Army were to suffer its attacks on their own homes.

'I might rain men on you'

Following the fall of Tsarism in March 1917, the liberal socialist Provisional Government had kept Russia in the war. However, its own downfall in October to the Bolshevik Revolution had led to Soviet Russia's armistice with the Central Powers in December. This allowed the Germans to switch forty-seven divisions from eastern Europe to the western front, where on 21 March 1918 they launched their calculated gamble for a decisive victory – their Spring Offensive with a total of 199 divisions against 158 BEF and French divisions. The gamble was to make a maximum effort to break through the Allied lines in the west before the United States Army could concentrate in France to tip the balance of forces. The risk was that failure would so weaken the German Army it would be unable to keep the Allies from Germany's borders. Behind the Spring Offensive were the Prussian generals Paul von Hindenburg and Erich Ludendorff, who since 1916 had been the masters of the German high command and become effective military dictators ruling Germany itself.

In London, the Prime Minister David Lloyd George responded to the Spring Offensive by reinvigorating the British Empire's war effort, in the Indian Empire's case by sending the Government of

India a public appeal by telegram on 2 April. 'I wish to ask the Government and people of India to redouble their efforts,' his telegram announced:

> Thanks to the heroic efforts of the British Armies, assisted by their Allies, the attempt of the enemy in the West is being checked. But if we are to prevent the menace spreading to the East and gradually engulfing the world, every lover of freedom and law must play his part. I have no doubt that India will add to the laurels it has already won, and will equip itself on an even greater scale than at present to be a bulwark which will save Asia from the tide of oppression and disorder which it is the object of the enemy to achieve.

The Viceroy, Lord Chelmsford, sent a public reply in kind three days later, declaring that 'all India is stirred to the depths by the noble sacrifices now being made by the British people in the cause of the world's freedom'. He went on to avow that Lloyd George's 'trumpet call at this crisis will not fall upon deaf ears', and that he would look to 'the people's leaders' – meaning the Indian nationalist politicians – 'for the fullest effort ... to secure the final triumph of those ideals of justice and honour for which the British Empire stands'.

From 27 to 29 April Chelmsford duly hosted a three-day emergency War Conference at Delhi. It was attended by the leading Indian politicians. They saw it as a stepping-stone towards the Montagu Declaration's promised 'self-governing institutions', as it offered a chance to raise the stakes in their traditional pursuit of political concessions from the British. They were prepared to back the colonial regime more than before to help realise the heightened mobilisation Lloyd George asked for, on the understanding that after the war they would get self-government all the sooner. They put this in writing at the Conference, tabling a resolution that they would 'invoke whole-hearted and real enthusiasm amongst the people of India' to mobilise more men, material and money to help win the world war, and in return the British government should 'without delay introduce a bill into Parliament meeting the demands of the people to establish responsible government in India within a reasonable period'. Such a bill, they proclaimed, 'will make our people feel that they are fighting ... for freedom in the defence of their own rights, rights in an Empire in which they possess the same status as other members thereof'.

Among the Indian politicians behind the resolution was a new national figure, back in British India after years away as a lawyer in England and South Africa: Mahatma Gandhi. 'I consider myself honoured to find my name among the supporters of this resolution,' he said in his Conference speech. 'I fully realise all that the resolution means and I tender my support to it with all my heart.' In private at Delhi, Gandhi in fact told a British civil servant that he was ready to become the Indian Army's 'recruiting agent-in-chief ... I might rain men on you.' His reasoning fitted the mainstream nationalist logic. 'Partnership in the Empire is our definite goal [and] the straightest way to win *swaraj* [self-rule] is to participate in the defence of the Empire,' he argued. 'If the Empire wins mainly with the help of our army, it is obvious that we would secure the rights we want.'

In June the Indian Army's annual target for new recruits was raised by 25 per cent to 500,000 men, with a quota of 200,000 for Punjab. The Indian politicians set out on public tours to make recruitment speeches, Gandhi for instance telling villagers of Gujarat north of Bombay that 'it is our duty to help' the British war effort and 'lay down our lives to defend the Empire'. The politicians' support put the Indian Army's territorial recruitment system into overdrive, with even closer cooperation between its quota-setting recruitment directorates, provincial civil authorities and Indian brokers in the villages. Meanwhile the Delhi War Conference had also produced the Central Publicity Board, whose offshoot provincial and district boards spouted new propaganda, centring on the material rewards and masculine fulfilment to be gained in the army. They produced 4 million recruitment leaflets and posters, rich in colour and cartoons, some caricaturing the German emperor as the demon-king Ravana from the *Ramayana*, and plastered them to the sides of buildings from Punjab to Madras. The publicity boards made recruitment films such as *Teja Singh Goes to War* showing Indian recruits enjoying a good army life of pay, food, games and teamwork, and telling stories of bravery overseas. They also commissioned patriotic performances across the country by local theatre actors, poets and wandering folk singers, who spoke and sang of the enlistment benefits and India's duty to fight a just war.

In the villages, all these initiatives contributed to increasing the Indian Army's monthly intake, the number of combatant recruits going up from 16,000 in May to 37,500 in September. This took the grand total of Indian wartime recruits by November 1918 to 1.27 million, including 60,000 Gurkhas from Nepal. But what were the Indian recruits' actual feelings behind the statistics?

'The help they render is not out of love for the country'

By 1917 there were some villages where soldiers who had returned from the fronts were well aware of India's existing legislatures, and in consequence almost certainly understood the nationalist debate flowing from the Montagu Declaration. For example, in early 1916 Charles Hardinge as Viceroy had reserved a seat in the Legislative Assembly of the United Provinces of Agra and Oudh for a Garhwali officer of the 39th Garhwals, as a reward for the regiment's sacrifices in France – one which its Garhwali officers themselves had asked for. Furthermore, by the end of 1916 Lord Chelmsford as Hardinge's successor had appointed a villager Indian officer to the Imperial Legislative Council at Delhi, to show British consideration for the Indian ranks by allowing a soldier-representative to comment in the council's debates on military service. Chelmsford's appointee was Subadar-Major Ajab Khan of the 76th Punjabis who had served with Indian Expeditionary Force D in Iraq and Iran in 1915. These Indian officers in the legislatures by 1918 would have heard of the nationalist arguments for more Indian recruits to join up in return for new self-governing institutions after the war, and they perhaps spread the word in their villages, inspiring some new recruits. Moreover, in 1917 the 49th Bengalis were raised as a new regiment not for villagers, but for young men of Calcutta's educated elite who entirely understood the nationalist idea of serving for constitutional reform. The initiative came from Bengali politicians to strengthen the province of Bengal's association with war service, and thereby the measure of self-government they could claim as a British concession.

But the majority of new Indian recruits in 1918, like those of 1917, were primarily attracted to military service by the material rewards. They lacked the education to invest much or anything in the nuanced nationalist argument for enlisting, even if they had heard the recruitment speeches of Gandhi and other politicians. Gandhi certainly thought this, writing in June that village recruits for the Indian infantry 'are rendering their services for their salt and for their livelihood ... they cannot be regarded as lovers of *swaraj*, their goal is not *swaraj*. The help they render is not out of love for the country.' Indeed, in London the former Viceroy Lord Curzon had advised the War Cabinet ahead of the Montagu Declaration that the Indian troops would be oblivious to its constitutional significance, and 'neither ask for nor want the particular reforms now under discussion'.

From November 1917 to April 1918, Edwin Montagu toured the Indian Empire to consult Indian opinion on what shape his Declaration's proposed 'gradual development of self-governing institutions' should take, in order to help him and Lord Chelmsford draft a joint report on reform proposals for Parliament. But on his tour Montagu did not consult a single village recruit or soldier family. It was just assumed by British officials and Indian politicians alike that the constitutional conversation was really between them.

In fact, all the evidence from the great British listening post for the Indian troops' thoughts – the censors office of Indian Expeditionary Force A in France that translated thousands of their letters – points to a communication gap still existing in mid-1918 between the educated urban Indian politicians and the uneducated rural Indian soldiers. The translated letters indicate among the Indian infantry and cavalry in France no nationalism as Gandhi and the Indian politicians articulated it at the Delhi War Conference. The letters' anthologiser, the British historian David Omissi, found this a 'deafening silence':

> The 'India' that they wrote about ... was very much a geographical expression, and one that was not central to a sepoy's main sense of self. Even in Europe, the sepoys left little evidence that they imagined themselves to be primarily 'Indians' ... Prominent people never mentioned in the letters read like a political *Who's Who* of the First World War: Woodrow Wilson, Lloyd George, Herbert Asquith, Lenin, Trotsky and Gandhi are among the many who failed to make any impression. [The] soldiers never discussed ... international politics, except in cases which, for Muslims, had an obviously 'Islamic' angle ... Nor were the troops aware of, or interested in, Indian 'high' politics ... Two men voiced a hope for self-government after the war, but neither were soldiers: one was a labourer and the other was clearly an educated man. The only letter which could in any way be described as subversively 'nationalist' was written by a storekeeper.

Indeed, far from subscribing to the nationalist politicians' argument in favour of the war, many village families were against military service for their own reasons. As the demand for recruits rose in 1918, so did villages' reluctance to send their men to fight. Rural pandemics of malaria and bubonic plague made helping hands at home all the more precious in the fragile rural economy, and the new publicity boards' propaganda posters and poetry only went so far to convince communities that had suffered losses at the fronts to give up more men. In some Punjabi districts volunteers became so unforthcoming that the local recruitment brokers, under pressure from provincial civil authorities to fill their quotas, grew desperate and strayed into unlawful coercion. Such brokers visited Punjabi villages with gangs to seize recruits against their will, and often took cash bribes to leave a village alone. There were also brokers who abused magistrates' powers of summons to court, by arranging for summons only to grab men for the Indian Army when they showed up.

In Punjab's Shahpur district, the young men of a number of villages stood up to the coercive brokers, entering into pacts to resist them with force. On occasion this led to violent fights and riots, leaving village streets running with blood. The active Punjabi resistance to recruitment deterred the Government of India from imposing conscription to make sure of reaching its new annual target of 500,000 recruits. This was despite local authorities' pleas for conscription because their stretched recruitment networks were, in the words of one British civil servant in Punjab in May, 'riding the voluntary horse to a standstill'.

There was also coercive recruitment in the Indian Empire's remoter hill and jungle tracts of the north-east called on for non-combatants for labour corps. The Kuki tribesmen of the Assam–Burma borderlands were so angered it sparked a local anti-colonial rising lasting throughout 1918. In response India's Commander-in-Chief Charles Monro sent in regiments of young Punjabi, Burmese and Gurkha recruits with Lee-Enfield magazine rifles, grenades, Lewis light machine guns and Stokes mortars, and backed by artillery. They were led by Henry Keary, one of the Indian Army's most experienced generals after three years in

France and Iraq. Keary's men burned and shelled to smithereens dozens of Kuki villages, inflicting hundreds of casualties; the Kukis retaliated by beheading captured Indian troops, in some instances cutting off their hands and feet too. Similar resistance to recruitment erupted in the desert of British India's north-western province of Baluchistan in February, among the Marri tribe. Some of the Indian units Monro sent against them were led by British and Indian officer veterans of the western front, men who had fought in the Indian infantry's offensive strikes of 1915 at Neuve Chapelle and Loos. They laid waste to the Marri lands up to May, killing hundreds of tribesmen.

The experiences of the Kuki and Marri tribesmen – for all Lloyd George's and the Indian politicians' talk of fighting the world war in defence of freedom – revealed that as colonial rulers the British had not changed their ugliest spots of colonial control from pre-1914 days. This was an ominous sign that behind the Montagu Declaration lay British expediency to secure the moderate Indian politicians' cooperation to see out the war on the home front, rather than complete commitment to the Allies' democratic ideals.

Montagu and Chelmsford's joint report to Parliament on their proposals for Indian constitutional reform, known as the 'Montford Scheme', was published in July. Its guiding intention was ongoing British executive control, albeit with greater self-government through more representative elected provincial legislatures, and a new national elected legislature modelled on the Westminster Parliament. There was nothing in the Montford Scheme for many Indian servicemen, whether independent Pukhtun or Gurkhas from outside British territory, or recruits from the British Indian provinces of Baluchistan, the North-West Frontier Province and Burma, which were excluded from the reforms as sensitive border zones where British control was to stay at pre-1914 levels in the interests of imperial security. Yet for Indian troops from Punjab and other British Indian provinces that were covered by the Montford Scheme, it did at least imply that their engagement in nationalist politics should increase after the war: it suggested they get the vote for the first time, to choose members for the expanded provincial legislatures.

But in order to win the vote the Indian troops first needed to help win the war. Where and how they would do this in 1918 were questions of grand strategy for the War Cabinet in London and its new Chief of the Imperial General Staff.

23

'WE ALONE HAVE GOT TO
KEEP SOUTHERN ASIA'

In February 1918, William Robertson's time as Chief of the Imperial General Staff in London was up. David Lloyd George had tired of his uncompromising, blunt style of delivering grand strategic advice to the War Cabinet. He gladly replaced him with a younger, more eager to please and readily humorous British Army officer, the Northern Irishman Henry Wilson, aged fifty-four and much the better debater. Robertson's preferred strategy for the British Empire's forces had still been concentration on the western front as the decisive theatre, but of late he had taken an increasingly rigid defensive approach towards other fronts where he did not want to fritter away resources. Wilson, however, like Lloyd George, was a more expansive strategist positively in favour of Asian operations, inevitably involving the Indian Army whose reins he now held like Robertson before him.

Wilson was all for efforts 'to try and knock out the Turk', meaning annihilating the Turkish Army and collapsing the Ottoman government. This was in fact now a formal and pri-oritised Allied war aim to help isolate Germany, decided on in January at Versailles by the new Supreme War Council, the

Allies' highest forum for coordinating their military effort. 'We ought to push about like the devil in the Caucasus, and if possible push on in Palestine,' thought Wilson of the British Empire's best tacks for Turkey. 'Also we must try and get command of the Black Sea.'

For Wilson, knocking out the Turk had value partly as an alternative to the BEF's slow progress in Flanders in late 1917, where Douglas Haig's disappointing offensive at the Third Battle of Ypres – Passchendaele – had cost 260,000 casualties for just a five-mile advance. Yet it also seemed vital for the British Empire's position east of the Mediterranean, a fresh focus of British strategic fear that had emerged during Robertson's tenure but which only crystallised in War Cabinet minds in March 1918. 'We have a new campaign which really extends from the Mediterranean shore of Palestine to the frontier of India,' wrote one of Lloyd George's most senior Cabinet ministers, Alfred Milner, on 20 March. 'We alone have got to keep Southern Asia, and we are lucky if our line only extends from the Mediterranean to the Caspian and does not have to double back from the Caspian to the Himalayas.' The risk of failing to keep such a line, Milner warned, was that 'the Central bloc under the hegemony of Germany will control not only Europe and most of Asia but the whole world'.

This doom-laden outlook had been in the making since the Bolshevik Revolution of October 1917. Soviet Russia had confirmed its withdrawal from the war by signing the Treaty of Brest-Litovsk on 3 March 1918. Crafted by Germany, the treaty was a conqueror's charter that allowed German troops to move into a vast swathe of the old western Russian Empire, from Poland and Ukraine to the Caucasus. On Russia's southern fronts, meanwhile, from the Turko-Georgian borderlands by the Black Sea coast to Iran, the Bolshevik Revolution's anti-war policy had left the Russian Army without a war to fight, and the Russian divisions had disintegrated, their men heading for home.

All in all, the Allies' Russian-held eastern flank from Poland to Iran had melted away, opening land routes to Central Asia for the Germans and the Turks to exploit. Once the German Spring Offensive on the western front had started on 21 March, capturing 100 square miles in the first twenty-four hours and shelling the streets of Paris two days later, the BEF appeared in mortal danger of being driven off the continent through Dunkirk and the other Channel ports. It therefore seemed to the War Cabinet and Henry Wilson that if the Germans kept up their momentum, both in the west and in the east in alliance with the Turks, Alfred Milner's vision of worldwide disaster could become the reality – a prospect that indeed fired Lloyd George's public telegram appeal to India for a redoubled war effort.

From early 1918, then, British imperial defence demanded not just concentration on the western front, but also a plan to stop the Central Powers from advancing eastwards into Asia. For Wilson, the primary means of Asian defence on land was the Indian Army, operating in secret missions and in conventional offensives. Wilson advised the offensives, above all in Palestine, as the best method of forward defence for India, and they would be the Indian Army's most conspicuous contribution to Allied victory in 1918. Come November, victorious Indian troops held a line across Southern Asia much as Milner had envisaged, from Greece to Gallipoli, Syria to Jerusalem, on to northern Iraq and Iran up to the western border of Afghanistan and into the desert of Soviet Turkestan. The British Empire had won a global victory, and had only done it with the help of the Indian Army.

The 'hush-hush shows'

The Indian Army's secret missions to block the Central Powers in Central Asia were of the highest secrecy, each spoken of with a nod by those in the know as a 'hush-hush show'. There were three of them on War Cabinet orders. They lasted throughout 1918, spread 1000 miles west to east from the Caucasus to

Soviet Turkestan (or what is now primarily Turkmenistan and Uzbekistan). Their fortunes varied, but what success they did have was down to their wily British officers and Indian troops, many of them veterans of France, Gallipoli and East Africa who spied, shot, bribed and lied a world away from the trenches.

The first hush-hush show was a military mission of 1400 men to the Caucasus. It was called 'Dunsterforce' after its commander Lionel Dunsterville, the fifty-two-year-old former commandant of the 20th Punjabis who had served on the western front in 1914–15. Energetic, charming and polylingual, he had been chosen for the Caucasus mission at Christmas 1917 by George Kirkpatrick, the Chief of the Indian General Staff, as the best brigade commander in British India. Dunsterforce itself was affiliated to Indian Expeditionary Force D in Iraq. Its objective was to infiltrate the Caucasus – which was in chaos amid the ruins of the Tsarist empire as the Bolsheviks and other factions vied with one another for political control – up to the Georgian capital Tbilisi, in the process raising pro-Allied local paramilitary forces to oppose any German or Turkish threat. The War Cabinet's particular fears for the Caucasus were that the Central Powers could export war resources from the region, in particular oil from Baku, or exploit it as a corridor to Central Asia for trade or an advance towards the Indian Empire.

Dunsterforce's base was Baghdad, where it gathered from January 1918. Its main component was around 100 white officers of the Indian, British, Australian, Canadian and South African armies, plucked from their regiments in India, Iraq, Thessaloniki and France, with around 200 white NCOs to raise and train the intended paramilitaries. Dunsterforce also had Indian and British regimental detachments drawn from Iraq. Its Indian troops included men of the 128th Pioneers and the Madras Sappers and Miners required to improve or build roads from Iraq through north-west Iran towards the Caucasus for motor transport of cars, vans and lorries, and the 2nd Gurkhas to protect the roads. 'I have to get my party through 600 miles ... on a bad road with few supplies, which means thinking out food and petrol schemes far ahead and measures for protection against Kurds, Germans and Turks,' Dunsterville wrote at Baghdad on 24 January of the initial Iranian leg of his mission to Georgia. 'My task is as difficult for one man as any Napoleon ever undertook ... I wonder if anyone will ever realize what a forlorn hope my mission is?'

In February, Dunsterville led his vanguard of British officers on their drive from Baghdad through the winter snows in the mountains of north-west Iran, with 'Turkish, German and Austrian agents, all over the place, and hostile Bolshevik soldiers several thousand, blocking the road'. He talked and bought their way to the Iranian port of Enzeli on the Caspian Sea's southern shore, where they began looking for ships to carry Dunsterforce over the Caspian to Baku, only to be turned away by mistrustful Bolsheviks. By mid-March they were stuck 200 miles back at the Iranian city of Hamadan, waiting for reinforcements from Iraq. 'What a Babel,' Dunsterville wrote on 8 April of a typical day at his Hamadan headquarters:

> I talk English to my orderly in the middle of my Persian lesson, I receive a letter from the Governor which I have to answer in French and a Russian soldier calls in the middle to complain of a loss of money – and two days ago I was talking German to a German prisoner. I read last night a letter in Gurmukhi from Sunder Singh, a Subadar in the 36th Sikhs, and I spoke Pushtu yesterday to the one and only Afghan in Hamadan, and Hindustani to two Indian deserters!

The 2nd Gurkhas joined Dunsterforce in north-west Iran in May. They had driven from Baghdad in Ford vans through the mountains as the winter snows thawed, hauling the vans over passes deep in mud. Into the summer they dispersed about the rugged country on the Iranian side of the Azerbaijani border to ward off attacks on Dunsterforce's supply roads. They clashed repeatedly with Iranian guerrillas of the German-assisted Jungle Movement of Gilan, which opposed the British imperial presence in their homeland south-west of the Caspian. The Gurkhas dealt brutally with the Jungle Movement, entering villages to kill with *khukuri*s and torch houses. By October, reinforced by the 6th Gurkhas and other units from Iraq, they held a string of outposts across north-west Iran – a Nepalese safety net to catch Central Powers' infiltrations from the Caucasus.

Dunsterville and his main body of British officers, meanwhile, made it to Baku in August, crossing the Caspian after Royal Navy agents had seized control of Russian shipping. They went no further than Baku, however. There they encountered Azerbaijani and other local paramilitaries who accepted their money but not their orders, before they were forced out by the Turkish Army's imminent capture of the city in September. They made a night-time getaway in blacked-out ships back across the Caspian to Iran, thus never making it to their original objective of Georgia. To score at least some success in the Caucasus, the War Cabinet had ordered Dunsterville to blow up Baku's 2000 oil wells, but he refused to attempt this as it ran contrary to his mission of winning over local allies. Nearby, one of Dunsterville's young Indian Army officers did strike a blow to the Central Powers' search for war resources. He was Reginald Teague-Jones, a fluent Russian speaker since his childhood in St Petersburg who could therefore travel the Caspian area with relative ease. In July he single-handedly sabotaged a large German shipment of cotton, which was needed in Germany as an ingredient for various war materials including explosives, the Allied blockade in the North Sea having created serious shortages. Teague-Jones bribed the Soviet Russians controlling the eastern Caspian port of Krasnovodsk, preventing the shipment's delivery to German officers at the northern port of Astrakhan.

'Magnificent material'

The second Indian Army hush-hush show was to north-east Iran. Its leader was Wilfrid Malleson, a pre-war senior intelligence officer of the Indian General Staff known for his sly sense of self-preservation. Malleson, according to his colleague Richard Meinertzhagen on the staff of Indian Expeditionary Force B to East Africa in 1915–16, was a cad, a bully and a liar. He had been sacked from East Africa by Jan Smuts for ducking duties in the field when the enemy was near, not only by faking abdominal pains to warrant a chauffeur-driven ride to the rear on the Kilimanjaro front, but also by temporarily absconding on the pretence of being chased up a tree by a pride of lions. In June 1918, when Malleson was idling unemployed in India, the Chief of the Indian General Staff George Kirkpatrick chose him to head the Indian mission to north-east Iran because despite being surplus to requirements on the main fronts, he was still a useful old hand at intelligence work. At the time, the Germans were at the northern end of the Caspian Sea and the Turks were pressing towards Baku. Malleson's task was to frustrate any Central Powers' plans for Soviet Turkestan east of the Caspian, whether for extracting war resources or spreading anti-Allied propaganda in the direction of the Indian border.

Based in the north-eastern Iranian city of Mashhad, Malleson had a free hand. At his disposal were the 19th Punjabis and 28th Light Cavalry; both regiments had moved up from south-east Iran in 1917 to cover the abandoned Russian half of the Allied cordon previously set up to screen the Afghan border from German and Turkish agents. In Malleson's eyes, they were 'magnificent material and led by exceptionally able and gallant officers', with a good number of their well-trained pre-war British officers and Punjabis intact. Up to November 1918, while Malleson remained rooted in the comfort of Mashhad, he sent his two Indian regiments over the Iranian border into the desert of western Soviet Turkestan (now Turkmenistan) to deny Bolshevik use of the Russian Trans-Caspian Railway's western branch. This terminated at the Caspian port of Krasnovodsk, and could help the Bolsheviks deliver Turkestan's harvested cotton available for export, an estimated 200,000 tons, to Central Powers buyers.

In western Soviet Turkestan, Malleson's Indian troops fought the Bolsheviks alongside the local counter-revolutionaries known as the Mensheviks. Together they duelled with the Bolsheviks from armoured trains, their own being complete with wagons for mounted artillery, kitchens, water storage, horses, hospital beds and prostitutes. The Indians depended on the Mensheviks for supply and other logistics, eating Russian black bread in the searing desert heat, and receiving old Russian Army gas masks after rumours of poison gas cylinders on the Bolshevik trains. They travelled over 200 miles down the Trans-Caspian line on the Menshevik trains, establishing trenches in the desert with barbed wire and Vickers heavy machine gun posts to secure sections of the railway and a few oases. Occasionally the Bolshevik Red Army made frontal assaults over the open desert on the Indians' trenches. Its ranks included German and Austrian soldiers –who had joined the Bolsheviks on their release from Turkestan's Tsarist prisoner of war camps – and the Indian machine gunners shot down hundreds of them.

The Indians themselves suffered heavy losses in fights for railway stations in west Turkestan, for example at Dushakh on 14 October when the 19th Punjabis lost 200 men under Red Army machine gun and artillery fire. One of the 19th Punjabis' casualties was a young non-independent Pukhtun, a Yusufzai from British India's North-West Frontier Province, who had twice been wounded in France in 1915 while attached to another regiment. 'He was somewhat supercilious and inclined to jeer at side-shows,' his British officer said of his comments in early October on how much easier the railway war in Turkestan was compared to the western front. Yet at Dushakh, the Yusufzai was wounded again, 'a nasty one, and publicly recanted' in view of the Mensheviks' lack of medical care, making the western front with all its modern hospitals suddenly seem the easier option.

In the first week of November, Malleson's Indian troops remained with the Menshevik armoured trains deep in west Turkestan, entrenched in the tree-lined grounds of a former Tsarist agricultural college at Bairam Ali. Unlike Dunsterforce in the Caucasus, they had accomplished their mission, snuffing out the possibility of Bolshevik use of the Trans-Caspian Railway to deliver Turkestan's resources to the Central Powers.

'Immediately all was hustle'

The Indian Army's third and final secret mission was the smallest, and it had the most delicate task: slipping into eastern Soviet Turkestan from Allied China to gather intelligence on any assistance its new Bolshevik central government – the Tashkent Soviet, an unknown quantity – might be providing the Central Powers. It was to take counter-measures as necessary, such as raising pro-Allied local paramilitaries just as Dunsterforce had been supposed to. Not least among the possible threats specified in the mission's instructions from George Kirkpatrick at Simla was the Tashkent Soviet's arming en masse of Turkestan's released German and Austrian prisoners of war, totalling some 40,000 men, enabling them to resume fighting the Allies.

This third mission was led by three junior British officers of the Indian Army. They were all in their thirties, had served on the western front or at Gallipoli, and been selected by Kirkpatrick mainly for their travelling experience in pre-war Central Asia. Their natural leader was Frederick Bailey of the 32nd Sikh Pioneers, a meticulous lepidopterist and Tibetologist. Analytical, circumspect, unflappable, he spoke several languages including German and Tibetan, and was the best suited to intelligence work. The other two were Stewart Blacker of the Queen Victoria's

Own Corps of Guides, who was a gregarious, monocle-wearing eccentric, and Percy Etherton of the 39th Garhwal Rifles, the more watchful and self-possessed. Indeed, to Bailey and Blacker, Etherton was not quite an officer and a gentleman; he had plagiarised much of his 1911 book *Across the Roof of the World* about his travels across the Russian Empire.

The mission also had sixteen pre-war professional Indian soldiers, fourteen of them Guides with experience of multiple fronts since 1914. 'The exact part that this cadre would play could not be foreseen, so care was taken to include men with the most varied accomplishments,' wrote Blacker. 'There were linguists, speakers of Russian, Persian, Arabic, and even of French; a bomber, a machine-gunner, a signaller, a carrier-pigeon expert, two or three skilled topographer-scouts, a first-aid man, and a veterinarian, whilst practically every N.C.O. carried on him scars of a protracted sojourn on the Western Front, and others had seen varied fighting.' One of the Guides was Awal Nur, a Pukhtun well known to Blacker as 'a sprig of perhaps the most aristocratic family of Yusufzai ... He had a brilliant war record, having been three times wounded in France, where he went through the murderous ordeal of half a dozen Flanders battles. Added to this a small frontier campaign, and the better part of a year in East Africa, in one of the battalions that shared the praise of their generous enemy, von Lettow-Vorbeck.'

Setting off from India in April 1918 disguised as Himalayan merchants, the mission marched from Kashmir in a caravan of camels and ponies with concealed firearms, skis, a Triumph motorcycle and a flock of carrier pigeons. Among the British officers, Etherton's chatter in his affected drawl soon grated with the others. 'D'yer know anything abaht the wimmin at Kashgar?' the British agent at the Indian frontier station of Gilgit recalled Etherton asking him with a knowing look, in a typical exchange Bailey and Blacker had already tired of, as the mission passed through. 'I've been told they're top-'ole ... By Jove, wot a lovely time I'm going to 'ave!'

The mission arrived in June at the western Chinese town of Kashgar, the desert trading hub and base for their onward journey to Soviet Turkestan. They tried out the carrier pigeons there, releasing them on test flights south to Hunza, the nearest Indian border post. 'The experiment did not work,' Bailey rued. 'The pigeons mostly served to fatten the beautiful falcons of the Hunza Valley.' Another problem was gasoline for the Triumph, which was in short supply at Kashgar; Blacker used the local vodka instead. His Guides, meanwhile, mooched about the streets of Kashgar off-duty. Blacker caught a glimpse of their personal world as he rounded a corner in the town one afternoon. 'The good-looking Awal Nur and Abdulla Shah sat on their ponies chatting in the most Occidental fashion with a brand-new acquaintance – a roguish-eyed, velvet-cheeked flapper of Kashgar, with her raven tresses in long plaits,' he recalled. 'She seemed to find the upstanding soldier strangers not unattractive, whilst they explained laboriously to me that they were just buying an apple or two.'

In the last week of July, the mission's work started in earnest. Bailey and Blacker left Kashgar for Tashkent in civilian clothes, posing as a British diplomatic delegation to the Tashkent Soviet, and leaving their Indian troops behind with Etherton to avoid any hint of hostility. The only casualty of their journey to Tashkent was Blacker's Triumph, which bounded through the border valleys and mountains until, he wrote, 'with the rarefaction of the air, the boulder-strewn track, and the steep gradient, it met its Waterloo, and went back to Kashgar in a Chinese cart'.

In August, Bailey and Blacker found Tashkent under a Soviet reign of terror. Armoured cars clattered down the dusty tree-lined boulevards and tramways of Tsarist times, scattering pedestrians, and secret police executed counter-revolutionaries at the roadside. The two British officers soon mixed in Tashkent's cafés and restaurants with the released German and Austrian prisoners of war. The latter were still in their 1914 uniforms they had worn in battle against the Russians in eastern Europe, replete with the Austrian cap badge branded 'F.J.I.' ('Franz Josef Imperator') in homage to their old emperor who had died in 1916. 'Fresh from the Western Front, it gave us a sort of "Alice-through-the-Looking-Glass" feeling to walk among a jostling crowd in field-grey,' thought Blacker. 'We met a few Austrian officers, many of whom were by nationality Serbs, Romanians, Italians, or Czechs.' In buying their rounds of beer and coffee to the sounds of Austrian orchestras, Bailey and Blacker picked up some of the information they sought. They learned that the freed prisoners of war were not inclined to rally to fight the Allies, but were desperate to go home. This was why a minority had joined the Red Army to fight on the western branch of the Trans-Caspian Railway, hoping to force their way past the Mensheviks to the other side of the Caspian for repatriation.

On meeting with the Tashkent Soviet's Chairman and Foreign Commissar in late August in search of other intelligence they were after – on the Soviet's relations with the Central Powers – Bailey and Blacker learned that the Soviet did indeed hope to sell as many war materials as it could to the Central Powers. Yet at the same time their cover as a friendly mission was blown with news of the Indian troops fighting the Bolsheviks on the railway in west Turkestan. The Tashkent newspaper the *Sovietski Turkistan* soon called for Bailey and Blacker's execution as anti-Bolshevik conspirators. Blacker returned to Kashgar, while Bailey remained to take his chances helping the city's counter-revolutionaries, who might depose the Soviet, cutting off Turkestan as a potential source of supply for the Central Powers. In October, however, British and other Allied interventions against the Bolsheviks from Arctic Russia to eastern Siberia served to confirm that Bailey was an enemy agent. He was tipped off by a note from friends in the local anti-Bolshevik resistance that the Tashkent Soviet had definite orders from Moscow to arrest him. 'For Bailey the position is especially dangerous and shooting is not out of the question,' the note warned.

Bailey had his escape plan prepared. 'The essence of this plan was speed,' he later said. 'Immediately all was hustle.' He changed at a safe house into an Austrian uniform with an F.J.I. cap, fled through back gardens to shake off six Soviet informants who tracked him daily, and emerged down the street to walk calmly away as they continued to watch the safe house front door. 'I now had to adopt in every way I could think of the habits and manners of an Austrian prisoner,' Bailey recalled:

> I thought of the advice old Peter Pienaar gave David Hannay in *The Thirty Nine Steps* and how he fell into his background, and I tried to melt into the field-grey mass of Austrian prisoners of war … It is a curious feeling to walk about in a foreign uniform; I was very conscious of the F.J.I. on my hat. I knew there were some thirty thousand Austrian prisoners about who had been together for four years, and was not sure whether a strange face would be noticed, and, though I met a few in the street, I never looked at them.

By the turn of November, Bailey had escaped 60 miles to the north-east of Tashkent, and was in hiding in the mountains among peasant farmers.

Back at Kashgar over the summer, Etherton had become the new British consul. He had sent the mission's Indian soldiers out to the China-Turkestan border to look for any Bolshevik propaganda that could possibly spread to India, but they found none. His own intelligence work into the autumn was limited as he developed a reputation at Kashgar for his dealings with a local pimp who provided him with prostitutes at the British consulate. 'He kept it up the whole time, until our name stank,' wrote one of his British consular colleagues, Clarmont Skrine, 'he had different bazaar women in every week or so'.

Blacker, meanwhile, investigated a group of German officers rumoured to be in the mountains south of Kashgar. He chased after them throughout October with the Yusufzai Awal Nur and most of the original mission's Guides. They crossed sixteen mountain passes above 15,000 feet, some days going without food or water and sleeping in the snow. 'We had during the summer and autumn chafed furiously under the feeling that we were not doing our full to win the War, and it was this bottled-up fury that carried us through,' Blacker thought. He and his band of Guides burst into an inn in early November to discover the truth about the supposed Germans. 'To our great disappointment, there was no German in the party,' Blacker admitted. He had caught up only with nine Afghan opium smugglers. Two parties of German officers had in fact passed through those mountains in 1916, possibly giving rise to the rumours he had heard.

The Indian Army's three secret missions, therefore, achieved only a few of their objectives, and they were of course tangential to winning the war – it was on the battlefields of the Middle East that the Indian Army made its greatest contribution of 1918.

24

'EACH ONE OF US MUST
FIGHT ON TO THE END'

In the first week of the German Spring Offensive on the western front from 21 March, Indian servicemen were among the BEF's initial casualties behind the front line in the Somme valley. They were Catholic hill-men of a Ranchi Labour Company from the Indian Empire's far north-east. 'Our life has been a veritable hell,' their Belgian Jesuit officer, Father Frans Ory, wrote at the end of the month of their retreat from German stormtroopers. 'We have been shelled and bombed night and day … The Germans being twice on us we had to run for dear life, leaving nearly everything … the shells went bang, bang every minute, with pieces flying over our heads.'

Meanwhile another Indian labour company from India's north-east, of Lushai tribesmen, retreated alongside British, Chinese and Italian units through the Somme department's capital of Amiens, as the city shook under German bombardment on 26 March. 'We could hear the rumble of houses falling down,' wrote the Lushais' company clerk, Sainghinga Sailo. 'People, women with babies, and children all filled with fear … and in tears.' The Lushai labourers so pitied the people of Amiens that they told Sainghinga

Sailo they wanted to fight for the city as soldiers, if only they had guns. 'We don't want to go,' they said, 'we are returning to fire at the Germans.' As non-combatants, however, the Lushais were denied guns and never did fire at the stormtroopers.

No Indian Army combatants in fact fought in the BEF's desperate retreat over 40 miles in the Somme valley during the Spring Offensive, nor in its wider defensive line in France and Belgium up to June which stopped the German attacks, rallied by Douglas Haig's Special Order of the Day on 11 April: 'With our backs to the wall and believing in the justice of our cause each one of us must fight on to the end.' That day the only Indian combatant units still active in a German theatre were those of Indian Expeditionary Force B in East Africa, where Muslim and Sikh batteries of the Indian Mountain Artillery, armed with new howitzers, were pursuing the Schütztruppen in the jungles of Portuguese Mozambique with British African troops. As for the 10,000 Indian cavalrymen in France, they had completed their final tours of duty in the BEF's front line in February on the Somme, and been withdrawn from north-eastern France entirely in March. Their last regiment out, the 20th Deccan Horse, had missed the Spring Offensive assaults by one day, quitting the Amiens area on 20 March.

Unlike the Indian infantry's haphazard withdrawal from the western front in 1915 when the British Empire had had no properly unified supreme command, the Indian cavalry's withdrawal in 1918 was carefully planned by David Lloyd George's War Cabinet. It was a buttress of London's overarching strategy for the year, to strike a new intercontinental balance between the empire's forces on the main overseas fronts of France, Palestine and Iraq. The key was thickening the concentration of the British, Australian, South African and other white imperial armies in western Europe against the Germans, and that of the Indian Army in western Asia against the Turks. The pivotal front for the Indians was Palestine, where, in keeping with the spirit of Haig's Order of the Day, they were to fight on to the end.

'Well-tried veterans, to whom nothing was now strange'

In 1917 Palestine had been the British Empire's most fruitful theatre on the Mediterranean. The Egyptian Expeditionary Force, largely of British, Australian and New Zealand divisions with only a few Indian regiments, had crossed the Sinai Desert to capture Jerusalem by Christmas – at the express wish of Lloyd George, who wanted the holy city taken to offset Passchendaele much as he had wanted Baghdad after the Somme. In January 1918, then, the Egyptian Expeditionary Force held a front line arcing around Jerusalem to the north and the east, facing the Turkish Army and the German Army's Asia Corps.

That month it was the Allied Supreme War Council's decision at Versailles to prioritise knocking Turkey out of the war that initiated London's concentration of the Indian Army in western Asia. On the advice of William Robertson, then still the Chief of the Imperial General Staff, the War Cabinet chose India and the Indian forces overseas as the main sources of reinforcements to enable the Egyptian Expeditionary Force to kick on northwards towards Syria. By February, the War Cabinet had triggered the transfer of large numbers of Indian troops to join the white imperial troops already in Palestine. It called mostly on British India for Indian battalions to fill out four divisions, as well as Iraq for the 7th Indian Division, and France for all the Indian cavalry there.[*]

London's decision to reinforce Palestine with specifically Indian rather than British troops was recommended by Robertson partly as a matter of shipping. British shipping shortages were grave by early 1918 after Germany's unrestricted U-boat warfare had sunk some 6 million tons in 1917. Sending more of the British Army to the Middle East would only increase the shipping required between England and Egypt in the most U-boat-infested waters,

---

[*] The Indian reinforcements sent to Palestine were for Indian Expeditionary Force E to Egypt, and were loaned to the Egyptian Expeditionary Force.

whereas the Indian sea lanes south of Suez were little affected by the submarine threat. More significantly, however, Robertson aimed to maximise the BEF's white Anglo-Saxon racial profile. Since Soviet Russia's exit from the war in late 1917 and the consequent freeing of German divisions in eastern Europe for the western front, Robertson had been determined to strengthen the BEF with its own extra British divisions, so far as Lloyd George would let him. Robertson took it for granted that the empire's best chance in the fight for survival against the Germans in the west lay with its white troops as racially the fittest, so that the Indians' natural place was on secondary fronts against the Turks. He had his eye at the start of 1918 on getting further British, Australian and New Zealand divisions into France from among the twenty of them in the outlying theatres from Thessaloniki to Iraq, swapping them for Indian troops from Iraq or India. But by February Lloyd George had not approved any such swapping. At that point he was less western front-focused than Robertson, and wanted to mass more troops in the eastern Mediterranean – British, Indian or otherwise – to smash Turkey.

For many of the Indian cavalrymen transferring from the western front to Palestine in February and March, half their journey was overland to save on shipping. They took trains from France into Italy along the Indian Army's trail blazed by the Indian Labour Corps in 1917. As they gazed out of their train windows through Italian provinces from Emilia-Romagna in the north down to Puglia in the south to catch their troopships to Egypt, some were unenthused by the move. 'We wanted to live for a longer period in France,' Ranjodh Singh, a Sikh cavalryman, said in later life of his squadron's mood – they already missed their French friends in the villages of the Somme valley. Some had of course left wives, girlfriends and babies behind, in a few known cases parting with gifts of personal portrait photographs, toys and promises to stay in touch by mail.

The Indian cavalry also departed France for Palestine by ship from Marseilles. Off the French coast they saw Allied Japanese servicemen for the first time, as Japanese Navy destroyers escorted their convoys through an enemy minefield, and protected them from lurking German and Austrian U-boats in the Mediterranean. On one of these Indian troopships, the cavalrymen of the 19th Fane's Horse on the lookout for U-boats proved particularly skittish, giving many a false alarm. 'To the amateur,' wrote their tutting British officer, 'anything floating, from a salmon-tin upwards, might be a submarine.' Fane's Horse's convoy stopped by Malta, where the men took in the sight of the island's great medieval fortifications down to the water's edge, and stepped ashore at the Grand Harbour of the Maltese capital Valletta. For locals on Valletta's baroque waterfront, there was the peculiar sight of a Pukhtun cavalryman of the regiment walking a French sheepdog, a pet from the Somme valley. The princely States unit the Jodhpur Lancers, meanwhile, had sailed from Marseilles for Palestine with a special four-legged cargo of their own from England, in twelve young thoroughbreds from Newmarket. The horses were the personal property of their commandant Sir Pratap Singh, who had bought them on leave from the western front, hoping to take them home to India to race them.

For the British officer William Watson of the Palestine-bound 38th Central India Horse, also sailing from Marseilles to Egypt, his men travelled with a new air of worldly wisdom from their western front experience. 'Anyone who had known them not later than 1914 would have been amazed at the difference,' he remembered of how they now carried themselves. On their arrival on the western front in December 1914 they had been 'somewhat bewildered by the novel experience', but they had left it exuding a heightened self-confidence as 'well-tried veterans, to whom nothing was now strange'. Anthony Filose, another officer of the Central India Horse, wrote that his men's talk on their troopship in the Mediterranean showed how their years in France had given them 'a very different and much broader outlook on life', as 'all were full of ideas of what they intended to do' when they got home. 'Quite a few of the Indian officers declared that they would no longer live in huts after the style of their forefathers.'

The Indian cavalry from France disembarked at Alexandria from mid-March. They went into camp for a month by the village of Tell El Kebir in the desert north-east of Cairo to re-gather and acclimatise. For some, their immediate impressions of Egypt swung against it compared to France. 'It is hot and dusty,' an uncomfortable trooper of the 18th Tiwana Lancers complained of their desert camp, adding that the Egyptian locals, unlike the French with their fixed market prices, were 'a pack of swindlers who ask double price for everything'. The Indians' horses were troubled too, having to adapt not only to new muzzles against the blustery desert's dust and sand, but also to the Egyptian equine ration of coarse hay, barley and bran, harsher than their old French equivalent of grassy hay and oats.

Sir Pratap Singh saved his thoroughbreds from the desert conditions by stabling them in Cairo with an old friend, an Indian Army general commanding the British garrison of Egypt. For several days in fact Sir Pratap gave his horses more attention than he did his men of the Jodhpur Lancers – including his two sons – at camp in the desert. He slept in the saddle room at the Cairo stable, lovingly watching over his thoroughbreds' recovery from their journey from Newmarket.

In late April, the Indian cavalrymen travelled up to the Palestine front on the Egyptian Expeditionary Force's purpose-built railway across the Sinai Desert, passing burnt-out British tanks in the desert at Gaza where the Force had broken through in late 1917. From May into the summer they rotated on defensive duty in the Jordan Valley east of Jerusalem, in what is now Israel and Jordan. The front line in the valley consisted not of continuous trenches through flat farmland as in France, but intermittent outposts down to 1200 feet below sea-level among craggy hillsides with green trees, scrub and numerous gorges. Although the terrain gave good cover, it was crawling with scorpions, six-inch centipedes and stinging spiders, and plagued by flies and mosquitoes. The valley's summer atmosphere was almost suffocating, with heat up to 46°C in the shade and intense humidity from evaporation of the Dead Sea at its southern end. The density of military forces per mile was lower than the Indian troops had experienced on the western front, as the British Empire, Ottoman and German armies were more spread out, and their lines were generally much further apart. Still, day to day the Indians faced persistent if relatively light bombardments, both from Turkish artillery and German air raids.

Sir Pratap Singh turned down a hotel in Jerusalem in order to stay with his Jodhpur Lancers in the Jordan Valley. He coped with the heat by being up and about only at sunrise and in the cool of the evening, spending the day at rest under the shade of a tarpaulin tied to some shrubs. There was not much society for him in the valley, but he found what he could, calling mainly on senior British officers. He drank whiskies at sundown with the British staff of the Jodhpur Lancers' brigade – the Imperial Service Cavalry Brigade, exclusively of princely States units – letting himself go over dinner as he repeated his mantra 'Me not liking propaganda, me fighting man' and his reminiscences of Buckingham Palace.

Sir Pratap also dined at the Egyptian Expeditionary Force's headquarters at Ramla north of Jerusalem with its Commander-in-Chief, Edmund Allenby. A tall, thickset British Army cavalryman nicknamed 'The Bull', Allenby had been a contemporary of Douglas Haig's at the British Staff College, served on the western front from 1914 to 1917, and led the breakthrough at Gaza and the advance to Jerusalem. Allenby was one of the most imposing personalities of British high command with his infectious enthusiasm, unflinching will and explosive temper.

'His mind is like the prow of the *Mauretania*,'* said one British major. 'There is so much weight behind it that it does not need to be sharp like a razor.' Besides horses, Allenby and Sir Pratap had teenage sons in common. 'Have you any news of my little boy today?' Allenby had asked his staff every night in France to see if the casualty lists named his only child Michael, aged eighteen, and with the BEF's artillery. It was after leaving Michael behind on the western front and moving to Palestine that Allenby got the telegram he dreaded most from his wife, working on at his desk in tears that fell to smudge the paper he sent out.

Back in the Jordan Valley, on 14 July Sir Pratap's Jodhpur Lancers' moment to gallop at the enemy finally arrived. It came at short notice after a Turkish and German attack towards bridges the Lancers were defending at El Hinu on the east bank of the River Jordan, a mile north of the Dead Sea. Sir Pratap's cavalrymen quickly countered under the late-morning sun, sneaking up on a Turkish column through some low hills before using their training in France. They combined Hotchkiss heavy machine gun fire from their dismounted troopers with a mounted charge of 125 horsemen in the open, their lances lowered over ground of dusty, dry mud. The charge was led by two aristocratic Indian officers who found some extra pace from their well-bred mounts. One of them was Major Dalpat Singh, known for his English-style manners having spent most of his youth in England at private school. He charged down a Turkish machine gun post, killed the gunners with his revolver, and took prisoner a Turkish officer by the scruff of the neck. His men lanced and shot dozens of Turks, driving off their attackers and taking fifty prisoners. The Lancers returned to the Indian lines at noon dripping in sweat having suffered twenty-eight casualties, matching their costliest day on the western front.

Sir Pratap Singh happened to miss the action as he had not

---

* A famous steamship of the age, for some years the world's largest and fastest.

been in the front line that morning. He rushed up to congratulate Dalpat Singh and the men, and eagerly asked after the part of his seventeen-year-old son Sagat, whose squadron had charged. To his fury he found that Sagat had missed the fight too – he had been manning a telephone at regimental headquarters. Sir Pratap publicly scolded Sagat, raging that he had not brought his sons to war to talk but to die for their King-Emperor. 'All British sahibs getting their sons killed, why not I getting some killed?' he sputtered. 'Nothing would make me happier to know they are dead on the battlefield.' Sir Pratap refused to speak to Sagat for several days, and when a British staff officer disclosed he had ordered Sagat to work the telephone on the morning of the charge, Sir Pratap refused to speak to him as well.

'Troops and animals had never had it so good'

Events in France, meanwhile, had prompted the War Cabinet in London to rearrange the Egyptian Expeditionary Force's fighting units. It did so not just by extracting British troops, but also by adding further Indian troops. The German Spring Offensive on the western front had caused a British Army manpower crisis in France and Belgium by inflicting 225,000 casualties within a month, a rate that required the BEF in the short term to draw replacements from other theatres. The new Chief of the Imperial General Staff Henry Wilson most wanted white British reinforcements, for the same shipping and racial reasons as his predecessor William Robertson. So Wilson took 60,000 British troops out of Palestine by August, nearly all those that were there. To replace them, he 'Indianised' – to use the General Staff term at the time – the Egyptian Expeditionary Force by drawing on Iraq and India for Indian reinforcements. Thereby he raised the Force's number of assault troops in Palestine to 70,000, the majority Indian infantry and cavalry in eight divisions, and the minority white British, Australians and New Zealanders in three divisions.

However, more broadly on the Palestine front and on its supply lines stretching back to the Sinai, Suez and Egypt, the Indian troops were themselves a minority. The total Allied force from the Jordan Valley to Egypt's Western Desert in summer 1918 totalled some 340,000 men, a global gathering of wider British Empire servicemen from Egyptians, black South Africans, Jamaicans, Barbadians and Guyanese to Jews of new British Army battalions recruited from Palestine, Russia, Argentina, the United States and elsewhere, alongside French imperial units of Algerians, Senegalese, Syrians and Armenians.

To feed and otherwise care for the Egyptian Expeditionary Force with its Indians and other British Empire elements, Allenby with his logistics staff officers, who were rich in western front and Gallipoli experience, did everything they could – or what 'ingenuity could suggest or money could pay for', wrote one of his staff, Cyril Falls, so that in Palestine 'troops and animals had never had it so good'. The staff ensured that in the Jordan Valley and nearer Jerusalem extensive anti-malarial measures were taken, principally the drainage of breeding waters, to leave the troops in generally good health. Hospitals and other medical units were improved, as were the Egyptian Expeditionary Force's self-built railways, which now ran up to Jerusalem and worked as well as on the western front. Then the railways in tandem with motor lorries, mule packs and horse carts delivered 2000 tons a day of supplies from Suez to the regiments in Palestine: lentils, beans, barley, smoked fish and fodder from Egypt; sheep and goats from Sudan; potatoes from Cyprus; grain from India; frozen meat from Argentina; and flour from Canada. Palestine itself was a provider of vegetables and fruit, especially from the orange orchards of Jaffa.

As for rest and recreation, the Indians were frequent visitors to rest areas in the cool air of the Jerusalem hills, where there were cinemas, concerts and sports. They also had regular leave, to Jerusalem, Cairo or India. In Jerusalem, the Indian Muslim troops flocked to the twelfth-century Mosque of Omar. The Muslim cavalrymen of the 19th Fane's Horse went there in a large group, leaving piles of their boots, spurs and uniforms outside, washing and changing into loose white cotton overalls, and going in to pray together.

Allenby's chief purpose with the Egyptian Expeditionary Force – the offensive in Palestine to help eliminate Turkey from the war, as approved by the Allied Supreme War Council, and originally pencilled in for April or May – was inevitably delayed when the German Spring Offensive in the west led to his force's Indianisation. As Allenby's combat units became largely Indian up to August, their readiness to fight was mixed. He had a few good-quality Indian battalions such as the 58th Vaughan's Rifles, which had left France in 1915 for Egypt before fighting in the Sinai up to Jerusalem in 1916–17, in the process becoming seasoned operators of Lewis light machine guns and other new equipment under their western front veteran officers and NCOs. And in the Indian cavalry from France Allenby had some of the world's most experienced and best-trained regiments of long-service professionals. But most of the incoming Indian infantry, spread across dozens of new battalions created in India for the expanded Indian Army since 1916, were fresh and under-trained wartime recruits hurried to Egypt with inexperienced British and Indian officers.

Allenby's solution to get these new Indian battalions battle-ready in short order was twofold. Firstly, he injected them with experienced British and Indian officers from Iraq and India. These included, for instance, the 129th Baluchis' British officer and veteran of France and East Africa in 1914–17 Harold Lewis, now second-in-command of the 2nd/127th Baluchis in Palestine. This time Lewis had none of his beloved independent Pukhtun recruits, however. Allenby banned them from Palestine in case they deserted, kicking them out of twelve of his Indian regiments after a mysterious affair at Gaza among the independent Pukhtun of the 58th Vaughan's Rifles involving the murder of a Yusufzai, the attempted murder of British officers and desertions. Indeed, Allenby sent some of the independent Pukhtun of his Indian cavalry recently arrived from France back there, not to fight but to help look after BEF replacement horses.

Secondly, Allenby arranged intensive training camps and schools of instruction from Cairo to Jerusalem for all the Indian infantry in Egypt and Palestine. The teachers were British and Indian officers and NCOs chosen for their eloquence and battle knowledge from various fronts. They gave lessons in the individual specialisms for attacking Turkish trenches in cooperation with artillery: how to use Lee-Enfield rifles, Lewis light machine guns, grenades and trench mortars, telephones and signalling equipment.

By September, Allenby's Indianised Egyptian Expeditionary Force was ready for his delayed offensive north of Jerusalem, against the Turkish Fourth, Seventh and Eighth Armies and the German Asia Corps. It proved a masterstroke of modern mobile warfare on a front 45 miles wide, as he combined all his force's arms by tapping his own and his British, Indian and Australian General Staff subordinates' experience of operations since 1914 in Europe and the Middle East.

'I would not have changed places with President Wilson himself'

Allenby's maxim for success in battle was 'Thorough preparation. Deception. Concentration of strength; with strong feints.' As his offensive unfolded north of Jerusalem, it achieved all these things. His artillery was a collection of approximately 550 heavy, field and mountain guns, mainly in British but also in South African, Indian, Hong Kong and Singapore batteries. For the Indian troops, this was by far the strongest firepower support they had had beyond the western front – over treble that available in Iraq to Indian Expeditionary Force D's commander Stanley Maude on the Tigris in late 1916.

The offensive opened on the morning of 19 September in the last of the moonlight. The artillery unleashed a hurricane bombardment lasting just fifteen minutes to neutralise Turkish and German trenches, achieving accuracy with British target-finding techniques developed in France and passed on to Palestine. The bombardment fell most devastatingly where the Turks and Germans least expected it, on a 20-mile front running inland from the Mediterranean coast across the plain of Megiddo (the name in fact of the offensive, being the Hebrew for the Biblical location of Armageddon). They had been deceived by Allenby's ruses further inland to simulate preparations for a main strike eastwards out of the Jordan Valley to capture the city of Amman. The deceptions had included fake radio traffic from Jerusalem, dummy camps near the River Jordan prepared by Australian, West Indies and Jewish troops with empty tents and 15,000 canvas horses, and dust clouds nearby thrown up by mules dragging sleds back and forth to give the appearance of busy regimental movements.

After the bombardment ripped open the Turkish and German trenches on the coastal plain of Megiddo, the weight of Allenby's assaulting infantry divisions – four Indian and one British – fell on them at around 5 a.m. His troops rapidly captured their target positions just as they had been trained to do with their rifles, light machine guns, grenades and trench mortars. Inland to the east up to 25 miles away, meanwhile, Indian, British, black South African, West Indies, Jewish and Australian units executed Allenby's feints not only towards Nablus in the Judaean Hills above Jerusalem – where Allenby drove in his motor car up to tired Dogra, Kashmir and Punjabi battalions to inspire them to keep going – but also in the Jordan Valley towards Amman. In both these inland areas Allenby's men held down potential Turkish reinforcements for the more beleaguered coastal plain.

The first morning of Megiddo was a model of modern infantry-artillery cooperation such as the Indian Army had tried, with generally improving results, in its offensives since 1915 in France, Gallipoli and Ottoman Iraq. The day has been better known, however, for something else: mobile shock tactics by Allenby's cavalry, who were mainly Indians with a minority of British and Australians.

The mounted Indian cavalry of Allenby's 4th and 5th Divisions emerged from orange groves by the Mediterranean at 6 a.m. to exploit the infantry's break-in on the plain of Megiddo. They passed them to break through in the direction of Haifa and Nazareth, galloping to get behind the retreating Turkish and German forces and to swing inland to encircle them. The Indian cavalry was packed with the regiments that had been in France for at least three years, and they made the most of their exceptional horsemanship and discipline to ride and fight over 80 miles in two days. As they went they cooperated closely with the reconnaissance and bomber aeroplanes of Britain's newly instituted Royal Air Force (superseding the Royal Flying Corps), with British armoured cars, and with mechanised transport including motor lorries with food and ammunition that trundled after them. Sir Pratap Singh rode with the Jodhpur Lancers, at last getting his chance at the mounted charge he had talked of daily since 1914. Incredibly for a seventy-four-year-old, he stayed in the saddle continuously for twenty-four hours, although it did for him – he had to retire sick.

Among the other galloping veterans of France at Megiddo on 19–20 September, the 19th Fane's Horse took cover one moment in an olive grove, the red soil spitting up between their horses' hooves from the machine gun fire of swooping German aeroplanes; at another they captured a Turkish motor lorry convoy carrying chests of gold, one sowar surreptitiously swiping a haversack-full before his British officer impounded the chests as official treasure. Meanwhile, the 2nd Gardner's Horse with an armoured car behind them charged down several Turkish machine gun posts near a German aerodrome, lancing forty-six Turks and capturing 470 more. They galloped on into the aerodrome itself, rounding up a hundred German mechanics trying to escape on lorries. 'An aeroplane bringing the German mails landed in our midst,' recalled George Barrow, the 2nd Gardner's Horse's jovial divisional commander. He was riding with them as one of the Indian Army's most respected senior officers, having been transferred to Palestine from the western front where he had been the BEF First Army's Chief of Staff. 'The pilot and observer got the surprise of their lives when they found themselves greeted by Indian troopers instead of their own countrymen. They bravely tried to get their M.G. into action but were soon silenced.' Among the 2nd's haul at the German aerodrome were three aeroplanes, several lorries, a large store of petrol, a hospital fully stocked with drugs, and a food store complete with champagne and hock. 'I have never enjoyed any time of my life half as much,' one of the regiment's exhilarated British officers told Barrow. 'Having settled down to a Boche cigar and a bottle of ditto hock, I would not have changed places with President Wilson himself.'

'Lawrence Sahib was a great snob'

To the east of the Egyptian Expeditionary Force's attacks at Megiddo, in what is now Jordan and southern Syria, the Indian Army secretly fought as part of a parallel advance by 3000 Bedu irregular freedom fighters from Arabia. These Arabs were cooperating with Allenby to harass the Turkish inland flank under the banner of Sharif Hussein of Mecca, to whom the British had pledged independent Arab statehood.

The famous British imperial link with Sharif Hussein's Arab forces was of course the archaeologist, Arabic scholar and liaison officer Colonel T. E. Lawrence. Their lesser known Indian contingent had British officers and men of the 9th Hodson's Horse, 18th

Tiwana Lancers, 34th Poona Horse, 116th Mahrattas and 3rd Gurkhas. The Indian troops here included well-trained machine gunners, some of them Pukhtun who had volunteered on the western front for secret service in Arabia, and Gurkhas picked from Palestine. They had fought under Lawrence since 1917, riding camels with him all the way from what is now Saudi Arabia into Syria to provide covering fire from sand dunes during his desert raids on Turkish railways. At times they were indispensable to him. The senior Pukhtun officer Hassan Shah won his respect in particular as 'a firm and experienced man [and] great-hearted' – for never complaining about the hardships of the desert, sharing his Indian tea around the camp fire with a smile, and resourcefully doing all he was asked in action. But Hassan Shah was less flattering. 'Lawrence Sahib was a great snob,' he said. 'Unless you were of good family, he had no use for you. He thought the world of me, but only because I am a Qureshi, descended from the Prophet's own tribe.'

Lawrence certainly had less time for his Gurkhas, speaking to them so little that after the war one of them, Manbahadur Gurung, a veteran of France, Gaza and Jerusalem in 1914–17, did not even know his name. 'It was not good but not bad ... not worse than the rest of the war,' Gurung said of his day-to-day camel-riding aches, telegraph wire-cutting and machine gunning with the Arab forces, compared to his previous service against the Germans and Turks. The main danger, he added, was that 'Turkish aeroplanes came right down on top of us, till they were only about five yards above our heads, to drop bombs and to fire machine guns at us, but they were very bad shots and we had very little damage ... Not like when our aeroplanes attacked the enemy, as I saw them do in Palestine.'

On 28 September 1918, Lawrence, the Arab forces and their Pukhtun and Gurkha attachments joined up with the main body of Allenby's Indian cavalry at the southern Syrian town of Dera, a Turkish railway junction between Amman and Damascus.

Over the following four days, Lawrence had a series of personal run-ins with the Indian cavalry at Dera that were to leave him with a lifelong contempt for the Indian Army. Indeed, in his autobiographical masterpiece *Seven Pillars of Wisdom* (1926) he would belittle the Indian troops in Palestine as 'not worthy of the privilege of space' in the desert, being 'something puny' with minds 'like slow sheep'.

The sourness started outside Dera when Lawrence, on horseback, trotted up to the advance guard of the 2nd Gardner's Horse. Freshly shaved and in clean Arab robes with a white headdress, intending to impress as an authoritative Arab military leader, he called out, 'I am Colonel Lawrence. Where is your General? Take me to him at once.' The young British officer of the guard, Dysart Whitworth, had not slept for fifty hours on the march, and did not like Lawrence's tone; he snapped back that he was commanding in action, was not a guide, and Lawrence was 'a bloody fool'. A yelling impasse ensued which Lawrence backed down from, riding off in fury shouting, 'I'll have you court martialled!' Shortly afterwards, while the robed Lawrence was driving in his Rolls-Royce with a Bedu escort, he came upon another Indian advance guard – this time of the 34th Poona Horse under their senior Indian officer Hamir Singh, a veteran of First Ypres. Mistaking Lawrence and his Bedu for Turkish irregulars, Hamir Singh's guard charged mounted at them, driving off the Bedu and taking Lawrence prisoner as a suspected spy. Another heated argument broke out, with Hamir Singh refusing to let an apoplectic Lawrence go for some time.

Then one morning at Dera railway station the Indian cavalry divisional commander George Barrow, with men of the 2nd Gardner's Horse and 38th Central India Horse, had encountered Lawrence on the platform next to a long Turkish ambulance train, whose driver was slumped in his cab shot dead. Through the carriage windows they saw some of Lawrence's Arabs going down the train tearing off every shred of clothing from groaning

Turkish patients, who lay helpless with open wounds and broken limbs, and slitting the throats of every naked man – 'a revolting scene', Barrow wrote, 'far exceeding in its savagery anything that has been known in the conflicts between nations during the past 120 years'. Barrow told Lawrence to get the Arabs off the train, but Lawrence said he could not 'as it was their idea of war'. Barrow replied, 'It is not our idea of war, and if you can't remove them, I will.' He sent his Indian cavalrymen to turn the Arabs out, guard the station, and do 'all that lay in their power for the unfortunate Turks still alive' by giving them water, dressing their wounds and making them as comfortable as possible. 'In the whole course of this war, in France and in Palestine,' Barrow reported soon after, surely speaking for his men as much as himself, 'I have never seen such a sight of dreadful misery.'

That night Lawrence's relationship with the Indian cavalry got even worse. He stormed into the 2nd Gardner's Horse camp by Dera railway station as the sowars slept, accusing them of thieving his Arabs' holy standard (a green and silver flag from Mecca) from outside their headquarters down the street. Lawrence insisted on searching every sowar's belongings, but found no standard; the thief, it seems, was a British soldier from Dorset brigaded with the Indians.* George Barrow resented this latest episode with Lawrence as 'a gratuitous insult to the Indian soldiers', and 'an unwarranted reflection on their fine discipline'. Lawrence for his part would always mistrust Indian soldiers, writing in his *Revolt in the Desert* (1927) of 'the Indian trooper who stole' as their mark as men.

On 1 October Lawrence drove into Damascus triumphantly in his Rolls-Royce with his Arab irregulars as liberators, just ahead of the Egyptian Expeditionary Force's Indian and other Allied troops. The capture of the city, 120 miles north of Allenby's

---

* The standard apparently flapped at a farm in the southern English county after the war.

Megiddo start line on 19 September, confirmed the crushing success of the offensive. In weighing up the contribution of Lawrence's Arabs, George Barrow would always repeat what a captured Turkish divisional commander told him: 'The Arabs gave us pin pricks; the British – blows with a sledge hammer.' The Arabs had indeed been marginal, and the hammer blows had been struck most frequently by the Indian infantry and cavalry.

In the week leading up to Lawrence's entry into Damascus, Indian cavalry regiments had been decisive in the pursuit of the retreating Turkish divisions and German Asia Corps all the way up from Megiddo. They had taken the majority of the Allies' 75,000 predominantly Turkish prisoners, along with several towns – for instance, the Mysore and Jodhpur Lancers had seized Haifa on 23 September with two squadrons galloping through the streets under fire from the houses, lancing a few Turkish troops in their path, and helping to capture 689 Turks and Germans, ten machine guns and twelve artillery pieces.

The Turks' own part in their downfall in Palestine was rooted not so much in their inferiority in numbers, guns or aircraft, all of which they had in good quantities for defence, as in their sapped spirit. This accounted for the large numbers of prisoners who surrendered easily. By mid-1918 the resolve of the Turkish Army was not what the Indians had seen at Gallipoli in 1915, on the Tigris in 1916 or at Gaza in 1917. The long war had gradually worn down them and their supply system, and by Megiddo they had little energy to carry on. Some of the Turkish troops there had fought hard, but many had lost heart, with no boots on their feet and almost no food to eat, at one with their artillery horses who were too under-nourished to pull back half their guns on the retreat. On account of the Turkish Army's scrawny appearance and reduced fighting capacity at Megiddo compared to the well fed, trained and equipped Egyptian Expeditionary Force, one British staff officer remarked that Allenby's offensive had ultimately been that of an Indian tiger against a Turkish tomcat.

'To score as heavily as possible before the whistle blew'

In London over the summer, the Chief of the Imperial General Staff Henry Wilson had continued to manage the Indian Army's overseas distribution to help the British Army on the western front. In August, anticipating the war carrying on into 1919, he decided to Indianise the Greek front at Thessaloniki more than he had Palestine, by withdrawing all its British divisions for France and replacing them with Indian troops. In September the Indian battalions (thirty-six of them) selected for Thessaloniki began to sail from Iraq and India, along with Indian hospitals and labour units. Yet as they sailed, the Greek front opened up from its stalemate of 1915–17. The French Army broke out northwards into Serbia, Bulgaria signed an armistice with the Allies, and the British forces at Thessaloniki advanced east into Thrace, heading for Istanbul. Added to Megiddo, these developments compelled the Turkish government to seek its own armistice with the Allies, and by early October it had opened talks at Paris with the Allied Supreme War Council.

By then, the British objectives in the war on Turkey had crystallised into securing post-war influence in the Middle East in the interests of imperial defence. The War Cabinet in London hoped to convert much of the region's conquered lands into British-controlled buffer states, an ambition already documented in an Anglo-French understanding of 1916 (the 'Sykes-Picot Agreement' to divide the Middle East between British and French spheres of influence, kept secret until Tsarist Russia's copy was published in anti-imperialist outrage by the Bolsheviks in November 1917; notoriously it was irreconcilable with Britain's earlier assurance to Sharif Hussein of Mecca of independent Arab statehood, which itself conflicted with 1917's British 'Balfour Declaration' of intent to establish a national home for the Jewish people in Palestine). The prospect of an imminent armistice with Turkey, therefore, focused British ministers' minds on developing in the limited time left of active hostilities their military control of the Middle East for post-war advantage. The consequence for Indian Expeditionary Force D in Iraq was an urgent mission to complete before the Turks signed in Paris. It was to advance 100 miles to secure Iraq's northern city of Mosul for control of its surrounding oil deposits, in order to guarantee Britain's post-war supply of fuel for the Royal Navy and the increasingly mechanised British Army. This was a matter of Force D making 'every effort ... to score as heavily as possible on the Tigris before the whistle blew,' as Arnold Wilson, the officer of the 32nd Sikh Pioneers who was now at Baghdad as the senior administrator of Iraq's Occupied Territories, put it.

The British commander of Force D's revival in Iraq by 1917, Stanley Maude, had died that November from cholera, caught from milk in his coffee during a Baghdad school performance of *Hamlet*. His replacement was a meticulous British Army general, William Marshall, experienced on the western front, at Gallipoli and under Maude in Iraq. Marshall organised the necessary desert offensive of October 1918 towards Mosul, to be carried out by Force D's I Corps. Like Allenby at Megiddo, Marshall efficiently combined his available means of modern mobile warfare – short artillery bombardments in cooperation with a majority of young Indian infantry recruits, trained with the latest small arms and led by a sprinkling of seasoned British and Indian officers who had seen most fronts since 1914, together with cavalry, armoured cars, Royal Air Force bombers, Ford vans and other mechanised transport. Force D's I Corps advanced the 100 miles to Mosul in twelve days, annihilating the Turkish Sixth Army and taking 11,000 prisoners. Indian cavalry occupied the city on 3 November, despite Turkish complaints of bad faith – the Allies and the Turkish government had signed their armistice on 31 October.

On the western front, the Allies launched their decisive offensives in France from August on a front of around 200 miles, with Douglas Haig's BEF on the left on the Somme, the French Army in the centre, and the American Expeditionary Force on the right, attacking through the Argonne forest. After four years of trial and error for the BEF and the French, and months for the Americans, the Allies found their winning combination of offensive techniques: close infantry-artillery cooperation with accurate and overwhelming curtains of shell fire just ahead of advancing troops (the British and French alone fired a million shells on 27 September); tanks keeping up momentum alongside men; low-flying attack aircraft, and more. By October these elements were combining to inflict a series of outright local defeats on the German Army, leading to Allied advances of several miles a day, and the desertion of over 100,000 war-weary German troops. The Indian Army's part in these BEF strikes was played by a small minority. There were only a few Indian Labour Corps companies, most having insisted on going home by June with their saved pay on the expiry of their one-year service contracts; the handful of independent Pukhtun cavalrymen Allenby had sent from Palestine to handle British Army replacement horses; and 18,000 further Indian combatants who had arrived in France in 1917 at London's request, and who mainly drove British artillery and Australian supply wagons.

In the first week of November, with 2 million men of the United States Army in France tipping the numerical balance in the west, with Bulgaria and Turkey already out of the war, and with Austria-Hungary agreeing an armistice with the Italians on the plains north of Venice and the Alps beyond, the German General Staff and Berlin completed the Central Powers' collapse in Europe by asking the Allies for their own armistice. And so the guns on the western front finally fell silent on 11 November at 11 a.m.

That day the Indian Army had approximately 500,000 men posted overseas. In Europe, beyond the western front, there were 18,000 Indian servicemen on the Greek front at Thessaloniki, and two Himalayan regiments at Gallipoli occupying the peninsula (the 6th Gurkhas and 39th Garhwals). Across the Mediterranean in Egypt, Palestine and Syria, Allenby's Egyptian Expeditionary Force had an Indian total of 103,000 troops and 15,000 non-combatants, now extending north of Damascus and occupying Beirut, Homs and Aleppo. In East Africa there were 4500 Indian ranks helping to secure German territory, and at Aden and on Red Sea islands 7500 Indian troops, confirming Britain as the dominant Allied power in western Arabia. In Iraq, the Occupied Territories from Basra to Mosul were held by 296,000 Indian servicemen. In Iran, from the Gurkha outposts in the north-west facing the Caucasus, to Punjabi units in the southern Persian Gulf hinterland and in the east along the Afghan border, there were detachments of thirty Indian regiments with Indian non-combatant support, altogether some 25,000 men. Then in Soviet Turkestan, Indian troops remained on the western branch of the Trans-Caspian Railway, and the Indian Army's Frederick Bailey was still hiding from the Soviets in the mountains north of Tashkent. Bailey was indeed not to learn the war was over for another month. But what were the feelings of the Indian Army's officers and men who did know on 11 November?

That evening among the 9th Gurkhas at camp in the Punjabi countryside on a route march, the news of the German armistice was announced on parade. 'Though a feeling of relief and grat-ification was apparent in all ranks,' wrote their British officer Frederick Poynder, 'it must be admitted that this stupendous announcement was received with little enthusiasm.' This was 'not altogether surprising', he thought, as many of the men were recent recruits who had not seen active service. Equally, for the regiment's Nepalese veterans of France and Iraq still serving, the war had seemed over since their return to British India in late 1916, and they 'lacked the imagination and knowledge to appreciate the stirring events that had happened in France and elsewhere' in 1917–18.

The Indians' British officers were typically more taken aback and relieved. 'Wonderful news of <u>PEACE AT LAST!</u> and this GREATEST WAR is over,' wrote Lionel Dunsterville, the Indian commander of the ill-fated Dunsterforce mission to the Caucasus, now back in British India's North-West Frontier Province. 'We are so accustomed to war in this fifth year that we can hardly believe the news.' For the younger British officer Harold Lewis, in Palestine with the 2nd/127th Baluchis, the news brought on a curious withdrawal symptom from his almost constant regimental service since 1914 on three continents. 'Personally I am not a bit excited and not even pleased,' he wrote. 'It will be so dull.'

How significant, then, had the Indian Army been to the Allied military victory over the Central Powers? The obvious answer is that in 1918 it was of slight importance compared to the British, Australian, Canadian, French and American armies' active roles in the decisive western theatre, at best having an indirect effect on the result there by serving in Palestine to release British Army reinforcements for France. But the more revealing measure is what the Indian Army achieved for the British Empire as the Allies' greatest power, a context in which the Indian role takes on a global significance.

The Indian Army's grand total of 1.5 million servicemen was equivalent to all the empire's military forces from Australia, New Zealand, the Pacific Islands, South Africa, the Caribbean, Canada, Hong Kong and Singapore put together; it in fact accounted for one in every six of the empire's military servicemen in the war. While the British Army on the western front made up the bulk of the remainder, the Indian Army had a consistently important support role across the theatres. In 1914, the arrival of Indian Expeditionary Force A to France saved the British Army from running too short of men to survive at First Ypres, and being run off the continent with disastrous consequences for the Allies. In 1915–16, the Indian Army was the most widespread military extinguisher of the flames of the Sultan of Turkey's jihad from the Sahara Desert to the independent Pukhtun tribal areas. In

1917–18, the Indian divisions in the Middle East were vital to the Turkish Army's defeat and the integrity of British imperial defence in Asia. By the time of the German armistice, the Indian Army bore the hallmarks of an effective modern force: it had adapted to learn lessons in mountain, trench, desert and bush warfare, developed a logistical facility to fight to the very end, and had never disintegrated with mass desertions or mutinies. Ultimately, its part in the Allied victory was sustaining the British Empire's global rather than European campaigns on land. For all that it contributed little to the decision in Europe in 1918, it had shaped much of the war's worldwide course.

Since 1914, the Indian troops themselves had of course had all sorts of new, life-altering experiences. 'The Indian Army has changed from what she was before,' said the 15th Ludhiana Sikhs' long-serving Subadar-Major Laxman Singh in 1920. 'The world has seen the Indian sepoy and the Indian sepoy has seen the world ... They have got their aspirations, desires and grievances.' Quite what these were in the post-war years, and what they meant for the Indian veterans' relationship with the British as the Indian independence movement developed from 1919, would confound any basic notions of loyalty or disloyalty to colonial rule.

Seven

VETERANS

'WHICH SIDE THEIR BREAD
IS BUTTERED'

'My Dear Nephew,' the Jodhpur Lancers' commandant Sir Pratap Singh began his telegram of 12 November 1918 to George V, from Jodhpur State and using his old term of endearment for the King-Emperor, 'Of all the soldier princes of India, I think I am the only soldier who has stuck to his post at the front throughout the war.' The 'fitting and gracious recognition of my loyal and humble services to the King and his Empire', he was sure, would be for George to 'leave no stone unturned' to secure his personal invitation to the Allies' Peace Conference in Paris. He wanted not just to represent India's princely States alongside President Wilson and other leaders of the free world, but actually to join them in 'settling and signing the terms' with the Central Powers. Sir Pratap's proposal, however, was not taken remotely seriously. His eccentric style of spoken English and propensity for pointed outbursts told against him as much as his tendency in his mid-seventies to fall asleep in his chair during long conversations.

Instead, the British chose a younger Hindu soldier to represent princely India in the negotiations at the Palace of Versailles from January 1919: the thirty-eight-year-old Maharajah Ganga

Singh of Bikaner. He had been an aide-de-camp to the King-Emperor, held an honorary King's Commission, and proudly wore the uniform of a British major-general, his tunic so beautifully cut that no British general wore finer. His princely States regiment, the Bikaner Camel Corps, had served since 1914 from the Sahara to Suez and Sinai, and in 1918 he had raised an Indian Army battalion in his own state, the 141st Bikaners. But what really qualified Bikaner for the Peace Conference was his politics. While Sir Pratap was self-confessedly 'a man of strict aristocratic ideas, and not at all a believer in equality', Bikaner swore by the wartime nationalist argument of backing the imperial war effort to the hilt in order to gain concessions towards Indian self-government. Furthermore, he was already trusted as a safe pair of diplomatic hand. From 1917 he had represented India at the Imperial War Cabinet in London, proving himself a master of the quiet, courtly deference and carefully chosen word the British liked most in a maharajah. At Versailles, Bikaner would be an assistant to both the Indian Empire's delegation chief, the Secretary of State for India Edwin Montagu, and its member for British India, Satyendra Prasanna Sinha, a Bengali civil servant and former President of the Indian National Congress.

Yet none of the Indian delegation at Versailles had much say as President Wilson and the major western leaders took charge, deferring a settlement with the Ottoman Empire to focus on the Treaty of Versailles with Germany, signed on 28 June. Montagu signed the treaty for British India, and Bikaner for the princely States. 'I do not think the Germans are in a position to fight us again,' Bikaner wrote approvingly of the treaty's punitive terms: shrinking Germany's borders with a measure of occupation, including by the British Empire's Army of the Rhine (which numbered some Indian Army officers and men still in France at the armistice, and who helped in 1919 to clear up the battlefields in Flanders); converting Germany's colonial territories from

Qingdao to East Africa and Cameroon into possessions of Allied powers as 'mandates', or areas of control under the auspices of the League of Nations, the forerunner of the United Nations; decimating Germany's armed forces; obliging 'reparations' or payments for war damage so colossal they were beyond computation for the time being; and a declaration that German aggression was the war's cause. Back in Jodhpur State, Sir Pratap Singh read the Treaty of Versailles quite differently to Bikaner, suggesting that his presence at the Peace Conference would indeed have caused a memorable scene. No fool, he thought the treaty most unwise. 'Politically, it was a mistake,' he wrote. 'I am sure the Germans would not rest without taking revenge some day.'

That summer, in celebration of victory and the Versailles peace, the Allies held triumphant parades with captured German guns and tanks through packed streets from New York City and Toronto to Cape Town and Sydney. In Paris an Indian Army contingent paraded down the Champs-Élysée in the Allies' great Victory Parade of 14 July, passing through the Arc de Triomphe next to New Zealanders. The Indian Army's own victory parade was in London on 2 August. Long columns of 1500 still-serving Indian veterans marched in the sunshine, the representatives of every Indian regiment that had gone on active service, each man selected for his distinguished service. Among them was the Afridi officer Arsala Khan of the 57th Wilde's Rifles as the regiment's subadar-major, aged forty-five or so, despite his wounds from Belgium and East Africa.

Arsala Khan and the other Indian veterans marched from Waterloo Station over the River Thames, past Big Ben and Parliament, up Whitehall past the original Cenotaph to Trafalgar Square, and on to the Mall towards Buckingham Palace. They processed to the sounds of drums and brass bands, and were cheered on by exuberant crowds who showered flowers on them from the street-sides and windows above. They carried tall pale-blue banners, each with a silver star, a laurel wreath and thick black lettering naming a place where they had served since 1914, from France to Gallipoli, the Caucasus and beyond. The crowds hurrahed them right through the palace's front gates chanting 'God Save the King', and the veterans lined up with their banners on the secluded back lawn for an intimate meeting with George V and the Queen-Empress Mary. 'I heartily thank all my Indian Soldiers for their loyal devotion to me and to my Empire, and for their sufferings cheerfully borne in the various campaigns in which they have served in lands and climates so different from their own,' the King-Emperor told them from his garden steps, in a speech that was repeated in Urdu on the spot by a British officer:

At times their hearts must have been sad at the long separation from their homes; but they have fought and died bravely ... for the defence of the Empire and for the cause in which the Allies have fought and conquered. I know you all unite with me in gratitude to God for the victory that we have achieved ... May you return in safety and take with you to your homes and villages my personal message of thanks and good will.

After the King's speech, the Indian soldiers roared three cheers for him, and another three for the Queen. They then watched him award the Victoria Cross to a nineteen-year-old Gurkha, Karanbahadur Rana – who had enlisted from Nepal in December 1916 and survived a hail of German grenades in Palestine in 1918 to knock out a German Asia Corps machine gun post – before they stood easy and mingled at a tea party in the garden in their honour. For the Afridi officer Arsala Khan, in his only known recorded words as written down by a *Times of India* interviewer, the Indians' victory parade and palace gathering were a worthy tribute to their allegiance. 'I have seen much service for the Badshah,' he said, using an Urdu word for 'emperor'. 'Now I am very happy and contented ... for I have seen the Badshah and he has thanked me and my comrades for our patriotism.'*

As the Indians marched away from Buckingham Palace after their tea party, it seemed Arsala Khan's bond with the British was shared by others. They passed a tall, tanned British man in plain clothes who had watched them march into the palace, and had waited by the road outside to watch them leave. Some of the Indian veterans recognised him, one shouting excitedly the Sikh war cry of 'Fateh!' in his direction. A group broke ranks and ran over to him, exclaiming, 'Here is our General!'

'It was a very short greeting,' the tanned man later said, 'but it was none the less both moving and splendid.' It was James Willcocks, on leave from governing Bermuda but still something of a social outcast, not invited like Douglas Haig and other generals to the garden party. A few days later, Willcocks drove in his motor car to the Indians' camp a few miles from London, in a meadow at Hampton Court Palace on the banks of the Thames. 'I clearly knew those faithful comrades would never forget their old Commander,' he wrote of his long chat on old times with the veterans at the camp's coffee bar. 'It is my final and highest reward.'

From Jodhpur State to the Palace of Versailles, Paris and London, then, the Indian Army seemed in the summer of 1919 to have come through the world war in unity under the British. Whether older soldiers who had fought the longest, such as Sir Pratap Singh and Arsala Khan, or the younger generation from the Maharajah of Bikaner to the teenage Gurkha VC Karanbahadur Rana, they gave Willcocks ample reason to conclude in the memoir he was writing at the time, *With the Indians in France*, that they were 'brave, loyal gentlemen'.

In British India, meanwhile, the Indian nationalist politicians'

---

* Like the Indian servicemen at Brighton Pavilion hospital in 1915, those parading through London and visiting Buckingham Palace on 2 August 1919 were filmed to make one of the several films shot in 1914–19 of them overseas and which survive today.

wartime alliance with the British had started to unravel. In March the British had tightened the colonial state's security laws, above all extending into peacetime the Defence of India Act of 1915 with its powers to detain without proof and sentence to death without appeal. To the Indian politicians this was a sickening betrayal. The Montagu Declaration in 1917 had promised them gradual self-government, and the British Prime Minister David Lloyd George's public telegram in 1918 had wooed them for their help to win the war in the cause of freedom, yet the first thing they got after the war was restricted civil liberties.

Mahatma Gandhi led the nationalist backlash, slamming the security laws as 'devilish' and 'a determined policy of repression', and exposing the Montagu Declaration as 'camouflage, humbug, and honeyed words'. He jettisoned his wartime platform of promoting Indian Army recruitment and obedience to the British, instead embarking on a new path to 'fight the greatest battle of my life'. This was his campaign of non-violent civil disobedience, which he called 'a duty imposed upon every lover of personal and public liberty', inspired by the idea that Hindu-Muslim non-cooperation with colonial rule would make it inoperable, bringing self-rule in its place. Gandhi began encouraging anti-British protests, sparking unrest from Bombay to Delhi and Punjab, much of it fuelled by India's distressing post-war living conditions caused by inflation, rising prices and the deadly worldwide Spanish influenza pandemic.

As Gandhi's civil disobedience marked the beginnings of India's mass independence movement into the 1920s, the Indian veterans of the world war faced a choice between supporting the nationalists or marching on behind the British. By the early 1930s, their decision had become clear to one British civil servant commenting on the Hindu Dogras of Punjab's eastern Kangra hill district. 'Their faith is pinned to the British government, which had provided an outlet for profitable employment,' he wrote. 'To put the matter on the lowest plane, a class in which practically every homestead had some connection with the military and government service ... is fully aware of which side their bread is buttered.'

There was a great deal in what he said, but the veterans' post-war feelings about the British were much knottier. Rather than being simply loyal or disloyal, they burned with inner turmoil over serving the British, choosing a number of post-war paths to fight their own battles with them. Many veterans chose ostensible obedience, continuing to serve the British and sending their sons into the Indian Army, yet quietly squirming as colonial servants wanting more self-respect and better treatment. There were others, however, who as ex-servicemen were actively resistant to the British – even helping to kill hundreds of Indian soldiers sent against them under their old British officers from France and East Africa.

'The war is not over'

In London in January 1919, the Chief of the Imperial General Staff Henry Wilson grappled with what the armistices of late 1918 meant for the Indian Army beyond the obvious ceasefires across the fronts. Essentially, as he put it, 'the war is not over'. The British Empire's conquests of German and Ottoman lands in Africa and Asia had bloated it by 27 per cent compared to 1914, its biggest extent. For David Lloyd George and his Cabinet, planning to defend the empire by holding on to most of the gains, Wilson's view that Asia 'from the left bank of the Don* to India is our interest and preserve' was about right. To secure Britain's imperial position in Asia, the British Army in Europe was largely unavailable, preoccupied with bringing troops home from France and fighting the Irish War of Independence. The burden fell heavily on the Indian Army, which mixed its own demobilisation – its

---

* The river of western Russia, north-east of the Black Sea.

grand total of Indian combatants reduced from 500,000 in 1918 to 120,000 by 1923 – with continuing overseas service. This was to be the most palpable sign of the Indian veterans' post-war support for the British, as in many respects they kept up and deepened their close relationship of the war years.

The bulk of the Indian Army's ongoing overseas service centred on occupying the Ottoman Empire as the Allies' peace negotiations with the Turks dragged on until 1923. Thousands of Indian troops served in the British Empire's Army of the Black Sea, its post-war garrison of the northern Ottoman areas. They guarded munitions stores, railways, cities and ports from Istanbul to inland areas of Turkey's Anatolian heartland, Georgia, Azerbaijan and Armenia. The Army of the Black Sea's most experienced Indian regiment was the 89th Punjabis who could count nine fronts in Europe and Asia on their roll of duty since 1914. Into 1920 in Georgia, they had with them veterans of France, Gallipoli and Iraq including the long-serving Punjabi Muslim, Shahamad Khan, who in early 1916 at Kut had won the Victoria Cross.

Meanwhile, Indian troops garrisoned Syria, Palestine, Jordan, Iraq, Iran and western Soviet Turkestan, often clashing with local opponents of British occupation. This was especially the case in Iraq and its mountainous Kurdish fringe north of Mosul. There were 65,000 Indian soldiers in Iraq in the summer of 1920 pitted against Arab and Kurdish rebels, and they sacked, burned and killed in numerous villages and valleys. In Syria, several of the Indian cavalry regiments who had served in France and Palestine were only to return to India after six years away. The 38th Central India Horse, for instance, reappeared at their depot at Guna, in what is now the central Indian state of Madhya Pradesh, in February 1921 with 150 sowars and one British officer who had departed for war in November 1914.

The Indian forces of occupation in the former Ottoman Empire and its environs were substantially pulled out by 1924 – not by Henry Wilson, whom the Irish Republican Army had assassinated in 1922, but by his replacement as Chief of the Imperial General Staff, the Earl of Cavan. This followed the Treaty of Lausanne to end the war with Turkey, and a post-war British policy of military economy, entailing cutbacks to the Indian Army's overseas commitments. Still, Indian units remained in some areas of the Middle East such as Palestine, a British mandate, up to 1928. Throughout the decade of post-war Indian Army occupation in the Middle East, the Indian troops proved reliable agents of imperial power, almost always following British orders and deserting very rarely.

The same was true of them on duty in the Indian Empire. In 1919–20 they had a number of grievances in the electric post-war political atmosphere as Gandhi's civil disobedience movement took off. Some 150,000 Indian recruits of 1918 were demobilised in British India in the first half of 1919 having not been abroad, which many resented as robbing them of the chance to earn the material rewards they had enlisted for, in particular land. Furthermore, Muslims of Indian regiments were acutely concerned about the fate of Islam's Holy Places as the Allied peace negotiations with the Turks seemed likely to bring an end to the Ottoman Caliphate, creating doubts as to who would protect the Holy Places in its absence. The issue sparked the popular Khilafat Movement, bringing Indian Muslims together with Gandhi to agitate for the British to preserve pre-1914 Ottoman borders and the Sultan of Turkey's authority within them. Then Indian officers widely received seditious leaflets and letters from pro-violence Indian revolutionaries, calling on them to fight the colonial regime. 'Kill these English, win the whole army to your side,' said one leaflet of 1919 sent to the 45th Sikhs' subadar-major in Punjab. 'Hindus and Muslims are now united. What does Gandhi say? . . . Don't lose time. Kill, Kill. The English are tyrants and if they remain they will treat you brutally. Save the country.'

Yet in 1919 it was the Indian troops who guaranteed the colonial regime. Most notoriously in Punjab, men of the 54th Sikhs, 59th Scinde Rifles and 9th Gurkhas – Hindus and Muslims, young

Baluchi, Gurkha and Pukhtun recruits, some in their teens – carried out the massacre at Amritsar in the Jallianwala Bagh on the afternoon of 13 April. At the signal of a whistle blown by their British commander Reginald Dyer, who was out to deter protests across British India against the extension of wartime security laws into peacetime, they opened fire with their Lee-Enfield rifles. They shot at a peaceful crowd of 20,000 Punjabis who stood, strolled or sat about, some waiting to meet friends, playing dice or sleeping, others listening to poetry and speeches. They fired 1650 bullets in ten minutes to kill some 500 Punjabis and wound 1200 more; indeed, some of the casualties were Indian Army veterans, Sikhs and Hindu Jats who had served in France and Iraq. The only recorded comment of the troops involved was made by a Gurkha soon afterwards to a British civil servant. 'Sahib,' the Gurkha said, 'while it lasted it was splendid, we fired every round we had.'

In Gandhi's eyes, the Amritsar massacre revealed the Indian soldiers as serving purposes far from those of self-rule he had advocated as an army recruiter a year earlier. 'I refuse to call the profession of the sepoy honourable when he has no choice as to the time when and the persons or people against whom he is called upon,' he wrote. 'The sepoy's services have more often been utilized for enslaving us than for protecting us.' Yet Gandhi's criticisms did nothing to stop Indian troops in British India going to war for the empire only a month after the Amritsar massacre.

From May on the Indo-Afghan border, India's Commander-in-Chief Charles Monro amassed 340,000 servicemen, the majority young and partially trained Indian recruits of 1918, for the Third Anglo-Afghan War. Afghanistan's new Emir Amanullah initiated the war after his father Habibullah had been assassinated. Amanullah disavowed his father's policy of official friendship with the British, and was intent on freeing Afghanistan from the British treaty control over its foreign relations in place since 1879. He declared a jihad against the British as tyrants of India, and ordered a large part of the Afghan Army – a semi-modernised force of about 50,000 regular soldiers all told – to advance towards British India, hoping that it would be supported by tribal irregulars.

In the first week of May 1919, therefore, Monro mobilised Indian and British troops to defend India's frontier with Afghanistan. Some of the Indian troops were palpably disappointed at their orders to go to the frontier. The men of the 3rd/124th Baluchis, for example, had just landed at Karachi after three years in Iran and were 'war weary', one of their British officers could see; 'Three months leave home was expected and would have been granted but for the outbreak of the Third Afghan War.' Nonetheless, the 3rd/124th and the Indian units as a whole selected by Monro for the war, including a hundred battalions and twenty-one cavalry regiments, promptly obeyed their orders to board trains or march to the frontier.

The same cannot quite be said of the British troops in India. They were mainly Territorials who had been on continuous Indian garrison duty since 1914–15, and whose hopes of imminently sailing home were dashed by their mobilisation for the Afghan war. This 'created a feeling of discontent ... which held the menace of mutiny', a British general later said of them. The Territorials openly talked of rejecting orders to fight the Afghans, and at least 2,000 of them refused to leave Punjab in the direction of Afghanistan. 'They had joined up to fight the Germans', a British officer reported of their mood, 'but, if India was going to conduct a new war against Afghanistan, it was none of their business and beyond what they had contracted for.' Many Territorials only agreed to serve against the Afghans after Monro held a personal audience at Simla with their representatives, tactfully but firmly appealing to their sense of duty to the empire. He persuaded them to go to the frontier, to join British regulars who like the Indian troops had accepted their mobilisation orders at the first time of asking.

For four weeks into June, in cooperation with Royal Air Force bombers (among them the world's largest aircraft at the time, the Handley Page V/1500, originally built to bomb Berlin), Indian, British regular and Territorial units repelled the invading Afghan Army at various points along 400 miles of the frontier. Using armoured cars, mountain artillery howitzers, Lewis light machine guns, Mills grenades and other weapons that had become familiar to Indian forces in France, Iraq and elsewhere up to 1918, they achieved a series of local successes rather than any decisive victory. Often digging trenches and laying barbed wire in front as they went, they secured control of several mountain passes, roads, fortresses and villages on both sides of the Indo-Afghan border.

Many Indian officers showed determined leadership. For instance, there was the 9th Gurkhas' Subadar Shibdhoj Mal, a decorated veteran of the western front in 1914–15. On 17 May in Afghanistan's Nangarhar Province, near the village of Loe Dakka on the banks of the Kabul River, he led his platoon up a rocky hill against an Afghan position on the crest, heading into substantial shell fire from the Afghan Army's German-made artillery. As he persevered with his men to gain and hold ground near the hill's crest, terrified young recruits alongside of the 35th Sikhs, who had lost their officers to Afghan fire, fled in the opposite direction.

To the south in the Afghan province of Kandahar later in May, the 22nd Punjabis and other battalions captured the fort of Spin Boldak, a minor but creditable feat of arms against the 600 Afghan defenders. It involved the Punjabis improvising with their entrenching tools and bayonets to make a breach in a thick mud outer wall fifteen feet high, sticking to the task even though the Royal Air Force bombed them by mistake, killing five of the regiment and wounding ten. The Punjabis pushed on under Afghan fire to climb with ladders an inner fort wall; they then pursued Afghan riflemen making a stubborn fighting retreat into dark rooms at the heart of the fort, and lobbed Mills grenades into these to finish the fight. The Territorials at Spin Boldak were the 1st/4th West Kents. They were comparatively hesitant to fight, their hearts already back in their home county. Contrary to repeated orders to attack, they deliberately stalled for over two hours outside Spin Boldak at an appreciable distance from its walls, in effect choosing to leave the fort for the Indian Army and British regulars to take.

In the wake of Spin Boldak and other Afghan battlefield setbacks both in Nangarhar and Kandahar provinces and in the independent Pukhtun tribal areas, besides Royal Air Force bombings of Kabul and the nearby Afghan city of Jalalabad, Amannullah sought an armistice. The Viceroy Lord Chelmsford agreed to one on 3 June; he was eager to avoid a long war, to limit ongoing border skirmishes with tribal irregulars supportive of Amanullah, and to re-establish official Anglo-Afghan friendship. The armistice formally stopped the fighting for the Afghan Army, which had lost an estimated total of 2,000 casualties against the Indian and British units on the ground, and more in Royal Air Force attacks. The war had cost the Indian Army around 380 officers and men wounded or killed by Afghan regulars (excluding a few casualties of the 15th Sikhs accidentally shot by British regulars in Nangarhar), and the British Army around 150.

The balance of the imperial losses reflected that once again Indian troops had obediently taken the strain of a frontier war for the British. The much heavier Afghan losses proved the price of Amannullah's eventual diplomatic victory. Under the war's peace settlement of 8 August 1919, the Treaty of Rawalpindi, Amannullah got the terms he sought: cancellation of all previous Anglo-Afghan treaties, and a British guarantee that Afghanistan was 'officially free and independent in its internal and external affairs'.

In 1921–2, in the coastal Malabar region of south-western India, Indian troops continued to follow British orders by suppressing the rural Moplah Rebellion by Muslim villagers. These Moplah rebels, concealed among their coconut palm groves by the coast and their hills inland covered in jungle interspersed with rice fields, were armed with little more than swords and a small number rifles and clay grenades filled with gunpowder. The British sent against them the 39th Garhwal Rifles and six other Indian battalions with artillery and armoured cars, which together swept through Moplah territory. The Indian troops, led at times by veteran Indian officers who had been promoted in 1914–18, did what the British wanted. They helped to take 45,000 Moplah prisoners, some of whom were publicly executed. They also shot rebels in houses, threw grenades into mosques occupied by rebels who would not surrender, and looted villages. Overall, the imperial forces killed approximately 2350 Moplahs and wounded 1650.

Throughout the 1920s and into the 1930s, many Indian regiments relied on Indian officer veterans of 1914–18 as their senior Viceroy's Commissioned officers. These veteran officers were known for their calmness as experienced men who had seen the western front, Gallipoli, East Africa, Iraq or Palestine, and for their distinctive language from the world war – one Gurkha officer of the 10th Gurkhas barked orders littered with obscenities picked up from the Australians. For numerous veteran Indian officers, their commitment to the Indian Army extended to sending their sons into it up to 1939.

What, then, contributed to Indian soldiers' willingness to carry on serving the British from 1919? For many there was an underlying spirit of togetherness with the British born of shared experience and heartfelt comradeship at the fronts. When Subadar Ramsarup Singh of the 97th Deccan Infantry recalled after the war the day on the Tigris beneath Kut in January 1916 when his company 'was turned to ashes', by Turkish machine gunners as they attacked over desert slush, he still felt a bond with his British officer, Captain Jenkins. The captain had seen Ramsarup Singh wounded, 'stopped by my side' with words of reassurance, saying 'everything he could short of crying for me', and tended to his wound, giving up his own field dressing. 'Today as I sit,' said Ramsarup Singh, 'it's as if I can see Jenkins sitting next to me just like he was that day and as I think of his kindness and behaviour towards me, it brings tears to my eyes. The poor fellow was actually killed that day.'

The veterans' sense of togetherness with the British came with a pride in their war service as a trial of their honour in arms, and they looked back on it with a feeling of achievement for themselves and their communities. 'We fought true,' said Lala Ram, a Hindu Dogra awarded the Victoria Cross in Iraq in 1916, who served in the Third Anglo-Afghan War and in the 1920s. At one Punjabi Muslim village, men of the Awàn tribe coined folk song phrases that took pride in their western front service while taking a swipe at their neighbouring villagers the Janjua. 'To German guns we bared the breast, / And they ran like men possessed,' they sang. 'But, Janjua, Janjua, where were they? / Skulking at home night and day.' The veterans' pride was tangible in the war trophies that flooded back to India with them from the fronts, such as German flags, bugles, shell cases and rhino horns from East Africa in Kashmiri, Mahsud and Punjabi hands. Equally, hill tribesmen of the Naga Labour Corps from India's far north-east brought back German spiked helmets from the Somme, adorning them with bison horns signifying bravery, and dancing in full war paint while wearing them. And Indian officers returning from the Indian Army's London victory parade in August 1919 carried framed signed copies of the King's speech to them at Buckingham Palace.

The Indian veterans often came together with their British officers in the 1920s and 1930s at emotional reunions. These were popular at regimental depots, usually on the anniversary of a battle; for example the 40th Pathans commemorated Second Ypres in 1915 with their annual Ypres Day on 26 April. The veterans proudly wore their medals of 1914–18, which were a bewildering array alongside their Indian awards such as the Indian Order of Merit. In addition to the Victoria Cross, their

British medals included the 1914 Star, 1914–15 Star, Military Cross, Distinguished Service Order and British War Medal. They had the Allied Victory Medal too, as well as foreign medals given by individual Allied countries, from the French Croix de Guerre and Légion d'Honneur to the Romanian Crucea Servicul Credincois, the Russian Cross of the Order of St George and the Serbian Silver Medal.

At their initial reunions they joined their British officers in donating funds for regimental memorials, before these were opened at ceremonies attended by all serving ranks and most retired. The 40th Pathans opened their memorial in March 1920, a 30-foot-high replica in stone of a Lee-Enfield cartridge, on a rocky hillock on the banks of the River Indus in British India's North-West Frontier Province. The ceremony was organised as a funeral service, with the regiment's own lament 'The Fortieth's Farewell to France' played on the Scottish Highland bagpipes accompanied by muffled drums, followed by an Indian officer reading out the regimental roll of honour, three volleys of rifle fire, and a bugler playing the Last Post. 'Each mourns his own dead,' the 40th's commandant Alexander Glasfurd said in the closing oration to the gathered British, Dogra, Pukhtun and Punjabi Muslim officers and men:

> But all are united in honouring the fallen heroes of the whole Regiment, no matter what their race or creed may be. We ascended this mound sorrowfully and shall stand here awhile with bowed heads as we think of the friends we have lost. But presently, our mourning finished, we shall march cheerfully away with our heads up and drums beating in quick time, to show our pride in our comrades' valour and our determination to prove ourselves worthy of their example.

In England, meanwhile, parties of still-serving Indian veterans of the western front, Iraq and East Africa took annual turns as orderlies to George V. In the 1920s, several accepted invitations to the house in Essex of James Willcocks, who was living permanently in England for the first time having finished his term as Governor of Bermuda. Willcocks showed them around his garden, where in the summer of 1924 he was growing willow trees from cuttings he had taken from France in 1923 at the derelict château of Hinges, his old Indian Corps headquarters and the scene of Douglas Haig's acceptance of his resignation. 'One of them, who had been with me in France,' Willcocks wrote of an Indian officer on his garden tour, 'asked me to send him a cutting later on to India, as he said it would serve to remind him that he had done his Hell on earth and was now assured of Heaven.'

Willcocks soon returned to India himself, in 1926 with his wife. It was during their tour of northern British India that December that he unexpectedly died of heart failure at the city of Bharatpur. According to a report in *The Times* of the procession taking his body to a cremation ground, 'a remarkable feature was the emergence from the city of thousands of Indians desiring to pay homage to a general whose Indian career was well known'. Willcocks' funeral was on 22 December at Delhi, where British and Indian veterans who had served under him on the western front – of the 59th Scinde Rifles, 69th Punjabis and 9th Gurkhas – accompanied his coffin on a gun carriage through the streets to St James' Church. His ashes were interred there. 'The buglers of the Battalion sounded a very fine Last Post and Reveille outside the church,' recorded the Scinde Rifles' regimental history. 'James Willcocks had been associated with the old 59th for many years, and was known personally to all those who had served in France. His loss was felt keenly.'

The Indians' post-war will to serve the British, however, was motivated most, as it was during the war, by material rewards. Many veterans received the promised land grants from the 178,000 acres of canal-irrigated land in Punjab earmarked for them during the war. The Government of India split the land between the regiments according to how long they had served overseas and how many casualties they had suffered, before regimental panels of British and Indian officers made individual allocations of up to 50 acres per soldier into the 1920s, based on service record, merit and family need. The recipients of particular regiments were awarded land next to retirement villages or 'canal colonies' named after their units – Hodsonabad for the 9th Hodson's Horse, or Fanepur for the 19th Fane's Horse – to which comrades of the western front or other theatres relocated with their families and grew old together. For deserving veterans too low down their regimental list of preference for land grants, the British gave consolation awards of monthly cash grants inheritable over two generations. In addition, the veterans got their pensions at the increased rates set during the war. Some indeed entered into lengthy correspondence with the Government of India to press their claim for the maximum pension entitlement. A retired Afridi of the 4th Cavalry named Awal Khan spent nine years from 1926 sending letters arguing that he had been unfairly denied a higher grade of pension over false allegations of his complicity in some Afridi desertions in Iraq in 1916, only to lose his case.

The veterans' allegiance to the British was also rewarded by special care from 115 local government organisations, the District Soldiers Boards, set up from 1919 across India. These dispensed state care for demobilised or retired soldiers and their families, favouring men with long service records and the best recommendations from their British officers. In the 1920s and 1930s, they handed out a steady flow of cash grants on a case-by-case basis on personal application from veterans or war widows. They sought out veterans blinded in battle, finding a total of forty-eight, and gave them special payments of their own. They also sponsored technical schools to teach veterans new skills for post-army life, from carpentering to tailoring, to help them earn money for themselves. A few of these technical schools were specially adapted for disabled veterans, teaching them skills appropriate to their physical capacity, for instance driving Ford lorries and motor buses for the lightly wounded. The District Soldiers Boards then found civilian employment for veterans, often for them to use the skills taught in the technical schools, or for unskilled work, such as guarding railways. Up to 1939, they found jobs for a total of 86,000 veterans.

All the while, the Indian soldiers' relationship with Gandhi and his fellow leading politicians of the Indian National Congress developed awkwardly. The initial constitutional reforms promised by the Montagu Declaration came in December 1919, when Parliament in London passed the Government of India Act. This granted the expanded but limited representative government proposed under the Montford Scheme of 1918, and completion of military service became a qualification to vote in elections for members of the provincial legislatures. Popular political parties and associations were soon promoting their provincial candidates and chasing after votes in the widened franchise, transforming village engagement with mainstream politics. The main bloc of Indian Army veteran voters was in Punjab, forming around a third of the province's total vote. Into the 1930s they generally kept their distance from the increasingly progressive and stridently anti-British Indian National Congress, alienated in part by some of its leaders' consistent criticism of soldiering in British pay. 'Our Army is a mercenary army employed by foreigners to put down their own countrymen, and to keep them under foreign heels,' declared Motilal Nehru, the father of Jawaharlal Nehru, in 1928. Instead the Punjabi veteran voters flocked to the conservative Punjab Nationalist Unionist Party, which cooperated closely with the colonial regime through its leaders of the traditional rural elite, landowners and the like, who had long supported military recruitment as a lever of official favour. The Unionist Party attracted the military vote with its policies to protect and improve soldiers' pensions, District Soldiers Boards' care and other government benefits, securing a conservative rural-military voting bloc to marginalise the Congress party in Punjab.

The Punjabi veterans' voting pattern, however, was intertwined with powerful tensions between them and the British. The Indian Army servicemen of 1914–18 were not just pliable payees in the post-war political world. They had their own vibrant ideas of racial equality, resistance and freedom sharpened by their experiences overseas in fighting the Central Powers, which inspired them to new self-assertion in the face of colonialism.

'We felt that we should be given liberty and freedom'

In the independent Pukhtun tribal areas' mountains of Waziristan by 1920, most of the Mahsud tribe's Indian Army veterans were back home. Besides those who had fought in France and East Africa, there were men of the 130th Baluchis who had spent the war in a Burmese jail for mutinying at Bombay and been released after the German armistice. Altogether the Mahsud veterans would prove the most violently anti-British of all the Indian servicemen. Since 1914, their tribe's long tradition of resistance to the British had continued with many raids into British India's North-West Frontier Province, involving murders or woundings of 502 British subjects, kidnaps of a further 378, and 257 offences against property, mainly thefts. In late 1919, stirred by the Afghan Emir Amanullah's call to jihad that had reached them at the time of the Third Anglo-Afghan War, the Mahsud mullahs roused the tribe to their own follow-up jihad. They gathered thousands of Mahsud volunteers in *lashkars* well-armed with modern rifles, including hundreds of war veterans.

The Government of India tried to force the *lashkars*' disbandment by sending the Royal Air Force to drop 10,000lb of bombs a day on Mahsud villages, but to no effect. It therefore invaded Waziristan from December 1919 with an almost exclusively Indian Army punitive force of approximately 100,000 men. As had been the case in the Third Anglo-Afghan War, they were largely fresh young recruits of 1918, and had some experienced British and Indian officers – among them the twenty-five-year-old John Smyth of the 15th Ludhiana Sikhs who had won the Victoria Cross in France, and the Afridi Arsala Khan, campaigning once again with the 57th Wilde's Rifles on his return from the Indian victory parade in London.

The leading Indian troops wound their way into the mountains of central Waziristan on a sunny mid-December afternoon, up the Tank Zam valley. As they went, Smyth was shot by a lone Mahsud sniper firing by the naked eye from over half a mile away, possibly a veteran of East Africa who had frequently sniped Germans at long distance. 'It seemed ridiculous,' Smyth wrote, 'he got me in one.' Smyth had just a hand-wound, but it was an ominous sign of what his inexperienced Indian troops were up against. Over the next few weeks, Mahsud *lashkar*s led by war veterans drawing on their years of fighting knowledge against the British at home and the Germans abroad made attacks of unprecedented sophistication. They fired and moved in such intricate and aggressive combinations that even the Indians' experienced officers had never seen anything like it. In one attack of 19 December on the 119th Mahrattas, within minutes the Mahsud killed ninety-five and wounded 140 of the regiment. In the following weeks they inflicted a total of 2600 Indian casualties, including Muslims, bringing the Indian assault troops to the verge of defeat. But they did not forget their old British officers in the field against them, in fact feeling a true comradeship with them. One Mahsud veteran of France and East Africa sought out his former officer Harold Lewis of the 129th Baluchis, talking his way blindfolded into an Indian camp for a friendly reunion.

Common conclusions among the British officers fighting the Mahsud were, as one wrote, 'the conditions are far harder ... than on the western front', and another 'commanding a Company in Waziristan was far more difficult than commanding a Battalion in France'. The difference was that in Waziristan a soldier needed to match the Mahsud and their war veterans individually – in its mountains there was no room for the tactics of France, Iraq or Palestine, dependent on fixed enemy positions being flattened by artillery. But matching the Mahsud man for man was practically impossible. 'I have fought against Germans, Japanese, Wazirs, Mohmands, Arabs and Senussi,' John Smyth was to write in the 1950s, 'and I have fought alongside many other races, but I think that the Mahsud ... fighting in defence of his own tangled mass of mountains, was the most formidable fighting man of them all.'

The Mahsud stopped fighting in April 1920 as they lacked the numbers to keep up their attacks against the heavier Indian and British firepower of machine guns, grenades, artillery and aerial bombing. They had been driven by their own long-standing independent tribal mentality of resistance to the British, which was quite separate from Gandhi's teachings or Indian nationalism. The chasm between the lines of thought still gaped up to 1946 when the Mahsud were visited by Jawaharlal Nehru on behalf of the Indian National Congress and Abdul Ghaffar Khan, a Muslim of British India known as the 'Frontier Gandhi' for his non-violent nationalism. Nehru and Ghaffar Khan gravely offended a Mahsud audience including war veterans of 1914–18 by offering them the patronage of an independent India, in order to set them free from 'the slavery' of their economic ties with the British. The Mahsud took this as an affront to their free will as men who had always been independent. One angry elder retorted, 'We are not the slaves of the British and we are certainly not going to be your slaves,' before insulting Nehru and Ghaffar Khan as *kortunai*, a Mahsud slur for Indians as outsiders. 'Hindu, if the British pay us money, there's a good reason,' snapped another Mahsud elder as the meeting ended in disorder. 'Our private parts are of an extraordinary size, as you will find out to your cost before too long.'

Elsewhere in the independent Pukhtun tribal areas after

1918, the Afridi war veterans in their homeland of Tirah were also distanced from Indian nationalism. Mir Mast who had travelled to Afghanistan with the Germans in 1915–16 played no part in this, dying of Spanish influenza in 1919. His brother Mir Dast VC, however, became a leading Afridi elder in the 1920s who championed the tribe's majority policy not to fight the British like the Mahsud, but to improve their employment opportunities in British India, both in the Indian Army and in railway-building and other civilian work. In doing so, Mir Dast (who was to live until 1945) put his name to diplomatic letters from the elders to the British reminding them of age-old Afridi independence, making a point that they did not wish to give the British trouble through common cause with the nationalists in British India, whether Muslim or Hindu. The Afridi troops in the Indian Army, meanwhile, continued to be a prickly quantity. In the 1930s, when a British officer suggested to one of his Afridi that he might like to visit Tirah's high forests, previously only seen by white men during the Anglo-Afridi small war of 1897–8, he got a cold response. 'If you did,' said the Afridi, 'I would shoot you.'

·   As for the Indian veterans of British India, their relationship with the British was shaped by their new senses of an improved racial status alongside white men, and of deserving more respect – referred to by one Indian officer as 'the silent change' among his men. The change flowed from how the Indian servicemen's pre-1914 perspective on their inferior lot compared to white men had developed through their life overseas from 1914 to 1918, which had widely given them fresh tastes of racial equality. While the Indian soldiers' kind treatment by the civilians of France from Marseilles to Calais had been the strongest wind of this change, there had been many gusts of wider experience. In battle, the Indians had been on a level with white men, seeing them fight, weep or die as they did, and they wore the same medals. Their terms of service had improved to approach or equal the white soldier's, for instance their pay rise for European service or their hospital treatment in France, England and eventually Iraq. They had had friendly encounters with white troops much more than before 1914, in particular with the Australians and New Zealanders at Gallipoli, in Egypt and in Palestine. As prisoners of war, some had been treated like white men for the first time, for instance by the Turks who had fed Indian officers at the same table as British officers. And there was of course the British announcement in 1917 of King's Commissions for Indians.

From the comments of Indian veterans recorded second-hand or in interviews from 1919 to the 1970s, a pattern emerges that in the immediate aftermath of the world war they generally spoke of enhanced racial status and respect as their due from the British, and only gradually became more articulate in expressing hopes of national freedom as the nationalist struggle grew into a mass independence movement. 'Those who have been in France,' observed a Punjabi policeman in April 1919, 'say that the British officers do not treat them as well as the French did.' For the Jodhpur Lancers' commandant Sir Pratap Singh writing at around the same time, the war had 'everywhere ... produced a spirit of equality'.

In old age, Indian veterans of the western front said this was exactly how they had felt. 'I felt that Indians were deprived of their rights,' said a Sikh, Subedar Singh, of his post-war mood. 'We felt that our social set-up should be on the new lines like that of France and Europe,' said Ram Singh, another Sikh. 'We felt that we should be given liberty and freedom which the French people were enjoying.' Many veterans in the 1970s in fact spoke of having been 'slaves' under the British. Mansa Singh, who had served in France for three years with the 6th King Edward's Own Cavalry, recalled how 'the French told us that we should fight for our own country, and advised us to be free from the British yoke ... We came to know that the British had been treating us as slaves.'

There are indications that such ideas among war veterans prompted some actively to join in the surge of anti-British protests as Gandhi's civil disobedience programme caught fire from 1919. On the day of the Amritsar massacre that April, a Sikh NCO of the 54th Sikhs with an exemplary service record since 1905 led a mob that burned down a railway station in Punjab. At one count, a total of eighteen serving or retired Indian soldiers were convicted of anti-government disorder offences during the nationalist unrest of 1919. Then in 1921, a still-serving Indian veteran of the 9th Bhopals, Brijpal Singh, who had served in France in 1914, organised a rural protest invoking Gandhi in the United Provinces of Agra and Oudh; it turned violent with an attack by hundreds of villagers on a police station. When Brijpal Singh was arrested by the police and handcuffed, he complained that he deserved better, having been a prisoner of war in Germany where the Germans did not handcuff him. He would also have remembered the anti-British propaganda of his German captivity, which might of course have influenced his initial protest. Indeed, the British feared that returning Indian prisoners of war who had been exposed to such propaganda in Germany would be prone to anti-government protest. Accordingly, British intelligence officers interrogated several at Marseilles and Bombay on their way home in 1918–19, discharging a few from the army under suspicion of conspiring with the enemy. Moreover, it seems that in the 1920s a number of Sikh veterans in Punjab who were inclined by their war experiences to be more demanding of their rights joined the Akali reform movement, which was primarily concerned with changes to how Sikh temples were controlled, but was also supportive of Gandhian civil disobedience.

In Punjabi villages, meanwhile, war veterans spoke regretfully of having served the British. Some told their families of feeling guilt over fighting for the colonial regime they increasingly understood as denying them and their countrymen civil rights. One post-war Punjabi Muslim village song perhaps reflected this in its tone of disillusionment: 'We went to war and fought, / For little or nought.'

'My only desire is to die under the flag of Islam'

Rather than actively turn against the British, however, it seems that the great majority of Indian veterans decided to try working with them on new terms. For some, the prospect of revolution was in itself unattractive. 'A revolution is a very bad thing', one Punjabi veteran commented having served in Georgia in 1919–20. 'I saw the Russian revolution,' he explained, 'and how the people struggled for the food we threw to them.' The Indian veterans appear to have widely prioritised stability for their families, and making the most of their British links by channelling their enhanced senses of self-respect and racial equality into seeking better terms of employment. When a Government of India committee of 1919–20 investigated proposals for army reform, it was told by several Indian officers who had fought in France that Indian soldiers should be treated the same as white troops. 'We have fought shoulder to shoulder with the soldiers of other nations and are capable of doing more if simply cared for like the soldiers of other nations,' argued Subadar-Major Laxman Singh of the 15th Ludhiana Sikhs. The Indian officers said they wanted equal pay and pensions for Indians, British, Australians and New Zealanders, equal bonuses for Indian and British officers for learning languages, and Indian Army barracks up to European standards with electricity and baths with hot water in winter. Many Indian troops had of course had similar thoughts before 1914, but now, boosted by their war experiences, they came out with them more regularly and forcefully as their due.

The way in which Indian war veterans delicately combined their developing senses of racial equality, civil rights and nationalism with serving the British for the good of their families was described in the 1960s by Mohammad Ayub Khan, the second

President of Pakistan. Ayub Khan was seven years old in 1914 when his Muslim father, a Viceroy's Commissioned officer of the 9th Hodson's Horse, had left their village of Rehana in British India's North-West Frontier Province to fight in France. By 1920, his father had returned to their village with 'vague but strong' ideas of nationalism, which he discussed with a local religious scholar. The scholar, wrote Ayub Khan, said to his father, 'India is *darul harb* [not under Islamic rule]. The rulers of this part of the world are *kafir*s, we should therefore migrate from here.' To which his father replied, 'My only desire is to die under the flag of Islam, but where is that flag? There is no Muslim country today which is free. They are all dominated by colonial powers.' Also in 1920, during a visit of a British civil servant to their village, Ayub Khan noticed how his father kept his distance from the colonial ruler and maintained his pride as a Muslim equal. 'There was only one chair for the Deputy Commissioner and the audience had to squat on a carpet. My father, who had been invited to this meeting, resented this and stood under a tree.'

Ayub Khan's father, however, still wanted him to join the Indian Army. Like many war veterans, his father had hopes for his son getting a King's Commission and rising to be the equal of British officers. The main obstacle was a good secondary school education, a prerequisite for British selection for the King's Commission officer cadet training for Indians that had started at Indore in central India in 1918. This was in fact a source of considerable resentment among veterans because for all that the war had in principle opened the King's Commission to Indians, most village families could not afford to pay for the preliminary schooling. Still, Ayub Khan's father managed to steer him through junior school in the North-West Frontier Province and in the early 1920s into the Muslim college of Aligarh in the United Provinces of Agra and Oudh. From there Ayub Khan went for officer cadet training in England at Sandhurst, which by 1920 had replaced Indore as the training centre for Indian officer cadets for King's

Commissions with an initial annual quota of ten, and he got his King's Commission into the Indian Army in 1928.

While Ayub Khan's story shows that his father's generation's sacrifices in the world war did soon lead to villagers possessing equality of command with white officers, most of the Indians with King's Commissions from 1919 to the 1930s nonetheless came from privileged backgrounds, and in practice they were treated as racially inferior. The Indian Army's British officers believed virtually as much as ever in their natural superiority as leaders, and were loath to relax the old strictures of prestige. For the Hindu diarist Thakur Amar Singh, post-war regimental life with the 16th Cavalry as the most senior serving Indian officer with a King's Commission was therefore packed with frustrations. At Delhi in 1919, after the Amritsar massacre, on suggesting to his British regimental peers that the shooting of civilians to maintain civil order might not be right, they at once turned against him. They fully supported the measure as the colonial power's prerogative to preserve prestige, and were suspicious of any hints of nationalistic thought in Indian soldiers as a sign of disloyalty. That summer Amar Singh took command of a squadron, but his junior squadron British officer, Captain Wilkes, refused to accept his orders as a racial inferior. Amar Singh raged on his diary page after his commandant had declined to enforce equal respect for him among the British officers, venting that Wilkes was 'a dirty low down swine for whom I do not care in the least though I keep up appearances'.

In April 1921, Amar Singh's commandant wrote him a bad annual report that he felt was unfair, being framed to damage his advancement as an Indian among British officers. 'I had some hot words with the Colonel,' he wrote. 'I am so fed up and annoyed at all their treatment I have ceased to care for anything at all. It looks to me as if I am supposed to be here as if by grace.' That June, as a mark of protest, he deliberately missed a special parade with the British officers to celebrate the King-Emperor's birthday.

He quit the Indian Army soon after, arranging extended leave to fill the time to qualify for his pension, and gladly left British India to retire to his estate in Jaipur State. Amar Singh was to spend the 1920s and 1930s happily at home with his wife, Rasal, and their daughter, who lived into adulthood. He achieved his long-held ambition of commanding Jaipur State's domestic forces, securing the appointment with British approval based on his Indian Army service. He continued writing his diary until he died at home in 1942 at the age of sixty-four, having written 89 volumes by hand since the 1890s, making it one of the longest diaries ever written.

Amar Singh and his pre-war generation of King's Commissioned Indian officers had always been too old to advance far in the Indian Army with equality of command. But for the wartime class of young Indian cadets for King's Commissions who graduated from their college at Indore in December 1919, were prospects any brighter? By 1939 there was a total of 250 Indian officers with King's Commissions (a small minority of the officer corps). At Sandhurst they had suffered humiliations from the British officers in charge who strove to uphold pre-war codes of prestige, such as telling them not to dance with white girls at the annual ball. Amid daily racial slights in their Indian regiments from British seniors such as a refusal to countenance Indian food on the British officers' table, some had wanted to resign their commissions. Yet they had persevered on the advice of Indian politicians who told them the free India of the future would need them to lead its Indian Army. The first of them to enter the Indian Staff College only did so in 1933, so little were they encouraged to apply.

When the Indian Army went to world war once again in 1939, its older King's Commissioned Indian officers were not the only men of 1914–18 still with it. Many of its former young British officers of the western front, East Africa, Gallipoli, Iraq and Palestine – including John Smyth VC of the 15th Ludhiana Sikhs and Harold Lewis of the 129th Baluchis – were now senior commanders. It also had some of its Indian troops of 1914, for instance a Gurkha who had enlisted in 1908 and fought at Gallipoli; he returned to Europe with his Indian regiment to fight the Nazis, going into action in Italy in 1944 at the Battle of Monte Cassino. It would be the Second World War that foreshadowed Indian independence in 1947, with a Hindu officer cadet of the First World War – Kodandera Cariappa, who had enlisted at the age of seventeen in 1918 – becoming the independent Indian Army's first Indian Commander-in-Chief. Among the Indian ranks of 1914–18, several unknown, potential Indian commanders-in-chief or chiefs of staff must of course have been killed on the western front and elsewhere, or retired in the 1920s and 1930s as veteran Viceroy's Commissioned officers who had had all the ambition yet always been subordinate to their British officers. It was a tragedy for them that in order to rise as high as Cariappa, or for that matter Douglas Haig, Stanley Maude, Edmund Allenby and the other British generals of 1914–18, they had simply been denied the education and opportunity.

EPILOGUE

'A new humanity'

According to British official records of the First World War compiled in the 1920s, a total of approximately 34,000 Indian soldiers and 16,000 Indian non-combatants were killed from August 1914 to November 1918, altogether some 3.3 per cent of the Indian Army's servicemen. Today the graves of many are tended by the Commonwealth War Graves Commission, with headstones of white Portland stone, engraved with name, number and regiment. These headstones with Indian names on them can be found in particular in Europe, for instance in France at Mazargues outside Marseilles or further north close to the battlefields of the western front; in England in Hampshire and Surrey near the old Indian hospital sites on the south coast; in Germany at Zehrensdorf close to the location of Camp Crescent Moon; in Italy at Faenza not far from where the Indian Labour Corps' camp was; or in Greece at the Monastir Road Indian Cemetery in Thessaloniki.

The same type of headstones atop individual Indian war graves of 1914–18 can be seen outside Europe, from Egypt and Israel to Kenya. But these are much scarcer, despite the majority of Indian war dead having died outside Europe. During and shortly after the mobile campaigning in non-European theatres, especially

Iraq and East Africa, British resources were unavailable for or not devoted to recording and burying individually the Indians killed. This left most to be buried by regimental comrades on the battlefield in graves now lost (often following deliberate British abandonment as individual Indian graves were officially deemed not worth marking or maintaining), or by colonial authorities in mass graves with a joint local stone memorial added later, such as outside Basra.

On the First World War's grim global scale of casualties, the estimated total Indian war dead – 50,000 men – was comparatively low. Belgium, Greece, Japan, New Zealand, Portugal, South Africa were among the countries which had fewer servicemen killed than India. However, the United States lost approximately twice as many servicemen killed as India, and the British, Turks, Germans, French, Russians, Italians, Austro-Hungarians and Serbians many times more each. The officially recorded total of Indians wounded during the war was around 64,000, again a comparatively low figure; the British suffered over 1.6 million wounded, the Russians perhaps 3.8 million, and the Germans over 4 million.*

After the war, a few Afridi and Mahsud soldiers arrived home in the independent Pukhtun tribal areas from France or East Africa only to be shot dead in blood feuds held over since they had left in 1914. Some had in fact discussed this possibility with their British officers. On telling his officer Harold Lewis, one Mahsud of the 129th Baluchis received Lewis' revolver to aid his cause; to no avail, as things turned out in Waziristan. Another Mahsud veteran of the regiment died in his feud, doomed beforehand because of his wound on the western front – he had lost an arm to a German shell.

---

* It is unclear to what extent the British official statistics for Indian casualties count victims of disease including the influenza pandemic of 1918–19 – which killed 17–18 million Indians, approximately 350 times as many Indian servicemen as estimated killed in the First World War.

Yet many Indian veterans home from the fronts by 1921 were determined not to fight, but to change their customary family or village life using ideas inspired by foreign cultures, above all in France. This was to be the most personal legacy of their war experiences. 'The war killed many splendid men from the Punjab,' reflected Malcolm Darling, a civil servant there from 1904 to 1940 who met thousands of war veterans as he rode on horseback from village to village, 'but in widening the minds of those who served abroad and returned it gave the province something of value to balance the loss. It has even helped to introduce a new humanity into village life.'

'The prosperity of the soldier family is one of the most striking features of the Punjab landscape,' Darling observed in 1934. He saw that compared to villagers who had not earned the material benefits of military service, many veterans – some sporting a tell-tale moustache coiffed in French style – had appreciably more money and land. They had a greater self-confidence from their war days which helped them manage their private affairs with more verve, for instance investing in business opportunities such as local shops, or becoming moneylenders. They also made good their wartime intention of moving their families out of traditional mud huts and into new brick homes they built for themselves, modelling them on the farmers' houses they had known in the Pas-de-Calais and Somme valley. 'The war,' Darling heard from veterans, 'revealed to the Indian villager who served in France an entirely new standard of housing and comfort. He saw there with astonishment and envy how well the peasant proprietor can live, and, returning to his village, beheld its cattle-shed life with a tinge of disgust.' The veterans' new brick houses had stone steps at the front doors and wooden window frames made by local artisans, and inside were kept neat and clean as western-style lamps, chairs, cooking utensils, crockery and clocks gradually accumulated. Indeed, Darling saw that some veterans' new houses had bottles of red wine on the table, a taste acquired in France, and were adorned with rugs from Iran or Iraq if they had served there too. The eastern Punjabi village of Kosali, which had sent 243 soldiers to the war, even gained a new name after its veterans' brick houses: 'Baawan Bangley ki Kosali', or 'Kosali of fifty-two bungalows'.

Other changes to Punjabi home life stemmed from soldiers' experiences abroad meeting Indians or Europeans beyond the social limits of their pre-1914 lives. Through eating and generally mixing on overseas service with men of different castes or religions in ships, railway carriages, cities, villages, trenches and hospitals, and seeing many a habit unusual to them – for some, the sight of Muslims in the Middle East enjoying whisky contrary to their own Islamic custom of abstaining from alcohol was eye-opening – the soldiers' pre-war senses of social and religious difference had softened, shaping a new appreciation of human togetherness. 'We must forget our absurd prejudices of castes and religions,' said one Hindu cavalry officer who had served in France for three years before Palestine:

There is no such thing as caste. I myself come of a family which is proud of its high caste. I say in the sight of God there is no difference between man and man because of caste. Religion also must not be a matter of difference and disunity. Be a Hindoo or a Mahommeddan, a Christian or a Jew, a Parsi or a Buddhist, as you like, and be true and pure and faithful to whatever religion you belong. Do not look down upon a man of another religion with prejudice and enmity ... we must love one another. If we learn that ... there will cease to be differences and ill feeling among ourselves, and we shall be a united and progressive people.

'Our minds have opened up,' agreed Jemadar Tek Chand, a Hindu Jat, of the consequences of western front service. A number of Punjabi veterans were now minded to break down pre-war rural barriers of caste and custom. Some Sikh veterans began growing vegetables with their own hands, which before the war had been strictly taboo for their caste, as a menial task fit only for their inferiors. 'We saw very good men growing them in France,' explained one Sikh in the fields near the Punjabi town of Tarn Taran, 'and the thought came to us – why is it a shame to grow them here?'

Veterans also started to grow fruit. 'A pleasant sight are the young orchard gardens springing up round the village, with their promise of oranges, bananas and loquats,' Malcolm Darling noticed. 'The taste for gardens is spreading and is in part a result of the war, when many a Punjabi enjoyed the luscious fruit of France.' At the village of Beri in Punjab's Rohtak district, Hindu Jat veterans also spread new ideas of marriage based on what they had seen in France. 'When they came back they called a *panchayat* [village council], and it was decided that there should be no more funeral feasts, that dowries should not exceed Rs. 100 ... and that Jats should no longer sell their daughters,' Darling related.

Such innovations were part of Punjabi veterans' spreading of better treatment for women in general. 'Since the war we have been trying to give them less work,' one Hindu Jat veteran of Beri village said of their womenfolk. 'The cutting of the thorn bushes for fuel and for hedges has been forbidden by the *panchayat*. The soldiers have more care for these things. Before the war women had no *izzat* and men beat them with shoes ... but now much light has spread, and beating is stopped. That is because we went to Europe.' In a Sikh village, Darling described the veterans' new attitude to women as 'Strike not your wife even with a flower'. A Sikh subadar-major told him with a smile of the decline of wife-beating in his village, 'Now if anything it is the other way.' For one Muslim Rajput veteran as Darling recorded his words in 1932, 'Man and wife (*Mian* and *Bibi*), each honours the other more than when I was young: they take counsel together, and woman is no longer looked down upon ... Before, we did not know the world, but we served in the army and saw other countries. Now we have civilization.'

Some Punjabi soldiers truly had France in their hearts as they kept in touch with their old French girlfriends from afar, one sending a gift of embroidered red leather shoes to a French girl who treasured them for the rest of her life in her Somme village. Although several Punjabi veterans said they had comrades who brought home their wartime brides from France, evidence of this actually happening has not been found.

One Afridi, however, is known to have taken his German wife back to the independent Pukhtun tribal areas. He was the NCO Guli Jan of the 58th Vaughan's Rifles who in March 1915 had deserted in France with Jemadar Mir Mast. In 1916 he had gone to the Middle East with the Jihadist Legion raised among the Allied Muslim prisoners of war at their propaganda camp south of Berlin, before returning to Germany once the Legion had fallen apart. By 1919 he was running a Berlin tobacco shop, said to have doubled as a brothel with him as the pimp. Two years later he reappeared in Tirah not just with a Mauser pistol but also with a well-educated middle-class German girl, in her late twenties. She had left Germany with him as his new and pregnant wife, travelling at his side to his mountain home largely on the Russian railways via Moscow and Tashkent. They spent a year living in Tirah with their baby girl, but their marriage broke down during this time, probably under cross-cultural strains; the details are a mystery. She was last heard of alone at Kabul in 1923 having fled Tirah, desperate and torn, she told a British diplomat, between going home to Germany or back to the Afridi mountains for her baby girl, now aged two and a half, and still with her husband there.

In Punjab, meanwhile, the Indian veterans' greatest hope for their children had become clear: they wanted education for them, both boys and girls. Mir Dad Khan, the western front veteran of the 9th Hodson's Horse and father of the future President of

Pakistan Ayub Khan, was just one of many Indian soldiers across the Indian Empire whose war in Europe, as some had written home from France, had grown their ambitions for the next village generation. During the war, Punjabi soldiers in France, Iraq and Palestine had joined together, organising themselves by letter, to send home a cut of their wages to help build new schools in their home districts, which stand to this day with the names of their regiments carved in stone on the walls. From 1919, as veteran Viceroy's Commissioned officers spoke to British committees advising on army reforms, they repeatedly asked for provincial schools to be opened for their children. The colonial regime responded from 1922 to 1939 by spending millions of rupees on new free schools for soldiers' children. There were rural primary schools from Punjab to the Himalayas, and secondary schools, including five King George's Royal Indian Military Schools, set up specially for the sons of Viceroy's Commissioned officers and offering the education needed for a cadetship to become a King's Commissioned officer.

Indian veterans from outside British territory were no less eager for their children's education. In Waziristan, a Mahsud veteran of the 127th Baluchis named Mir Badshah, who had lost an eye in 1914 at First Ypres and served in East Africa, founded a primary school. He did it at the risk of his own life, having to defend the school against armed mullahs who wanted to burn it down as a symbol of British influence. Mir Badshah's school prospered, sparking the military career of his son Alam Jan Mahsud, who became a general in the Pakistan Army. As for Gurkha veterans, they too established schools in their villages of Nepal.

All the while, many children of Indian war veterans had new routines at home born of the world war. One daily ritual seen in Punjab was the family sitting together to share milky British-style tea – a habit ingrained in fathers of the Indian cavalry whose tea habits had taken their milky turn at British tea urns on the western front. At such family gatherings, veterans' war stories also poured out. Before the war Indian soldiers had brought home their tales of China, Tibet and elsewhere, but active service across the fronts between 1914 and 1918, along with the victory parades in Europe in 1919 and the post-war occupations of Germany and the Ottoman Empire, now left them with countless more wonders to relate.

Besides Marseilles, Paris and submarine attacks, the veterans regaled their families with accounts of crumbling ancient ruins, from the Great Sphinx of Giza on the River Nile's west bank to the tombs and halls at Pasargadae and Persepolis in central Iran, where in 1916 an Indian Army general had given the 124th Baluchis and 15th Lancers guided tours; of Saint Catherine's Monastery in the Sinai Desert, housing the world's oldest surviving library, and visited in 1917 by the 58th Vaughan's Rifles with the Egyptian Expeditionary Force; or of the men and women from Lake Victoria in East Africa who had gone about naked and told censorious Muslim troops from Punjab's Salt Range, 'You wear clothes, but how can you tell who is man and who is woman?'

The veterans who had marched in the Indian victory parade in London in August 1919 had their stories of everything they had seen on that visit to England, from a First Division football match at London's Stamford Bridge stadium between Chelsea and Everton, a trip to the West End to Maskelyne's Theatre of Mystery where magicians turned ink into drink and made ladies levitate, to specially organised flights on the Royal Air Force's heaviest bombers that had flown missions over Germany in 1918. Then there were Muslim veterans who when occupying the Ottoman Empire had walked the streets of Baghdad, or gazed up at the enormous domed ceiling of the Hagia Sofia in Istanbul. Others stationed to the south, down to Amman and Jerusalem, had been given leave for pilgrimages at government expense to Islamic Holy Places. They could talk to their families as Hajis, or those who had made the annual pilgrimage to Mecca, where Britain's wartime ally Sharif Hussein of Mecca had welcomed, lodged and fed them. By 1920, according to Subadar-Major Ajab Khan of the 76th Punjabis, Sharif Hussein's generosity was proverbial among Muslim veterans' families: 'the old folk of the Soldier Hajis in India have heard of the kind and fatherly treatment extended to their boys.'

But Indian veterans' proudest stories for their families, which they might tell wearing their old regimental tunics, were of battle. In Punjab, Ude Singh of the 14th Sikhs frequently told of saving his wounded British officer in 1915 at Gallipoli under Turkish fire by slinging him over his shoulder and carrying him to safety; he won no medal for this, only the officer's warm friendship for decades. Other Sikh veterans of Gallipoli told of its evacuation by early 1916, describing Allied troops withdrawing in the dark from their trenches on the peninsula for their ships, having left something behind to trick the Turks: rifles wedged among sand-bags and primed to fire across no man's land hours later, the triggers being tied to a delayed pulling mechanism (which had tins hanging below slowly filling with water dripping from containers above), a ruse to lull the Turks into thinking the Allied trenches were still manned. The Indian veterans recounted hardships in Iraq; the siege of Kut entered Punjabi folklore with memories of the starving garrison eating horse meat to survive. Further the Hindu cavalryman Gobind Singh told of his tenacity in France to win the VC at the Battle of Cambrai in December 1917, carrying messages as German shells blew his horse from under him.

As they told their war stories at home, many Indian veterans would bring out their cherished mementos from the fronts, such as their own Princess Mary Gift Box, a five-inch brass box sent at Christmas 1914 on behalf of George V's daughter to all the British Empire's soldiers in the front line. Some opened their boxes to take out and unfold their certificates of honourable discharge with wounds, signed by the King-Emperor and prized as proof of the fight in them.

Veterans also showed pride in their war service through their personal choices of memorials in their local communities. In the Himalayas to commemorate their courage and losses on the western front, Garhwali veterans clubbed together for a silver memorial *trishula*, the three-pronged weapon of Shiva, which they put on the altar of their ancient Hindu temple of Badrinath. At the Punjabi village of Dulmial, the British asked the Muslim headman, a veteran Indian officer called Ghulam Mohammed, what reward the villagers would like for contributing 460 recruits, the largest number for a single village in all India. Ghulam Mohammed asked for a cannon, which was duly provided on a plinth in front of which Dulmial's veterans posed proudly for a photograph wearing their uniforms and war medals. It was also with feelings of pride that Indian veterans attended unveilings of the numerous imperial war memorials of the 1920s and 1930s in Europe, Africa and Asia dedicated to the Indian Army's war dead. For example, veterans of the western front went back to France in 1927 for the opening of the Indian memorial at Neuve Chapelle, reuniting with French families in local villages, while others went to the opening in 1931 of New Delhi's All India War Memorial, the triumphal arch better known as the India Gate.

Down the decades into the early 2000s, Indian veterans' pride in their war service often lived on with their families. In Chandigarh, capital of northern India's Haryana and Punjab states, the eighty-year-old son of a Sikh soldier of 1914 daily honoured his father's war service; he lit a lamp in a corner of his home in front of his father's regimental badge, which he kept by photographs of his father and his father's British officer. In India's western state of Maharashtra, Mohan Nikam, the grandson of a Hindu soldier of the 103rd Mahrattas who had fought in Ottoman Iraq in 1914–16, treasured his grandfather's Princess Mary Gift Box. 'Don't you think this small box is witness to a very significant period in our history?' said Mohan Nikam in a newspaper interview at his home. 'For others, these could be just some metal objects or old pieces of paper, but for us, they are symbols of our glorious past.'

In the Himalayas a whole village kept alive the courage of a posthumous Indian VC, Gabar Singh Negi of the 39th Garhwal Rifles. In March 1915 the twenty-two-year-old had been among the leading assault troops of the Indian Army's first BEF offensive on the western front, at Neuve Chapelle, and had been killed. In his village shortly afterwards, his widow Satoori Devi had received his VC medal. Her husband's name was inscribed on the back, although she could not read it. Nor could she read the letter the Queen-Empress Mary sent from London to Gabar Singh's old regimental depot near their village, offering her condolences for the loss of 'a very brave Indian of the Empire who died for you and for us in the glorious fight for truth and freedom against tyranny'. Yet Satoori Devi commemorated her husband all by herself until her dying day in 1981, wearing his VC while cooking over the family stove or gathering wood in the forest, and initiating an annual memorial fair on his birthday which the whole village got together for. Gabar Singh VC's descendants carried on the memorial fair in their village into the 2000s, complete with his VC story re-told proudly over loudspeakers.

Across British India's old recruitment grounds, however, there were descendants of Indian troops or their fellow villagers for whom pride in war service for the British was problematic as a pat on the back for reviled colonialism. In Pakistan's Punjabi village of Dub, the descendants of the first Indian VC – Khudadad Khan of the 129th Baluchis at First Ypres in October 1914 – still had the medal, but his grandson described it as the family's 'cross to bear ... It is a lightning rod for crazies. There are those who call us from unknown numbers and say "Khudadad Khan was a British stooge".' The family apparently received violent threats from these callers who scolded them for harbouring the medal as a token of their sympathy for the old colonial regime, prompting them to wash their hands of it by sale to a British collector in 2016.

The family of the Afridi VC Mir Dast, who held on to their grandfather's medal for bravery at Second Ypres in 1915, had similar trouble in Pakistan's northern province of Khyber Pakhtunkhwa. Mir Dast's family had moved to its administered areas on the plains below his ancestral home in Tirah, but they were not always welcome. 'They consider us British here, they don't like us,' said his grandson of typical village reactions to them. There were of course many reasons not to remember the British kindly in the villages, not least the widespread coercion into military service in 1917–18.

What, then, did it really mean to be an Indian soldier of the world war of 1914–18? It could be said that it was a life of honour, duty and valour with the British providing the curries, clothing and medical care respectful of the Hindu, Muslim and Sikh religions, while the Indian ranks stoically suffered the western front's rain and mud, cruelly catapulted by the fates into a war far from home that was never their own yet winning their fair share of VCs. And that by the time they returned home they had evolved from politically uninformed villagers into more worldly-wise freedom fighters, helping to spur the nationalist cause and pave the way for Indian independence. Yet such a view would be a contemporary convenience, dealing in the most recognisable terms of the war in Europe and the human right to be free, rather than a probe into the darker chaos and horror of the Indian soldiers' colonial world.

It is telling that in the summer of 1917, the hour of the Montagu Declaration, the leading Indian nationalist politicians were conspicuously silent on the Parliamentary report into the war in Ottoman Iraq. The report's findings on the Indian Army's extreme suffering on the Tigris related to a constituency of villagers whose support they were not actively seeking, and whose British service some of them would soon vilify on giving up their fragile wartime politics of cooperation, in effect marooning the Indian soldier as the ship of Gandhian nationalism sailed on. But to be an Indian soldier was mostly to do with suffering and cooperating with the British – whether suffering themselves through trials of racial inequality, prestige and war, or making others suffer in the Indian Army's massacres of civilians from India to Iraq.

The Indian servicemen's self-inflicted wounds, mutinies and murders of British officers are only the most obvious indications of how they were not so willing and eager to work for the British as it could seem. For the British, these things were black marks on service records; for the Indians, they were expressions of despair and rage among men who took money and land in return for their bodies, ultimately fighting not for the Allies' democratic ideals but for their families' livelihoods. Their achievement was bearing their humiliations at the hands of the British with such strength in adversity, and not letting go of their humanity to return from the war full of hopes that their wives and children would live better lives in a more equal world to come.

NOTE ON NAMES AND PLACES

For place-names, I have generally used those that would seem most familiar today and that in some cases were in use in 1914, albeit not always in English. Hence 'Istanbul' and not 'Constantinople', 'Iraq' not 'Mesopotamia', 'Iran' not 'Persia' and so on. I have used 'Punjab' (and not 'the Punjab') to mean the former British imperial province or the area it covered. For Indian Army units, I have used their titles of 1914–18 rather than refer to their pre-1903 or post-1922 titles, and have streamlined regimental or battalion titles.

ENDNOTES

These Endnotes are a general guide to the sources I have used. They are divided into three parts: first, archival or previously unpublished sources; second, published sources of statistics and general information on the war, particular theatres and the Indian Army; and third, published sources per chapter on more specific themes.

1 Archival or previously unpublished sources

A major source of interviews with Indian veterans is a set of transcripts kindly given to me in 2006 by DeWitt Ellinwood, the late American historian of the State University of New York. In the 1970s and early 1980s, DeWitt co-led an Indo-American team in the countryside of northern India and southern Pakistan interviewing Indian veterans of 1914–18. DeWitt then kept his interview transcripts in his attic in Albany, New York State, before he sent them to me. In November 2018 I donated them to the British Library in London (DeWitt's wish), and copies to the United Service Institution (USI) of India in Delhi.

I have drawn extensively on the India Office Records and Private Papers collections at the British Library, in particular the Indian Army records for the Boxer Rebellion in 1900–02 (in L/MIL/17/20); the Indian General Staff records of conferences and staff reports (L/MIL/17/5 and 11); the Indian Expeditionary Force War Diaries (L/MIL/17/5); the wartime telegrams between the India Office and Viceroy (L/MIL/17/16); reports on desertion, above all by independent Pukhtun (L/MIL/7 and L/PS/10–11); transcripts of interviews with Indian officers by Government of India commissions and committees (for instance see the papers of the Esher Committee of 1919–20, in L/MIL/5); and the records for Indian Army logistics such as the Proceedings of the Indian Soldiers Fund General Committee (Mss Eur F 120). The India Office Records on Indian prisoners of war – including the files on the Indian camps in Germany, Romania, Turkey and East Africa (in L/MIL/7) – have been indispensable.

While the National Archives at Kew (formerly the Public Record Office) have provided me with many further sources on Indian prisoners of war such as Foreign Office records (FO/383), I have mainly used the War Office records – from Reports of the Censor of Indian Mails in France (in FO/383/288), the Papers of Lord Kitchener (PRO/30/57/52) and medical papers on the Indian wounded (WO/32/5110 and WO/159/16, which include the highly detailed letters and reports of Walter Lawrence, Kitchener's chief inspector of Indian troops' medical care in France), to Indian Army War Diaries (WO/95), Correspondence of the Chief of the Imperial General Staff (WO/106), and the Western Front Diaries of Field Marshal Sir Douglas Haig (WO/256). I have also used Haig's pre-1914 diaries at the National Library of Scotland in Edinburgh, besides his many letters for the period 1909–18 in the archived collections of his correspondents, in the British Library's India Office Private Papers collections (Mss Eur F 116/37–38), the Liddell Hart Centre for Military Archives at King's College London (see the Howell and Kiggell Papers), and the Imperial War Museum's Department of Documents in London (see the Papers of Field-Marshal Sir Henry Wilson, 2/69/70–71).

I have drawn on the Imperial War Museum's Papers of Major-General Harold Lewis (Con Shelf), Lieutenant-Colonel Kenneth Henderson (DS/MISC/2), and Lieutenant-General Sir Henry Keary (Con Shelf). For the Viceroy Charles Hardinge, my main source has been his private papers (the Papers of Baron Hardinge of Penshurst) at Cambridge University Library's Department of Manuscripts and Archives. I have also used sources from the National Archives of India at New Delhi for reports on the independent Pukhtun border tribes, the German Foreign Office Archives in Berlin for reports on Indian prisoner interrogations in German captivity, and the Royal Military College of Canada, Kingston, Ontario for the private papers of George Kirkpatrick, Chief of the Indian General Staff 1916–20.

The private papers of James Willcocks are spread about the archived collections of his correspondents, especially in the Papers of Baron Hardinge of Penshurst at Cambridge, the Papers of Lord Kitchener at the National Archives, and the Papers of Field Marshal Sir William Robertson at the Liddell Hart Centre for Military Archives.

2 Published sources: statistics and general histories

My main guides as general histories of the war have been James Edmonds' *A Short History of World War I* (London, 1951); Cyril Falls' *The First World War* (1960); Ian Brown's *British Logistics on the Western Front* (Westport, 1998); Michael Howard's *The First World War* (Oxford, 2002); Hew Strachan's *To Arms* (Oxford, 2003) and *The First World War, A New Illustrated History* (London, 2003); Mark Harrison's *The Medical War: British Military Medicine in the First World War* (Oxford, 2010); and the *International Encyclopedia of the First World War* at http://www.1914-1918-online.net.

As guides for the various theatres, I have used British official and semi-official histories including J. Merewether and F. E. Smith's *The Indian Corps in France* (London, 1919); W. Macpherson's *Medical Services* (London, 1921–23); Charles Lucas' *The Empire at War* (Oxford, 1921–26); James Edmonds' *Military Operations: France and Belgium* (London, 1922–48); F. Moberly's *The Campaign in Mesopotamia* (London, 1923–27) and *Operations in Persia* (1929); C. Falls and G. MacMunn's *Military Operations: Egypt and Palestine* (1928–30); A. Henniker's *Transportation on the Western Front* (London, 1937); C. Hordern and H. Stacke's *Military Operations: East Africa* (London, 1941); and James Edmonds' *The Occupation of Constantinople* (1944).

For major statistics such as the size of the Indian Army or Indian Expeditionary Forces, or casualty totals, I have used the War Office's numerous Despatches published as *Supplements to the London Gazette* (1914–1920), and the British Empire and British India's official post-war records in *Statistics of the Military Effort of the British Empire during the Great War, 1914–1920* (London, 1922); *India's Services in the War* (Lucknow, 1922); *The Punjab and the War* (Lahore, 1922); *India's Contribution to the Great War* (Calcutta, 1923); and *The Army in India and Its Evolution* (Calcutta, 1924). I have also used more recent compendia or tables from Niall Ferguson's *The Pity of War* (London, 1999); S. Saxena's *Role of Indian Army in the First World War* (Delhi, 1987); and B. Pati's *India and the First World War* (New Delhi, 1996).

For general histories of the Indian Army, I have mostly turned to H. Dodwell's *Cambridge History of India* (Cambridge, 1922–32); E. Benians' *Cambridge History of the British Empire* (Cambridge, 1929–61); D. Ellinwood and S. Pradhan's articles in their *India and World War I*

(New Delhi, 1978); G. S. Sandhu's *The Indian Cavalry* (New Delhi, 1981); E. Proud's *History of the Indian Army Postal Service* (privately published, 1984); A. Ghosh's *History of the Armed Forces Medical Services, India* (Hyderabad, 1988); David Omissi's *The Sepoy and the Raj* (1994); S. Cohen's *The Indian Army* (New Delhi, 2001); S. H. Rudolph and L. I. Rudolph with M. S. Kanota, *Reversing the Gaze, Amar Singh's Diary, A Colonial Subject's Narrative of Imperial India* (Boulder, 2002); S. Menezes' *Fidelity and Honour* (New Delhi, 2004); and D. Ellinwood, *Between Two Worlds: A Rajput Officer in the Indian Army, 1905–1921, Based on the Diary of Amar Singh of Jaipur* (Lanham, 2005).

I have used many newspapers and service journals published between 1900 and the 1940s with reports, interviews or articles or lectures on the Indian Army, among them *The Daily Mirror*; *The Times*; *The New York Times*; *The Times of India*; the *Army Review*; *Blackwood's Magazine*; *The British Medical Journal*; *The Indian Antiquary*; *The Geographical Journal*; *The Journal of the Royal Artillery*; *The Journal of the Royal Central Asian Society*; and *The Journal of the United Service Institution of India*.

I have often referred to the more detailed Indian Army regimental histories often written by British officers of 1914–18 describing events they witnessed, including W. Watson's *King George's Own Central India Horse* (Edinburgh, 1930); W. Thatcher's *The Fourth Battalion, Duke of Connaught's Own Tenth Baluch Regiment* (Cambridge, 1932); A. Lind's *A Record of the 58th Rifles F.F. in the Great War 1914–1919* (Dera Ismail Khan, 1933); R. Waters' *History of the 5th Battalion (Pathans), 14th Punjab Regiment* (London, 1936); H. Hudson's *History of the 19th King George's Own Lancers* (Aldershot, 1937); E. Sandes' *The Indian Sappers and Miners* (Chatham, 1948); C. Graham's *History of the Indian Mountain Artillery* (Aldershot, 1957); and H. Huxford's *History of the 8th Gurkha Rifles* (Aldershot, 1952).

For the Indian soldiers' letters, my main sources beyond the archives have been S. van Koski's article 'Letters home, 1915–16' in the *International Journal of Punjab Studies* (1995); D. Omissi's *Indian Voices of the Great War* (Basingstoke, 1999) and his article 'Through Indian Eyes' in the *English Historical Review* (2007); R. Visram's *Asians in Britain: 400 Years of History* (London, 2002); and G. Singh's *The Testimonies of Indian Soldiers and the Two World Wars: Between Self and Sepoy* (New York, 2014).

For the Indian political context, I have used J. Brown's *Gandhi's Rise to Power: Indian Politics 1915–1922* (Cambridge, 1972); A. Rumbold's *Watershed in India 1914–1922* (London, 1979); Sumit Sarkar's *Modern India 1885–1947* (Delhi, 2001); B. and T. Metcalf's *A Concise History of India* (Cambridge, 2005); and T. Metcalf's *Imperial Connections: India in the Indian Ocean Arena* (Berkeley, 2007).

3. Published sources per chapter

Introduction

For the Delhi Durbar, see *Scheme and Orders for the Military Arrangements at Delhi in Connection with the Coronation Durbar* (Calcutta, 1911); J. Fortescue's *Narrative of the Visit to India of Their Majesties* (London, 1912); *Military Report on the Military Arrangements for the Coronation Durbar Held at Delhi in December 1911* (Calcutta, 1913); D. Cannadine's *Ornamentalism: How the British Saw Their Empire* (London, 2001); and J. F. Codell's *Power and Resistance: The Delhi Coronation Durbars* (New Delhi, 1912). For the individual parts of the Hindu diarist Thakur Amar Singh, see D. Ellinwood, *Between Two Worlds: A Rajput Officer in the Indian Army* (Lanham, 2005); of Mir Dast, see 'The Piffer' or *The Journal of the Punjab Frontier Force Officers' Association* (1963); and of James Willcocks, see J. Willcocks' *The Romance of Soldiering and Sport* (London, 1925). The full list of Durbar attendees is in the British Library's India Office Records.

On the Indian Army's officers and men speaking more languages than any other army, I have evaluated this on the initial basis of E. Upton's *The Armies of Asia and Europe: Embracing Official Reports on the Armies of Japan, China, India, Persia, Italy, Russia, Austria, Germany, France, and England* (Portsmouth, 1878), which provides a comparative analysis of the number of languages that Indian Army soldiers were examined in or spoke on duty. I have compared Upton's assessments against the languages spoken in the Indian and other armies of 1914–18, including the Austro-Hungarian Army, which acknowledged eleven languages (not including Yiddish). I have concluded that the Indian Army of 1914–18 acknowledged or used at least fifteen languages, being more than any other army. In reaching this conclusion, I am grateful to Alexander Watson, Professor of History at Goldsmiths, University of London, for his guidance on the Austro-Hungarian Army.

The Prime Minister Herbert Asquith's speeches are taken from *War speeches by British ministers* (London, 1917); and J. Spender and C. Asquith's *Life of Herbert Henry Asquith* (London, 1932). For F. E. Smith and Rudyard Kipling's post-war observations, see S. Price's *Neuve Chapelle* (London, 1927); for George Barrow, see his *The Fire of Life* (London, 1942); and for Mahatma Gandhi, see the *Collected Works of Gandhi* (New Delhi, 1958 onwards).

For the initial critical comments on the Indian soldiers on the western front, see J. Buchan's *Nelson's History of the War* (London, 1915–19); A. Conan Doyle's *The British Campaign in France and Flanders* (London, 1916–19); F. Richards *Old Soldiers Never Die* (London, 1933); D. Lloyd George's *War Memories* (London, 1938); and M. Brock and E. Brock's *H. H. Asquith, Letters to Venetia Stanley* (Oxford, 1985).

For the later ideas of Indian military failure, see J. Greenhut's 'The Imperial Reserve: The Indian Corps on the Western Front, 1914–15' in the *Journal of Imperial and Commonwealth History* (1983) and 'Sahib and Sepoy: An Inquiry into the Relationship between the British Officers and Native Soldiers of the British Indian Army' in *Military Affairs* (1984); John Keegan's *First World War* (London, 1999); P. Barua's *Gentlemen of the Raj* (Westport, 2003); and N. Gardner's *Trial by Fire: Command and the British Expeditionary Force in 1914* (Westport, 2003).

For the political comments on the Indian troops, see P. Spear's *A History of India* (London, 1965) and David J. Silbey's chapter on the Indian Army in Timothy C. Dowling's *Personal Perspectives: World War I* (Santa Barbara, 2006).

For the Afridi brothers Mir Dast VC and Mir Mast, see C. Chenevix Trench's *The Indian Army and the King's Enemies* (GDR, 1988); S. Das *Race, Empire and First World War Writing* (Cambridge, 2011); and the Brighton Pavilion blog 'Mir Dast – the Man Behind the Plaque' at https://brightonmuseums.org.uk/discover/2016/06/03/mir-dast-the-man-behind-the-plaque/.

For perspectives on the Indian soldier as a colonial subject, see W. E. B. Du Bois' *The Souls of Black Folk* (Chicago, 1903); J. Nehru's *An Autobiography* (New Delhi, 1936); J. C. Scott's *Domination and the Arts of Resistance: Hidden Transcripts* (Yale, 1990); S. Bose's *A*

Hundred Horizons: The Indian Ocean in the Age of Global Empire (Harvard, 2009); H. Liebau, K. Bromber, K. Lange, D. Hamzah and R. Ahuja's *The World in Wars, Experiences, Perceptions and Perspectives from Africa and Asia* (Leiden, 2010); F. Roy, H. Liebau and R. Ahuja's *'When the War Began We Heard of Several Kings': South Asian Prisoners in World War I Germany* (New Delhi, 2011); and L. Tarazi Fawaz's *A Land of Aching Hearts: The Middle East in the Great War* (Harvard, 2014).

PART ONE: THE ROAD TO WORLD WAR

Chapter 1: 'The peasant's university'

For the Indian villages, see D. Ibbetson's *Panjab Castes* (Lahore, 1916); O. Creagh's *Indian Studies* (London, 1919); M. Darling's *Rusticus Loquitur: Or the Old Light and the New in the Punjab Village* (Oxford, 1930), *Wisdom and Waste in the Punjab Village* (Oxford, 1934), and *At Freedom's Door* (Oxford, 1949); and the various works of C. Dewey including *Arrested Development in India* (New Delhi, 1988). For the 'martial races' as social groups, see G. MacMunn's *The Martial Races of India* (London, 1933); and H. Streets' *Martial Races: The Military, Race and Masculinity in British Imperial Culture* (Manchester, 2004).

For the Indian recruits' pre-1914 army life, including overseas travel, see M. Conway, *The Alps from End to End* (London, 1895); P. Etherton's *Across the Roof of the World* (London, 1911); A. Stein's *Ruins of Desert Cathay* (London, 1912); N. Woodyatt's *Under Ten Viceroys* (London, 1922); O. Creagh's *The Autobiography of General Sir O'Moore Creagh V.C.* (London, 1924); C. Bruce's *Himalayan Wanderer* (London, 1934); A. Wilson's *SW. Persia: a Political Officer's Diary, 1907–1914* (Oxford, 1941); R. Parkinson, *The Auk: Auchinleck, Victor at Alamein* (London, 1977); R. Maxwell's *Villiers-Stuart on the Frontier 1894–1914* (Edinburgh, 1989); S. H. Rudolph and L. I. Rudolph with M. S. Kanota, *Reversing the Gaze, Amar Singh's Diary* (Boulder, 2002); and T. Metcalf's *Imperial Connections: India in the Indian Ocean Arena, 1860–1920* (Berkeley, 2007).

Chapter 2: 'Inferiors in the scale of humanity'

For the Indian soldiers as colonial subjects, see G. Younghusband's *Two Lectures to The Guides* (Poona, 1908); J. Ker, *Political Trouble in India 1907–1917* (Calcutta, 1917); E. Candler's *The Sepoy* (London, 1919); O. Creagh's *Indian Studies* (London, 1919); M. Channing's *India Mosaic*

(Philadelphia, 1936); Frank Richards' *Old-Soldier Sahib* (London, 1936); T. Metcalf's *Ideologies of the Raj* (Cambridge, 1995); and S. H. Rudolph and L. I. Rudolph with M. S. Kanota, *Reversing the Gaze, Amar Singh's Diary* (Boulder, 2002). I have made my own calculations on the Indian soldiers' basic pay as unequal to British soldiers' in 1914, comparing the sepoy wage of 11 rupees a month and the British private wage of 1 shilling a day, and using the 1914 exchange rates of 15 rupees to the pound sterling or 1s. 4d. to the rupee. On Indian soldiers' pensions I have drawn on O. Creagh's *The Autobiography of General Sir O'Moore Creagh V.C.* (London, 1924).

On the Sikh soldiers specifically up to 1914 including their political views, see *Political Trouble in India* and *The Autobiography of General Sir O'Moore Creagh* (as above); British officers' statements in *Proceedings of the Army in India Committee, 1912, Volume II, Minutes of Evidence* (Simla, 1913); R. J. Popplewell's *Intelligence and Imperial Defence: British Intelligence and the Defence of the Indian Empire, 1904–1924* (London, 1995); R. K. Mazumder's *The Indian Army and the Making of the Punjab* (Delhi, 2003); and Tan Tai Yong's *The Garrison State* (New Delhi, 2005).

For the independent Pukhtun, the outstanding source is E. Howell's *Mizh: A Monograph on Government's Relations with the Mahsud Tribe* (Simla, 1931). I have also used several of A. Ahmed's books including *Pukhtun Economy and Society* (London, 1980) and *The Thistle and the Drone* (Washington DC, 2013); and D. M. Hart's including *Guardians of the Khaibar Pass: The Social Organisation and History of the Afridis of Pakistan* (Lahore, 1985). Further, see H. Hutchinson's *The Campaign in Tirah 1897–1898* (New York, 1898); T. Holdich, *Indian Borderland, 1880–1900* (London, 1901); C. Callwell's *Small Wars* (London, 1906) and *Tirah 1897* (London, 1911); O. Creagh's *The Autobiography of General Sir O'Moore Creagh V.C.* (London, 1924); G. Barrow's *The Fire of Life* (London, 1942); O. Caroe's *The Pathans* (London, 1958); L. Baha's *N.-W.F.P. Administration Under British Rule* (Islamabad, 1978); O. Roy's *Islam and Resistance in Afghanistan* (Cambridge, 1986); C. Allen's *Plain Tales from the British Empire* (London, 2008); V. Schofield's *Afghan Frontier* (London, 2010); and O. Khan Afridi's *Pukhtanah: A Concise Account* (Karachi, 2014).

Chapter 3: 'He merely obeys orders'

For the Indian Army's pre-1914 campaigns in China and around the Indian Ocean, see the Indian General Staff's *Frontier and Overseas Expeditions from India* (Simla & Calcutta, 1907–13). Also see the U.S. Army's *Reports of the War Department, Year Ended June 30, 1900: Part 7* (Washington DC, 1900); A. Landor's *China and the Allies* (New York, 1901); E. Norie's *Official Account of the Military Operations in China, 1900–1901* (London, 1903); E. Candler's *The Unveiling of Lhasa* (London, 1905); D. MacDiarmid's *The Life of Lieutenant-General Sir James Grierson* (London, 1923); J. Elliot's *Some Did it for Civilization; Some Did it for Their Country: A Revised View of the Boxer War* (Hong Kong, 2002); S. H. Rudolph and L. I. Rudolph with M. S. Kanota, *Reversing the Gaze, Amar Singh's Diary* (Boulder, 2002); D. Ellinwood, *Between Two Worlds: A Rajput Officer in the Indian Army* (Lanham, 2005); and R. Bickers and R. G. Tiedemann's *The Boxers, China and the World* (Lanham, 2007).

For the massacre of the Bhil people, see F. James' *History of the 1st Battalion 6th Rajputana Rifles* (Aldershot, 1938); H. Rawlinson's *History of the 3rd Battalion 7th Rajput Regiment* (Oxford, 1941); U. Mahurkar's article 'Descendants of Mangad massacre seek recognition for past tragedy' in *India Today* (30 November 1999); and M. Zama's *Emerging Literatures from Northeast India: The Dynamics of Culture, Society and Identity* (New Delhi, 2013).

For the Indian Army's small wars in the independent Pukhtun tribal areas, see A. Yate, *Lieutenant-Colonel John Haughton* (London, 1900); C. Callwell's *Small Wars* (London, 1906); I. Hamilton's *A Staff Officer's Scrap Book* (London, 1906); the India Office's *East India (North-West Frontier) Papers Regarding Orakzais, Zakka Khel Afridis and Mohmands* (London, 1908); C. Miles, *The Zakka Khel and Mohmand Expeditions* (Rawalpindi, 1909); C. Enriquez's *Pathan Borderland* (Calcutta, 1910); H. Nevill's *Campaigns on the North-West Frontier* (London, 1912); J. Willcocks' *The Romance of Soldiering and Sport* (London, 1925); Anonymous, *Regimental History of the 4th Battalion 13th Frontier Force Rifles* (London, 1932); C. Bruce's *Himalayan Wanderer* (London, 1934); M. Channing's *India Mosaic* (Philadelphia, 1936); and T. Moreman's *The Army in India and the Development of Frontier Warfare* (New York, 1998).

For Douglas Haig and the Indian General Staff, see J. Willcocks' *The Romance of Soldiering and Sport* (London, 1925); J. Charteris'

Field-Marshal Earl Haig (London, 1929); G. MacMunn's *Behind the Scenes in Many Wars* (London, 1930); C. Hardinge's *My Indian Years, 1910–1916* (London, 1948); J. Gooch's *The Plans of War: The General Staff and British Military Strategy c.1900–1916* (London, 1974); D. French and B. Holden Reid's *The British General Staff: Reform and Innovation, 1890–1939* (London, 2002); J. P. Harris' *Douglas Haig and the First World War* (Cambridge, 2008); and Gary Sheffield's *The Chief: Douglas Haig and the British Army* (London, 2011).

PART TWO: 1914

Chapter 4: 'Vivent les Hindous!'

For mobilisation and the voyage to Marseilles and Flanders, see *The Times History of the War* (London, 1914–19); M. Bibikoff's *Our Indians at Marseilles* (London, 1915); H. Alexander, *On Two Fronts, being the Adventures of an Indian Mule Corps in France and Gallipoli* (New York, 1917); J. Willcocks' *The Romance of Soldiering and Sport* (London, 1925); B. van Wart's *The Life of Lieutenant-General H. H. Sir Pratap Singh* (London, 1926); G. Curtis, *Monograph on Mahsud Tribes* (Peshawar, 1947); C. Hardinge's *My Indian Years, 1910–1916* (London, 1948); J. Terraine's *Douglas Haig* (London, 1963); M. Brock and E. Brock's *H. H. Asquith, Letters to Venetia Stanley* (Oxford, 1985); G. Corrigan's *Sepoys in the Trenches* (Staplehurst, 1999); D. Ellinwood, *Between Two Worlds: A Rajput Officer in the Indian Army* (Lanham, 2005); D. Dendooven and P. Chielens' *World War I, Five Continents in Flanders* (Tielt, 2008); and G. Morton-Jack's *The Indian Army on the Western Front* (Cambridge, 2014).

Chapter 5: 'In the nick of time'

For the Indian Army's arrival on the western front and impact on the balance of forces, see J. French, *1914* (London, 1919); J. Merewether and F. E. Smith's *The Indian Corps in France* (London, 1919); J. Willcocks' *With the Indians in France* (1920) and *The Romance of Soldiering and Sport* (London, 1925); W. Lawrence's *The India We Served* (London, 1928); F. Maurice's *The Life of General Lord Rawlinson* (London, 1928); John Charteris' *Field-Marshal Earl Haig* (London, 1929), and *At G.H.Q.* (London, 1931); F. Smith's *Frederick Edwin, Earl of Birkenhead* (London, 1935); J. Smyth's *The Only Enemy: An Autobiography* (London, 1959); M. Brock and E. Brock's *H. H. Asquith, Letters to Venetia Stanley* (Oxford, 1985); A. Home, *The Diary of a World War I*

Cavalry Officer (Tunbridge Wells, 1985); A. Farrar-Hockley, *Death of an Army* (Chatham, 1998); and G. Morton-Jack's *The Indian Army on the Western Front* (Cambridge, 2014). For Qingdao, see E. Knox's article 'The Siege of Tsingtao' in the *Journal of the United Service Institution of India* (1915).

Chapter 6: 'The riff-raff'

For East Africa, see R. Meinertzhagen's *Army Diary 1899–1926* (Edinburgh, 1960); S. Pradhan's *Indian Army in East Africa 1914–1918* (New Delhi, 1990); R. Anderson's *The Forgotten Front: The East African Campaign 1914–1918* (Stroud, 2004); E. Paice's *Tip and Run* (London, 2007); and Andrew Kerr's *I Can Never Say Enough About the Men: A History of the Jammu and Kashmir Rifles throughout their World War One East African Campaign* (London, 2010).

For the early campaign in Iraq, see C. Murphy, *Soldiers of the Prophet* (London, 1921); Anonymous, *Historical Records of the 20th (Duke of Cambridge's Own) Infantry, Brownlow's Punjabis 1908–1922* (London, 1923); C. Townshend's *When God Made Hell: The British Invasion of Mesopotamia and the Creation of Iraq, 1914–1921* (London, 2010). For the 130th Baluchis' British officer murder, see the British Library's India Office Records file 'Mutinous Conduct of the 130th Baluchis' (L/MIL/7/18846) and Evelyn Howell's *Mizh: A Monograph on Government's Relations with the Mahsud Tribe* (Simla, 1931).

Chapter 7: 'That God-forsaken ground'

For the Indian Army's winter of 1914 on the western front, see J. Merewether and F. E. Smith's *The Indian Corps in France* (London, 1919); J. Willcocks' *With the Indians in France* (1920) and *The Romance of Soldiering and Sport* (London, 1925); F. Smith's *Frederick Edwin, Earl of Birkenhead* (London, 1935); David James' *The Life of Lord Roberts* (London, 1954); and George Morton-Jack's *The Indian Army on the Western Front* (Cambridge, 2014).

Chapter 8: 'Enterprises and surprises'

For the Indians in the trenches of France up to Christmas 1914, see *The Times History of the War* (London, 1914–19); J. Merewether and F. E. Smith's *The Indian Corps in France* (London, 1919); J. Willcocks' *With the Indians in France* (1920) and *The Romance of Soldiering and Sport*

(London, 1925); D. Drake-Brockman's *With the Royal Garhwal Rifles in the Great War* (Haywards Heath, 1934); G. Corrigan's *Sepoys in the Trenches* (Staplehurst, 1999); D. Ellinwood, *Between Two Worlds: A Rajput Officer in the Indian Army* (Lanham, 2005); M. Brown's *The Imperial War Museum Book of the Western Front* (London, 2013); G. Morton-Jack's *The Indian Army on the Western Front* (Cambridge, 2014); and P. Hart, *Fire and Movement: The British Expeditionary Force and the Campaign of 1914* (Oxford, 2015).

PART THREE: 1915

Chapter 9: 'An anti-British crusade'

For Germany's revolutionary strategy, see G. Wyman-Bury's *Pan-Islam* (London, 1919); D. McKale's *War by Revolution* (Kent, 1998); and S. McMeekin, *The Berlin-Baghdad Express* (London, 2010). For the Indian Army in Egypt, see C. Bruce's *Himalayan Wanderer* (London, 1934); and M. I. Qureshi's *History of the First Punjab Regiment 1759–1956* (Aldershot, 1958).

For the Indian Army in Iraq and Iran, see A. Wilson's *Loyalties: Mesopotamia, 1914–1917* (London, 1931); C. Townshend, *When God Made Hell: The British Invasion of Mesopotamia and the Creation of Iraq, 1914–1921* (London, 2010); I. Rutledge's *Enemy on the Euphrates: The British Occupations of Iraq and the Great Arab Revolt, 1914–1921* (London, 2014); and E. Rogan's *The Fall of the Ottomans: The Great War in the Middle East, 1914–1920* (London, 2015). For the desertions and mutinies including the 5th Light Infantry and 130th Baluchis, see the British Library's India Office Records file 'A Conference of General Officers' (L/MIL/17/5/1769); L. Baha's 'The Trans-Frontier Pathan Soldiers and The First World War' in *Islamic Studies* (1986); and G. Singh's *The Testimonies of Indian Soldiers and the Two World Wars: Between Self and Sepoy* (New York, 2014).

Chapter 10: 'I could not bear the news'

I have drawn the circumstances of the Afridi officer Mir Mast's desertion in France from the papers on the matter in the British Library's India Office Records and Private Papers collections, the National Archives at Kew, the German Foreign Office Archives in Berlin and the National Archives of India at New Delhi; I have also used A. Lind's *A Record of the 58th Rifles F.F. in the Great War 1914–1919* (Dera Ismail Khan, 1933).

For the German propaganda camp and diplomatic mission to Kabul, see D. J. McCarthy's *The Prisoner of War in Germany* (New York, 1918); H. Dayal's *Forty-Four Months in Germany and Turkey* (London, 1920); Mahendra Pratap's 'My German Mission to High Asia, or How I Joined Forces with the Kaiser to Enlist Afghanistan against Great Britain' in the *Asia Magazine* (1925) and his *My Life Story of Fifty-Five Years* (Dehradun, 1947); A. Bose's *Indian Revolutionaries Abroad, 1905–1922* (Patna, 1971); Gerhard Hopp's *Muslime in der Mark: Als Kriegsgefangene und Internierte in Wurnsdurf und Zossen, 1914–1924* (Berlin, 1997); Matthias Friese and Stefan Geilen's *Deutsche in Afghanistan* (Köln, 2002); Werner Otto von Hentig's *Von Kabul nach Shanghai* (Tübingen, 2003); Gottfried Hagen's 'German Heralds of Holy War: Orientalists and Applied Oriental Studies' in *Comparative Studies of South Asia, Africa and the Middle East* (2004); N. Barooah's *Chatto, The Life and Times of an Indian Anti-Imperialist in Europe* (New Delhi, 2004); and Jules Stewart's *The Kaiser's Mission to Kabul* (London, 2014).

For the further details of the individuals of the diplomatic mission to Kabul, see in particular 'Dr. Becker's Diary' in the British Library's India Office Records (IOR L/PS/11/133), and the MI5 files on Werner Otto von Hentig and Said Ahmed of the 129th Baluchis at the National Archives at Kew (KV2/393–394).

Chapter 11: 'Just like the photos'

For the Indians at Gallipoli, the outstanding book is P. Stanley's *Die in Battle, Do Not Despair: The Indians on Gallipoli, 1915* (Solihull, 2015). Also see I. Hamilton's *Gallipoli Diary* (London, 1920); C. Callwell's *The Dardanelles* (London, 1924); C. Bruce's *Himalayan Wanderer* (London, 1934); H. Davies's *Allanson of the 6th: An Account of the Life of Colonel Cecil John Lyons Allanson, 6th Gurkha Rifles* (Worcester, 1990); and M. Arthur's *Forgotten Voices of the Great War* (London, 2002).

For British India and Ghadar in 1915, see F. Isemonger and J. Slattery's *An Account of the Ghadar Conspiracy, 1913–1915* (Lahore, 1919); M. O'Dwyer's *India as I Knew It, 1885–1925* (London, 1925); C. Hardinge's *My Indian Years, 1910–1916* (London, 1948); B. Busch's *Hardinge of Penshurst* (Hamden, 1980); S. Sarkar's *Modern India 1885–1947* (Delhi, 2001); R. J. Popplewell's *Intelligence and Imperial Defence: British Intelligence and the Defence of the Indian Empire, 1904–1924* (London, 1995); and P. Stanley's *Die in Battle, Do Not Despair* (Solihull, 2015).

On the Sikhs in particular in 1915, I am grateful to Squadron Leader Rana Tej Pratap Singh Chhina (retd.), Secretary of the Centre for Armed Forces Historical Research at USI, Delhi, for his guidance, including on potential reasons why the British did not award any Sikh a Victoria Cross in 1914–18 (an idea which I owe to him).

Chapter 12: 'Keskersay'

For the Indian regiments on the western front including at Second Ypres and in hospital, see J. Merewether and F. E. Smith's *The Indian Corps in France* (London, 1919); J. Willcocks' *With the Indians in France* (1920) and *The Romance of Soldiering and Sport* (London, 1925); C. Campbell's *Chapters from a Soldier's Life* (privately printed, 1941); W. Condon, *The Frontier Force Rifles* (Aldershot, 1953); D. Thapar's *The Morale Builders, Forty Years with the Military Medical Services of India* (London, 1965); G. Corrigan's *Sepoys in the Trenches* (Staplehurst, 1999); D. Omissi's *Indian Voices of the Great War* (Basingstoke, 1999); R. Visram's *Asians in Britain: 400 Years of History* (London, 2002); G. Cassar's *Hell in Flanders Fields* (Toronto, 2010); Vedica Kant's *'If I die here, who will remember me?', India and the First World War* (New Delhi, 2014); G. Morton-Jack's *The Indian Army on the Western Front* (Cambridge, 2014); and S. Das' *1914–1918 Indian Troops in Europe* (Paris, 2015).

The source for Kasturba Gandhi and Sarojini Naidu as volunteers in the Indian hospitals in England is D. Thapar's *The Morale Builders* (as above). This is the only source that has come to light of their volunteering (Naidu's biographers do not mention it). Thapar was a doctor of the Indian Medical Service, before becoming independent India's Director-General of the Indian Armed Forces Medical Services.

For further analysis of the Indian hospitals in England as sites of propaganda, see S. Das' *India, Empire and First World War Culture* (Cambridge, 2018).

Chapter 13: 'As when the leaves fall off a tree'

For the Indian Army's battles in France, see J. Merewether and F. E. Smith's *The Indian Corps in France* (London, 1919); J. Willcocks' *With the Indians in France* (1920) and *The Romance of Soldiering and Sport* (London, 1925); R. Blake's *The Private Papers of Douglas Haig,*

1914–1919 (London, 1952); A. Clark, *The Donkeys* (1991); G. Corrigan's *Sepoys in the Trenches* (Staplehurst, 1999); D. Omissi's *Indian Voices of the Great War* (Basingstoke, 1999); D. Ellinwood, *Between Two Worlds: A Rajput Officer in the Indian Army* (Lanham, 2005); and G. Morton-Jack's *The Indian Army on the Western Front* (Cambridge, 2014).

PART FOUR: 1916

Chapter 14: 'The Pasha of Baghdad'

For the decision to advance on Baghdad in 1915 and the withdrawal of the Indian infantry from France, see *Hansard* (House of Commons) (London, 1915); *Report of the Commission Appointed by Act of Parliament to Enquire into the Operations of War in Mesopotamia* (London, 1917); W. Robertson's *From Private to Field-Marshal* (Boston, 1921) and *Soldiers and Statesmen* (London, 1926); G. Cassar's *Kitchener's War: British Strategy from 1914 to 1916* (Washington DC, 2004); and G. Morton-Jack's *The Indian Army on the Western Front* (Cambridge, 2014).

For the Indian infantry's journey to Iraq, the fall of Kut and the 6th Indian Division in captivity, see *Report on the Treatment of British Prisoners of War in Turkey, Presented in Parliament by Command of His Majesty* (London, 1918); E. Candler's *The Sepoy* (London, 1919) and *The Long Road to Baghdad* (London, 1919); A. Wilson's *Loyalties: Mesopotamia, 1914–1917* (London, 1931); C. Campbell's *Chapters from a Soldier's Life* (privately printed, 1941); M. FitzHerbert, *The Man Who Was Greenmantle: A Biography of Aubrey Herbert* (Oxford, 1985); D. Ellinwood, *Between Two Worlds: A Rajput Officer in the Indian Army* (Lanham, 2005); C. Townshend's *When God Made Hell: The British Invasion of Mesopotamia and the Creation of Iraq, 1914–1921* (London, 2010); N. Gardner's *The Siege of Kut-al-Amara, At War in Mesopotamia 1915–16* (Bloomington, 2014); P. Crowley's *Kut 1916, The Forgotten British Disaster in Iraq* (Stroud, 2016); and A. Ghosh's blog on the war in Iraq at http://amitavghosh.com/blog.

Chapter 15: 'A tin full of kerosene'

For the failure of the German mission to Afghanistan, M. Pratap's *My Life Story of Fifty-Five Years* (Dehradun, 1947); L. Adamec, *Afghanistan, 1900–1923: A Diplomatic History* (Berkeley, 1967); M. Friese and S. Geilen's *Deutsche in Afghanistan* (Köln, 2002); W. von

Hentig's *Von Kabul nach Shanghai* (Tübingen, 2003); and J. Stewart's *The Kaiser's Mission to Kabul* (London, 2014).

For the Afridi officer Mir Mast's return to Tirah, I have used the official and private reports of the Chief-Commissioner of British India's North-West Frontier Province and his agents held in the British Library's India Office Records and Private Papers collections, and at the National Archives of India at New Delhi (which include the reports of Mir Mast's speeches to his tribe). For the desertion of Mir Dast VC, the source is 'The Piffer' or *The Journal of the Punjab Frontier Force Officers' Association* (1963) – see 'Extracts from a letter of Colonel J. P. Villiers-Stuart to Lt.-Col. E. D. Galbraith'.

For the Indian prisoners in Germany and the jihad otherwise, see J. Smyth's *The Only Enemy: An Autobiography* (London, 1959); H. von Glasenapp, *Meine Lebensreise* (Wiesbaden, 1964); G. Hopp's *Muslime in der Mark* (Berlin, 1997); D. Omissi's *Indian Voices of the Great War* (Basingstoke, 1999); N. Collett's *The Butcher of Amritsar: General Reginald Dyer* (London, 2007); and G. Singh's *The Testimonies of Indian Soldiers and the Two World Wars: Between Self and Sepoy* (New York, 2014).

Chapter 16: 'Looking for Germans'

For East Africa, see C. Campbell's *Chapters from a Soldier's Life* (privately printed, 1941); R. Meinertzhagen's *Army Diary 1899–1926* (Edinburgh, 1960); S. Pradhan's *Indian Army in East Africa 1914–1918* (New Delhi, 1990); R. Anderson's *The Forgotten Front: The East African Campaign 1914–1918* (Stroud, 2004); E. Paice's *Tip and Run: The Untold Tragedy of the Great War in Africa* (London, 2007); A. Kerr's *I Can Never Say Enough About the Men: A History of the Jammu and Kashmir Rifles throughout their World War One East African Campaign* (London, 2010); T. Crowson, *When Elephants Clash: A Critical Analysis Of Major General Paul Emil Von Lettow-Vorbeck* (Damascus (Maryland), 2012).

For the Indian cavalry in France, see G. S. Sandhu's *The Indian Cavalry* (New Delhi, 1981) and D. Omissi's *Indian Voices of the Great War* (Basingstoke, 1999).

Chapter 17: 'A cemetery of reputations'

For the Parliamentary Report on Iraq, the Parliamentary debate on it and the underlying causes of the failed advance on Baghdad of 1915 and the fall of Kut in 1916, see *Hansard* (House of Commons and House of Lords) (London, 1917), in particular the July debates; *Report of the Commission Appointed by Act of Parliament to Enquire into the Operations of War in Mesopotamia* (London, 1917); W. Robertson's *From Private to Field-Marshal* (Boston, 1921) and *Soldiers and Statesmen* (London, 1926); M. Hankey's *The Supreme Command* (London, 1961); B. Busch's *Hardinge of Penshurst* (Hamden, 1980); C. Townshend's *When God Made Hell: The British Invasion of Mesopotamia and the Creation of Iraq, 1914–1921* (London, 2010); A. Syk's 'The 1917 Mesopotamia Commission', *RUSI Journal* (2009); K. Roy's *The Indian Army in the Two World Wars* (Leiden, 2012); and R. Johnson's *The British Indian Army: Virtue and Necessity* (Newcastle upon Tyne, 2014).

Chapter 18: 'An ambulating refrigerator'

For the Indian high command following the fall of Kut, see C. Callwell's *The Life of Stanley Maude* (London, 1920); J. Willcocks' *With the Indians in France* (1920) and *The Romance of Soldiering and Sport* (London, 1925); W. Robertson's *From Private to Field-Marshal* (Boston, 1921) and *Soldiers and Statesmen* (London, 1926); G. Barrow's *The Life of General Sir Charles Carmichael Monro* (London, 1931); A. Syk's *The Military Papers of Lieutenant-General Frederick Stanley Maude,1914–1917* (Stroud, 2012); and P. Crowley's *Loyal to Empire: The Life of General Sir Charles Monro, 1860–1929* (Stroud, 2016).

For Indian recruitment and the home front, see *War speeches of his honour Sir Michael O'Dwyer* (Lahore, 1918); Tan Tai Yong's article 'An Imperial Home-Front: Punjab and the First World War' in the *Journal of Military History* (2000) and his *The Garrison State* (New Delhi, 2005); and R. K. Mazumder's *The Indian Army and the Making of the Punjab* (Delhi, 2003). Also see Mahmood Awan's article 'From the war front' in *The News on Sunday* (3 August 2014).

Chapter 19: 'No longer a Cinderella'

For the Indian Army in Iraq, see C. Callwell's *The Life of Stanley Maude* (London, 1920); W. Robertson's *From Private to Field-Marshal* (Boston, 1921) and *Soldiers and Statesmen* (London, 1926); G. Barrow's *The Life of General Sir Charles Carmichael Monro* (London, 1931); A. Wilson's *Loyalties: Mesopotamia, 1914–1917* (London, 1931) and *Mesopotamia 1917–1920, A Clash of Loyalties* (London, 1931); G. MacMunn, *The Martial Races of India* (London, 1933); E. Latter's article 'The Indian Army in Mesopotamia, 1914–18' in the *Journal of the Society for Army Historical Research* (1994); E. J. Erickson's *Ottoman Army Effectiveness in World War I* (London, 2007); I. Beckett's *Beyond the Western Front* (Leiden, 2009); C. Townshend's *When God Made Hell: The British Invasion of Mesopotamia and the Creation of Iraq, 1914–1921* (London, 2010); K. Roy's *The Indian Army in the Two World Wars* (Leiden, 2012); A. Syk's *The Military Papers of Lieutenant-General Frederick Stanley Maude, 1914–1917* (Stroud, 2012); K. Coates Ulrichsen's *The First World War in the Middle East* (London, 2014); R. Johnson's *The British Indian Army: Virtue and Necessity* (Newcastle upon Tyne, 2014) and *The Great War & the Middle East: A Strategic Study* (Oxford, 2016); and P. Crowley's *Kut 1916, The Forgotten British Disaster in Iraq* (Stroud, 2016).

Chapter 20: 'Why did I leave my little trench in France?'

For East Africa, I have primarily used the British Library's India Office Records' Indian General Staff reports on East Africa in 1916–17. Also see C. Campbell's *Chapters from a Soldier's Life* (privately printed, 1941); R. Anderson's *The Forgotten Front: The East African Campaign 1914–1918* (Stroud, 2004); and E. Paice's *Tip and Run: The Untold Tragedy of the Great War in Africa* (London, 2007).

Chapter 21: 'Bonjour petite fille Louise'

For the Indians otherwise in France, Italy, Germany, Switzerland and Thessaloniki, see H. Picot's *The British Interned in Switzerland* (London, 1920); W. Doegen's *Kriegsgefangene Völker* (Berlin, 1919) and *Unter fremden Völkern* (Berlin, 1925); E. Casadio and M. Valli's *Il Campo Inglese a Faenza nella Grande Guerra* (1917–1919) (Faenza, 2007); H. Liebau, K. Bromber, K. Lange, D. Hamzah and R. Ahuja's *The World in Wars, Experiences, Perceptions and Perspectives from Africa and Asia* (Leiden, 2010); and F. Roy, H. Liebau and R. Ahuja's *'When the War Began We*

Heard of Several Kings': South Asian Prisoners in World War I Germany (New Delhi, 2011). I have depended on H. Fecitt's articles at www.kaiserscross.com for the story of Santa Singh at Thessaloniki.

For 28,000 as the total number of the Indian Labour Corps in France, I have referred to the *Fourth Supplement to the London Gazette* (28 July 1919). Otherwise for the Indian Labour Corps – in particular for their joining up in India; their experiences from there to Italy; the reminiscences of their officers William Alderson and Frans Ory along with the company clerk Sainghinga Sailo; their experiences in France in camp and elsewhere – I have depended on the original or primary research of Radhika Singha, Professor of Modern Indian History at the Centre for Historical Studies, Jawaharlal Nehru University, New Delhi. My main sources for the Indian Labour Corps have been Professor Singha's articles 'Finding Labor from India for the War in Iraq: The Jail Porter and Labor Corps, 1916–1920' in *Comparative Studies in Society and History* (2007) and 'The Short Career of the Indian Labour Corps in France, 1917–1919' in *International Labor and Working-Class History* (2015). In addition, I am extremely grateful for her general guidance on Indian non-combatants of 1914–18. Without her research and kind assistance, this book's account of the Indian Labour Corps would not have been possible. Professor Singha's book *The Coolie's Great War: Indian Labour in a Global Conflict, 1914–21* (forthcoming, 2020) promises to be the definitive work on Indian labourers in the First World War.

PART SIX: 1918

Chapter 22: 'The political self-development of the people'

For Indian politics and the Indian Army including the development of King's Commissions for Indians, see *Speeches by Lord Hardinge of Penshurst, Viceroy and Governor General of India* (Calcutta, 1916); *Speeches by Lord Chelmsford, Viceroy and Governor General of India* (Simla, 1919); C. Hardinge's *My Indian Years, 1910–1916* (London, 1948); the *Collected Works of Gandhi* (New Delhi, 1958 onwards); B. Busch's *Hardinge of Penshurst* (Hamden, 1980); D. Omissi's *The Sepoy and the Raj* (1994); B. Pati's *India and the First World War* (New Delhi, 1996); G. Sharma's *Nationalisation of the Indian Army, 1885–1947* (New Delhi, 1996); D. K. Palit's *Major General A.A. Rudra: His Service in Three Armies and Two World Wars* (New Delhi, 1997); C. B. Khanduri, *Field Marshal KM Cariappa: a Biographical Sketch* (Delhi, 2000) and *Field Marshal KM Cariappa: His Life and Times* (Delhi,

2013); S. Sarkar's *Modern India 1885–1947* (Delhi, 2001); P. S. Gupta and A. Deshpande's *The British Raj and Its Indian Armed Forces* (New Delhi, 2002); P. Barua's *Gentlemen of the Raj* (Westport, 2003); R. K. Mazumder's *The Indian Army and the Making of the Punjab* (Delhi, 2003); D. Ellinwood, *Between Two Worlds: A Rajput Officer in the Indian Army* (Lanham, 2005); Tan Tai Yong's *The Garrison State* (New Delhi, 2005); K. Roy's *War and Society in Colonial India* (New Delhi, 2006); Mahmood Awan's article 'From the war front' in *The News on Sunday* (3 August 2014); and J. Francis' *Short Stories from the British Indian Army* (New Delhi, 2015). For the Indian Army's operations against the Kuki and Marri, I have drawn on several regimental histories and H. Fecitt's articles at www.kaiserscross.com.

Chapter 23: 'We alone have got to keep Southern Asia'

For the supreme command, grand strategy and the Imperial General Staff, see W. Robertson's *From Private to Field-Marshal* (Boston, 1921) and *Soldiers and Statesmen* (London, 1926); C. Falls' *Military Operations: Egypt and Palestine, Volume 2, Part II* (London, 1930); M. Hankey's *The Supreme Command* (London, 1961); C. Callwell's *Field-Marshal Sir Henry Wilson: His Life and Diaries* (London, 1927); K. Jeffery's *The British Army and the Crisis of Empire, 1918–1922* (Manchester, 1984) and *Field Marshal Sir Henry Wilson: a Political Soldier* (Oxford, 2006); D. French's *British Strategy & War Aims, 1914–1916* (London, 1986) and *The Strategy of the Lloyd George Coalition, 1916–1918* (Oxford, 1995); and J. Darwin's *The Empire Project: The Rise and Fall of the British World-System 1830–1970* (Cambridge, 2009).

For the Indian Army's 'hush-hush shows', see L. Dunsterville, *The Adventures of Dunsterforce* (London, 1920); S. Blacker's *On Secret Patrol in High Asia* (London, 1922); F. M. Bailey's *Mission to Tashkent* (Oxford, 1946); A. Swinson's *Beyond the Frontiers: The Biography of Colonel F.M. Bailey Explorer and Special Agent* (London, 1971); P. Hopkirk's *The Spy Who Disappeared: Diary of a Secret Mission to Russian Central Asia in 1918* (London, 1991) and *On Secret Service East of Constantinople: The Plot to Bring Down the British Empire* (Oxford, 1994); M. Sargent's article 'British Military Involvement in Transcaspia (1918–1919)' in the Conflict Studies Research Centre's *Caucasus Series* (2004); B. Blacker's *The Adventures & Inventions of Stewart Blacker* (Barnsley, 2006); G. Milton's *Russian Roulette: How British Spies Defeated Lenin* (London, 2013); T. Ter Minassian's *Most Secret Agent of Empire: Reginald Teague-Jones, Master Spy of the Great Game* (Oxford, 2014).

Chapter 24: 'Each one of us must fight on to the end'

For the Indian Army in France, Palestine and Iraq in 1918, see C. Bean's *The Official History of Australia in the War of 1914–1918* (Sydney, 1920–42); T. E. Lawrence's *Seven Pillars of Wisdom* (Oxford, 1922) and *Revolt in the Desert* (London, 1927); B. van Wart's *The Life of Lieutenant-General H. H. Sir Pratap Singh* (London, 1926); W. Marshall, *Memories of Four Fronts* (London, 1929); G. Barrow's *The Fire of Life* (London, 1942); C. Falls' *Armageddon 1918* (London, 1964); B. Gardner's *Allenby* (London, 1965); N. Saroop, *Gardner of Gardner's Horse: 2nd Lancers, Indian Army* (New Delhi, 1983); C. Chenevix Trench's *The Indian Army and the King's Enemies* (GDR, 1988); R. Holmes' *The Western Front* (London, 2008); L. James' *Imperial Warrior: The Life and Times of Field-Marshal Viscount Allenby 1861–1936* (London, 2015); R. Johnson's *The Great War & the Middle East: A Strategic Study* (Oxford, 2016); and J. Kitchen's *The British Imperial Army in the Middle East: Morale and Military Identity in the Sinai and Palestine Campaigns, 1916–18* (London, 2014).

On the Indian labourers in France, including the account of Frans Ory, the experiences of the Lushai tribesmen, and Indian Labour Corps departures from France, I have again depended on the research of Professor Radhika Singha – above all her article 'The Short Career of the Indian Labour Corps in France, 1917–1919' in *International Labor and Working-Class History* (2015). For further information on the Indian labourers, see Professor Singha's 'Finding Labor from India for the War in Iraq: The Jail Porter and Labor Corps, 1916-1920' in *Comparative Studies in Society and History* (2007), and *The Coolie's Great War: Indian Labour in a Global Conflict, 1914–21* (forthcoming, 2020).

PART SEVEN: VETERANS

Chapter 25: 'Which side their bread is buttered'

For Sir Pratap Singh and the Maharajah of Bikaner at Versailles, see B. van Wart's *The Life of Lieutenant-General H. H. Sir Pratap Singh* (London, 1926) and H. Purcell's *Maharajah of Bikaner, India* (London, 2010). For the Indian victory parade in London, see the British Library's India Office Records' file L/MIL/17/5/4290. The surviving film of this parade is a British Pathé newsreel; other surviving Pathé newsreels show Indian servicemen in England, France and Greece. I understand that the Imperial War Museum has further contemporary film footage of the Indian Army of 1914–18.

For the Indian Army's post-war service, rewards and politics, I have drawn on veteran interviews and many Indian regimental histories; the Indian General Staff's *Operations in Waziristan, 1919–20* (Calcutta, 1921); H. de Watteville, *Waziristan, 1919–1920* (London, 1925); J. Willcocks' *The Romance of Soldiering and Sport* (London, 1925); M. Darling's *Wisdom and Waste in the Punjab Village* (Oxford, 1934); the *Collected Works of Gandhi* (New Delhi, 1958 onwards); J. Smyth's *The Only Enemy: An Autobiography* (London, 1959); T. Moreman's *The Army in India and the Development of Frontier Warfare* (New York, 1998); D. Killingray and D. Omissi's *Guardians of Empire: The Armed Forces of the Colonial Powers C. 1700–1964* (Manchester, 1999); R. K. Mazumder's *The Indian Army and the Making of the Punjab* (Delhi, 2003); D. Ellinwood, *Between Two Worlds: A Rajput Officer in the Indian Army* (Lanham, 2005); Tan Tai Yong's *The Garrison State* (New Delhi, 2005); H. Liebau, K. Bromber, K. Lange, D. Hamzah and R. Ahuja's *The World in World Wars, Experiences, Perceptions and Perspectives from Africa and Asia* (Leiden, 2010); F. Roy, H. Liebau and R. Ahuja's '*When the War Began We Heard of Several Kings': South Asian Prisoners in World War I Germany* (New Delhi, 2011); and Mahmood Awan's article 'From the war front' in *The News on Sunday* (3 August 2014).

For the Third-Anglo Afghan War in particular, see General Staff Branch, Army Headquarters, India, *The Third Afghan War: Official Account* (Calcutta, 1926); G. Barrow's *The Life of General Sir Charles Carmichael Monro* (London, 1931); F. Poynder's *The 9th Gurka Rifles 1817–1936* (London, 1937); G. Molesworth, *Afghanistan, 1919* (London, 1962); L. Adamec's *Afghanistan, 1900–1923: A Diplomatic History* (Berkeley, 1967); B. Robson's *Crisis on the Frontier: The Third Afghan War and the Campaign in Waziristan, 1919–20* (Staplehurst, 2004); and P. Stanley's *Terriers in India: British Territorials 1914–19* (Exeter, 2018).

For the Moplah Rebellion, see J. Evatt's *Historical Record of the 39th Royal Garhwal Rifles, Volume I, 1887–1922* (Aldershot, 1922); O. Chaldecott's *The Tenth Baluch Regiment* (London, 1935); H. Huxford's *History of the 8th Gurkha Rifles* (Aldershot, 1952); and Sumit Sarkar's *Modern India 1885–1947* (Delhi, 2001).

Epilogue

For the Indian and other casualty statistics of the First World War, I have used the British official records in *Statistics of the Military Effort of the British Empire during the Great War, 1914–1920* (London, 1922) and *India's Contribution to the Great War* (Calcutta, 1923); imperial era Government of India records cited in S. Saxena's *Role of Indian Army in the First World War* (Delhi, 1987) and B. Pati's *India and the First World War* (New Delhi, 1996); the Commonwealth War Graves Commission's (CWGC) records at http://www.cwgc.org/find; and academic analysis including Niall Ferguson's *The Pity of War* (London, 1999) and in the *International Encyclopedia of the First World War* at http://www.1914-1918-online.net.

It is important to recognise that the study of Indian casualty statistics has been relatively neglected. A figure of 74,000 Indian soldiers killed in the First World War was widely used for the 2014 centenary (by the BBC, gov.uk and others), but this figure can mislead if it is applied to 1914–18. The 74,000 figure appears to have been based on CWGC records for the period 1914 to 1921, so that it includes campaigns such the Third Anglo-Afghan War 1919 and Waziristan 1919–20; in addition, it includes a significant number of British casualties in Iraq and at sea. My search of the CWGC records for *Indian* war dead of the Indian Army for the period August 1914 to November 1918 indicates a total figure of around 50,000, which aligns with the official British statistics of the 1920s and the imperial era Government of India records. A forensic modern study of the Indian casualty statistics of the First World War – how they were compiled per theatre, how accurate they are, and how correctives might apply – seems yet to be carried out.

For a detailed survey of Indian war graves and memorials, see R. Chhina's *Last Post: Indian War Memorials Around the World* (Delhi, 2014). Also see S. Price's *Neuve Chapelle* (London, 1927). On British abandonment of Indian war graves outside Europe, see R. Chhina and A. Chhina's article 'Commemoration, Cult of the Fallen (India)' (as updated on 5 March 2018) at http://www.1914-1918-online.net.

For the Indian veterans' post-war lives, I have drawn mainly on M. Darling's *Rusticus Loquitur: Or the Old Light and the New in the Punjab Village* (Oxford, 1930), *Wisdom and Waste in the Punjab Village* (Oxford, 1934), and *At Freedom's Door* (Oxford, 1949). Further details of veterans come from Rana Chhina (including veteran stories of Gallipoli and Kut), and from articles in the UK and US media, in particular M. Aikins' article 'The Doctor, the CIA, and the Blood of Bin Laden' in *GQ* (2012), and articles in the Indian and Pakistan media for the First World War's centenary in 2014, for instance in the *Indian Express* (by P. Kulkarni and S. G. Kashyap), in the *Sunday Guardian* (by B. Raman and A. Sakorkar interviewing Professor K. C. Yadav), and in *The News on Sunday* (by Mahmood Awan). Also see S. Basu's *For King and Another Country: Indian Soldiers on the Western Front, 1914–1918* (London, 2015) – this is my source for the story of Satoori Devi (who is on the front cover of this book), the wife of Gabar Singh Negi VC (posthumous).

GLOSSARY

Afridi a Pukhtun tribe, residing largely in their homeland of Tirah in the independent Pukhtun tribal areas ('Afridi' is used to mean the singular or plural for individuals of the tribe).

army corps a body of divisions; a British Army or an Army in India army corps usually had two divisions.

Army Headquarters the Army in India's headquarters, attached to the Government of India.

Army in India the garrison of British India, including all the Indian Army and part of the British Army posted from the Home Army, and administered by the Government of India.

battalion a body of soldiers composed of companies (which sub-divided into platoons or sections); an Indian battalion had approximately 750 men in 1914, increased to 1000 men by 1917; a British battalion had 1000 men in 1914 and after. A 'battalion' usually refers to an infantry unit – the Indian cavalry regiments were smaller with around 600 men each.

brigade a body of battalions; an Indian brigade usually had three Indian Army battalions and one British Army.

British Expeditionary Force (BEF) the Home Army expeditionary force sent from England to France in 1914, which expanded to include Indian Expeditionary Force A, British Army units from pre-war imperial garrisons from the Caribbean to China, and the forces of Australia and other British Empire territories.

British General Staff a British Army institution also known as the Imperial General Staff and based in London; it was responsible for planning British Army or British Empire operations directed by the War Office; from 1916, it controlled the Indian General Staff.

British government the government of the United Kingdom with executive power over the Government of India, normally exercised through its Secretary of State for India.

British India the part of the Indian Empire (some two thirds) directly ruled by the British through the Government of India, and excluding the Indian princely States.

company a unit of infantry within a battalion; up to 1914 there were eight companies per Indian regiment (this gradually changed to a four-company system from 1914).

dharma a religious term delineating broad behaviours needed to preserve the natural order; an individual's dharma could give a sense of personal duty or conduct appropriate to social status – equivalent to a righteous path through the universe.

division a body of brigades; an Indian division usually had three brigades.

durbar a royal court, a state reception given by a King or a public audience.

Egyptian Expeditionary Force the British Empire's expeditionary force that attacked the Ottoman Empire out of north-eastern Egypt, reaching Syria by 1918; it was directed by the War Office and incorporated Indian Expeditionary Force E.

Frontier Force the Indian Army's body of elite regiments; they served in or near the independent Pukhtun tribal areas between 1850s and 1914, making them the most active of all Indian regiments and as a rule the most professional.

Government of India British India's local administration, headed by the Viceroy; its offices moved with the seasons, from 1914 spending the winter in Delhi and the summer at the Himalayan town of Simla.

Home Army the garrison of the British Isles, made up of the British Army on duty in the United Kingdom (with a small number of British staff officers seconded from the Indian Army); in the scheme of British imperial defence it did not include the British Army's units posted on overseas garrison duty to British India and elsewhere.

Imperial Service Troops the domestic military forces of the Indian princely states, maintained at their own expense in readiness for foreign service under British command alongside the Indian Army.

independent Pukhtun tribal areas the collection of independent tribal lands between Afghanistan and British India (and part of the area known as the north-west frontier); their independent status was recognised by treaties with the British; Britain did not administer their territories and had no legal rights in them; their border with Afghanistan was recognised by international treaty.

India Office the British government department in London responsible for, and with direct control over, the Government of India and the Indian Army.

Indian Corps the Indian infantry army corps in France in 1914–15 (its full name was the 'Indian Army Corps').

Indian Empire the sub-section of the British Empire comprising British India, the Indian 'princely' States, and outlying territories such as Aden on the Arabian Peninsula under the control of the Government of India.

Indian Expeditionary Force an expeditionary force sent overseas from the Army in India at the British government's request through the India Office, of which there were seven in 1914–18:

Force A – to France;

Force B – to German East Africa;

Force C – to British East Africa;

Force D – to Ottoman Iraq;

Force E – to Egypt;

Force F – to Egypt;

Force G – to Gallipoli.

Indian General Staff the Army in India's (and by extension the Indian Army's) General Staff, based at Army Headquarters; it was traditionally separate from the British General Staff, being subordinate to the India Office rather than the War Office; its officers, all British, belonged to both the Indian and British armies; it assisted in the planning of all Indian operations from 1914; from 1916, it became directly controlled by the British General Staff as the British Empire's supreme command was reorganised in London.

Indianise a British term used in 1918 for the process of significantly increasing the Indian proportion of a British Empire expeditionary force to release white troops for the western front. The term was also used to describe the post-war increase of Indian officers in the Indian Army's (traditionally white) officer corps holding King's Commissions.

Indian Medical Service the Government of India's medical service, some of whose doctors were assigned to the Indian Army.

Indian officer an Indian officer usually serving in an Indian regiment and holding a Viceroy's Commission (but sometimes a King's Commission); Indian officers occasionally held non-regimental posts, such as in a division as an aide-de-camp.

Indian 'princely' States the nominally independent Indian States of the Indian Empire, outside British India and ruled by their own hereditary leaders (as allies of the British by treaties, which made their territories client-states of the British Empire without responsibility for their own foreign relations).

Iraq see Ottoman Iraq.

izzat honour, reputation, prestige or social standing.

jemadar the most junior Indian officer in an Indian regiment.

jihad a holy or religious war against non-believers in Islam.

kafir meaning 'one who covers the truth' by rejecting, disbelieving or otherwise not following the teachings of the Prophet Muhammad; also translated as an 'unbeliever' in Islam, and used by some Muslims as a derogatory term.

King's Commission an officer's commission in the British Army or the Indian Army, held mostly by British but also by some Indian officers; when held by British officers, it always carried a power of command over British and Indian troops; when held by Indian officers, it always carried a power of command over Indian troops but not necessarily British (depending on the conditions attached to the commission, whether it was granted as an honorary or otherwise). The ranks of King's Commissioned officer in regiments were lieutenants, captains, majors, colonels, with generals above.

lashkar a Pukhtun war party.

Mahsud a Pukhtun tribe, residing in Waziristan in the independent Pukhtun tribal areas ('Mahsud' is used to mean the singular or plural for individuals of the tribe).

Mediterranean Expeditionary Force the British Empire's expeditionary force that fought on the Gallipoli Peninsula in 1915–16; it was based on Egypt and Aegean islands, and incorporated Indian Expeditionary Force G.

Mesopotamia see Ottoman Iraq.

Occupied Territories the areas of Ottoman Iraq under British occupation from 1914 by Indian Expeditionary Force D.

Ottoman Iraq the Ottoman imperial territory of 1914 (consisting of the Turkish *vilayets* or provinces of Basra, Baghdad and Mosul) that was known to its own people in 1914–18 as Iraq, and to the British as Turkish Arabia or more commonly Mesopotamia (the ancient Greek name for the area, essentially meaning 'the land between two rivers' – the Tigris and Euphrates); its area corresponds to the Iraq of 2018.

princely States battalion, regiment or unit see Imperial Service Troops.

Pukhtun a speaker of Pushtu, a member of a Pukhtun tribe and a Muslim (also referred to as Pathan, Pashtun and other variants in English of the term; Pushtu is the same as Pashto or other variants).

Ramadan the ninth month of the Muslim year, observed as a fast during the hours of daylight.

regiment the basic lower-level fighting unit of the Indian Army, comprising one or more battalions; up to 1914, most Indian regiments were single-battalion, but by 1917 had two or three battalions.

sahib the main Indian term of address to a white European, used in the Indian Army to refer to a British officer.

Secretary of State for India the British government minister at the India Office, and the Viceroy's direct superior.

sepoy an Indian infantryman (equivalent to a British private or Tommy); 'sepoys' is used to refer to a body of Indian infantry.

Sirkar the government or a presiding authority.

sowar an Indian cavalryman (equivalent to a British cavalry trooper); 'sowars' is used to refer to a body of Indian cavalry.

squadron a unit of cavalry within an Indian cavalry regiment; there were usually four squadrons per cavalry regiment.

subadar-major the most senior Indian officer in an Indian regiment, holding a Viceroy's Commission.

Tirah the homeland of the Afridi (among others) in the independent Pukhtun tribal areas.

Viceroy (of India) the Governor-General of British India – its local ruler on behalf of the British monarch, and subordinate to the Secretary of State for India at the India Office.

Viceroy's Commission an officer's commission in the Indian Army held exclusively by Indian soldiers; it carried a power of command over only Indian troops (and never British); it was therefore inferior to a King's Commission, and had its own ranks, in the Indian infantry between jemadar and subadar-major.

War Office the British Government department (succeeded by the Ministry of Defence in 1964) responsible for administering the British Army, but ordinarily not that part of the British Army with the Army in India.

Waziristan the homeland of the Mahsud (among others) in the independent Pukhtun tribal areas.

Yusufzai a Pukhtun tribe, residing largely in British India's North-West Frontier Province ('Yusufzai' is used to mean the singular or plural for individuals of the tribe).

DRAMATIS PERSONAE

Ahmed, Said an Indian Muslim soldier of the 129th Baluchis and prisoner of war in Germany who joined a secret German mission from Berlin to Afghanistan, and on to China.

Allenby, Edmund also known as 'the Bull', the British Army general who led the British Empire's Egyptian Expeditionary Force to victory against the Turks in Palestine and Syria in 1918.

Asquith, Herbert Henry the British Prime Minister from 1908 to 1916.

Bailey, Frederick a British officer of the 32nd Sikh Pioneers who served on the western front and Gallipoli in 1915, before a secret Indian Army mission to spy in Soviet Central Asia in 1918.

Barrow, Edmund a British general of the Indian Army infantry who served in London from 1914 to 1917 as the Military Secretary to the India Office; he was particularly influential in 1914 over Indian Expeditionary Forces B and C to East Africa, shaping their plans to invade Germany East Africa.

Barrow, George a British general of the Indian Army cavalry who commanded in France, Palestine and Syria.

Bikaner, Maharajah Ganga Singh of the Indian princely States representative at the Paris Peace Conference in 1919 who signed the Treaty of Versailles; he was selected partly for his support of the British war effort.

Blacker, Stewart an eccentric, monocle-wearing, motor-bicycle-riding British officer of the elite Indian unit the Queen Victoria's Own Guides – he fought on the western front in 1915, then in China and Soviet Central Asia in 1918 as a spy.

Bruce, Charles a British officer of the 5th Gurkhas (Frontier Force) who before 1914 trained his men in mountaineering from Scotland to the Himalayas, and in 1914–15 served in Egypt and at Gallipoli.

Campbell, Charlie a model, multi-lingual young officer of the 40th Pathans who served in France and East Africa.

Candler, Edmund a British war correspondent whose war memoir *The Long Road to Baghdad* (1919) is one of the few eye-witness civilian accounts of the Indian Army's campaign in Ottoman Iraq.

Chelmsford, Lord the Viceroy of India from mid-1916 who oversaw India's revitalised war effort up to 1918.

Dast, Mir an Indian Muslim officer of the 55th Coke's Rifles (Frontier Force) and the second Indian Muslim VC – in Belgium in 1915 – whose brother, Mir Mast, deserted in France and entered secret German service.

Devi, Satoori the wife of the posthumous Indian Hindu VC Gabar Singh Negi of the Himalayan Garhwal region; her husband's VC was for bravery in France in 1915, and she wore it all her life.

Duff, Beauchamp a Scottish general and the Indian Army's Commander-in-Chief in 1914, he was recalled to London in disgrace in 1916.

Dunsterville, Lionel an Indian Army general who led a secret British Empire mission to the Caucasus in 1918, including Indian Army officers and men.

Etherton, Percy a British officer of the 39th Garhwals who served in France with his regiment in 1915, then in China in 1918 as an intelligence officer with Indian veterans of the western front.

Gandhi, Kasturba the wife of Mahatma Gandhi and wartime nurse in Indian hospitals in England.

Gandhi, Mahatma the Indian nationalist leader – he supported the Indian war effort, in particular in 1918 as an Indian Army recruiter.

George V the Indian Empire's King-Emperor and the Indian Army's ceremonial commander-in-chief.

Habibullah, Emir the Emir of Afghanistan who received a German secret mission in 1916 with Indian Army prisoners of war in German service.

Haig, Douglas the British Army general and Commander-in-Chief of the BEF – the British Empire's forces in France and Belgium – from 1915 to 1918; before the war, he was the Chief of the Indian General Staff.

Hamilton, Ian a British Army general and in 1915 the Commander-in-Chief of the British Empire's Mediterranean Expeditionary Force – whose Indian troops had a majority of Nepalese Gurkha units at his special request.

Hardinge, Charles the Viceroy of India from 1910 to 1916 and local leader of the Indian Army's early war effort – and its disaster in Ottoman Iraq in 1916 when the entire 6th Indian Division surrendered to the Turks.

Henderson, Kenneth a Glaswegian officer of the 39th Garhwals who sailed to France with his regiment in 1914, later writing an unpublished memoir of the earliest days in the Indian front line.

Hentig, Werner Otto von a German officer who led Indian prisoners of war from Germany to Kabul on a secret mission to turn Afghanistan against the Allies.

Herbert, Aubrey the British Member of Parliament who in 1916, as a former intelligence officer of Indian Expeditionary Force D in Iraq, led calls for an independent Parliamentary inquiry into the mismanagement of operations there – leading to the scandalous Mesopotamia Report of 1917.

Khan, Ajab an Indian Muslim officer of the 76th Punjabis; in Ottoman Iraq and Iran he led Indian Muslim troops against local Muslims.

Khan, Arsala an Indian Muslim officer of the 57th Wilde's Rifles (Frontier Force) who served in France, Belgium, Egypt and East Africa – he led the first Indian soldiers into the trenches against the Germans in 1914.

Khan, Ayub an Indian soldier of the 129th Baluchis who spied deep behind German lines on the western front and later fought in East Africa.

Khan, Mohammad Ayub (not the soldier of the 129th Baluchis) the second President of Pakistan from 1958 to 1969; the son of an Indian veteran of the western front, he was one of the new generation of Indian officers after 1918 who held a King's Commission.

Khan, Khudadad an Indian Muslim officer of the 129th Baluchis – he was the first Indian VC, in Belgium in October 1914.

Kirkpatrick, George a Canadian officer of the Indian Army, and the Chief of the Indian General Staff from 1916.

Kitchener, Lord the British Secretary of State for War at the War Office from 1914 to 1916 with responsibility for British operations in the west, and therefore Indian Expeditionary Force A to France in particular.

Lawrence, T. E. the British liaison officer with anti-Ottoman Arab forces up to 1918; he commanded his own, little-known, Indian contingent in the desert.

Lettow-Vorbeck, Paul von the Prussian commander of the German forces in East Africa which the Indian Army fought for four years.

Lewis, Harold a young British officer of the 129th Baluchis who served in France, East Africa and Palestine from 1914 to 1918.

Lloyd George, David the British Prime Minister from 1916.

Malleson, Wilfrid a British Army intelligence officer who led a secret Indian Army mission to north-east Iran in 1918.

Mast, Mir an Indian Muslim officer of the 58th Vaughan's Rifles (Frontier Force) and the brother of Mir Dast VC; he deserted in France in 1915, going on to enter German secret service.

Maude, Stanley the British Army commander of Indian Expeditionary Force D to Iraq in 1916–17.

Meinertzhagen, Richard a British Army intelligence officer with Indian Expeditionary Force B to East Africa in 1914–16.

Monro, Charles a British Army general and the Indian Army's Commander-in-Chief from 1916.

Mukherji, Dr Kalyan a Bengali of the Indian Medical Service who was captured in Ottoman Iraq in 1916; he was a prisoner of war in Syria in the same camp as Dr M. L. Puri.

Naidu, Sarojini the Bengali poet and wartime nurse in Indian hospitals in England.

Nasrullah, Sardar the brother of Emir Habibullah of Afghanistan.

Pratap, Mahendra an Indian revolutionary who enlisted Indian prisoners of war in Germany in 1915 for a secret mission to Afghanistan.

Puri, Dr M. L. a Bengali of the Indian Medical Service who was captured in Ottoman Iraq in 1916; he was censured after the war for his inhumane treatment of Indian prisoners of war in Syria.

Roberts, Lord the British general of the Indian Army and Victorian Commander-in-Chief of the Indian Army, who spent time with the Indian troops in France in 1914.

Robertson, William the Chief of the Imperial (or British) General Staff from 1915 to 1918, with control over the Indian forces overseas.

Singh, Gobind an Indian Hindu cavalryman who won the VC in France in 1917, at the Battle of Cambrai.

Singh, Sir Pratap the oldest serving Indian soldier during the First World War – in his seventies – who led the elite princely States' regiment the Jodhpur Lancers continuously in France and Palestine (apart from briefly returning to Jodhpur in 1915).

Singh, Thakur Amar an Indian Hindu officer in France, Iraq and British India from 1914 to 1918, who was the most senior Indian Army officer on active service. His diary, which he kept between 1898 and 1942, may be the longest continuous personal diary ever written. Today it is kept at his ancestral home at Kanota in Rajasthan State, and is published in part.

Smuts, Jan the South African politician and general, in 1916–17 the commander-in-chief of the British Empire forces in East Africa which included Indian Expeditionary Force B.

Smyth, John a young British officer of the 15th Ludhiana Sikhs who in 1914 spent his twenty-first birthday in the trenches of France with his men, won the VC there in 1915, and went on to serve in the Sahara Desert and elsewhere up to 1918.

Thapa, Harkabir an Indian officer of the 5th Gurkhas (Frontier Force) who went mountaineering with his British officer Charles Bruce prior to 1914, and served in Egypt and Gallipoli in 1914–15.

Townshend, Charles a British Army general infamous as the commander of the Indian 6th Division who surrendered it in Iraq in 1916.

Willcocks, James a British Army general born outside Delhi who commanded the Indian Corps in France in 1914–15. He lived in India as a boy and before the First World War was the British soldier most decorated for active service. On the western front he took an unusual approach to command – he tried to save his men's lives in Douglas Haig's offensives by keeping them from attacking. While Willcocks felt a close comradeship with the Indian troops, he should not be romanticised to obscure his trenchantly expressed beliefs in white racial superiority – for instance that an Indian officer could never match a British officer: 'no argument decked in rhetoric will alter the fact,' he wrote in 1920, 'that you can never replace the British officer in the Indian Army.'

Wilson, Arnold a British officer of the 32nd Sikh Pioneers who served in

Iraq and Iran from 1915 as both a military intelligence officer and an administrator of Iraq's British Occupied Territories.

Wilson, Henry the Chief of the Imperial (or British) General Staff from February 1918, overseeing the Indian Army's victories in Palestine and Syria.

ACKNOWLEDGEMENTS

First and foremost my thanks must go to Jonathan Conway and Richard Beswick, my literary agent and editor, for their enthusiasm and inspiration to bring this book into being. I am also very grateful for the superb contributions at Little, Brown of David Bamford, Nithya Rae, Tracey Winwood and Linda Silverman, and for all seven maps so expertly crafted by John Gilkes. For their generosity of time and spirit in discussing ideas for this book, I am most indebted to Santanu Das, Radhika Singha, Akbar Ahmed, Rana Chhina and Hew Strachan. I would like to thank for their help and advice – in India, Pakistan, the United States, Canada, Australia, Belgium and the UK – Adil Chhina, Dominiek Dendooven and Tom Donovan (who have been especially kind in pointing me towards sources), along with Omar Khan Afridi, Irfan Malik, Gajendra Singh, Kaushik Roy, David Omissi, Doug Delaney, Peter Stanley, Peter Duckers, Cliff Parrett, Alan Jeffreys, Harry Fecitt, Gordon Corrigan, Andrew Jarboe, Barnaby Blacker, Matthieu Aikins, Jo Scofield and Andrew Yarme. I also owe sincere thanks to readers who notified me of some errors in the original text that I have corrected in this edition. Finally, I thank my wife, Mia, for her help every step of the way.

INDEX

To buy any of our books and to find out
more about Abacus and Little, Brown, our authors
and titles, as well as events and book clubs,
visit our website

www.littlebrown.co.uk

and follow us on Twitter

@AbacusBooks
@LittleBrownUK